TITUS COAN

TITUS COAN

"Apostle to the Sandwich Islands"

PHIL CORR

WIPF & STOCK · Eugene, Oregon

TITUS COAN
"Apostle to the Sandwich Islands"

Copyright © 2021 Phil Corr. All rights reserved. Except for brief quotations in critical publications or reviews, no part of this book may be reproduced in any manner without prior written permission from the publisher. Write: Permissions, Wipf and Stock Publishers, 199 W. 8th Ave., Suite 3, Eugene, OR 97401.

Wipf & Stock
An Imprint of Wipf and Stock Publishers
199 W. 8th Ave., Suite 3
Eugene, OR 97401

www.wipfandstock.com

PAPERBACK ISBN: 978-1-6667-1393-0
HARDCOVER ISBN: 978-1-6667-1394-7
EBOOK ISBN: 978-1-6667-1395-4

10/15/21

I dedicate this book to:

- My beloved family: Karin, Don, Sarah, Betsy and Don. They happily adopted Titus Coan as a member of the family from late 2009 onward. Their understanding, encouragement, and listening were priceless as I researched, wrote, edited, and finalized this book.
- The readers of this book: present and future; general and scholarly. This book is for you.
- Titus Coan: without his amazing life this book would not have been written!
- My Lord and Savior Jesus Christ, whose Holy Spirit I fervently pray will use this book, along with other resources, to bring revival in Hawai'i and around the world and through time. Two people unknown to each other told me they believed God would use this book in such a way.

Contents

Acknowledgments | ix
Abbreviations | xvi
Chronology of Titus Coan's Life and Times | xvii
Preface | xix

    Introduction | 1
1 Early years | 15
2 Patagonia | 33
3 Call to and Arrival in the Sandwich Islands | 67

REVIVALIST

4 Prelude to Revival | 105
5 The Great Awakening | 133
6 The Great Awakening, Part 2 | 162

RENAISSANCE MAN

7 Scientist | 195
8 Vulcanologist | 222
9 Vulcanologist, Part Two | 259

10 Missions, Part 1 | 284
11 Missions, Part 2 | 313
12 Expatriate Ministry | 335
13 Peace Man | 365
14 Other Religions | 396
15 The Coans Visit America, 1870–71 | 424
16 Final Years, 1872–82 | 455
17 Legacy | 483

Bibliography | 515
Index of Scripture | 531
Index of Subjects | 537

Acknowledgments

THE ACKNOWLEDGMENTS SECTION IS the one place in a work where the author may use the word "I" and related pronouns. I first met Titus Coan when working on my dissertation, which examines the first thirty years of the American Board of Commissioners for Foreign Missions and its emphasis on preaching in policy and practice.

As the leader of the Hawaiian Great Awakening, Coan showed a robust leadership and passion in proclaiming the gospel of Jesus Christ. Over the years he continued to intrigue me. When in September of 2009 I began to research in depth the life of Titus Coan, I started making new friends and appreciating old friends even more.

Before thanking individuals and groups, however, I would like to acknowledge three technological developments that have greatly contributed to the quality of this book: the internet, the personal computer, and digitization. While individuals have been involved with the invention and development of each item, I do not know any of them! The internet has brought a revolution in technology that is as great in its own way as the invention of moveable type, as represented by the Gutenberg Bible.

The use of the internet by private citizens was in its infancy while I worked on my dissertation between 1989 and 1993. By the time I began researching Titus Coan, I could search for anything with lightning speed. What a time saving device it is. With Coan's knowledge of the Bible,[1] I deemed it important to provide the Bible book, chapter, and verse(s) references in brackets whenever possible. The internet astronomically sped up that process. Below I list two of the major internet assists Ed Coan provided me. When it comes to small yet important aspects of the biography, Wikipedia[2] was invaluable. Launched by Jimmy Wales and Larry Sanger in January of 2001, Wikipedia has become a quick reference internet encyclopedia for scholar and general user alike.[3]

The personal computer is known to every reader of this page. The more observant know that "personal computer" is the name for one brand of what was initially a desktop. Then came the laptop and many other variations, including a computer on what came to be called a "smartphone," which itself was a brand developed by a

---

1. See Preface.
2. Which has become increasingly accurate and reliable on the subjects I needed.
3. Wikipedia, "Wikipedia."

non-personal-computer company. With yellow words on a black screen and a dot matrix, I estimated that I saved forty hours per quarter while working on a chapter of my dissertation. The numbers of hours saved on the entire dissertation as well as this book are incalculable and I am very grateful for that.

I am grateful for so much research material being brought to the home by digitization. Made possible by the internet and the computer, all of the Coan correspondence at the Mission Houses has been digitized, based in turn on microfilmed material, which was in turn based on many typed letters from the original handwritten letters and documents, and the handwritten items themselves.

By early 2012 my autobiographical Coan chapter appeared in the two hundredth anniversary of *The Role of the American Board*. That chapter would not have seen the light of day were it not for the yeoman work of a then-Camp Pendleton Marine, Brandon Quarles, who, along with his wife Susan, joined my Escondido church in 2011. He was able to work with both co-editors and format the chapter to the publisher's guidelines.

I turned that chapter into the anchor for a new title proposal with the publisher of the anniversary book—Wipf and Stock. Because you are reading this published book, obviously Wipf and Stock accepted the proposal and for that and all their assistance I am deeply grateful. I first worked with Christian Amondson. In recent years Matthew Wimer has provided invaluable assistance. And for those helping in the preparation of the book for publication and in getting the word out on the book, I express a heartfelt thank you to: Caleb, for formatting; Griffin, for copy-editing; Ian for typesetting, Shannon for designing the cover; and everyone else!

When researching Coan online I came across the digitized version of Coan's autobiography. At that site I found a functioning e-mail for a descendant of Titus Coan by the name of Ed Coan. Ed has been unfailingly encouraging and helpful, as he provided images, links to online works (such as an interactive map of the Big Island, and a Coan Google search that led to even more leads!), and introductions to other people. Email friendship has been wonderful.

The other people include his two cousins Alison Dibble and Sarah Stephens. Alison has expressed interest in this project all along. She has enthusiastically requested copies, such as Margaret Ehlke's thesis and many other items. At one point she indicated that I was "becoming the world expert on Titus Coan."

Sarah Stephens shared that assessment. She sent me items that she found in her mother's effects. She and Alison have provided insights into the life of various Coans, as well as input on the possible chain of possession of the Titus Coan papers. The latter led to her being named in 1969 as the holder of the literary rights of "the unpublished writings of Titus Coan and other members of the Coan family" in the custody of the Library of Congress.

Ed also introduced me to Paul Rapoza. Using the same email I had to first contact him, Ed said he thought the two of us would "develop an interesting synergy."

Acknowledgments

He started out with a website dedicated only to the Titus Coan autobiography. That soon expanded to Lydia Bingham's *Memorial Volume*. Then he went beyond Coan and provided memoirs by other missionaries to Hawai'i, including Hiram Bingham's. I recommend Paul's website to all.[4] During my researching and writing of this book, Paul happily found and shared links that I requested and helped me with technical questions I had. He also posted online a comparison of two versions of Titus's Patagonia journal: one side the journal from Coan's *Adventures in Patagonia*, the other the digitized, typed, transcribed journal found at the Library of Congress.

At the Library of Congress, Lewis Wyman provided unstinting help from late 2009 up to the sending of the manuscript to the publisher. In the early weeks of my Coan research, he sent me a potpourri of selected material from the Titus Coan Papers. Among those items was a typed page copy listing Coan's letter articles in *The Advocate of Peace* and related journals. This one page and the subsequent copies made of the letters off of a microfilm copy machine at the Vista, California, public library, became the heart of the "Peace Man" chapter—exploring a previously unexamined aspect of Titus Coan's varied interests and passions. He was unfailingly prompt in responding to my various email queries.

Lewis was also unstinting in his assistance to my cousin William Philip Corr III during his three visits there. Bill enjoyed securing his own Library of Congress card. He provided perfect images of countless pages of letters and journals. In particular, he greatly strengthened with these primary sources the first Great Awakening chapter and the chapter on the Coans' trip to America in 1870–71.

At the Mission Houses in Honolulu, I first worked with Carol White, then John Barker, and finally Kelsey Karsin. Somewhere along the line a correspondence developed with Tom Woods, who headed up the Mission Houses for some years. His insights have been invaluable with regard to individuals and organizations. Tom, along with two others, published in 2019 the priceless *Partners in Change*, with information both about Hawaiian Christian leaders and the American Board missionaries. Since his retirement he has continued to be unflagging in his support and encouragement.

Even though I was not able to go on a 2020 or 2021 Hawai'i research trip due to the COVID-19 situation, I had begun an email friendship with Peter Young, the president of the Mission Houses and a descendant of Hiram Bingham.

Carol introduced me to Joan Hori at the University of Hawai'i, Manoa, Voyagers library. She was unfailingly helpful, including processing the second copy of Ehlke's thesis for my use through the Charles City, Iowa, public library.

Upon her retirement, Joan introduced me to Jodie Mattos, who provided me with a PDF of Nancy Morris's dissertation on Hawaiian missionaries to other island nations. Nancy in turn has provided me with leads, tips, background information, and, at times, specific names—such as the brother and sister High Priest and Priestess of Pele who became Christians during the Hawaiian Great Awakening. In 2019,

---

4. Titus Coan Memorial library, www.tc-lib.org.

Acknowledgments

Nancy, along with Robert Benedetto, published *Nā Kahu: Portraits of Native Hawaiian Pastors at Home and Abroad, 1820–1900*.

In Hilo one finds the Lyman House. First Libby Burke was very helpful, including electronically transmitting material about the Wetmore family. Since Libby returned to the mainland, Miki Bukos and others have made themselves available to help.

Two Big Island pastors have shared friendship and information. Brian Welsh is the pastor of Coan's church, Haili.

Brian introduced me to Alan Tamashiro, the pastor of Puna Baptist Church. Early on in my research, Alan sent me a copy of his English-Hawaiian dictionary, which has been a helpful reference work. Along with Brian, he provided most helpful input. Brian introduced me to Alan because Alan was at the time working on his Doctor of Ministry dissertation on revival. Alan's reflections on Titus Coan fitting the categories of revivalist contributed greatly to the conclusion of the second chapter on the Hawaiian Great Awakening. Along with many others mentioned in this part of the book, Alan was a great encouragement as I slogged through the hours of research and preparation of the book.

Along with Paul, Alan and Patricia Bjorling were prayer warriors during difficult times in my life since 2010. I was glad to return the ministry when possible. Patsy has been a friend since the 1990s, when she served on the staff of the Hawaiian Conference of the United Church of Christ. At the time she was assisting Hawaiian Evangelical Churches write grant proposals for funds from the Coan Endowment.[5] She has graciously provided insights and leads, as well as sent me some printed and published material. Further, she took time out of a very busy work schedule to research letters by Lydia Bingham Coan at the Yale Bingham Papers. Something she shared with me in 2010 led to the Coan chapter in *The Role of the American Board*.

Two more Hawaiian scholars are Regina Pfeiffer and Nancy Morris. Regina twice visited the Mission Houses on my behalf. She provided excellent and precise summaries of the not-yet-digitized correspondence. Nancy Morris graciously responded to my initial email. She occasionally commented on writings I sent her. Her specialty has to do with Hawaiian missionaries to Micronesia and Marquesas, as well as Hawaiian pastors of Hawaiian churches. My undergraduate friend, Craig Ing, also visited the Missison Houses for me.

Two other renowned scholars—one connected to Gordon-Conwell Theological Seminary and Fuller Seminary—Garth Rosell and James Bradley—have helped. Garth was a faculty member and administrator during my Master of Divinity days at GCTS and we have stayed in touch since then. Among many other specialties, Garth is the premiere expert on Charles Finney, whose life and labors intersect Coan's, especially during the Upstate New York Great Awakening years of the late 1820s and early 1830s, as well as late 1870 at Oberlin College.

---

5. See "Legacy" chapter.

Acknowledgments

Jim Bradley served as my PhD mentor at Fuller when I examined the first thirty years[6] of the American Board of Foreign Missions. His was the final paragraph in the dissertation's acknowledgments. His training and mentoring formed me into a scholar. The training and mentoring inform the scholarly part of this book. In 2016, he and Richard Muller published their revised and updated historical research and methods.[7] For the Coan biography, Jim counseled me to choose which audience I was going to write for—general or scholarly—then write accordingly. In that matter I diverged from him, coming up with a synthesis of the two as explained in the "hybrid" introduction. Throughout both processes—the dissertation and the biography—he has remained a great friend.

For most of the research, writing, and pre-publishing of this book, there has been a small group averaging around 20 who actually enjoyed receiving emails from me about my latest work on the project. A few asked to be removed from the mailings. A few were added over the years. Many of the recipients have already been mentioned.

As of this writing, two have gone to be with the Lord: Lucy Lincoln[8] and Paul Toms. On July 22, 2011, Dr. Toms sent me an email which read in part, "Hi Phil: I am discouraged to read that your material on Titus Coan may not be published for some years. That means I will have to lean over the battlements of heaven[9] to read it. I appreciate the short burst of material you sent on his life. His ties with Park Street[10] are so interesting—and he really did have a flair for lovely words in writing."

Other Coan email recipients include Steve Carmany, Steven Gammon, and Kathy Bruns. Too the rest I apologize, as I do for anyone else whom I have not acknowledged by name.

In 2020, two documentaries were released independent of each other. *Witness to Aloha* tells the story of Hawaiian Christians, ABCFM missionaries, and the first church on Oahu.[11] Karin and I were scheduled to attend the two hundredth anniversary service at Kawaiahao Church. By viewing the video, we had a deeper understanding of and love for the current congregation without having yet met them.

The other documentary is about the Hawaiian who, more than anyone else, is viewed as the inspiration for the first American Board missionary company to depart

---

6. 1810–40.

7. Bradley, *Church History*.

8. A Bible translator extraordinaire and Conservative Congregational Christian Conference missionary.

9. Dr. Toms died in early 2015.

10. Dr. Toms had the unique distinction of being the only person to have ever lived who both served Titus Coan's church in Hilo and the church—Park Street in Boston—where Titus Coan was ordained to be a missionary scout to Patagonia and two years later commissioned to serve the Sandwich Islands.

11. It can be seen here: www.youtube.com/watch?v=nJOTS81wErQ. Produced by Kawaihao Church and Rev. Kenneth Makuakāne, senior pastor of the Kawaiaha'o Church.

the United States and arrive in the Hawaiian Islands in 1820: ʻŌpūkahaʻia[12] With his name providing the title, the documentary was produced by Michael Lineau and his Global Net Production company. I first learned of Michael when my friend Alan Tamashiro called to let me know he had told Michael (then living on the other side of the Big Island from Alan) that I was the Titus Coan expert. There followed some phone calls and texts. We have continued to stay in contact.

In the weeks prior to the manuscript submission, George Demetrion provided priceless counsel. In his 2014 book, he writes the following about me: "It is not an exaggeration to say that, without the critical editing that Phil provided in 2013, this book would not have been published."[13] In many ways, for different reasons, the same could be said about George for this book that you are now reading.

In the months leading up to submitting the manuscript to the publisher, Ed Coan again provided invaluable assistance. After I had worked through the manuscript in detail, he similarly worked his way through using the Review function. He has also been very helpful and encouraging in the details of final preparation.

In the year before the book was published, Christopher L. Cook became a friend who helped me as well. His email address actually includes "obookiah"! He sent me the two books he has published on related matters. He also helped with technical matters, including tracking down bibliographic references.

I thank the church where I have so far had the privilege of serving for more than six years: The Church of the Living Savior in McFarland, California. In addition to being wonderful people and eager to reach out to the community and the world with the gospel of Jesus Christ, they allowed continued education time between September of 2015 and April of 2016 for me to write the bulk of the manuscript. Then in early 2021, the church granted me a stay-at-home partial sabbatical/pastor's sabbath enabling me to prepare the manuscript for submission to the publisher.

Next to last, I thank my family, as does Margaret Ehlke in her next to last paragraph in her acknowledgments. As the love of my life wife, Karin has encouraged me in researching the American Board all the way back to our honeymoon on Maui. It was on the last day that she encouraged me to check the small headstones near a church. It turned out to include six of the first Hawaiian Christians, including "Blind Bartimeus"[14] She has encouraged my research and writing ever since.

All three of my children—Don, Sarah, and Betsy—helped me with technical issues leading up to the submission of the manuscript. Don while on a visit. Sarah and Betsy lived at home due to COVID-19 and helped in various ways. I have dubbed Betsy "Auntie Em."

I join with Margaret Ehlke in her final thanks, with two additions. "But most of all, I have to say thank you to Titus and Fidelia Coan for providing such fascinating

---

12. Anglicized in the nineteenth-century as Obookiah.
13. Demetrion, *In Quest*, xii.
14. Bartimeus Lalana Puaʻaiki.

ACKNOWLEDGMENTS

material and to their descendants for preserving their letters for posterity."[15] I am grateful for other intriguing primary materials that provide further information for posterity, as well as examinations by secondary sources. The other thanks goes to Lydia Bingham Coan,[16] who lived quite a life and whom Titus thanked for helping her publish his autobiography near the end of his life, as well as put together and published the Titus Coan *Memorial Volume*.

---

15. Ehlke, "Enthusiastic Religion," iii.
16. I hope that someone will write a thesis, dissertation, or book on Lydia's life and labors.

Abbreviations

ABCFM	American Board of Commissioners for Foreign Missions
BFP	Bingham Family Papers, at Yale University, New Haven, Connecticut.
HEA	Hawaiian Evangelical Association
HMH	Hawaiian Mission Houses. Formerly known as Hawaiian Mission Children's Society Library, Honolulu, Hawai'i. Multiple collections.
LOC	Library of Congress, Washington, DC. Titus Coan Papers.
NYHS	New York Historical Society, New York. Titus Munson Coan Papers
LH	Lyman House Museum, Hilo, Hawai'i.
USGS	United States Geological Society, Big Island of Hawai'i.

Chronology of Titus Coan's Life and Times

COAN'S LIFE	COAN'S TIMES
1801: February 1: Born at Killingworth, Connecticut	Unitarian/Trinitarian split
	1806: Haystack Prayer Meeting
	1810: King Kamehameha unites Hawai'i
	War of 1812
	1812: First ABCFM Company departs for the Indian subcontinent
	1818: Death of Henry 'Ōpūkaha'ia
1819–26: Teaches school in Connecticut	1820: First ABCFM Company departs for the Sandwich Islands
1826–30: Teaches school at Riga, New York	Upstate New York Revivals with Nettleton and Finney
	1830: LDS Church established in Upstate New York
1831–33: Attends Auburn (New York) Theological Seminary	
1833: Licensed as a minister by Cayuga (New York) Presbytery	
Ordained a missionary by American Board of Commissioners for Foreign Missions	
1833–34: Goes on missionary expedition to Patagonia	
1834: Marries Fidelia Church (1810–72)	
1834: December 1: Departs Boston Harbor on *Hellespont*	1834: December 24 Lydia Bingham born
1835: June 6: Lands in Honolulu	1835: June Annual Meeting of ABCFM Hawaiian Mission
1835–82: Serves as missionary at and from Hilo, Hawai'i	
1836–40: Leads Hawaiian Great Awakening	

Chronology of Titus Coan's Life and Times

COAN'S LIFE

1836: Birth of son, Titus Munson Coan (died 1921)

1839: Birth of daughter, Harriett Fidelia Coan (died 1906)

1843: Birth of daughter, Sarah Eliza Coan (died 1916)

1846: Birth of son, Samuel Latimer Coan (died 1887)

1860 & 67: Makes voyages to Marquesas Islands for Hawaiian Missionary Society

1870 & 71: Visits the United States

1873: Marries Lydia Bingham (died 1915)

1880: Publication of *Adventures in Patagonia*

1882: Publication of *Life in Hawaii*
1882: December 1: Dies at Hilo, Hawai'i

COAN'S TIMES

1850: Mormon missionaries arrive in Hawai'i

1859: Darwin's *Origin of the Species* published

1860: Abraham Lincoln elected president of the US

1861–65: American Civil War

1865: Abraham Lincoln assassinated

1869–73 U. S. Grant president

1881: Chester A. Arthur becomes president

Preface

THE PURPOSE OF THE Preface is to explain various matters—both great and small in importance—to assist in the reading and understanding of this book. It will move from the lesser to the greater in the order of subjects. Abbreviations are found in the originals of Coan's and other's writings. Examples of these abbreviations include: "&c." for "etc."; "wh." for "which," "Bro." for "Brother"; "ch." For "church"; and so on. Some scholars such as Ehlke and Putney usually keep the original abbreviations. When Chester S. Lyman published his journal in *Around the Horn*, he put brackets with the letters to complete the words he had abbreviated. That is the pattern I follow—putting the rest of the word in brackets.

In handwritten documents, such as letters and journals, it was not possible to use italics, so they underlined words. Similarly, Ehlke did not have italic capability for her typewriter in the 1980s. So, she underlines the words as well. In this volume, I italicize underlined items. Occasionally I add italics for emphasis, at which point I indicate such.

When it comes to the Hawaiian language, there are three things to remember: early fluidity, liquidity, and updated spelling, etc. In the early years of the Board missionaries, there was fluidity in spelling the language. They provided an alphabet with Roman letters. An example of this fluidity was Owyhee for Hawai'i.

When it comes to liquidity, Polynesian languages and Japanese mix interchangeably "l's" and "r's." In the case of Hawaiian there could be Honoruru for Honolulu and Mona Roa for Mona Loa. When a Westerner writes such words, I do not correct it. During the early part of the twenty-first century, diacritical marks were added to correct spelling of Hawaiian words, including names.

However, I do not correct writers of any age who characterized the word as "Hawaii" without a diacritical mark. Or, take a name such as Henry Obookiah. I keep the writing of that name by nineteenth-century and early twentieth-century writers. But in the text when there is no quotation, I use Ōpūkaha'ia. The diacritical spelling of the place Kilauea is Kīlauea. In this volume every effort has been made to spell Hawaiian words correctly with diacritical marks when warranted.[1] I take full responsibility for any mistakes of omission or commission in this area.

1. Including the 'oikana, as in Hawai'i.

Preface

Titus Coan "learned his letters" during the first twenty years of the nineteenth century. As such, he occasionally used English spelling as opposed to what has developed in American English. The most often used is spelling words ending in the English "our" instead of the American English "or," such as "labour" and "Saviour." When Coan or others use such spellings or archaic versions of words no "sic" is put in brackets.

Bible quotations and, when identifiable, near quotations, allusions, and paraphrases are put in brackets after the verse or passage. The Bible book abbreviations used follow the publisher's guidelines. Even though the early generations of Puritans in New England used the Geneva Bible,[2] by the time of Titus Coan the King James Version was universally used.[3] First printed in 1611, the "Authorized Version" came to be called that because the king authorized its use in the Church of England over which he was the temporal head.[4]

"By the mid-eighteenth century the wide variation in the various modernized printed texts of the Authorized Version, combined with the notorious accumulation of misprints, had reached the proportion of a scandal, and the Universities of Oxford and Cambridge both sought to produce an updated standard text. The first of the two was the Cambridge edition of 1760, the culmination of twenty-year work by Francis Sawyer Parris, who died in May of that year. This 1760 edition was reprinted without change in 1762 and in John Baskerville's fine folio edition of 1763. This was effectively superseded by the 1769 Oxford edition, edited by Benjamin Blayney, though with comparatively few changes from the 1760 edition, which became the Oxford standard text, and is almost unchanged in most current printings."[5] Coan used the 1769 Oxford edition, which came to be called the "standard text of 1769." As far as an American printing of the KJV, he might have used the Noah Webster edition.[6]

Titus Coan immersed himself in the Bible. He saturated himself in it. He drew from the entire Bible, including what many today might view as obscure Minor Prophet references. His knowledge of the Bible was similar to that of John Bunyan, the author of *Pilgrim's Progress*. What Charles Spurgeon wrote about Bunyan can be said of Titus Coan: "I would quote John Bunyan as an instance of what I mean. Read anything of his, and you will see that it is almost like the reading the Bible itself. He had read it till his very soul was saturated with Scripture; and, though his writings are

---

2. The first full edition was printed in 1560.

3. Later in life he would comment on the E. R. V., the English Revised Version. It was published the year of Coan's death.

4. See the page near the beginning of the original KJV and the Standard text (below) that Coan had.

5. Wikipedia, "King James Version."

6. First published in 1833, "the Webster Bible" was characterized as containing "a more familiar language than the original King James Version, without tampering with the meaning of the original Hebrew and Greek" (http://www.amazon.com/The-Webster-Bible-Noah/dp/0801096847). Perhaps it foreshadowed the New King James Version, the first complete Bible of which was published in 1982.

charmingly full of poetry, yet he cannot give us his *Pilgrim's Progress*—that sweetest of all prose poems—without continually making us feel and say, 'Why, this man is a living Bible!' Prick him anywhere—his blood is Bibline,[7] the very essence of the Bible flows from him. He cannot speak without quoting a text, for his very soul is full of the Word of God. I commend his example to you, beloved."[8]

To twenty-first-century ears and eyes, some of the words and perceived attitudes of Titus Coan and others can sound harsh, even condescending. Even granting his and other missionaries' views on Christianity as being the one true faith, such words as "savage" and "heathen" come across as demeaning and inappropriate. Before descending on nineteenth-century individuals with indignation, it is well to remember that they were immersed in their culture and not aware of what we see from the rearview mirror of history.

Another example might be to understand the views of African Americans following the Civil War. In the 2012 movie "Lincoln," actors speak many words and phrases used in the House of Representatives while debating the Fourteenth Amendment. Words that grate on the contemporary ear were progressive in their day. The noble goal of that amendment was reached with what now appear as convoluted logic and painful arguments.

It is the same with Western views of peoples around the world during the nineteenth century. At times, Christianity and civilization could get intertwined. But, unlike many vested Western interests, missionaries put their charges first. No one less than Titus Coan dearly loved the Hawaiians that he went to as a missionary, but became their beloved "Papa," pastor, and mentor.

The word "savage" has to do with uneducated[9] members of primary cultures. The word "gentile" is drawn from the Old Testament and it means any nation other than Israel. In the New Testament it has to do with groups of people—"nations"—who have not heard the gospel.

When it comes to the copious use of quotations by Titus Coan and his contemporaries, the author has two reasons. The first has to do with the revising of history by some, all of whom were not present. While broader and deeper understandings are often welcome and needed, sometimes they twist the truth of history. The second reason ties in with the first one and that is to allow Titus Coan and others to speak for themselves and to listen to them—their goals, their struggles, their loves.

---

7. In the Bible, wine and blood are closely related. Here is one definition of "Bibline": "Bibline is believed to have been made in a style similar to the Phoenician wine from Byblos, highly regarded for its perfumed fragrance by Greek writers." Wikipedia, "Ancient Greece and Wine."

8. Uncited Spurgeon, tidesandturning.wordpress.com/tag/charles-spurgeon/. Another way it has been put it is that "wherever you pricked Bunyan, he bled Bible."

9. From the perspective of the West.

Preface

As readers peruse this missionary biography, they are encouraged to remember "Corr's Golden Rule of History": "Judge those in the past with the same understanding by which you would like people in the future to judge you!"

INTRODUCTION

WHY I WROTE THIS BOOK

I WROTE MY DISSERTATION—EXAMINING the first thirty years of the American Board of Commissioners and how it emphasized preaching in policy and practice—to combine my two passions of congregational renewal and world missions. In the course of the research and writing of the dissertation, a dynamic missionary caught my attention: Titus Coan. In 2009, sixteen years after the completion of the dissertation and the same year it was published as is (with a new cover) online,[1] I began looking into this man's life. As chronicled elsewhere,[2] I began to make many fascinating connections and to dig, dig, dig in research.

This led to a Coan biographical chapter in the two hundredth anniversary volume on the Board entitled *The Role of the American Board*.[3] From 2012 through 2015, I placed my research in a catena[4] entitled "The Coan Chronicles." The Chronicles are more than a catena, however, because I do add commentary and follow-up research notes.

During those years, between fifteen and twenty-two friends and family received Coan Chronicle updates via email.[5] Every year or so, I would send the full updated

---

1. Corr, *"Field Is the World."*
2. See "Acknowledgments," unpublished chronological essays "Titus Coan and Me," and elsewhere.
3. Corr, "Titus Coan."
4. On page *xii* of his "General Introduction" to the *Ancient Christian Commentary* Series, Thomas Oden talks about the Talmud and catena commentaries, "The Talmud originated largely from the same period as the patristic writers, often using analogous methods of interpretation. In the Talmud the texts of the Mishnah are accompanied by direct quotations from key consensual commentators of the late Judaic tradition. The format of the earliest published versions of the Talmud itself followed the early manuscript model of the medieval *glossa ordinaria* in which patristic comments were organized around Scripture texts. Hence the ACCS gratefully acknowledges its affinity and indebtedness to the early traditions of the catena and *glossa ordinaria* and of the tradition of rabbinic exegesis that accompanied early Christian Scripture studies" (Oden, "Introduction"). Freedictionary.com defines it in this way: "ca·te·na (kə-tē-nə) *n. pl.* **ca·te·nae** (-nē) or **ca·te·nas**. A closely-linked series, especially of excerpted writings or commentaries."
5. The numbers varied based on people learning about the project, one being asked to be removed

Chronicles. For the years I have worked on this biography, I have had two audiences in mind: general readers and scholars. At times I struggled over how I could write a biography that would meet the needs and interests of those occasionally disparate readers. Occasionally I was encouraged to pick one and focus on it, but I did not give up on somehow producing a hybrid biography.

Then one evening in late 2014, an idea came to me on how to combine the two, or at least juxtapose the two audiences with some connecting interests. When it came to choosing between the general reader and scholars, I decided that the answer is yes! Hence this chapter.

FOR THE EDIFICATION OF THE GENERAL READER

General readers themselves come with two potentially overlapping interests: biography and Christian inspiration. For them, this book is mostly in chronological order, with some themes (such as peace) warranting a separate chapter.

For the general reader, I now provide paragraph chapter summaries. Chapter 1 (of seventeen) begins with Coan's birth and continues through his attending Auburn Seminary. Born in Killingworth, Connecticut, he grew up with a military bent. Later in life, with his peace emphasis, he regretted organizing fellow eleven-year-old boys into a troop after watching War of 1812 soldiers parade through town. He also regretted his involvement in a militia as a young adult. He moved to Upstate New York and became a teacher. One day while riding his horse past another schoolhouse, he looked through a window and saw a young woman teacher "with the face of an angel." He beheld Fidelia Church, who would later become his wife. Under the leadership of Asahel Nettleton (a relative of Titus Coan) and (more significantly) the attorney-turned-evangelist Charles Finney, Fidelia and Titus Coan participated in the Second Great Awakening in that part of the country. They both joined Auburn Presbyterian Church and Titus began attending Auburn Seminary (Presbyterian). He believed that God was calling him to be a missionary.

That sense of call took an unexpected turn when the American Board of Commissioners asked Titus together with William Arms to travel to the southernmost part of South America, known as Patagonia. Chapter 2 examines the agonized parting of the close but not yet betrothed Fidelia and Titus, who secures a passport, is ordained as a missionary at Park Street Church (Congregational) in Boston, and takes ship for Patagonia. This sojourn is significant for several reasons: the visit overlaps with the travels of Charles Darwin on the *Beagle*; the "what-if" scenario: Had the two missionary scouts recommended a mission company go to Patagonia and asked Coan to head that company, would he have never gone to Hawai'i?; the silence of the months

---

from the list and, sadly, deaths.

INTRODUCTION

between Patagonia and the United States; and, upon his return, Fidelia's strong influence upon Titus for them to go to Hawai'i rather than Patagonia.[6]

After their return, the American Board agreed with Coan and Arms, who recommended that a mission not be sent to Patagonia. Chapter 3 looks at Coan and Fidelia from their marriage to their journey to the Sandwich Islands (as Hawai'i was then called) to their arrival at Honolulu on June 6, 1835, to their arrival in Hilo to their language learning to his first sermons in Hawaiian. Not long after getting married, they embarked on the merchant ship *Hellespont*, which took them around the horn of South America. Titus drew a sketch of the ship. At a stop in Lima, the Catholic bishop gave them a tour of the cathedral. This was the first of several times (others being the Marquesas and Salt Lake City) when Coan would show courtesy on the turf of representatives of other religions, as Catholicism was viewed in those days. Upon arrival at Honolulu, he learned that the annual general meeting of the ABCFM missionaries along with their families was underway. Among the many to greet the Coans would be the Binghams, including Lydia, who was less than six months old at the time. The Coans stayed with the Binghams for a week. The missionaries decided that Sarah and David Lyman would return to Hilo on the Big Island of Hawai'i. They assigned the Coans to that village and island as well. The Lymans shared their small home with the Coans (with a blanket being put up in the middle for privacy) for a time. The Coans would eventually move into the home of the recently departed (leaving Hilo in November 1835) Goodrich family. With modifications and improvements to the house over the years, the Coans would refer to the home and surrounding property as their "Emerald Bower." Titus took the baby steps of learning the Hawaiian language and after a few months gave his first sermon—at the First Church of Hawai'i, Hilo.

Not long after that, he began his tours of the Kau, Puna, and Hilo districts. Before examining Coan's role in what came to be called the Great Awakening or Great Revival, developments that set the stage for the revival will be considered. Chapters 5 and 6 come under the heading of "Coan the Revivalist." The preceding period (chapter 4) goes back to the mists of time well before any Europeans passed through or "discovered" the islands, going all the way back to the treks of "the Voyagers" who traveled from elsewhere in Polynesia to the islands over the course of some years. Tamashiro presents the theory that the Voyagers were monotheistic in belief. However, eventually polytheism developed, which included human sacrifice. The Hawaiian word for temple is *heiau*. Different heiaus had different purposes, including many other than human sacrifice. Heiaus (including at least one where human sacrifice was practiced) are found on the Big Island and other islands. Pele worship and attempts to placate the volcano goddess developed over the years. Captain Cook arrived in the late 1700s and left a representative to advise the royalty. King Kamehameha further prepared the ground for the arrival of missionaries in two ways: through the abolishing of the *kapu* system and the unification of the islands into one kingdom under one ruler.

---

6. For reasons of her health.

The first company of ABCFM missionaries arrived in 1820, under the leadership of Hiram Bingham. They and subsequent companies were the morning stars of the Great Awakening (through conversions of royalty, education of Hawaiians by giving them their language in writing and having schools, printing, translating of the Bible, and preaching the gospel), as were the Hawaiian evangelists who worked with the missionaries and served their people by living and preaching the gospel.

Pua'aiki—otherwise known as "Blind Bartimaeus"—spent a few years in Hilo prior to Titus Coan's arrival and prior to Pua'aiki's settling in Maui until his death. Missionaries in Hilo and other islands write of harbingers of revival in the fifteen-plus years leading up to the Great Awakening and set the Great Awakening in context. Chapter 5 focuses on Coan and his leadership of the Great Awakening. It appears to have started during a preaching tour in Puna in 1836. Lorenzo Lyons—an ABCFM missionary in Waimea and responsible for points north (Kohala) on the Big Island—became close friends and a harvest laborer with Titus Coan, as revealed in correspondence. The Great Awakening spread throughout the islands, with various missionaries reporting on it through station reports and other means. Much of it was written about publicly in the American Board's official journal, *The Missionary Herald*. Coan's letters were published in the *Herald*, and he wrote about it extensively in his private correspondence, including the Hawaiians' responses to his sermons. A brother and sister, priest and priestess of Pele, became followers of the living and true God, as did thousands of other people. On one Sunday in 1838, Titus Coan used a bucket and paint brush to baptize 1,705 adults that he had examined and considered for up to a year. Two days later he baptized several hundred children. Criticisms of the great work developed. Coan needed to admonish the head of the ABCFM—Rufus Anderson—in a private letter. Coan and some others were criticized for using Finney's New Measures and for hasty membership (which was anything but). The Great Awakening came to a crushing and crashing end (in the area of Coan's influence, at least) after the US Exploratory Expedition (known as the Ex Ex) arrived in Hilo harbor. This scientific expedition, while noble in purpose, led to some disheartening developments among the Hawaiians. Coan points to it as the end of the time of revival.

Coan continued to preach the rest of his life—at the church(es) and on tours. He was always a revivalist. He was also a "Renaissance man," as chapters 7 through 9 reveal. Chapter 7 looks at every scientific aspect of Coan's work except for that of volcanoes, which are discussed in chapters 8 and 9. For thirteen years, Titus provided the only western-style medical care for the Hilo and Puna districts. Once Dr. Charles Wetmore arrived in 1849, Coan happily turned the medical responsibilities over to him. Coan kept weather records, including temperature and rainfall. He reported on tidal waves (tsunamis) and earthquakes. Through the use of the internet, I have linked up at least two of the tidal waves during Coan's residence with major earthquakes that occurred a day or so before: one off the western coast of South America and another off the southern coast of Alaska.

INTRODUCTION

Coan put together an earthquake and a tidal wave with an eruption in 1868. A 6.8 earthquake on the Big Island led to a tsunami and occurred just before a major eruption. This was the thirty-second year of Coan's visits to, observations about, and writings of volcanoes and related matters. Though a handful Westerners, such as Ellis, made a few observations, Coan provided observations and measurements—sometimes at risk to his life—over a forty-five-year period. Such material found its way into *The Missionary Herald*, *The American Journal of Science*,[7] his autobiography, and (posthumously) in the Lydia Coan *Memorial Volume* (letters and journal entries). nineteenth-century authors looked to Coan when it came to the volcanism of Hawai'i. Twentieth- and twenty-first-century specialists as well draw on the volcano labors of Titus Coan.

While Coan was very much a Renaissance man, his focus was always on bringing the gospel to Hawaiians and people on other Pacific islands. "Missions" could be Coan's middle name. That is the focus of chapters 10 and 11. They examine his relationship with the American Board of Commissioners for Foreign Missions and the transition to the Hawaiian Evangelical Association, of which he was the first president and president for at least twenty years. He played a role in all three of the *Morning Star* ships that took people and provisions to and from Micronesia. As a representative of the Hawaiian Missionary Society he took two trips to the Marquesas Islands.

As much as he was devoted to Hawaiians and missions, Titus Coan did not forget others in his midst in the Hilo area. Chapter 12 examines his outreach to the sailors, captains, and officers who came into Hilo harbor. Coan had his own ocean travels, be they long-distance, to the Marquesas, or between the Hawaiian Islands. He wrote letters to and wrote an article entitled "The Sailor's Sabbath" in a sailor's magazine. He supported the full-time ministry of Samuel Chenery Damon to sailors at and through the Sailor's Bethel Chapel in Honolulu. Coan had conversations with sailors and preached to sailors and other foreigners on Sunday afternoons (after multiple services to the Hawaiian congregation in the morning). He distributed written material to the sailors from such organizations as the American Tract Society, the American Bible Society, and the Missionary and Tract Societies.

Coan also provided material from the American Peace Society, including *The Peace Book*. He became a prolific writer of letters over several decades that were published in *The Advocate of Peace* journal. These letters become the spine or foundation of chapter 13, which shows Coan's emphasis on the pursuit of peace. He once wrote, "If I ever became a disciple of Christ, I then became a *peace man*." He addressed boys, saying that he was not pround of his activities as an eleven-year-old who imitated soldiers or of his service in the militia in his twenties. After he became a full disciple of Jesus, he became a peace man. Around 1850 his letters began to appear in the journal *The Advocate of Peace*. The same journal held up Coan's congregation as an example of

---

7. See title in bibliography of Corr, "Titus Coan," 28, where the journal is called *The American Journal of Science and Arts*.

giving. Coan continued to write letters to the journal during the Civil War and after. He wrote his Quaker friends—Mr. and Mrs. Bean—explaining the nuances of being a peace man while supporting the Union effort. His view was that the "War of Rebellion" (as he called it) would not have needed to occur if pastors (especially those in the South) had done their jobs. Coan was deeply moved by the death of Abraham Lincoln.

Coan had strong views about "other religions," as chapter 14 is entitled. In an era long before Vatican II and the Mormon-Evangelical Dialogue, he had very definite positions concerning the views and messengers of those two religions. Priests arrived and eventually established a parish. Mormon missionaries arrived on the Big Island in 1850. I seek to understand the situations from the other faiths' viewpoints. I have a particularly large amount of material on that subject from the Latter-day-Saint perspective. Coan would again show his ability to be gracious while on the other person's turf when he and Fidelia visited Salt Lake City early in their 1870–71 trip to and through the United States.

That trip is the subject of chapter 15. Charles Finney had turned down an invitation to visit the Hawaiian Islands. Titus had been writing for two or three years that he could not possibly get away from his manifold responsibilities. Then Fidelia's health took a turn for the worse and they decided to seek medical help on the continent. After corresponding with their son, Samuel Latimer Coan, who was in San Francisco, they arrived by ship in May of 1870. After visiting with him for a couple of weeks, they began a cross-country train journey, with the Transcontinental Railway having been recently completed (except for the Missouri River, which still required a boat crossing). After a weekend in Salt Lake City, they continued eastward. They would stay more than once with Fidelia's relatives in Niles, Michigan. Coan spoke in many locations. The chapter focuses (in addition to Salt Lake City) on Oberlin, Brooklyn, and Washington City. In Oberlin, Ohio, he attended the Ohio Congregational annual meeting, hosted by the transitioning-to-retirement Charles Finney. In addition to speaking to and conversing with many people, Coan came full circle by officiating at communion with Finney and a pastor from Texas. The annual meeting of the ABCFM took place in Brooklyn, New York. Both the *Brooklyn Beagle* and the *New York Times* newspapers reported on events attended by thousands of people. Coan spoke and led during these meetings. In what is now called Washington, DC, the Coans were busy—visiting government and colleges (Howard), as well as seeing the sites, such as Mount Vernon. While in the United States, Coan visited several seminaries—receiving an honorary Doctor of Divinity degree from one. The winter cold proved to be too much for Fidelia, so the Coans worked their way back west and ultimately to Hilo.

Fidelia died (of cancer, I believe) in Hilo within the year. Titus grieved the death of his angel to such an extent that he poured himself into a multi-page "Ode." Fidelia's death ushers in chapter 16, which looks at the last ten years of Titus's life. In another year he would marry Lydia Bingham, a union that Titus's daughter Henrietta "Hattie" opposes. Hattie is only four years younger than Lydia. Nevertheless, Titus shows

INTRODUCTION

himself capable of deep love for a second time. They have a happy ten years together. In the 1870s, Titus Coan develops into a senior mission statesman and even more beloved pastor. Lydia encourages and helps him in the writing of two books—*Adventures in Patagonia*, followed by his autobiographical *Life and Adventures in Patagonia*. She struggles in the last months of Titus's life, after his stroke.

After the death of Titus Coan, Lydia pulls together a memorial service which becomes part of the Titus Coan legacy. That is focus of chapter 17. Coan's legacy immediately following his death down to the present day will be traced, with the understanding that he was and is "the Apostle to the Sandwich Islands."

TO ASSIST THE SCHOLAR

General readers can also be scholars. There are lay historians and professional historians. Sometimes lay historians achieve scholarly levels in their work, or their interest in the subject carries over to wanting as much information on sources and leads as possible. Additionally, see the final section of this introduction: "What the Two Audiences Have in Common."

When it comes to the subject of historical research—and church history in particular—James Bradley and Richard Mueller provide an invaluable resource in *Church History: An Introduction to Research, Reference Works, and Methods*. Bradley and Mueller describe the need for an existential interest in the subject that carries the researcher through many hours of what would otherwise be viewed as drudgery. Digging into the texts, asking questions, and following leads to other material all provide the scholar with an ever deeper understanding of the subject.

The historian needs to interact with the scholarship on the subject up to the time of publication. As he or she does so, the gap in the scholarship, the need for the work, and the thesis of the book must be presented.

In the case of Titus Coan, there is a large gap with minimal scholarly work on the subject. To date, Margaret Ehlke's thesis is the only full-length work on Titus Coan. While also looking at Fidelia Church Coan and providing priceless primary material and analysis, there are many gaps in her work, as no doubt gaps will be found in this work. The gaps in Ehlke's work include: limiting herself almost exclusively to correspondence; and limited interaction with scholarship, except for the background of the Coan's life, times, and beliefs. Ehlke provides little or no original research in such areas as: Coan's Patagonia sojourn; his peace emphasis; his interaction with Catholic and Mormon leaders; his and Fidelia's trip to the United States; and his relationship with his second wife, Lydia Bingham.[8]

---

8. Ehlke, "Enthusiastic Religion." See the bibliography of this text for full citations on every work mentioned.

In turn, the current work does not spend as much time as Ehlke on: Coan's early years, Fidelia, the Coan family, and other details of life. With so much primary and secondary material, one must prioritize. Ehlke did so, and so do I.

Two other Coan scholarly works include Gavin Daws's early 1960s paper on the Great Revival[9] and Nancy Morris's 1990s PhD look at the Hawaiian pastors and missionaries, including those whom Titus Coan mentors.[10] Daws's paper is not digitized while Morris's is.

Online and Digitized Material

Bradley and Mueller's 2016 revised edition on church history research examines the explosion of available online and digitized material. Between the late 1990s online digitized and searchable versions of Coan's autobiography[11] and the publication of this biography, Coan online and digitized material has burgeoned. Boston University has links to both primary and secondary sources.[12] Paul Rapoza developed a Coan web site that became far-reaching in its scope.[13] The Titus Coan Family Papers have only a PDF online finders' guide.[14] The only known online digitized Coan material from the Library of Congress is his Patagonia journal.[15] The Mission Houses of Honolulu has digitized all of its Coan correspondence.[16]

A search of Google Books provided many sources which in turn provided other leads. A digitized map of Hawai'i enabled the author to identify almost every location listed by Coan and C. S. Lyman regarding his tours of the Puna district.[17]

With regard to the broader missionary and Hawaiian contexts that tie in with Coan, Paul Rapoza has provided an invaluable service by pulling together[18] missionary

---

9. Daws, "Evangelism in Hawaii."

10. Morris, *Hawaiian Missionaries Abroad*. See also Morris and Benedetto, *Nā Kahu*.

11. Coan, *Life*. Unknown to each other, Beryl Walter, a member of Coan's church (now called Haili) was inspired to print Coan's autobiography in paperback form. She reprinted it in approximately 2002 ("Here it is, 120 years later—unabridged").

12. http://www.bu.edu/missiology/missionary-biography/c-d/coan-titus-1801-1882/.

13. http://www.tc-lib.org/TCoan/links.html.

14. http://rs5.loc.gov/service/mss/eadxmlmss/eadpdfmss/uploaded_pdf/ead_pdf_batch_17_june_2010/mss009306.pdf.

15. See Rapoza link.

16. https://hmha.missionhouses.org/items/browse?collection=105.

17. Ed Coan provided both the Google Books link and the USGS map.

18. At http://www.helps7.com/Books/paperback.html.

INTRODUCTION

autobiographies[19] and biographies,[20] material on Hawaiians,[21] Hawaiian history,[22] and missionary appeals.[23] Using the internet, digitization, and other technological tools, Rapoza makes available both ebooks[24] and print-on-demand books.

In virtually every chapter, one or more links to sources are given. Additionally, the increasingly accurate and reliable Wikipedia is cited for basic facts and background material on numerous subjects.

Discussion of Select Bibliography

Through a discussion of a select bibliography, the interaction with the scholarship and gaps in the Coan scholarship continue. As with the chapter-specific online and digitized material, an examination of bibliographic material specific to chapters is left to those chapters.

Taking a wide-lens view of the Hawaiian Islands, formerly known as the Sandwich Islands, two scholarly twentieth-century general histories are of particular assistance to this Coan biography.[25] The first and longest is the three-volume work by Kuykendall. The first volume includes the fifty-seven years Titus Coan lived and labored in the Hilo region.[26] The second work is by Gavan Daws.[27]

When it comes to the ABCFM missionaries to Hawai'i, there is one reference work with short summaries of each one and his spouse, as well as children and service

---

19. Bingham, *Residence of Twenty-One Years*; Coan, *Life* and *Patagonia*; Lydia Bingham Coan, *Memorial Volume* [mostly Titus's letters and journal entries; letters and with Lydia compiling and providing bridge passages]; Judd, *Sketches of Life*; and Thurston, *Life and Times*.

20. Alexander, *Mission Life*; Gulick et al., *Pilgrims*; Humphrey, "Titus Coan."

21. Dwight, *Memoirs*; and Pacific Commercial, *Kalakaua's Tour*.

22. Anderson, *Heathen Nation*; Bartlett, *Historical Sketch*; Dibble, *History*; and Hallock, *Hawaii under King Kalakaua*.

23. Ellis, *Vindication and Appeal*; and Alexander, "Duty to Evangelize."

24. Rapoza combines three mini-ebooks into a print-on-demand volume entitled *Three Native Hawaiians*. These mini-books include: William Richards, "Memoir of Keopuolani"; Rufus Anderson, "Kapiolani Heroine of Hawaii"; and Hiram Bingham, "Bartimeus of the Sandwich Islands."

25. Nineteenth-century histories of various lengths and focus are helpful to greater or lesser degrees and will be noted when cited in the body of this work.

26. Kuykendall, *Hawaiian Kingdom*.

27. Daws, *Shoal of Time*.

information. The *Missionary Album*[28] also provides portraits, daguerreotypes,[29] photographs, and even a watercolor[30] of the missionaries, their wives, and single female teacher/missionaries. The summaries, though short, provide a wealth of information, as do other facets of the book.

In 2018, the magisterial *Partners in Change* transcended the *Missionary Album* in many ways, but most importantly by examining the Hawaiian and Tahitian colleagues of "the American Protestant Missionaries."[31]

That a few scholarly biographies of ABCFM missionaries to Hawai'i have seen the light of day points all the more to the gap in the scholarship with regard to Titus Coan. The only leader ahead of Coan in prominence is Hiram Bingham.[32] Char Miller published his dissertation on the three Hirams,[33] as well as the letters and other writings of Hiram Bingham I.[34] At various points in this work I will interact with Miller's very fine scholarship.

---

28. Judd, *Missionary Album*. This edition is "enlarged from the first edition of 1937," which in turn is based on the 1901 first edition, published when some of the missionaries and spouses were still alive, such as Lydia Bingham Coan. The "Introduction from the 1937 Edition" provides a window on the challenges to the missionary legacy swirling at the time Kuykendall was working on his first volume. Albert F. Judd II writes, "In the turmoil of the conflicts between civilization and the clash of interests of foreign nationals, it was to be expected that violent criticisms of the missionaries would be voiced. The missionaries fought injustice, arrogance, selfishness, licentiousness, and ambitions directed against Hawaii's independence. This aspect of the mission is described in Judge Walter F. Frear's 'Anti-Missionary Criticism with Reference to Hawaii.' See as well the 2018 greatly expanded and updated Forbes et al., *Partners in Change*. This book is a re-visioning of three previous books that commemorated the Protestant missionaries sent to Hawai'i by the American Board of Commissioners for Foreign Missions." This book "takes a deeper look at the missionaries and their Hawaiian and Tahitian colleagues who worked with them to achieve common goals," xii. "This book also intends to help readers begin to understand missionaries as individuals, rather than combine them into one all-encompassing label as 'the missionaries,'" xiii.

"That the missionaries 'stole the land' is an often-repeated untruth. The record of all their land transactions have been brought together by Miss Jean Hobbs in 'Hawaii, A Pageant of the Soil,' in which any seeker of the truth can read for himself the official documents.

"The story of the mission is one for which no apologia needs be written. The noble men and women who gave their strength, prayers and lives for the gospel in Hawaii, have left their own monument. '*Si monumentum quaeris, circumspice* [If you seek his monument, look around].'" Judd, *Missionary Album*, 5.

29. Many were provided in 1850 by a gentleman recommended by Coan.

30. *Memorial Volume*, 58, has the following under Angeline Loraine Tenney Castle's name: "Watercolor portrait by member of Wilkes's Expedition about 1840." Angeline would die the following year at the age of thirty.

31. Forbes et al., *Partners in Change*.

32. Vilified by many, Hiram Bingham I is caricatured in both the book and movie entitled "Hawaii." In response, Cecil M. Robeck writes the following on the back cover of Corr's published dissertation, "In '*Field Is the World*,' Phil Corr provides a careful historical study of early Congregational missionary life and work in the Hawaiian Islands. It is long overdue as an antidote to many of the spurious claims that Michener made popular in his treatment of early missionaries in Hawaii."

33. Miller, *Fathers and Sons*.

34. Miller, *Selected Writings*.

INTRODUCTION

A similarly excellent work is Clifford Putney's biography of a husband-and-wife team, the Gulicks.[35] This work will be referenced as well.

Both Miller and Gulick provide insight and leads to this author. Ehlke has already been mentioned as the only twentieth-century scholarly work on Coan, along with Daws's and Morris's works that look—either directly or tangentially—at one aspect of Coan's career. Also mentioned has been the author's own chapter on Coan. In the twenty-first century, Alan Tamashiro wrote a Doctor of Ministry dissertation that includes a look at Coan's life, especially his role as a "revival leader."[36]

Titus Coan Primary Source Material

A prolific "pen painter," Titus Coan wrote over his lifetime thousands of pages of material that was either unpublished, printed, or published. His unpublished material is found primarily in two locations: the Library of Congress and the Mission Houses Library. Except for some printed and published material, most of the Library of Congress Titus Coan material is handwritten and either loose[37] or bound with a string.[38] In addition to many letters to and from Titus and Fidelia and family members and friends, Coan's journals are preserved from his Patagonia exploration, the period of the Great Awakening, and his two missionary trips to the Marquesas. All items are in containers, called boxes.

Scholarship has lost most of Coan's handwritten sermon material and all of his lectures. The lectures covered decades, going through every book of the Bible,[39] as well as Roman Catholicism and other subjects.

A Bible verse and a short quotation from the verse are found in Coan's journal covering his early years in Hawai'i. When he first preached in Hawaiian he noted such verses. He preached the first Hawaiian sermon several times, probably due to his not having a full facility and fluency in the language. Not long after that, Coan stopped recording the verses and references.

At the Mission House library, the correspondence has gone through various forms of preservation. Some of the letters were first typed.[40] In the 1930s, the entire collection—over twenty file folders—was microfilmed. By 2015 all of the microfilmed

---

35. Putney, *Missionaries in Hawai'i*.

36. Tamashiro, "Original Monotheism." Pahoa is in the Puna district, which Coan toured and where the Great Awakening broke out.

37. Mostly letters, but also his holographic manuscript of his autobiography in LoC Box 18.

38. Such as journals and "Waymarks."

39. Coan makes reference to completing the Bible lecture series. In one letter he thanks a person for sending him a book on the excavation of Nineveh and how it tied in with a recent lecture.

40. By his children Harriet and Titus Munson?

Coan correspondence was digitized and available for searching online. A few of Lydia's letters reside at the Mission House Library as well.[41]

One important handwritten document found neither at the Library of Congress nor the Mission Houses is Titus Coan's Last Will and Testament. After some sleuthing, the author learned it resides on microfilm at the state archives in Honolulu. See the legacy chapter for the format description, paragraphs, and paragraph analysis.

The Mission House Library also has Coan's two printed items: "A Sailor's Sabbath: or, a word from a friend to seamen" and "The Appropriate Duties of Christian Females, in Public and Social Worship."

An annual printed document prepared by Titus Coan most years from the late 1830s through the 1860s was the Hilo station report. Most of these are available online and digitized at the Mission Houses' web site.[42] The Mission House Library Digital Collection also includes a newspaper and a journal. *The Friend*[43] was begun by Samuel Damon who was in Honolulu as the American Seamen's Friend Society chaplain. He was *The Friend's* editor from 1842 through 1884, as well as the pastor of Bethel Union Church, the Seamen's Chapel.[44] Coan published reports and letters and was reported about in *The Friend*.

Similarly, letters and reports by Coan are published in the American Board's journal, *The Missionary Herald*.[45] The Library of Congress has articles by and about Coan from *The Missionary Herald* and other publications.[46]

In the "Peace Man" chapter, it is noted that over twenty letters by Coan appeared in *The Advocate of Peace* and related journals. As a scientific Renaissance man, articles by Coan appeared in *The Journal of American Science*.

In the last years of his life, Titus Coan published two books. Within two years of his death, Lydia published a book with more primary material, mostly by Titus. He first published *Adventures in Patagonia: A Missionary's Exploring Trip*.[47] In the Patagonia chapter the transcribed original journal from the Library of Congress is compared with the published version of the journal found in the first thirteen chapters of the book. The remaining four chapters pass along the writings by other people on Patagonia, as well as an update on missions to Patagonia almost fifty years later.

---

41. More letters written by Lydia are found at the Bingham Papers in the Yale University Manuscript Collection.

42. http://74.50.122.17:8282/Greenstone/cgi-bin/library.cgi?site=localhost&a=p&p=about&c=missions&l=en&w=utf-8.

43. HMH, http://server.honstudios.com/mhm-friend/cgi-bin/mhm-friend.

44. Judd, *Missionary Album*, 76–77. See also Forbes, *Partners*, 206–12.

45 HMH, http://74.50.122.17:8282/Greenstone/cgi-bin/library.cgi?e=d-01000-00--off-omission1-00-1--0-10-0--0--0direct-10--4----0-1l-11-en-50--20-about--00-3-1-00-0-4-0-0-0-11-10-0utfZz-8-00&a=d&c=mission1&cl=CL2&d=HASH01f83cb4cd24c052420b3bb8.

46. LOC.

47. Coan, *Patagonia*.

INTRODUCTION

Coan was so encouraged by the response to *Patagonia* that at the age of eighty he wrote his autobiography. *Life* travelled a long history: from jotting down reminders in the string-bound "Waymarks";[48] to handwriting the draft;[49] to Munson proofing the work;[50] to the first edition; to Ed Coan and Mark Levin of the USGS making it available and searchable online during the second half of the 1990s; to Beryl K. B. Walter's paperback reprint in approximately 2000; to being available as print-on-demand; to Paul Rapoza's online version.

Lydia compiled and did some writing for the vital complementary work to the autobiography: what is called *The Memorial Volume* as shorthand.[51] She writes very important bridge passages that provide further invaluable information. It consists primarily of a representation of Titus's correspondence and journals.[52] There is much retrospective and laudatory material by others from the March 1883 memorial service at the Hilo church.

Sarah Lyman was still living in Hilo at the time. Her journal and letters provide another primary source.[53] Her writings are representative of many missionaries and others. A distant relative of David Lyman—C. S. Lyman—wrote a book that qualifies as both a primary and secondary source. Within years of the conclusion of the Great Awakening, Lyman accompanied Coan on a Puna tour, visited a volcano, and came to Coan's defense on the matter of Captain Wilkes and the *Vincennes* Exploratory Expedition and its affect on the Hawaiian people and the Great Awakening. He both participates and observes.[54] It is a book that can be enjoyed by the general reader and scholar alike.[55] With that, we come to:

WHAT THE TWO AUDIENCES HAVE IN COMMON

Access to the Internet and Digitization

Paul Rapoza provides a bridge between general readers and scholars by his website, which includes many reworked and digitally available nineteenth-century Hawaiian missionary works. He wrote the following to the author in late 2014: "One of the

48. LOC.

49. LOC.

50. Including three reference to his mother in the index, but not a single one to his stepmother, although she is mentioned at least twice.

51. Lydia Coan, *Memorial Volume*.

52. The journal entries are mostly from his two mission trips to the Marquesas Islands.

53. Martin et al., *The Lymans of Hilo*.

54. Lyman, *Around the Horn*.

55. See also two documentaries that came out in 2020, the two hundredth anniversary of the arrival of the ABCFM Pioneer (or first) Company to the Sandwich Islands. Kawaiahaʻo Church in Honolulu produced *A Witness to Aloha*, which weaves together the ABCFM missionaries, the life of that church, and Hawaiian Christians, including ʻŌpūkahaʻia. See also Michael Lienau's documentary on ʻŌpūkahaʻia.

things that grew on me was the sense that *Life in Hawaii* and *Titus Coan—A Memorial* were two companion editions. That they are as inseparable as Titus and Lydia were in marriage. Both birthed out of the same mutual heart and effort. Since Lydia worked alongside him on *Life* she was uniquely qualified knowledge-wise and spiritually to write *Memorial*. She was already the most familiar with all that material and of course with Titus.

"That kept growing on me, and although I resisted it for some time I found myself gravitating towards *Memorial* as well. With some assurance from Cornell University Library's statements, I was able to take the rough OCR text and work on repairing it to match a scan copy I have of the book from the same source. Ended up formatting it for the web as well and although I haven't done much on that second site beyond corrections to the text it is standing there. No quotes, links, or info but just the contents of the book in web version."[56] Since then, as has been noted, he has expanded far beyond those two works.

The Future

The two kinds of readers are united by the future, because that is when they will read this work.[57] Whatever the reason for reading this book, it is hoped that general readers will be inspired and scholars will be assisted in their research.

Now that the two hundredth anniversary of the arrival of the 1820 Pioneer Company has passed, it is hoped that a look to the past of the vibrant life of Titus Coan will help inform the future.

Interest in Titus Coan

Whichever kind of reader you are on whatever level, you are reading this because of your interest in the missionary to Hawai'i. May your interest deepen and your insight increase as you continue on the journey of his life, seeing that Titus Coan was an "Apostle to the Sandwich Islands."[58]

---

56. Paul Rapoza, email to author, December 2, 2014.
57. Though you are in the present if you are reading this right now!
58. *New York Times*, January 4[?], 1883.

1

Early years

"I was born on the first day of February, Sunday morning, 1801, in the town of Killingworth, Connecticut. My physical constitution was good, my health was perfect, and my childhood happy."[1]

"Not satisfied with my knowledge of English grammar derived from Murray and unskilled teachers, I had private lessons from a teacher fresh from a grammar school[2] in the city of New York, and under his instructions gained a more satisfactory insight into the construction of my mother tongue than from all my winter's study in what seemed to me dry Murray."[3]

"Let me tell you then, that it is but a little time since I found my sins an oppressive load. My Saviour hid his face [Isa 59:2][4] for a moment. I sought him at twilight [Song 5:6], at midnight, I inquired of the watchman [Song 5:7]. I wandered over the field of truth. I looked, I listened, I fainted, My Beloved spake [Song 2:10], my soul melted, I caught him, and held him by his feet, and bathed them with my tears [Luke 7:38, 44]. I would not let him go till [Gen 32:26] he pardoned and smiled. 'Twas a sweet hour. My heart often softens at the recollection. Do you ask where I found him? I will tell you. It was in Jeremiah, 3:19.[5] At first his voice was indistinct, but it arrested my attention.

---

1. Coan, *Life*, 2.

2. The original, medieval grammar schools taught Latin. Greek and Hebrew were eventually added. "In 1755 Samuel Johnson's *Dictionary* defined a grammar school as *a school in which the learned languages are grammatically taught*; However, by this time demand for these languages had fallen greatly. A new commercial class required modern languages and commercial subjects." Wikipedia, "Grammar School."

3. Coan, *Life*, 5.

4. "But your iniquities have separated between you and your God, and your sins have hid his face from you."

5. "But I said, 'How shall I put thee among the children, and give thee a pleasant land, a goodly heritage of the hosts of nations?' and I said, 'Thou shalt call me, My father; and shalt not turn away from me.'"

I listened and he spake again. Is this, said I, the voice of My Father? Again the notes became more distinct, and tender and earnest. [H]e was inquiring how he should 'put me among his children.' He stated the condition, 'Thou shalt call me, My Father, and shalt not turn away from me.' My heart responded, My Father, My Father, thou art the guide of my youth [Jer 3:4]. I have read these words before, but I never 'found and ate them' [Ezek 3:3; Rev 10:9] with such relish as now. The condition,—Thou shalt not turn away from me, seemed equally precious as the privilege of adoption [Rom 8:15] I thought I made, or renewed, an unreserved, unconditional, cheerful, eternal surrender of myself to God."[6]

INTRODUCTION

In her *Memorial Volume*, Lydia Bingham Coan writes the following about Titus's brief description of his first thirty-one years in his autobiography. "Through all this history the reader is hurried forward over sixteen short pages,[7] as if the narrator were eager to enter upon the main business of his life, his earnest work on a mid-ocean isle."[8]

Lydia devotes nine pages[9] to this first period of Titus's life. Yet, she relates that "the experiences of those earlier years were of untold value to the future. He was never to lose through life the influence of his childhood, which passed in a home so beautifully ordered by pious parents that obedience, truthfulness, and filial and fraternal affection were the characteristics of the eight children reared there.

"His vigorous youthful sports, and the severer toils upon his father's farm, developed and strengthened his sturdy frame." That would certainly prepare him for rigorous travel throughout his parish on the Big Island of Hawai'i. "Military drill in the militia ranks[10] of the state confirmed his natural promptness and precision,[11] while self-reliance and quiet dignity were the outgrowth of responsibilities early assumed at the teacher's desk of the village school."[12]

Titus would eventually travel to Upstate New York where he taught. As he rode by another school house one day, he would espy another teacher through a window.

---

6. Titus Coan to Fidelia Church, December 22, 1832, HMH, in Ehlke, "Enthusiastic Religion," 46–47.

7. Out of 340, including index.

8. Coan, *Memorial Volume*, 1.

9. Out of 248. Ehlke devotes thirty-two pages out of 298 (including endnotes and bibliography) to these years of Coan's life.

10. He would later forswear his military involvement as he became a partial (He favored the Union fight in what he called "the War of Rebellion") pacifist and complete "peace man" (see chapter by that title).

11. See his precision in keeping a pocket book that kept track of the progress of possible candidates for baptism and church membership during the Hawaiian Great Awakening.

12. Coan, *Memorial Volume*, 2–3.

He would write that he beheld "the face of an angel" and would call her his "angel" throughout their life together and even after her death in 1872.

Together they would participate in the Second Great Awakening in Upstate New York. Influenced somewhat by his maternal cousin, Asahel Nettleton,[13] they would be most affected by the attorney-turned-evangelist Charles Grandison Finney. In 1871, Titus would co-officiate a Communion service[14] with Finney at Oberlin College, where Finney was President Emeritus.[15] Fidelia and Titus would join Auburn Presbyterian church. Titus would enroll in Auburn seminary, resolved to become a missionary. While at Auburn Seminary, the American Board of Commissioners would invite him to join William Arms to go on a scouting mission to Patagonia. This adventure would become the next chapter in his life.

GROWING UP

Titus devotes the first paragraph of the first chapter of his autobiography to his father, "Gaylord Coan, of Killingworth, Middlesex Co., Connecticut."[16] The son describes his father as a God-fearing man, who lived his life based on Christian principles. One can see much of the father in the son. "He was a thoughtful, quiet, and modest farmer, industrious, frugal, and temperate, attending to his own business, living in peace with his neighbors, eschewing evil, honest in dealing, avoiding debts, abhorring extravagance and profligacy, refusing proffered offices, strictly observing the Sabbath, a regular attendant on the services of the sanctuary, a constant reader of the Bible, and always offering morning and evening prayers with the family. He was born August 4, 1768, and died September 24, 1857, in his ninetieth year."[17]

He devotes a paragraph to the life of the mother in which he reveals that Titus was the youngest of seven children. "My mother was Tamza Nettleton, sister of Josiah Nettleton and aunt of Asahel Nettleton, DD, the distinguished Evangelical preacher. She was the tender, faithful, and laborious mother of seven children, six sons and one daughter. Of these I was the youngest."[18]

In the next paragraph he relates the death of his mother and the ramifications of that tragic, though not uncommon in those days, event. "While still in the vigor of

13. 1783–1840.

14. At an annual meeting of the Ohio Congregational churches.

15. A third man would help lead this service—a pastor from Texas.

16. Coan, *Life*, 1. For more on Gaylord Coan and his descendants, see Fulton, *Coan Genealogy, 1697–1982*. The partial online copy shows a copyright date of 1983. Mrs. Fulton donated the copy to the Utah Genealogical Society. A filled-out permission form to microfilm by the Society is dated February 13, 1984, with an indication that "errata" would be provided in 1984. Part Three is entitled "George Coan and Descendants." Chapter 7 is the first of two chapters in that part and is entitled "The George, Mulford, Gaylord Line." That chapter runs from page 327–86.

17. Coan, *Life*, 1.

18. Coan, *Life*, 1.

womanhood, she was cut down January 14, 1818, by typhus fever, aged fifty-eight. Her death left the house desolate, and the loss was deeply mourned by all the children,"[19] even though all but Titus were eighteen or older.

Titus Coan was born February 1, 1801, one month and three days before Thomas Jefferson was inaugurated the first time.[20] Originally named Hammonasset, Killingworth is nineteen[21] to twenty-seven[22] miles from New Haven, where Yale College and Divinity School were located.[23] It is five to seven miles from the Atlantic coast. In 1820, the census showed 2,342 residents. By 1850 it had dropped to 1,107. When Titus visited there in late 1870, there were approximately 856 residents.[24]

As for his first eight years of formal education, he would attend a one-room schoolhouse. "From the age of four to twelve I was sent to the district school, where the boys and girls were drilled in Webster's spelling book[25], The American Preceptor, writing, arithmetic (Daball's), Morse's geography,[26] Murray's grammar, and the Westminster Shorter Catechism."[27]

Lindley Murray lived from 1745 until 1826. A grammarian and textbook author, Murray was an American Quaker. Young Titus Coan probably used an edition published later than the original 1795 *English Grammar Adapted to the Different Classes of Learners. With an Appendix, Containing Rules and Observations, for Assisting the More Advanced Students to Write with Perspicuity and Accuracy.*[28] The Westminster Shorter

---

19. Coan, *Life*, 2. Titus notes that after "this our father married Miss Platt, of Saybrook, by whom he had one daughter, who died at the age of eighteen."

20. Titus died almost eight months after the inauguration of James A. Garfield; and less than three months after Chester A. Arthur became President.

21. As the crow flies.

22. By road.

23. The Killingworth area was the first location of Yale College and Divinity School. "In the late seventeenth century, Killingworth became the birthplace of what would eventually become Yale University. The Rev. Abraham Pierson, the college's first president, taught some of the first classes in his Killingworth home - which is actually in present-day Clinton, Connecticut." Wikipedia, "Killingworth, Connecticut."

24. Wikipedia, "Killingworth, Connecticut."

25. Noah Webster first published his "Blue-Backed Speller" in 1783. Wikipedia, "Noah Webster." =

26. Jedidiah Morse, whose son Samuel would invent the telegraph, "strongly influenced the educational system of the United States. While teaching at a school for young women, he saw the need for a geography textbook oriented to the forming nation. The result was skimpy and derivative, *Geography Made Easy* (1784). He followed that with *American Geography* (1789), which was widely cited and copied. New editions of his school textbooks and the more weighty works often came out annually, earning him the informal title, 'father of American geography.' His postponed gazetteer for his work of 1784 was bested by Joseph Scott's *Gazetteer of the United States* in 1795. With the aid of Noah Webster and Rev. Samuel Austin, Morse published his gazetteer as *Universal Geography of the United States* (1797)." Wikipedia, "Jedidiah Morse."

27. Coan, *Life*, 2.

28. Wikipedia, "Lindley Murray."

Catechism is a Presbyterian faith document. Coan was a lifelong Presbyterian who served in a predominantly Congregational mission organization.

Ehlke paraphrases Coan's decades-later reflections on the then-shuttered school house. "Titus attended a district school in a typical rural schoolhouse with a warm fire in the broad fireplace and benches made of slabs of lumber, with the 'round side down' and no backs."[29] He characterized his childhood as a happy one. 'Days and weeks and years went quietly along, with the usual experiences of joyous childhood spring, summer, autumn, and winter each had their peculiar charms, their duties and diversions, and I moved along the stream with only now and then a ripple.'[30]

Discontented with the Murray grammar and unskilled teachers, at age thirteen he retained a well-educated tutor. Coan relates it in this way: "Not satisfied with my knowledge of English grammar derived from Murray and unskilled teachers, I had private lessons from a teacher fresh from a grammar school in the city of New York, and under his instructions gained a more satisfactory insight into the construction of my mother tongue than from all my winter's study in what seemed to me dry[31] Murray."[32] This study would contribute greatly to Coan being dubbed a "pen painter."

Coan already evinced a life-long habit of reading widely and deeply, which would put him in good stead with fellow missionaries, educated sea captains, government officials, and others. He also indirectly recognized the accelerating number of publications between his teen years and the conclusion of his eighth decade. "I also read eagerly such worthy books as I was able to buy or borrow; few indeed, compared with the overwhelming flood of literature of the present time. I read history, rhetoric, astronomy, philosophy, logic, and the standard poets."

Reflecting his nature as a Renaissance man,[33] Coan also attended a school near the Atlantic coast, not far from Killingworth. Most, if not all, subjects would stand him in good stead in Hawai'i. "I joined an Academy in East Guilford, now Madison, where I studied with delight geometry, trigonometry, surveying, etc., under the instruction of the Principal, an active graduate of Yale College."[34]

TEACHING AND FIDELIA

Having been prepared by formal education, tutoring, and broad reading, Titus writes that at "the age of eighteen I was called to teach a school in the town of Saybrook, and from this time onward my winters were occupied in teaching in Saybrook,

---

29. Ehlke, "Enthusiastic Religion," 35, summarizing Coan, *Life*, 219.
30. Coan, *Life*, 2.
31. In all subjects Coan and others were "drilled" in the district school.
32. Coan, *Life*, 5.
33. See three chapter section by that title.
34. Coan, *Life*, 5–6.

Killingworth, and Guilford, until I left New England for Western New York."[35] Coan relates his service in the militia, which will be examined in the "Peace Man" chapter.

Months before he turned twenty-five, Titus first beheld Fidelia. "During this summer of 1826 I often rode by a school-house in a western district of Riga, and through the windows I saw a face that beamed on me like that of an angel. The image was deeply impressed, and is still ineffaceable." Eight years after her death, Fidelia's face is still vivid to Titus.

Taking the initiative, Titus found out the name that went with the face. "On inquiry, the young lady proved to be Miss Fidelia Church of Churchville. I often saw her sunlit face in the choir on the Sabbath, for she was a sweet singer, but I did not make her acquaintance for many months."[36] Was he shy?

As with Titus Coan's extended a family, there is a book on Fidelia Church's family.[37] Ehlke draws from that book to provide background on Fidelia. "Fidelia Church's family were pioneers in western New York. Her father, Samuel Church, came from Berkshire, Massachusetts, in 1805, to explore the densely wooded tract of West Pultney, later Riga, with his brother Elihu, who had emigrated to New York in 1796. The founder of Churchville, Samuel Church is remembered as 'a man of ceaseless activity, resourceful, skillful with tools; a man's man on the frontier.'"[38]

Ehlke continues to summarize the life of Fidelia's father.[39] "A farmer as well as a millwright, Church built the first sawmill in Churchville in 1808, and a grist mill in 1811. Commissioned as a captain in the first militia company organized in Riga, Church participated in the frontier war at Lake Erie during the War of 1812."

Ehlke relates Samuel Church's church involvement, including a further change a few years after Titus and Fidelia met. Samuel "was a trustee of the First Congregational Society of West Pultney around 1809–10. Dissolved under the Plan of Union several years later, the Society was reoganzied under the Presbytery of Ontario and later transferred to the Presbytery of Rochester. After a religious revival in Riga in 1831, Church joined the Methodist Episcopal Church, which later ordained his two sons."[40]

Ehlke next writes about Fidelia's mother and children. "Fidelia's mother, Abigail (Munson) Church, at age thirty-five, had moved to western New York with her husband, four daughters, and a son, ages thirteen to three. Three more children were born to the Church family, Maria—the first white child born in Riga—Fidelia, and Jared. Fidelia was born on February 17, 1810. She and Maria were close companions, sharing the experience of going away to school in Candaigua, New York. Fidelia's desire

---

35. Coan, *Life*, 6.
36. Coan, *Life*, 9.
37. Ettta A. Emens, comp., *Descendants*.
38. Emens, *Descendants*, 27, in Ehlke, "Enthusiastic Religion," 38.
39. Paraphrasing Emens without attribution?
40. Ehlke, "Enthusiastic Religion," 38–39.

to learn set her apart from her companions at the Ontario Female Seminary. Her classmate, Sophia T. Johns, wrote: 'I suppose your school days are over. This must be a melancholy reflection to you.'"[41]

Ehlke notes that "Fidelia's educational ambitions led her to continue her studies while teaching in neighboring towns, and her letters to Titus Coan contain many requests for guidance in selecting evangelical reading material."[42] In addition to physical attraction, Fidelia and Titus were compatible in the important area of intellectual curiosity and pursuits.

One year after Titus noticed Fidelia and began attending her church, Titus opened a "select-school" in Riga and Fidelia "applied for admission." Coan writes in his autobiography: "In this I rejoiced greatly, for it gave me a good opportunity to mark the character of her mind, which proved bright and receptive, and to become acquainted with her moral and social characteristics."[43]

Coan reaches the point where four possible vocational ways are open to him. "I had not chosen my life-work. Four paths lay before me. My brother wished me to become his partner in the mercantile business. A good physician in Rochester, and several in other places, advised me to become a physician, offering to teach me free of charge. Some said I was made for a school teacher, and many clergymen and Christian laymen urged me to go into the gospel ministry."

Lydia Coan decades later addressed herself to Titus's ethical business talents. For "such a career, doubtless, his talents fitted him. His perfect integrity, his abhorrence of debt, which led to an early formed and conscientiously practiced rule of his life, never to owe a farthing which he had not means to pay, his sound judgment, unflagging energy and uniform urbanity of manner, would have secured for him a leading place in business circles, and guaranteed pecuniary success."[44]

Coan's business acumen would stand him in good stead during his decades in Hilo; and continue to bless others long after his death with the Hawaiian Evangelical Association Titus Coan Fund. His medical knack, along with some basic training, would assist Hawaiians for fourteen years until the arrival of Dr. Wetmore. As far as teaching, pastors are called to be "pastor-teachers," "equipping the saints for ministry" [Eph 4:12]. And his gospel ministry abilities became well known.

He asks himself profound questions and shares his internal dialogue. "What should I do? What could I do? The subject pressed heavily upon my mind and heart. I said that teaching is pleasant in youth, but for *life* it would not satisfy me. As for the medical profession, I was not adapted to it, and I dared not make the trial. But how of the sacred ministry? I felt utterly unfit and unworthy—my natural talent, education,

---

41. Sophia T. Johns to Fidelia Church, September 12, 1828, LOC, in Ehlke, "Enthusiastic Religion," 39.

42. Ehlke, "Enthusiastic Religion," 39.

43. Coan, *Life*, 9.

44. Coan, *Memorial Volume*, 3.

piety, were all unequal to the exalted calling. As Moses [Exod 3], Isaiah [6:1–13], and Jeremiah [1:4–10] shrank from the offices of legislator and prophet, so I from being an ambassador of Christ, yet I was willing to work hard as a layman, and even longed to go as a servant among the heathen, to help the honored missionaries. Thus my spirit labored under a burden which none but God knew, and to find relief, I decided to be an active and devoted layman; to return to Connecticut, finish up my business there, and then settle down to a mercantile life in Medina."[45]

"ETERNAL SURRENDER" AND AUBURN SEMINARY

Ehlke picks up the story. "At age twenty-eight, Titus Coan still had not decided on his life's work. In April 1829, Coan set out with his friend, the Rev. H[erman] Halsey,[46] to attend a meeting of the General Assembly of the Presbyterian Church in Philadelphia. On the canal boat from Rochester, Coan began to shake, his temperature shot up and, by the time they reached Syracuse, chills had overtaken him.[47] At Albany, he reluctantly agreed to leave the party and go to Madison, Connecticut, where he had friends who could care for him."[48]

Ehlke continues her build up to the major spiritual experience of Coan's life. "By fall the disease which had disrupted his journey abated sufficiently to allow to return to his father's house in Killingworth. He had regained his strength sufficiently by October to allow him to take over the district school at Killingworth for the winter. During that winter a revival of religion in the town and in his school brought Titus to place his future in God's hands."[49]

In a letter at a later time, "he described his emotional turmoil as he wrestled with the decision to become a minister." He wrote about it to Fidelia more than three years later. It is quoted from Ehlke at the beginning of this chapter. Drawing from Isaiah, the Song of Solomon, Luke, Genesis, Jeremiah, Ezekiel, and Romans, he concludes, "'I thought I made, or renewed, an unreserved, unconditional, cheerful, eternal surrender of myself to God.'"[50]

45. Coan, *Life*, 11–12.
46. With whom Coan will correspondence throughout their lives.
47. What Coan calls "ague," *Life*, 12.
48. Coan, *Life*, 12, in Ehlke, "Enthusiastic Religion," 46.
49. Ehlke, "Enthusiastic Religion," 46.
50. Titus Coan to Fidelia Church, December 22, 1832, HMCS, in Ehlke, "Enthusiastic Religion," 46–47. "With this first reference to Titus's letters, here is a note on the kind of ink he probably used for the many letters during his life time. The rust brown color of his letters indicate he used iron gall ink." On xxii of George Q. Cannon's Hawaiian *Journals*, editor Chad Orton writes: "The majority of Cannon's Hawaiian mission journal entries were written in iron gall ink, the most common ink of the day. Initially almost colorless, iron gall ink becomes deep brown, almost black, in color when exposed to air. However, because the formulation of ink was often not scientific, the composition of the same type of ink varied from batch to batch. Over time the ink used by Cannon oxidized to various shades of brown, depending upon the composition of the batch he used." Wikipedia, "Iron Gall Ink," defines

Titus Coan is not sure whether he has previously surrendered his life to Christ before. He was raised in a pious Christian home. He has increased his involvement in church. But this spiritual event is the watershed of his life. Before this event, he was not sure what his life's work would be. After this event he decided to enroll at Auburn seminary. Not long after that he would determine to be a missionary and be in contact with the American Board.

Lydia Coan puts it this way. "Thoughtful and sober as he had been for years, he had as yet come to no fixed determination to enlist on the Lord's side. When at last this resolve was made, it was one, he says, in which he was greatly helped, comforted, and established, so that duty done for Christ was a sweet and joyous pleasure."[51]

Titus received wise counsel, being encouraged to do some preparatory study before matriculating at Auburn Seminary. "Returning to western New York, Coan consulted with his friends, who advised him to take a short preparatory course before entering the Theological Seminary at Auburn, New York. The Rev. Lewis Cheeseman, pastor at Byron, invited Titus to study and assist him in revivals. In January Titus Coan went to Knolesville to study with the Rev. David Page and assist him in revivals."[52]

Titus explained "his move to his brother George: 'Mr. Page, who is preaching there, and the brethren of the church urge me very strictly to abide with them, and pursue my studies; they offer me room, my board, etc. I think I shall spend a few months there, at least. Brother Page I find to be a good classical scholar, and think he will teach me as well probably as any one. I am still reading Greek. In respect to my future plans I am not entirely decided: my prevailing impression however is that I shall enter Auburn Seminary next summer or fall. A brother of Mr. Mead is now here from that institution; he says that a great many of the students there are not graduates, and that if I can only read the Greek Testament, they will receive me with my present attainments in other things.'"[53]

Ehlke relates Coan's efforts at study and ministry, as well as his enrollment at Auburn. "He spent the winter and spring there, conducting evening meetings, leading the Sunday school and continuing his classical studies. Titus thought himself ill-prepared in Latin and Greek, reporting, 'I know nothing of Latin, and hardly anything of Greek.'"[54] "Despite these scholastic deficiencies, Titus Coan entered the Theological Seminary at Auburn, New York, in June 1831 to prepare for the ministry."[55]

---

it as follows: "Iron gall ink (also known as iron gall nut ink, oak gall ink, and common ink) is a purple-black or brown-black ink made from iron salts and tannic acids from vegetable sources. It was the standard writing and drawing ink in Europe from about the fifth century to the nineteenth century, and remained in use well into the twentieth century." The article provides other information, such as preparation and use, chemistry, history, and other areas.

51. Coan, *Memorial Volume*, 2.
52. Ehlke, "Enthusiastic Religion," 47.
53. Titus Coan to George Coan, March 31, 1831, HMH, in Ehlke, "Enthusiastic Religion," 47.
54. Ehlke, "Enthusiastic Religion," 47–48.
55. Ehlke, "Enthusiastic Religion," 48.

Auburn Seminary took a middle way: between Presbyterian seminaries such as Princeton that were uncomfortable with some of the expressions of the Second Great Awakening[56] and "'revivalistic training schools [that] sprang up at Troy, Whitesboro, and Rochester.'"[57]

Ehlke relates Coan's thinking that led him to enroll at Auburn. "He had written his brother George of this decision in March: 'My mind has been nearly established to go to Auburn for some time, but I don't think it will be best for me to take a full course there, as much of the time is spent in the study of Hebrew. This knowledge I want, but to obtain it, you know I must neglect other studies more essential to my usefulness. I therefore think of trying to enter the Seminary at the commencement of the second term, which will be on the twenty-fifth of May, when they come more directly on the study of theology.'"[58]

Lydia Coan writes that in "June 1831 he entered the middle class of Auburn Theological Seminary. He is remembered by those who knew him there as 'unostentatious, devoutly pious, and possessed of a very sweet spirit.'"[59] She relates an extended remembrance by Rev. Newton Reed, who was one of Titus's fellow students. "'My memory is full of pleasant recollections of Mr. Coan. When I returned to the Seminary in 1832, I found him the superintendent of the Prison Sunday School, a position that must have been conceded to him spontaneously. I immediately became acquainted with him, and had many occasions to know the value of his wise counsel and his tender sympathy."

Foreshadowing Coan's middle way in the Hawaiian Great Awakening, despite the accusations of some, Reed writes of Titus's temperance regarding the excesses of a revival at a local church. "There was a revival in the First Church that winter, under the ministry of the Evangelist, Burchard,[60] attended with great extravagance, and some of the students as well as the citizens lost their discretion. Mr. Coan attended the meetings with the others, but without being critical or captious, or in opposition to a work which seemed to some a marvel of grace, he was very useful to many. Dr. Richards himself could hardly have taken a wiser course."[61]

56. Especially relating to Finney and Upstate New York.
57. Cross, *The Burned-over District*, 156, in Ehlke, "Enthusiastic Religion," 50.
58. Titus Coan to George Coan, March 31, 1831, in Ehlke, "Enthusiastic Religion," 50.
59. Uncited in Coan, *Memorial Volume*, 3.
60. Is this he? Or too young to have led revival in 1832? Samuel Dickerson Burchard (September 6, 1812—September 25, 1891) was a nineteenth-century Presbyterian minister from New York. Born in Steuben, New York, Burchard moved to Kentucky with his parents in 1830, attended Centre College, and graduated in 1837. He was licensed to preach in 1838. He was pastor of several Presbyterian churches in New York City. Burchard was chancellor of the Ingham University, and president of Rutgers female college. He died at Saratoga, New York. Burchard originated the phrase, "Rum, Romanism, and Rebellion" and applied it to the Democratic Party near the end of the Blaine-Cleveland campaign in the United States presidential election, 1884. The phrase was said to have cost Blaine the presidency. See Rossiter, *The Twentieth-Century Biographical Dictionary*. Also Wikipedia, "Samuel D. Burchard."
61. Coan *Memorial Volume*, 4–5.

Rev. Newton writes of Titus's Renaissance man nature. "'The great beauty of Mr. Coan's character was in its symmetry. He was all over alike, not greatly above his fellows in any one thing, but in the combination, physical, intellectual and emotional, and even in the imagination, he was head and shoulders above them.

"The first constituent of his character was remarkable common sense, and the completeness of it was his intelligent piety, his faith. In all the men I have ever met I don't think I have known one so well proportioned.'"[62]

Ehlke relates that the "subjects listed for the middle class when Coan entered included: Didactical Theology, Biblical Antiquities, Canon of Scripture, Principles of Interpretation, Hebrew, and Critical Reading of the New Testament continued from the first year."[63] So Coan began in the second year of a three-year program, based on his preparation for starting seminary.

As much as Titus the student wanted to study Hebrew, he was aware of a time consideration before being deployed as a missionary. Being a doer, a man of action, he wanted to take those courses which most prepared him for a life of ministry.

Ehlke writes about the third-year courses. Students "took Polemick[64] and Pastoral Theology, including the Composition of Sermons, Ecclesiastical History, Church Government, and more of the Principles of Interpretation. Speaking and Composition were studied throughout the course."[65]

Ehlke provides the names of the Auburn professors while he was a student there. "When Coan studied there, Dr. James Richards was superintendent of the Theological Department; Dr. Matthew LaRue Perrine was in charge of the Ecclesiastical Department; and Dr. Henry Mills taught Sacred Literature. Dr. Richards, a moderate Edwardsean, was tolerant of minor 'doctrinal innovations' but found himself at odds with the New Measures of Charles G. Finney.[66] Dr. Perrine was an avowed Hopkinsian[67] who had been involved in the early nineteenth-century controversy in the Presbyterian Church when Hopkinsianism was deemed a heresy by many Presbyterians."[68]

Coan emphasizes and takes the lead in prayer while at Auburn. "Coan found his niche in the Seminary as 'The brethren at the seminary are generally lovely men, and seem to live in perfect harmony and to love each other with pure hearts fervently. I find some of them very devoted and prayerful . . . I have taken a catalogue of the brethren in the seminary and commenced presenting them individually to God in my closet, and I find it has a most happy effect on my mind . . . I suggested this course to

---

62. Coan, *Memorial Volume*, 5.
63. Ehlke, "Enthusiastic Religion," 51.
64. Now known as "Polemics," having to do with "the refutation of errors." Freedictionary.com, "Polemics." This would assist Coan in his efforts against polytheists, Catholics, Mormons, and others.
65. Ehlke, "Enthusiastic Religion," 51.
66. Plumley, *Presbyterian Church*, 373, in Ehlke, "Enthusiastic Religion," 52.
67. Samuel Hopkins was a protégé of Jonathan Edwards.
68. Ehlke, "Enthusiastic Religion," 52.

the brothers at a prayer meeting, and it seemed to excite one cordial and simultaneous echo.'"[69]

Returning to the theme of Coan being a doer, Ehlke unearths a letter wherein Titus expresses his frustration with his coursework. He would later proclaim that the Bible was the creed of the church in Hilo. "'After examining the various and contending theories, the magisterial dogmas, the abstruse and subtle disquisitions, the vain and unsatisfying speculations, and grave and confident conclusions . . . of numerous theological disputants, I gain relief from their perplexing speculations by taking my precious Bible, and stealing away to the feet of Jesus [Luke 10:38–42][70].'"[71]

Lydia provides more of Titus's letter to his brother George. "I am pent up here amid the venerable lore of ages, and hurried from field to field of metaphysical, ethical, and theological research . . . [Jesus] has told me, when I want anything, to ask him, and his promise never fails, he never upbraids. He does not, indeed, answer all my irreverent inquiries, but he teaches me not to dive beyond my depth, nor soar amid brightness too dazzling. Here I learn that I cannot trace the mysterious phenomena of my own mind, then why should I think to find out the Almighty to perfection? Thus I can run to my Bible, and when the billows begin to beat around me, I can lay my hand upon that and find it *'Rock,'* and thus with Jesus for my teacher, I can sit and quiet myself as a weaned child [Ps 132:2].'"[72]

While a student, Titus continues to express his passion for the salvation of men's souls, to "do the work of an evangelist" [2 Tim 4:5]. He never waited to go to the mission field to reach out to others. It was a big part of who he was. He became the Sunday School Superintendent to the prison in Auburn. "'O Fidelia,' he wrote, 'I love to go unto that prison because Jesus loves to go there.'"[73] And it was also successful, as he told his father, 'Out of 200 scholars, more than 130 profess to hope they have passed from death to life and many of them give very pleasing evidence of a saving change.'"[74]

Reverend Newton writes of Coan's leadership in the prison. "'In the prison school he became acquainted, through the teachers and by his own personal enquiries, with the religious condition of the prisoners. Those whose time was about to expire were invited to come to his room, when released, and he would give them advice and encouragement which was suited to their case. He was very discerning of their true character, and was led to a reasonable hope in the conversion of some.'"[75]

---

69. Titus Coan to Fidelia Church, June 23, 1831, HMCS, in Ehlke, "Enthusiastic Religion," 53.

70. Jesus tells Martha that her sister, Mary, has "chosen the better part," namely sitting at the feet of Jesus and learning from him.

71. Titus Coan to George Coan, March 21, 1832, HMCS, in Ehlke, "Enthusiastic Religion," 53.

72. Titus Coan to George Coan, March [21], 1832, in Coan, *Memorial Volume*, 6.

73. Titus Coan to Fidelia Church, February 2, 1832, HMH, in Ehlke, "Enthusiastic Religion," 54.

74. Titus Coan to father, May 18, 1833, LOC, in Ehlke, "Enthusiastic Religion," 54.

75. Coan, *Memorial Volume*, 4.

At this point in Reverend Newton's narrative, Lydia Coan provides a footnote, which might be based on personal conversation with Titus Coan. "A discharged prisoner, who professed to be converted, came to his room, and they had a prayer together. When the prisoner prayed, he said 'I' instead of 'We.' 'That is an evidence,' said Coan, 'that he has been accustomed to pray in his cell.'"[76]

He writes to Fidelia about his prison ministry. "'I have now another class in the Prison. Most of them I hope are converted. ''Tis truly affecting to hear some of them confess their former sins and with bursting hearts tell of the love of Jesus. I love to go into that prison because Jesus loves to go there. I often feel as if I wanted to wash the feet of those who are Christ's free men there, for it seems as if my Master would do it. Jesus visits their dungeon, lights up their dark cells, communes with them at midnight and converts their dreary mansion into a sanctuary of their souls.'"[77]

Coan yearned to see everyone become a Christian in Upstate New York. Ehlke writes about Titus and Fidelia participating in revivals.[78] Their involvement would inform their leadership in the Hawaiian Great Awakening. "The Rev. Charles G. Finney came to Rochester, New York, in September 1830 and preached for six months in the Presbyterian churches of that city. His revivals coincided with Titus Coan's work with the Rev. Lewis Cheeseman in Byron."[79]

"Titus wrote his brother George of the revivals: 'The revival in Byron moves on as usual—Brother Cheeseman remains there yet. Revivals are bursting forth on every hand in this region and throughout the State, and in fact all over our land. It is truly a day of wonders. The sound of Jehovah's footsteps is heard moving onward in majesty before his sacramental hosts, and the lighting down of his arm is seen, while his awful voice sends terror and dismay among his foes.'"[80]

Ehlke notes that the "Finney revivals in Rochester, New York, from September 10, 1830, until March 6, 1831, were, according to Lyman Beecher, 'the greatest revival of religion that the world has ever seen.'[81] The Presbyterian General Assembly, after examining the records, announced that 'the work has been so general and thorough, that the whole custom of society has been changed.'"[82] The Hawaiian Great Awakening would transform Hawaiian culture.

The New Measures of the Second Great Awakening played a role in Hawai'i. "Since the introduction of Finney's New Measures, the method of conducting revivals had become increasingly important; so Fidelia's remarks about a four-day meeting in LeRoy in February 1831 dealt with methodology as well as content. 'Christians are not

---

76. Coan, *Memorial Volume*, 4.
77. Titus Coan to Fidelia Church, January 1832, in Coan, *Memorial Volume*, 5–6.
78. Ehlke, "Enthusiastic Religion," 55–61.
79. Ehlke, "Enthusiastic Religion," 56.
80. Titus Coan to George Coan, January 21, 1831, HMH, in Ehlke, "Enthusiastic Religion," 56.
81. Johnson, *Shopkeeper's Millenium*, 109, in Ehlke, "Enthusiastic Religion," 57.
82. Johnson, *Shopkeeper's Millenium*, 109, in Ehlke, "Enthusiastic Religion," 57.

expecting a revival unless they have been praying in their closets for one, at least five or six weeks, and then in prayer meetings as long, and then been doing something else as much longer.'"[83] Protracted meetings would take place in Hilo, Puna, and throughout the Islands.

"During vacation from the Seminary, [Titus] found himself once more assisting in revivals, going far away as Lower Canaan in the fall of 1831. 'Since that time I have received letters from there informing me of numerous protracted meetings held in that province, particularly in the district of Niagara. These meetings have all been attended with signal blessings; that field is truly ready for the sickle; and there are few reapers—they depend chiefly upon ministers from our state.'"[84] In Hawai'i, Titus would lament the low number of reapers and witness "signal blessings" of God's grace and the outpouring of his Holy Spirit.

Revival would strike close to home, in Auburn itself. "In January 1832, Coan, remaining at Auburn during the vacation to study, was drawn into attending a seven-day revival at the First Church. Reporting to his father, he said: 'There has been a powerful revival in Auburn during this winter past. The whole village trembled beneath the footsteps of Jehovah, the Lord thundereth upon the gates of death, and the bars of hell gave way, while the Redeemer rode triumphantly through the hosts of his foes. More than one thousand were hopefully converted. About the same number has been hopefully born again in Rochester.'"[85] Coan would baptize over 1700 people in one day in Hilo in 1838.

Coan's passion for souls extended to the whole world. He joined the "Society of Inquiry," which was an organization at various evangelical seminaries "composed of young men interested in foreign missions."[86] The leaders of the American Board regularly visited Congregational and Presbyterian seminaries, cultivating students as future missionaries. "Broadsides sent out by the Board to the seminaries outlined the need for missionaries for specific fields around the world and appealed to '*ministers of the gospel* and to *candidates for the holy office*' to apply for openings."[87]

Harvey R. Hitchcoks and Mr. and Mrs. Lorenzo Lyons would join Titus Coan in late 1834 as part of the Seventh Company of missionaries to the Sandwich Islands.[88] Lyons in particular would be very close with Titus in their labor in the vineyard during the Hawaiian Great Awakening.

In January 1832, "Titus reported to Fidelia: 'Our Sem. is now in health and prosperity. I think a missionary spirit is rising among us. Three of the senior class, Viz.

---

83. Fidelia Church to Titus Coan, February 3, 1831, HMH, in Ehlke, "Enthusiastic Religion," 57–58.
84. Titus Coan to George Coan, March 22, 1832, HMH, in Ehlke, "Enthusiastic Religion," 60.
85. Titus Coan to father, May 18, 1833, HMCS, in Ehlke, "Enthusiastic Religion," 60.
86. Ehlke, "Enthusiastic Religion," 54.
87. ABCFM Broadside, February 1833, LOC, in Ehlke, "Enthusiastic Religion," 54.
88. Ehlke, "Enthusiastic Religion," 54.

Charles Robinson, Charles Johnson, and Lowell Smith, are accepted by the A. B. as missionaries to go out within a year. One or more of that class will soon offer themselves to the Board. How many of the middle class will decide on a missionary life I know not. Some are already decided and I think the Lord will take others."[89]

Near the end of 1832, Titus writes Fidelia of his own passion for the lost. "As Titus Coan continued his studies the plight of the 'heathen' came to occupy his thoughts more and more, as this emotional response indicates: 'But oh! The heathen! No Sabbath! No Bible! No Savior! No one to point them to the morning-star [Rev 2:28] faintly twinkling through the midnight of sin which hangs heavily on their eyelids.'"[90]

In early 1833, Fidelia writes Titus about her growing sense of call to the mission endeavor. "I am thinking almost incessantly on the subject of missions in connection with our prospects. My anxiety to engage in the work is daily increasing. Life seems so short and the advancement of the Redeemer's Kingdom on earth, an object so infinitely worthy of all that I can do that I anticipate the moment which will land me among my wretched fellow-beings, whose miserable condition excites so little compassion in the bosoms of Christians. I have not dared to think or speak thus until lately: but my dear I have strong hope that the Lord will yet permit me to labor on mission ground."[91]

Titus in no way considered being a missionary a sacrifice. "He almost rebuked the candidates for the foreign mission field for speaking of their going as a *sacrifice*. He evidently had a steady delight in the anticipation of going, and for the true reason—love of the Master. The only thing for which I ever heard him criticised [sic] was a sharp expression against the unbecoming rivalry of ministers of different names crowding each other in a little village, while the great field of the world [Matt 13:38] is calling for laborers" [Matt 9:38].[92]

At this point in her narrative, Lydia bridges to Titus Coan's correspondence during this period of preparation and consecration. "With characteristic ardor and fidelity, Mr. Coan devoted himself to every duty of the classroom, while he improved each opportunity that offered for direct work for the Lord. Time he had none for keeping a private diary; nor in those days of slow mails and expensive postage, was his correspondence large. But to his nearest kin, and to her whom he had chosen, his heart must speak. Extracts from these letters will reveal the lovely spirit that irradiated his whole life."[93]

In the first such letter to Lydia, he alludes to John 4 and Jesus saying the fields are "white unto the harvest." "From this consecrated spot I sometimes attempt to survey the vast whitening harvest field [John 4:35] as it spreads around me to the east and west, to the north and south. My eye affects my heart and I exclaim, Lord, send me

---

89. Titus Coan to Fidelia Church, January 22, 1832, HMH, in Ehlke, "Enthusiastic Religion," 55.
90. Titus Coan to Fidelia Church, December 22, 1832, HMH, in Ehlke, "Enthusiastic Religion," 55.
91. Fidelia Church to Titus Coan, March 23, 1833, HMH, in Ehlke, "Enthusiastic Religion," 66.
92. Reverend Newton, in Coan, *Memorial Volume*, 4.
93. Coan, *Memorial Volume*, 5.

where thou wilt, only go with me, lay on me *what* thou wilt, only sustain me. Cut any cord but the one which binds me to *thy cause*, to thy heart."[94]

Ehlke returns to the relationship of Titus and Fidelia. "By 1831 Titus Coan was thirty years of age and Fidelia Church twenty-one. These two young people knew that their friendship had developed into a serious personal commitment. At this time Titus Coan left Riga to prepare to enter Auburn Seminary and their correspondence began. The separation emphasized their growing dependence upon one another as they related the daily events of their lives, discussed revivals, recalled the happy times they had experienced together and began to discuss plans for the future. Their shared commitment to evangelical causes seemed to provide a solid basis for future happiness."[95]

Ehlke also describes how both were physically attractive. She provides a description of Titus, based on his passport for Patagonia.[96] Turning to Fidelia, she writes that "Fidelia Church was reported to be the most beautiful of all the Church sisters, with her light eyes, arched brows and a straight well-proportioned nose set in an oval face."[97]

Ehlke contrasts the physical abilities of the two. Titus "was a man of action whose body demanded hard, physical work to keep his restless energy within bounds." His Hilo posting and tours were ideal for that need. "Fidelia, on the other hand, needed calm, quiet times to keep her healthy."[98] While Hilo was certainly preferable to Patagonia,[99] the constant interruptions, the working with others, and the demands of mission life took their toll.

Fidelia reported a significant physical challenge and worried it might end their future together. "In 1832 the vision of a future together seemed to be shattered as Fidelia wrote with the startling news that 'my health . . . may prevent our becoming mutual helpers during our wandering in this vale of tears.' She went on to explain that her shoulder, which had given her so much pain some months before, was still aching whenever she did any hard labor, leading her to wonder if 'my usefulness may be greatly hindered on that account.'"[100]

Titus's response was swift and firm. His "impassioned response to the thought of being permanently separated from his beloved Fidelia reveals the depth of his attachment. 'I have formerly been afraid that I should never have affection for any one

---

94. Titus Coan to Fidelia Church, July 1831, in Coan, *Memorial Volume*, 5.

95. Coan, *Memorial Volume*, 48.

96. See the next chapter.

97. Emens, *Descendants of Captain Samuel Church*, 39, in Ehlke, "Enthusiastic Religion," 48. While the facial description is still evident in a daguerreotype seventeen years later, Fidelia looks older than her then-thirty-eight years of age. She had been affected by childbirth, the demands of the missionary life, her various ailments, and so on.

98. Ehlke, "Enthusiastic Religion," 48.

99. See the next chapter.

100. Fidelia Church to Titus Coan, February 18, 1832, HMH, in Ehlke, "Enthusiastic Religion," 48–49.

strong enough to warrant a connection for life, but now I feel the force of the adage, 'You'll never know the strength of a cord till you try to break it' . . . when I read of your health and of separation from my better-life, every cord around my heart was tremulous and sent out moaning sounds."[101]

Fidelia worked on rehabilitation of her shoulder and saw some improvement. Their relationship remained as strong as ever. Ultimately the shoulder problem would not affect their relationship. It would, however, play a role in their deciding against going to Patagonia and requesting a posting to the Sandwich Islands.

By early 1832, Titus was seriously considering becoming a missionary. "Coan's evangelical persuasion led him to set his sights on becoming a missionary although he felt, as he wrote Fidelia, 'I know I am unfit for a missionary and sometimes think it presumption for me to look that way.'"[102]

By this time, Fidelia and Titus were united in heart and united in desire to be missionaries together. "Telling Fidelia of the band of seminary students who met each week to converse and pray on the subject of missions, he asked: 'And now, Fidelia, to what field of labor shall we direct our eyes?'"[103]

Ehlke writes that "Fidelia's acceptance of the partnership indicated by Coan's use of 'we' and her own emotional investment in the cause is evident in her reply: 'I am glad there is a missionary spirit among you,—a spirit that shrinks not at the idea of leaving America.'"[104]

Titus knew Lowell Smith, who had departed with the Sixth Company to the Sandwich Islands. "The departure of his friend Lowell Smith for the Sandwich Islands in the fall of 1832 reinforced Coan's desire to make a firm commitment. He poured out his anguish in a letter to Fidelia: 'God's dealings with his missionaries have of late been mysterious—his ways are wrapt in clouds, but I think I never felt more delight in the thought that 'The Lord reigns [Psalms 96, 97 and 99].' When meditating on the subject of missions I often feel that 'I cannot rest.' I feel about ready to say, 'And I will go,' if I may be counted worthy. I wish you dear, to keep your heart much on the subject. Examine it. Pray over it. Examine it.'"[105]

An American Board recruiting decision would play a role in Titus making firm his plan to become a missionary. "In February 1833, the Prudential Committee of the American Board dispatched an urgent message to the nations' seminaries—fifty

---

101. Titus Coan to Fidelia Church, date not certain (Ehlke has date one day before Fidelia's letter), HMH, in Ehlke, "Enthusiastic Religion," 49.
102. Titus Coan to Fidelia Church, January 22, 1832, HMH, in Ehlke, "Enthusiastic Religion," 63.
103. Titus Coan to Fidelia Church, January 22, 1832, HMH, in Ehlke, "Enthusiastic Religion," 63.
104. Fidelia Church to Titus Coan, February 10, 1832, HMH.
105. Titus Coan to Fidelia Church, November 10, 1832, HMH, in Ehlke, "Enthusiastic Religion," 63.

ministers would be needed for the coming year as the Board worked to attain its goal—'The Speedy Conversion of the Whole World.'"[106]

The date is not known when the broadside arrived at Auburn Seminary, nor when Titus Coan read it. But the fact remains that Titus responded to the call in less than two months. "On April 12, 1833, Titus Coan answered this appeal, offering his services as a missionary to the 'heathen.'" Dr. Benjamin B. Wisner replied on the Board's behalf on May 3, 1833. He " informed Coan that the letter had been laid before the Prudential Committee, but that no further action could be taken until there had been a personal interview with the candidate 'as you will not go on a mission if appointed until fall.'"[107]

Titus writes near the end of the first chapter of his autobiography about his licensure. "On the seventeenth of April, 1833 [five days after the letter referenced above], I was licensed to preach the gospel by the Presbytery of Cauyga County, at a meeting in Auburn.

"I was then invited to preach during the summer vacation in one of the churches in Rochester, while the pastor was absent as a delegate to the General Assembly of the Presbyterian Church in Philadelphia.

"At the close of the vacation, as I was about to return to Auburn, the elders of the church in which I had labored put the following paper into my hands:

ROCHESTER, July 8, 1833.

REV TITUS COAN:

Dear Sir:—In behalf of the First Free Presbyterian Church and Congregation of Rochester, we present you this testimonial of our entire satisfaction of your ministerial labors among us during the absence of our beloved pastor, Rev. Luke Lyons,[108] who was called from us to attend the General Assembly of the Presbyterian Church in Philadelphia.

You may rest assured that we shall remember you in our prayers, and may the Lord abundantly reward you for your labors of love among us, guide you by his counsel, and make you eminently useful in promoting the Redeemer's Kingdom in whatever situation you may be place.

We are, dear sir, your friends and brethren in Christ our Lord.

"The four elders signed the letter."[109]

During the first chapter in his autobiography, Coan relates his birth, growing up, meeting Fidelia, being born again, enrolling in Auburn Seminary, ministering in the surrounding communities, deciding to become a missionary, and being licensed. He is on the cusp of being called to be a mission scout in a land far away.

---

106. ABCFM Broadside, February 1833, LOC, in Ehlke, "Enthusiastic Religion," 63.
107. Benjamin B. Wisner to Titus Coan, May 3, 1833, LOC, in Ehlke, "Enthusiastic Religion," 64.
108. Brother of Lorenzo Lyons, Ehlke, "Enthusiastic Religion," 64.
109. Coan, *Life*, 16.

2

Patagonia

"Missionary Rooms, Boston, June 19, 1833.

"Mr. Titus Coan,

"*Theological Seminary, Auburn.*

"My Dear Sir: an exploring mission has been resolved upon by the Committee, Providence permitting, on the western coast of Patagonia. The vessel in which the mission must go, if it goes during the present year, is expected to sail on the last of July, and two missionaries can have a free passage. Two men ought by all means to go, and not one alone. One—Mr. Arms, of the Theological Seminary of Andover—has been engaged for the enterprise, and another is wanted. It occurred to us that perhaps you were the man. We received your testimonials, and made inquiries, and the result is that the question has been brought before the Committee, and they have unanimously appointed you a missionary of the Board, with special reference to this important expedition. Mr. Arms, the bearer of this letter, will explain to you the nature of the mission."[1]

"The following notes of a visit to Patagonia and the Falkland Islands are offered to the public in response to the call of many friends who desire to see the simple narrative in print.

These sketches of daily life at sea and among the wild savages of Patagonia were written for friends, and to assist personal recollections, and are now offered with diffidence simply as a plain record of facts and experiences."[2]

---

1. Letter from Rufus Anderson of the ABCFM, in Coan, *Patagonia*, 9–10. NB: Ed Coan has an 1880 first edition of *Patagonia*, published by Dodd, Mead, and Company in New York.

2. Coan, *Patagonia*, 10.

Titus Coan: "Apostle to the Sandwich Islands"

MAIN SOURCE: TITUS COAN'S JOURNAL

Unlike other areas of his adult life, Titus Coan wrote very little in his autobiography about his Patagonia adventure. While Lydia Coan devotes nine pages to the pre-, during-, and post-Patagonia trip, it is negligible compared to the space devoted to his time in Hawai'i.[3] Margaret Ehlke writes eight pages about the Patagonia chapter of his life.[4] Nevertheless, neither the compiler nor the scholar spend much direct space on Coan's time in Patagonia itself. This could well be for two reasons: the focus of both is on Coan's time in Hawai'i; and they defer to Titus who wrote a book on the subject.[5] The Missionary Herald's seemingly[6] frank discussion of the recommendation to *not* send further missionaries will be woven in near the end of the chapter.

The "Darwin Project" provides this summary of the scouting trip as it ties in with Charles Darwin. "As a young missionary, Coan had spent a few hazardous weeks among the indigenous peoples of Patagonia on the north shore of the Magellan Strait. The thirty-two-year-old Coan had landed at Gregory Bay (now in Chile) on November 14, 1833, and left again on January 25, 1834. Just one day later, the twenty-two-year-old Darwin arrived in the Strait on board HMS *Beagle*. In his diary entry for January 29, 1834, Darwin described anchoring in Gregory Bay and going ashore with Captain FitzRoy where they were met by a group of Toldos: their appearance, he wrote, was rather wild, with long hair and faces painted red and black, but they gave the *Beagle* crew a kind reception.

Coan and his fellow missionary, William Arms, were also made welcome, but they were poorly equipped and unprepared, and after sharing the daily lives of the natives for two months without being able to communicate beyond a few shared words of Spanish, they abandoned their mission. Extracts from their diaries were published in *The Missionary Herald* in 1834 and 1835, and a complete transcript of Coan's diary, now in the Library Congress, is available online.[7]

Titus writes only this paragraph at the end of his first chapter. "It was but a few days after my entrance upon my last term at the Seminary, when a letter from the Rev. Rufus Anderson, Secretary of the ABCFM, called me to Boston to be ordained, and to sail on a mission of exploration to Patagonia, on which expedition I embarked on the sixteenth of August 1833. An account of this trip may be found in my *Adventures in Patagonia*."[8]

---

3. Coan, *Memorial Volume*, 12–21.

4. Ehlke, "Enthusiastic Religion," 67–74.

5. Ehlke, "Enthusiastic Religion," also devotes three pages, 72–75, in this section to Fidelia spending the duration of Titus's absence at the Middlebury, Connecticut, Female Seminary with Arms's fianceé Maria S. Goodwin.

6. See the end of this chapter for the real reason the Board recommended against establishing a mission in Patagonia and, instead, sending Titus and Fidelia (clue) to Hawai'i.

7. Darwin Correspondence Project.

8. Coan, *Life*, 16. Under "Missionaries" is found: "1833: Arms and Coan"; "Titus Coan—Journal";

Coan's Patagonia journal is the main source for this period in his life. There are two formats of his journal: the original journal and the journal as Coan arranged it in his book. How can there be two formats of the same journal? It turns out that, as part of the "Patagonia Bookshelf,"[9] Douglas S. Campbell and Gladys Grace-Paz transcribed the original journal at the Library of Congress, and it is juxtaposed with what Coan put in the book, beginning with November 11, 1833, and continuing with eleven weeks[10] of journal entry comparisons. In the process, they noted significant differences between the handwritten journal and the journal as presented in the book.[11] As he begins his journal the first day on the vessel carrying him south, Coan writes about making extracts from "my journal."[12]

Paul Rapoza observes: "He did add to some entries more detail than was in the Journal but almost anyone who is familiar with his writings,(books and letters, etc) will verify that he had a penchant for vivid, accurate descriptions with an incredible memory for detail even in his later life. Those added insights on some dates very likely is a product of that quality peculiar to him."[13]

The only drawback to this excellent resource is that it provides neither chapter titles nor transitions between chapters.

CORRESPONDENCE

Prior to his departure for Patagonia, Coan receives a letter of request from Rufus Anderson, recently[14] appointed General Secretary of the American Board. On the subject

---

"1845 Gardiner and Hunt"; "1896 South Am. Missionary Society."

9. Grace-Paz, "Patagonia Bookshelf."

10. The eleven weeks while Coan and Arms were in Patagonia.

11. At the top of page 9, one finds:
"A Date-by-Date Comparison"
Of Missionary Titus Coan's Patagonia Journal with
Comparable Entries in His Book *Adventures in Patagonia*."
Under the left-hand column "Original Journal," one reads: "Journal text of Titus Coan's travels with the indigenous natives in Patagonia is an extracted version from the his original handwritten journal located at the Library of Congress and this extraction has been provided by: http://patlibros.org © Duncan S. Campbell & Gladys Grace-Paz, 2004–2015. Reproduction for commercial gain is not authorized. Used by permission in this comparison for educational non-commercial purposes." Under the right-hand column "Book Contents": "Text from Titus Coan's book written in 1880, much of which was written from extracts from his private journals. Note: Journal and Book entries are from November 10, 1883, to January 25, 1884. (The dates of their arrival and departure.) Book content is public domain. Formatting © 2015 Helps Communications. Personal, Educational use permitted." Free copies of this book are available in various formats or to read online at the Titus Coan Memorial Library, http://www.tc-lib.org.

12. *Patagonia*, 30.

13. Paul Rapoza, email to author, March 2, 2016.

14. 1832; Wikipedia, "Rufus Anderson."

of going to Patagonia, correspondence indicates the agony for both who loved Christ and whose hearts were becoming knit together.

The first letter on the subject was the June 19, 1833, missive from Anderson to Coan.[15] In that letter, Anderson introduces Mr. Arms and indicates that he brings the Anderson letter to Coan and Arms who "will explain to you the nature of the mission."[16]

Not much is known of William Arms after the sojourn in Patagonia. The following is found in an 1838 *Missionary Herald* notice.

> MISSION TO BORNEO.
> Sambas[17]—William Arms and Samuel P. Robbins,
> Missionaries, and Mrs. Robbins.
> (1 station; 2 missionaries, and 1 female assistant missionary;—total, 3.)

As he had with Patagonia, Mr. Arms made a survey of two areas in Borneo. "Mr. Arms spent four months of the last year in Borneo, at Pontiana and Sambas; travelled interior a hundred miles; saw the Dyaks in their villages; and collected such information as he could respecting their numbers, religion, languages, character, customs, and the practicability of a mission among them. He made a second visit to Borneo at the close of the year, with the expectation of remaining at Sambas. Mr. and Mrs. Robbins were on the point of proceeding from Singapore in March to join Mr. Arms."[18] Elsewhere the *Herald* notes that Arms graduated from Andover Seminary in 1833[19]. He would have graduated from that Seminary just before leaving with Coan for Patagonia.

Ehlke relates the name of Mr. Arms's fiancée. Even as Coan departed Fidelia and his country, he "opened doors to the future by suggesting a correspondence between Fidelia and Maria S. Goodwin, Mr. Arms's intended wife."[20]

Returning to his letter to Coan, Anderson lays out the project. "The plan is, in brief, that two men, willing to endure hardship, be landed on the coast, at a place which is resorted to by sealing[21] vessels, and spend a suitable time, probably a year or more, in travelling among the tribes of that coast; that they shall ascertain what can be done for them—where a mission had better be located, what should be the nature

---

15. See the first page of this chapter.

16. Letter from Rufus Anderson of the ABCFM in Coan, *Patagonia*, 10.

17. Sambas was a traditional Malay state in Indonesia in modern Borneo. Wikipedia, "Sultanata of Sambas."

18. *Missionary Herald* 34, 10.

19. *Missionary Herald*, 34, 18.

20. Ehlke, "Enthusiastic Religion," 71.

21. "The Valdes Peninsula, in Argentine Patagonia, is home to the only continental reproductive Southern Elephant Seal colony in the world. This species (Mirounga Leonina) is distributed throughout the Sub-Antarctic region with an estimated population of 700,000 individuals. It is calculated that approximately twenty thousand reach the Valdes Peninsula each year between August and March to mate, give birth, and molt." Hotel Del Nómade, "Elephant Seals."

of the mission, etc.—and at the same time make arrangements for a mission, and then come home and report to the Committee."[22]

In his letter, Anderson does not suggest, as would ultimately be the case, that Coan and Arms might recommend against the establishment of a mission. Anderson recognized that this request is sudden and gives Coan some time to think about it. "As this subject comes before you unawares, and you have but little time to reflect upon it, we do not ask you to decide now whether you will ultimately be a member of the Patagonian mission."[23]

But Anderson does continue on with questions and a request. "The question now before you is, whether you will accompany Mr. Arms to the Patagonian coast and spend a couple years, if necessary, among the Indian tribes of that coast?" Coan and Arms would be there less than a year. Anderson paints an inspiring vista of purpose for Coan. "The expedition now proposed to you is one full of privations; but it opens a prospect of bringing the gospel to the minds and hearts of the poor degraded natives of Patagonia."

Anderson presses home the request to decide as soon as possible and let him know. The letter does not seem to brook a response of "no." "I beg you to take this important subject into immediate and prayerful consideration. Let me hear from you as soon as possible. I earnestly hope you will go. If you do not, I see not how the mission can go during the present year."[24]

After the Anderson to Coan letter, Titus lists what materials Mr. Arms brought with the Anderson letter. They included letters to Rufus Anderson, dated January 24 and February 25, 1833. Captain Morrell's first letter is in response to one written to him by Anderson on January 17. These letters and accompanying material provide both the seeds leading to the scouting mission and, as Captain Morrell's misleading representations became known, what would ultimately be the seeds of the mission's outcome and recommendation against establishing a mission.

Coan writes that Captain Benjamin Morrell lived in New York and "had recently published a very attractive narrative of a cruise along the eastern coast of Patagonia, also through the Magellan Strait and up the Pacific coast as far as the island of Chiloe. In this journal he had given a glowing description of the harbors, the forests, the climate, soil, clover-meadows, and the numerous and peaceful inhabitants of the western coast of Patagonia. He had also taken occasion to hint that this coast would be a favorable field for missionary enterprise."[25]

Morrell's writings contained seeds both for there being a scouting mission and, because of misrepresentations, the seeds of the mission's outcome and recommendation against establishing a mission. After arriving in New York City, there "came

22. Letter from Rufus Anderson of the ABCFM, in Coan, *Patagonia*, 10.
23. Coan, *Patagonia*, 10.
24. Coan, *Patagonia*, 11.
25. Coan, *Patagonia*, 12. Morrell's letters are found on 13–18.

a shock of disappointment. Captain Clift assured us that the officers of the Board had been misled by the recently published book of Captain Morrell. He denied the statements as to the fine climate, the beautiful lands, the luxuriant meadows of clover, the considerable number of the inhabitants, their quiet habits and their amiable disposition."[26]

Returning to the theme of correspondence, Titus and Fidelia would engage in excruciating interaction over this opportunity, with its requisite separation. In his letter to Coan, Anderson writes without any efforts to sympathize or empathize: "Of course you will both have to go unmarried. Mr. Arms leaves an intended wife behind him, and we understand that your circumstances are similar to his."[27]

Ehlke seems to indicate that there is more to Anderson's letter than what Titus put in his book. "I trust that you will never have occasion to regret the decision you have been enabled to make: and that both you and your intended wife will hereafter find it an occasion of joy and of gratitude to God."[28] Coan makes a request of Anderson that Rufus would not be able to fulfill. "Titus asked Anderson to notify Fidelia of any news relating to him that 'would be important for you to know and which you can get from no other source.'"[29]

In 1838, there is no mention of Mrs. Arms in *The Missionary Herald*.[30] Coan does indicate Anderson being correct with regard to Coan having an intended wife. He writes that the communications regarding Patagonia came when he "was then entering on my last term in the Theological Seminary. At its close I was engaged to marry Miss Fidelia Church, and I hoped to go with her as a missionary to some foreign land. We had been betrothed for years, and this call, if accepted, would throw a cloud over the prospects of our union for a long time at least, perhaps forever."[31]

Ehlke notes that a "letter dated June 19, 1833, addressed to Titus Coan at the Theological Seminary at Auburn abruptly altered the lives of Titus Coan and his beloved Fidelia."[32] James McDowell wrote Fidelia, exhorting her "to rejoice in 'the opportunity of exhibiting your supreme love for Jesus and his cause.'"[33] Looking back on their parting on July 8, Fidelia writes her sister Maria. She "bade him farewell 'perhaps to see him no more until we meet in our Father's house to go no more out forever.'"[34]

---

26. Coan, *Patagonia*, 25. See below for further information from Clift, that proved to be true in the going and experiencing.

27. Coan, *Patagonia*, 11.

28. Anderson to Coan, June 19, 1833, LOC, in Ehlke, "Enthusiastic Religion," 70.

29. Titus to Fidelia Church, August 14, 1833.

30. See above re: Borneo scouting mission.

31. Coan, *Patagonia*, 20.

32. Ehlke, "Enthusiastic Religion," 67.

33. James McDowell to Fidelia Church, June 26, 1833, LOC, in Ehlke, "Enthusiastic Religion," 69.

34. Fidelia Church to Maria C. Robinson, August 7, 1833, HMH, in Ehlke, "Enthusiastic Religion," 69–70.

Ehlke continues. "The depths of their evangelical commitment did not make the decision to separate any easier as Fidelia's first letter [to Titus], written that night as she began to experience her sense of personal loss, reveals: 'I have just begun to learn how necessary you are to my happiness—how all my plans have been formed with some reference to you—and how the thought of being one day united to you for life has rendered study, labour, every employment pleasant.'" Fidelia works her way to a position of disinterested benevolence, a teaching first developed by Samuel Hopkins. "Still I think I am willing to give you up entirely to the Lord's disposal, but O the life, the soul of my earthly joy has departed! Good night, dear, dear T—I leave you reluctantly. The Lord keep you in perfect peace."[35]

Three days later, Titus wrote to Fidelia. "Dearly beloved of my soul, the thought that I am seated at my desk, where I have spent many sweet seasons of communion with you, to address you for the last time from these consecrated walls, causes some tender struggles and gushings of nature; but my heart does not faint, it is still fixed. The cords which twine around kindred and country and friends twinge and complain a little. But I must not indulge. The Lord is good, immeasurably good, and I am happy. I contemplate the arduous enterprise before me with pleasure rather than otherwise."[36]

Three days later Coan describes more of a heaviness as he reflects upon the ever-nearer departure to the mostly unknown. "This is the Sabbath—the sweet Sabbath of rest. Recollections sweet and tender are finding avenues to my heart, and making deep traces there. Associations solemn and moving are thickening around my soul and making strong impressions there. Less than a year ago I was here under circumstances and prospects very different from those which now arrest my attention. Then I was with my loved one, traveling with her to a peaceful home—to the bosom of friends and the blessings of the sanctuary. Now I am journeying without her toward a land of strangers whose tender mercies are cruel—to a region where the daylight of life never dawned."[37]

Four days after that letter he is in Boston[38] and visited with Rufus Anderson in his home. Titus wrote to Fidelia of his longing for them to share such marital and familial bliss. "I took the stage last evening and went out to Dorchester, and spent the night with Dr. A.'s family. It was a delightful season to me. Mr. Anderson is one of the most amiable men I ever saw—kind, affectionate, with a piety sweet and clear, consistent and winning. He is also equally yoked to a lovely, affectionate, and constant companion, *another self*. The family is truly a scene of domestic piety and peace. So, by

---

35. Fidelia Church to Titus Coan, July 8, 1833, in Ehlke, "Enthusiastic Religion," 70.

36. Titus Coan to Fidelia Church, July 11, 1833, in Coan, *Memorial Volume*, 14-15. Written in Auburn?

37. Titus Coan to Fidelia Church, July 14, 1833, in Coan, *Memorial Volume*, 15. Written in Albany, New York.

38. Technically, Dorchester. See next sentence.

the grace of God, *we* will live, dearest F. I still feel happy in my mission, and nothing but a solemn sense of duty could induce me to turn back."

After expressing his gratitude "for the privilege of endeavoring at least to seek out some of the lost tribes of Adam" and bring them the news the angels announced in Bethlehem, he seeks to comfort and encourage Fidelia. "My heart pants to give you some assistance or counsel or consolation before I go. But I can only throw you on the bosom of our best beloved, and pray him to keep you in perfect peace. Though we never meet on earth our feet will soon stand upon Mount Zion, whence we shall look down upon a world regenerated and filled with the glory of God. So fare-you-well. The Lord Jehovah shield you [Ps 28:7]—the everlasting arms sustain you."[39]

More than a month after Fidelia's last known letter to Coan before his departure, Titus writes her, "'Thus my dear, I believe I have made all the arrangements for you before my departure which one that loves you more than his own life can make. I have told you my desire in relation to the little money etc. which I leave in your hands,[40] provided I should not return.'"[41]

DECISION, PREPARATION, ORDINATION, AND DEPARTURE

In *Patagonia*, Coan relates visiting with Fidelia soon after receiving the initial letter from Dr. Anderson. The two of them quickly, though painfully, reached a decision. He took a redeye stage from Auburn to Rochester. "Early the next morning I was in Rochester, where I had left my espoused but a few days before."

He was able to eat food and participate in morning prayers without saying anything to Fidelia about the life-altering letter from Dr. Anderson. He then placed the material in Fidelia's hands. "She was at breakfast when I entered her house. After salutations I took breakfast with the family; then came morning prayers, during all which time nothing had been said as to why I had returned so soon to Rochester. All was mystery to Miss Church and her friends.

"After prayers we retired to a separate room, and I, without a word of explanation, put Dr. Anderson's letter into her hands. As she read, her emotion deepened, her tears flowed. What a change of situation! What an uprooting of fondly and long-cherished hopes! For seven years we had waited, and now only three or four months before our nuptials were to be celebrated, and we were to go forth into some foreign field, to toil, to suffer, and to rejoice together in the vineyard of our Master."

Coan continues to relate both Fidelia's emotions and her decision. "For a minute she was dumb. The struggle was intense. Soon, however, faith gained the victory. That full consecration which, long before, she had made to her Master and Lord assumed

---

39. Titus Coan to Fidelia Church, July 18, 1833, in Coan, *Memorial Volume*, 15–16.
40. A verbal will and testament?
41. Titus Coan to Fidelia Church, August 14, 1833, LOC, in Ehlke, "Enthusiastic Religion," 71.

its power; her soul rose from the stern conflict of emotion—of hope deferred, perhaps slain. She took my hand and said, '*My dear, you must go.*'"

Coan had literally placed the decision in Fidelia's hands. She made the decision and let him know that it was imperative that he go on the mission to Patagonia. "Henceforth it was preparation in earnest." Part of his preparation was to apply for and receive a passport. At the top center is an American Eagle image surrounded by thirteen stars. On the left diagonal is "UNITED" and right diagonal "STATES." Underneath the Eagle is "OF AMERICA" in a gentle curve. Underneath those two words is a line that says "To all to whom these Presents shall come, Greeting."

The left-hand column with a vertical line two inches to the right is headed "DESCRIPTION." Coan fills in handwritten information in the blanks next to cursive printed words.[42]

> *Age* 32
> *Stature* 5 Feet 7 Inches
> *Forehead* high & retreating
> *Eyes* Blue
> *Nose* Prominent
> *Mouth* Middling Size
> *Chin* Long
> *Hair* Brown
> *Complexion* Light
> *Face* Long
> *Signature of the Bearer*
> [Titus Coan]
> GRATIS

On the right side is "No 3142."[43] He then fills in his name under the passport number with printed wording: "*I, the Undersigned, Secretary of State of the* United States of America, *hereby request all whom it may concern to permit safety and freely to pass* [Titus Coan signature] [wavy line for a little over two lines] *a Citizen of the* **United States**, *and in case of need to give him all lawful Aid and Protection.*"

Under the word "Protection" is a circular "Secretary of State's Office" seal with the image of an Eagle and shield. To the right of the seal are the words, "*Given under my hand and the impression of the Seal of the* **DEPARTMENT OF STATE**, *at the City of Washington the* [wavy line handwritten] Twenty Second day of July 1833, *in the Fifty-Eighth Year of the Independence of these United States.*" The passport is signed by Louis McLane, who was a recess appointment as Secretary of State by President Jackson. McLane served in that capacity from May 29, 1833, through June 30, 1834.[44]

---

42. Note this is done before going to Patagonia, not the Hawaiian Islands.

43. Does that mean the total number since the establishing of the Republic? Or that many so far that year?

44. Wikipedia, "Louis McLane."

In the midst of his preparations, Coan learned that Captain Morrell's glowing reports did not match reality. "Captain William Clift, of Mystic, Connecticut, the Master of the *Mary Jane* . . . [confirmed his denial of Morrell's claims when] he stated that he had sailed up and down the whole western coast of Patagonia several times; had seen the bays, channels, islands, the mainland, and the natives; that he had sealed from the western entrance of Magellan's Strait to the island of Chiloe, and that the description of that coast by Captain Morrell was far from being correct."

Clift gets specific in his explanation of the region. He "described the coast as broken, mountainous, wild, and the climate as often stormy. The ravines, headlands, cliffs, spurs, and precipitous sea-walls . . . rendered travelling by land along the shore impossible, and by sea in a boat very difficult and dangerous."

He relates the dwellers in that land. "As for the inhabitants . . . they amount to only a few scores, and these are the most wretched and squalid creatures I have ever seen in human form: small in size, nearly naked." Others confirmed Clift's views. "Furthermore, Captain Clift said that on the present voyage he should not visit that coast at all." He also indicated he could not carry out his instructions as presented. "To take the missionaries to the west coast of Patagonia would change the whole plan of his voyage, and probably make it an entire failure; and that to land us where we were instructed to go, to look after us along that coast, and to pledge himself to take us off and return us to the United States when our explorations were ended, was out of the question. He also said that to land and leaves there, without care or means of escape, would be but to abandon us to a cruel death."

Arms, Coan, and the American Board officials faced a dilemma. "All this put a new and dark aspect on the Patagonian mission. What could be done? Must we go back to Boston? Must we acknowledge failure, return our instructions, and seek another field of labor?"

As he would throughout the rest of his life, he ties in a Bible verse to the situation. "This seemed like 'putting the hand to the plough and looking back' [Luke 9:62]. We looked at one another, but all was blank. We looked to the Lord for guidance, and in half an hour the problem was solved."

The problem was solved by the agency of Captain Clift who said, "Gentlemen, if you wish to *Eastern Patagonia*, I will take you into the Strait of Magellan and land you on the north shore, among the Horse Indians, and then pursue my voyage, which may be one or two years. My object is to fill my vessel with seal-skins, whether the time be longer or shorter. Should you be on the shore, where I can reach you, when I return, I will take you home, but more than this I cannot promise."

This course would be used as part of a negative recommendation by Arms, Coan, and the Board in *The Missionary Herald* regarding the efficacy of a permanent mission to Patagonia.[45] And the two missionaries would be taken off the Patagonian coast

---

45. See Fidelia letter, presented after *Missionary Herald* discussion near the end of this chapter, for her role in the decision.

by an officer and vessel other than the one that took them there. The missionaries wonder. "Our instructions from the Prudential Committee had cautioned us to avoid, if possible, getting among the Eastern Patagonians, as they were reputed to be fierce savages of gigantic size, and cannibals withal."

Captain Clift sought to allay those fears by indicating that while they were "hard fellows," they nevertheless would allow shipping to pass through the Strait "unharmed." The missionaries gathered with members and friends of the American Board who were in New York City at the time. "After prayer and due consultation, the following question was put to the young missionaries: 'Are you willing, in view of all the circumstances and conditions of the case, to go to Eastern Patagonia?' The reply was, promptly, 'Yes.'" Those gathered unanimously approved the missionaries' "desire to embark on this untried enterprise."[46]

Prior to this change in situation, Coan had travelled from Rochester where the grieving yet affirming Fidelia lived and served to join Mr. Arms in Boston. On "Sunday evening, July 28, 1833, we were ordained in Park Street Church. On the twenty-ninth we received our instructions for the Patagonian expedition from the Prudential Committee of the ABCFM, in the house of the venerable chairman, the Hon. S. Hubbard.[47]

"All things being now ready, we took passage for New York to embark for Patagonia." Coan relates the further preparations that took place, both financial and with the US Navy. "In order to assist us in any further necessary preparations, Mr. Henry Hill, Treasurer of the Missionary Board, accompanied us to New York. He also furnished us with ample letters of credit on banking houses in Valparaíso and London, and the Secretary of the Board gave us letters of introduction to the commodore commanding the US squadron on the Pacific station."

Coan explains that this "was precautionary, in case we should find it necessary to reach Valparaíso in order to obtain passage to the United States, and perhaps *via* England or France." In New York City, Arms and Coan met with others, including the owner of the *Mary Jane* vessel that would take them to Patagonia, as well as Captain Clift, whose views have already been presented.[48]

Perhaps the missionaries felt pressured to continue with the project because of everything that had already happened: the good-byes to fianceés, the ordination, and preparations in New York City.

JOURNEY TO PATAGONIA AND ARRIVAL AT WRONG LOCATION

"Having completed our outfit, written our last letters to distant correspondents, and bidden adieu to many kind and faithful friends in New York, we went on board the

---

46. Coan, *Patagonia*, 25–29.
47. Coan, *Patagonia*, 24.
48. See above.

little schooner *Mary Jane* on the sixteenth of August, 1833, and sailed for one of 'the ends of the earth.'"[49]

Coan's first journal extract[50] is "August 16, 1833, *Schooner* Mary Jane, *off Sandy Hook*[51] . . . By the good hand of God, our voyage to the far south is now commenced. We have bidden smiling and weeping friends farewell. The city, with its turrets and towers and lofty spires, has faded in the distance. Its busy hum is hushed. With favoring breeze and pilot at the helm, our little bark has sped down the channel, and now the great ocean opens on our sight. The sun is setting behind the western hills of my beloved country. The wind has died away. A placid calmness rests on the deep.

"Captain Clift calls all hands, exhorts them to observe the rules of morality, and to obey orders *promptly* and *cheerfully*. He then invited one of us to offer up prayer to Almighty God."[52]

Thus begins a journey southward of almost three months.[53] During this time he describes weather, reports coordinates, indicates occasional sickness, and reports admiringly of Captain Clift's navigating the seas and other elements in the far south of the American continent, including navigation of the Straits of Magellan. Under Captain Clift's leadership and with the approval of Coan, Sabbath services were held on board.

He provides early evidence of being a "pen painter," such as this description after being out of sign of New York City and any other coastal towns. "All is ocean around and under us, and our little cockle-shell is ploughing a white foaming furrow along the bosom of the deep.

"On the eighteenth we had a heavy gale. Our light shallop danced and leaped and staggered, and plunged like a mermaid into the foaming billows, and like a duck or a swan received the spray and the leaping waves upon her deck."[54]

Foreshadowing his later writing on "The Sailor's Sabbath," Coan relates this example of worship services, Bible reading, and personal reformation. "We have religious services on board when the weather is good, and a part of the crew seem attentive and thoughtful. Some retire to quiet places on deck to read the Bible and religious books and tracts, and to converse. Others are hard and heathenish. A few seem resolved to reform and lead new lives."[55]

His entries reflect his scientific bent as a Renaissance man. He writes about sailing below the equator. "October 9—lat 6° S . . . We shall now run south of the sun for

---

49. Coan, *Patagonia*, 30.

50. Journal material in the book will be cited as Coan, *Patagonia*, while the original journal entries will be cited as LOC and drawn from the Titus Coan Memorial Library.

51. A name that would become infamous when the 2012 superstorm struck.

52. Coan, *Patagonia*, 30–31.

53. Thirteen pages of journal extracts in Coan, *Patagonia*, 30–42.

54. Coan journal entry, August 17, 1833, in Coan, *Patagonia*, 31.

55. Coan, *Patagonia*, 31–32.

a long time, and may often long for his nearer visits."[56] On October 12, Coan writes about the Magellan nebula. "One of the Magellan clouds is in full view, hanging about 10 degrees above the horizon. The appearance of this nebula is like that of the galaxy, and it is, no doubt, formed by the blended rays of unnumbered stars." He recognizes that our "seasons are now all reversed. We are in the midst of an opening spring, while the blasts of autumn are sweeping over the north. It seems odd to look north for the sun, and to see our tiny shadows fall southward."[57]

He writes about birds "of the 'south seas' gather[ing] thick about us. The lively little stormy-petrel, called by sailors 'Mother Cary's Chickens'[58] and the Cape pigeons are very numerous and sportive. The soaring mollemoke (*Procellaria glacialis*) and the proud albatross (*Diomedia exulans*) sail gracefully above and around us, often lighting and dancing on the rolling waves. The albatross is very large, often measuring from 12 to 13 feet from tip to tip of his outspread wings."[59]

He sees the southern constellations. "The Southern Cross, also, rises higher and higher to remind us of the Sacrifice and of our great errand into the wild and dreary realms of the south."[60] Over several pages he relates a horrific storm of two days that "was a wind-storm from the great Buenos Ayres pampas, or prairies.[61]

Coan provides coordinates at beginning of his November 8 journal. "Lat. 48 °S., lon. 65° 14' W." While the online original journal entries do not begin until two days after Coan's notation, there is no reason to believe that he would misrepresent that measurable detail.

He indicates the sighting of land: "At 10 a.m. the cry 'Land ho!' rang from all parts of the vessel." He describes what he sees of the coast. "The low, sandy shores of Eastern Patagonia near Cape Blanco are in full view about thirty miles to westward. The day is delightful; the sky unclouded, the air soft and bland, the rays of the sun mild and grateful, all giving indications of the vernal season." In the southern hemisphere, the calendar spring would have begun on September 21 with summer arriving on December 21.

It will be remembered that Coan and Arms went to Eastern instead of Western Patagonia for two reasons from Captain Clift: he debunked Morrell's rosy description of the western part; and Clift was insistent that he was going sealing on the eastern side and that was where he would drop them off or not at all.

---

56. Coan, *Patagonia*, 33.
57. Coan, *Patagonia*, 33–34.
58. "Mother Carey is a supernatural figure personifying the cruel and threatening sea in the imagination of eighteenth- and nineteenth-century English-speaking sailors. She was a harbinger of storms, and a similar character to Davy Jones (who may be her husband... Storm petrels, thought by sailors to be the souls of dead seamen, are called Mother Carey's Chickens." Wikipedia, "Mother Carey."
59. Coan, *Patagonia*, 35.
60. Coan, *Patagonia*, 34.
61. Coan, *Patagonia*, 36–42.

Coan describes everything he sees and what he does not see. "But we see no fields smiling under the hand of the husbandman; no gardens and orchards dressed in the blooming beauties of spring; no harbors adorned with the waving flags of commerce; no cities lifting their towers against the sky; no peaceful villages and dainty hamlets sprinkling the extended plains; no glittering church-spires pointing the weary pilgrim to 'a better country" [Heb 11:16].

He writes about the inhabitants' need for a Savior. "Art and science have never shed their kindly influences over this benighted land; nor has the 'Light of Life' [John 8:12] yet dawned upon it. Here the fierce savage has roamed from age to age, tearing the flesh and drinking the blood of his prey. Generation after generation has gone down to the shades of death without a beam of light to cheer the dark valley, or a 'morning star' [Rev 2:28, 22:16] to give promise of 'an eternal day.'"

Before continuing with Coan's time in Patagonia, further information on the name, location, and people are provided.

BACKGROUND ON PATAGONIA

While this chapter has provided some of Captain Clift's description, here is some more information on the name, geography, climate, and people. As far as the etymology of the place name, "The name 'Patagonia' comes from the word *patagón* used by Magellan in 1520 to describe the native people that his expedition thought to be giants. It is now believed that the people he called the Patagons were Tehuelches, who tended to be taller than Europeans of the time.

"The Argentine researcher Miguel Doura observed that the name Patagonia possibly derives from the ancient Greek region of modern Turkey called Paflagonia, possible home of the *patagon* personage in the chivalric romances *Primaleon*, printed in 1512, ten years before Magellan arrived in these southern lands. The hypothesis was accepted and published in the *New Review of Spanish Philology* in the 2011 article... The original word would mean (*patagón*). It has been interpreted later as 'big foot' but the etymology refers to a literary character in a Spanish novel of the early sixteenth century."

As far as the referenced novel and further discussion of *patagon*'s etymology: "According to Antonio Pigafetta, one of the Magellan expedition's few survivors and its published chronicler, Magellan bestowed the name '*Patagão*' (or *Patagón*) on the inhabitants they encountered there, and the name 'Patagonia' for the region. Although Pigafetta's account does not describe how this name came about, subsequent popular interpretations gave credence to a derivation meaning 'land of the big feet'. However, this etymology is questionable. The term is most likely derived from an actual character name, '*Patagón*,' a savage creature confronted by Primaleón of Greece, the hero in the homonymous Spanish chivalry novel (or *knight-errantry tale*) by Francisco Vázquez. This book, published in 1512, was the sequel of the romance 'Palmerín de

Oliva,' much in fashion at the time, and a favorite reading of Magellan. Magellan's perception of the natives, dressed in skins, and eating raw meat, clearly recalled the uncivilized *Patagón* in Vázquez's book. Novelist and travel writer Bruce Chatwin suggests etymological roots of both Patagon and Patagonia in his book, *In Patagonia*, noting the similarity between 'Patagon' and the Greek word παταγος, which means 'a roaring' or 'gnashing of teeth' Iin his chronicle, Pigafetta describes the Patagonians as 'roaring like bulls')."[62]

The broad geographic description of Patagonia is that it is the southernmost part of South America's cone. Here is a more detailed account: "Patagonia is a sparsely-populated region located at the southern end of South America, shared by Argentina and Chile. The region comprises the southern section of the Andes mountains as well as the deserts, steppes, and grasslands east of this southern portion of the Andes. Patagonia has two coasts; a western one towards the Pacific Ocean and an eastern one towards the Atlantic Ocean. The Colorado and Barrancas rivers, which run from the Andes to the Atlantic, are commonly considered the northern limit of Argentine Patagonia. Tierra del Fuego is sometimes included as part of Patagonia. Most geographers and historians locate the northern limit of Chilean Patagonia at Reloncaví Estuary."

"The overall climate is cool and dry." As is mentioned above, the area was and is sparsely populated. The average per square kilometer population as of 2013 bears that out, as this chart indicates:

Country/region	Area	Population	Density
Argentina	2,780,400 km2	40,091,359	14.4 per km2
Chile	743,812 km2	16,601,707	22.3 per km2
Patagonia	1,043,076 km2	1,999,540	1.9 per km2

Here is a map showing the Patagonia area, including the Straits of Magellan in the southernmost part of the landmass:

---

62. Wikipedia, "Patagonia."

TIME IN PATAGONIA AND FALKLANDS

November 10, 1833, marks the first date that both the book journal extracts and the full Library of Congress journal transcription are available. In the book extract, Coan writes: "***November* 10.** We have had divine service on board to-day, for the last time probably. Our next Sabbath we expect to spend among the Patagonian savages. We have enjoyed religious worship on the Lord's Day when it has been fine weather during the voyage, and our little congregation is dear to us. Some of the crew express faith in Christ, and others have appeared sober-minded and impressible under the sound of the gospel."[64]

By contrast, here is the more extensive original and full journal entry: "**Lord's Day. November 10.** Since my last date we have not seen land as the wind has kept us off from the shore. The weather being comfortable we attended worship on deck this afternoon. Brother Arms preached from Song of Solomon 2:15 'Take us the foxes' etc. The services were much interrupted by the swell of the sea which broke completely over the decks to our no little inconvenience. As we hope to land during the week this is probably the last Sabbath we shall spend on board. Though our little congregation

---

63. Wikipedia, "Patagonia." Coan provides a map of Patagonia on page 8 of the book with the same name. Map Janitoalevic, Wikimedia Commons.

64. Coan, *Patagonia*, 43–44.

for the most part are only nominal Christians still it is affecting to think that we shall no more be permi[tted][65] to worship even in such a circle for months or years; perhaps not till we en[ter] on the eternal Sabbath. Perhaps all these men with whom we have come preachi[ng] the kingdom of God will see us, and be seen by us no more till we meet them at the bar of our final Judge. God grant that we may be able to say when called to separ[ate] [Matt 25:23] that we are clean from the blood of all these men [Acts 20:26], that we have not failed to decl[are] to them the whole counsel of God [Acts 20:27]. Many of them are yet in their sins though they have long had the word of God preached to them and though our hearts are moved for them we must say to them 'Your blood be on your own head, from henceforth we turn to the gentiles' [2 Sam 1:16; Ezek 33:4; Acts 18:6]. Where our next Sabbath will be spent is all unknown to us, but I feel no anxiety on the subject as the place and circumstances will all be arranged by that infinitely wise and gracious God who has promised to be a 'little Sanctuary' to his children in all places where they wander."

In this case the original journal entry is longer than the extract in the book. In many subsequent entries covered by the eleven weeks Coan was in Patagonia itself,[66] the greater detail is found in the book. This reality reflects Rapoza's comments about Titus's phenomenal memory and desire to fill out the details and/or some other written resource that Coan used. The general reader and scholar welcome the extra detail, regardless of the source.

The fourth and eleventh chapters of *Patagonia* include Arms and Coan being on Patagonian land (arrival and departure). The fifth through tenth in their entirety take place in Patagonia. A total of approximately 173 pages are devoted to their time there.

After efforts of two days—including headwinds and laying at anchor—the *Mary Jane* made it through the Straits of Magellan and arrives at Gregory Bay. "**November 14.** On awaking this morning we found the *Mary Jane* quietly anchored in Gregory's Bay, some seventy miles from the entrance of the Strait.

"Thus our voyage of just ninety days is ended, and the land for which we sailed is before us. We look out upon a beach of white sand, upon sand-cliffs, sand-dunes, the grassy pampas, and distant snow-crowned hills; but neither man nor beast nor human habitation is visible: all is drear solitude."[67] They set foot on land the same day. They first saw inhabitants the next day. They were back on the vessel and the man was on the sand: "After noon we descried one savage on the beach, and shortly after he was joined by three more, all mounted on horseback and attended by more than twenty dogs. In a little time Mr. Arms and the Captain appeared on the bank above the beach when a boat was sent from the schooner to bring them on board. Three of the savages came off with them, one of whom is a son of an aged chief whom they call *el capata le grande*, the grand captain. The young man is of more than middling size, firmly built,

---

65. Brackets by transcribers.
66. The number of weeks covered by the transcribed journal.
67. Coan, *Patagonia*, 46.

of an open countenance, and, for a savage, of modest and pleasant manners. He can speak a few words in English and more in Spanish. By signs and a little Spanish we signified to him that we wished him to furnish us with two horses and be our guide to the Indian camp among the northern hills, where we could spend the night, and return with him to the shore in the morning.

"This we were very anxious to do, that we might learn what we could about Patagonian life before the *Mary Jane* leaves us. The young chief seemed to understand and to consent to our desires. So we took him on shore, where he selected two horses for us, and, mounting his own, we set off on full gallop, leaving three Indians and one horse on the shore. After riding rapidly for four or five miles, our guide dismounted, drew out two pebbles from his skin pouch, struck fire and kindled the dry grass around us. This soon made a dense smoke, which was the signal for the other savages of his clan to come down."[68]

Arms and Coan were not the first to make contact with this group of people. The two Americans knew some Spanish and the indigenous people knew some Spanish, because the first Spaniards had arrived approximately three hundred years prior. Additionally, vessels of various European nationalities passed through the area to seal or travel to distant lands.

Arms and Coan were eager to learn about Patagonian life before the vessel left, perhaps to make sure there was not any threat to their lives before their scouting mission had begun. "On we galloped, but shortly we descried dark forms coming down the side of the mountain from a pass among the hills, one or two miles distant. Then another and another squad followed, while we rode on to meet them. The first detachment came up like a whirlwind, their long, coarse black hair streaming and their rough skin mantles flapping in the wind, while all were shouting in savage glee. The ground shook under the rush of their horses, and the atmosphere was clouded with dust. They surrounded us; they yelled and grinned; they were as noisy as a flock of loons, and as active as a swarm of bees. They talked with our guide; they tried to talk with us; they examined and counted our garments; they opened our vests, felt in our pockets, pulled up our trousers and thrust their hands into our boots. This was rough courtesy and a savage reception.

"Probably all this examination was to ascertain whether we had arms or tobacco. The former would have excited suspicion; the latter aroused their cupidity.

"They were large, strong, and bold men, quite independent in their bearing, and perfectly conscious that they were 'masters of the situation.' They were dark and filthy, ignorant and brutal in the last degree; and yet each man was a king in his own estimation, and their country was the greatest, the richest, and the best in the world. It had never been conquered, and these proud men were lords who knew no masters." While the Spaniards controlled the continent, as the Pathans of the Northwest Frontier

---

68. Coan, *Patagonia*, 49–50.

Province and the groups of Afghanistan were to the British, they had not conquered the Patagonians.

"They laughed, showing splendid rows of white teeth, and in five minutes the interview ended. Every man put spurs to his horse, and, with yells and an uproarious shout, the whole band, of about twenty, rushed toward the Strait, leaving a long cloud of dust behind them.

"Our guide wished to turn back and go with them to the shore, but we still urged him to proceed to the camp. This he did reluctantly, often lingering, dismounting, and showing a desire to return. We met a few more straggling companies of savages, and when the last came up it was impossible to press him forward any longer. We judged ourselves to be ten or twelve miles from the sea, with no signs of an Indian camp in sight. So when our guide turned his horse's head toward the shore, we had no alternative, and we wheeled also. This was near sundown. We gave our coursers the rein and followed our savage friends without stopping to think, to wink, or to breathe."[69]

On November sixteenth the journal entry indicates learning of a "Queen," with whom they hoped to meet. "Through seamen who have visited the Strait and seen numbers of this tribe of savages, we learn that a chief whom the sailors called Maria and dubbed the Queen was somewhere in this region. Supposing that this woman was invested with high authority, and wishing to have an early interview with her, we inquired of our old chief and his son where she was. They signified that she was gone far north to her winter quarters, but that she would return in about 'one moon' to her southern rambles. We then made them understand that we wished to leave our vessel to live with them for a season. The three Indians consulted together for about ten minutes, when the aged sire signified their assent to our proposal, promising by signs to put food into our mouths, to give us horses to ride, to carry our luggage, and to take good care of our persons."[70]

Even though they early on had these group and individual meetings, the missionary scouts wanted to observe and interact with a gathering of the Patagonians. Titus relates such an opportunity in the chapter entitled "Visiting the Indian Camp." He relates their arrival at the camp. He describes the geographical location, what they lived in, and something about their nature. "We found the savages encamped in a narrow valley between two ranges of hills which screen them from the strong winds of this country.

"On our approach to this first real Indian lodge which we had seen, all the savages, old and young, men, women, and children, with a new pack of dogs, rushed out to hail us. The dogs howled, the horses neighed, the men shouted and yelled, the children screamed and ran to and fro, hiding in and behind the tents, peeping out to get a sight of the strangers and then withdrawing through fear, while the whole camp was astir with noisy interest. There were remarkable sights and sounds, and wonderful

69. Coan, *Patagonia*, 50–51.
70. Coan, *Patagonia*, 54–55.

garrulity; and what odors too! In this camp we found a large number of Indians who were not on the shore. The lodge contains ten skin tents like the one on the beach. These hovels are arranged in a slightly curved line, all facing the east, as the prevailing winds are from the west. The tent in which the chief and his family live is larger and better than the rest, and is a little separated from them on the right."

He expresses appreciation for a stream with fresh water, as such was "extremely scarce in this land." He also notes that there is no wood. Bushes were the only plant suitable for burning. The missionaries are welcomed as family members and the Patagonians give tangible expressions of hospitality. "These chiefs seem to have adopted us as their children, and to feel a peculiar responsibility for our protection and comfort. All our baggage was brought safely up, even to the smallest article, and delivered to us in good condition.

"Everything being thus arranged, we took possession of our little 'tabernacle in the wilderness,' and felt almost at home once more, though 'in a strange land.' Sitting in our tent door as the winds were hushed and the mild sun was sinking behind the hills, the people gathered around us, full of smiles and beckonings and wakeful curiosity; and even the little children, naked as Adam in Eden, were running and leaping and giggling in their evening gambols, often venturing near our tent, looking in upon us with curious eyes, and then with a jolly shout returning again to their plays upon the turf.

"The old mother, wife of the aged chief, brought us a piece of guanaco[71] and of pork from the *Mary Jane*. It was cooked in an old iron pot, and upon this we made our first meal in the inland camp of the Indians; after which we offered up our evening thanks and petitions to him whose guardian love and care had led us thus far, and then, resting from care, enjoyed a peaceful sleep."

In the morning the curiosity continues. "**November 21.** Early in the morning the whole camp was astir, and the people flocked around our tent to watch our movements. Our hero, Louis, also came, and seeing me in the act of shaving, he begged me to take off his beard. This I did, apparently much to his gratification. Our breakfast, like our supper, was given us by the good old motherly chief, though this was evidently nearly the last morsel of meat in the tent.

"Thus far we have not suffered severely from hunger, as our Indian hosts divide their scanty pittance with us. This we eat without bread or vegetables." Coan relates how he spent his day and his interaction with the Patagonians, longing for an interpreter and lamenting that they are probably the only ones in the world who understand their language. "I spent the day in our little tent surrounded as usual by the natives, who take great pains to communicate with us, and who seem to wonder who and what we are, whence we came, and why we have voluntarily located ourselves among them. We long to converse with them, but there is no interpreter. Probably no

---

71. The guanaco is an animal native to the arid, mountainous regions of South America. Wikipedia, "Guanaco."

man on earth understands their language but themselves. They seem fond of their little children, and love to have us notice them. The children also are losing their shyness, and flock around us in a smiling and confiding way. We brought out many coarse combs, with finer ones for their use, and the little naked urchins seem delighted to have us teach them how to comb their swampy heads."

With typical Coan precision and detail he writes about the tribe's tents. "We have been examining their tents, or wigwams, and find they are made thus: Three or four rows, according to the size of the wigwam, of small stakes are set vertically in parallel lines in the ground. The first or front row may be five, six, or eight feet high, the second a foot or two shorter, and the third or fourth about two feet. On the tops of these upright stakes are slender longitudinal poles that reach from end to end of the hovel; they are lashed to the stakes with strips of skin or with the tendons of animals. This completes the frame. Over this a large covering of skins is spread and secured by thongs. The ends of the hut are secured by skins fastened to upright stakes or horizontal poles. The front is left open in fair weather; but in winter and during storms it is enclosed like the ends with curtains of skins. For this covering they use the skins of old guanacos, or those of the puma, cougar, or gray lion of South America. These skins are cut and well matched and sewed together with the sinews of animals, making blankets of convenient size, to be rolled, unrolled, spread on the tent, and removed at will. All the tents, including frames, coverings, partitions, etc., are made with reference to packing and transporting from one part of the country to another; for when a tribe or clan or division removes, nothing is left behind."

Next he describes what the natives wear. "The dress of these people in its primitive state was, of course, exclusively of skins. For this purpose the skins of the calves or young guanacos were selected because of the lightness of the material, but especially on account of the softness of the fur, or rather wool. This is short, thick, and soft, like lamb's wool, interspersed with thin scattering hairs. The Indians have the art of dressing these skins with the wool on, so that they are soft and pliable like dressed deer-skin.

"Thus prepared, they are cut by 'dovetailing' so as to secure the greatest economy of the material, and then sewed together with a small awl of iron, which they call *hodle*, according to the size desired. The form is that of a shawl or blanket, and it is often ornamented on the flesh side with various figures colored in pigment. This is the only garment of the males, except a narrow belt of skin or cloth to cover their nakedness. It is wrapped around the person like a blanket, and in cold and stormy weather it is drawn up so as to cover the head like a hood and fastened around the waist with 'a girdle of skin' like the mantle of John the Baptist [Mark 1:6]. When the weather is cold the wool side is turned inward, and outward when it is warm. When hunting, the Indian girds it tight about his loins to save it from being swept off by the wind, but lets it fall from his shoulders to flutter in the wind, while the arms and upper part of the body are free for the management of the reins, the lasso, the bolas, the spear, the bow and arrow, or the knife.

"The women dress like the men except that they wear a broader garment around the waist, extending from the hips to the knees. Over this the mantle is like that of the man. The foot is usually bare, but sometimes protected by moccasins made of the skin of a horse's or guanaco's leg, dressed soft and worn like a boot or stocking. They wear no head-dress but their long, coarse black hair. The small children wear 'Adam-skin.'"

Arms and Coan receive visitors and provide medical treatment. "We receive visitors as usual from morning to night, and endeavour to converse with them by signs, but it is hard to. Old Captain is groaning with pain and we apprehend that he may have a severe illness. Brother Arms has administered some medicine to him."

In the book as opposed to the original journal, Coan has much to write on a Sabbath day, November 24. He observes a Patagonian game, discusses Chief Louis not playing the game, discusses their moral code, and explains Coan's and Arms's efforts to educate them. He also relates how they view them as superior beings. "**Sunday, November 24.** The Indians had a long game at ball-play this forenoon; otherwise the day has been quiet. We have never seen our young chief Louis at a game of ball. Is it because he regards his dignity too highly? We cannot say. As yet we have seen nothing which looks like religious rites among this people, nor do we know whether they have any notions of a Supreme Being or a future state of existence. They have crude ideas of right and wrong. They praise and blame. The thief is shy and shows a sense of fear and guilt; and the man who has lost a knife, a file, or a piece of meat by a thief is full of rage and cursing. Of course their moral code, or their distinction between right and wrong, is very imperfect. We are forcibly impressed, however, with the truth asserted by Paul in regard to the heathen who have not the Scriptures: 'These having not the law, are a law unto themselves; who show the work of the law written in their hearts, their conscience also bearing witness, and their thoughts the mean while accusing or else excusing one another' [Rom 2:14].

"Most of this day we have spent in our little tabernacle, where we have been visited by many of the Indians, who have been very civil; and we have tried to interest them by signs. But ah! it is hard to be surrounded by these gazing, chattering savages without being able to teach them of 'the true God and Eternal Life' [1 John 5:20]. We long for an interpreter, to open an avenue to their understandings and hearts. But our desires are vain.

"These savages seem to look upon us as of a superior race of beings, and they are more and more careful not to do things which appear to displease us, often quietly asking liberty to come into our tent, and carefully avoiding meddling with our furniture without leave.

"We show them maps and pictures, and interest them with object-lessons so far as we have the means to teach them. The effect of checking them when noisy and rude, and in every effort to commit petty depredations, appears favorable; and thus we are enabled to impress them with some moral lessons and to lead them in some degree. We look upon them with pity and compassion, and they gaze upon us with unceasing wonder."

At one point, Coan climbs a small mountain and describes the panorama. This foreshadows in a small way his Renaissance man exploration of mountains and volcanoes in Hawai'i.

Coan and Arms worked on learning Spanish so they could better communicate with the Patagonians. They hoped to meet runaway sailors to help them communicate. The natives continued to be curious and sit at their feet. How Coan and Arms must have yearned to communicate the gospel. "Cold and dreary. We spend a large portion of our time in reading, writing, and studying Spanish.

"We hear that there are some Indians in other clans who know more Spanish and English words than any we have yet met. We learn, also, that there are several runaway captive sailors among the northern clans, and that these clans will soon visit us, with the queen, Maria, and these English and American captives. We therefore await with great interest their arrival, hoping to find some better medium of communication than we now have, and thus to learn more of the country and its inhabitants.

"The Indians come to us in crowds, filling our tent, squatting before the door, and straining their black eyes to look in and see what we are doing. Many of them are pleasant in their demeanor, and bring us pieces of meat. But we depend chiefly upon our host, Louis, to supply our wants."[72]

Eventually Coan and Arms were affected by a family feud and had to leave. Coan describes a strong storm, what he calls "a squall." Years later while reflecting on Darwin's visit to the same area at the same time as Coan and Arms, Titus would write: "It seems that the *Beagle* was at Port Desire and Port St. Julian in December 1833 and January 1834 while we at the same time were travelling in the region of the Strait of Magellan, surrounded by large clans of savages."[73]

By late December he meets "The Great Chief Congo and His Clan."[74] On December 23 he describes him and his visit. "Soon after his arrival this grand captain came and introduced himself to us as the great chief of the tribe, and spent several hours with us. He is a splendid specimen of physical organization, about six feet three inches high, well formed and graceful in figure and movements. He has a mild, open countenance with an intellectual stamp, and full of kindness and good-nature. His manners are easy and natural, and one might at first sight take him for a half-civilized native.

"He rides a splendid horse, and dressed in his skin leggins [sic] and rich fur mantle he makes a fine appearance for a Patagonian. He speaks many Spanish and some English words, and thinks himself quite a learned man, especially as he can count ten in English.

72. Coan, *Patagonia*, 64–89.
73. Coan, *Patagonia*, 271.
74. Coan, *Patagonia*, 124.

"He told us that a large part of this tribe were with Santa Maria, and that they would be here in one moon.

"He inquired of us about our country. Was it great? Were there plenty of guanacos? How we came to Patagonia; how many moons we were on the water? How long we had been here; how long we would remain? What goods we had brought? Whether we were not great captains and owners of many vessels? And many such like questions. To all these inquiries we gave him truthful answers that seemed to satisfy and please him. He was also curious to know the English name of almost everything around. After a social interview he invited us to visit him at 'de casa le grande'—the great house—and presenting his hand in all the apparent cordiality of civilized etiquette, he left us and returned to his own tent."

Coan describes the tribes as Bedouins in charge of their destiny. He met a man subordinate to Chief Congo. This man spoke Spanish and gave evidence of having been with Catholic priests. As with Congo, he was inquisitive. He told Coan about Queen Maria, who was at Port St. Julian, north of Santa Cruz, on the Atlantic coast.

Things go well for the time being and apparently Coan views his success as sufficient to eventually find a vessel to return to Boston and make a recommendation to have missionaries establish themselves permanently in Patagonia. "All things now look bright and cheering, and in our connection with this large company we hope to increase our knowledge of the country, and of the numbers, character, and habits of its inhabitants. These facts once obtained we shall be ready to embrace the earliest opportunity to return to our country and report, agreeably with our instructions, in Boston. But as no provision has been made for a vessel to come for us, the time of our departure from this country is altogether uncertain: whether in a month, a year, or never is all unknown to us."

Coan writes about the physical stature of the indigenous people. He notes that while they are tall they are not giants. He responds to the "romantic" reports of nine- or ten-foot-tall savages. "The Indians of this land are physically a noble race. They are tall, well formed, and strong. They are not, however, gigantic. None of them are over six feet six inches, and few of them will weigh over two hundred pounds; and there is not a large proportion of them that will measure over six feet in height. Owing to the nature of their food, their great exertions to procure their game, and their roaming habits, there is little tendency to obesity among them. I have seen taller and much larger men among Americans and Europeans than among Patagonians. We are inclined to estimate the average height of what are called by sailors the 'Horse Indians,' or the pampas tribes, at five feet ten inches, and their average weight at 170 pounds. We think the extravagant estimate so often made of the size of the Patagonians has arisen from seeing them standing, walking, or riding on the shore, wrapped in their immense mantles of skin with the wool on, and with the upper end of this mantle rising above the head like a hood.

"Some strangers have estimated the height of these savages at nine or more feet, and it may not be improbable that some of them have indulged in a touch of romantic exaggeration."[75]

Christmas day passes without notice. Coan and Arms continue their usual activities. Again, foreshadowing some of his ministry to Hawaiians, when he writes on December 26, "The day has been filled up with our usual round of duties; entertaining the savages, making little articles of use to them, distributing small presents, attending to the sick, etc."[76]

January 1, 1834, dawns dreary both in the sky and the heart. Arms and Coan greet each other with New Year felicitations yet their thoughts turn toward home. We salute each other with 'a happy new year,' while our thoughts turn to the dear friends in the land of our fathers. We are here among savages, shut out from all the tender and precious endearments and priceless privileges of social and Christian civilization. No whispers of sympathy come to us on the night air, no voice of love echoes along these everlasting mountains from the northern winter to the regions of southern summer. No white-winged messenger-bird comes over the wide waste of waters to tell us of our loved ones' welfare. No morning greetings and evening benedictions of 'kith and kin' come to our ears. No voices arrest us but the harsh sounds of the savages, the neighing of horses and baying of dogs, the roar of winds, and the rush and rattle of rain and hail."[77]

Chief Congo rouses the camp and the group begins the trek to Gregory Bay. January third is a more pleasant day than the first. "Our present location is pleasant. On our left is a range of low mountains, overlooking a broad extent of country, including the Magellan Strait and the distant and dim shores of Tierra del Fuego. In our rear is a hill to break the force of the wind, with an open champaign[78] in front."

Word reaches the group that "Queen Maria is advancing with a very large train, and our camp is all astir."[79] Coan devotes the next chapter[80] to "The Arrival of the 'Queen.'" The first people Coan relates meeting in that chapter are "two young sailors, named Henry Boruck and Harry Hassel."[81] They had been with the Patagonians for eight months. While Coan feels a "painful sympathy" for them, he is concerned over the deleterious affect they are having on the Patagonians, not unlike some sailors in the Sandwich Islands.

Next, Nicholas Druery comes on the scene. He was rescued with the rest of the schooner *Transport* crew after it wrecked on Tierra del Fuego. He tells of another man

75. Coan, *Patagonia*, 124–31.
76. Coan, *Patagonia*, 136.
77. Coan, *Patagonia*, 143–44.
78. "An expanse of level open country." Merriam Webster, "Champaign."
79. Coan, *Patagonia*, 147.
80. Coan, *Patagonia*, 148–59.
81. Coan, *Patagonia*, 148.

who lives among the Patagonians, one Daniel Smith.[82] Coan observes the "treatment" by a Patagonian doctor of the Spaniard, Santo Rio. "By what we saw on this occasion we are led to think that these savages, like many of the more civilized races, believe in possession by evil spirits, and that these wild and superstitious measures are practiced to exorcise them."[83]

On January 6, Coan records his and Arms's first meeting with the Queen. "The long-looked-for Patagonian Queen has at last arrived. She comes to us not in regal pomp and royal splendor, attended with a brilliant retinue of 'peers of the realm,' but as a savage squaw with a few straggling attendants, and escorted hither by Mr. Arms, who went up to her camp this morning.

"Santa Maria is an aged woman, tall, large, and well formed, with a mild and somewhat intelligent face. She is partially civilized; has visited the Falkland Islands, and converses tolerably well in Spanish. She appears amiable in her disposition, and we are pleased with her. She is now living, as we are told, with her fourth husband, whose name is Kahatech. She has four sons, viz., Parpon, Toorloon, Checo, and Bistante. The oldest is a captain in the clan.

"On entering our tent the Queen offered me her hand with civility and kindness, and then introduced her husband, for whom she manifests much affection.

"We prepared a dinner of boiled meat, and our royal guests partook with us in the best style we could offer. They seemed to relish the savory meat, and, as we furnished but one course, the dinner was soon despatched. Our conversation then turned on various subjects, and she inquired of us how long we would remain in her country, what goods we had brought, when there would be more vessels at the bay, etc., etc."[84]

Coan describes a gift he and Arms give the Queen. He relates a visit to her tent, the gifts she gives them, and her service to them including bringing a bucket of water for them to wash in the morning. Upon seeing an individual referred to as "padre," he inquires as to burial and marriage customs. The burial customs are minimal. Marriage involves purchase and polygamy is practiced by most Patagonian men.[85]

In the next chapter,[86] Coan reports a French brig from Valparaíso that passes through on the way to Havre, France. He relates that there is no correspondence for them[87] while understanding that he accepted the commission to Patagonia with the understanding there would be no sending or receiving of mail during the scouting trip. "Thus the first vessel we have seen has come and gone without a letter or a paper from our dear country, or 'a wish or a thought' from friends who are dear to us as life.

---

82. Coan, *Patagonia*, 148–52.
83. Coan, *Patagonia*, 154.
84. Coan, *Patagonia*, 154–56.
85. Coan, *Patagonia*, 157–59.
86. Chapter IX, "Sail Ho!"
87. The odds of transferring of correspondence to such a ship are quite high.

This is tantalizing, but we bear it patiently, for it is one of the conditions of our mission to Patagonia."

In the same journal entry of January 8, Coan and Arms decide not to take advantage of this return opportunity, wanting instead to meet more Patagonians before heading home. "'Though the vision tarry' [Hab 2:3] we will wait for it, because it will come in due time. We are not prepared to leave this country as yet... The good Lord will send us a direct conveyance back to our country and friends. So we wait the will of our Master."[88]

But Titus does let his human side show. He offered to buy sea biscuit and a few edibles from the captain, who says he has none to spare. Coan asks to sleep on the transom. First he goes to the galley where everyone has already eaten. He espies one pancake. He then relates this poignant scene complete with stream of consciousness. "Now we are forbidden to covet, but I found it hard to suppress my desire to eat that cake. Still I held back till near bed-time, trying hard to entertain the captain with conversation, especially on matters pertaining to his profession as a seaman and on my experiences of Patagonian life, hoping that my remarks on these experiences in the matter of eating would be rightly interpreted. At last forbearance seemed to cease to be a virtue, and I became desperate and burst out with 'Captain, I am very hungry; I have eaten nothing since morning, and have eaten nothing made of flour for many weeks. I see a cake on your table and with your permission I would like to eat it.' He gave his consent, and immediately, called out, 'Steward! here, bring on some grub; this man is hungry.' In rushed the steward with a plate of 'cold junk' (salt beef) and another of 'hard-tack' (sea biscuit). The feast was sweeter to my taste than the best Thanksgiving dinner I ever ate, though it might have been sweeter still. I thanked the captain for my delicious repast and lay down on the transom for the night."[89]

In his January 11 journal entry, Coan relates a conversation with "Captain Congo and the Spanish Indian into our tent to-day, to inquire more at length of them about the country and the people. These men tell us that they have travelled all over Patagonia, and their descriptions accorded so nearly with our maps that we were satisfied that they had seen what they reported."

After talking about the Atlantic coast going north from the Strait, they eventually inquired about the interior of the land. "Having thus followed our guides along the Atlantic coast, where we had data and way-marks to detect errors, we next requested them to lead us through the interior, which, to all the world beside the Patagonian, is a terra incognita, and a land of romantic conjecture."

After discussing that area, they discussed lands farther west, including the mountain ranges and spurs. When they asked about populations, they received the following

---

88. Coan, *Patagonia*, 161–62. The LOC journal indicates that the French schooner captain offered Coan and Arms free passage to Havre. In addition to wanting to do more scouting, Coan might have wondered about the length of the journey home when it was by way of the west coast of France.

89. Coan, *Patagonia*, 163–65.

response. "On the northern borders are what he called the Oucas[90] tribe, numbering several thousands. These live in tents of skin like the southern clans, and are partly agricultural and partly nomadic. They have horned cattle, horses, and sheep, and they also cultivate the earth to some extent. Occasionally they remove to short distances to obtain grass for their cattle when it is exhausted near them."

Coan provides analysis of the information he has received from these two men. "This account of the inhabitants of this great and wild country, with its islands and smaller islets, may be approximately correct or it may be erroneous. I give it as received on the best authority we now have. But our data are few and our sources of information imperfect. If corrected by further researches we shall be glad."

He next discusses his views of the Patagonians' ideas on immortality of the soul, the future state, and the Supreme Being. "About the immortality of the soul and the character of the future state, subjects which we brought forward in this conversation, we find their notions somewhat similar to those of the North American Indians. They believe in the existence of the soul after death, and in a distinction between the good and bad. When a good Indian dies they say he will go to a land where there is no night, no winter, no pain, and no death, but where there is constant sunshine and eternal beauty, and where all will be supplied with fine horses and with everything which the heart desires; but as there will be no hunger or thirst there will be no need of hunting and striving for food. When the bad Indian dies, they say he will descend deep to an evil land, filled with darkness and barrenness and thorns, where there is much fighting and sorrow.

"We could not feel sure that these crude notions of the future state, with its rewards and punishments, originated with the Patagonian savages. It seems more probable that they are the result of imperfect information on the Christian religion communicated to them by sailors or Spaniards with whom they have come in contact.

"We could not find that they have any distinct notions of a Supreme Being who created and who sustains and governs all things. When we called their attention to tangible objects, as mountains, waters, the sun, moon, etc., and inquired who made all these things, their minds seemed utterly blank, as if it were a subject on which they had never bestowed a passing thought. As yet we have seen nothing which appeared like religious worship among them. One day, while riding out in company with Captain Louis, on coming to a clump of bushes he dismounted, and with his knife cut off a portion of his horse's mane, rolled it into a little wisp, dug a hole among the bushes and carefully buried it. He then remounted his horse and we rode on without explanation, so that I was left only to conjecture as to the meaning of the act."

Coan asks them if they would like American teachers to read. "On inquiring how they would like to have American teachers come and teach them to read and write, as we did, and to instruct them in all things useful and good, they seemed delighted with the idea, and said it was 'much bono.' And when we suggested the thought of building

---

90. Auca? AKA Huaroni tribe? They are in Ecuador. Wikipedia, "Auca." Perhaps homonym.

a large mission-house at Gregory's Bay, where their children might remain and be instructed while the parents roamed for sustenance for themselves and their horses, 'they became much animated with the subject, and said that the Indians would all leave their children with the Americans, and would come now and then to see them and bring them 'much guanaco and much mantle.'"

"They seemed very anxious to know if missionaries would be sent, and how many moons it would be before they would come; also whether they would build 'casa grande'—a large tent—with many other things relating to the subject. Of course we could make them no definite promise, but we thought it well to put these questions in order to ascertain their minds with regard to them though they little understood their import, in order to have something to report to the friends of missions in the United States."

This discussion was followed by despairing "of ever being able to reach the western coast by land in the vicinity of the peninsula of Tres Montes, and we can only wait the developments of Providence of our future course." An English boat arrived within a few days. Coan and Arms converse with "H. Penny, of Liverpool, England, owner of the schooner Sappho and cargo, bound to Mazatlan, California."

When Penny inquires about cannibals, Coan assures him that he is safe. Penny then "inquired earnestly as to our situation and life among this people, and I gave him the principal facts briefly." Days later Coan presages his Hawaiian "peace man" perspective when he comments on why he did not carry a firearm. "And just here it may be proper to remark that from personal experience, observation, and reflection, I have been led to the firm conviction that carrying weapons, whether at home or abroad, whether travelling in civilized or savage countries, is seldom a protection of life, but the contrary. Among savages the armed man is watched, suspected, feared, and this jealous fear often provokes attack. As with nations, so with individuals, arming on one side leads to arming on the other side, suspicion excites suspicion, fear awakens fear, and intimidation provokes intimidation, until blow responds to blow, and there is war in the wigwam, in the camp, and in the field.

"When selecting an outfit in Boston and New York, some of our kindest friends advised us to take arms as protectors in times of emergency and danger. This counsel we rejected and went unarmed, and as unprotected as children. And this weakness we believe to be our strength. This defenceless condition is our defence. This lack of firearms is as 'a wall of fire round about us'"[91] [Zech 2:5].

After another chapter entitled "Camp Life,"[92] Coan describes his departure from Patagonia. While he does not point to any one event leading to a decision to recommend against a mission or a decision to leave Patagonia, he does relate dysfunction within and between clans. At the end of that chapter, Coan notes in his January 24 entry that Mr. Arms arrived "with the report that the schooner Antarctic, of New

---

91. Coan, *Patagonia*, 165–83.
92. Coan, *Patagonia*, Chapter X.

York, Captain James S. Nash, of Rhode Island, had anchored in the bay, and that the captain would take us on board to-morrow, requesting us to be down at the sea at 9 a.m."[93]

As they took their leave, one Patagonian "held up a religious tract and called out to us to look on while he dashed it into the sea." The Queen followed suit and the captain explained what was behind her action. "This token of contempt was at once imitated by the Queen, who raised a bundle of tracts in the air and in a spiteful manner threw them over-board, exclaiming 'Malo! malo!' The captain afterwards told us that these tracts were stolen from his cabin, that Maria said we had a chest full of them, that they were very bad, and that by means of our paper we prevented them from getting rum and tobacco; that she had also complained of Mr. Arms that he was very bad, and had declared that as soon as she got on shore she would tear up the papers before his eyes, and then stab him with a knife which she drew from her bosom and showed him. These threats had led the captain to take the precaution of sending her and her people on shore while we were coming off, that thus a meeting might be avoided, as he had no doubt she would execute her threat should she find an opportunity. It might have happened so had we met the old Queen, but as we were blissfully ignorant of this danger until safe on board, we were saved from fear and anxiety. We are under great obligations to Captain Nash, who has treated us with much kindness, and who has shown firmness and discretion in getting us on board."

Apparently the Queen was upset that Coan and Arms were leaving. Captain Nash informed Titus that the previous captain, on whose schooner Titus had eaten and slept, had chatted with him two weeks prior. That captain let him know of the mistreatment he had received from the Patagonians.

Near the end of the "Farewell to Patagonia" chapter, Coan writes some comments that might hint at his eventual recommendation against the Board sending a permanent mission there. "And now our prow was pointed eastward towards the great Atlantic and we were really 'home-ward bound.' We saw the savages on the shore all astir, getting up their horses, packing, mounting, and moving off to their dismal homes. This to us was a sad picture; for though we are joyful at the thought that our exploring mission is accomplished, and that we show compassion; their kindness kindles our gratitude; and the blindness of their moral and spiritual natures awakens our sympathies and our love. are now on our way back to our thrice-blessed native land, and to our precious friends from whom we have received no tidings for nearly six months, yet it was painful to see these poor, dark-souled human beings for whom the Saviour died left in their darkness and ruin, and with little hope that the blessings of Christianity and civilization would ever come to their generation."

The above paragraph is in the book, but not the original journal. Could this be an addition by Coan to help explain or justify the ultimate recommendation not to return to Patagonia?

93. Coan, *Patagonia*, 208.

The book "journal entry" continues, with some phrases that are found in the original journal.[94] "Thus **commingled emotions** of joy and pity **move our** hearts. **The remembrance of their abominations pains and sickens our souls; their wretchedness excites our compassion; their kindness kindles our gratitude**; and the blindness of their moral and spiritual natures awakens our sympathies and our love."[95]

"**Ah! when will the day dawn and the day star arise upon them?**" [2 Pet 1:19].

He concludes with a paragraph that it is the end of the chapter and the end of the eleven weeks' transcribed Library of Congress journal. "Well, we are in the cabin of the swift clipper Antarctic, a beautiful schooner of 173 tons, running like a racer, while the shores of Patagonia are gathering the mantle of night over them and fading from our view."[96]

In chapter XII, Coan relates his brief "Life at the Falkland Islands." His January 29 journal entry is labeled "*Albermale Harbor, Falkland Islands.*" On March 8 he writes, "We have now been at these islands forty days save one, and expect to leave on the fortieth. We have met hundreds of our fellow-men of about twelve different nationalities. We have received nothing but respect and kindness from all; and we have endeavored so to live among them as to convince all of our earnest desire for their welfare here and forever."[97]

Chapter XIII relates his being "Homeward Bound." They depart the Falklands on March 9. They arrived at New London Harbor at 1 a.m. on May 6.[98]

Humphrey summarizes Arms and Coan's sojourn in Patagonia. Perhaps reflecting what Coan calls the romanticism of the place and people of Patagonia, Humphrey writes, "With one companion, the Rev. Mr. Arms, he was set ashore among the savages of Gregory Bay. Their little vessel had sighted the *Beagle* in the straits, the vessel on which Charles Darwin was making his famous voyage of exploration. It is a suggestive thought that the missionaries of science and of religion should thus have crossed each other's tracks at the outset. Mr. Coan and Mr. Arms lived and roamed with the ferocious nomads of the eastern coast of Patagonia, striving in vain to communicate to them something of their message. The savages grew suspicious of their motives, and at last it became evident that there was nothing to do but to escape with their lives, if possible. A chance vessel gave them the opportunity; they evaded their captors by stratagem and were returned to New London [Connecticut] in May 1834, after an absence of four months."[99]

---

94. Original journal overlapping book entry words in bold letters. Book words only in non bold.
95. The original journal has these words: "**their immortal souls enkindle my love.**"
96. Coan, *Patagonia*, 211–20.
97. Coan, *Patagonia*, 223, 253.
98. Coan, *Patagonia*, 254, 265.
99. Humphrey, "VI. Titus Coan," 4–5.

Titus Coan: "Apostle to the Sandwich Islands"

EARLY RETURN TO US AND RECOMMENDATION AGAINST SENDING ABCFM MISSIONARIES THERE

After putting in at New London, Connecticut, Titus went to Fidelia at the Female Seminary in Middlebury, "much re-duced by my arduous labors."[100] Coan never referred to the physical toll the trip took on him.

The Arms and Coan journey concluded on May 8, 1834, when they "took stage" from New London "to Boston this morning to meet the Prudential Committee of the ABCFM and report" on their mission on which they had been sent by the Prudential Committee. Those at the Mission House were dumbfounded, because there had been no communication received from the two missionary scouts. "All were surprised to see us, as nothing had been heard from us from the day of our embarkation in New York until we entered the rooms of the Board in Boston to-day."[101]

Humphrey, perhaps paraphrasing Coan, writes, "It was like a reappearance from the dead. Not a word from Mr. Coan had reached family or friends during all this time; and to the heart of one whom he had left behind the separation was perhaps as bitter as death, because of its uncertain duration and fate."[102]

Coan concludes his journal extracts with an understated yet profound sentence of recommendation: "Our report was unfavorable to the present establishing of a mission in Patagonia."[103] It is not known whether those words are in the original handwritten diary.[104]

The *Missionary Herald* provides a four-part serialization of Coan and Arms in Patagonia. But the most revealing portion is found on pages 20 and 21 of the 1835 volume 31 wherein a destination change allegedly leads to both a shortened time in Patagonia and to the recommendation that the Board take no action, that it send no Board missionaries there for permanent settlement and ministry.

"For prudential[105] reasons the [Prudential] Committee did not describe the plan of this mission last year, thinking the publication of it might in some way embarrass their missionaries." This is rare candor on the pages of the official organ of a mission organization. What follows is excruciating detail. "The destination of these brethren was to the western coast of Patagonia, and it was expected that they would land about latitude 47 or 48 degrees south."[106] Remember the change to the east affected as a result

---

100. Fidelia Church to Maria C. Robinson, August 31, 1834, LOC.
101. Coan, "VI. Titus Coan," *Patagonia*, 267–68.
102. Humphrey, 5.
103. Coan, *Patagonia*, 268.
104. See Fidelia Church letter, below.
105. No pun intended?
106. *Missionary Herald* 1835, vol. 31, 20.

of Captain Clift's input. Coan notes in his journal after the sighting of land: "lat. 48 ° S., lon. 65° 14."[107] It will be noted that the latitude is within the range provided—48°.

Returning to *The Missionary Herald*: "[B]ut owing to a misunderstanding in regard to the destination of the vessel, that could not be carried to that point, and were landed at Gregory's Bay near the eastern entrance of the Straits of Magellan . . . And as the population of the accessible country amounted to but a few hundreds, they thought it expedient to return to the United States." After a thank you to the shipmasters who did not charge the two men for the return voyage, "the Committee refer the Board for the results of this mission."[108]

Next comes the payoff, with the wondering of what might have been and how history might have been changed if they had debarked where they planned. Unlike the Pilgrims, who stayed in the Plymouth Rock area, what might have happened (and not happened) if the Board had assigned Coan to Patagonia and, therefore, he had not gone to the Sandwich Islands? "Their early return has been approved by the Committee. Mr. Arms has since been designated to the Indian Archipelago, and Mr. Coan to the Sandwich Islands. No farther [sic] measures are proposed, for the present, in Patagonia."[109]

Lydia writes about a historical "what if" in a bridge section at the conclusion of the Patagonia chapter in *Memorial Volume*. "Who can doubt that he himself would have made the self-denial [of returning to Patagonia on a long-term basis], had the guiding Hand led him to retrace his steps to that field?

"There were other paths for him to follow."[110] Do these words belie information Lydia had been given by Titus or, years before, by Fidelia? Ehlke relates a portion of a letter from Fidelia Church to her sister Maria. This letter provides the real reasons behind the recommendation to not send missionaries by the Board. "Fidelia confided to her sister Maria: 'When he returned from Patagonia he had the Indian mission in view.'" That certainly sounds like Titus was ready to recommend a permanent mission and to volunteer to be part of that mission.

But "on a prayerful & I trust impartial examination of the subject we came to the conclusion . . ."—Notice that Titus and his fianceé came to a mutually agreed to decision—". . . that in view of my disability [inability?] to perform manual labour to any considerable extent, some other field gave promise of more usefulness in my sphere.'" She also presents a drawback for Titus—language learning—that might underlie other concerns, such as difficulty to have a steady diet of food[111] and psychological duress of

---

107. Coan journal entry, November 8, 1834, in Coan, *Patagonia*, 46.

108. *Missionary Herald* 1835, vol. 31, 21.

109. *Missionary Herald* 1835, vol. 31, 21.

110. Coan, *Memorial Volume*, 20.

111. In a March 11, 2016, email, Tom Woods then of the Mission Houses in Honolulu writes the following about a tragic mission effort fifteen years later in Patagonia: "The Patagonian Missionary Society was established in London to bring Christianity to Patagonia, and seven missionaries accompanied Capt. Gardiner there on the *Ocean Queen* in 1850. The next year the English crews of the

living among this group of people. "'And as his health seemed an obstacle to the severe mental application wh[ich] the acquisition of an oriental language requires we came to the conclusion that the most promising field for us as the S. Islands.'"

A specific area was selected by the couple and, within two months of Titus's return from Patagonia, the Board would agree with it.[112] It is possible that the Board felt the couple had already made great sacrifices and wanted to honor their legitimate request.

The Fidelia quotation in Ehlke concludes with these words: "I hope that the revelation of the *Great Day* will show that we were honest in our reasoning and correct in the result."[113]

In one year and a little less than a month, Mr. and Mrs. Titus Coan would arrive after a long ocean journey in Hilo, beginning what would be for Fidelia thirty-seven years of ministry, and for Titus, forty-seven. His journey to, in, and from Patagonia would provide insight for his decades of service in Hawai'i as "Papa Coan."

E. Davidson and the *Dido* found the remains of the missionaries. Death was presumed to be from starvation after having been 'shunned' by the Patagonian natives." Coan writes about this situation in chapter XVI, entitled "The Story of Capt. Gardiner, RN," 291–310.

112. See the next chapter for the Board's appointment of the Coans to the Sandwich Islands.

113. Fidelia Church to Maria Church Robinson, August 31, 1834, LOC, in Ehlke, "Enthusiastic Religion," 75.

3

Call to and Arrival in the Sandwich Islands

"The bay of Hilo is a beautiful, spacious, and safe harbor. The outline of its beach is a crescent, like the moon in her first quarter. The beach is composed of fine, volcanic sand, mixed with a little coral and earth. On its eastern and western sides, and in its center, it is divided by three streams of pure water; it has a deep channel about half a mile wide, near the western shore, sufficiently deep to admit the largest ship that floats. Seaward it is protected by a lava reef one mile from the shore. This reef was formed by a lateral stream of lava, sent out at right angles from a broad river of molten rocks that formed our eastern coast. This reef is a grand barrier against the swell of the ocean. Lord Byron, who visited Hilo, when he brought home the corpses of King Liholiho and his queen, gave the name of "Byron's Bay" to this harbor, but that name is nearly obsolete."[1]

"The beach was once beautifully adorned with the coca palm, whose lofty plumes waved and rustled and glittered in the fresh seabreeze. Beyond our quiet bay the broad, blue ocean foams or sleeps, with a surface sometimes shining like molten silver, tumbling in white foam, or gently throbbing as with the pulsations of life."[2]

"Inland, from the shore to the bases of the mountains, the whole landscape is 'arrayed in living green,'[3] presenting a picture of inimitable beauty, so varied in tint, so

---

1. Coan, *Life*, 24–25.
2. Coan, *Life*, 25.
3. "On Jordan's stormy banks I stand,
   And cast a wishful eye
   To Canaan's fair and happy land,
   Where my possessions lie.
   O the transporting, rapt'rous scene,
   That rises to my sight!
   Sweet fields arrayed in living green,
   And rivers of delight!"
        Lyrics by Samuel Stennett, 1787.

grooved with water channels, and so sparkling with limpid streams and white foaming cascades, as to charm the eye, and cause the beholder to exclaim, 'This *is* a scene of surpassing loveliness'" [1 Cor 12:21].[4]

"From the shore the land rises upon a uniform angle to the foot of Mauna Kea and Mona Roa,[5] a distance of thirty miles. Behind all this in the background tower the lofty, snow-mantled mountains, Kea and Loa, out of one of which rush volcanic fires. At the first sight we were charmed with the beauty and the grandeur of the scene, and we exclaimed, 'Surely the lines are fallen to us in pleasant places, and we have a goodly heritage'" [Ps 16:6].[6]

"From this the mountains raise their majestic summits amidst the clouds, and stand as everlasting monuments of the power of their creator. Their height [has] been computed to eighteen thousand feet, but later measurements make them less.[7] At the foot of Mauna Roa is the great volcano of which you have heard.[8] We often see its awful fires throwing their lurid glare upon the clouds at night, and we are sometimes visited by earthquakes which make us feel our impotence in his hands who shakes the earth out of her place, and makes the pillars thereof tremble" [Job 9:6].

"The climate of Hilo is cool. In the day-time the heat is moderated by a sea breeze, and during the night by a pure wind from the mountains. The soil is a mixture of decomposed lava and vegetable mould,[9] and being watered by abundant rains produces a great variety of rich and luxuriant vegetation, such as cocoanuts, breadfruit, plantain, bananas, pine apples, citrons, lemons, limes, (oranges don't do well) guavas . . ."[10]

"The first thing I would say in addressing you is to record the unmeasured goodness of God in bringing me into the field of labor to which I have long looked with strong desire."[11]

INTRODUCTION

After his return from Patagonia, events moved quickly for Titus and Fidelia. As noted in the previous chapter, Titus and Fidelia consulted and prayed together, reaching a decision to not go to Patagonia. This led to an official public recommendation against establishing a mission there. The Coans requested a posting to the Sandwich Islands and the board honored that request. After making a recommendation of no mission to Patagonia, the Board appointed Titus to go to the Sandwich Islands. In short order

4. Coan, *Life*, 25.
5. Mauna Loa. See discussion in Preface of fluidity of pronunciation and spelling in the early years.
6. Coan, *Life*, 25–26.
7. See Ed Coan and USGS estimates on elevation.
8. Kilauea?
9. See Preface discussion of spelling.
10. Letter, np nd.
11. Titus Coan to George and Mabel Coan, October 20, 1835, in [?]

they were married; he was commissioned; and they boarded the *Hellespont* for the arduous journey, including the previously-navigated Straits of Magellan. After the passage of some time they continued on to Honolulu, arriving there midyear 1835 during the annual meeting of the Board missionaries in Hawai'i. After attending the meetings and staying with the Binghams, the Coans were sent to the small town of Hilo on the Big Island. They lived in close quarters with the Lymans until the Goodriches vacated their dwelling. This structure would become known as "The Emerald Bower" as Titus made improvements to it over the years. They both engaged in language study. Titus did some preaching in English. He began preaching in Hawaiian, first at the Hilo church, then on tours, including the Puna district. The first tour would bring him to the cusp of the Hawaiian Great Awakening.

PRE-DEPARTURE

After Titus and Fidelia agreed to not go to Patagonia, they requested that the Board send them to the Sandwich Islands. Instead of no support system, Hawai'i had fifteen years of mission infrastructure ready to receive and assist them. The Board granted their request. "A letter from Dr. Benjamin B. Wisner, Secretary of the American Board, announcing their appointment to the Sandwich Islands Mission arrived in July to set the evangelical network in motion."

Approximately two months after returning to the United States from Patagonia, Titus and Fidelia received word that the Board had confirmed their hoped-for mission location. Lydia Coan provides a bridging comment and a quotation from an undated and uncited letter. "In July he was informed of his appointment to the Hawaiian Mission. 'I received this announcement,' he writes, 'with great joy, for, although I was willing to go to any missionary field on the face of the earth, yet the Sandwich Islands had ever been a field of peculiar and special interest to me.'"[12]

Titus began the process of requesting needed materials for the trip and their initial time in Hawai'i. He "dispatched a letter to Miss Sarah Oliphant of Auburn, addressing her as 'the Missionary Oracle.' 'You doubtless know better than any one within the circle of my acquaintance what is necessary to our outfit. Will you be so kind as to sit *immediately* down (if your health and circumstances permit) and give me in a letter as complete a list of articles for this mission as you can.'"[13]

He continues his letter to Sarah Oliphant with specific requests. "The ladies of the Second Church in Rochester donated 'cloth for wearing apparel to the amount of $40.00—the ladies in Riga above $20.00 besides donations of various descriptions and values from different individuals in these and other places.'[14] The First Church in Rochester assisted Titus with his outfit, and friends in Medina put together a box

---

12. Undated and uncited Titus Coan letter in Coan, *Memorial Volume*, 21.
13. Titus Coan to Sarah Oliphant, July 25, 1834, LOC, in Ehlke, "Enthusiastic Religion," 75.
14. Titus Coan to Sarah Oliphant, July 25, 1834, LOC, in Ehlke, "Enthusiastic Religion," 75.

valued at $95.00. Fidelia's shoulder gave her no trouble as she sewed the light garments she knew she would need in the Sandwich Islands."[15]

Titus and Fidelia may well have used the "Outfit for the Sandwich Islands," which was "Prepared by the Mission in 1834." Within quotation marks it is noted that "Articles necessary as an outfit to the Sandwich Islands; it being deemed a sufficient supply for three years." The following are the major categories, with numbers and specific items listed under each category: "Gentlemen's Outfit for the Voyage, of 150 days"[16]; "Gentleman's Outfit for the Islands"; "Lady's Outfit for the Voyage"; "Lady's Outfit for the Islands"; "Furniture"; "Crockery"; "Kitchen Furniture"; "Iron Ware, etc." Almost two hundred distinct items are listed in approximately 8-point print on one page in the *Missionary Album*.[17]

The Board had hoped to send Titus and Fidelia by sail vessel as soon as possible, but delay developed. Dr. Wisner showed the control the Board had over couples under its care when he "wrote in late September that no passage had yet been obtained, adding these instructions: 'You will be notified as soon as it is settled. You will defer marriage till you get such notice.'"[18]

Ehlke notes that almost one "month later Dr. Rufus Anderson wrote from Boston that they were to leave 'in the ship *Hellespont*, which sails from this port on Monday Nov[ember] 24. We shall expect you to reach Boston on the nineteenth or twentieth.'[19] The Coans were beginning to experience the tight control exercised by the American Board of Commissioners for Foreign Missions over the lives and actions of missionaries of the Board."[20]

Titus and Fidelia had waited for years to be married. Then they had the physical and time separation during the Patagonia sojourn. They were kept apart by the Board until a vessel could be found for their transport. Finally the blessed day came. They did not waste any time after receiving Anderson's letter. "Titus Coan and Fidelia Church were married at the Monthly Concert of Prayer the evening they received Anderson's letter, on November 3, 1834, at Churchville, New York. The following day they departed, taking the packet boat down the Erie Canal destined for New York City."[21] Lydia puts it in this way: "Once more he journeys eastward, but not alone. With him is his chosen helpmeet, to whom he had been united in marriage on the evening of November 3, 1834, at the Monthly Concert of Prayer for Foreign Missions."[22]

---

15. Ehlke, "Enthusiastic Religion," 75.
16. This number does not count for stops along the way.
17. Judd, *Missionary Album*, 2.
18. Wisner to Coan, September 30, 1834, LOC, in Ehlke, "Enthusiastic Religion," 75–76.
19. Anderson to Coan, October 24, 1834, LOC, in Ehlke, "Enthusiastic Religion," 76.
20. Ehlke, "Enthusiastic Religion," 76.
21. Ehlke, "Enthusiastic Religion," 76.
22. Coan, *Memorial Volume*, 21–22.

Ehlke relates a letter Titus writes while on the canal and to which Fidelia adds a note. "As they passed Sarah Oliphant's house, they addressed a letter to her, with Titus writing: 'I cannot refrain from dropping you a passing note as I am borne by your residence for the last time. I am on my way to Boston with my dear Fidelia—now Mrs. Coan—for the purpose of embarking, on the twenty-fourth inst[ant], for the Sandwich Islands.'[23] Fidelia added a note telling of her sadness at leaving home and family. 'Mother felt deeply at being called to part with another child for life. Still I hope she has no wish to keep me at home.'"[24]

The Coans visit various people in New York City and on the trip up the coast to Boston. "The couple visited Mr. and Mrs. Whittlesey, the publishers of *Mother's Magazine*, in New York City; stopped off at New Fairfield and Killingworth, Connecticut, to bid farewell to George and Mabel Coan and Titus's parents before proceeding to Boston."[25]

Coan writes about the commissioning and instructions for the Seventh Missionary Company to the Sandwich Islands. "On [Sunday] the twenty-third of November we received our instructions as missionaries to the Sandwich Islands, in Park Street church, together with Miss Lydia Brown,[26] Miss Elizabeth Hitchcock,[27] Mr. Henry Dimond and wife,[28] and Mr. and Mrs. Edwin O. Hall."[29]

He writes his parents about their time in Boston. "We have now been here nearly two weeks, waiting for the ship to be ready. We hope to go to-morrow." He writes about the service at Park Street Church. "The meeting was crowded, solemn, and impressive.

---

23. Titus Coan to Sarah Oliphant, November 6, 1834, HMH, in Ehlke, "Enthusiastic Religion," 76.

24. Ehlke, "Enthusiastic Religion," 76.

25. Ehlke, "Enthusiastic Religion," 76–77.

26. 1780–1865. She was a teacher in Wailuku, Maui, and Kalauaaha mission station. Judd, *Missionary Album*, 57.

27. A sister of the Molokai missionary Harvey R. Hitchcock, Miss Rogers married Edmund Horton Rogers on July 12, 1836. Mr. Rogers was a Board printer was serving in Lahainaluna when they married. In 1840 they moved to Honolulu to work at the printing office there. Judd, *Missionary Album*, 164–65. See also Forbes et al., *Partners in Change*, 529–33.

28. Henry Dimond and Ann Maria Anner Dimond lived in Honolulu, where he served as a bookbinder. Because his services were no longer needed, he was released from the Board and became a mercantile business until his death. Judd, *Missionary Album*, 82–83. See also Forbes et al., *Partners in Change*, 27.

29. Coan, *Life*, 18. Mr. Hall was a printer and assistant secular agent for the Board. "In 1850 he was released from the ABCFM to take charge of the Department of Finance of the Government during the absence of Dr. Judd." He went on to establish the E. O. Hall and Son mercantile business that was eventually "absorbed into Theo. H. Davies Ltd." Sarah Lyon Williams Hall was slight and frail but was able to work as a milliner upon her couch. Judd, *Missionary Album*, 112–14. See also Forbes et al., *Partners in Change*, 298–303. Further, Coan notes that another group received its instructions during the same service. "On the same occasion a company of twelve missionaries, destined to Southeastern Africa, received their instructions. The house was packed and the occasion was one of great interest." Looking back over the years, Coan describes the members of the Company: first the two single women, then the couples in 19, 20 of Coan, *Life*.

The people of Boston take a deep interest in the cause of missions, and are very hospitable to missionaries. We have been kindly entertained since our arrival here."

He writes of the pain he causes his parents by his departure. "You will forgive me all the pain an unworthy son has ever caused you, and you will not cease to remember me at the throne of grace. I shall never cease to bear you on my heart, though in distant realms, until we meet in a better country" [Heb 11:16].[30]

JOURNEY TO HONOLULU

The *Hellespont* got closer and closer to Honolulu. "'On the morning of the fifth inst[ant], just six months from the time we lost sight of our native land, we first descried the island of Hawaii, at the distance of sixty or seventy miles. On the morning of the sixth we made this island (Oahu), and at 10 a.m. dropped anchor in the harbor.'"[31]

"Anchoring two miles off the harbor because of the wind, the passengers on the *Hellespont* saw Honolulu spread out before them, a mixture of wooden, adobe, and thatched dwellings and shops, with cool green hills beyond, and towards Waikiki, a dry, dusty plain with a fringe of palm trees and rolling surf."[32]

The members of the Seventh Company would get to know each other well during their journey of six months and one day. They departed Boston on Friday, December 5, 1834, and anchored off of Honolulu on Saturday, June 6, 1835. Coan made a basic sketch of the *Hellespont*.[33] He briefly describes the vessel to his father in a letter before his departure. "'Our ship, the *Hellespont*, is a very good one, of 340 tons burden, but she is deeply laden. We shall be pent up in small rooms, but they will be large enough to hold our Bibles and our God, if our spirits are contrite.'"[34]

He provides more detail of the vessel to his brother Ezra. "Our ship is one hundred and eight feet long, twenty-eight feet wide, and eighteen feet deep. The lower hold extends the whole length of the ship, and is twelve feet deep. This is filled with freight. Over this is a floor, making a space between the lower hold and the deck six feet deep. On this floor a little room is built in the bows for the sailors—the forecastle. In the stern is the officers' cabin, twelve feet by six feet, and at each end of it, opening to the sides of the ship, is a stateroom, six feet square, for sleeping. Forward of the cabin, about five feet, a partition is thrown across from side to side of the ship, forming a space for the stairway, pantry, and a baggage room. Between this and the forecastle, a space nearly ninety feet long, and embracing the whole width of the ship is the upper hold, which is usually occupied with the cargo, and as we missionaries are

---

30. Titus Coan to his parents, December 3, 1834, in Coan, *Memorial Volume*, 22.
31. Titus Coan to brother Heman Coan, June 26, 1835, in Coan, *Memorial Volume*, 34.
32. Coan, *Memorial Volume*, 34.
33. LOC.
34. Titus Coan to his parents, December 3, 1834, in Coan, *Memorial Volume*, 22.

esteemed a sort of 'merchandise' or burden to be borne, we are put in the place where cargo is usually stored.'"

Continuing his frank and vivid description that he did not give to his father, Coan provides information on their living quarters. "We have four temporary rooms, six feet by five feet, built directly in front of the steerage, and into these rooms we entered "two and two." Our rooms are lighted only by one solid piece of glass, six inches by two inches, set in the deck over our heads."

He writes about what they brought with them for their use during the trip. "In our room we stowed all that we can have access to on the voyage. We have two chests, four trunks, a medicine chest and writing desk, several bags, bundles, boxes, etc.; a looking-glass, some book shelves, a chair, a lamp, a pitcher suspended in a cot like a swallow's nest, a berth, garments hung around the walls, etc., etc."

After telling his brother how happy he and Fidelia are as husband and wife, he continues. "As our rooms are built two on each side of the ship, opposite each other, there is a little space in the middle between them which is our common sitting room. This is walled up on one side with pipes of water, barrels of beef, pork, and potatoes, boxes and bales of goods, etc.—a formidable bulwark! In this space you would see a few chests, boxes, trunks, and chairs lashed for seats, a washstand or board, a pail, an old lantern suspended overhead to render darkness visible, and multitudes of loose garments dangling from rusty nails, and waving in graceful measure with the motion of the ship. The light of heaven can enter this room in no way but by opening the door or removing the hatch overhead."

He explains to his brother why he gives such descriptions. "Now, I do not give you this description to show you how hard we fare, but to gratify you with the picture of facts which I know you want. We are all well off, and our accommodations are as good as they could conveniently be made."[35]

In a letter to his brother Ezra, Titus writes specifics about the sendoff the Company received. "It was a day of deep interest. A large company of friends collected on the wharf to witness our embarkation, and to unite in one last prayer and one final song of praise with us, until we bow around the throne of our Common Father, and mingle our voices with the 'great multitude' [Rev 7:9, 10, 13–17], whose notes are like 'many waters and like mighty thundering' [Ps 93:4]. As the sails of our gallant ship were unfurled to the breeze, and we glided down the smooth bay, and as we exchanged the last signals of adieu with weeping friends, and gazed upon the city, the temples and hills of the pilgrims, as they faded in the distance, we *thought* and *felt* and *wept*. But we were not sad. Oh, no! though our emotions were tender and strong—they were joyful. Our Master left a better country for our sake, and his example and the pledges of his presence and fellowship were enough to cheer us."[36]

---

35. Titus to Ezra Coan, January 27, 1835, in Coan, *Memorial Volume*, 24–26.
36. Titus to Ezra Coan, January 27, 1835, in Coan, *Memorial Volume*, 23.

In his autobiography he further describes their departure from Boston and heading out to sea. "On the fifth of December, 1834, we embarked on board the merchant ship *Hellespont*, Capt. John Henry, and bade farewell to Boston, to hundreds of dear and precious friends, to our dear country, not expecting ever to see them again. On the sixth we awoke and looked in vain for land. City, hills, mountains, had sunk in the ocean, and nothing outside of the dancing *Hellespont* was seen but the ethereal vault and the boundless blue sea."

Seasickness struck the voyagers, but then passed. "We plunged into the Gulf Stream and were handled roughly by current and wind and foaming wave. The wild winds howled, the clouds thickened and darkened, and the tempest raged.

"Our good ship labored, plunged, rose, trembled, plunged, and rose again amidst the foaming billows, shaking off the feathery spray like a sea-lion, and rushing along her watery way with grandeur. In the night her shining pathway was all aglow with countless, sparkling brilliants. Our voyage soon became pleasant. The weather was favorable, the captain attentive and kind, the officers faithful, and the crew obedient and respectful. Our seasickness vanished, our skies brightened, and we were a happy family, daily becoming better acquainted with each other."[37]

Fidelia writes her sister Abigail about how she turned the long cruise into a beneficial time for her. "These months of leisure are the last I expect to have at present, indeed they are the last I ever expect while I am able to discharge the duties of a missionary; and although I shall rejoice when we arrive at our field of labour, and though a long voyage is in many respects undesirable, yet I do highly value this uninterrupted season, for mental and moral improvement. I devote my time chiefly to reading, yet have knit three cotton stockings and studied some Greek."[38]

Titus relates prayer times and how the captain and crew would join them in Sabbath services. "This united circle held morning and evening devotions, and our days were spent in reading, writing, and social intercourse. On Sabbaths when the weather was favorable we had preaching, at which service the captain, officers, and crew were present."[39]

In a letter to his brother Ezra, Titus deepens his description of the principals and prayer on board, as well as the first part of the challenges of the earlier part of the voyage. "Captain Henry is very kind, and does all he can to make us comfortable. She is a temperance ship. The captain allows preaching on the Sabbath and the distribution of tracts, but no personal conversation with the sailors. In the mission family we have prayers morning and evening, and a Bible-class exercise twice a week."

---

37. Coan, *Life*, 18–19.

38. Fidelia Coan to Abigail Church Smith, March 18, 1835, HMH, in Ehlke, "Enthusiastic Religion," 19. Titus adds a prospect: "I need not tell you how happy my dear F. and I are in our union and in our prospects of laboring among the heathen."

39. Ehlke, "Enthusiastic Religion," 19.

He relates the difficulties of the first two or three weeks of the voyage. "The first two or three weeks of our voyage were dreadfully boisterous—a violent storm raged almost without intermission. The wind howled, and the sea roared and foamed, and rolled its angry billows to the clouds. Our ship is heavily laden, and every wave seemed to sweep over her like a log. She labored and creaked and groaned as if in the agonies of dissolution. But what was worse than this, we found that her decks leaked, and during the whole storm the cabin and all our rooms were constantly drenched—even our beds were insecure; but we were obliged to sleep in them wet, with the water dripping in our faces. There was no remedy; to calk was impossible, and every seaman was at his wits' end to manage the ship and keep her above water. For two or three days our company were all seasick, and unable to rise or to help one another. But out of all these troubles the Lord delivered us, and we are now in good health and pursuing our voyage prosperously."[40]

He writes briefly of their journey southward. "I need not detain the reader with a third voyage in the Atlantic. Enough to say that we passed pleasantly along to the south, sinking the northern constellations one by one, and raising the southern, seeing no equatorial line, no Neptune, and no land until the hills of Terra del Fuego lifted their snowy heads upon us above the clouds."

He expresses his unfulfilled wish to see Patagonian land and his grief for the people of that land. "I had longed to see the wild coast of Patagonia and the Falkland Islands, where only a year before I had roamed with the savage tribes, or found more comforts among the whalers and sealers of those southern islets. But we passed between the Continent and the Islands, descrying neither.

"My heart mourned for this land of Patagonia, a land on which the shadows of death had always rested and where no day had yet dawned."[41]

Coan writes about the challenges of traversing from the Atlantic to the Pacific. "We passed through the Strait of Le Maire, and with all sails set, in a balmy and bright summer day sailed very near the dreaded Cape Horn.

"Only a day after we had set our studding sails[42] and spread all our canvas, a stormy wind took us far toward the Southern Cross and the ice mountains of the Antarctic. But in a few days, more favoring gales hurried us northward again, and on

---

40. Titus to Ezra Coan, January 27, 1835, in *Memorial Volume*, 226–27.
41. Coan, *Life*, 18–20.
42. A studding sail, studsail or stunsail (traditionally pronounced stuns'l) is a sail used to increase the sail area of a square rigged vessel.

the eighth of March the joyful sound of 'land ho!' thrilled all on board and the lofty Cordillera chain stood out in grandeur before us."[43]

They had arrived in Valparaíso,[44] Chile. In 1810 the first pier in the country was built there, and it soon became a major stopover point for ships rounding South America via the Straits of Magellan and Cape Horn.[45] The *Hellespont* stayed in port for twenty days, accounting for most of the time beyond the estimated five-month voyage to the Sandwich Islands. Ever the peripatetic explorer, Titus joined Henry Dimond in engaging "a carriage and driver, and made a trip to Santiago, the capital of Chili [sic], about a hundred miles inland and near the foot-hills of the Andes. Our ride was very exhilarating. This city is one of the most beautiful in South America, well watered from the mountain snows, and well shaded with trees." Coan continues to describe his jaunt.[46]

The vessel continued on to the harbor of Callao, Peru. The *Hellespont* stayed in that port for 21 days. Titus visited Lima and attended "the gorgeous ceremonies of Passion Week."[47] His amicable time with the Bishop of Lima is related in the "Other Religions" chapter later in this volume.

One month and one day from arriving off the coast of Honolulu, Titus writes a letter to his father. He relates his sadness of leaving family. He provides an extensive report on his visit to Santiago.[48]

HONOLULU

The *Hellespont* gets ever closer to Honolulu. "On the morning of the fifth inst[ant], just six months from the time we lost sight of our native land, we first descried the island of Hawaii, at the distance of sixty or seventy miles. On the morning of the sixth we made this island (Oahu), and at 10 A. M. dropped anchor in the harbor."[49]

The new arrivals waited a bit while word reached the missionaries on shore that reinforcements had arrived. It turned out that the annual General Meeting of the Island missionaries was being held at the time of the Seventh Company's arrival. All but two missionaries and their families were present. "On hearing of our arrival, Messrs.

Diagram showing how a studding sail attaches to a yardarm, Wikimedia commons, public domain.

It is an extra sail hoisted alongside a square-rigged sail on an extension of its yardarm. It is named by appending the word *studding* to the name of the working sail alongside which it is set. Wikipedia, "Studding Sail."

43. Coan, *Life*, 20–21.
44. In his *Around the Horn*, Chester S. Lyman writes several pages about his time in Valparaíso.
45. Wikipedia, "Valparaíso."
46. Coan, *Life*, 21–22.
47. Coan, *Life*, 22.
48. Titus Coan to his father, May 5, 1835, in Coan, *Memorial Volume*, 27–33.
49. Titus Coan to brother Heman, June 26, 1835, in Coan, *Memorial Volume*, 34.

Bingham, Chamberlain, and Armstrong came off to the ship in a boat, to welcome and to take us on shore.'"[50] Ehlke notes that a "boat came alongside bringing Brothers Bingham, Armstrong and Chamberlain to welcome them ashore."[51]

In his autobiography, Coan notes that the "mission appointed a committee of three to meet us on board, while the meeting was adjourned, and a large part of the members with wives and children came down to the wharf to welcome us, and to escort us to the house of the Rev. Hiram Bingham."[52] Either at the wharf or at the Bingham home, Titus and Fidelia would have met less-than-six-months-old Lydia Bingham, who would become Titus's wife thirty-eight years later, one year after Fidelia's death.

Titus notes that when "we landed, we found the band of brethren and sisters at the seaside awaiting our arrival and ready to embrace us. Every heart seemed to feel more than it could utter. What first struck me with peculiar force was the plain attire and simple manners of the missionaries, but, above all, the wasting inroads which climate and toil had evidently made on the constitutions of this beloved band of disciples."[53]

In his autobiography he writes that the "welcome was warm and warmly reciprocated, and the meeting was joyful. It seemed to us *apostolical*. We regarded these veteran toilers with a feeling of veneration. Some looked vigorous and strong, others seemed palled and wayworn." Coan expresses his deep respect for the missionaries, spouses, and families. "Here the fathers and mothers in Israel, and here the brothers and sisters, with flocks of precious children. We rejoiced that we were permitted to be numbered with this honored and happy family." As they had departed Boston with songs of praise, they sang praises to God upon their arrival in Honolulu. "'We all united in a hymn of praise and thanksgiving to God, and then knelt in prayer.'"[54] "From the shore we walked up through the town one mile to the mission-houses, where all joined in a song of praise and thanksgiving to God, and then united in prayer.'"[55]

Titus goes with Hiram Bingham to the chapel. "At half-past four P. M. I went with Brother Bingham to the chapel. After services Mr. B. introduced me to the governess and some of the high chiefs, who expressed much joy at the arrival of more teachers on their shores. When we turned from our interview with the chiefs, the common people pressed around me in crowds, each one striving to grasp my hand and express his warm welcome. For a long time I stood and received the hands of individuals in rapid succession, each one expressing his 'aloha' (love to you) and retiring before the crowd that were pressing for the same privilege."[56]

50. Ehlke, "Enthusiastic Religion," 94.
51. Ehlke, "Enthusiastic Religion," 95.
52. Coan, *Life*, 12.
53. Titus Coan to brother Heman, June 26, 1835, in Coan, *Memorial Volume*, 34, 35.
54. Coan, *Life*, 22–23.
55. Titus Coan to brother Heman, June 26, 1835, in Coan, *Memorial Volume*, 35.
56. Coanm *Memorial Volume*, 35.

Next develops something similar to a presidential or papal visit for the one who would come to affectionately be known as "Papa Coan." It reflects upon the kind nature of the Hawaiians, as well as their respect for the missionaries that had already been established. "As a great many were unable to get near me in the chapel, they arranged themselves by the wayside the whole distance from the church to Mr. B's house, and held out their hands as I passed. It was an affecting scene, and never have I seen before a people who expressed so much gratitude and affection."[57]

"Mr. and Mrs. Bingham took the Coans into their home in the mission frame house; and, while Bingham took her husband to hear him preach in Hawaiian to a congregation of four hundred islanders,[58] Fidelia became acquainted with Mrs. Bingham, observing for the first time the operation of a missionary home."[59]

During the time the Coans stayed with the Binghams, "Fidelia became acquainted with Mrs. Bingham, observing for the first time the operation of a missionary home." Fidelia and Titus were both struck by the spiritual lack in so many of the missionary children. Thus began a life-long passion by both for the welfare of those children. "Titus in his forthright manner suggested that he conduct a meeting for the children of missionaries at 8 a.m." during the annual General Meeting "with an inquiry meeting for the children between 1 and 2 p.m. Many of the sixty missionary children were gathered with their parents in Honolulu and 'An interesting work commenced among them, and some are now rejoicing with hope; others are struggling with conviction.'"[60] The Sabbath School teacher in Coan would not let the uncoverted souls of missionary children rest.

S. E. Bishop writes of Coan's impact upon him as a child. "When he first arrived at Honolulu in 1835, he held meetings with us children of the older missionaries, which are recalled as very moving and winning. We youngsters used to hang upon Mr. Coan's words, and formed a deep personal attachment to the new missionary. Three of the older ones made public profession of religion in 1836, in consequence."[61]

Lydia Bingham, who would grow up attending General Meetings, writes about Titus's gift with children. "There was in Mr. Coan's nature a remarkable adaptability to minister to the little ones. This endeared him to them. Throughout his missionary life his almost yearly attendance at the general meeting was hailed both by parents and children as a special blessing to the young, many of whom will never forget his tender earnestness to lead them to Jesus."[62]

57. Coan, *Memorial Volume*, 35.

58 Kawaiahaʻo, or "first church," in Judd, *Missionary Album*, 41–42. See also Forbes et al., *Partners in Change*, 40–42, 110–12, 180–81, 411–12, 504–06, and *passim*. Kawaiahaʻo was founded in 1821, one year after the Pioneer Company arrived on Oahu. See the 2020 documentary *A Witness to Aloha*.

59. Ehlke, "Enthusiastic Religion," 96.

60. Titus Coan letter to brother Heman, June 26, 1835, HMH. This letter does not appear in Coan, *Memorial Volume*.

61. Bishop, *Reminiscences*, 54.

62. Coan, *Memorial Volume*, 71.

Call to and Arrival in the Sandwich Islands

Such attention toward and care of children extended to the Hawaiian children that would come to be under his care. "The children of his own flock received him with joyous acclamations as he came among them on his tours, and in Hilo and Puna there were frequent duplicates of the scene so pleasantly described on page 170 of *Life in Hawaii*."[63] On page 170 of his autobiography, Coan relates the welcome he receives from children in the Marquesas. "On landing, I found myself surrounded with merry and bright-eyed boys and girls, all shouting in glee, 'Kaoha, kaoha, ka mikiona'— Love, love, to the missionary. Many struggled to get hold of my hands to lead me to the house, and to please as many as possible, I offered a finger to one and another. Thus I was led by ten laughing children, while others caught hold of my arms, and elbows, and of the skirts of my coat, shouting *kaoha*, until we entered the house of Kaivi. Surely, thought I, here is material for a Christian civilization, and with wise and faithful training, these boys and girls may become kind and good men and women, and never kill and eat one another. I have not seen brighter or sweeter looking children than these on the Hawaiian Islands."[64]

Returning to June of 1835, "On the Sabbath we attended worship with a company of some fifteen hundred. The chapel is one hundred and eighty feet long and sixty feet wide. Its framework is of posts and poles, and it is thatched all over with long grass."[65]

The Coans' stay in Honolulu and the stay of the others in the Company was a busy time. Less than three weeks after their arrival, the members of the Seventh Company composed and sent a letter to Rufus Anderson, Secretary General of the American Board. Dated June 25, the writers were listed first in married alphabetical order,[66] followed by the two single women.[67] The letter comes across as both formulaic and in concert with the enthusiasm of the first arrival to the place to which they have been called to serve.

It has dateline "Honolulu, S." The letter opens with "Very dear Sir: It is with great joy that we now record the goodness of God in bringing us in safety and health to this field of labor." They write of their arrival. "On Friday morning the fifth [of June] . . . just six months from our embarkation we made the mountains of Hawaii sixty miles distant, and on the following morning entered the port of Honolulu."

They relate their arrival during the General Meeting of the missionaries. "We found the dear Brethren assembled in general meeting, with their wives and little ones. They all received us on the shore with open arms, and after rapid and warm hearted salutations, we walked up to the house of Mr. Bingham, where a season was

---

63. Coan, *Memorial Volume*, 71.
64. Coan, *Life*, 170.
65. Titus Coan to brother Heman, June 26, 1835, in Coan, *Memorial Volume*, 35, 36. See Bingham's architectural sketches of the chapel structure in Judd, *Missionary Album*, 42.
66. Coan, Dimond, and Hall.
67. Brown and Hitchcock.

spent in prayer and praise." After fifteen years in the Islands, Mr. Bingham continued to be viewed as the leader of all the American Board missionaries.

The newly-arrived company spent time with Hawaiian leaders. "We have been invited to an interview with the king and chiefs, and they welcomed us to their Islands, and given us the assurance of their protection." The company describes its journey from western South America to the Sandwich Islands. "We were forty days from Callao to this place, and the voyage was uniformly pleasant."[68] In his separate letter to "Brother Anderson," Coan writes, "I would suggest to you that in giving private instructions to missionaries before they sail, it may be well to caution them on the subject of diversions at sea, such as checkers, chess, etc."[69]

Foreshadowing of his powerful decades of Christian leadership and his positive influence on children is seen in the later reflections of one of the missionary children. "From the time of his entrance in 1835 upon missionary labor in Hawaii, Titus Coan had shown exceptional spiritual fervor, combined with a rarely[70] winning manner. He would anywhere have proved an evangelist or revivalist of unusual force. When he first arrived at Honolulu in 1835, he held meetings with us children of the older missionaries, which are recalled as very moving and winning. We youngsters used to hang upon Mr. Coan's words, and formed a deep personal attachment to the new missionary."[71]

Continuing to the joint letter, the new company laments the death of two missionaries. They reported "[i]ntelligence of the shocking fate of Brs. Lyman[72] and Munson[73] have just reached our ears."[74] The letter returns to an upbeat outlook. "We find the Miss[ionarie]s here a very dear band, and our attachment to them is daily increasing. The field before us is wide and white for the harvest [John 4:35], and we rejoice in the privilege of going into it as laborers for our Lord" [Matt 9:38].

On a practical matter, the missionaries note that their "goods are in good order as far as we know."[75] Then there is a break in the letter.[76] In Coan's separate letter, he gives evidence of his precision as a "pen painter" in requested corrections to a *Missionary*

---

68. Seventh Company letter to Rufus Anderson, June 25, 1835, HMH.

69. Titus Coan to Rufus Anderson, June 26, 1835, HMH.

70. E.g. "Rare."

71. Bishop, *Reminiscences*, 55, in Forbes et al., *Partners in Change*, 185.

72. Any relation to David Lyman? Henry Lyman's "parents were Theodore Lyman and Susan Willard Whitney, his wife Eliza Pond," Wikipedia, "Henry Lyman." Sarah and David did honor the two martyred missionaries by naming their second child "Henry Munson" in 1835, Judd, *Missionary Album*, 143.

73. The person after whom the Coans would name their first born a year later? Titus Munson Coan. He would eventually be called, by his family at least, "Munson."

74. "Henry Lyman (Northampton, Massachusetts, November 23, 1809–Sacca village, Lobu Pining, Tarutung, Sumatra, June 28, 1834) was an American Baptist missionary murdered in Sumatra together with his colleague Samuel Munson." Wikipedia, "Henry Lyman."

75. Seventh Company letter to Rufus Anderson, June 25, 1835, HMH.

76. This break was confirmed by Carol White of the HMH library.

Herald article.[77] It has to do with pages 377, 400, and 432. "If you think the above worthy of correction, you will please show this to Mr. Green.[78] The last error [instead of 'buried' it should be it should be 'burned'][79] is the only one of importance, & I should not have mentioned the others had it not been for that. It may be called a 'false fact.'"[80]

As inspiring and informative as Honolulu was for the Coans, it was a transit point for them. They awaited their assignment to a mission station. "On June 25, 1835, the Coans learned that their missionary station would be in Hilo on the island of Hawaii, one of the most remote posts in the Sandwich Islands, two hundred and fifty miles from Honolulu."[81]

In a letter to his brother Heman, Coan recognizes that missionaries can be redeployed in the Sandwich Islands. He writes of being in Hilo for 1835. "Our location for the present year will be at Hilo, on the island of Hawaii." He notes that our "associate is to be Rev. Mr. Lyman. We shall probably be two hundred and fifty miles[82] from medical aid, and can expect *none*. We can only . . . trust in God."[83]

The Lymans had had similar concerns after being in Hilo for the four years since their arrival there. They had hoped that at the General Meeting of 1835 they would be reassigned somewhere closer to medical care and other amenities. Instead, the Lymans would share their then very small home with the Coans and for decades share ministry with them in and around Hilo.

Sarah Lyman writes in her June 27, 1835, journal. "Another week has passed, and to me it has been one of unusual excitement. The subject of a change in our location was brought before the meeting. Once there was a prospect of our being located with Mr. Greene at Wai'ili' afterwards a proposition was made for us to engage in a boarding school at Waialua.[84] It is however overruled by the mission that we return to Hilo, and by request Mr. Coan is to be our associate. We feel tried in view of returning without a prospect of our medical wants being supplied the ensuing year."

She explains why the leadership objected to any movement by the missionaries. "The mission objected to any change, on account of the influence it might have on the natives. Since it is the will of Providence that we still remain at that distant point of the field, I trust that we will return cheerfully to our work."[85]

---

77. Undated.

78. Someone involved in *Missionary Herald* editing? Someone other than the Maui missionary Green?

79. Brackets inserted by Coan.

80. Seventh Company letter to Rufus Anderson, June 26, 1835, HMH.

81. Ehlke, "Enthusiastic Religion," 97.

82. By ocean.

83. Titus Coan to brother Heman, June 26, 1835, in Coan, *Memorial Volume*, 36–37.

84. Northeastern Oahu.

85. Lyman, *Lymans of Hilo*, 78.

Titus Coan: "Apostle to the Sandwich Islands"

HILO

Sometimes the last, shortest part of a journey can be the most intense and negative. Such was the case for the Coans and others as they travelled from Honolulu to Hilo. In his autobiography, Titus relates the agonizing trip, due to the poor eyesight and lack of sobriety of the captain. "We embarked at Honolulu, in the schooner *Velocity*, falsely so-called, on the sixth of July. The schooner was small, a slow sailer, dirty, crowded with more than one hundred passengers, mostly natives, and badly managed. The captain was an Irishman given to hard drinking.

"We sailed from Honolulu on Monday. The sea was rough and nearly all of the passengers were very seasick. Our first port was Lahaina, eighty miles from Honolulu, where we were to land Mr. and Mrs. Richards, Dr. and Mrs. Chapin, Mr. and Mrs Spaulding, and other families. On Wednesday morning the captain announced that the land just ahead was Maui, and that we should all land in about an hour at Lahaina, where we might rest a day, bathe, eat grapes and watermelons, and be refreshed for the rest of the voyage, about 150 miles further.

"But the poor captain's eyes were dazed, and he had lost his reckoning. We had gone about in the night and we were back at Honolulu! This fact came upon us with a shock of agony. After such seasickness as some of us had never before endured, the dreadful thought came over us, 'Shall we ever reach our homes on this vessel and with this master?' Many of us had tasted neither food nor water from Monday to Wednesday, and all had lain crowded on a dirty deck, exposed to wind, rain, and wave, and how could we live to reach our destination? But there was no alternative. We said *go*, and the dull *Velocity* went about and headed again for Lahaina, where we landed passengers, and on the twenty-first we saw the emerald beauty of Hilo, and disembarked with joy and thanksgiving. Hundreds of laughing natives thronged the beach, seized our hands, gave us the hearty '*Aloha*' and followed us up to the house of our good friends, Mr. and Mrs. Lyman, who were with us to comfort and inform us all the way."[86]

Hilo harbor was called Byron's Bay when Titus Coan arrived.[87] Here is what Hiram Bingham writes about it. "Lord Byron, with his scientific corps, visited Hilo, the great crater of Kilauea, and Kealakekua Bay, and caused accurate surveys of Waikiki Bay, Honolulu harbor, and Hilo Bay, which has since been called Byron's Bay."[88] Lord Byron was in Hawai'i in 1824.[89]

The American Board Hilo Station was established in 1824. It eventually became one of six such stations on the Big Island. Robert W. Andres tabulated "Missionary

---

86. Coan, *Life*, 23–24.
87. See Coan, *Life*, 24–25, at the beginning of this chapter.
88. Bingham, *Residence*, 270–71.
89. Wikipedia, "George Byron, 7th Baron Byron."

Stations in Hawaii" as part of the 1901 *Missionary Album*.[90] "Hilo, E.—the center of a well watered and fertile district of great extent."[91]

Some decades later, the Englishwoman Isabella Bird would wax lyrical about her approach to and description of the Hilo area. "Ten miles from Hilo we came in sight of the first sugar plantation with its patches of yet brighter green, its white boiling house and tall chimney house, then more churches, then more plantations, more gulches, more houses, and before ten we sailed into Byron's, or as it is now called Hilo Bay.

"This is the paradise of Hawaii. What Honolulu attempts to be, Hilo is without effort. Its crescent-shaped bay, said to be the most beautiful in the Pacific, as a semi-circle of about two miles, with its farther extremity formed by Cocoanut Island, a black lava islet on which this palm attains great perfection, and beyond it a fringe of cocoanuts marks the deep indentations of the shore. From this island to the north point of the bay, there is a band of golden sand on which the roar of the surf sounds thunderous and drowsy as it mingles with the music of the living waters of the Waiakea and the Wailuku, which after lashing the sides of the mountains which give them birth, glide deep and fern-fringed into the ocean."

Bird continues the theme of Hilo and greenery as she continues her description. "Native houses, half hidden by greenery, line the bay, and stud the heights above Wailuku, and near the landing some white frame houses and three church spires above the wood denote the foreign element."

She then focuses on the elements that combine to make Hilo so green, which would lead the Coans to call their home and the surrounding area the "Emerald Bower." "Hilo is unique. Its climate is humid, and the long repose which it has enjoyed from the rude volcanic upheavals has mingled a great depth of vegetable mould with the decomposed lava. Rich soil, rain, heat, sunshine, stimulate nature to vigorous efforts, and there is a luxuriant prodigality of vegetation which leaves nothing uncovered but the golden margin of the sea, and even that above high-water mark is green with the Convolvulus maritimus."[92]

Bird becomes even more thorough in her explanation of greenery and other colors. "So dense is the wood that Hilo is rather suggested than seen. It is only on shore that one becomes aware of the bewildering variety of native and exotic trees and shrubs. From the sea it looks one dense mass of greenery, in which the bright foliage of the candle-nut relieves the glossy dark green of the breadfruit—a maze of

---

90. Judd, *Missionary Album*, 14–16, 1969 Edition. "While the 'Sandwich Islands' were missionary ground, seventeen missionary stations and two schools were successively chosen and occupied. There were many other preaching stations—some of great importance—which were not the residences of missionaries. The following enumeration of stations begins at the northwest end of the group, and gives some characteristics of each place, at the time the station was established." Judd, *Missionary Album*, 15. See also Forbes et al., *Partners in Change*, xxii, for map; and 15–47 for descriptions of each station. The Hilo station is discussed on pages 16 and 17.

91. Judd, *Missionary Album*, 15.

92. Flowering plants by the sea.

preposterous bananas, out of which rise slender, annulated trunks of palms giving their infinite grace to the grove. And palms along the bay, almost among the surf, toss their waving plumes in the sweet, soft breeze, not 'palms in exile,'[93] but children of a blessed isle where 'never wind blows loudly.'"[94]

She lifts her eyes above Hilo to describe "broad lands sweeping up cloudwards, with their sugar cane, *kalo*,[95] melons, pine-apples, and banana groves suggest the vast liberality of Nature."[96]

Wikipedia provides the following history of Hilo. "Circa 1100 AD, the first Hilo inhabitants arrived, bringing with them Polynesian knowledge and traditions. Although archaeological evidence is scant, oral history has many references to people living in Hilo, along the Wailuku and Wailoa Rivers during the time of ancient Hawaii. Oral history also gives the meaning of Hilo as 'to twist.'

"Originally, the name Hilo applied to a district encompassing much of the east coast of the Island of Hawai'i, now divided into the District of South Hilo and the District of North Hilo. When William Ellis visited in 1823, the main settlement in the Hilo district was Waiākea on the south shore of Hilo Bay. Missionaries came to the district in the early-to-middle nineteenth century, founding Haili Church, in the area of modern Hilo.

"Hilo expanded as sugarcane plantations in the surrounding area created new jobs and drew in many workers from Asia, making the town a trading center."[97]

George Q. Cannon, the leader of the first Latter-day Saint missionaries to the Sandwich Islands, describes Hilo in his journal: It "is situated on a beautifully[98] bay of

---

93. Gerald Massey poem, "Jerusalem the Golden."

> "JERUSALEM the Golden!
> I weary for one Gleam
> Of all thy glory golden
> In distance and in dream!
> My thoughts, like Palms in Exile,
> Climb up to look and pray
> For a glimpse of thy dear Country
> That lies so far away!"

94. The only reference this author could find to this quotation is by Mrs. Charles Cowman in *Springs in the Desert*. However, she was born in 1870 so if these words were quoted by Isabella Bird, Mrs. Cowman would have had to have drawn them from a previous author.

"Security in Storms," By Mrs. Charles Cowman

In *Streams in the Desert* "The wind was contrary [Matt. 14:24]. Rude and blustering the winds of March often are. Do they not typify the tempestuous seasons of my life? But, indeed, I ought to be glad that I make acquaintance with these seasons. Better it is that the rains descend and the floods come than that I should stay perpetually in the Lotus Land where it seems always afternoon, or in that deep meadowed Valley of Avalon where never wind blows loudly." Back to the Bible, "Security in Storms."

95. Taro plant.

96. Bird, *Hawaiian Archipelago*, Letter IV, 36.

97. Wikipedia, "Hilo, Hawaii."

98. As will be noted in the "Other Religions" chapter, most of the young LDS missionaries had their unique spelling and syntax. As with the American Board missionaries, the word "sic" is not

considerable extent, called Byron's Bay, it is well sheltered and affords good anchorage, so I am told by the natives, at all times for vessels; it is a port of entry and often visited by whalers for recruits of provisions and water &c. It is an extremely fertile place, bread fruit, cocoa nut, banana, and other trees grow in profusion, and all vega[ta]tion flourishes luxuriantly there."[99]

Four decades after his arrival, Titus would write of his enduring joy of living and serving where he did. Lydia introduces it with "Hilo was to them at the first 'a picture of loveliness' and forty years later Mr. Coan could write:

"The ecstatic romance with which I first saw these emerald isles has not abated by familiarity or by age. The picture is photographed in unfading tints upon my heart, and it has become to me the romance of reality. Where can you find within so small a space such a collecting, such massing, such blending of the bland, the beautiful, the exquisite, the gorgeous, the grand and the terrific as on Hawaii? Along the summits of our lofty mountains the God of glory thundereth [Ps 29:3], while the overhanging clouds send down the rattling hail and drop the fleecy snow. There telluric[100] fires find vent and send up columns of melted rocks to the heavens, spreading out in baleful glare like a burning firmament. The crashing thunder, the vivid lightning, the rending earthquake and the bursting volcano we have in the near proximity of the peaceful village, the grassy landscape, the sweet flower garden, the cultivated field, the babbling brook, the tropical fruits and ferns, the waving palm, the golden sunshine, the stellar vault above, and the surrounding ocean whose swelling bosom moves with the zephyr and the tempest, while her white foam girdles with glory our rock-bound shores."[101]

"Fidelia expressed relief at reaching the end of her long journey. 'It would be impossible for me to describe my feelings as I laid me down to rest that night, and thought that after more than eight months of constant shifting and changing, embarking and debarking, packing and unpacking, I had at last arrived at a spot which for a while[102] I could call my home. I trust I was not entirely destitute of emotions of gratitude that my ardent wishes were accomplished with regard to a field of labor, nor without desires to occupy faithfully this portion of the Lord's vineyard.'"[103]

The Coans enjoy the climate and luxuriant greenery. "Despite its distance from the center of population, they found the beautiful lush scenery and cooling rains of Hilo to their liking. 'This climate,' Fidelia wrote, 'though very wet, agrees with me quite well as yet; and what is of more importance to me, my dear Titus is quite as well as he was at home in warm weather.'"[104]

---

repeatedly used so that it does not get in the way of reading the substance of a quotation.

99. Sunday, May 7–8, 1854, in Cannon, *Journals*, 465.

100. "Esp in reference to natural electrical or magnetic fields." Dictionary.com, "Telluric."

101 Coan undated journal or letter [1875? 1876?], in Coan, *Memorial Volume*, 38.

102. Little knowing that she would live in Hilo for her thirty-six remaining years.

103. Fidelia Coan to her parents, September 9, 1835, in Ehlke, "Enthusiastic Religion," 98.

104. Ehlke, "Enthusiastic Religion," 99.

Sarah Lyman writes about sharing their small home with Titus and Fidelia. First she talks about how difficult it is to put her home back in order after being away. More challenging, she writes, is squeezing the Coans into their modest home. From her July 23, 1835, journal. "I find it no little work to put my house again in order after so long an absence. But what renders it more difficult is that we were obliged to give up a part of our house to Mr. and Mrs. Coan, or at least we prefer doing this to having their health exposed in a native house."

Sarah is understated as she relates the housing situation. "We find ourselves very much cramped for room and have no conveniences at all in the little room there is, there not being a cupboard or a closet in the house. As there was but one room partitioned off, Mr. Coan has to-day thrown up a mat partition, which makes them one comfortable room in one end of the house. At present they are to board with us."[105]

Ehlke notes that the house occupied by the Lymans had been built "by Mr. Dibble but not completed. [I]t was a long narrow building with rock walls laid up with mud, a firm dry floor, a thatched roof and thin walls that shook when the winds blew." The Lymans were living in this structure after living in "native houses" for three years. Their "permanent wooden house" "was expected to be completed in a few months."[106]

Lydia writes this bridge passage on their housing. "Amid such surroundings the earthly home was established."[107] Titus writes in his July 30, 1835, journal, "Having prepared a room in Brother Lyman's house, we have this day commenced housekeeping and established ourselves as a distinct family. The Lord be gracious to us." And in his autobiography: "Mr. Lyman's home into which we were received was a small, stone house, with walls laid up with mud, and a thatched roof. Each family had but one room about fifteen feet square."[108] He writes his brother George about his preliminary living situation and creatures with whom they shared the habitation. "We live in one end of a long narrow house of rough walls of stone laid in with mud, with roof of thatch—and occupy but one room separated from the rest by a mat partition. Our home is rather open. Hens come in, now and then, to find their newest with us, and rats, mice, and lizards frequently play their merry gambols on our floor, walls and roof." He nevertheless says how happy he and Fidelia are together and in their service to their Lord. "None of the tenants of our rude habitation are as happy as we. We are happy in our union, happy in our work, and happy in our Redeemer."[109]

Months before the Coans' arrival, the 1835 station report indicates that "Mr. Goodrich's health [an already-established Hawaiian missionary] has failed rather than

---

105. Lyman, *Lymans of Hilo*, 78.
106. Ehlke, "Enthusiastic Religion," 99.
107. Coan, *Memorial Volume*, 38.
108. Coan, *Life*, 26.
109. Titus to George Coan, undated, in Coan, *Memorial Volume*, 39.

improved during the year."[110] Martha Barnes Goodrich died in Kewanee, Illinois, on November 6, 1840.[111] Mr. Goodrich died in the same town on February 19, 1852.[112]

However, in September, 1835, Titus doubts the Goodriches will leave. "We live in one end of Bro. L's house and occupy but one room for all purposes. Bro. Goodrich and family are well. It is not my opinion that they intend to leave Hilo this year if ever."[113] Near the beginning of this letter, Coan indicates how happy he is. It is hard to say if that is truly what he felt, because it is easy to read between the lines and wonder if the Goodriches would ever leave Hilo in the context of his discussion of the cramped one-room quarters he and Fidelia shared with the Lymans. I do not think there is irony in his happiness statement for two reasons: Coan's faithful outlook, and his happiness at arriving at what he believed (correctly) would be his base of missions for the rest of his life. Further, consider what he had already persevered through before his arrival in Hilo: Auburn seminary; intense and dangerous time in Patagonia; return to the US, call to Sandwich Islands, marriage to Fidelia, long journey around the Cape and arrival in Honolulu.

But Joseph Goodrich had been talking about leaving. "Rev. J. Goodrich is here, but he talks of returning to the United States this fall."[114] In his November 16, 1835, journal Titus writes of co-signing of a letter of commendation to ABCFM General Secretary Rufus Anderson on behalf of Brother Goodrich, with his and his family's departure imminent. "Signed a letter on behalf of Bro. G. prepared by Bro. L[yman] and addressed it to Mr. Anderson Sec. of the A. Board. In the evening held a special prayer meeting of the Mission families at the station in reference to the departure of Bro. G. and family on the morrow."[115]

On the next day, a Tuesday, "Mr. G. and family left their house at noon, and dined with Br. L and us expecting to go on board immediately after dinner;[116] but the wind not favoring they remained to supper." After supper "we united in prayer with Br. G. and then accompanied the family down to the beach, where we sang the hymn 'Blest be the dear uniting love.'[117] Prayer was then offered in native, and another in English."

---

110. Unsigned Hilo station report, May of 1835, 1/15, HMH.

111. At the age of forty-one.

112. At the age of fifty-seven. Judd, *Missionary Album*, 102–03; and Forbes et al., *Partners in Change*, 446–51,

113. Titus Coan to Levi Chamberlain, September 14, 1835, HMH.

114. Titus Coan to Levi Chamberlain, September 14, 1835, HMH.

115. Coan journal entry, November 16, 1835, LOC.

116. Lunch, with the evening meal being called "supper."

117. Charles Wesley, lyrics. First verse:

"Blest be the dear uniting love,
That will not let us part!
Our bodies may far off remove,
We still are one in heart."

After prayer in two languages, "Mr. G. made a short address to the crowd of people collected to witness the departure. With many affectionate farewells and commendations to the protection and blessing of God they were [went?] into the boat. And just as the twilight of the evening was gathering around we waved a reciprocal adieu, not expecting to see them again on earth. The scene was solemn and affecting and rarely have my feelings been wrought up to deeper sympathy than in seeing them bid a reluctant final farewell to the people and place where they had so long sojourned, and to wh[ich] they appeared to cling almost with the tenacity of life. Bro. Rogers[118] left with them to return to Maui."[119]

The Goodriches were in Hilo on the November 1 Sabbath of 1835 when Mr. Goodrich baptized his son "Charles Barns [sic].[120] One of the native children [was also] baptized by Bro. Goodrich."[121]

Titus notes that "Mr. Goodrich, with his family, left Hilo in November for the United States, not to return, and we were advised to occupy his house, which with later additions and improvements has been our habitation ever since."[122] In a bridge passage, Lydia writes that to "the many guests who through the passing years had been entertained with cordial hospitality at the Emerald Bower."[123]

Eventually Titus and Fidelia would move to the home formerly occupied by the missionary Goodrich family at the location which Titus often fondly called their "Emerald Bower." "Hilo had then but one framed house. It was a low, two-story building in the style of a New England farmhouse, built and occupied by the Rev. Joseph Goodrich, a good and faithful missionary of the ABCFM."[124]

Titus writes about Fidelia and him moving into the Goodrich home. "For two days past we have been occupied most of the time in preparing the house in wh[ich] Br. G. lives for our habitation, and today we removed into it, to make it the place of our residence so long as it shall please God to permit us to occupy it. With us this is all uncertain, as the missionaries in these Islands have for the most part no certain

---

118. Edmund Horton Rogers was an ABCFM printer who was apparently visiting in Hilo and transferring to Lahainaluna, Maui; Judd, *Missionary Album*, 164.

119. Coan journal entry, November 17, 1835, LOC.

120. "Barnes," Judd, *Missionary Album*, 103.

121. Coan journal entry, November 1, 1835, LOC.

122. Coan, *Life*, 26.

123. Coan, *Memorial Volume*, np. Kahu (Pastor) Brian Welsh—pastor of Haili church—indicates in an August 2012 email to the author that the phrase "Emerald Bower" is used for both the Coan home and the Hilo area. He also suggests that Lydia was especially fond of using that phrase. In *Life*, 25, Coan gives evidence of Kahu Welch's theory when he quotes Stennett's "On Jordan's Stormy Banks": "arrayed in living green." See beginning of this chapter.

124. Coan, *Life*, 26.

abiding place"[125] [Heb 11:10]. To an unnamed correspondent he writes, "We now live in a good two story house, built by brother Goodrich."[126]

Fidelia adds her input in a letter to her sister Maria in May of 1836. "Since I last wrote you we have left the thatched cottage which was at first our residence, and removed into the house formerly occupied by the Rev. J. Goodrich now on his way to America. It is a wood building two stories in height, with a 'native room,'[127] two sleeping rooms, and kitchen—all small—and a large dining room and sitting room on the ground; above are two sleeping rooms, study, and store room."

She describes how it is furnished and notes the "frailty" of the construction. "The house is finished in plain English style and accommodates us at present. But it is a frail tenement and has already been injured by earthquakes which are not uncommon here

---

125. Coan Journal entry, November 20, 1835, LOC.

126. Titus Coan letter to unnamed recipient, no date, HMH. Sometime in 1836? (based on evidence a little later in the letter): "I believe I told you that I commenced preaching in this language in about three months after our arrival at the station."

127. Paul Rapoza wrote the author an email on the subject of a native room: "The 'native room' has been mentioned in several of the missionaries' writings and has always meant a room for native domestic helpers that they had in their employment. I believe it was Lucy Thurston [author unable to find reference] that also mentioned that they had a special room to meet with natives that was built to keep their private housing quarters separate but that was a fairly large room/building and that was their particular outlook in keeping their children separate from the natives to avoid negative influence. I don't think that Coans were quite that aloof in that respect and because it was a small room it is likely to be the former I mention (the norm). Most of the missionaries eventually had live-in native domestic helpers as the task of preparing food on an open fire was arduous for the missionary women along with getting water, etc. It also allowed many of them to participate in missions work as well to some degree, i.e., Fidelia taught school for some time." According to Ehlke, Fidelia was not so sanguine about indigenous influence. In an 1837 letter (HMH), Fidelia explains to Titus one-year-old Munson's propensity to learn Hawaiian, "He will learn native in spite of us, unless we seclude him more." Ehlke continues, "Mrs. Coan felt that children should not learn the language 'until their moral principles were well established,'" Fidelia Coan letter to her sister Maria C. Robinson, May 8, 1843, LOC, in Ehlke "Enthusiastic Religion," 182–83. From 1829 *Lucy Thurston* letters and journal entries, 129: "The first rule to be attended to with regard to children is that they must not speak the native language. It is an easy thing to make such a law, but it is a mother's duty to guard it from being violated, and to form in her children fixed habits of doing as they are required. It, of course, follows that they are never left to the care of natives after reaching the age of prattling. No intercourse whatever should exist between children and heathen. On this point I am very particular. Establish a loose system here, and I would say with every one else, 'Send children to America, no matter how soon.'" From 83, 84, and 85: "Five acres were enclosed with a stone wall three feet wide and six feet high, with simply the front gate for entrance running from the outer wall each side of the front gate, close up against the side of the house, each side of the front door. A large thatched house was erected. Space was allowed for a yard twenty-five feet in breadth. Two close partition walls were built six feet high … At the back side of the house is a hall which leads both from the dining room and study to a door, the only entrance into a retired yard of three acres. There stands another thatched house, built after the custom of the country. The frame is tied together with the very strong bark of a certain tree. Then from the ridge-pole to the ground, the frame is entirely covered with long slender poles, tied within a few inches of each other, over which the long lauhala leaves are laid, leaving the two ends to hang down on the outside. That house is the home of our children. There is our family sitting room, eighteen feet square, and there are our sleeping apartments. And inasmuch as I often wish to invite my native friends to that sitting room, we enclosed the further bed room in a yard sixty feet square, with a wall six feet high."

though rarely severe. Besides, the heavy rains which often continue for weeks in Hilo, soon undermine and destroy wood buildings. Zinc is considered the most suitable for roofs, at our station. Mr. Lyman's house and ours both have it, but they leak."[128]

Titus Coan writes Levi Chamberlain about zinc having been applied to the roof of his new home. Chamberlain had oversight of the "Depository" in Honolulu from which missionaries requested and withdrew sundry materials. This process changed after missionaries began receiving salaries later in the 1830s. Coan's heart for men's souls is found in the midst of the mundane.

"I have to-day paid Mr. Higinson for painting my house last winter and for giving it a second coat since General meet[ing]. Also for soldering the roof by giving him an order on our Secular Agent of $21.62. I have also given an order of $12.75 to Mr. Hall for putting on the Zink[129] [sic] a second time. These orders will probably be sold to Mr. Paty and you will of course honor them when presented. Mr. Hall worked for seventy-five cts per day including the voyage from Lahaina to Hilo. He has been very faithful and has done well. I think the roof will be tight. But what is worth more than all we hope Mr. Hall has turned to the Lord since he has been with us. Behold he prays."

Coan writes about needing more sheets of "Zink." "Fearing that I had not Zink enough, Bro. Clark gave me forty sheets of his, and I have now only four sheets left out of the eighty. The old Zink was very poor at first and much of it could not be put on a second time. It was well that I took some of Bro. C[lark] as my workman would otherwise have come to Hilo in vain."[130]

Ehlke provides a further description of the home and Joseph Goodrich's legacy of that home. "Mr. Goodrich's legacy to the Hilo station, reflecting his mechanical skills, became the two-story wooden house the Coans moved into after the family's departure. Their new home was a snug, low-frame house painted red with white trim, the paths lined with fruit trees. Writing to her aunt and uncle in Canandaigua, New York, Fidelia compared their new home 'many farm houses I have seen in Ontario Co.—looks about as *foreign* at these Islands as do its inmates.'"[131]

---

128. Fidelia Coan to Maria Robinson, May [blank], 1836, HMH.

129. "Pure zinc was used for roofing in Belgium, France, and Germany, where it replaced more expensive copper and lead in roofing. Starting in the 1820s, Belgian sheet zinc was imported in America, used by builders in New York City and elsewhere. Pure zinc is subject to creep at ordinary temperatures.

"Zinc-coated metals were first patented in 1837, separately by M. Sorel in France and H. W. Crawford in England. The methods employed a 'hot dipping' process to coat sheet iron with zinc. By 1839 'galvanized' sheet iron roofing was being used in New York City. The Merchant's Exchange in Manhattan was one of the first buildings to have both a galvanized roof and galvanized gutters. Some galvanized sheet roofing was pressed with designs, a popular technique in the Victorian era." Wikipedia, "Architectural Metals."

130. Titus Coan to Levin Chamberlain, September 10, 1838, HMH.

131. Fidelia Coan to Mr. and Mrs. Horace Church, October 21, 1842, LOC, in Ehlke, "Enthusiastic Religion," 101–02.

Call to and Arrival in the Sandwich Islands

Mr. Goodrich's mechanical ability is further evidenced in a letter from Titus to Levi Chamberlain about his watch. "I believe the chain is broken perhaps nothing more, though I have not examined it carefully. Bro. Goodrich would repair it but he is now on the eve of leaving us, and has no time. Perhaps he may find time at Honolulu. The watch wants cleaning and regulating. It has run too slow for some time. I wish her to be put in perfect order if possible, as she will be the only time piece on which we can depend at this station."[132]

A little over a month later, Titus writes Chamberlain about bookshelves, his happiness at the mission, lumber, and other items. Titus continues to improve the home he and Fidelia have moved into. While the 1834 "Outfit for the Sandwich Islands" includes "one bookcase" that is listed first under furniture,[133] it is possible that the list was a counsel of perfection and not everything could be fitted within the *Hellespont*.[134] Additionally, Titus was a voracious collector and reader of books and other printed publications.

"I have given a young man, of the Ship *Mayflower*, by the name of Tho[mas] Anthony, an order on you of *.50 for making me a book-case. I cannot hang the doors for want of trimmings. Can you send me some by the first opportunity.

"Eight pair of butts, 1 ½ in. or 2 inches. Locks also. If you can send 2 doz butts. And ½ doz or a doz. of cupboard locks, they may not come amiss at this Station.

"We are all well here . . . Love our Station and our labor, contented and happy. God is good and hope we are thankful . . .

"For a #10 lot of refuse lumber (800 or 900 feet) for lime, sand, and native labor on my house, for stone fence, repairing of native houses, etc. etc. not included in the former calculation, we shall probably need one bale of cloth more than was mentioned in our last order."[135]

Coan notes there are extinct craters near the "cottage." "About half a mile in the rear of our cottage are three extinguished craters, standing in a line at right angles with the shore, each more than half a mile in circumference and elevated many hundred feet above the plain on which they are based."[136]

Coan did a great deal of work on the home, especially in the early years. He made "the Emerald Bower" more and more living as well as welcoming to others. Nevertheless, in their early period the Coans experienced a great deal of loneliness.

---

132. Titus Coan to Levin Chamberlain, September 10, 1838, HMH.
133. Judd, *Missionary Album*, 2.
134. See descriptions of close quarters, above.
135. Titus Coan to Levi Chamberlain, October 24, 1836, HMH.
136. Titus Coan to Levi Chamberlain, October 24, 1836, HMH.

LONELINESS

Before the internet age, most cross-cultural missionaries were cut off from most contact with their home countries. At best, it could take months for letters to be delivered... one way. Such was the case for the Coans in what was then the backwater of Hilo. Letters could take six months to go in one direction, so round trip with receipt, response, and sending could be well over a year. Given the few ships from Honolulu to Hilo after the Coans arrived, it could be much longer than a year. And then there were the letters lost when ships sank during the long ocean journey.

During their early weeks, months, and pre-Great Awakening[137] in Hilo Fidelia and Titus felt particularly acutely the lack of correspondence. After their arrival in Honolulu and excitement of being with other missionaries; and their initial arrival in Hilo, they ached for communication from home. Whether between towns or states, correspondence was the primary way of staying in regular touch with friends and family.[138]

The absence of correspondence was painful. While letters could not have arrived before they did, the wait wore on them and seemed to expand or slow down the days. In early October 1835 Titus writes "To Reverend Herman Halsey of Middleport in Niagra county, New York... With hands and head and heart full of labors I arrest a passing moment to pen a hasty line to a dear and distant brother. To this I am prompted by at least three considerations; Christian affection, the encouragement I gave of writing when I last saw you, and the hope (selfish perhaps) that I shall receive a hundredfold reward from your pen. When I see the immense work before us in this dark land, I sometimes groan out and say, O that our dear friends in America would cheer and strengthen our hearts by full and frequent letters without waiting to be addressed first, or even insisting on answers to their communications, according to the usual rules of epistolary correspondence!"[139]

In their early letters to loved ones, they requested or drew from memories prior to their departure. Lydia Bingham Coan relates an undated letter in which Titus writes about what he would like to hear about. "Tell us of those events which would form the subject of inquiry and conversation were we to meet. This brings *Home* right before us, with its bright fireside, its endearing circle, and all its cherished scenes."[140]

As late as 1840, Titus asks Levi Chamberlain to have Rufus Anderson[141] let correspondents know of the vagaries of handwritten and printed material sent by sea. He writes of the extensive loss of letters in a recent ship wreck. Because "of a great number of American letters [that] have been lost by the late wreck I would suggest to you the

---

137. A period from late summer of 1835 through late 1836.
138. See the Library of Congress correspondence, that begins well before departure to Hawai'i.
139. Coan to Halsey, October 7, 1835, HMH.
140. Coan to Halsey, October 7, 1835, HMH.
141. General Secretary of the American Board.

expediency of writing a notice [indecipherable] of the fact, stating the names of all the Brethren whose letters were lost, also the ship by which the letters were brought to the Islands, and forward it to Mr. Anderson with the special request that it be published in the Herald, the N. Y. Observer, the Evangelist and such other papers as they may think best. Our friends who have written us will thus learn the fate of their letters and not input[142] their want of answers to neglect on our part. They will thus be induced to write us again and as soon as may be, fill the painful blank made in their correspondence by the loss of their letters. We do not yet hear whether the Hilo letters were on board the vessel which was wrecked, but we suppose this was the fact.

"If you will have the kindness to write to the [Missionary/ABCFM] Rooms [in Boston] on this subject you will oblige at least *two*, and I doubt not *many* friends."[143]

Lydia writes of fireside and memories in a letter to Mrs. Rufus Anderson, the wife of the ABCFM General Secretary. "My dear Mrs. Anderson,—Ever since our short but pleasant interview in Boston I have been purposing to write you, but want of time—an apology which sometimes means something—has hitherto prevented."[144]

In early 1836, Fidelia writes her sister Amanda Church of a disappointingly small bundle of letters as well as how it got there. "Your letter which bears the date of March 19–23, came to the island of Oahu by the *Don Quixote*. It left Boston in September 1835 but brought but one letter from the state of New York for us. I will not yet believe that you alone of all my brothers and sisters and friends had written me when I had been absent nine months. I do confidently expect a parcel still. I cannot think that it took the family from March to September to read and copy sister Maria's letter which you said you should send me as soon as that was done. I receive two sheets of foolscap closely written from Mrs. Cooke, and one from a daughter of Dr. Bates, Middlebury [CT?]. Titus received one from a minister in Vermont, and this comprised our bundle."

She continues to describe the travel of the ship. "We saw the vessel pass here, several miles at sea, about five weeks since—were sure that it was the *Don Quixote* which we knew was daily expected by her owners in Oahu, and been waiting and watching and longing for some word from Oahu ever since. So you see we have to exercise patience in waiting for letters after they arrive at the Islands. I think letters are still behind, and should wait awhile before writing to you that I might acknowledge them, but an opportunity occurs of sending part way, at least, to Oahu on Monday, and I felt as though I should drop a line, though in much haste, as it is Saturday afternoon."

Titus was gone so he was not yet aware of the letters. "Our dear Titus has been gone nearly a week on a tour of a distant part of the field, examining schools, so he is not here to rejoice and weep with me that the prayer that I have so often heard him

---

142. Impute.
143. Titus Coan to Levi Chamberlin, February 10, 1840, HMH.
144. No citation.

offer so frequently of late, is to some extent answered—a prayer for intelligence from dear friends, and especially tidings of the prosperity of Zion"[145] [Ps 128:5].

She writes Maria in November of 1836 about the continued lack of any letters received from her sister. Maria is a missionary in Siam, hence Fidelia's question. "I have taken more time and paper than I intended in writing about our [volcano] tour, but it is not much to be regretted perhaps, as I wrote you not long since, and here nothing particularly new to communicate. It will not be new to you that I am waiting with intense desire to hear from you. More than fifteen months since I have heard a word—so long that all the enquiries seem to be merged in this, are you yet alive? This is the third time I have written you since my arrival, but perhaps you have received nothing yet."[146]

She also laments to her sister that she has received no letters during autumn of that year. "There have been no arrivals from the United States this fall, so we have had no letters. We are expecting to hear however by every message from Honolulu. Are our people faithful in writing to you? They are cruel if they are not."[147]

In December of 1836, while Titus is on a Puna tour, she writes to her parents of being alone and the dearth of letters. "I am quite alone now, or at least I feel so though there is no lack of noise and natives about me from daylight till bed time . . . We received letters from parts of the Islands the other day, but none from home as we are constantly expecting to. Two years have elapsed since I left home, and I have received two letters!"

She writes of knowledge of a box of letters for the Coans in Honolulu. She is adamant about not sending letters in boxes. "There is a box for us at Honolulu from Siam. Whether from Maria or from home, sent that way by the Board, I cannot tell. I am extremely anxious to get it, but must wait until a vessel sails to come here. Vessels from Honolulu frequently touch at the other side of this island, so that letters can be sent across the island by land. Boxes cannot be: so don't put letters in boxes."[148]

Within a month of the date of Fidelia's letter, Titus writes Levi Chamberlain about receiving many letters in one delivery. "How do you all do at the leeward? We have had a long long blockade at Hilo, till a few days ago when we had thirty or forty letters all in a lump bearing dates from September to December 20. So you see we sometimes get things new and old at our Station. Our letters came over the Continent, Hawaii, and of course brought us no supplies."[149]

---

145. Fidelia Coan to Amanda Church, March 12, 1836, HMH.
146. Fidelia Church to Maria Robinson, November 11, 1836, HMH.
147. Fidelia Church to Maria Robinson, November 11, 1836, HMH.
148. Fidelia Coan to Samuel and Abigail Church, December 8, 1836. HMH.
149. Titus Coan to Levi Chamberlain, January 7, 1837.

CALL TO AND ARRIVAL IN THE SANDWICH ISLANDS

Remembering a Boston fireside visit from two years before, Fidelia writes Mrs. Rufus Anderson. "Were I by your pleasant fireside this evening, you perhaps would ask me how missionary life appears after having tried it for a year and a half."[150]

LANGUAGE LEARNING AND EARLY MINISTRY

In her letter to Mrs. Anderson, she next writes about language learning. "[N]otwithstanding all that is said—and with truth perhaps—of the ease with which this language is acquired, it has been to me a source of more strain than anything else since we left America. Getting it is not the trouble but being without it. I did not anticipate what my feelings would be to be speechless when it would seem the stones must cry out [Luke 19:40]. It is not the work of six months or a year to acquire the Hawaiian language. Persons of tolerable capacity for language will acquire sufficient knowledge in a year to be understood on common subjects: but I greatly mistake if it is not a labor of years to become so familiar with it as to know readily how natives think; how to analyze their characters; how to apply truth to them, as Hawaiians, I long for the time when I shall feel at home in the Hawaiian language. 'O Lord, open thou my lips, and my tongue shall show forth thy praise'"[151] [Ps 51:15].

Coan writes of similar challenges in language learning. "We are studying the language as the first thing, of course, and I assure you it is no small task to acquire even the Hawaiian tongue. The language is still rude, and in a great measure unformed, and the oldest missionaries on the ground confess that they still know little of it. No grammar or lexicon is yet prepared. One can obtain a smatter of this language in a short time by care and attention, but a thorough knowledge of it will require a man's lifetime."[152]

In a bridge passage, Lydia writes of Titus ministering to sailors almost daily during his first three months of language learning and his reaching the point of preaching in Hawaiian. "He found work at once, and with him, as with Fenelon,[153] it was ever: 'Do the duty that lies nearest [the] unknown tongue,' from direct efforts for the natives, he had, as his own words record, 'close, personal conversation with captains and sailors,' of ships stopping at the port of Hilo. There were calls every day from sailors enquiring the way of life, and solemn meetings when he preached to them. But when the new language had been to some degree acquired, and three months after landing, he had preached his first Hawaiian sermon, he began the touring which was to be a marked feature of his after life."[154]

---

150. Fidelia Coan to Mrs. Rufus Anderson, January 20, 1837, HMH.

151. Fidelia Coan to Mrs. Rufus Anderson, January 20, 1837, HMH.

152. Unspecified Coan journal entry, in Coan, *Memorial Volume*, 38.

153. François de Salignac de la Mothe-Fénelon, 1651–1715, was a French Roman Catholic archbishop, theologian, poet and writer. Wikipedia, "François Fénelon."

154. Coan, *Memorial Volume*, 39. Uncited Coan journal entry.

On September 20, 1835, Coan writes in his journal about preaching on the Sabbath. "Preached in English. Text, 'For the redemption of their souls, etc.'"[155] ["is precious"; Ps 49:8]. A week later, his "ship's company [were] nearly all present." The "meeting" was "solemn." He "preached from text 'Because sentence.'"[156] In this sermon, Coan did call for a response from the listeners. "After sermon gave invitation to all who would now turn to the Lord to signify by arising. Three young men arose. Several have called for private conversation on the subject of religion."[157]

Three days later he writes about calls "from sailors every day to enquire the way of life. Four [?] John Moore, Henry Biddell, Charles Burdick [?], and Hosea Elliott, appear much changed in their feelings and seem truly determined to follow Christ." He also notes that the ship master's wife, "Mrs. [Joseph] Paddock also seems fixed in her purpose of serving the Lord."[158]

On the Sabbath October 11, "Nearly all the sailors on shore. Preached to them from t[he] text 'What must I do to be saved' [Acts 16:30]. Conversed with some after meeting. One promised to serve the Lord."[159]

Titus writes about language learning and preliminary efforts at working on a sermon. "It is not quite three months since I commenced study, and I have just completed one written Hawaiian sermon, so that I can now preach from paper (a thing which I never did) but it will be a great while before I can preach extemporare.[160] Some don't attempt it in less than two years. It is one thing to read and translate a foreign language, and quite another to make it so much our own as to be able to speak it fluently without premeditation. We read twice a day with native teacher, write for correction, teach a school of eighty scholars, attend meetings, etc."

After being in Hilo for three months, he writes about language learning and preaching in the mother tongue. "I believe that I have told you that I commenced preaching in this language in about three months after our arrival at the station. I can now preach with a good degree of ease and fluency, but I have much yet to learn before I have a thorough knowledge of the Hawaiian tongue."[161]

On the same page he perhaps modestly compares himself to other missionaries in their learning and preaching in Hawaiian. "The same is true to a greater or less

---

155. Coan journal entry, September 20, 1835, LOC.

156. Coan journal entry, September 27, 1835, LOC. Could the "because sentence text" refer to Ecclesiastes 8:11 King James Version (KJV): "Because sentence against an evil work is not executed speedily, therefore the heart of the sons of men is fully set in them to do evil."? Or perhaps Acts 17:31, "*Because* [God] hath appointed a day, in which he will judge." [emphasis added.] See below, first sermon in Hawaiian.

157. Coan journal entry, September 27, 1835, LOC.

158. Coan journal entry, September 30, 1835, LOC.

159. Coan journal entry, October 11, 1835, LOC.

160. It wouldn't be too long before he did.

161. HMH miscellaneous letters. Undated unnamed recipient because letter begins in midst.

extent with all the missionaries here." And then this: "It takes years of patient study and practice to gain a thorough knowledge of any foreign language."[162]

Though challenging to learn the language and daunting to preach in it, Titus Coan had the dual benefits of an established station with Hawaiian Christians; and the New Testament already translated into Hawaiian.[163]

Fidelia wrote to a friend at Andover about "her feelings at [her] initial hindrance" in language learning. She also indicates some instruction she and other missionaries had received before leaving Boston. "Since our arrival our attention has been devoted primarily to the language, and secondarily to school teaching. Before leaving home I had been accustomed to reckon the acquisition of a foreign language among the trials of a missionary. While in Boston, Mr. Abeel[164] spoke to us particularly and affectingly on that point. But my mind dwelt rather on the difficulty of *acquiring* a language than the trial of being ignorant of it . . . Our hearts ache and we often cry out, when shall we speak plain?"[165]

Fidelia writes about continuing language learning in an October letter to her brother, S. C. Church. "The language still embarrasses us, so that we feel we are accomplishing little at present, but we look forward with hope that [the?] time will arrive—if God spares us—when we shall be able to declare plainly to this people the unsearchable riches of Christ [Eph 3:8]. It is a delightful work even now, but we long to bring more efficiency into it."

She continues by talking about Titus's labored efforts in preaching in Hawaiian. She then presents a theory that Wycliffe Bible Translators in the twentieth and twenty-first century have shown to be incorrect. "Mr. Coan preaches but is obliged to write every thing. Talking is hard work—it requires a labor of years to enable one to express himself on all subjects with force and precision if, indeed, it can ever be done in pure native . . . The language, like that of all[166] heathen nations, is barren [of] religious terms."[167]

Fidelia might not have had a bent toward translation. She may well have developed a more nuanced view over the years, though she was aghast when her son Munson was speaking Hawaiian fluently to the house helper by the time he was one

---

162. HMH miscellaneous letters. Undated unnamed recipient because letter begins in midst.

163. The first Hawaiian New Testament (*Buke 2*) was printed in Honolulu in 1832. The entire Bible—including the Old Testament (*Buke 1*)—was printed in 1839. Citizendum.org, "Hawaiian Bible."

164. An American Board missionary, David Abeel promoted interest in missions within the Dutch Reformed Church between 1835 and 1838. Apparently he was in Boston at the time the Coans were there before debarking for the Sandwich Islands. http://www.bdconline.net/en/stories/a/abeel-david.php.

165. Fidelia Coan to William H. Parker, October 23, 1835, HMH, in Ehlke, "Enthusiastic Religion," 101.

166. A regrettable sweeping generalization.

167. See also discussion in pre-Great Awakening chapter on theory of monotheistic backgrounds of Polynesians who voyaged to the Hawaiian Islands.

year old! She provides examples of this situation. "Words by the missionaries which are used to express the attributes of God are exceedingly defective until by long and constant usage the natives learn to attach the real meaning to them. The native word for holiness—*hemolele*—would as soon be applied to a good straight stick of wood as to that attribute in the character of God.[168] There is but one word[169] to express what a man ought, and is solemnly bound, to do, and what he may do or do not as he chooses. Thus it is *pono* for a man to repent from his sins, and *pono* to wash his hands when they are dirty, to bathe himself, or anything equally indifferent."[170]

Fidelia indicates that these examples compound the embarrassment a Christian Hawaiian language learner experiences. "So after all, there will be embarrassment until the language improves, which will be the case if the people improve."

She does acknowledge prayer for language learning and help in the language from Hawaiians. "The natives pray that we may soon acquire a knowledge of their language, and are always ready and sometimes skillful in helping us out of difficulties. Sometime since I took a member of the church and went around to the houses of the people to get the mothers to a maternal meeting. In one house I found an old woman and a girl. I asked my guide if the former was mother to the girl: she said no, she was *kupana*. I told her I did not understand the meaning of the word. After thinking half a moment she replied it was like Lois to Timothy."[171] [2 Tim 1:5].[172]

Coan records his first sermon in Hawaiian in his November 8, 1835, journal. Considering the Hawaiian Great Awakening that would break out within a year or two and that Titus Coan would lead it, this is a historic day. It was on a Sabbath and he preached it at the Hilo church. "Preached for the first time in the Hawaiian language. Text Acts 17:30 'But now [God] commandeth all men' etc. 'And the times of this ignorance God winked at; but now commandeth all men everywhere to repent [verse 31 begins]: 'Because he hath appointed a day in which he will judge the world in righteousness by that man whom he hath ordained; whereof he hath given assurance unto all men, in that he hath raised him from the dead.'"[173]

---

168. This example would now be shared approvingly as a "dynamic equivalent" translation. A "translation which attempts to produce a dynamic rather than a formal equivalence is based upon the principle of equivalent effect. In such a translation one is not so concerned with matching the receptor-language message with the source-language message, but with the dynamic relationship, that the relationship between receptor and message should be substantially the same as that which existed between the original receptors and the message." Nida, *Toward a Science of Translation*, 159.

169. But there *is* a word.

170. The Apostle Paul would be grateful for such an opportunity and link.

171. Fidelia Coan to brother S. C. Church, January 19, 1836, HMH.

172. Could instead have to do with the Greek word *doula*, which has to do with an older woman mentoring a younger woman.

173. Coan journal entry, November 8, 1835, LOC.

Call to and Arrival in the Sandwich Islands

On the Sabbath of March 6, 1836, Titus "preached from 1 Cor 16:22 'If any man love not' etc."[174] The "Sacrament of the Lord's Supper administered in the afternoon.

"Four persons admitted to the church on profession of faith in Xst [Christ]." He provides the names of the four adults: "Mr. Kekuhoupio, Kapiano, Kuuani, and Akahi." He notes that he had "the privilege of baptizing them all." He also baptized the children of all four. Coan goes into some depth about Kekuhoupio, who "was formerly a priest of one of the Heiaus, or idol Temples, of this Island. In his person and manners he is one of the most interesting of the nations. Tall, well formed, of a sweet and prepossessing countenance, powerful in his manners and cultivating habits of neatness, he appears much more advanced in civilization than most of his neighbors."

Coan continues with a description of Kekuhoupio's priestly background, his style of dress, and his faithful pursuit of Christian knowledge and teaching. "He must have been a mere stripling in the days of his priesthood, as he does not appear over thirty-five years old at the present time. He dresses in English style, and is diligent in the pursuit of knowledge. We employ him as a teacher, and in this department he is very faithful."[175]

On the Sabbath March 13, 1836, Coan preached at a 9 a.m. service.[176] He used the same passage he did the previous Sunday in Hilo: 1 Corinthians 16:22, "If any man love not our L[ord] J[esus] C[hrist], etc." This became his first and repeated Hawaiian language sermon in his early days. He notes that "immediately after the sermon" there was a Bible class. Then Lyman preached on "whosoever will, let him take of the water of life freely" [Rev 22:17].

In his autobiography, Titus Coan describes the area where he would minister for decades. "The field in which I was called to labor is a belt of land extending by the coast-line one hundred miles on the north-east, east, and south-east shore of Hawaii, including the districts of Hilo and Puna, and a part of Kau.

"The inhabited belt is one to three miles wide, and in a few places there were hamlets and scattering villages five to ten miles inland. Beyond this narrow shore belt there is a zone of forest trees with a tropical jungle from ten to twenty-five miles wide, almost impenetrable by man or beast. Still higher is another zone of open country girdling the bases of the mountains, with a rough surface of hill, dale, ravine, scoriaceous lava fields, rocky ridges, and plains and hills of pasture land. Here wild goats, wild cattle, with hogs and wild geese feed. Still higher up tower Mauna Kea and Mauna Loa, nearly fourteen thousand feet above the sea, the former being a pile of extinct craters, often crowned with snow, and the latter a mountain of fire, where for unknown ages earthquakes that rock the group and convulse the ocean have been born, and where volcanoes burst out with awful roar, and rush in fiery rivers down the mountain sides,

---

174. The complete KJV verse is, "If any man love not the Lord Jesus Christ, let him be Anathema. Maranatha" [Aramaic for "Come Lord"].

175. Coan journal entry, March 6, 1836, LOC.

176. In Puna?

across the open plains, through the blazing forest jungle and into the sea. All but the narrow shore belt is left to untamed bird and beast, and to the wild winds and raging fires of the mountains, except when bird-catchers, canoe-makers, cattle-hunters, or volcano visitors are drawn thither by their several interests from the shore."

Coan estimates the number and demographics of his district in 1836. "The population of this shore belt was probably at that time about fifteen thousand to sixteen thousand, almost exclusively natives. Very few foreigners had then come here to live." He writes about making tours on foot and the difficulties of travelling. He writes about the challenges of crossing swollen streams. Many years later he would purchase a horse and roads were somewhat improved.[177]

Titus and Lyman commit to send a Hawaiian to minister to a Puna district area. "The sight of these sheep without a shepherd affected our hearts, and as they seemed tender and anxious for instruction we determined to leave one of the native converts to labor with them for a few weeks."[178]

On April fourth, a Monday, he reports on return from Kuolo "where I spent the Sab[bath]. Preached two sermons from 1 Cor. 16:22."[179] Again there is a Bible class between Coan's sermon and Lyman's sermon. Kuolo was where he first prayed "in nation[180] for the first time, in public, one week ago."[181]

He writes of the High Priest of Pele who would eventually become a Christian. His sister, the High Priestess, would do so later. "On the evening of this day several natives of Puna, forty miles distant, called to enquire the way of life [Jer 21:28]. Among others were the old hereditary High Priest of Pele."

Foreshadowings of the Great Awakening's beginning near the end of 1836 are evident during earlier months. I met "many people on the way. Sometimes one, sometimes ten, twenty, fifty, etc. at a time. Spoke to them on the things pertaining to the kingdom of God." He shared the gospel with everyone, including prisoners. He met "a large company of prisoners, perhaps sixty or seventy, going onto Hilo to be put in custody. Pointed them to the Lamb of God"[182] [John 1:29; Rev 5:6].

On the Sabbath of April 17, 1836, at "10 a.m. preached to the people from the words, 'To day if ye will hear his voice etc. [Heb 3:7, quoting Ps 95:7]. He "retired for ½ an hour, and left the native professor who was with me to talk and pray with those who chose to tarry." Coan preaches again. "At half past 11 I preached from these words, 'Come unto me' etc." [Matt 11:28–30].

Three months later, Coan preached "two sermons in the native chapel. Texts 'Come for all things are now ready—' [Luke 14:17] and 'Therefore whosoever heareth

---

177. Coan, *Life*, 29–36.
178. Coan journal entry, March 13, 1836, LOC.
179. Coan journal entry, April 4, 1836, LOC.
180. Native language.
181. Coan journal entry, April 15, 1836, LOC.
182. Coan journal entry, April 15, 1836, LOC.

Call to and Arrival in the Sandwich Islands

these sayings of mine and doeth them' etc. [Matt 7:24–27]. Br [Ephraim] Spaulding[183] preached at our station."[184] One month after that, Coan relates his sermon topic for a Sabbath sermon in Hilo. "Preached this morning from the words, 'Now then we are ambassadors for Christ'"[185] [2 Cor 5:20–6:2]. A week later he "preached from the words, 'Be not deceived, God is not mocked'"[186] [Gal 6:7].[187] On August 28, he preached "from the words, 'God is angry with the wicked every day'"[188] [Ps 7:11].[189]

In one of his early Puna tours, Coan occasionally noted the Bible passage he used in his preaching. He wrote in his journal on December 16, 1836, "We found the people collected in a school house on the shore where I addressed them from the words, 'Thy King[dom] come'"[190] [Matt 6:10].

Titus would eventually return to Hilo.

After preparing for and traveling to the Sandwich Islands, Fidelia and Titus arrived in Honolulu on June 6, 1835. After being assigned to the Hilo mission station, they would live in small quarters with the Lymans, then move to the nearby Chamberlain home, which would become the Coans' Emerald Bower. After three months of language learning, Titus began to preach the gospel in Hawaiian at the Hilo church and in the districts of Hilo, Kau, and Puna. He was on the cusp of what would come to be called the Great Awakening. Before examining this movement of God's Holy Spirit, the centuries of preparation for that event will be considered.

---

183. Stationed in Lahaina, Spaulding would leave Hawai'i with his family due to ill health in late 1836. He would die in June of 1840 in Westborough, Massachusetts. Judd, *Missionary Album*, 183.

184. Coan journal entry, July 24, 1836, LOC.

185. Coan journal entry, August 14, 1836, LOC.

186. The rest of the verse is "whatsoever a man soweth, that shall he also reap."

187. Coan journal entry, August 21, 1836, LOC.

188. The full verse is "God judgeth the righteous, and God is angry with the wicked every day."

189. Coan journal entry, August 28, 1836.

190. Coan journal entry, December 16, 1836, LOC.

REVIVALIST

4

Prelude to Revival

"Morning Star of the Great Awakening"

INTRODUCTION: INTERACTION WITH SCHOLARSHIP AND OVERVIEW OF CHAPTER

THE FOUNDATIONS OF THE Hawaiian Great Awakening developed from the mists of time. From the arrival of Polynesian Voyagers to the development of royalty and the taboo system to the arrival of Cook to King Kamehameha's uniting the people of the islands and elimination of *tabu*,[1] the preparations were being made for the arrival of the first Protestant missionaries. The Pioneer Company and others were inspired by Hawaiians who became Christians, such as Henry 'Ōpūkaha'ia.[2]

After their arrival and in concert with subsequent Companies and other Hawaiian leaders—such as Lalana Pua'aiki,[3] royalty (*ali'i* in Hawaiian), and others—the gospel was preached and members were gathered into congregations. To accompany such efforts, the missionaries provided the Hawaiian language with letters and words. This led to literacy, which made possible the translating and reading of the Bible in Hawaiian. All of these, together with missionaries and Hawaiians cultivating the Hilo field, prepared the ground for the harvest of the Great Awakening.

When it comes to scholarly history of Hawai'i, Gavan Daws—himself the author of *The Shoal of Time*[4] history of Hawai'i—wrote the fifth-edition[5] of the first modern objective history, the magisterial four-volume set on *The Hawaiian Kingdom*.

1. Also called *kapu*.
2. With the westernized name of Henry Obookiah.
3. Nicknamed "Blind Bartimaeus/*Bartimea*."
4. Daws, *Shoal of Time*.
5. Kuykendall, *Hawaiian Kingdom*.

Kuykendall "spent four decades of his life writing the history of Hawaii. He came to the Islands in 1922 as executive secretary of the newly-formed Historical Commission of the Territory of Hawaii. The commission planned, among other projects, to publish a large-scale history: a general narrative of a thousand pages or more, sufficiently documented to ensure 'authoritativeness.'"[6]

Two paragraphs later, Daws writes of Kuykendall's temperament and philosophy of history. "Kuykendall's work for the Historical Commission was to be 'official' as well as authoritative. This suited his temperament. He seems to have been well content to regard himself as a reliable chronicler rather than as an interpreter or re-interpreter of events. He never found it necessary to put much on paper about his own philosophy of history. Indeed we have to go to his private correspondence to find even so brief and unexceptionable a statement as this one: 'It is *the business of the historian* to tell the truth, the whole truth, and nothing but the truth—to draw a faithful picture (a moving picture, if you please) of the past ... Until comparatively recent times, the exploits of kings, diplomatic intrigues, religious controversies, and wars were about the only things that historians wrote about.'"

Kuykendall continues. "'That, of course, gave a very one-sided, incomplete picture of human life. Nowadays, historians try to give a *complete picture*, with proper attention to all factors, including social, economic, and psychological conditions and developments. Hence it happens that kings, priests, diplomats, and battle have to share the scene with trade guilds, explorers, inventors, business men, farmers, educators, stevedores, and all the rest of us and our doings.'"[7]

"In another way Kuykendall was temperamentally well suited to the writing of 'official' history. His view of his role as chronicler was *equable and uninflected*. He was content to see the past diligently documented and (in a sense) laid to rest. 'As events recede into the past,' he wrote in a letter composed only a few months after he began

---

6. Daws, "Preface," *Hawaiian Kingdom*, vi. On ix, Kuykendall writes more about the Commission and volume 1, in the Preface, xi. "This volume is one of the fruits of a project undertaken more than a dozen years ago by the Historical Commission of the Territory of Hawaii and carried on since 1932 by the University of Hawaii. The project called for the preparation of a comprehensive general history of Hawaii based upon a thorough study of original sources.

"The first phase of the undertaking was to discover the source material not already available in Honolulu and to obtain copies of as much of it as possible, particularly of documents which shed new light on the history of the islands. For this purpose, extensive research has been carried on in the national archives of the United States, Great Britain, and France ... May thousand [pages?] of transcripts have been obtained from these places, supplementing at many points and in many important respects the materials previously available in Honolulu." After thanking various institutions, Kuykendall writes, "Next in value, from the point of view of such an enterprise as this, are the library of the Hawaiian Mission Children's Society, which is not by any means exclusively missionary in character, the library of the Hawaiian Historical Society, which is especially rich in voyages, and the library of the Bernice P. Bishop Museum."

On xi, Kuykendall notes that a "very special acknowledgment is due the Hawaiian Mission Children's society and the officers who have been connected with its library from time to time, Mr. H. M. Ballou, Rev. B. T. Sheeley, Miss Bernice Judd, Miss Harriet G. Forbes, and Mrs. Violet A. Silverman."

7. Uncited Kuykendall letter, in Kuykendall, "Preface," *Hawaiian Kingdom*, vi–vii.

work in Hawaii, 'we are able to see them in truer perspective. And so, many controversies gradually lose the sharp edge of bitterness. Many actions which at the moment seemed due to malice are at length seem to have been the result of misunderstanding.'"

While Daws does not fully agree with Kuykendall's assessment on that matter, he writes, "On subjects concerning the establishment of the frame of government of the kingdom, and on Hawaii's early political and economic relations with the outside world, he remains authoritative. On a host of other topics he remains instructive. As a guide to sources his work is invaluable. He could never have claimed—modest man that he was—that his work was definitive. But certainly it was the best that had been done up to his time."[8]

While other sources and resources will be used, Kuykendall provides helpful information for each major section of this chapter. With that, we turn to the first such section.

PRE-EUROPEANS/AMERICANS

Before writing about the people who journeyed to the islands, Kuykendall writes about the islands themselves. "The Hawaiian islands, as a whole, consist of a chain of islands extending over a distance of nearly two thousand miles. If the ocean were drained of its water, this chain would appear as a lofty mountain range. The whole range is of volcanic origin, the separate islands having been built up by outpouring of lava from vents along a crack in the earth's crust. Raised up by volcanic action, they have been sculptured by geological processes and modified by growth of coral into their present forms. It is supposed that the volcanic action began at the northwest; the islands at that end have been reduced to the status of coral atolls, while the up-building by lava flows is still in progress at the other end of the chain, on the island of Hawaii."

Kuykendall writes about the new volcanic island that is forming southeast of the Big Island. "Eighteen miles southeast of the Big Island of Hawaii, there is a new island called Loihi forming, with lava erupting from its peak underwater and building it closer to the ocean surface. The top of Loihi is still three thousand feet underwater. It is estimated that it will take another fifty thousand years for it to rise up and form dry land for a new Hawaiian island."[9]

"The Hawaiian islands are situated in the north central portion of the Pacific Ocean. They lie almost wholly within the western hemisphere, the main islands being little more than two thousand miles distant from the American continent; however,

---

8. Kuykendall, *Hawaiian Kingdom*, vii. Kuykendall, x, on being objective: "The writer has made a conscientious effort to present the facts objectively and to treat impartially the numerous controversial questions that have to be dealt with."

9. In *Hawai'i*, Andrew Doughty expands on Lo'ihi. "This new volcano is still 3,200 feet below the ocean's surface, twenty miles off the southwestern coast of the island. Yet in a geologic heartbeat, the Hawaiian Islands will be richer with its ascension, sometime in the next 100,000," 13.

those two thousand miles of water are unbroken by any islands, while the seas to the south and west of Hawaii are dotted with thousands of islands lying in the ocean like stepping stones to the continents of Asia and Australia."[10]

While during the nineteenth century Hawaiian missionaries reversed the direction and took the gospel to Micronesia, it is from some of the Polynesian islands that groups migrated off and on for some centuries. Known as "voyagers," they brought their customs to the previously uninhabited islands. "So far as Hawaii is concerned, it is quite generally believed that there were successive arrivals of settlers extending over some hundreds of years. It is also believed that these ancestors of the modern Hawaiians came from the Society Islands (Tahiti); it is almost certain that the later ones came from there. The first human beings who came to Hawaii—the real 'discoverers' of these islands—may have come as much as a thousand years ago; they may have come from Tahiti or they and the earliest settlers may have branched off from a common stem somewhere along the route from Asia."[11]

An online source writes the following about the voyagers: "The Islands were uninhabited until sometime around 400 CE when Polynesian voyagers sailing double-hulled canoes arrived from the Marquesas Islands. Since the settlers had no written language and virtually no contact with the Western world until 1778, our knowledge of Hawaiʻi's prehistory comes primarily from archaeological investigations and oral legends."[12]

In his Doctor of Ministry dissertation, Tamashiro writes about the voyagers. "Sources exist on Polynesian voyaging. This information is important to understand Polynesian migration and their navigational routes." Tamashiro provides the following sources on this subject. "Abraham Fornander's *An Account of the Polynesian Race*,

---

10. Kuykendall, *Hawaiian Kingdom*, 1.

11. Kuykendall, *Hawaiian Kingdom*, 2. See also Doughty, *Hawaiʻi*, 12–13, on "The First Settlers": "Sometime around the fifth century AD a large, double-hulled voyaging canoe, held together with flexible sennit [Wikipedia, "Sennit": "Sennit is a type of cordage made by plaiting strands of dried fiber or grass. It can be used ornamentally in crafts, like a kind of *macrame*, or to make straw hats. Sennit is an important material in the cultures of Oceania, where it is used in traditional architecture, boat building, fishing and as ornamentation."] lashings and propelled by sails made of woven pandanus [See Wikipedia, "*Pandanus*": *Pandanus* is a genus of monocots with some 750 accepted species. They are palm-like, dioecious trees and shrubs native to the Old World tropics and subtropics. Common names include pandan (/ˈpændən/), screw palm, and screw pine They are classified in the order Pandanales, family Pandanaceae.], slid onto the sand on the Big Island of Hawaiʻi. These first intrepid adventurers, only a few dozen or so, encountered an island chain of unimaginable beauty.

"They had left their home in the Marquesas Islands, 2,500 miles away, for reasons we will never know. Though some say it was because of war, overpopulation, or drought, it was more likely part of a purposeful exploration from a culture that had mastered the art of making their way through the featureless seas using celestial navigation and reading subtle signs in the ocean. Their navigational abilities far exceed all the other 'advanced' societies of the time [Doughty's opinion]. Whatever their reasons, these initial settlers took a big chance and surely must have been highly motivated. They could not have known that there were islands in these waters since Hawaiʻi is the most isolated island chain in the world. (Though some speculate that they were led here by the gold plover [bird].)."

12. EH.net, "Economic History of Hawaii."

Volume One: Its Origins and Migrations and the Ancient History of the Hawaiian People to the Times of Kamehameha I and *Ancient History of the Hawaiian People to the Times of Kamehameha I*[13] and *Ancient History of the Hawaiian People to the Times of Kamehameha I.*[14] Fornander is a prominent authority in the history of Polynesian history and migrations. A second resource is K. R. Howe, who edited *Vaka Moana Voyages of the Ancestors: The Discovery and Settlement of the Pacific.*"[15]

As part of his research findings on "God's General Revelation to the Hawaiians,"[16] Tamashiro presents a theory that some of the Voyagers were monotheistic in belief rather than polytheistic. The first words of his dissertation indicate that theory: "The Original Monotheism of the Hawaiians." This presentation is part of Tamashiro's showing how God prepared the Hawaiian people for the arrival of Christianity in the person of the ABCFM missionaries in 1820.

He begins that section by quoting someone who indicates secret worship of a supreme being. "Ancient Hawaiians worshiped a supreme being called 'Io. Malia Carver, interviewed by the *Iolani* Newspaper (May 1993) explained how her family worshiped 'Io. Carver mentioned in the article that the worship of 'Io was kept secret."[17]

Tamashiro provides other sources to corroborate "Carver's interview about the worship of 'Io in Polynesia. In *King Potatau*, Pei Hurinui Jones tells the story of the first Maori King. In this narrative, chants from the House of Sacred Learning spill forth about 'Io. The narrative is recorded also in Frank J. Stimson's *The Cult of Kihotumu*, E. S. Craighill Handy's *Polynesian Religion*, Emma Ahueana Taylor's "The Cult of *Iolani*,' and H. T. Whatahoro's *The Lore of the Whare-Wananga.*"[18]

Tamashiro next describes several works that he characterizes as "insightful." One is Michael Kioni Dudley's *A Hawaiian Nation I: Man, Gods, and Nature*, which looks "at how ancient Hawaiians viewed the universe, God, and themselves."[19] Next, Tamashiro suggests William R. Gray's *Voyages to Paradise: Exploring in the Wake of Captain Cook*. Gray retraces Cook's travels throughout Polynesia."[20] He lists Herb Kawainui's *Ancient Hawaii, Voyage: Discovery of Hawaii*, and *Voyagers*.[21]

---

13. Fornander, *Account of the Polynesian Race.*, vol. 1.
14. Fornander, *Ancient History of the Hawaiian People.*
15. Howe, ed., *Vaka Moana*, in Tamashiro, "Original Monotheism," 82–83.
16. Tamashiro, "Original Monotheism," 82.
17. Tamashiro, "The Original Monotheism of the Hawaiians."
18. In an extended footnote, Tamashiro, "Original Monotheism," 84, provides the following citations: "Pei Te Hurunui Jones, *King Potatau: An Account of the Life of Potatau Te Wherowhero the First Maori King*; Frank J. Stimson, *The Cult of Kihotumu*; and Edward Smith Craighill Handy, *Polynesian Religion*, Co.; and H. T. Whatahoro, *The Lore of the Whare-Wananga*, pt. 1, vols. 3–4, Memoirs of the Polynesian Society."
19. Dudley, *Hawaiian Nation I*, in Tamashiro, "Original Monotheism," 84.
20. Gray, *Voyages to Paradise*, in Tamashiro, "Original Monotheism," 84–85.
21. Kane, *Ancient Hawaii*, in Tamashiro, "Original Monotheism," 85.

Mary Kawena Pukui compiled *Hawaiʻi Island Legends: Pikoi, Pele, and Others*,[22] which "is a source relating to the history and legends of Hawaii Island." Similarly, R. McBride writes about "the religious priests of ancient Hawaii in *The Kahuna: Versatil Masters of Old Hawaii. The Kahuna* were more than priests. Skilled artisans in various trades, they were the learned professionals of their time."[23]

Returning directly to the theme of monotheism, Tamashiro turns next to "God's Special Revelation to the Hawaiians."[24] In that section he demonstrates "the revelation of God's progression from general knowledge to special revelation, which is redemption through Jesus Christ. Ancient Hawaiians had a general knowledge of a supreme being called ʻIo. The arrival of the Tahitian high priest Paʻao corrupted the worship of ʻIo. Paʻao built temples and instituted new rituals, making the Hawaiian religion more rigid.[25] ʻIo's priests were killed or fled the islands. Monotheistic worship was replaced by polytheism."

Tamashiro finds support in Romans 1:20 to identify ʻIo with the God of the Bible. Since the Creation, God's "eternal power" and his "divine nature" have been made evident; men have no excuse for not knowing God and his character. God can be clearly understood by his creation.[26]

He links ʻIo to the God of the Bible. "The *name* ʻIo should not be minimized, because a different culture refers to God by another name. Melchizedek blessed Abraham by the 'God of the Most High.' Abraham gave a tithe to Melchizedek, although Melchizedek referred to God by the Canaanite name of *El Elyon* instead of the Hebraic form of *Yahweh* (Gen 14:18–20)."[27]

While there is evidence of ʻIo worship among Polynesians and early Hawaiians, polytheism became ascendant. Kuykendall notes that the "religion of the Hawaiians was essentially a nature worship. They were profoundly impressed with the mystery of nature, with the manifestations on every side of a power which they could not see and did not understand. The ceremonial system was designed to establish and preserve the right relationship between man and this unseen power. In writing about Polynesian deities, Handy says:

> The native's sense of the presence of his gods was by no means a vague feeling. In the elements and in nature about him he saw and felt the beings that he venerated . . . In Hawaii the rain clouds are referred to in prayer as the "bodies of Lono," the rain god. The more immediate features and objects of nature were all the children of the gods . . .

---

22. Pukuʻi, *Hawaiʻi Island Legends*, in Tamashiro, "Original Monotheism," 85.
23. McBride, *The Kahuna*, 3rd ed., in Tamashiro, "Original Monotheism," 85.
24. Tamashiro, "Original Monotheism," 85.
25. Kane, *Ancient Hawaii*, 18, in Tamashiro, "Original Monotheism," 85.
26. Daniel Kikawa, telephone interview by Alan Tamashiro, March 28, 2013, Hilo, HI, in Tamashiro, "Original Monotheism," 86.
27. Tamashiro, "Original Monotheism," 85.

> The gods of the Polynesians were personified concepts that, on the one hand, embodied the desires and needs, the hopes and dreads of their worshippers; and, on the other hand, individualized the elements and forces that they observed in nature.[28]

Kuykendall explains Handy, then extends the discussion with a quotation from W. D. Alexander. "As one might expect from this, there were many gods—one chant speaks of the four hundred thousand gods—and there was of necessity a gradation of rank and a difference of character among them. The great gods of Hawaii were Kane, Ku, Lono, and Kanaloa; 'each of these four gods were worshipped under various special attributes or functions, which afterwards came to be regarded as different persons.'"[29]

Kuykendall posits the possibility of the higher priests acknowledging a "Supreme Being." "The god Ku-kailimoku, a war god and the special god of the kings of Hawaii, was of great importance during the latter part of Hawaii's ancient history and in the reign of Kamehameha I. Pele, goddess of the volcano, was specially feared and worshipped in the southern part of Hawaii. Among the higher ranks of the Hawaiian priesthood there may have existed a conception of a Supreme Being, who overtopped all other gods."[30]

Kuykendall describes the places of worship for the worship of such gods. "The place devoted to the public worship of the gods was called *heiau*; it consisted of one or more stone-paved platforms or terraces enclosed by stone walls and containing various objects, houses, and other structures, each of which had some special use in the ceremonies. There were several classes of heaus, in one of which human sacrifices were offered."

In some 1836 journal entries, Titus Coan describes a *heiau* where human sacrifices had been offered in the not too distant past. Bingham and others write about human sacrifice.

With his reference to heiaus, Kuykendall transfers to a discussion of the kapu or tabu system. "There were certain kapu days in each month, when the rites of the heiau were attended to. Besides the formal services in the heiau, religious ceremonies were performed in connection with all important activities in which the Hawaiians engaged."

He ties it in with the Hawaiian royalty system. "Interwoven with the religion of Hawaii (and all Polynesia)[31] and with governmental and social organization was the kapu system." He looks at it from the perspective of the first Europeans to arrive and record their observations. "This was the feature of the Hawaiian culture which made

---

28. Handy, *Polynesian Religion*, 87–88, in Kuykendall, *Hawaiian Kingdom*, 7.
29. Alexander, *Brief History*, 36, in Kuykendall, *Hawaiian Kingdom*, 7.
30. Kuykendall, *Hawaiian Kingdom*, 7.
31. Parentheses by Kuykendall.

of the Hawaiian culture the deepest impression upon most of the early foreign visitors, who saw only the outer manifestations of the system and who in their descriptions emphasize its bizarre restrictions and cruel sanctions. In one aspect, the kapu system was a system of rules which regulated the daily life of the different classes of society and insured the subordination of the lower to the higher, the maintenance of an aristocratic type of government and a caste system."[32]

Kuykendall presents what he considers to be a deeper level of understanding of kapu, tying it back in with polytheism. "From a more fundamental viewpoint, the kapu system grew out of a dualistic conception of nature which placed on the one side that which was sacred and divine, the male principle, light, life, etc.; while on the other side were the common and unsacred, the female principle, darkness, death, etc."[33]

Citing Hand, Kuykendall explains the meaning of tapu/dapu/kapu/tabu. "'In its fundamental meaning tapu [dapu] as a word was used primarily as an adjective and as such signified that which was psychically dangerous, hence restricted, forbidden, set apart, to be avoided, because: (a) divine, therefore requiring isolation for its own sake from both the common and the corrupt; (b) corrupt, hence dangerous to the common and the divine, therefore requiring isolation from both for their sakes.'"[34]

While Kamehameha I "held to the religious beliefs until his death . . . Kaahumanu, Keopuolani and Liholiho (Kamehameha II) broke the eating kapu, one of the fundamental elements of the kapu system that held society together."[35] The documentary *A Witness to Aloha* explains the ending of the system and how at least one reason was that foreign visitors to the Islands broke it all the time and nothing happened to them.[36]

An understanding of tabu and the tabu system is important in order to realize the magnitude of its elimination not long before the Pioneer Company arrived. Kuykendall continues his discussion of kapu. "As a substantive, the word kapu means a prohibition or restriction.

---

32. Kuykendall, *Hawaiian Kingdom*, 8.

33. Footnote in Kuykendall, *Hawaiian Kingdom*: "David Emerson, with notes by the translator (Honolulu, 1903), 186–210. There are references to the arrival and departure of the god (obviously referring to the kamahi [?] god) and to boxing and other sports which began just after the god's departure, in the diary of Francisco de Paula Marin (translated extracts made by R. C. Wyllie, in AH [Archives of Hawaii]), under the dates Dec. 10, 29, 1811, Oct. 19, 26, Nov. 27, 1812, Nov. 5, 7, 9, 27, 1814, Dec. 3, 4, 1817, Nov. 21, 1818] . . . Don Francisco de Paula Marin (1774–1837) was a Spaniard who became influential in the early Kingdom of Hawaii. Often called Manini, Marini, or other variations, he became a confidant of Hawaiian King Kamehameha I. Marin acted as a jack-of-all-trades, sometimes even acting as a physician, probably without any formal education, and is credited with introducing many agricultural products." Kuykendall, *Hawaiian Kingdom*, 8.

Marin would oppose the continuation of the Pioneer Company in 1820. See below.

34. Handy, *Polynesian Religion*, 34–43, in Kuykendall, *Hawaiian Kingdom*, 8.

35. Nancy Morris, email to author, June 13, 2020.

36. *Witness to Aloha*.

PRELUDE TO REVIVAL

"Anything associated with the gods acquired sacredness; hence there were kapus relating to the priests, heiaus, and all other things dedicated to the gods. The ali'i (chiefs) were believed to be descended from the gods, hence there were many kapus referring to them; there were, however, degrees of sacredness among the ali'i; the highest of all, the *ali'i-kapu*, was thought of as being, in some sense, an actual god through whom the nation was kept in rapport with the supernatural realm; hence he was surrounded with many and very rigid kapus, in order to prevent any interruption of good relationship between the people collectively and the gods; in this manner the interests of all were deeply involved and there was little likelihood of these kapus being voluntarily violated. In the fundamental conception noted above can be discovered, likewise, the reasons for the eating kapus and the restrictive kapus affecting women."[37]

Kuykendall continues to relate kapus and the privileged class. "Besides the permanent kapus, there are kapus of a periodical character; and the chiefs and priests might impose special and temporary ones . . . At the top of the social scale were the ali'i or chiefs, a highly privileged class. Closely associated with them were the priests. Below the chiefs were the mass of the people, collectively called the *makaainana*, those who lived on the land."[38]

COOK THROUGH 1819

It is this kind of system that Captain James Cook and his crew discovered when they arrived in the Hawaiian Islands. He first arrived in 1778 at Waimea on the island of Kauai of the chain he dubbed the Sandwich Islands. During his second visit in 1789 he was murdered. But books have been written about Cook's voyages, including the one noted by Tamashiro, Gray's *Voyages to Paradise*. Kuykendall notes the idyllic natural state of the islands. "It is a pleasant land in which to live, and hence it is no matter of surprise that the Hawaiian people, who dwelt close to nature in the 'paradise of the Pacific,' were a healthy, robust, intelligent, and good-tempered folk."[39]

A few years after Cook's death, George Vancouver arrived in Hilo. Sheldon Dibble writes that on "his third trip[40] he arrived in Hilo Bay on January 9, 1794, but could not enter the Bay because of the prevailing wind. Kamehmeha was in Hilo at the time. He got on board with Vancouver off the coast of Hilo and traveled to Puna and Ka'u, where they anchored on the twelfth" of January.[41]

Vancouver had a conversation with Kamehameha that would have implications for the later arrival of the Congregational missionaries. "Observing the king was

---

37. Kuykendall, *Hawaiian Kingdom*, 8.
38. Kuykendall, *Hawaiian Kingdom*, 9.
39. Kuykendall, *Hawaiian Kingdom*, 2.
40. Exploration.
41. Dibble, *History of the Hawaiian Islands*, 46–47.

religiously inclined, Vancouver said, 'There is a God above in heaven[42] and if you desire to worship him, then I will entreat his majesty[43] to appoint for you a clergyman, and when he comes hither you must renounce your tabu system, which is false—there are no earthly deities—but there is a God in heaven.'"[44]

Dibble notes the seed that Vancouver the Anglican plants in the king. "There is no evidence that these remarks of Vancouver had any influence on the heathen notions of Kamehameha; but the advice was not lost. In the progress of events an occasion was afforded, on which it proved of immense importance."[45] Vancouver had during a 1793 visit recommended John Young, among other men, to the king. Young would play a role in later royalty's acceptance of the Pioneer Company of missionaries.[46]

Young assisted Kamehameha in uniting the islands. "In 1794 each island of the group was a separate kingdom. About this time Kamehameha made war on the other islands [besides Hawai'i] and eventually conquered all of them, becoming the first King of the Sandwich Islands. In these wars he was greatly aided by Young, by the firearms and the military instruction he had received from Vancouver," and a vessel.[47] Kamehameha's unifying of the islands helped prepare the way for the Pioneer Company.

As significant for the arrival of intentional Protestant missionaries was Kamehameha's son's ending of the kapu system. The same article just referenced also has the following: "King Kamehameha died May 8, 1818,[48] in the presence of John Young and all his chiefs."[49] Prior to that death, the king had done away with the kapu system described above. "Like his famous father Kamehameha, Liholiho became an agent of change for the Hawaiian people. However, unlike his father, the changes that Liholiho helped bring about changed the very fabric of society. Whereas Kamehameha the Great practiced the religion of his ancestors and followed the strict guidelines of the *kapu* system, Liholiho would usher in dramatic changes that would alter daily life and worship in Hawai'i. Shortly after the death of Kamehameha in 1819, Liholiho brought both the *kapu* system and the ritual system to an abrupt end."[50]

Coan writes about father and son in the following way. "Tradition and history alike tell us of Kamehahmeha I, the Caesar of Hawaii, the iron-framed warrior, the

---

42. Hymn, "In Heaven Above," Laurinus; Deut 4:38, and other verses.

43. George III, ruled 1760–1820. Wikipedia, "List of British Monarchs."

44. Dibble, *History of the Hawaiian Islands*, 47. For a short Sheldon Dibble biography, see Forbes et al., *Partners in Change*, 212–16.

45. Dibble, *History of the Hawaiian Islands*, 47.

46. See Dibble, *History of the Hawaiian Islands*, 160, and below.

47. "Boatswain John Young," in *New York Times*, February 14, 1886. http://query.nytimes.com/mem/archive-free/pdf?_r=1&res=990CE5D61F3BE532A25757C1A9649C94679FD7CF.

48. Kamehameha died on May 8 or May 14, 1819.

49. "Boatswain John Young," in *New York Times*, February 14, 1886. http://query.nytimes.com/mem/archive-free/pdf?_r=1&res=990CE5D61F3BE532A25757C1A9649C94679FD7CF.

50. US National Park Service, "Kamehameha II."

first legislator, and the first law-giver of the Hawaiian race. We are told how he warred and conquered, and how he united all the islands and all the petty principalities under one chief." Writing in 1881, Coan notes that there "are men still living who have seen this stern old king. He died in 1819."

Coan writes briefly about "Liholiho, styled Kamehameha II, [who] was the reigning sovereign when the first band of missionaries arrived in 1820." Perhaps deferring to Bingham and others to write about that event, Coan spends the rest of the paragraph discussing the death of the king and his queen, as well as the return of their ashes to Hawaiʻi. He writes about "Kamehameha III, son of Kamehameha I, [who] was on the Hawaiian throne when I arrived at the Islands, having been proclaimed not long before."[51]

In its outstanding documentary about the first church on Oahu and Protestant Christianity coming to the islands, the Kawaiahaʻo church's *Witness to Aloha* uses an agricultural metaphor. Focusing on the life cycle of a particular Hawaiian plant, it shares the following parts: "Preparing the Soil"; "Planting the seeds"; "Growth"; "Uprooting and Replanting"; and "Blooming." For the purposes of this chapter, the first two parts are germaine.[52]

Changing (or mixing!) the metaphor, preparing the soil before the arrival of the Pioneer Company involved another piece of preparation that needs to be put in place. It is the human piece of the puzzle that inspired the missionaries to make the Sandwich Islands their aim. Several Hawaiians became Christians during the decade leading up to the arrival of the Pioneer Company. One in particular is best known.

Tamashiro writes: "Henry Opukahaiʻia's life and untimely death are important components enabling God's special revelation to be communicated to the Hawaiian people. Sources supporting this aspect of God's redemptive plan include Edwin W. Dwight's *Memoirs of Henry Obookiah: A Native of Owhyhee, and a Member of the Foreign Mission School; Who Died at Cornwall, Connecticut, February 17, 1818, Aged 26 Years*, and Cornwall Historical Society's *Cornwall in Pictures: A Visual Reminiscence 1868–1941*."[53]

Christopher L. Cook has provided an outstanding pictorial narrative of pre-Hawaaian Great Awakening, weaving together early Hawaiian Christians and ABCFM missionaries. The title and extended subtitles explain the work—*Preparing the Way: A Pictorial History for the Hawaiʻi Mission Bicentennial 1820–1920; Featuring Images of Events Held in New England in 2019; How Native Hawaiians Joined with American Protestant Missionaries in New England and Together Brought Christianity and the Bible to Hawaiʻi*.[54]

---

51. Coan, *Life*, 127.
52. *Witness to Aloha*.
53. Dwight, *Memoirs of Henry Obookiah*; and Brecher, *Cornwall in Pictures*. See also Forbes et al., *Partners in Change*, 484–88.
54. Dwight, *Memoirs of Obookiah*.

While the entire volume is invaluable as an introduction to the Hawaiian Great Awakening, here are some of the pertinent chapter titles: "'Ōpūkahaʻia,"[55] "Hopu,"[56] "Auna,"[57] "Hawaiʻi Mission Bicentennial,"[58] and "Band Missionary Awakening Timetable."[59]

I wrote about ʻŌpūkahaʻia[60] and the Cornwall school[61] in my dissertation. The following is fair use material from that publication. Hutchison characterizes Henry ʻŌpūkahaʻia and the other Hawaiians at the Cornwall school as "matinee idols."[62] Henry Obookiah was a prototype and martyr to whom the board drew attention between 1815 and 1825. At least thirteen editions of his memoirs have appeared.[63] This slender and simple "book shaped the future of Hawaii."

ʻŌpūkahaʻia, the son of a Hawaiian priest, requested and received passage on a ship to the United States after both of his parents died. President Timothy Dwight[64] and other members of the Yale College community befriended him. Becoming fully convinced of the truth of Christianity, he proclaimed the gospel in his prayers, letters, and conversations; he preached through his life and his death.

While a student at the Foreign Mission School he, as a pastor to the other Hawaiians, met weekly on Saturday evenings with his companions and "questioned them individually concerning the state of their minds, and addressed to them such observations as the particular situation of each seemed to demand."[65]

As early as April of 1817 at the Foreign Missions School, ʻŌpūkahaʻia had made up his mind to prepare as soon as possible to preach the gospel in Hawaiʻi. "He paid particular attention to preaching, and made many remarks upon the subject of sermons and the manner of preaching them." He did not worry about offending American

---

55. Dwight, *Memoirs of Obookiah*, 1–49.

56. Dwight, *Memoirs of Obookiah*, 50–85.

57. Dwight, *Memoirs of Obookiah*, 86–95. Auna was a Tahitian Christian leader who "arrived in Hawaiʻi with a party from the Tahiti station of the London Missionary Society. They arrived in Hawaiʻi at a time of great need among the American missionaries in developing a written Hawaiian language, and in bonding with the *aliʻi nui*," 87. For more on Auna, see Forbes et al., *Partners in Change*, 80–84.

58. Dwight, *Memoirs of Obookiah*, 130–32.

59. Dwight, *Memoirs of Obookiah*, 133–36.

60. See also Global Net production's 2020 documentary, *ʻŌpūkahaʻia*. See also *Witness to Aloha* for excellent ʻŌpūkahaʻia material; and Forbes et al., *Partners in Change*, 484–88; and Cook, *Providential Life and Heritage*.

61. As do Benedetto and Morris more extensively in *Nā Kahu*, 3–5, 29–30, 29–54.

62. Hutchison, *Errand to the World*, 67, in Corr, "Field Is the World," 154. Benedetto and Morris, *Nā Kahu*.

63. Andrew, *Rebuilding the Christian Commonwealth*, 102, writes that Dwight's *Memoirs of Obookiah* went through twelve editions and sold over fifty thousand copies. He cites 84–85 of Spring, *History of Williams College*. The 1968 edition, 97, lists editions of 1818, 1819, 1830, undated, 1867 (in Hawaiian), and one in Choctaw. It is available online.

64. Grandson of Jonathan Edwards, leader of the Second Great Awakening, and one of the early leaders of the American Board.

65. Dwight, *Memoirs of Obookiah*, 85, in Corr, "Field Is the World," 155.

preachers when he provided observations on homiletics, averring that people "can't carry *dictionary to meeting*."[66]

All scholars of the Board's mission to Hawaii[67] agree that 'Ōpūkaha'ia's death influenced individuals and organizations to move forward with sending the first group of missionaries.[68] In his concluding exhortation at the October 11, 1819, Bingham wedding, Thomas H. Gallaudet called his listeners to be "faithful unto death. And may the mantle of Obookiah descend and rest upon you—Farewell!" The memory of Obookiah was used as a motivation in the instructions to the missionaries and the Hawaiians accompanying them.[69]

1820-35

Twelve days after Sybil Mosley and Hiram Bingham were united in holy matrimony, "Mr. and Mrs. Bingham,[70] members of the Pioneer Company, sailed from Boston" in the "brig *Thaddeus*." On March 30, 1820, they "sighted Mauna Kea. . . . and anchored at Kaiulua, Hawaii, April 4, 1820."[71]

Much has been written of the Pioneer Company's first year[72] and the arrival of subsequent Companies, including the Seventh, which included Fidelia and Titus Coan. The priest Hewahewa "foresaw that the one true God will soon land yonder" on a Honolulu beach. And the missionaries arrived within days.[73] Dibble writes about the struggle over whether the king would allow the Pioneer Company to remain. John Young, who became an adviser first to King Kamehameha I, then his son, Liholiho, made a difference. After first introducing Young, Dibble writes that "*it seemed to turn the scale in the question whether the first missionaries should be permitted to land and reside upon the islands.*"[74]

---

66. Dwight, *Memoirs of Obookiah*, in Corr, "*Field Is the World*," 155–56.

67. For a beautifully illustrated history of the Board in Hawai'i, see Cook, *Preparing the Way*.

68. Andrew, *Rebuilding the Christian Commonwealth*, 114; Bingham letter, July 16, 1819, in Miller, *Selected Writings*, 100, in Corr, "*Field Is the World*," 156.

69. Miller, *Selected Writings*, 121 and 140, in Corr, "*Field Is the World*," 157. NB: The authors of *Partners in Change* indicate that the work is dedicated "to the Memory of Henry 'Ōpūkaha'ia," vii. *Partners in Change* further recognizes 'Ōpūkaha'ia's place by having a full-page image of him, xvii. The only other full-page image found is that of previously noted Hiram and Sybil Bingham, 105.

70. Whose youngest daughter, Lydia, would marry Titus Coan in 1873. Judd, *Missionary Album*, 71.

71. Judd, *Missionary Album*, 41. An 1819 portrait of the young couple is found on 40. Forbes et al., *Partners in Change*, on the couple, 104–19, with full page image of same portrait on 105.

72. For example, see the heavily historical novel by Loomis, *Grapes of Canaan* [Num 13:23].

73. *Witness to Aloha*.

74. Dibble, *History of the Hawaiian Islands*, 47. Emphasis by Dibble. See also *Witness to Aloha*. See as well May 4, 2020, email to author from Thomas Woods: "Regarding Hewahewa's prediction, it is included in several publications, but I think you would enjoy this reference that is very detailed about Hewahewa's prediction and has other information about very early Christianity, I think you would

Titus Coan: "Apostle to the Sandwich Islands"

Dibble picks up the story more than one hundred pages later. The arrival of the missionaries in 1820 caused several difficulties to Hawaiian royalty. Among them were that these missionaries were from America while Vancouver had spoken of missionaries coming from England. The chiefs "were in doubt whether it was consistent to receive missionaries from another country. This doubt was removed by John Young, the Englishman . . . who had fought in the battles of Kamehameha and who had been commended to their confidence by Vancouver. He gave his decided advice in favor of the missionaries and said to the chiefs: 'Missionaries from America are the same as missionaries from England; they worship the same God and teach the same religion.' The difficulty being thus solved, the whole weight of Vancouver's advice turned in favor of receiving the missionaries who had arrived, and the king and chiefs had but little further hesitation in giving them a welcome on shore"[75] from the harbor of Kailua.[76] This welcome was apparently over the objection of the Spanish Catholic adviser "Manini."[77]

During the early months and possibly years, the missionaries focused on the royalty—*aliʻi*—as the key to reaching the population. Kuykendall notes that before "the missionaries were well settled in their thatched houses, built for them by the king, at Honolulu, they gathered some of the people into a school. The same thing was done at Kaiula and at Waimea."[78]

While they preached to all and welcomed all levels of society into church membership, the royalty received a great deal of attention. Two *aliʻi*[79] women in particular would have the greatest impact on the spread of the Christian faith throughout the islands.[80] "Bingham points to Keōpūolani one of the wives of Kamehameha I who was one of the first converts and whose stance among her people influenced openness (especially among the aliʻi class)."

Bingham also writes about Kaʻahumanu, the queen regent who ruled while the child-king Kamehameha III was growing up. "She was at first very distant about the things of Christianity for years but she liked what she saw in the way that the missionaries brought a written language and education to the people and so she greatly supported them. When she had a rather profound conversion experience, she became a cheerleader for Christianity in her later years (pre-Great Awakening) and went about speaking to her people on most of the islands."[81]

---

enjoy this publication by John Charlot, 'Two Early Hawaiian-Christian Chants'": Charlot, "Two Early Hawaiian-Christian Chants."

75. Dibble, *History of the Hawaiian Islands*, 160–61.
76. Just south of Kona on the Big island.
77. See above.
78. Kuykendall, *Hawaiian Kingdom*, 104.
79. The Hawaiian word for royalty.
80. *Witness to Aloha*.
81. Paul Rapoza, email to author, May 9, 2020. See also *Witness to Aloha* and Forbes et al., *Partners in Change*, 412–13 (Keōpūolani) and 372–77 (Keōpūolani). See also Thomas Woods, email to author,

Returning to the Corr dissertation and the Hawaiians who were friends of ʻŌpūkahaʻia in New England, Thomas Hopoo [*Hopu*] listened to the instructions to the Pioneer Company along with John Honoore [*Honoliʻi*] and William Tennooe [*Kanui*]. Hopu and Obookiah's souls had "'appeared to be knit together like those of David and Jonathan'" [1 Sam 18].[82] In 1815, Hopu said, "'I want to serve [Christ];—I want my poor countrymen to know about Christ.'"[83] When in the United States, Hopu converted Honoliʻi to Christianity.[84]

Not long after returning to the Sandwich Islands, Honoliʻi visited the blind and ill jester of the royal Hawaiian court, Puaʻaiki. Honoliʻi told him about "the great and good Physician who alone could heal his maladies, and restore his sight." Puaʻaiki crawled out of his house, accompanied by Honoliʻi, "to the place of worship, and for the first time he listened to the glad tidings of great joy which, the heavenly messenger declared, should be 'to all people'" [Luke 2:10].

Soon after Puaʻaiki became a Christian, he was summoned by the court to perform the hula, which was his sole talent. He indirectly preached his first sermon when he returned an answer that "'he had done with the service of sin and Satan, and that henceforth he should serve the King of heaven.'" The new vocation of Bartimeus[85] the blind preacher had begun.[86]

Born in 1785, Lalana Puaʻaiki[87] became almost completely blind while a teenager. Although his poor eyesight severely limited his ability to read, he nevertheless spoke of being educated twice. In an autobiographical reference, Puaʻaiki explained to Christian families the two ways in which he had been educated. In an appeal for payment to Christian Hawaiian teachers, he reminded his listeners that "I have been *twice* educated. In the time of dark hearts, I learned the *hula*"—the amusement above described and which was accompanied with shocking licentiousness—"and the *lua*"—the art of murder and robber—"and the *kake*"—a language unintelligible to any but those initiate in its mysteries. "I learnt mischief in those days."

May 15, 2020: "I'd also include Kinaʻu [Forbes et al., *Partners in Change*, 414–18] in that list, though, she wasn't mentioned in [*Witness to Aloha*]. She succeeded Kaahumanu as kuhina nui. Lots more were very helpful, and most of them are covered in *Partners in Change*."

82. Dwight, *Memoirs of Obookiah*, 90, in Corr, "Field Is the World," 157. Quotation from Mrs. Stone, who nursed Obookiah during his last illness.

83. Tracy, *History*, 57, in Corr, "Field Is the World," 157.

84. Miller, *Selected Writings*, 568, in Corr, "Field Is the World," 157. For Hopu, see Forbes et el., *Partners in Change*, 326–333; and Honoliʻi/Honorii or Honoree, Forbes et al., *Partners in Change*, 322–36.

85. "Batimea" in Hawaiian.

86. The best biography of Bartimeus is found in Green, *Notices*. Quotations thus far are from 8 and 9, in Corr, "Field Is the World," 157–58. In addition to passing references in his *Residence*, Bingham penned *Bartimeus, of the Sandwich Islands*. Green worked closely with Bartimeus. The nickname "Bartimeus" or "Bartimaeus" is from the blind man healed by Jesus in Mark 10:46–52. See also Forbes et al., *Partners in Change*, for Bartimeus/Batimea Lalana Puaʻaiki, 511–15.

87. See Forbes et al., *Partners in Change*, 511–15.

Titus Coan: "Apostle to the Sandwich Islands"

Instead of being punished for his refusal to perform the *hula* as it was practiced in those days, many members of royalty gave Christianity its first serious consideration. After he refused to do the dance, some of the chiefs became seriously disposed toward spiritual matters, and all of them became friendly to the mission.[88] He learned to make his way to the little thatched church in Honolulu, where he began to memorize Bible themes and passages.

Known for his retentive memory, eloquence, and knowledge of Hawaiian culture,[89] Bartimeus worked effectively with individuals and groups of all sizes and ages.[90] He assisted missionaries in pastoral visits[91] and went on itinerant evangelistic preaching tours.[92]

Bartimeus used plainness as his overriding principle for preaching. As with Obookiah, his organizing theme and main priority involved simplicity, understandability, and applicability. He used a wide variety of topics in his sermons. Characterized as "an uncommonly original thinker," he "often discoursed upon the following topics: The law of God—its extent, spirituality and penalty; the nature, necessity, and evidence of repentance; the power of faith; the mediation of Christ; the guilt of unbelief; the overwhelming ruin of the impenitent, and the blessedness of the righteous, etc."[93]

Bartimeus will be heard from again later in this chapter with regard to his time in Hilo and in the next chapter with regard to his service in Maui during the Great Awakening.

As was previously mentioned, he knew his culture, the Hawaiian culture. The Voyagers brought culture with them, including oral history and other oral presentations. Kuykendall notes that although "the Hawaiians had not reduced their language to writing, they had an extensive literature accumulated in memory, added to from generation, and handed down by word of mouth. It consisted of *meles* (songs) of various kinds, genealogies[94] and honorific chants, stories and traditional lore in which

---

88. Green, *Notices*, 9, in Corr, "Field Is the World," 158–59.

89. On Bartimeus's memory, see Bingham, *Residence*, 482. Green, *Notices*, discusses his eloquence on 42, 44, and 49. On 44, Green avers that Bartimeus matched and surpassed the skills of American Indian evangelical orators. "But he cannot write, and it is difficult for him to gather up his precise remarks after they have flown from his lips." Anderson, *Heathen Nation*, 219, and Bingham, *Residence*, 482 indicate his knowledge of his own culture. In Corr, 159.

90. On the diverse content and audiences of Bartimeus, see Green, *Notices*, 42–50, in Corr, "Field Is the World," 159.

91. Green, *Notices*, 20, in Corr, "Field Is the World," 159.

92. On the diverse content and audiences of Bartimeus, see Green, *Notices*, 42–50. Green writes of his pastoral visits on 20. On 24–26, Green details Bartimeus's preaching tours. In Corr, "Field Is the World," 159.

93. Green, *Notices*, 47–48, in Corr, "Field Is the World," 161.

94. The Hawaiians may well have enjoyed hearing and, eventually, reading, the genealogies found in the Gospels of Matthew and Luke.

were imbedded fragments of history and biography. Much of this was composed in the form of poetry characterized by imaginative art and literary skill of a high order."[95]

He quotes N. B. Emerson on Hawaiian poetry. "The poetry of ancient Hawaii evinces a deep and genuine love of nature, and a minute, affectionate, and untiring observation of her moods, which it would be hard to find surpassed in any literature. Her poets never tired of depicting nature; sometimes, indeed, their art seems heaven-born. The mystery, beauty, and magnificence of the island world appealed profoundly to their souls; in them the ancient Hawaiians found the image of man the embodiment of Deity;[96] and their myriad moods and phases were for him an inexhaustible spring of joy, refreshment, and delight."[97]

As beautiful as the oral culture of the Hawaiians was, studies have shown that cultures without a written language accelerate toward extinction. It was to such a culture, with western civilization poised to overwhelm it, that the ABCFM missionaries came. For the educational efforts of the missionaries among the Hawaiian people, see, among others, Corr's published dissertation.[98]

Kuykendall notes that the missionaries realized that if "the Hawaiians were to be made literate within a reasonable period it must be in their own language. If the work of the missionaries was to be effective, it must be carried on in the native tongue. Their first task was to learn the language and reduce it to written form."[99]

The *Witness to Aloha* documentary in the "Preparing the Soil" section praises ʻŌpūkahaʻia and the early missionaries for providing the Hawaiians with their own written language.[100]

The Board missionaries gave the Hawaiian language an alphabet, using Roman letters. They faced the dilemma of learning and reducing to writing the language of the Sandwich Islands. "The missionaries had but slender helps in forming their alphabet."[101] Bingham[102] contacted as many missionary linguists as possible on the subject of orthography.

After listing Hawaiian language helpers and translators, Kuykendall writes, "Of much value likewise was the help received from Rev. William Ellis. The latter had been for six years engaged in missionary work in the Society Islands under the London Missionary Society; in 1822 he came to Hawaii as a visitor and at the urgent invitation of the American missionaries and the native chiefs remained for two years. His

---

95. Kuykendall, *Hawaiian Kingdom*, 10.
96. Cf Richardson, *Eternity in Their Hearts*.
97. Emerson, *Unwritten Literature* 263, in Kuykendall, *Hawaiian Kingdom*, 10.
98. From which fair used sections are now used.
99. Kuykendall, *Hawaiian Kingdom*, 104.
100. *Witness to Aloha*.
101. Stewart letters [Second Company] in *Missionary Herald* 23 (September 1827) 272.
102. In addition to Char Miller's work on the three Hiram Binghams, see Forbes et al., *Partners in Change*, 104–15, for Hiram Bingham I.

familiarity with the Tahitian language, so much like the Hawaiian, enabled him to gain an early command of the latter language, and he was the first foreigner to preach to the Hawaiians in their own tongue. By reason of his knowledge and experience his cooperation was especially helpful in the important work of reducing the Hawaiian language to written form."[103] Most scholars recognize the herculean effort exerted by the early Board missionaries. Judd speaks positively of their printing before settling on a standardized alphabet and orthography.[104]

According to Bingham, the spelling book was for the use of the schools and contained "about a thousand words of the Owyhee Language, adopting as the basis of the alphabet what is termed the *foreign sounds*[105] *of the vowels*, unless some new light on that point should induce us to commence printing with a different plan."[106]

In 1824, Bingham pleaded with the editor of *The Missionary Herald* to use consistently the orthography developed by the missionaries. Despite this appeal, Bingham and others did not finalize the Hawaiian orthography until 1826. A year or two later, Charles Stewart listed the three rules used in establishing the Hawaiian orthography: choose the requisite number of letters from Roman characters; "each letter should have but one invariable sound; and ascertained that every syllable ended with a vowel."[107]

As the primary translator, Bingham explained Hawaiian orthography and pronunciation in his biography. He listed three classes of letters in the Hawaiian alphabet. Class one were those sounds existing in Hawaiian: a, e, i, o, h, k, l, m, n, and p, with u and w being optional. Class two had to do with sometimes interchangeable letters: b and p, k and t, l and r, v and w. Class three included "unmixed foreign terms," whether biblical or English terms. A few examples of Bible terms included "Sabbath" becoming *Sabati*; for "baptize," *baptetizo*; and the verbal noun *bapetizo ana*.[108]

With a written language, literacy became a need. Hawaii provided the most fertile field for literacy education. Within four years of the arrival of the Pioneer Company, the Hawaiian mission contained more students than any other Board location. Four years after that, in 1828, adult and child students progressed from basic spelling

---

103. Kuykendall, *Hawaiian Kingdom*, 103. See Ellis's *Narrative*. See also Forbes et al., *Partners in Change*, 236–41.

104. Judd et. al, [get title], xiii. Bibliography of Judd, *Missionary Album*, includes Spaulding, "Adoption of the Hawaiian Alphabet," in Corr, *"Field Is the World,"* 235–36.

105. Imported from mother languages.

106. Bingham letter, November 25, 1821, in Miller, *Selected Writings*, 201. The transitional nature of the orthography was evident in the use of "Owyhee," which would soon become "Hawaii." In Corr, *"Field Is the World,"* 236.

107. *Missionary Herald* 24 (January 1826) 26; extract from Stewart's letter in *Missionary Herald* 23 (September 1827) 272, in Corr, *"Field Is the World,"* 236–37.

108. Bingham, *Residence*, xiv, 152–56, and 530–32. On the Hawaiian alphabet, Nida, *Book of a Thousand Tongues*, lists 12 letters: a, e, i, o, u, w, h, k, l, m, n, and p. In Corr, *"Field Is the World,"* 237.

primers to *The Thoughts of the Chiefs* and finally the Sermon on the Mount.[109] Adults outnumbered children as literacy students until the early 1830s.

Two presenters in *Witness to Aloha* indicate that 92 percent of Hawaiians were literate in their language in 1832, and 97 percent were by 1837. For a while the Hawaiian people had the highest literacy level in their own language of any group in the world.[110] Depending on the scholar, the Hawaiian Great Awakening began either mid-1836[111] or 1837.

Hawaiian students caused a great demand for printed material. Between 1822 and 1842, the Hawaiian-based mission press produced more than one hundred million copies of assorted and publications. By 1840, the press published in Hawaiian 206 distinct items, at least eighty-four of which directly pertained to education. Although most of the early books published in Hawaiian contained religious offerings, numerous other subjects were printed as well.[112]

The ability for the Hawaiians to read was foundational to being able to read the Hawaiian New Testament and, by 1838, the entire Bible. This in turn was foundational to the Great Awakening. As a written language is to a culture, so is Bible translation to a new church among a people group. Again, studies have shown that a newly-begun

---

109. Corr, "Field Is the World," 284. For his source on the progressive difficulty of reading materials, see Tollefson, "Schools for Cyprus," 219, citing 254–63 of Anderson's *Hawaiian Islands*. Judd, *Missionary Album*, 24, lists a total of 170,000 copies of *A E I O U*—the earliest and most enduring speller—published by March of 1831. The Board also published such literacy works as *First Lessons for Children: A Book Teaching the Children Who Do Not Know How to Read Books* [O ke/kkumua/na/ na kamalii,/he palapala e ao aku ai I na kamalii/ike ole I ka/ heluhelu palapala./Ka ha o ke pai ana], Judd, *Missionary Album*, 56. On the other items mentioned by Tollefson, see Judd, *Missionary Album*, 9, *Thoughts of the Chiefs* [Ka mao o na alii] and *Jesus' Sermon on the Mount, Recorded by Matthew* [Ka/ olelo a Iesu ma ka mauna,/I kakauia'I e Mataio].

110. *Witness to Aloha*. Peter Young (descendant of Hiram Bingham) provided the 1832 number. Dr. Ron Williams Jr. (on staff at the Hawai'i State Archives) provided the 1837 number. See also Thomas Woods, May 4, 2020, email to author: "My citation for the higher rates would come from an unpublished document by John Laimana, 'The Phenomenal Rise to Literacy in Hawai'i: Hawaiian Society in the Early Nineteenth Century' (91% to 95% by 1834 on pages 12–13 and Appendix 1). John's figures are an estimate based on school attendance, Hawaiian population, and mission-reported rapidity at which Hawaiians learned to read. And a less detailed published account by John, by 1829, 'possibly 90 percent of the population were in possession of a pī'āpā.'" (Lamaina, "Hawaiians Begin," 27.) "You should also be aware of a complicating statistic by Robert C. Schmitt, *Demographic Statistics of Hawai'i, 1778–1965*, Table 3. Based on population census and from school attendance and illiteracy from Hawai'i Department of Public Education data in 1853—75 percent of population was literate; in 1878, 80 percent was literate. The determination of literacy is also a complicated issue. How do you define literacy? The ability to sign your name? The ability to read and understand what you are reading? This is not a simple question or answer. For a detailed look at this—Albert J. Schültz, *Hawaiian, Past, Present and Future: Things Every Teacher and Student of the Hawaiian Language Might Like to Know*, University of Hawai'i Press. Al does not cite a percentage, but he covers the issue of literacy in great detail throughout, especially 85–88 (pages in manuscript). I don't have the published book yet, but I see that the manuscript has finally been published and is available for purchase."

111. This author will present evidence that the Hawaiian Great Awakening began in June of 1836.

112. Corr, "Field Is the World," 284–86.

church will not last much beyond its first generation if it does not have the Bible in its own language.

The Bible translated into the Hawaiian language was foundational to the Great Awakening. Hiram Bingham took the lead in the "painstaking, at times tedious, labor of creating a written Hawaiian language and then translating portions of the Bible into it."[113] Bingham's first translation and publication of scripture appeared in a volume of hymns he worked on with William Ellis, an English evangelist-printer in Tahiti before visiting Hawaii in 1822.[114]

Bingham listed translating the Scriptures as second only to preaching the gospel as contributing to the fulfillment of the missionaries' great aim of winning the nation to Christ.[115] Miller, giving a backhanded compliment, asserts that Bingham, "not the most prolific scholar in this regard, nonetheless completed seven books of the Old and New Testaments."[116] Darlow credits Bingham with translating seven New Testament books and committee reports indicated that Bingham translated a significant number of Psalms together with Ephraim Clark,[117] William Richards,[118] and Lorrin Andrews.[119]

Partners in Change provides the full picture of missionaries working with Hawaiians to translate the Bible. Jeffrey Lyon's "*Na Ka Baibala Hemolele*: The Making of the Hawaiian Bible"[120] is the best source used to describe the translation efforts of Bingham, Richards, and Bishop with ʻIʻi,[121] Malo,[122] Hoapilli,[123] and Kuakinni and Kamak-

---

113. Miller, *Selected Writings*, 33, in Corr, "Field Is the World," 223.

114. Bingham letter, March 6, 1824, in Miller, *Selected Writings*, 260. Also Corr, "Field Is the World," 223.

115. Bingham, *Residence*, 491 (quoting from an 1836 memorial written by all the Board's missionaries in Hawaii), in Corr, "Field Is the World," 224.

116. Miller, *Selected Writings*, 33.

117. Forbes et al., *Partners in Change*, 179–81.

118. Forbes et al., *Partners in Change*, 521–27.

119. Darlow, *Historical Catalogue*, 699, in Corr, "Field Is the World," 224. For Lorrin Andrews, see Forbes et al., *Partners in Change*, 62–66. Darlow, *Historical Catologue*, 699, lists Bingham as the translator of Luke, 1 Thessalonians, Colossians, and Hebrews. In 1832 Bingham translated 2 Thessalonians, 1 and 2 Timothy, Titus, and Philemon. Translation assignments for Bingham and others on the Psalms are found in general letters in *Missionary Herald* 28 (March 1832) 73. On 699, Darlow lists the translators of all the New Testament books in Hawaiian. In Corr, "Field Is the World," 224. Judd, *Missionary Album*, lists which Bible books which missionary translated. On 41, it confirms that Bingham translated the seven New Testament books referenced above. It specifies that he translated Psalms 1–75, as well as 1 Kings and Ezekiel. Each of those is a significant accomplishment, showing Bingham's God-given abilities and the quality of education he received at Andover Theological Seminary. Such talents were found in each missionary doing such translation from the Old Testament Hebrew and/or New Testament Greek into the Hawaiian language.

120. Jeffrey Lyon, "*No Ka Baibala Hemolele*," 113–51.

121. Forbes et al., *Partners in Change*, 345.

122. Forbes et al., *Partners in Change*, 467–72.

123. Forbes et al., *Partners in Change*, 313.

au.[124] The missionaries did a rough translation from the original Bible languages which the Hawaiians developed into beautiful printed Hawaiian. The Bible books translated by each team are listed in *Partners*.

After completing a revision in 1835 (published in 1836)[125] of the New Testament, the missionaries believed that they could "unhesitatingly recommend the New Testament to the American [Bible] Society as a good translation from the Bible original." The ABS, in turn, accepted the 1839 publication of the entire translation in Hawaiian as a "faithful" version of the Holy Scriptures.[126] Bingham wrote of providing Hawaiians with "the living oracles in their own tongue."[127]

These translations needed to be printed. The ABCFM printing presses for some time were the only ones west of the Mississippi.[128] During its first twenty years, the Hawaiian mission employed at least five printers, with Elisha Loomis being the first and most important.[129] Loomis brought with him a second-hand Ramage press, which was used in Honolulu for six years and later at Lahainaluna, Maui.[130] For health reasons, Loomis had to return to the United States, where he printed Hawaiian books, including Scripture portions, for the American Bible Society.[131] After Loomis's departure, the

124. Forbes et al., *Partners in Change*, 381–84.

125. At the beginning of the Hawaiian Great Awakening.

126. *Missionary Herald* 32 (March 1836) 102; Lacy, *Word-Carrying Giant*, 88, in Corr, "Field Is the World," 225.

127. Bingham, *Residence*, 156, in Corr, "Field Is the World," 225.

128. In Corr, "Field Is the World," 249: Day, "Pioneer Presses of Hawaii," 33–40; Day and Loomis, "Ka paʻi palapala: Early Printing in Hawaii"; Ballou and Carter, "The History of the Hawaiian Mission Press," 10–11; Tracy, *History*, 112; Bingham letter, July 29, 1827, in Miller, *Selected Writings*, 282; *Missionary Herald* 22 (March 1826) 73; 24 (January 1828); 8 (June 1828) 103; 26 (January 1830) 9–10; 27 (April 1831) 115–15 ["History of the Press at the Sandwich Islands"] and 116–17 ["Influence of the Press"]; 28 (March 1832) 73; 32 (September 1836) 353; 33 (July 1837) 273; 35 (January 1839), 12; 36 (January) 13; 37 (January 1841) 13; and Lingenfelter, *Presses of the Pacific Islands*. Lingenfelter lessens the value of his work with a biased and undocumented attack in his "Preface," vii-ix, on all missionaries and their use of the press as a tool for conquest of the peoples of the islands. Ignoring for the time being the tensions between some merchants and the missionaries, Lingenfelter avers that publications published by missionaries helped "make the islands safe for the exploitation of [by?] European whalers, traders, blackbirders, and plantationers." Lingenfelter concludes his unfounded attack by writing, "Thus it was in opening the way for the expansion of European commercial and political interests in the Pacific, that the missionary and his press were of greatest importance."

129. In his chapter on printing in Hawaii, Lingenfelter, *Presses of the Pacific Islands*, lists the following printers in Honolulu: Loomis from 1820–26; James Carey, a sailor, in 1827; Stephan Shephard, 1828–30; Edmund H. Rogers, 1832–36 (when he went to relieve Andrews at the Lahaina High School printing establishment); and Edwin O. Hall, beginning in 1836 (with assistance from Henry Dimond, bookbinder). See Albertine Loomis, *Grapes of Canaan*; Judd, *Missionary Album*, xiv; Lingenfelter, *Presses of the Pacific Islands*, 34, in Corr, "Field Is the World," 250; and Forbes et al., *Partners in Change*, 442–44.

130. Lingenfelter, *Presses of the Pacific Islands*, 34; Judd, *Missionary Album*, xiv, in Corr, "Field Is the World," 250.

131. Chamberlain letter, March 2, 1826, *Missionary Herald* 23 (July 1827) 226; Judd, *Missionary Album*, xiv–xv. On sending and printing Hawaiian Scriptures in New York, see *Missionary Herald* 24

operation at first lagged, but then more work was performed on the press in the next six months than in the previous two years.[132]

In the case of the Hawaiian people, the "printed page was the magic key giving access to the hearts and minds of the people."[133] In an article during which he lays a foundation for the Great Revival, Sereno Edwards Bishop[134] shows how the seventeen or so years of mission efforts leading up to the Great Revival prepared for the powerful outpouring of the Holy Spirit. "From the beginning of the Mission in 1820, a vast amount of diligent and successful labor had been performed and great results accomplished."

Bishop's list of accomplishments includes: a majority of islanders had been taught to read; the New Testament and most of the Old Testament had been printed; many school books were published; and Lahainaluna[135] Seminary had been active training teachers and pastors. He expresses the need for the Great Awakening. "There was always a grave danger of recrudescence[136] of the ancient idolatry towards which the heathen nature of the race preserved an inveterate proclivity, only held in check by the powerful authority of the large band of faithful pious chiefs, like Kalakiea, Kinau, Hoapili, Kuakai, and many others."[137]

In a different work, Bishop observes that while the missionaries of the pre-Revival Companies were not fully understanding of the Finney revivals, they nevertheless laid the foundation for the Hawaiian Great Awakening. "I think that the older pioneers of our Mission had but limited experience, if any, of the intense Revival activity which roused and multiplied the American churches between 1825 and 1845. Those devoted and faithful fathers, however, laid deep foundations."[138]

Nevertheless, Bingham writes of an awakening throughout the islands, beginning in 1824. "The outpouring of the Spirit of God upon the islands in 1824 and 1825, and his continued favor which followed, brought hundreds at first, and thousands at length, into praying circles or societies, the meetings of which occurred weekly at the different missionary stations, or other places." He next provides church membership

---

(July 1828) 210; 25 (January 1829); 26 (June 1829) 183; 26 (January 1830) 9–10, in Corr, "*Field Is the World*," 250.

132. *Missionary Herald* 25 (January 1829) 9; Hiram to Calvin Bingham letter, July 29, 1827, in Miller, *Fathers and Sons*, 282, in Corr, "*Field Is the World*," 250.

133. Kuykendall, *Hawaiian Kingdom*, 104.

134. While he provides a great deal of information about pre-Great Awakening missionary efforts and the Great Awakening itself, Bishop has an in some ways deserved horrible reputation among Hawaiians because of his duplicity during the events of the late nineteenth century. See Bishop's article on "Kamehameha" at the HMH and the work of Ron Williams on this subject. For short biography, see Forbes et al., *Partners in Change*, 133–36.

135. Up the hill from Lahaina, Maui.

136. "Return of an undesirable condition." Merriam Webster, "Recrudescence."

137. Bishop, "The Great Revival of 1837–38," in *The Friend*, December 1, 1902.

138. Bishop, *Reminiscences*, 55.

statistics by the beginning of 1830. "About the commencement of 1830, these associations at three of our stations, Honolulu, Lahaina, and Kailua, embraced more than ten thousand men and women; and at three other stations, Waiamea on Kauai, Kaawaloa, and Hilo, five thousand more, making the aggregate about fifteen thousand."[139]

In contrast to the boisterousness of the Great Awakening, this was a quiet move of the Holy Spirit, probably reflecting the personalities and training of the early missionaries. Men and women met separately. "Multitudes were, by these associations, brought under a good influence; and their meetings conducted in a good and orderly manner facilitated the access of missionaries to numbers, and afforded good opportunities to inculcate upon them, with freedom, the doctrines and precepts of the Bible. They professed to take the Word of God for their guide, to desire to be instructed by the doctrines, to abstain from known immoralities, and to pray for God's blessing on their inquiries and labors."[140]

Ehlke relates an 1832 revival on Kauai. "In 1832, the Rev. Peter J. Gulick,[141] husband of Finney convert Fanny (Thomas) Gulick, sent word to Honolulu that an awakening was in progress. Hiram Bingham hastened to Kauai to assist, personally conversing with many who felt they had changed their hearts, instructing them, putting questions to them in order to judge each case. Hundreds gathered to listen, to pray, and on the Sabbath two thousand, one-fifth of the population of Kauai, filled the church at Waimea. 'During the summer and autumn while we were alone at the Station, we were permitted to witness the effusion of the Spirit, in power and extent, far surpassing anything that we have seen in any other period of the five years that we have been on Missionary ground,' noted Mr. Gulick."[142]

Bingham provides the background of and his travel to Kauai regarding the revival. "During the absence[143] of Mr. [Samuel] Whitney[144] from Kauai, there were striking indications of the revival spirit among his flock. A little before his departure, he preached to them a sermon on the life and death of Kaahumanu,[145] and then a parting sermon, and in company with Kaiu, one of the principal members of his church, left them in an interesting state in the care of Mr. Gulick, his associate, who shortly after speaks of the outpouring of God's Spirit there.

"Who can doubt that the consistent manifestation of Christian solicitude for distant tribes is adapted to awaken attention to the value of the gospel and the salvation of

---

139. Bingham, *Residence*, 365.

140. Bingham, *Residence*, 365.

141. On Gulick, see Forbes et al., *Partners in Change*, 292–94. For a complete biography see Putney, *Missionaries in Hawai'i*.

142. Gulick, Kauai station report, 1833, 1, HMCS (typewritten), in Ehlke, "Enthusiastic Religion," 108–09. See also Bingham, *Residence*, 438–43.

143. Assisting in a survey of the Washing Islands, Bingham, *Residence*, 437–38.

144. Judd, *Missionary Album*, 198–99; and Forbes et al., *Partners in Change*, 632–35.

145. A recently deceased Hawaiian Christian queen. See Bingham, *Residence*, 431–36.

the soul among those who have been already evangelized? Or that any church which endeavours duly to water, shall itself also be watered?"

Bingham writes about his learning of the revival and his departure, with two Hawaiians, to assist in the Kauaian harvest field. "I hastened to assist Mr. G. in the important duty of pointing sinners to the Lamb of God, and sailed from Honolulu with two native assistants, Paulo Kanoa and Daniel Oleloa, in a vessel of twenty tons,[146] which we imagined to be about the size of the ships used by the fishermen of Galilee, on the sea of Tiberias."[147]

Focusing on the 1820 through 1835 period in Hilo, Ellis visited Hilo in 1822. The American Board Hilo mission station was established in 1824.[148] Joseph Goodrich and Samuel Ruggles arrived in Hilo together with their wives Martha and Nancy on January 24, 1824. Goodrich was in Honolulu twice—1826 through 1828; and 1830 through 1832—"to superintend the press and book bindery in the absence of the Honolulu printer.

"Mr. Goodrich was the missionary from Hilo who met the Chiefess Kapiolani and her retinue at the brink of Kilauea volcano on the occasion of her courageous defiance of the fire-goddess Pele which served to strengthen the faith of her people in the new Christian religion."[149] This power encounter would be at the back of Hawaiian minds during the Great Awakening.

Goodrich was a licensed[150] preacher, as well as "a good mechanic and agriculturist, keenly interested in teaching the people how to grow coffee and other food products necessary to life in the Islands. He decided against entering into a contract to manage Koloa Plantation because of the disapproval of the American Board and, instead, left with his family for the United States from Honolulu, January 26, 1836."[151]

As part of the Pioneer Company, the Ruggles were assigned first to Waimea, Kauai. They served with the Goodriches in 1824 and 1825, returning there from 1826 through 1828. "Mr. Ruggles was so loved by the Hawaiians that they called him 'Keiki' (child)." Due to ill health, he left Hawai'i in early 1834, dying in 1871 in Wisconsin.[152]

Hiram Bingham visited with the Goodriches and the Andrews in Hilo in 1830, apparently before the arrival of the Greens. Bingham writes that we "took our course

---

146. A first-century Sea of Galilee fishing vessel was discovered in 1986. While no estimated weight is provided, the other dimensions are as follows: "The remains of the boat, 27 feet (8.27 meters) long, 7.5 feet (2.3 meters) wide and with a maximum preserved height of 4.3 feet (1.3 meters)."

147. Bingham, *Residence*, 438.

148. Judd, *Missionary Album*, 16; and Forbes et al., *Partners in Change*, 16–17.

149. Judd, *Missionary Album*, 102.

150. I.e., not an ordained pastor or "Reverend."

151. Judd, *Missionary Album*, 102–03; and Forbes et al., *Partners in Change*, 271–76. On the Goodriches' departure, see the previous chapter and the Coans' moving into the Goodrich home that would become the "Emerald Bower."

152. Judd, *Missionary Album*, 168. For further Ruggles biography, see Forbes et al., *Partners in Change*, 540–44.

to Hilo, where a wonder-working God had begun especially to record his name." He writes that, one evening in Hilo, "several presented themselves as candidates for admission to the church, and were carefully examined as to their faith and experience. Several appeared to understand, believe, and love the fundamental doctrines of the gospel, and to be built on the solid foundation; but some failed to give the requisite evidence of true conversion."[153]

Bingham notes that on the ensuing Sabbath in Hilo "I endeavored to unfold to a great assembly[154] the instruction contained in Romans viii., 1: 'There is, therefore, now no condemnation to them which are in Christ Jesus, who walk not after the flesh, but after the Spirit'; and assisted Mr. Goodrich in the ordinances. We had occasion for thankfulness in receiving to fellowship five new members,[155] and in witnessing there such demonstrations of the Christian religion, where, a little before, unbroken darkness, degradation, and alienation from God had prevailed. The company of believers appeared to be refreshed, and it was remarked by one of the missionaries that Hilo had never before had such a Sabbath."[156]

Jonathan and Theodotia Green arrived in Hawai'i in 1830. He served in Lahaina during 1830 and 1831. He served in Hilo during 1832 and then Wailuku, Maui, from 1832 through 1836. He eventually became "an independent pastor in connection with the American Missionary Association" at the Makawao church[157] on the slopes of Haleakala.

Jonathan Green writes about blind Bartimeus (Pua'aiki) in Hilo. After ministering in Lahaina, Maui, he was invited to Hilo in 1829 by some of the chiefs on the Big Island. "Here a wider field of usefulness than he had hitherto [sic] occupied."[158] Green characterizes the Hilo area as "a field of Christian toil and self-denial well adapted to the zeal, energy, and perseverance of Bartimeus."[159]

Green relates the visit of a Christian Hawaiian queen and her support of Bartimeus. "In 1830, Kaahumanu the excellent Queen Regent of the islands, visited Hilo.

---

153. Bingham, *Residence*, 384. How does this examination compare with the accusation against Coan of "hasty admissions" during the Great Awakening? Coan carried a book with him and kept records on individuals for a *year* until some were admitted to membership in a church.

154. Bingham, *Residence*, provides no numerical estimate. See below re: Green's reference in *Notices* to the "little" Hilo church asking Bartimeus to remain. Had most members dispersed/left the church by then? If so, was it because of missionary turnover—several different missionaries over a short period of time?

155. Compared with how many during previous receptions? What was the total membership of the church at that time?

156. Bingham, *Residence*, 384–85.

157. Judd, *Missionary Album*, 104. See also Forbes et al., *Partners in Change*, 278–81. Green left the ABCFM because he did not believe that organization was strong enough in its opposition to slavery.

158. Green, *Notices*, 17.

159. Green, *Notices*, 17.

She seconded by her influence as a ruler, and what was of vastly most importance, by her example as a *Christian*, the efforts of Bartimeus. This extraordinary woman gave very pleasing evidence of 'possessing the mind which was in Christ Jesus' [1 Cor 2:16]. She seemed earnestly to desire the salvation of all her people; and to secure this great object, she made many and costly efforts. Great good to the people of Hilo obviously resulted from the visit of the chiefs, especially Kaahumanu."[160] Near the time of the departure of the royalty from Hilo, one missionary invited Bartimeus to stay in Hilo, while another shared with him reasons to stay in Hilo or to return to Maui. When the chiefs were about to leave Hilo during the summer of 1830, "the resident missionary of Hilo, Mr. Goodrich, gave Bartimeus an invitation to stay in Hilo, and aid in the labors of the station. The little church united in the invitation. Mr. Andrews, who was at that time residing at Hilo for a little season, assisted Bartimeus in coming to a decision by spreading before his mind the reasons for staying at Hilo, and the reasons for returning to Lahaina. Those for remaining, to a man who was not averse to labor and who loved the souls of perishing men, preponderated. Accordingly, with the advice of Kaahumanu, he took up his residence at the station, and entered, with his accustomed energy, upon the labors that devolved upon him."[161]

Green shares his year and a half of service with Bartimeus in Hilo. "Early in 1831, I removed to Hilo; became pastor of the church following June, and continued my relation till August 1832. During those eighteen months, my interest in Bartimeus greatly increased as I became more intimately acquainted with his character as a man and a Christian. I saw him daily. I communed with him on subjects which had a bearing on the interests of the Redeemer's kingdom. He stood by my side and held up my hands [Exod 17:12] in my labors and my trials as pastor of that infant church."[162]

Bartimeus labored with Green to have the people repent of their sins. He was a proponent of literacy and of the need to search the Scriptures. "He co-operated with me in my efforts to break up the sottish ignorance of that people, and especially to convert them from the errors of their ways, and save their souls from death. He not only exhorted the people to learn to read, so that they might be able to search the Scriptures, and thus become wise unto salvation [2 Tim 3:15], but he actually gave them an example of learning himself."[163]

Perhaps what would be characterized as being legally blind, the Hilo climate proved salubrious for his eyesight. Green relays this as he explains Pua'aiki's efforts to learn to read and, therefore, read the Bible for himself. Ephraim Clark, during his brief stint in Hilo provides Green with a description of Pua'aiki's painful labors at literacy. "Though so nearly blind at Lahaina as to grope his way at noon day, and sometimes to be lead [sic] by the hand, yet the cool climate of Hilo, the ever verdant fields[,] the

---

160. Green, *Notices*, 17.
161. Green, *Notices*, 17–18.
162. Green, *Notices*, 18.
163. Green, *Notices*, 18.

cloudy skies, and frequent rains of that station, all contributed to the restoration, in some measure, of his sight. Mr. Clark, in giving me some reminiscences of Bartimeus, writes me thus: 'My first acquaintance with him was in the summer of 1829. I was laboring for a short season in Hilo, on Hawaii, where he, at the time, resided. He was beginning to recover his eye sight a little, and was making a painful effort to learn how to read. So eager was he to acquire knowledge of the word of God that he was willing to subject himself to the most painful labor of his spelling book that he might have free access to the word of God.'"[164]

In 1830, Bartimeus learned that Mary Clark was starting a school in Hilo in 1830, and he applied to be a student. Mrs. Clark tried to dissuade him because the school was only for children. But the benefit of the Board's efforts at literacy were going to bear fruit in the life of Bartimeus, who wanted to deeply study and teach the principles and truths of the Bible. He "had made up his mind to do what in him lay to be able to read for himself to read the word of God." He answered Mrs. Clark that he "was a child, and must insist upon attending the school. He did so; and by literally *digging*, for he was so dim of sight—that he used to bury his face in his book—he became able to make out a verse in the Bible."[165]

After the Greens arrived in Hilo, Theodotia started a class for adult females. Bartimeus asked to attend with his wife. That request was granted. He continued to do so until his eyesight became "aggravated." Because of his eye disease, "he reluctantly abandoned altogether his design of becoming a reader." Green points out that Puaʻaiki's ability to remember Bible verses and passages he heard overrode his truncated efforts to learn to read. "The arrangement of Providence by which he was obliged to 'hide the word of God in his heart' [Ps 119:11] was a wise and benevolent arrangement, for he never could have become so eloquent and mighty in the scriptures as he actually became had he depended upon his imperfect vision instead of his extraordinary vision."[166]

Bartimeus's example of trying to read would endure into the Great Awakening after the arrival of Titus Coan in Hilo. "Still, his example at Hilo as a learner, putting himself in the place of a little child, learning his letters, and spelling out sentences till he could actually read, was of incalculable value. It was also to him a matter of unfeigned delight that he had been able, though for a short season only, to trace with his own lines, of the book of God, which he loved for his daily food."[167]

Green returns to Bartimeus's pastoral role, including the subject of home visits. These would also help prepare for the Great Awakening. First Green relates Sabbath Schools and small meetings. Then he relates Bartimeus's value in accompanying him on home visits. "He engaged with much energy and delight in the labors of the Sabbath

---

164. Green, *Notices*, 18–19.
165. Green, *Notices*, 19.
166. Green, *Notices*, 19.
167. Green, *Notices*, 19.

School. He used to attend little neighborhood meetings with me, and these he would assist in making very interesting."

Sounding very similar to Coan, Green notes that Bartimeus "frequently accompanied me on my pastoral visits, and I can testify to his happy talent in securing the wakeful attention of persons of every variety of character, to his faithful admonitions or his searching inquiry. He used to visit the people either alone or accompanied by his wife or a Christian brother. His own house too was always open for the reception of all who either sought instruction, or desired fraternal intercourse. Being of a social affectionate disposition he attracted many to his house and seldom did anyone leave without having received benefit in the shape of instruction, warning or encouragement. In short he was 'instant in season and out of season' [2 Tim 4:2]; he was the laborious servant of Jesus Christ, 'always abounding in the work of the Lord'" [1 Cor 15:58].[168]

Green left Hilo for Wailuku, Maui, in August of 1832. Bartimeus remained in Hilo. Green would see him on Maui approximately two years later.[169] So, Bartimeus left Hilo approximately one year before the Coans' arrival. So great would his impact be that Coan would write about a "Bartimeus" with whom he worked, though he would indicate as valued as that Hawaiian Evangelist was, he was not on the same level as the original Bartimeus.

Puaʻaiki—"blind Bartimeus"—left his mark on Hilo. With his example of becoming as a little child and learning to read; his tender and challenging home visits; and his powerful visits, Puaʻaiki would leave his imprint on Hilo during the Great Awakening and beyond.

While the first Bartimeus still lived in Hilo, David and Sarah Lyman arrived in 1832, having reached the Sandwich Islands with the Fifth Company. They have already figured in the Coan story and will be woven with them in some of the future chapters, including the next two on the Hawaiian Great Awakening.

168. Green, *Notices*, 20.
169. Green, *Notices*, 20.

5

The Great Awakening

1836–40 in the Hilo and Puna Districts

"At one time, when I was holding a series of outdoor meetings in a populous part of Puna, a remarkable manifestation . . . occurred. A very large concourse were seated on the grass, and I was standing in the center preaching 'Repentance toward God and faith in the Lord Jesus' [Acts 20:21]. Of a sudden, a man who had been gazing with intense interest at the preacher, burst out in a fervent prayer, with streaming tears, saying: 'Lord have mercy on me; I am dead in sin.' His weeping was so loud and his trembling so great, that the whole congregation was moved as by a common sympathy. Many wept aloud, and many commenced praying together. The scene was such as I had never before witnessed. I stood dumb in the midst of this weeping, wailing, praying multitude, not being able to make myself heard for about twenty minutes. When the noise was hushed, I continued my address with words of caution, lest they should feel that this kind of demonstration atoned for their sins, and rendered them acceptable before God. I assured them that all the Lord required was godly sorrow [2 Cor 7:10] for the past, present, faith in Christ, and henceforth faithful, filial, and cheerful obedience. A calm came over the multitude, and we felt that "the Lord was there" [Ez 48:35].[1]

Father Coan and Father Lyman had Eastern Hawaii for their field and the evangelization of fifteen thousand native heathen for their task, and they wrought it well. Three hundred miles in circumference, Hawaii was traversed again and again by these men on foot, preaching from two to four times each day in successive native villages. There was not a horse on the island, and often they swam streams with ropes round their waists or were let down and drawn up otherwise inaccessible cliffs by natives.

---

1. Coan, *Life*, 59–60.

Their success increased as they learned the language and habits until in 1839, the people cried for "more gospel!"[2]

INTRODUCTION

The Hawaiian spiritual soil had been prepared for revival by over sixteen years of American Board missionary service.[3] The awakening took place throughout all the Sandwich Islands. But many people traveled to Hilo to hear Titus Coan preach and to join the church there. Best known for this period of intense ministry for approximately four years, Coan gave human leadership to this outpouring of the Holy Spirit. "His evangelistic and dramatic style of preaching expanded rapidly—and particularly during what was known as the Great Awakening."[4]

First, comes a question.

WHAT'S IN A NAME?

At least two names are attached to this movement of God: The Great Awakening and the Great Revival. In his autobiography, Coan refers to it primarily as "the Great Awakening," while also referring to "the work" (of the Holy Spirit).[5] Coan and some others probably selected that phrase because of its echoing the title given to a movement of God's Holy Spirit in Britain and the American colonies approximately a hundred years before.[6]

In her summary of chapter V, Lydia Bingham Coan does not use either phrase with regard to Hilo, but rather: "A visitation from God," "continued manifestations of the Spirit's presence," and "continuous labors." She does write of "tidings of revival in Honolulu," then "the great ingathering."[7] Lydia notes that S. J. Humphrey writes of "Four Memorable Years at Hilo."[8] In another format, Humphrey provides the heading "REVIVAL SCENES," which is centered on the page.[9]

---

2. Hallock, *Hawaii under King Kalakaua*, 62–63.

3. See documentary *A Witness to Aloha* for metaphor of preparing the soil.

4. Forbes, et al., *Partners in Change*, 185.

5. Coan, *Life*, 42 and 48 ("the work deepened").

6. Historically, what is now known as the First Great Awakening took place during the 1730s through 1743. Wikipedia, "Great Awakening."

7. Coan, *Memorial Volume*, i–ii.

8. Humphrey, "Four Memorable Years at Hilo," in Coan, *Memorial* Volume, 41. Lydia notes the chronology of Humphrey's writings: "'[I]t was first printed in the *Advance* and in *Missionary Papers* No. 16, and was then reproduced in the *New York Independent*. Years afterward it was issued in tract form by the 'Friends' Tract Association,' Wilmington, Del."

9. Humphrey, "VI. Titus Coan," 8.

The Great Awakening

In his biography on the Gulicks, Putney indicates that in May of 1838 Peter Gulick first heard "'about Hawaii's 'Great Revival.'"[10] In his autobiography covering forty years of service, Hiram Bingham includes in his summary of chapters XVII and XVIII on 1837 and 1838 the phrases "Progress of the Great Revival on Hawaii" and "Progress of the Great Revival" respectively.[11] In 1846, C. S. Lyman writes of "the Great Revival."[12] Writing some thirty years later, Rufus Anderson labels chapter XVIII "The Great Awakening.—1836-1838" and chapter XIX "Results of the Great Awakening.—1838-1841."[13]

In the 1887 *Jubilee Celebration* volume,[14] Charles Wetmore writes of the event that concluded almost ten years before his arrival in Hilo. He entitles his lecture "The Revival of 1837 at Hilo, with Personal Recollections by Dr. C. H. Wetmore."[15] Also in *Jubilee*, Castle has the heading "Great Revival" in "A General Review of the Mission Work in Hawaii."[16]

Many decades after the event, an elderly S. E. Bishop writes of "The Great Revival of 1837-38."[17] Bishop writes of his childhood experiences during that time, labeling it "THE GREAT REVIVAL" and relating the "intense Revival activity." He also refers to it as a "Religious Awakening of the years 1838 and 1839."[18] Not many years after those two publications, the Reverend and Mrs. Orramel Hinckely Gulick[19] provided explanatory and illustrative material compiled and verified from original sources. One section examining 1838 and 1840 is entitled "The Great Revival."[20]

After Bishop and before Kuykendall, Emily Hawley characterized the event as "the 'great religious awakening'" in her 1922 *The introduction of Christianity into the Hawaiian Islands and the development of these islands through the agency of the missionaries and their descendants, 1820-1920*.[21]

During the 1930s, Kuykendall in his scholarly and objective history of the islands characterizes the event as the "great revival."[22] In a 1960 paper published in 1961, Gavan Daws entitles his presentation on the period as "Evangelism in Hawaii:

---

10. Putney, *Missionaries in Hawai'i*.
11. Bingham, *Residence*, xii.
12. Lyman, *Around the Horn*, 99.
13. Anderson, *Heathen Nation*, xix.
14. Which publishes presentations given to commemorate the arrival of the eighth Missionary Company in 1837.
15. Wetmore, "Revival of 1837," 61-75.
16. Wetmore, "Revival of 1837," 61-75.
17. Bishop, "The Great Revival," in *The Friend*, December 1, 1902.
18. Bishop, *Reminiscences*, 49, 53, 55.
19. See Forbes, et al., *Partners in Change*, 288-92.
20. Gulick et al., *Pilgrims*, 161-72.
21. Hawley, *Introduction of Christianity*, 33.
22. Kuykendall, *Hawaiian Kingdom*, 115.

Titus Coan and the Great Revival of 1837."[23] Daws combines the words "awakening" and "revival" as he introduces Coan and his leadership of the movement throughout the islands. "The place Hawaii; and at the center of the excitement there stood Titus Coan." Daws believes that Coan's life and thought prepared him for the Revival and "an examination of his work during the years of his greatest achievement helps to explain the form taken by the Great Revival in Hawaii."[24] He also writes of "the awakening impulse of the Great Revival [that] radiated was the district of Hilo on the island of Hawaii." Christopher L. Cook wrote a 2019 article that has "Revival" in its title and in the article as well as citing Coan's phrase "great awakening."[25]

In his biography of the three Hiram Binghams, Char Miller writes of Coan's "Great Revival in 1837."[26] Ehlke has a section entitled "The Great Awakening."[27] Morris writes of "the Hawaiian Great Awakening,"[28] while writing of Finney's revivals as "frenzied affairs."[29] Tamashiro labels a section "Hawai'i's Great Awakening,"[30] while repeatedly using the word "revival," including a discussion of Titus Coan's characteristics as a "Revival Leader."[31]

So, there is ample evidence for the use of both phrases in both primary and secondary sources and among both participants and historians. Some writers interchange the words. Unless one accepts Tamashiro's theory of pre-Western arrival Hawaiian monotheistic beliefs, the phrase "The Great Awakening" makes more logical sense, because one cannot revive what has not previously been alive, in the meaning of the Christian faith. On the other hand, to the extent that individuals who had sometime during the previous fifteen years of mission activity made a profession of faith returned to that faith, it could be called revival. As shorthand, "Great Awakening" will be used. Nevertheless, in this and related chapters, the various authors' own words will be provided without comment.

---

23. Daws, "Evangelism."
24. Daws, "Evangelism," 22.
25. Cook, "When Revival Swept Hawaii."
26. Miller, *Fathers and Sons*, 47.
27. Ehlke, "Enthusiastic Religion," 107–36.
28. Morris, "Hawaiian Missionaries Abroad," 54.

29. Morris, "Hawaiian Missionaries Abroad," 54. As will be noted later in the chapter, there is no evidence of Coan whipping his audiences into frenzies. While he was a passionate preacher of the gospel who expected the Holy Spirit to fall upon the people, he worked to not whip up the crowds. He would make efforts to have the listeners not spin out of emotional control.

30. Tamashiro, "Original Monotheism," 198–204. In an email to the author, Tamashiro indicated that Pastor James Moracco's *Hawaii's Great Awakening* influenced him in the usage of the phrase "The Great Awakening."

31. Tamashiro, "Original Monotheism," 200–204.

The Great Awakening

SOURCES

The above discussion provides a number of both primary and secondary sources, with a few providing both kinds of sources. What follows is a more in-depth and systematic presentation of sources for the Great Awakening.

Titus Coan holds pride of place in both primary and secondary sources on the Great Awakening. His autobiography and Lydia Bingham Coan's *Memorial Volume* provide material for that period. Coan focuses on the Great Awakening in twenty pages[32] and Lydia eleven.[33] Much more material is found in his journals and voluminous letters from that period, along with Fidelia's letters.[34] Contemporaneous letters from other revival leaders, such as Lorenzo Lyons, come into play.

Other primary and contemporaneous sources on the Great Awakening include station reports, articles in *The Friend*, and *The Missionary Herald*. Coan wrote or co-wrote with David Lyman the station reports. He also provided material to *The Friend* and *The Missionary Herald*, as well as other publications.

Char Miller provides primary source material in his *Selected Writings* of Hiram Bingham. Mostly correspondence, this work includes writings by Bingham during the Great Awakening.[35] In portions of chapter XVII and all twelve pages of chapter XIX,[36] Hiram Bingham writes about the Great Revival—both his involvement in it and that of Titus Coan and others. S. E. Bishop much later would write both as a primary source—his witnessing of revival experiences as a preteen—and as a secondary source.

C. S. Lyman is an almost contemporaneous source. During 1846, he visited the Hawaiian Islands, including the Big Island. In June he went on a preaching tour with Coan and relates the stories from the recent Great Awakening, including the location viewed as where the Great Awakening began.[37]

Lyman was a relative of Coan's Hilo co-laborer David Lyman. C. S. was also an academic, so his journal entries combine devotion and keen observation. In juxtaposition with Coan's writings, Lyman provides helpful material on Puna locations, the people, and other aspects related to the Great Awakening.

A little less than twenty years after Lyman published his book, Rufus Anderson would in 1870 provide both primary and secondary source material in his sanitized version of the tumultuous period of the Great Awakening. An example of the smoothing out of what went on is his emphasis on "Care in the Admission in the Church."[38] During the discussion of the internal conflict within the American Board on the

---

32. Coan, *Life*, 42–61.
33. Coan, *Memorial Volume*, 40–50.
34. Several locations, but especially (in order of amount) the Library of Congress and the Mission Houses Library in Honolulu.
35. Miller, *Selected Writings*.
36. Bingham, *Residence*, 520–31.
37. Lyman, *Around the Horn*, 94–109.
38. Anderson, *Heathen Nation*, xix.

subject of "hasty admissions," it will be seen how Coan wrote Anderson a letter chastising him for claiming such membership admissions were taking place without knowing Coan's very thorough process on that matter.

As was mentioned in the discussion of the event's name, numerous scholars have examined the Great Awakening. Kuykendall did so in 1930; Daws in the early 1960s over sixteen pages.[39] As with Daws, much of Ehlke's secondary source work includes primary sources with quotations from primary sources, particularly letters.

Tamashiro is mostly secondary. He quotes another secondary work that is devotional in nature.[40]

My previous work provides material on the Great Awakening in two works: his dissertation and a chapter biography of Coan. Corr examines Coan in his dissertation chapter on preaching by American Board missionaries.[41] Corr devotes four pages in the chapter.[42]

In the introduction of this book, an extensive presentation is made of online digital sources. For this chapter, the reader is referred to Paul Rapoza's web site.[43]

BEGINNINGS

As discussed in the previous chapter, there is much background to and preparation for the Great Awakening. In chapters preceding that one, Coan's preparation to be and arrival as a missionary in Hilo are presented. We come now to the beginnings of the Great Awakening.

Unlike dates of birth, the beginnings of a revival can be viewed with some fluidity, especially as the years, decades, and centuries go by. As indicated earlier in this chapter, some writers give the dates of 1837 and 1838 or 1838 and 1839. In the summary of the Great Awakening in his autobiography, Coan lists "1837–1838" as the years of the revival.[44] While Lydia Coan points to an eight-day protracted meeting in 1837, she also notes the early response of the Hawaiians to his preaching. In "the first year there were many inquirers and marked and manifestations of the Holy Spirit's presence."[45]

When it comes to preaching, Coan vividly described his goal in preaching by observing that he sought "to keep the holy law of the Everlasting God constantly blazing

---

39. Daws, "Evangelism in Hawaii," 20–35.
40. Piercy, *Hawaiian Missionary Saga*. Piercy also wrote *Hawaii: Truth Stranger than Fiction*.
41. Corr, *"Field Is the World,"* 56–130.
42. Corr, "'Apostle to the Sandwich Islands,'" 248–51.
43. Titus Coan Memorial library.
44. Coan, *Life*, 42.
45. Coan, *Memorial Volume*, 40–41.

before the midst of all the people, and to hold the claims and sanctions of the gospel in near and warm contact with their frigid hearts."[46]

As was the case in some of the frontier revivals in America, physical demonstrations occurred. Coan indicated that on "some occasions there were physical demonstrations which commanded attention." Such demonstrations occurred during very plain and kindly conversations at the Coan home, as well as during sermons preached to large groups. In the latter category, Coan was preaching on the subject of "Repentance toward God and faith in the Lord Jesus" when an emotional outbreak occurred.[47] See elsewhere in this chapter for a discussion of this event and Coan's response.

When it comes to Coan's view of preaching, near the end of his life he wrote the Reverend S. E. Bishop, "These days and years I never rose to address a native audience without feeling an assurance that a divine power rested upon me, and that 'Death and Hell' could not withstand the Word of God, but that it was the 'sword of the Spirit, quick and powerful' [Heb 4:12–13]; that it was the 'fire and hammer' [Jer 23:29]; and the gleaming battleaxe of Jehovah [Jer 51:20], ordained to conquer Satan and sin; and that it is in *deed* and truth, 'the power of salvation' to all who believe [Rom 1:16], whether speaker or hearer."[48]

Upon a close reading of Coan's Great Awakening chapter, one sees that its beginnings were in a late 1836[49] tour of Puna. This is confirmed both by his journal[50] and by C. S. Lyman's journal entries almost ten years later. Coan writes in his autobiography, "Giving a vacation to my pupils, I set off November 29, 1836, on a tour around the

46. *Missionary Herald* 36 (July 1840) 247, in Corr, "Field Is the World," 76.
47. Coan, *Life*, 76, in Corr, "Field Is the World," 76.
48. Coan to Bishop, nd, no citation, in Corr, "Apostle to the Sandwich Islands," 248.
49. At the precipice of the flaming of revival fires, the Hawaiian Islands Mission at its June 1836 annual meeting put together a booklet of twelve resolutions entitled the "Duty to Evangelize." The mission explains its purpose in the introduction: "The following resolutions, and the remarks connected with them, are designed for all the friends of Christ, but more particularly for his ministers, in the United States.

"The members of the Sandwich Islands mission, at a meeting in June 1836, were led to consider their duty in relation to the churches in Christian lands, who, possessing the means for saving a lost world, do not employ them. Almost none of the settled ministry hear the command, GO TEACH ALL NATIONS. Almost none of the candidates hear it. The number is very small who go abroad, notwithstanding agents at home and from the different missions have been laboring to awake the slumbering churches."

The introduction concludes with these words: "The resolutions and remarks which accompany them were prayerfully, patiently, and earnestly discussed by this mission for four or five days, and unanimously adopted. They are our united voice. They contain the sentiments of our hearts. We are willing to hazard our lives on the truth of them. We are voluntary exiles from our country because we believe them.

"The discussion, of which this document is the fruit, has done us good; we are led therefore to hope it will be useful to others. It is a token of our love to the cause of Christ. To him we dedicate it; to his blessing we commend it; praying that his way may be known on the earth, and HIS SAVING HEALTH AMONG ALL NATIONS" [Ps 67:2]. *Missionary Herald* 34 (July 1838) 261, in Ehlke, "Enthusiastic Religion," 107.
50. LOC Box 1.

island." Accompanying him were two or three Hawaiians, who acted as his guides and porters. He sailed to Kau and then worked his way back east through Puna and then ultimately back to Hilo.[51]

Ehlke summarizes this tour in her opening paragraph on the Great Awakening. "The instructions to the members of the Seventh Company, read before their departure from Boston, admonished them to be the 'Voice of God' in the Sandwich Islands, adding, 'There you may find multitudes of souls, for whom Christ died, who never heard of his redeeming love.'[52] In December 1836, Titus Coan set off on his first tour of Hawaii to preach in remote parts of the island, improve himself in the native language, obtain a knowledge of the condition of the people, and visit the other stations.[53] Preaching from five to eight times a day, often 'to congregations that listened with deep interest and many tears,' Coan found his voice."[54]

When Coan reached "the western boundaries of Puna, my labors became more abundant. I had visited this people before, and had noticed a hopeful interest in a number of them." So Coan himself had done some preliminary work in the people's lives. On this tour the numbers grew significantly. "Now they rallied in masses, and were eager to hear the Word. Many listened with tears, and after the preaching when I supposed they would return to their homes and give me rest, they remained and crowded around me so earnestly, that I had no time to eat, and in places where I spent my nights they filled the house to its entire capacity, leaving scores outside who could not enter." Coan would experience this often over the next several years, including in Hilo. "All wanted to hear more of the 'Word of Life.' At 10 or 11 o'clock I would advise them to go home and to sleep. Some would retire, but more remain until midnight. At cock-crowing the house would be again crowded, with as many more outside."[55]

Combining Coan's journal entries from his first tour of Puna with David Lyman and C. S. Lyman's notes, the following comparison of locations on the Puna tour can be considered.

PUNA TOURS

TC and DL	TC and CSL
March 1836	**July 1846**
Keaao	Keaau
Makuu	Makuu
——	Koae
Waiakahiula	——

51. Coan, *Life*, 42.
52. Bingham, *Residence*, 477–78, in Ehlke, "Enthusiastic Religion," 107.
53. *Missionary Herald* 34 (July 1838) 261, in Ehlke, "Enthusiastic Religion," 107.
54 *Missionary Herald* 34 (July 1838) 261, in Ehlke, "Enthusiastic Religion," 107.
55. Coan, *Life*, 42–43.

The Great Awakening

Kula/Kapoho[56]	——
Ahalanui	——
Pohoiki	Pohoiki
Kaimu	——
——	Kauaea[57]
——	Keekee
——	Kehena
Kalapana	Kalapana
Kahaualea	——
Leaupuki	——
——	Komoa
Kealakomo	Kealakomo[58]

C. S. Lyman reports two locations and times for the beginning of the Great Awakening. The earliest, in late 1836, was in Kalapana.[59] In a Saturday, July 11, 1846, journal entry, he writes, "It was in this place that the great Revival in the S[andwich][60] Ids commenced as far back as 1836 . . . When he came to this place he preached a plain sermon on the text 'The Wages of Sin is death' [Rom 6:23]. The people became very much affected, thronged around him for instruction, followed him from village to village to attend meetings and often were clustered by the wayside to meet him as he came along."[61]

Daws notes that "in 1836, Titus Coan of Hilo toured his district on foot and for several weeks spoke at crowded and interested meetings."[62]

Coan continues in his autobiography to relate the Puna tour of late 1836. "At one place before I reached the point where I was to spend a Sabbath, there was a line of four villages not more than half a mile apart. Every village begged for a sermon and for personal conversation. Commencing at daylight I preached in three of them before breakfast, at 10 a.m." In a time when there was no television, recordings, or internet, people wanted to hear sermons over and over again in person. "When the meeting closed at one village, and thus my congregation increased rapidly from hour to hour.

---

56. Coan suggests this area for a mission station, since it has "one thousand souls." Kapoho is the location of Pastor/Kahu Alan Tamashiro's Puna Baptist Church. As of the 2010 census, the entire district of Puna has 20,000 residents, Wikipedia, "Puna, Hawaii."
57. "A hamlet." No citation.
58. See USGS online interactive map of the Big Island.
59. Lyman, *Around the Horn*, 97.
60. Brackets were placed for publishing purposes.
61. Lyman, *Around the Horn*, 99.
62. Daws, "Evangelism in Hawaii," 21.

Many were 'pricked in their hearts' [Acts 2:37] and were inquiring what they should do to be saved" [Acts 2:38].[63]

Sunday in Puna coincided with Coan visiting the most populous part of the region. "Multitudes came out to hear the gospel. The blind were led, the maimed, the aged and decrepit, and many invalids were brought on the backs of their friends. There was great joy and much weeping in the assembly. Two days were spent in this place, and ten sermons preached, while almost all the intervals between the public services were spent in personal conversation with the crowds which pressed around me."

In his next paragraph he writes in a subdued way of the intensity of the people's response, as well as the fact that decades later some still lived who had taken part in the revival. "Many of the people who then wept and prayed proved true converts to Christ; most of them have died in the faith, and a few still live as steadfast witnesses to the power of the gospel."

Coan next discusses two well-known converts and what could be called power encounters.[64] It has to do with a major religious challenge to the Christian faith on the Big Island. The goddess Pele was greatly feared because hers was the power of the volcano, earthquake, and fire; destruction and land-building.[65] The two converts are brother and sister, priest and priestess of Pele. The brother becomes a Christian first, but the sister would eventually have a powerful witness.[66]

"Among these converts was the High Priest of the volcano. He was more than six feet high and of lofty bearing. He had been an idolater, a drunkard, an adulterer, a robber, and a murderer. For their *kapas*, for a pig or a fowl he had killed men on the road, whenever they hesitated to yield to his demands. But he became penitent, and appeared honest and earnest in seeking the Lord.

"His sister was more haughty and stubborn. She was High Priestess of the volcano. She, too, was tall and majestic in her bearing. For a long time she refused to bow to the claims of the gospel; but at length she yielded, confessed herself a sinner and under the authority of a higher Power, and with her brother became a docile member of the church."[67]

In his December 24 journal entry, Coan writes of having planned a meeting with one person that day. Instead, after he awoke in the house where he was staying at daybreak, he found "a full house of people collected who wanted me to stop long enough to address them once more. I therefore preached to them again, and with much effort I broke away from them." He writes about meeting the priest of Pele. A large group

---

63. Coan, *Life*, 44.
64. 1 Kings 18.
65. See volcano chapters.
66. In a March 20, 2016 email, Dr. Nancy Morris wrote the author, "Re Coan meeting the 'priest' and 'priestess' of Pele: there is a letter of Coan's dated April 17, 1845, to Greene [sic] in which Coan names these two: Iaea and Wahineomao. I have not seen this letter, just the reference."
67. Coan, *Life*, 43–45.

THE GREAT AWAKENING

of people followed him, "among whom were an old High Priest of Pali [sic], or the volcano, with his wife, who both seem much interested in attending to instruction."[68]

The same day, Coan preached to many more people. Once on the shore at Kalapana. "After examination [of school students] preached to the people. After more preaching and a 4 p.m. wedding ceremony, 'Multitudes of people still pressed around me to talk about the way of salvation.'" On the Sabbath (Sunday) the next day, Titus preached on December 25. Continuing in Kalapana in Puna, he "met the people . . . and preached Christ to them. Quite a full congregation. Preached again at 10 a.m. A large native house was devoted to . . . by the congregation and was crowded full . . . At 1 o'clock I preached again from the text, 'woe to the wicked' [Isa 3:11]. A good deal of apparent solemnity." He preached yet again that day. "At 4 p.m. I went out to Kaimu and preached to the people there. Many followed from Kalapana."[69]

Coan concluded his Puna tour and returned to Hilo. "After my return, congregations at the center increased in numbers. Meetings for parents, for women, for church members, for children, were frequent and full. Soon scores and hundreds who had heard the gospel in Kau, Puna, and Hilo came into the town to hear more."[70]

Coan writes contemporaneously about the protracted meeting in his journal. He presents a combination of meetings, individual inquiry, sermon texts, and other items. "This day is the commencement of a protracted meeting with our people. A large congregation assembled in the morning. [Meeting][71] House nearly full. Many came from the most distant parts of Hilo and Puna. I opened the meeting by preaching from the text, 'Verily, Verily, I say unto you, the hour is coming and now is here when the dead shall hear the voice of the Son of God' [John 5:25] etc. The word seemed to take effect and several and several came to me before night in evident distress, and seeming to feel they were dead in trespasses and sins." Coan notes that 250 children attended in the morning.[72] His text for them was "'except a man be born again' [John 3:3], etc."[73]

In his February 6 journal entry, Coan notes that Brother Lyman "preached in the a.m. from the text, 'Strive to enter in at the strait gate' [Luke 13:24] and in the p.m. I preached from the words 'How shall we escape[?]'"[74] etc. Coan writes of Concerts of Prayer and other matters. "At 4 p.m. we observed the Monthly Concert. Many people present."[75]

---

68. Coan journal entry, December 24, 1846, LOC Box 1.
69. Coan journal entry, December 24, 1846, LOC Box 1.
70. Coan journal entry, December 24, 1846, LOC Box 1.
71. See below.
72. See Ehlke, "Enthusiastic Religion," above.
73. Coan journal entry, February 5, 1837, LOC Box 1.
74. "How shall we escape if we ignore so great a salvation?" Heb. 2:3. Word somewhat difficult to decipher in original hand.
75. Coan journal entry, February 6, 1837, LOC Box 1.

Titus Coan: "Apostle to the Sandwich Islands"

In his journal, Coan provides the daily schedule in a way that parallels Bingham's report.[76] "The following is the order of daily exercises which we have adopted for the week.

"<u>1</u>. Prayer meeting at daylight conducted by the members of the Church.

"<u>2</u>. Preaching to children at 8 a.m. and a prayer meet[ing] of the Ch[urch] at the same hour.

"<u>3</u>. Preaching in the Meeting house at 10 a.m.

"<u>4</u>. Preaching again at 2 p.m.

"<u>5</u>. Meeting for the anxious and enquiring at 4 p.m. and Church prayer M[?] [at] the same hour.

"<u>6</u>. Prayer meeting of the mission family from 8 to 9."

Coan relates how God is at work in this process. "The Spirit of God is evidently with us, and the attention of many seems arrested. Three or four hundred in the anxious meeting. Many evidently impressed and many thoughtful. The attention of many children seems to be arrested."[77]

Coan writes about the continued protracted meeting in his next day's journal entry. The Bible text at the bottom of the page is illegible.[78] At the top of the next page he relates Brother Lyman's text:[79] "See that ye refuse not him that speaketh" [Heb 12:25]. He notes that the Coan and Lyman homes "are thronged during the intervals of [between] meetings. Multitudes press in [upon?] us to talk about their souls."[80]

On February 8, Coan begins his journal entry with, "Meetings still interesting. Feeling deeper." David Lyman's morning text is "'to as many as received him'[John 1:12] etc." Coan held forth on, "'So if ye live after the flesh ye shall die' [Rom 8:13] etc."[81] On the ninth, Coan spoke "from the text, 'Choose ye this day'[82] etc." [Josh 24:15]. Lyman's text was "seal not the sayings . . . for the time is at hand."[83] [Rev 22:7].

On the tenth, Lyman spoke on "the parable of the sower"[84] [Matt 13:1–23], while Coan spoke on "And this is the condemnation" [John 3:19]. Coan notes that there is much "inquiry, and many profess to have passed from death to life"[85] [John 5:24; 1

---

76. Bingham obviously learned of this schedule from Coan.
77. Coan journal entry, February 6, 1837, LOC.
78. Including some bleed through from the page on the other side.
79. It is helpful to consider the texts that each man used in concert with each over these days of intense consideration.
80. Coan journal entry, February 7, 1837, LOC Box 1.
81. Coan journal entry, February 8, 1837, LOC.
82. ". . . whom ye shall serve," i.e., the Lord or evil.
83. Coan journal entry, February 9, 1837, LOC.
84. Various soil types; response to the written word of God.
85. Coan journal entry, February 10, 1837, LOC.

The Great Awakening

John 3:14]. On the eleventh, Coan preaches from the text "'Enter not into the path of the wicked' [Prov 4:14], etc." Coan and Lyman made one nod to preparing for the Sabbath. "Omitted the meeting at 2 p.m. in order that the people might prepare for the Sab . . . All other meetings as usual."[86]

On Sunday, February 12, Lyman "preached in the morning. Subject. Christ cursing the fig tree"[87] [Mark 11:12–25]. In the afternoon Coan "preached from the text 'If any man be in Christ' etc." [2 Cor 5:17].[88]

The protracted meetings become more protracted out of consideration for the spiritual state of the children. On Monday, February 13, Coan writes that he is feeling "encouraged by the deep seriousness of some of the children. We have resolved to open this week in special effort for their conversion to God. We have therefore adopted the following order of exercises to be pursued daily through the week. First preaching to children at 9 a.m.

"2. Again at 2 p.m.

"3. [?] and also a Ch. prayer meeting on their behalf at the same hour. Fourth meet[ing] ourselves as usual, besides other incidental meetings. 250 children were present today and no little impression seems to have been made on the minds of some."[89]

Coan's next entry marks the conclusion of the protracted meetings. "Closed the pro[tracted] meeting for children today. Some we hope are born again, many are serious, and all seem to feel the effect of the meet[ing] in a greater or less degree."[90] On the next day, Coan indicates the initial impact on the church of the protracted meetings for children and adults. "Two hundred children in S[unday] S[chool]. Congregation large and attentive."[91]

Ehlke continues. "Titus Coan compared the revival with those they had witnessed in New York in a letter to his missionary neighbor and friend from Auburn Seminary days, the Rev. Lorenzo Lyons[92] at Waimea: 'There has been some cases of apparent conviction and conversion as distinctly marked as we find in our own land in

---

86. Coan journal entry, February 11, 1837, LOC.

87. "Hiram Bingham first reported the fig in Hawaii in 1825." Hawaii Fruit, "Figs."

88. "Therefore if any man be in Christ, he is a new creature: old things are passed away; behold, all things are become new." Coan journal entry, February 12, 1837, LOC Box 1.

89. Coan journal entry, February 13, 1837, LOC.

90. Coan journal entry, February 18, 1837, LOC. The bottom lines are illegible.

91. Coan journal entry, February 19, 1837, LOC.

92. Lyons, who will appear in the next chapter as using controversial measures in the Great Awakening, is described by Forbes et al. in *Partners in Change,* 455, as follows: "Of all the American missionaries to come to and labor in the Hawaiian Islands, none is remembered with as much affection by Native Hawaiians as Rev. Lorenzo Lyons. He was beloved for his humanity and, particularly, for his role as a hymnist and author of the lyrics of the well-known anthem 'Hawaii Aloha,' which expresses his love for his adopted homeland. 'Hawaii Aloha' is one of contemporary Hawai'i's most cherished songs."

times of a revival, and the state of things more nearly resembles that of an American revival than anything I have before seen at Hilo.'"[93]

Turning to late 1837, Lydia Bingham Coan writes a bridge passage, then quotes an undesignated writing of Titus Coan. "In November 1837 a protracted meeting of eight days was held at the [Hilo?] station [church building?]. Of that time Mr. Coan wrote: 'God wrought for us. I opened the meeting with a sermon from the text, 'Prepare ye the way of the Lord' [Mark 1:3]. Great effect was produced. On the second day of the meeting God came in terror. The sea rose suddenly to the perpendicular height of fifteen or twenty feet, and fell in one mountain wave upon the shore, sweeping away nearly one hundred houses with all their tenants. All was sudden as a peal of thunder. No premonitions were given. None had time to flee. The scene was awful. Hundreds were engulfed in a moment. Cries of distress were heart rending, and the roar of the raging sea was deafening. To the people the event was as the voice of God speaking to them out of heaven, 'Be ye also ready.'"[94] [Matt 24:44].

Daws notes that on November 6, 1837, "Titus Coan began a protracted meeting at Hilo before a congregation of several hundred. The next day a tidal wave struck the village, taking several lives and causing great damage. From then on his congregations were unique in size and fervor."[95]

Coan relates the same event in his autobiography. Providing more commentary and depth of description of the tidal wave[96] and its after effects he writes, "God visited the people in judgment as well as in mercy. On the seventh of November, 1837, at the hour of evening prayers, we were startled by a heavy thud, and a sudden jar of the earth. The sound was like the fall of some vast body upon the beach, and in a few seconds a noise of mingled voices rising for a mile along the shore thrilled us like the wail of doom" [Ezek 30:3].[97]

Coan explains how this tragic event was used for spiritual benefit among the living. "So sudden and unexpected was the catastrophe, that the people along the shore were literally 'eating and drinking' [Matt 24:38], and they 'knew not, until the flood came and swept them all away'" [Matt 24:39]. "This event, falling as it did like a bolt of thunder from a clear sky, greatly impressed the people. It was as the voice of God speaking to them out of heaven, 'Be ye also ready.'"

Coan ministers to the physical needs of the people and sees many hopeful conversions. "We fed, comforted, and clothed the living, and God brought light out of darkness, joy out of grief, and life out of death. Our meetings were more and more crowded, and hopeful converts were multiplied."

---

93. Titus Coan to Lorenzo Lyons, February 25, 1837, HMH.
94. Coan, *Memorial Volume*, 41.
95. Daws, "Evangelism in Hawaii," 21–22.
96. Tsunami.
97. For a discussion of the rest of this natural event and of earthquakes (near and far) causing tsunamis, see the "Renaissance Man" section, "Science" chapter.

The event affected English-speaking people present in the Hilo environs.[98] The English captain of a vessel that had been in the harbor "spent his nights in our family [home], and his intelligent and courteous clerk, professed to give themselves to the Lord while with us, and both kneeling with us at the family altar, silently united in our morning and evening devotions, or cheerfully led in prayer." The captain shared his religious background and the reality of his new life in Christ. "He gave us an interesting account of his eventful life, and confessed that he had enjoyed very few religious privileges and had thought little of God or the salvation of his soul. He now accepted the offer of life through Christ, with the spirit of a little child."[99]

Not long before claiming the Great Revival began in late 1836, C. S. Lyman avers that it took place in 1837 or 1838. Before Kalapana came Kehena. An elderly gentleman relates Coan's sermon from those days. The man related the following to C. S. Lyman: There "was an old man who c[oul]d hardly express his joy at seeing me and learning that I was from America. He thanked God that I had been preserved to get here and expressed great regret that we did not speak a common language. He repeated the text that he s[ai]d converted him or *killed* him—'The hour cometh &c when they that are in the graves &c and they that hear shall live [John 5:25, 28]. It was preached from by Mr. Coan at this place at the beginning of the great revival (1837 or 1838) and seemed to produce a deep impression; several swooned and fell prostrate and about fifty were hopefully converted and have all worn remarkably well."[100]

THE REVIVAL BUILDS

"When Coan had come to Hilo, church membership had stood at about twenty. By April 1837 there were eighty-four professed converts who had been received into the church. Coan had made a prolonged tour of his district at the end of 1836, with apparently good results; but in general the people of Hilo remained 'hard as a nether millstone' [Job 41:24].[101] By mid-1837, Coan was becoming impatient for the victory of Christ. 'This people are . . . dead but God can raise them. Is it not *time for him to work?*'"[102] [Ps 119:126].

"Writing to Levi Chamberlain in Honolulu in October on a business matter, Coan noted a stirring. 'State of things interesting here. Sinners anxious. The Word has power. Pray for us.'"[103]

---

98. For more on this and other foreigners influenced by Coan, see chapter on Coan's ministry to non-Hawaiians.

99. Coan, *Life*, 51–53.

100. Lyman, *Around the Horn*, 97–98.

101. "The nether millstone is the lower of the two millstones by which corn is ground." The Free Dictionary.com, "Millstone."

102. Italics in Daws original. Daws, "Evangelism," 25–26n12. Titus to Fidelia Coan, August 29, 1837, in Coan Letters, NYHS.

103. Daws, "Evangelism," 26n13. NYHS HMH.

Coan indicates that beginning in 1837, "Hilo was crowded with strangers" from Kau, Puna, and the Hilo districts. There is some indication that people travelled there from the other islands as well in order to hear Coan preach and participate in the Great Awakening.[104] He talks about the physical people movements that occurred during this people movement to Christianity. Whole "families and whole villages in the country were left, with the exception of a few of the old people, and in some instances even the aged and the feeble were brought in on litters from a distance of thirty or fifty miles. Little cabins studded the place like the camps of an army, and we estimated that our population that our population was increased to ten thousand souls."[105] By comparison, the first official census of Hilo in 1910 indicated 6,745 Hilo residents and 20,431 in 1920.[106] In addition to departures after the denouement of the Great Awakening, many Hawaiians would die due to illness.[107] So, the numbers are not known (how much up or down and when) between 1840 and 1910.

Coan continues his description of the situation at Hilo during the Great Awakening with regard to food growing and size of church building. "Those who remained some time fished and planted potatoes and taro for food. Our great native house of worship, nearly two hundred feet long, by about eighty-five feet wide, with a lofty roof of thatch, was crowded almost to suffocation, while hundreds remained outside unable to enter."

He continues with a description of the receptivity of the congregants by providing multiple Bible quotations and allusions. "This sea of faces, all hushed except when sighs and sobs burst out here and there, was a scene to melt the heart. The word fell with power [Acts 10:44], and sometimes as the feeling deepened, the vast audience was moved and swayed like a forest in a mighty wind. The word became like the 'fire and the hammer' of the Almighty [Jer 23:29], and it pierced like a two-edged sword [Heb 4:12]. Hopeful converts were multiplied and 'there was great joy in the city'" [Acts 8:8].

Because the place of worship had become "'too strait' for the increasing multitudes," the Hawaiians on their own initiative traveled for several materials to secure the building materials for a second facility. They did this "without the knowledge of their teachers." When Coan asked them about a large heap of timber, the "reply was, 'We will build a second house of worship so that the people may all be sheltered from sun and rain on the Sabbath.'" They had a further idea on this matter: and "this is our thought; all of the people of Hilo shall meet in the larger house, where you will preach to them in the morning, during which time the people of Puna and Kau will meet for prayer in the smaller house, and in the afternoon these congregations shall exchange places, and you will preach to the Puna and Kau people; thus all will hear the minister."

104. Tamashiro email to author.
105. Coan, *Life*, 45.
106. Wikipedia, "Hilo, Hawaii."
107. Diamond, *Guns, Germs, and Steel*; and Kuykendall, *Hawaiian Kingdom*.

The Great Awakening

Even with that idea and implementation, there were times when a further need developed to "economize room. So, some Hawaiians organized everyone to stand up and be as close together as possible. When "the house was thus filled with these compacted ranks, the word was given them to *sit down*, which they did, a mass of living humanity, such perhaps as was never seen except on Hawaii."[108] Imagine the sight. Imagine the sound.

NEW MEASURES AND THE GREAT AWAKENING

Coan presses on in his descriptions of the Great Awakening. "Time swept on; the work deepened and widened. Thousands on thousands thronged the courts of the Lord. All eastern and southern Hawaii was like a sea in motion. Waimea, Hamakua, Kohala, Kona, and the other islands of the group, were moved."

He refers to the New Measures under his cousin Asahel Nettleton and his mentor Charles Finney. He applies them to what is happening in Hawai'i. "I had seen great and powerful awakenings under the preaching of Nettleton and Finney, and like doctrines, prayers, and efforts seemed to produce like fruits among them."[109]

In June of 1839, Coan writes of himself regarding district tours and protracted meetings. "Since July last the pastor has made five separate tours through Hilo and Puna, holding numerous protracted meetings and preaching from twenty to thirty times a week."[110]

Protracted meetings were one form of New Measures. In her second paragraph on the Great Awakening, Ehlke notes that a "fifteen-day protracted meeting commenced February 5, 1837, following the same pattern as those held in western New York during the Finney revivals. The first week the program called for a prayer meeting at the break of day; preaching to children at 8 a.m. with a church prayer meeting at the same time; preaching to the whole congregation at 10 a.m. and 2 p.m., with anxious[111] and inquiry meetings at 4 p.m. and a church prayer meeting at the same time. The evening hours from eight to nine were spent in social prayer with the two mission families. Any spare time, Coan reported, was devoted to conversation with those 'who, in great numbers filled the houses, and beset the paths of the missionaries.'"[112]

Coan describes "actions meet for repentance" [Acts 26:20] resulting from a protracted meeting. "Pipes like the 'books of those who used curious arts' [Acts 19:19]

---

108. Coan, *Life*, 45–46. See Daws, "Evangelism," 27. Sounding a bit like early-twenty-first-century mega church volunteers, Daws describes the preparations made for Coan's sermons. "At the time of the Revival, every sermon he preached was eagerly anticipated; and at Hilo the big meeting-house had to be carefully prepared to seat the great crowds."

109. Coan, *Life*, 49.

110. Coan letter, June 6, 1839, in Gulick et al., *Pilgrims*, 172.

111. With the "anxious bench" being a New Measure. See Rosell et al., *Memoirs of Charles Finney*.

112. Bingham, *Residence*, 515, in Ehlke, "Enthusiastic Religion," 107.

were brought in great numbers and burnt, and most of the plantations of tobacco in Kohala were destroyed."[113]

Ehlke provides further material from Hiram Bingham on the protracted meeting of early 1837 in Hilo. "The meetings were full and solemn. Many came from the most distant parts of our field, fifty or sixty miles, to attend this meeting. The Holy Ghost came, at the commencement of the meeting, and many were awakened under the first sermons, which was preached from these words: 'Verily, verily, I say unto you, the hour is coming and now lo, when the dead shall hear the voice of the Son of God, and they that hear shall live'"[114] [John 5:25].

"With three hundred at the inquiry meeting, the people aroused, and the spirit of prayer among them, Coan felt the subjects showed as much evidence of 'conviction and hopeful conversion . . . as most cases in the United States.' The protracted meeting was continued another week to give special attention to the children, who were assembled three times a day to hear the gospel. The task of preaching during the meeting was divided between Mr. Lyman and Mr. Coan, who 'endeavored to strengthen each other's hands in the Lord.'[115] At the conclusion of the meeting, the church members were directed to bring in the aged, so that they might learn of God's promises for them."[116]

In an early 1837 letter to Lorenzo Lyons, Coan compares what is going on with what happened in Upstate New York. "There has been some cases of apparent conviction and conversion as distinctly marked as we find in our own land in times of a revival, and the state of things more nearly resembles that of an American revival than anything I have before seen at Hilo."[117]

One development in the First[118] and Second Great Awakenings, as well as earlier spiritual movements in the history of the church, were what he called "physical demonstrations which commanded attention. Among the serious and anxious inquirers who came to our house by day and by night, there were individuals who, while listening to a very plain and kind conversation, would begin to tremble and soon fall helpless to the floor."[119]

Whether in calm conversation with a few people or preaching to many people, Coan did not seek to whip his audience into a frenzy. "At one time, when I was holding a series of outdoor meetings in a populous part of Puna, a remarkable manifestation

---

113. Coan letter, nd, in Gulick et al., *Pilgrims*, 78.

114. Gulick et al., *Pilgrims*, 78.

115. Coan to Lyons, February 25, 1837, HMH, in Ehlke, "Enthusiastic Religion," 108. No direct Bible quotation found.

116. Bingham, *Residence*, 515–16, in Ehlke, "Enthusiastic Religion," 108.

117. Coan to Lyons, February 25, 1837, in Ehlke, "Enthusiastic Religion," 108.

118. See Jonathan Edwards's discussion of real and counterfeit spiritual expressions in *Religious Affection Vol. 2* and *The Great Awakening Vol. 4*, Yale.

119. Coan, *Life*, 49.

of this kind occurred. A very large concourse were seated on the grass, and I was standing in the center preaching 'Repentance toward God and faith in the Lord Jesus' [Acts 20:21]. Of a sudden, a man who had been gazing with intense interest at the preacher, burst out in a fervent prayer, with streaming tears, saying: 'Lord, have mercy on me [Luke 18:13]; I am dead in sin'[Eph 2:1]. His weeping was so loud, and his trembling so great, that the whole congregation was moved as by a common sympathy. Many wept aloud, and many commenced praying together. The scene was such as I had never before witnessed. I stood dumb in the midst of this weeping, wailing, praying multitude, not being able to make myself heard for about twenty minutes. When the noise was hushed, I continued my address with words of caution, lest they should feel that this kind of demonstration atoned for their sins, and rendered them acceptable before God. I assured them that all the Lord required was godly sorrow [2 Cor 7:10] for the past, present faith in Christ, and henceforth faithful, filial, and cheerful obedience. A calm came over the multitude, and we felt that 'the Lord was there'"[120] [Ps 18:18].

Coan relates how one man came to a meeting to ridicule what was going on and wound up having a physical manifestation and becoming a sincere Christian. "A young man came once into our meeting to make sport slyly. Trying to make the young men around him laugh during prayer, he fell as senseless as a log upon the ground and was carried out of the house. It was some time before his consciousness could be restored. He became sober, confessed his sins, and in due time united with the church."

He urges the people to guard against hypocrisy and to not trust in such manifestations. Rather, he tells them to focus on the main things of the Christian life. "Similar manifestations were seen in other places, but everywhere the people were warned against hypocrisy, and against trusting in such demonstrations. They were told that the Lord looks at the heart, and that 'repentance toward God and faith in the Lord Jesus' [Acts 20:21] were the unchangeable conditions of pardon and salvation, and that their future lives of obedience or of disobedience would prove or disprove their spiritual life, as 'The tree is known by its fruit'"[121] [Matt 12:33].

Ehlke notes that Lyons and Coan—the "two missionary brethren laboring in adjoining fields on the island of Hawaii—shared similar theological views and frequently compared notes on the most effective revival techniques. 'I preach daily, have anxious meetings, meet different classes, visit, talk with the multitudes at my house, send out church-members to work for God, use them in looking out [for] converts, &c., &c.' He told Lyons that he closed his sermons with a call for all to rise who resolved to serve the Lord, often calling upon different classes of church members such as young converts to respond to his question. 'Brother Lyman never uses any of these

---

120. Coan, *Life*, 49–50.
121. Coan, *Life*, 50–51.

measures. When his sermon is done he closes the meeting; though I know not that he disapproves of my eccentricities.'"[122]

KING KAMEHAMEHA III

Coan writes about Kamehameha III, who was a son of Kamehameha I. A man torn between loyalties, Coan indicates that the king had a wonderful disposition and, when he was sober and focused on the things of God, he was a great encouragement to people on every island and especially a blessing to those of the Hilo region. Ultimately, he would give in to what Coan characterizes as "spoilers."

Coan introduces Kamehameha III as having become king soon after the Coans arrived in Hawai'i. "Kamehameha III, son of Kamehameha I, was on the Hawaiian throne when I arrived at the Islands, having been proclaimed not long before.

"He was then a young and mild prince, greatly honored and loved by the whole nation. The natives loved to style him 'The Good King.' Bad men, both foreigners and natives, beguiled him into some unworthy habits; but his disposition was kind and amiable, and he was the king who gave to the people a liberal constitution with all its attendant blessings.

"During the great awakening which spread over the Islands in 1837 and onward, he was greatly impressed with the importance of spiritual things. He was not only an attendant on divine service on the Lord's Day, but he was often in the prayer-meetings, apparently an earnest seeker after truth. He was also willing to listen to wise counsels; and during his reign his Government enacted a law forbidding the introduction and sale of intoxicating liquours in this kingdom.[123] The nation became a great temperance society, with the king at its head; and it was reported that he said he would rather die than drink another glass of liquour.

"During his year[s?] of abstinence he seemed like a new man. He was awake to all the interests of his kingdom, visited the different islands, addressed large assemblies, and greatly increased the love and homage of his people.

"His visits to Hilo were like a benediction; the people flocked around him as they would around a father, and he seemed like a father to them. He visited our families, dined and supped with us, and gave us free opportunities to converse with him, not only on the interests of his kingdom, but also on his own spiritual interests and his personal relations to God and to the eternal future. He has gone with me into an upper chamber where we conversed together as brothers and knelt in humble prayer before the mercy-seat of the King Eternal. On one occasion, when he attended our Sabbath service, I preached from Jer 23:24, 'Can any hide himself in secret places that I shall

---

122. Coan to Lyons, January 29, 1838, HMH.

123. See next chapter and affect of this law on some of the sailors and officers of the *Vincennes* Exploring Expedition.

not see him? saith the Lord.' The doctrine of God's omnipresence and omniscience was the subject.

"The king seemed one of the most earnest hearers in the congregation, often bowing his head in assent to what was said. For months he seemed nearly ready to unite with the visible church, and his true friends rejoiced over him.

"But the spoiler came. He that 'goeth about as a roaring lion seeking whom he may devour' [1 Pet 1:8] was lying in wait for him. The French came with their fire and thunder, threatening his crown and kingdom if the prohibition law on intoxicants was not repealed; and the British lion was ready to stand by the French eagle.

"The king was called a fool for coming under the influence of Protestant missionaries. He was, as report said, advised to assert his royal prerogative of independence, and urged to drink with his official and distinguished friends. The poor man, through fear and flattery, yielded, and his doom from that hour was sealed." He would die in late 1854.[124]

As tragic as that was, he had encouraged the Great Awakening seventeen years before. And that movement of God's Holy Spirit continued and grew, cresting in 1838.

THE BIGGEST YEAR: 1838

While the Awakening had its first glimmerings in 1836 and grew significantly in 1837, most people agree that 1838 was the main year of the Revival. Coan notes that many "passed from death to life in 1836 and 1837"; most joined in the church in 1838 and 1839.[125] In the *Memorial Volume*, Lydia Bingham presents several letters from Titus Coan to his closest revival laborer, Lorenzo Lyons. Based in Waimea, he ministered in central Hawai'i and the northern district of Kohala, and wherever invited. He began there in 1832 and continued to serve until his death there in 1886.[126]

Lydia asked Lorenzo to review the revival letters before their publication in the *Memorial Volume*. One sees the closeness between the two men, forged in the crucible of revival fire. "'In reviewing these letters, the tears have flowed, and I could not refrain from crying aloud. I stood before the picture of my sainted brother, and it seemed as if I could almost hear him speaking in his soul-inspiring strains. We were in deep sympathy, and unbosomed our hearts, our joys, our longings to each other.'"[127]

The first letter in the *Memorial Volume* from Coan to Lyons is dated November 24, 1837. 1838 is in prospect. The first letter has a significant lacuna, discovered by Ehlke. What Elke found is omitted by brackets[128] by Lydia. To put the lacuna in context, it is provided in italics below. "Mr. Coan reports to Mr. Lyons:

124. Coan, *Life*, 127–30.
125. Coan, *Life*, 54–55.
126. Judd, *Missionary Album*, 144–45.
127. Coan, *Memorial Volume*, undesignated and undated writing by Lorenzo Lyons, 42.
128. "[. . .]"

"We have a glorious work of grace here. Hundreds think they are converted. How many will bring forth fruits meet for repentance remains to be seen. That very many are born of God is to my mind as sure as that the gospel is the power of God unto salvation [Rom 1:16]. If I can judge of my own feelings, I never took hold of the work of pulling sinners out of the fire [Jude 1:23] with more faith, and more unshaken confidence of success, than at this time, and I never saw God's work more manifest. *When my dear brother, I say again that we and this mission are red with the blood of souls. Our unbelief has sent thousands down to endless burnings . . . It is so and what we will now, we shall find it so in the day of Decision.*[129] Only let us preach the gospel in *living*[130] faith, and under the awful pressure of the powers of the world to come, and I defy the people, stupid as they are, to sleep. Why, they might as well sleep under a cataract of fire . . . Write me often, and we will not fail to pray for each other."[131]

It is not known for certain why Lydia left out that section. Perhaps she did not want to show him in a bad light or with agonizing self-flagellation. The rest of the letter portion indicates as well his passion for saving souls and working with Lyons toward that end.

Coan wrote his next letter to Lyons on Christmas Day of 1837. He exhorts both of them not to doubt, but instead to press forward in the work of God. He prophetically hopes that 1838 will be a Jubilee year [Lev 25:11–12] of drawing many souls into the Kingdom of God.

"The Captain of our salvation[132] is still riding through the field. He must conquer, for all power is his. Why should we ever doubt his power or his love? Why cherish that child of hell—that soul-murderer? Five hundred conversions in your field! I hope there are as many in ours. But what are they among the thousands left? Some may call this a great work, and it surely is glorious. It wakes up sweet and long songs in heaven. But this work is yet small compared to what God wishes to do, and to what he will do if our faith fail not. I am sometimes sorely tempted of Satan to doubt and fear, and say this may be all smoke. God forbid that I should yield to such soul-killing suggestions. This is God's work, and it *will go on*. Our meetings are more and more crowded. I preach and talk to multitudes every day. One hundred will probably be added to this church on the first Sabbath in January. Let 1838 be a year of Jubilee to these islands.

---

129. Ehlke, "Enthusiastic Religion," 117–18.
130. This word is italicized in Coan, *Memorial Volume*.
131. Coan to Lyons, November 24, 1837, *Memorial Volume*, 42–43.
132. Hymn by Charles Wesley, verse 1:

> "Captain of our salvation, take
> the souls that here are trained for thee,
> and fit for thy great service make
> these heirs of immortality;
> and let them in thine image rise;
> and then transplant to paradise."

NB: Originally a baptism hymn; Taditional Music Library.

God help you, my brother. Be strong, go on, do valiantly. Fear nothing but sin. Look up; listen to the voice that says, 'Lo! *I* am with you always' [Matt 28:20]. Preach boldly, plainly, in living faith, in burning love, and in high holy expectation of success. If thousands are not converted we shall be red with the blood of souls. If these things are so, how can we sleep?"[133]

Note that Lydia includes part of the phrase she omitted from the previous letter. Coan exhorts Lyons and himself to move forward in God's work. Lydia provides a bridge passage writing of protracted meetings in Puna and the "fearfulness" that took hold on sinners during every sermon by Coan. This leads to the next letter to Lyons, dated January 29, 1838.

"At the first village the Holy Ghost fell on many that heard the word, and they left all and followed from place to place, weeping as they went. I should hardly dare tell my brethren generally what I saw in Puna. Some would call it Methodism, some fanaticism, wildfire, etc. I call it the power of God unto salvation [Rom 1:16], for I felt it in my soul before it fell upon my congregation. And it fell upon them under the most bold and searching and simple truth which I could present to their minds, and as the most unequivocal answer to prayer."[134] He next discusses church membership and admission to same. That subject is discussed later in the chapter "Opposition and Response."

Daws notes the January tour in Puna. Coan "left this center of enthusiasm [in Hilo] to tour Puna in January 1838, and the contagion spread with him. Concurrently Lorenzo Lyons had been working zealously with his congregations at Waimea, and now he began to achieve results apparently as spectacular as Coan's."[135]

In his February 13 letter, Coan shares both his physical weariness and spiritual exaltation with the ongoing awakening in people's lives. "'It is late and I have just dismissed one hundred natives from my house whom I have been pointing to the Lamb of God [John 1:29]. My body is all weak and trembling with weariness, but my heart is full of love, joyful in God our Savior" [Titus 2:13; Jude 25].

He asks Lyons how the work goes in Kohala, which is the northern district of the Big Island. "What tidings from Kohala? Do the banners of salvation [Ps 20:5] wave in glory there? Are the devil's towers down? Are his bulwarks fallen? Tell me, Brother Watchman [Ezek 3:17], tell me, for my soul is in expectation."[136]

On August 28 he writes an exultant letter, noting that he is delayed two weeks in writing Lyons because of the tour he has been on. "I should have written sooner but have been absent touring two weeks. Have returned with arms full of sheaves [Ps 126:6]. Heaven shouts it home. The gospel was all triumphant. The prayers of some were wonderful—heaven-moving, heaven-opening. Jesus rode [Rev 6:2] all glorious

---

133. Coan to Lyons, December 25, 1837, in Coan, *Memorial Volume*, 43–44.
134. Coan to Lyons, January 29, 1838, in Coan, *Memorial Volume*, 44–45.
135. Daws, "Evangelism," 22.
136. Coan to Lyons, February 13, 1838, in Coan, *Memorial Volume*, 45–46.

all mighty to save [Zeph 3:17]. God girded a worm for the fight and the slain of the Lord were *many*."[137]

He writes about how he loves the spiritual battle in a September 9 letter. "Comparatively few fall here as yet, but O, the tug of battle; the watchings, the fightings, the toils necessary to keep such a church awake and at the post of duty. But I love the struggle and God helps me wonderfully. I want to fight on till I die. I wish to die in the field with armor on [Eph 6:10-18], with weapons bright."[138]

On October 15, Titus expresses his yearnings to Lyons to have Christ-like virtues to carry forth the service to others. "O for meekness, patience, faith; for a single eye that looks right on, and for a soul that *presses* toward the mark [Phil 3:14]. I pray for that meekness which commits one's self, motives, measures, actions, *all* to him who judges righteously"[139] [Ps 7:11].

Coan wraps up the year 1838 with a December 23 letter to Lyons, expressing his joy in the Christian battle against Satan. "I have been absent on a tour of eighteen days in Puna. I have returned weary, lame, and sore, but rejoicing. I was much cheered by the steadfastness of the church; nearly all appear well. Out of two thousand church members in that district only ten are wandering. May the Good Shepherd preserve them into his heavenly kingdom. This field, my dear brother, is all *battle ground*. It belongs to Jesus. Satan disputes the title, contends for every inch of the ground, and fights hard on the retreat. If you find any of my sheep scattered and wandering in your field, you will do me a great favor to look after them. I shall ever esteem it a privilege to do the same by the sheep and lambs of your fold who may chance to wander, or to feed in this field . . . I have many joyful feelings, and many which are solemn and almost overpowering. For some of my little children I travail in birth again and again until Christ be formed in them [Gal 4:19]. So it is with you. Let us hold on, my brother, for we shall reap if we faint not. There is glory in the prospect. The *crown of life!* O! I see it, all glittering, all glorious."[140]

At the end of the chapter on Coan's letters to Lyons during the revival years, Lydia Coan writes a bridge section indicating that, although "Mr. Coan's frequent correspondence with Mr. Lyons continued through his life," no other letters to Lyons were preserved. Lydia notes that the "notable characteristic steadfastness in Mr. Coan was strongly marked in his friendships. Names that occur on the first pages of his *Synopses of Letters*[141] are found on the last. It was only as friend after friend crossed the flood[142]

---

137. Coan to Lyons, August 28, 1838, in Coan, *Memorial Volume*, 46-47.
138. Coan to Lyons, September 9, 1838, in Coan, *Memorial Volume*, 47.
139. Coan to Lyons, October 15, 1838, in Coan, *Memorial Volume*, 47.
140. Coan to Lyons, December 23, 1838, in Coan, *Memorial Volume*, 48-49.
141. See LOC Box 17?
142. The River Jordan, symbolizing death.

and passed beyond the reach of voice or pen, that his name dropped out of the list of correspondents."[143]

Great excitement preceded both his sermons in Hilo and "visits to outlying villages. Sometimes church members would go out ahead to bring in sinners to hear the sermon, and very often the congregation would be waiting for him in perfect order. It was such a sea of faces or 'forest of heads' or 'field of wheat just ready for the sickle' [Joel 4:13; Mark 4:29] which produced the greatest numbers of weepers, prayers, fainters, and fallers.

"'I arrived [at Hakalau][144] yesterday at 8 a.m. Found a large company of children collected . . . in the met. house, besides several hundreds of adults. I was a little weary, but I felt the Spirit break upon my heart; so I went right in among the children and fell upon my knees and looked up to heaven. The H. Ghost fell **instantly**,[145] so soon as I opened my mouth. The place was shaken. The congregation was all in tears, and there was such a crying out as I had not heard before.'"[146]

STATISTICS

Thorough in all areas of his life, Titus Coan kept precise statistics relating to the Great Awakening, such as baptisms, membership, etc. He kept track of each person in the process of possibly becoming a member. "I had kept a faithful note-book in my pocket, and in all my personal conversations with the people, by night and by day, at home and in my oft-repeated tours, I had noted down, unobserved, the names of individuals apparently sincere and true converts."

He further relates the thoroughness of his tracking of prospective converts and church members. "Over these persons I kept watch, though unconsciously to themselves; and thus their life and conversation were made the subjects of vigilant observation. After the lapse of three, six, nine, or twelve months, as the case might be, selections were made from the list of names for examination. Some were found to have gone back to their old sins; others were stupid, or gave but doubtful evidence of conversion, while many had stood fast and run well."

The likeliest candidates for membership were instructed over a course of months. "Most of those who seemed hopefully converted spent several months at the central station before their union with the church. Here they were watched over and instructed from week to week and from day to day, with anxious and unceasing care. They were sifted and re-sifted with scrutiny, and with every effort to take the precious from the vile. The church and the world, friends and enemies, were called upon and

---

143. Coan, *Memorial Volume*, 50. NB: Some other Coan to Lyons correspondence is found in the HMH library.

144. Fourteen miles north of Hilo.

145. Bold and italics in Daws's text.

146. Daws, "Evangelism," 28. Titus to Fidelia Coan, March 11, 1838, in HMH.

solemnly charged to testify, without concealment or palliation, if they knew aught against any of the candidates."[147]

Once someone became a member he used another book. He explains his process in his autobiography: "In order to keep every member under my eye, and to find ready access to each, I prepared a book ruled thus . . ."[148]

In the table there are eight sections with words typed at 90 degrees to the horizontal. In order they are: "Date, Name, Residence, Dismissed by Letter, Received by Letter, Excommunicated, Died, Children Baptized." In the example he provides, Coan writes the following under each section: "1838. July 1 Sept. 2 1837; Kapule . . . Lonoakeawe[149]; Waiakea . . . [Waikea]; [Lonoakeawe?]; To Hana, June 1840; [no received by letter]; [no excommunication]; [Kapule died] Mar. 1841; Abenera, Joane."[150]

He provides statistics through 1880. For now, here are the numbers from a quarter through 1838 followed by the complete years of 1839, and 1840:

"Number received during year ending April 30, 1838,[151] 639[152]

" " " " " " " 1839, 5,244

" " " " " " " 1840, 1,499"

By comparison, 2,348 were admitted as members between 1841 and 1850. Well over half of the members received through 1880 were brought in during three years listed above.[153]

"DAY OF DAYS": BAPTISM OF 1,705

From his pocket list "of about three thousand, 1,705 were selected to be baptized and received to the communion of the church on the first Sabbath of July, 1838."[154] Coan discusses why this selection was made. "The selection was made, not because a thousand and more of others were to be rejected, or that a large proportion of them did not appear as well as those received, but because the numbers were too large for our faith, and might stagger the faith of others. The admission of many was deferred for the

---

147. Coan, *Life*, 54–55.

148. In the Coan-Levin digitized autobiography at this point it says "table," while the Rapoza version has something else.

149. Wife of Kapule? Coan notes that by "simple signs males and females were distinguished. This is important here, because the same name is often used interchangeably for the sexes." Coan, *Life*, 58.

150. Coan, *Life*, 57.

151. Cutoff date for annual station report. "At this period the ecclesiastical year of the mission began on the first of May. The reports of the churches were made up to the thirtieth of April, 1838." He draws from "the records of Hilo church." Coan, *Life*, 57.

152. Cf Daws, "Evangelism," 29. In the reporting year ending April 31, 1838, "Coan admitted 639 members and Lyons 2,600. Their two stations together accounted for 32,239 of 4,390 admissions for the year 1837–1838."

153. Coan, *Life*, 57.

154. July 1.

more full development of their character, while they were to be watched over, guided, and fed as sheep of the Great Shepherd" [John 10:14].

Coan explains that the people to be baptized had been gathered before July 1. "The 1,705 persons selected had all been gathered at the station some time before the day appointed for their reception." Sounding a bit like the ordering of the Israelites (Num 1), Coan notes that they "had been divided into classes, according to the villages whence they came, and put in charge of class leaders, who were instructed to watch over and teach them."

He comments on the beautiful weather of the day. "The memorable morning came arrayed in glory. A purer sky, a brighter sun, a serener atmosphere, a more silvery sea, and a more brilliant and charming landscape could not be desired. The very heavens over us and the earth around us seemed to smile."

Reverting to Old Testament descriptions again, Coan relates the gathering of the candidates for baptism. "The hour came; during the time of preparation the house [of worship] was kept clear of all but the actors. With the roll in hand, the leaders of the classes were called in with their companies of candidates in the order of all the villages; first of Hilo district, then of Puna, and last of Kau." Sounding now almost like a graduation ceremony and the handing out of diplomas, Coan writes, "From my roll the names in the first class were called one by one, and I saw each individual seated against the wall, and so of the second, and thus on until the first row was formed. Thus, row after row was extended the whole length of the house, leaving spaces for one to pass between these lines. After every name had been called, and every individual recognized and seated, all the former members of the church were called in and seated on the opposite side of the building, and the remaining space given to as many as could be seated."

Coan moves to a description of the baptism ceremony itself. Showing vestiges of his being a Presbyterian and doing everything decently and in order,[155] he relates, "All being thus prepared, we had singing and prayer, then a word of explanation on the rite of baptism, with exhortation. After this with a basin of water, I passed back and forth between the lines, sprinkling[156] each individual[157] until all were baptized. Standing in the center of the congregation of the baptized, I pronounced the words, 'I baptize you all into the name of the Father, and of the Son, and of the Holy Ghost[Matt 28:19]. Amen.'"

---

155. Acts 20:7. NB: Author's observation, not Coan's.

156. Showing his Presbyterian colors, Coan sprinkles the ones being baptized. One might also wonder at the ability of one pastor to immerse that many individuals in one day! Everyone wanted to be baptized by Titus Coan. Elsewhere he indicates that a deep-enough body of water is not always at hand. That argument seems a bit thin, given that the ocean was never far away, especially from Hilo. Perhaps modesty and his back were other reasons.

157. With a brush.

Coan shares the emotional feel of the occasion. "The scene was one of solemn and tender interest, surpassing anything of the kind I had ever witnessed. All heads were bowed, and tears fell. All was hushed except sobs and breathing."

Coan's journal entries significantly fall off during this period of 1838. All he wrote that day was, "This day I baptized and received to the Ch. at Hilo 1,705 individuals. A great and solemn day."[158]

Next came communion. "The nature of the Lord's Supper and the reasons for its observance were then explained, and the bread and cup distributed among the communicants." He concludes his reflections on that day by remembering and bringing it to the time of his writing his autobiography. "This was a day long to be remembered. Its impressions were deep, tender, and abiding; and up to the present time, the surviving veterans of that period look back to it as the *day of days* in the history of the Hilo church."[159]

Comparing his father's baptism of four hundred Hawaiians at the Ewa station, S. E. Bishop relates Coan's day of baptisms and baptisms throughout the year in the following way. Entitled "BAPTIZING WITH A BRUSH," Bishop writes of his father's baptisms that the "ordinance was deeply impressive, and was witnessed by six thousand people from Aianae and Ewa. In his parish of Hilo, the Rev. Titus Coan used much less ceremony in administering baptism to over five thousand persons in one year, and to twelve [sic] hundred at a single service. He sprinkled each group with a brush as a whole, without calling off their individual names."[160] Bishop does allow that it "might have been impossible to reach the whole twelve hundred by another method." Then Bishop asks a rhetorical indirect question based on Acts 2:39: "How the twelve apostles and their helpers baptized three thousand disciples on the day of Pentecost we are not told."[161]

The *Memorial Volume* has a letter from Coan to Lyons that speaks of the July 1 baptism Sabbath in the past tense.[162] Coan pushes the narrative forward by relating the baptisms of the children of the adults who were baptized.[163] "Sabbath was a glorious day here. I baptized and received seventeen hundred and five to this church. Yesterday I spent the afternoon in baptizing the children of the church, several hundreds[164] in number." He also relates the spiritual movement within people from around his area.

---

158. Coan journal entry, July 1, 1838, LOC Box 1.

159. Coan, *Life*, 54–57.

160. See where Coan calls out each name at one point.

161. Bishop, *Reminiscences*, 54.

162. Probably Tuesday, July 3, because he baptized the children on Monday the second. See reference to "yesterday" in letter.

163. Again Coan shows his Presbyterian beliefs. Instead of dedicating the children to the Lord as done in baptistic circles, he baptizes children and infants.

164. See Coan journal entry, July 2, 1838, LOC: "Today baptised 500 children of the church."

The Great Awakening

'Sinners are coming in from Kau and all parts of Hilo and Puna, and hardened rebels are constantly breaking down. Some fall, but God's work does not fall to the ground.'[165]

Leavitt Hallock summarizes the "day of days" in the following manner, looking back to his 1878 visit with Titus Coan. "The conch-shell would call together from four to six thousand hearers, and for two full years these faithful men preached three times each day to vast and eager throngs. It was not idle hearing: the first Sunday in July, 1838, was a glad day in Hilo: seventeen hundred and five converted men and women whose evidence of intelligent faith could not be doubted, the pick of many, were gathered and seated in rows on the grass, surrounded by a multitude of interested spectators. The missionaries read to them a simple creed, vic.: 'You do now truly and earnestly repent of your sins and steadfastly purpose to lead new lives in Christ Jesus?' To this they solemnly assented; these godly men then passed forth and back between the long rows of devout disciples, sprinkled each bowed head with water and said, amid the perfect but tearful silence, 'I baptize you all in the name of the Father and of the Son and of the Holy Ghost, Amen!' and then the Holy Communion was administered, within sight of the distant volcano, to twenty-four hundred Christian communicants! Pentecost [Acts 2] indeed!"[166]

This revival, this Great Awakening, would spread like wildfire throughout the Hawaiian Islands. And, as is often the case with revivals, controversy developed, which Coan and others would answer. There would be conflict, denouement, and vindication.

---

165. Coan to Lyons, July 3 [sic?], 1838, in Coan, *Memorial Volume*, 46.

166. Hallock, *Hawaii under King Kalakaua*.

6

The Great Awakening, Part 2
Islands-Wide; Controversy; Coming About; and Conclusion

THE REVIVAL THROUGHOUT THE ISLANDS

COAN WRITES ABOUT THE spread of the revival through the island chain. The "other islands of the group . . . were moved. Reporting and inquiring letters circulated from post to post, and from island to island."[1]

Bishop notes that the "revival spread like a fire from island to island, enveloping the whole people. It was a veritable national Pentecost, in which hundreds and thousands every week were converted to Christ, with intense manifestations of feeling."[2] A mission letter notes that the "past year has been one of uncommon interest throughout all the Sandwich Islands."[3]

Sereno Bishop, after writing about Hilo and the Big Island, broadens the lens to include all the islands. "The wonderful work became general *through all parts of the Islands*[4] . . . [A]ll of the churches and stations felt the power in a marvelous and pervasive degree."[5]

Bishop[6] writes about revival from the perspective of an eleven-year-old. "The present writer, then a lad of eleven, vividly recalls the immense and deeply moved congregations at his father's station at Ewa, and what seemed a supernatural power in

---

1. Coan, *Life*, 48.
2. Bishop, *Reminiscences*, 54.
3. June 4, 1838, Mission letter in Gulick et al., *Pilgrims*, 162.
4. Bishop emphasis.
5. Gulick et al., *Pilgrims*, np.
6. See Forbes et al., *Partners in Change*, 133–35.

the preacher's tones. He witnessed the baptism there of FOUR HUNDRED converts in the presence of six thousand people assembled under a vast alanai [sic]."[7]

Bishop provides further observations. "To enter deeply into the tremendous tide of feeling which enveloped and uplifted the whole nation for many months was not possible at my age of eleven, with my nearly entire ignorance of the native language. There was a great multiplication of religious meetings, attended by enormous congregations. Our great church on the hill would hold one thousand people, with four hundred more standing in the encircling verandas. It finally became necessary to cover the north side of the church yard with a lanai, which would seat six thousand people. On several occasions this space was well filled, the preacher standing near the church door, so as to be heard by those sitting inside of the church."[8]

Bishop continues relating what occurred in Ewa.[9] "One Sunday morning, before the removal to outdoors, an impression still vivid was made on my mind by a strange intensity of tone, and exaltation of feeling in my father in his pulpit. Ordinarily he had no forcible eloquence, his usual manner being rather mild and colloquial. On this occasion, he was entirely carried out of himself, and spoke in an impassioned strain of intense fervor, finally calling out in a strange tone to the crowd of sensual sinners before him, 'U'oki! U'oki!' (Stop! Stop!)'"

Bishop next moves on to apply a two-word phrase to his father. He would use it for himself, as well as Titus Coan, and other preachers. The phrase is "divine afflatus." The preceding paragraph already provides something of what Bishop means by the phrase. "Afflatus" can be defined as "a divine creative impulse or inspiration,"[10] so in this case it has to do with divine inspiration—literally "inbreathing" by God.

Referring to his father, Artemas Bishop, Sereno writes, "I have always felt that he was for the time a veritable prophet, uplifted above his human capacity by a supernatural inspiration. I have many times afterwards witnessed such a divine afflatus taking possession of preachers in times of revival, when the Holy Spirit was present in great power. At similar times it had been my own experience to be in the same way uplifted quite out of my usually inefficient delivery, and to be swept forward upon a divine tide which seized upon hearers and preacher alike. The supernatural and divine character of the phenomenon is a matter of personal conviction and certainty."[11]

Bishop relates the specifics of a mass baptism by his father. "A very notable incident of those days was my father's administration of baptism to four hundred converts on one Sabbath morning, the ordinance occupying two hours' time. Each

---

7. Forbes et al., *Partners in Change*, 133–35.

8. Bishop, *Reminiscences*, 53.

9. Artemas and Della Bishop served in Ewa from 1836 until 1856, when they moved to not far from Kawaiaha'o Church. Judd, *Missionary Album*, 46. For these two Bishops, see Forbes et al., *Partners in Change*, 125–31.

10. Oxford Dictionaries, "Afflatus."

11. Bishop, *Reminiscences*, 53–54.

person received a Christian baptismal name,[12] attended by the application of water to the forehead. There had been a thorough preliminary organization of the four hundred people into groups occupying a large space in the great lanai. The pastor moved among them with an attendant deacon carrying the font, a sponge being in the minister's hand. When he approached a group, they knelt down before him. Taking the prepared list, he named them in succession, applying the wet sponge to the forehead of each person when named, thus: 'John, Zebedee, Martha, Timothy, Dorcas, etc., I baptize you all (oukou apau) into the name, etc.' Generally each convert had selected a Bible name for himself, the pastor correcting any injudicious choice, such as Iscariot, or Herodias, or Beelzebub."[13]

Rufus Anderson presents Richard Armstrong[14] as a typical missionary during the Great Awakening. Armstrong "resorted to no special measures, except calling upon those who had chosen Christ to separate themselves, that they might be instructed in classes and carefully watched over, so as to learn what manner of spirit they were of."[15]

Anderson admitted, however, that while "it is true that at most of the stations there were no special efforts to excite the feelings, aside from plain, simple preaching, it was to be expected that there would be some exceptions among so many laborers, and at a time of so great interest."[16]

Sheldon Dibble[17]—an Auburn seminary graduate and one who had come to Hawaiʻi as a Board missionary during the Great Awakening—gave no names or places, yet he described special measures used by the "preaching of some. The pastor, in some instances, descended from the pulpit, and passed through the midst of the congregation, preaching and gesticulating with intense emotion. Sometimes all the members of a large congregation were permitted to pray aloud at once. And again, at times, many expressed their fears and sense of guilt by audible groans and loud cries."[18]

Dibble did admit that the special measures used by a few "were not probably so much designed, as naturally incident to a kind of uncontrollable state of tumultuous feeling, both on the part of the pastor and people."[19]

---

12. See Corr, *"Field Is the World,"* discussion of such naming in Sri Lanka.

13. Bishop, *Reminiscences*, 54.

14. He and his wife Clarissa Chapman were posted in Wailuku, Maui, during the Great Awakening years. *Missionary Album*, 30–31; and Forbes et al., *Partners in Change*, 73–80.

15. Anderson, *Heathen Nation*, in Corr, *"Field Is the World,"* 78.

16. Anderson, *Heathen Nation*, 143, in Corr, *"Field Is the World,"* 78.

17. As far as the Great Awakening years ago, Sheldon Dibble served in Lahainaluna, Maui, during 1836 and 1837 and returned to Lahainaluna in 1840. His wife, Maria Tomlinson, died in 1837. He married Antoinette Tomlinson, a relative of Maria, in 1839. Judd, *Missionary Album*, 78–79; and Forbes et al., *Partners in Change*, 212–17.

18. Dibble, *History*, 348, in Anderson, *Heathen Nation*, 143, in Corr, *"Field Is the World,"* 79.

19. Dibble, *History*, 348, in Anderson, *Heathen Nation*, 143, in Corr, *"Field Is the World,"* 79.

Hawley provides both a description of the Islands' wide awakening, as well as some statistics. "In the years 1836 to 1839 occurred what is known in Hawaii as the 'great religious awakening'; during the period the Hawaiian people changed from a heathen to a Christian nation." He continues with statistics. "The number of persons attending religious worship in some of the churches were as large as six thousand at a service . . . During the previous years the annual number of additions was about one thousand . . . At this period the congregations were often immense, at Ewa numbering four thousand, at Honolulu two congregations of twenty-five hundred each, and at Lahaina two thousand . . . Hilo had a congregation of five thousand, and in 1841 Rev. Titus Coan stated his church[20] numbered over seven thousand persons."[21]

Andelucia Conde wrote from Lahaina, Maui, of her hopes and prayers for revival. "O that a spirit of believing prayer might descend upon us all, until we should take *strong hold* upon the promises, and bring down a great blessing upon all this people."[22] Richard Armstrong writes from Wailuku, Maui, of protracted meetings. From January of 1838 "till May first I attended more than twelve meetings a week, besides almost constant conversation with individuals in private.'" He also writes that my "public labors during the past year have been more abundant than they have [been] any previous year of my missionary life.'"[23] Dwight Baldwin notes that "our congregations had increased in size before the protracted meeting. The house was almost always crowded to excess. Probably two thousand were generally present."[24]

William P. Alexander[25] writes from Kauai in 1838. "The showers of blessings which have been refreshing the garden of the Lord in these islands of the sea [Isa 24:15] have not been withheld from our field. I have never before witnessed among the people so earnest an attention to the means of grace and so deep concern for the salvation of the soul."[26]

In his book on "Blind Bartimeus,"[27] Jonathan Green[28] writes about the Great Awakening coming to the Wailuku area of Maui. "Near the close of 1837, it became evident to us who were watching the signs of the times[29] [Matt 16:2–3], and who had long been praying 'O Lord, revive thy work in the midst of the years' [Hab 3:2], that

---

20. Membership?

21. Hawley, *Introduction to Christianity*, 33.

22. Andelucia Conde to Fidelia Coan, December 8, 1837, LOC, in Ehlke, "Enthusiastic Religion," 114.

23. Armstrong letter, August 4, 1838, in Gulick et al., *Pilgrims*, 163.

24. Baldwin, in Gulick et al., *Pilgrims*, 165.

25. Judd, *Missionary Album*, 18–20 and Forbes et al., *Partners in Change*, 51–56.

26. Alexander letter, August 25, 1838, in Gulick et al., *Pilgrims*, 164.

27. Puaʻaiki.

28. Judd, *Missionary Album*, 104–05; and Forbes et al., *Partners in Change*, 278–82.

29. Reference to eschatology in the Gospels?

the gracious influences of the Holy Spirit were about to descend upon the congregation at Wailuku."

He continues with generalized statistics, the response of the people, and descriptions of the work of the Holy Spirit. "The members of the church, at that time few, awoke to a sense of their deficiencies of Christian character. They humbly besought God to pardon their sins for Christ's sake. They implored the gracious agency of the Holy Spirit, that, created wholly anew, they might henceforth live devoted to God. With many tears they confessed their faults one with another, and prayed one for another that they might be healed. God heard the prayer of his people, graciously pardoned them, and granted them the joy of his salvation" [Ps 51:12].

Bartimeus feels conviction of his own sin and grows even more passionate for the spiritual well-being of others. "Among the members of the church, no one seemed more deeply penitent than Bartimeus;[30] the most deeply penitent of all the people—no one more importunate in seeking for mercy on his own behalf, and on behalf of his brethren." Bartimeus "with some others in the church awoke to a deeper concern than before for the impenitent." Bartimeus and others "wrestled in prayer with God in behalf of sinners, blind to a sense of their guilt and danger, and deaf alike to the calls of mercy, and the thunders of the law—'dead in trespasses and sin' [Eph 2:1] and sinking rapidly to perdition."

Bartimeus and others "became more active also in efforts for the salvation of these dying men." When "during most of the year of 1838, the Spirit of God moved upon the mass of the population; and caused multitudes to bow to the scepter of the Son of God, the heart of the good old man seemed to overflow with joy. He poured out the emotions of his soul in language[31] not easily described. None but those who saw him during some of those interesting scenes can conceive the appearance of our friend. And yet no one that saw that glory—that index of unearthly joy, can cease to retain an effecting impression of it."

Green continues, "Often have I thought when seeing him seemingly laboring under the weight of holy emotion, of good old Simeon when he exclaimed, 'Lord, now lettest thou thy servant depart in peace,[32] according to thy word: for mine eyes have seen thy salvation'" [Luke 2:20].

Green notes the increase for a desire of instruction in the Lord. "In consequence of the outpouring of the Holy Spirit upon the people of Wailuku and vicinity, the desire for instruction in the word of God greatly increased." Protracted meetings were one answer to Green's rhetorical question as to how such instruction could be "met and gratified." These took place in the Wailuku area. As was the case with Hilo and the

---

30. Bartimeus had labored for the Lord's Kingdom since his conversion during the early days of the ABCFM missionaries in the Hawaiian Islands. See Pre-Great Awakening chapter, for his service in Hilo prior to returning to Maui.

31. Speaking in tongues?

32. *Nunc dimittis.*

surrounding districts, Wailuku became the gathering place for revival. "What ever the strength of the regularly constituted watchmen at Wailuku allowed them to do, they cheerfully attempted. Protracted meetings were held at [M.], at Kula, and at Honaaula. The people moreover from all these places frequently resorted to the station at Wailuku to listen to the messages of the Savior's mercy."

By the end of 1837, clear signs were seen of the Great Awakening. Bartimeus and others increased their prayers and became "more active in efforts for the salvation of these dying men." By 1838, a great increase was observed in the desire for instruction in the word of God. The missionaries Green and Armstrong selected "a class of our most devoted and talented church members, and taught them with a special reference to their being readers and exhorters at our out stations." Most of the men in the class were between the ages of thirty and fifty; most were "of very humble attainments" in economic and educational terms. The missionaries taught the class to read the Bible, removed difficulties in Genesis, read the gospels "after the manner of Newcomb's Harmony," discussed the "Elements of Moral Science," church history, and theology. Despite his inability to see to read, Bartimeus "was a prominent member of this class. He had indeed been regarded for many years, as in *fact*, though not in *law*, an Evangelist, yet no member of the church seemed so sensibly to feel the need of instruction as he—no one eagerly drank it in from our lips. He has been better qualified, as a matter of course, than any other individual of the class, and his labors have been more abundant, acceptable, and success[ful]."[33]

At a protracted meeting in Honolulu, Bartimeus spoke about a misunderstanding over repentance, conversion, and membership. In the audience, Bingham "heard Bartimeus, in an able plea, urge on his countrymen the duty of immediate repentance, and the practicability of instantaneous conversion."[34]

Bingham continues by relating that Bartimeus presented for Scriptural warrant on this matter the story in Luke 19:1–10 of Zacchaeus and Acts 16:25–40 of the Philippian jailer, responding to those who believed that a "considerable time" was requisite to pass through all the stages of conversion.[35]

From the nearby island of Molokai, Harvey Hitchcock[36] writes from Kaluaaha of Hawaiian Christians making an interesting discovery in a rural area of the island. Several "of the native brethren were sent out to the outstations to converse with the

---

33. Green, *Notices*, 21–23, in Corr, "Field Is the World," 159–60.

34. Bingham, *Residence*, 528, in Corr, "Field Is the World," 161. Footnote on same Corr page: "Finney had much to say about the need for 'instant submission,' the reality and necessity of immediate conversion, and the usual procedure of admitting applicants to church membership 'when they apply.'" See Rosell et al., *Memoirs of Charles Finney*, 321 and 570; and Finney, *Holy Spirit Revivals*, 353–54 and 389–90.

35. Bingham, *Residence*, 528.

36. Forbes et al., *Partners in Change*, 306–10.

people and they were astonished to find that the Lord had preceded them and had inclined the hearts of many to attend to his word."[37]

When it comes to Honolulu and the broader revival, Hiram Bingham notes that those "of us who have seemed to think the gospel could hardly gain a lodgment in the heart of this people . . . are now constrained to admit that they can be as readily affected by the Spirit of God as any class of men with whom we have been acquainted."[38]

"'Blessed news! More than twelve hundred converts in Honolulu. Blessed work. Blessed Savior. Blessed reward. I predict that this whole nation is about to be shaken.'"[39] Two months later Hiram Bingham wrote that the "protracted meeting here about the time of Nahienaeana's funeral appears to have been crowned with many fruits."[40] In late 1839, Juliette Cooke in Honolulu wrote Fidelia Coan "that they were expecting a protracted meeting in Mr. Bingham's congregation next week. 'Pray that the Holy Spirit may come down. Oh how much does this polluted city need its reviving influences. How I wish Mr. Coan would be present but we must look away from the help of men.'"[41]

Sereno Bishop makes a sweeping comment about the great revival and its implications for the Hawaiian Islands. "This great revival was the spiritual birth of the Hawaiian people. It truly regenerated them into a Christian nation from being in a large degree a heathen one. The whole mass of the people became permeated with a vital sense of the reality of Christ's Kingdom and of the heavenly power of his gospel. This great moral and spiritual renovation which changed and elevated their prevailing sentiments so as to render the nation capable of begetting and cherishing the vast civil reforms which followed in the next decade."[42]

Before writing about a protracted meeting, Titus Coan delivered a sermonic peroration with the theme "God was there" that summed up the all-encompassing nature of the work of God in the Great Awakening. "The presence of the spirit was indicated by the fixed eye, the gushing tear, the quivering lip, the deep sigh, and the heavy groan, God was there and the people were moved at the presence of the Lord of the whole earth. God was there. His power was felt. His arm was seen. His voice was heard [Rev 21:3]. His thunders [Ps 29:3–4] shook the hosts of hell. God was there and none but a sleeper could fail to see it—none but an infidel could deny it."[43]

---

37. Hitchcock letter, November 1838, in Gulick et al., *Pilgrims*, 168.

38. Bingham letter, April 26, 1838, in Gulick et al., *Pilgrims*, 171.

39. Coan to Lyons, February 13, 1838, in Coan, *Memorial Volume*, 45.

40. Bingham letter, April 26, 1838, in Gulick et al., *Pilgrims*, 171. "Harriet or Harrieta Keopuolani Nahienaena was a high-ranking princess during the founding of the Kingdom of Hawaii and the conversion of its royalty to Christianity." Wikipedia, "Nahienaena."

41. Juliette Cook to Fidelia Coan, October 4, 1838, LOC, in Ehlke, "Enthusiastic Religion," 114.

42. Corr, "Coan Chronicles," 83–84.

43. Coan letter in Gulick et al., *Pilgrims*, 172.

The Great Awakening, Part 2

OPPOSITION AND RESPONSE

Titus Coan wrote to Lorenzo Lyons that the greatest threat to revival was not an external threat, but that which comes from within. "You say there will be noise where there is fighting and conquering. This is true, and there will be much noise before the world is converted to God. But I have little fear of the noise of praying Christians and wailing sinners, if so be the wailing is confined to time. In eternity it will roll up fearful and augmenting notes forever and ever. *The most dangerous noise in a revival springs up*, not, perhaps, from the devil, nor from scoffers and open opposers, but *from false or timid, or dictatorial friends*.[44] I feel sure of this fact, and the whole history of the church presents an array of proof to this position."[45]

"The conservative attack on Coan and Lyons concerned two main questions: the means used to produce so-called conversions, and the speed with which converts were admitted to church membership."[46]

"Coan was convinced from the very beginning that the revival was a valid and glorious work of the Spirit. He affirmed the value of physical manifestations. 'Whatever others may say, *I* know and feel that such cries are tokens of the Spirit.'"[47]

Daws notes that the controversy "concerned two main questions: the means used to produce so-called conversions, and the speed with which converts were admitted to church membership." Daws documents unease by some missionaries with outward manifestations. "Sheldon Dibble, writing just a few years after the subsidence of the initial excitement, spoke of pastors whose 'excited minds' and 'peculiar views' led them to use 'special measures to operate upon the feelings of a congregation.' Praying aloud by members of the audience, audible groans and loud cries, shrieks and lamentations, were part of a pattern of dubious special measures operating in an 'uncontrollable state of tumultuous feeling.'"[48]

Dr. Baldwin in Lahaina writes of his ambivalent views on the matter of emotional expressions and faith. The station at Lahaina "had been among the earliest to experience revival symptoms, [and] made a clear distinction between outward signs and inward feeling." By August 1838, he noted, initial excitement had died down. "There was less running to the mountains and bushes to pray, but the 'real feeling' had not diminished. A protracted meeting in September 1838 produced a great deal of 'public exercise,' but he found himself unable to tell what good had come of it."[49]

On the subject of hasty admissions, see Coan's discussion of taking up to a year to admit Hawaiians as members of the church. Note his little book where he keeps track

44. Emphasis added.
45. Coan to Lyons, March 10, 1839, in Coan, *Memorial Volume*, 49.
46. Daws, "Evangelism," 28.
47. Daws, "Evangelism," 28. 34n22, Titus to Fidelia Coan, December 14, 1839, HMH.
48. Dibble, *History*, 348–49, in Daws, "Evangelism," 28. For short Dibble biography, see Judd, *Missionary Album*, 78–79.
49. Baldwin to Levi Chamberlain, August 6, 1838, HMH, in Daws, "Evangelism," 28.

of possible members. Regarding the baptism of 1,705 on one Sunday, as quoted above Coan indicates that more were not baptized "because the numbers were too large for our faith, and might stagger the faith of others."[50]

He also writes that some "said that the Hawaiians were a peculiar people, and very hypocritical, so debased in mind and heart that they could not receive any true conception of the true God, or of spiritual things; even their language was wanting in terms to convey ideas of sacred truth; we must not hope for evangelical conversions among them. But most of the laborers redoubled their efforts, were earnest in prayer, and worked on in faith. Everywhere the trumpet of jubilee sounded long and loud [Lev 25:8–10], and 'as clouds and as doves to their windows' [Isa 60:8] so ransomed sinners flocked to Christ."[51]

"Coan found ample justification for his policies in the urgency of the situation in the islands. He felt strongly that to leave people outside the protection of the church in the name of caution was to abandon them to 'wander in darkness, uncertain as to their own character, exposed to every temptation of earth and hell, unknown and unrecognized as the sheep and lambs of the Lord Jesus, and in danger from the all-devouring lion'" [1 Pet 5:8].[52]

In a January 29, 1838, letter to Lorenzo Lyons, Coan sets out their agreement on the church membership admission process, as well as explaining the specifics of his procedures. "On the subject of receiving converts soon into the church, you and I probably agree. There is neither Scripture nor philosophy, nor prudence, in the opposite practice. I mean when we get good evidence of conversion.[53] I avail myself of every help to learn the life of every one of the candidates, inquiring into the private and domestic habits of each individual, receiving no man simply on his own profession of love to Christ. I show the lists to Brother Lyman. If he knows anything good or bad of any one, he tells it. After this I call all these candidates together and examine them individually in my own house. If they appear well I invite them to the church meeting, and there they are again examined before the whole church."[54]

Near the end of 1838, in the midst of a letter he notes the "voice of agonizing prayer breaks the stillness of the evening on every hand. Let envy and malice sneer, let skepticism cavil, let cold prudence caution, and let timidity tremble. Still the work

---

50. Coan, *Life*, 55.

51. Coan, *Life*, 48–49.

52. Daws, "Evangelism," 30. 34n29, Coan in *1840 Annual Report of the American Board of Commissioners for Foreign Missions*.

53. One wonders why Coan apparently never cited Acts 8, wherein Philip is guided to the Ethiopian treasurer in his southbound chariot. Philip explains how a passage from Isaiah speaks of the death of Christ, leading the Ethiopian to ask, "There is water. What prohibits me from being baptized?" This took place within the course of a day and, as it is Holy Writ, would never be challenged by the American Board administrators or the negative ABCFM missionaries in Hawai'i.

54. Coan to Lyons, January 29, 1838, in Coan, *Memorial Volume*, 44–45.

goes on. To God only wise [Ps 150:6; Rom 16:27; Jude 1:25] be the glory. My lips shall praise him, my soul shall bless him" [Ps 63:4].[55]

He writes sharply about an unnamed "Brother," probably meaning a fellow missionary on the Islands, who reproves and remonstrates him for the measures he takes in his ministry. "Brother ——— writes me strong reproofs and remonstrances about measures, etc. I know that I am ignorant and foolish. Oh, that some of these kind and anxious brethren would show me 'a more excellent way'"[1 Cor 12:31b].[56]

While providing helpful information on the probationary period for membership candidates, Sereno Bishop is, at best, misinformed about Coan's methods of preparing potential members. "It had always been the practice of the missionaries in Hawaii to enforce a probation of six months upon candidates for membership in the church, before their admission by the rite of Baptism. During that probation, they were known as 'poe Hooikaika,' or strivers. Usually many of them would fail to stand fast through the six months without lapsing into the prevailing sin of [unchastity?]. During this Awakening my father, like most of his brethren, did not deviate from the old rule as to probation. I believe that Mr. Coan and Mr. Lyons baptized their converts very promptly, and experienced much falling away in consequence. The records show that these two ardent souls baptized as many converts as all the rest of the missionaries together. For a whole generation those two churches of Hilo and Waimea held precedence among the Hawaiian churches in strength and activity."[57] Bishop appears to contradict himself by inveighing against Coan and Lyons's probationary practices, then concluding with the observation that those two missionaries had the strongest and most active congregations in the entire island chain.

Titus writes his wife from the center of the action on May 10, 1838. "My dear Fidelia, my wife, my earthly all.

"The general letter of Mr. Anderson has occupied most of our time as yet. When we shall get through with it is not certain. It contains more than one hundred pages. It is on the whole written temperately, tho it throws blame on the mission. It seems evident that the prudential committee intend to keep the ground they have taken in regard to us. Some of the brethren feel strongly, tho we have kept pretty cool as yet. How we shall get on with *unhappy controversy*[58] I don't know. The Lord help us out of it soon, or it will kill our souls. Revivals and internal interests are forgotten and our conflict with the board is the all engrossing topic of our conversation. *They have not begun to handle me as a heretic.*[59] What will they do when they get through with the foreign war[60] I know not. I feel strong and hold for God."

---

55. Coan to Lyons, November 6, 1838, in Coan, *Memorial Volume*, 47.
56. Meaning the way of love. Coan to Lyons, November 6, 1838, in Coan, *Memorial Volume*, 48.
57. Bishop, *Reminiscences*, 55.
58. Emphasis added.
59. Emphasis added.
60. French v Hawaiʻi? US War? Board v Missionaries?

After a discussion of the financial side of things, Coan continues. "The general letter may be printed before the meeting closes. If so I shall take a copy to Hilo. Mr. Anderson rejoices in the work of God at the islands, but says he dare not tell it in the monthly concert! He warns us against hasty admissions, and advises us to go back to the good old way! *Auwe! Auwe!* [Alas? See below.] He says that our proceeding[s have] already awakened fears, and called forth severe remarks from some of their most judicious men! And furthermore he says that the board will no longer be able to appeal to the members in our churches as an evidence of the prayers of Christianity among the people etc.! Alas! Alas! 'By whom shall Jacob arise?' [Amos 7:5] I could say much on this subject [he already has!], but time forbids. I could demonstrate the weakness and folly of such reasoning [now waxing rhetorical!]. I could show that even our fathers and patrons at the [mission] rooms [in Boston] have not faith as a grain of mustard seed [Matt 17:20] in the conversion of the heathen. They professedly devote their powers to the immediate salvation of the world, and yet they plainly declare that they do not expect this result, and if it be announced to them as already in progress, they coolly and decidedly make up their minds not to believe it, and that before they have heard the evidence in the case! This is just what I expected from the Rooms. They do not mention Hilo, but they speak of hasty admissions into one or two churches at Hawaii, and say that our course is at variance with sound Christian discretion etc. 'Cease ye from man' [Isa 2:22].

"I want to write a pastoral letter to the church and people at Hilo, but cannot at this time. Hope to [at] the next opportunity."[61]

The above Coan letter is dated May 1838. Apparently the controversy did continue into 1839 and 1840. According to Ehlke,[62] Fidelia Coan was encouraged by a letter to Titus from Levi Chamberlain in November of 1839. "Yet Mr. Chamberlain had already reported to Dr. Rufus Anderson that 'many of the brethren think [Coan] admits professed converts to baptism and church membership on too slight evidence of conversion;[63] and they are afraid there will eventually be a great falling away.'[64] Yet, Chamberlain assured the Secretary of the American Board that 'Br. Coan is full of faith and is abundant in labors.'"[65]

In early 1838, Lyons "agreed with Coan on all points relating to membership . . . He insisted on his right to follow his own observations and experience. Though everybody else were against me—I have the Bible on my side."[66]

---

61. Titus Coan to Fidelia. HMH digitized correspondence to and from 0005 Part 4, pages 4 and 5.

62. Ehlke, "Enthusiastic Religion," 119.

63. See previous chapter, wherein Coan notes how he interviewed others regarding the character of each candidate for baptism and membership.

64. Chamberlain to Anderson, February 7, 1839, HMH, in Ehlke, "Enthusiastic Religion," 119.

65. Chamberlain, in Ehlke, "Enthusiastic Religion," 119.

66. Daws, "Evangelism," 31. 34n31, Lyons to Chamberlain, January 17, 1838, HMH.

Lyons differed from Coan in one important respect. Daws finally admits that "Coan had an elaborate follow-up system worked out for keeping a check on his converts and new members. His sense of personal responsibility for his parishioners was not shared by Lyons, who tended to abdicate in favor of God once he had brought sinners into the church. Lyons had a tendency toward millenniumism,[67] and one expression of this was that he could be less deeply concerned than Coan about attacks on his methods. He bristled, to be sure, but fell back on the defense that the final truth was not for him or anyone else to know. He could only use his judgment, until he was proved right on 'the last day . . . To which we are all rapidly hastening.'"[68]

Daws provides excellent analysis when he distinguishes between Lyons and Coan. "If the history of the Waimea church seemed to prove the conservative point completely, Hilo refuted it. Coan's great congregations continued into the early forties,[69] and his losses over less propitious periods were not appreciably greater, proportionately speaking, than those of stations where conservative ministers worked."[70]

Ehlke continues: "Dr. Anderson added his own words of caution after reading the General Letter of 1838 from the Sandwich Islands Mission and the accounts of the revivals sent in by the individual missionaries. Although relieved that the cutback of funds for the Mission, occasioned by the 1837 financial crisis in the United States, had not impaired the progress of missionary labor, Anderson was reluctant to relay the information concerning the large number of converts to supporters in Boston.[71] '[T]he intelligence of the early and extensive admissions into one or two of the churches on Hawaii would exceedingly alarm the fears of our most judicious and best friends. Indeed I have some painful apprehensions myself.'[72] Anderson told them frankly that their practice 'of admitting converts so speedily and on such slight evidence' would make it impossible for the ABCFM to look at numbers received into the churches as evidence of progress. He closed with the suggestion that they 'revert again to the more cautious policy of former times.'"[73]

Lorenzo Lyons was "astonished at this rebuke, questioning the reasons for such actions." Ehlke relates Anderson's response to Lyons's letter. "I know you felt as if you must write in haste; but it was unquestionably due to a work of such a nature which

---

67. Belief in the Christian doctrine of the millennium. The word is found in Revelation 20. See discussion of eschatology in Corr, *"Field Is the World,"* chapter on sermons preached at annual ABCFM meeting in the United States. Most of the speakers held to a post millennial view, namely that the millennium has already occurred.

68. Daws, "Evangelism," 31N33, 34, Lyons to Chamberlain, January 17, 1838, Lyons Letters, HMH.

69. In contrast to Lyons great fluctuations of numbers due to the high amount of excommunications and backsliding.

70. Daws, "Evangelism," 31.

71. See Coan letter to Fidelia above. Should Coan's letter be dated 1839?

72. Anderson to Sandwich Island Mission, October 2, 1838, ABCFM-HEA, HMH, in Ehlke, "Enthusiastic Religion," 119–120.

73. Anderson, in Ehlke, "Enthusiastic Religion," 120.

had brought nearly five thousand souls into your church, and it was due to your numerous and deeply interested patrons, that you should have take[n] time sufficient to draw up a calm and well mediated history of what the Lord had been pleased to do through your instrumentality. Mr. Coan took the right course, on receiving intimations from me of the doubts and fears entertained among the churches at home; and his admirable letter has been read by thousands and thousands in this land, with weeping, joyful interest, and has called forth thousands and thousands of prayers from God's people. I must say that I like the spirit and matter and manner of his letter."[74]

Ehlke next relates the letter in *The Missionary Herald*, to which Anderson refers in his letter to Lyons. "Titus Coan's explanation of the work in progress in the Islands was published in *The Missionary Herald* for June 1839[75] with this foreword: 'It is important that the Christian community should know in what labors the missionaries are engaged, by what means, and with what spirit and what hopes they prosecute them, and by what results, seen in the apparent conversion of great multitudes, surpassing any thing witnessed since the days of the apostles, they are cheered on in their work.' Coan outlined the process he used to determine who should become members of the church, admitting that there probably would be backsliders,[76] but added: 'It is true they are ignorant and without refinement, but I believe that a larger proportion of them possess a simple and saving piety, than of any other community of Christians with whom I am acquainted in any other land.'"[77]

Next Ehlke provides fascinating intelligence. "What the *Herald* did not print were the scathing remarks from Coan to Dr. Anderson on the subject of 'hasty admissions,' which prefaced the printed portions. Suggesting that when even the brethren in the Islands 'have been vastly misinformed and almost totally ignorant, as to many of my measures, and especially as to the principles on which I have received to my Ch[urc]h during the last two years past. Is it marvelous then that you, at the distance of eighteen thousand miles, should not be able at once to get all the facts and circumstances connected with our revivals, and all the reasons which modify and govern our conduct.' Coan said he had enough work to keep him busy without reporting for others, and suggested that judgments be withheld until the 'facts and circumstances in the case be fully known.' At the end of the thirty-six-page letter, Coan called upon the Board to acknowledge that the Sandwich Islands field was ready for conversion with a prediction: *This year more souls ought to be converted at the S. Isls. than have been converted here during all previous years. Such is my opinion . . . We are in danger of grieving the Holy Spirit of God* [Eph 4:30] *by jealousies, suspicious fears, and false alarms; or by a*

---

74. As opposed to the "spirit and matter and manner" of Lyons's letter? Anderson to Lyons, October 23, 1840, HMH, in Ehlke, "Enthusiastic Religion," 120.

75. One must keep in mind that letters at this time went both ways around the southern tip of South America via sail.

76. Were there no backsliders in American churches?

77. *Missionary Herald* 35 (June 1839) 197–98, in Ehlke, "Enthusiastic Religion," 121.

tenacious adherence to forms, and a disposition to limit his influences by our narrow views of prudence, and to select for him the exclusive agencies and measures by which he shall carry on his mysterious work.'"[78]

On the same date Coan wrote to Anderson, a letter from Titus is provided in a later book. Coan addresses the overwhelming (to many) numbers of the ingathering of the Awakening. "I suppose the great numbers added to our church is what staggers the faith of many. A beloved missionary sister in writing to us; on this subject says: 'If there were only a few hundreds we could believe, but there are so many it spoils it all.' That was a frank and honest confession . . . The fact is that the church is not prepared to see great things in the conversion of the heathen. Missionaries themselves are not prepared for it."[79]

Ehlke next provides a report on the 1839 General Meeting of the Hawaiian Association of the ABCFM missionaries. It specifically "addressed the question by appointing a committee on 'Hasty Admissions to the Churches.' The ministers who made up the Association, while gratefully acknowledging the hand of God in the work of grace which had been visited upon the Mission during the past two years, came to the painful conclusion 'that a few have erred . . .' Suggesting that 'the highest degree of watchfulness and mutual cooperation is required of us all to promote that highest interests of our churches,' the committee which included Titus Coan as moderator of the meeting, recommended the churches exercise prompt and rigorous discipline in all cases of defection from Christian standards."[80]

As moderator, Coan would have exercised significant influence over the outcome. Nevertheless, "Coan's delight at the mildness of the rebuke can[not] be concealed in this letter to his wife. 'My report of Hilo shut the mouths of gainsayers and none of the brethren have undertaken to prove me insane. I have been treated with kindness and respect, and in the minds of many of our brethren and especially of the sisters, there is a wakeful jealousy of anything which would impeach the revivals, the measures, or the men of Hawaii. I am happy that I came to general meeting. Had I not been there to explain, I am confident that severe and darkhearted strictures would have been passed on my movements. I think there may be individuals even now who would be glad to do it, but they are overawed by facts and arguments and by the decided and bold stand which is taken to vindicate the freedom of conscience and the work of God on these islands. On the whole all will probably pass pleasantly, and let God be praised.'"[81]

Ehlke relays the analysis and ultimate approval of what transpired by the leading missionary, the one who arrived with the Pioneer Company—Hiram Bingham. While expressing some mild concerns, he gives his imprimatur to the Hawaiian Great

---

78. Coan to Anderson, June 6, 1839, ABCFM, in Ehlke, "Enthusiastic Religion," 121–22.

79. Titus Coan, June 6, 1839, in Gulick et al., *Pilgrims*, 172.

80. *Minutes of the Hawaiian Association, Held at Honolulu, May and June, 1839*, 34, in Ehlke, "Enthusiastic Religion," 122.

81. Titus to Fidelia Coan, May 29, 1839, HMH, in Ehlke, "Enthusiastic Religion," 122–23.

Awakening. "Hiram Bingham's reply to a letter from Dwight Baldwin, in the midst of the 'Great Awakening,' gives a first-hand view of the dilemma posed for the missionaries on the ground. Asked if he regard his 'juniors' as gathering 'into the church too fast,' Bingham replied, 'I have faith to believe that Hawaiians can be converted while they have but little knowledge, and while they live in mean and filthy habitations, even without partitions, and when they give *evidence* that they are truly converted they may come in to the church in any numbers.' Bingham, however, had difficulties with the way that Lyons admitted church members, saying that many he proposed 'must be comparative *strangers* to him.'"[82]

Ehlke next relates Bingham's "methods for assuring that conversions were genuine." He has them give their testimony to him. He asks them questions. He looks for a life that was reformed and "to corroborate the testimony, then make up my mind whether their place should be in the church or out of it."[83] If anything, Coan's procedure seems even more thorough than Bingham's.

"Thus spoke the conservative older missionary, but one who still felt that the work was genuine. His faith was underscored by his prediction, relayed by Mrs. Wilcox to Mrs. Coan in 1838, that 'Mr. Bingham feels that the missionaries in these islands ought to expect that one hundred thousand will be converted this year.'"[84] Aside from the fact that that amount was not reached, that number begs the question as to how Coan, Bingham, or any other missionaries together could possibly personally vet that many individuals in the course of a year. That would involve more than two hundred a day for the year.

The long distance and time between Hawai'i and Boston as previously noted continued to cause difficulties and misunderstandings. "The difficulties of communicating over the thousands of miles made the receipt of critical letters from Boston difficult to accept. When Anderson wrote a conciliatory letter to the Sandwich Islands Mission dated June 10, 1840, on the subject of the many conversions in the islands, it was still viewed as a reproof. Saying that Mr. Coan's epistle of June 6, 1839,[85] would be 'read with interest,' Anderson continued: 'If we have done any injustice to any of the brethren at the islands by expressing fears that converts were admitted too hastily, the publication of this letter will serve as a reparation. It was not the *number* of admissions, however, which occasioned those fears; we had other grounds for approbation. Let the truth, whatever it is, be known.'"[86]

Ehlke notes that Fidelia did not view Anderson's letter as sufficient "amends for the earlier criticism of her husband's policies as she consoled him in this letter. 'O for

---

82. Bingham to Baldwin, January 15, 1838, in Ehlke, "Enthusiastic Religion," 123.

83. Bingham, in Ehlke, "Enthusiastic Religion," 124.

84. Lucy E. H. Wilcox to Fidelia Coan, March 8, 1838, LOC, in Ehlke, "Enthusiastic Religion," 124.

85. The fourth anniversary of the Coans' arrival in Honolulu.

86. Anderson to the Sandwich Islands Mission, June 10, 1840, HMH ABCFM-HEA, in Ehlke, "Enthusiastic Religion," 124.

living witnesses in the church members of this field that God and not Satan had the ground here in 1838–39! The churches cannot have everything done among the heathen just as they would at home. Why should there be such a dreadful reaction! The board claims to know best how missionaries can act upon the public mind at home. Do they also know best how they can operate upon the heathen? There never was a great revival yet probably which was not stigmatized and its instruments called enthusiasts, mad, drunk, etc. Perhaps Brainerd's was an exception, for he had no Christian [sic] brethren to report his measures.'"[87]

Some of the missionaries would not, however, let go of the subject. "Yet the brethren continued to discuss the Awakening. The Rev. Richard Armstrong in Honolulu answered questions from his former pastor, Rev. George Junkin, who had read of the revivals in a Presbyterian publication in the eastern United States. He hoped to set Junkin straight about the so-called 'indiscretions in promoting the excitement' which had occurred in only two stations[88] in the islands.[89] He blamed the difference in approach at these two stations on the fact that the pastors 'were schooled (inter nos) in Western New York and carry with them the peculiarities of that region.'[90] Although conceding that he had not witnessed those revivals personally, another missionary[91] had described thousands 'wailing, praying, groaning, and screaming all together very much as we used to see at Methodist meetings in the state of Pennsylvania and Maryland.'[92] Armstrong felt a '*new heart* and a holy life, or a new heart evinced by a holy life'[93] was needed before a Hawaiian could consider himself a Christian."[94]

Ehlke next cites multiple sources for the next sentence. "The use of language reminiscent of Finney shows the influence of Finney's *Lecture on Revivalism*,[95] which was being read and used as sermons in Hawaii as early as 1836.[96] To his credit, Arm-

---

87. Fidelia to Titus Coan, January 13, 1838, HMH, in Ehlke, "Enthusiastic Religion," 125. The reference is to David Brainerd, who served among Native Americans during the last years of his brief life during the eighteenth century.

88. Waiemea/Lyons and Hilo/Coan.

89. Armstrong to Junkin, October 12, 1841, HMH, in Ehlke, "Enthusiastic Religion," 125.

90. Armstrong to Junkin, September 23, 1841, HMH, in Ehlke, "Enthusiastic Religion," 125.

91. One person providing second-hand gossip without context or thoughtful analysis.

92. Armstrong to Junkin, September 23, 1841, HMH, in Ehlke, "Enthusiastic Religion," 125.

93. Armstrong, in Ehlke, "Enthusiastic Religion," 125.

94. One wonders how this differs from Coan's practices. It reminds one of the false dichotomy some try to set up between Paul's "saved by grace through faith alone" and James's "faith and works."

95. First published in 1835.

96. In one of her many fine expressions of research, Ehlke, "Enthusiastic Religion," cites multiple dates from the writings of three American Board missionaries to Hawai'i. Amos S. Cooke Journal, August 31, 1837; October 15, 1839; December 8, 1839, HMH; Reuben Tinker Journal, May 11, 18, October 12, 1836; February 22, March 8, 22, 1837, HMH; Gerrit P. and Laura F. Judd, Judd Fragments IV, *Family Records of the House of Judd*, 28–29. Footnote 124 in Ehlke, "Enthusiastic Religion," 157.

strong did share his opinion directly to Lyons and Coan during the awakening, but did not doubt that the revivals were genuinely 'a work of God.'"[97]

Cochran Forbes did debate the theory but not practice with Lyons on the subject of waiting to receive members.[98] Forbes said that "they didn't disagree in practice, however we may in theory, as to the main question, which is *to wait till we have satisfactory evidence of conversion.*"[99]

Ehlke allows Coan to respond. Two years after the Great Awakening effectively had ended, he "wrote to the American Board in May 1842 defending the practices in Hilo. 'At the revival at Hilo, which resulted in the professed conversion of several thousands of souls, it will be remembered that there were some exhibitions of feeling which, in civilized communities, would be disapproved and discountenanced. It is obvious, however, that our standard of propriety is not altogether suited to a simple and semi-barbarous people.'"[100]

He explains characteristics of the Hawaiians, as he understands them. "Explaining that Hawaiians expressed sorrow with wailing, that joy and other strong passions produced noisy demonstrations, Coan said he 'did not undertake to put down this excitement, because I had so much evidence that the thing proceeded from the Lord, that I feared to lay my unhallowed hand upon it, or rashly and hastily to forbid it under all circumstances whatever.'"[101]

Coan addresses the loud praying and the fact that he knows how to judge the "'work of the Lord.' He wrote his brother-in-law, the Rev. Charles Robinson, in Siam: 'I will not attempt to tell you all the new names and attributes which have been applied to me during the progress of the revival, not all the base, malicious, and subtle slanders which have been reported about this work. But this is not strange. It is in accordance with the history of great revivals in all ages. Indeed were it not so, I should feel that it lacked one distinguishing feature of a genuine work of God.'"[102]

Through a letter from Titus to Fidelia, Ehlke addresses religious tensions caused by such groups as Methodists and within Presbyterianism in the context of the Great Awakening. "Explaining the workings of God to his wife, Coan wrote from Puna in January 1838: 'God's hand is high here. His work is distinct and marvelous. I have not preached a sermon since I left home without clear evidence that the Holy Ghost fell on those who heard the word. There has been a shaking in every place where I have spoken. The church members with me have been searched, and have been in tears under almost every sermon. I hope many children are converted here; great weeping

---

97. Ehlke, "Enthusiastic Religion," 126. Confusing citation. No letter to either missionary mentioned in endnote.

98. Judd, *Missionary Album*, 98–99.

99. Forbes to Lyons, February 2, 1838, HMH, in Ehlke, "Enthusiastic Religion," 126.

100. *Missionary Herald* 39, in Ehlke, "Enthusiastic Religion," 126.

101. *Missionary Herald* 39, in Ehlke, "Enthusiastic Religion," 126.

102. Coan to Robinson, November 1, 1838, LOC, in Ehlke, "Enthusiastic Religion," 126.

among them. You have seen nothing like it at Hilo. So with the adults. They have broken out into spontaneous and loud wailings during a sermon of prayer so that their cries were heard afar off. Trembling has seemed to seize almost the entire congregation simultaneously.

"'You call it Methodism. I call it the power of God. Most that have attended the meeting here profess to be converted, and very many give as good evidence as can be had in so short a time. God has helped, and blessed be his name. I adore his power. I rejoice in his love, and in his name I raise my banners and go forward. "The Lord of Hosts" is with us [Ps 46:7]. My soul is all on fire, and I know that Christ's kingdom will come in Puna.'"[103]

Ehlke continues. "Did the mention of Methodism refer to the loud and enthusiastic response reminiscent of a Methodist camp meeting? Or did the doctrines presented by Coan bear some resemblance to those of John Wesley? His colleague, the Rev. Lorrin Andrews,[104] seemed to feel they did. Discussing the split in the Presbyterian Church[105] in the United States in a letter to his father, he wrote 'that some of our number are precisely of the stamp you speak of. They are half if not whole Perfectionists. We have no quarrel on doctrinal points, because the language in which we preach does not admit it. But in practice it comes out in the churches of Mr. Lyons and Mr. Coan and less so in two or three others.[106] You will perceive that the Board has censured Mr. Lyons and justified Mr. Coan.' Andrews concluded his discussion of his fellow ministers with this interesting observation: 'In reading the Report of the Board we[107] see and understand that there is a great deal of favoritism.'"[108]

Ehlke turns to a discussion of Finney and Perfectionism. "The Rev. Charles G. Finney also bore the 'Perfectionist' label, as he developed his ideas of sanctification along the same lines as Wesley. He came to believe that man could be perfect 'even as your Father which is in heaven is perfect' [Matt 5:48]. This perfection could be attained through 'a "second blessing" which would constitute an "assurance of faith" beyond that of the ordinary Christian.'"[109]

However, Ehlke provides no documentation of Coan adhering to perfectionist principles. Instead she discusses how Coan based his views on the Bible, perhaps suggesting Coan held the view of perfectionism and second blessing Finney had because of a verse that Finney used. "Coan remembered his involvement in the awakenings of Nettleton and Finney, saying 'like doctrines, prayers, and efforts seem to produce like

---

103. Titus to Fidelia Coan, January 16, 1838, HMCS, in Ehlke, "Enthusiastic Religion," 157.

104. Judd, *Missionary Album*, 22–23.

105. New Light and Old Light, with the New Light favoring revival measures. 1840 marked the last year a Presbyterian spoke at the ABCFM annual meeting in the United States.

106. Unnamed.

107. Emphasis by Andrews.

108. Lorrin Andrews to father, December 8, 1841, HMH, in Ehlke, "Enthusiastic Religion," 127.

109. McLoughlin, *Modern Revivalism*, 103–04, in Ehlke, "Enthusiastic Religion," 128.

fruits among this people.'¹¹⁰ Like that of the famous evangelist, Titus Coan's theology came straight from the Bible. He preached boldly, he said, 'in living faith, in burning love, and in high and holy expectation of success.'¹¹¹ At the beginning of his ministry, he assured the people 'that all the Lord required was godly sorrow for the past, present faith in Christ, and henceforth faithful, filial, and cheerful obedience.'¹¹² Coan's reference to Methodism does not indicate Fidelia's disapproval of her husband's methods. Her father had joined the Methodist church in 1831 and two of her brothers were Methodist ministers so she probably held positive views of the sect."¹¹³

Ehlke next interacts with Coan's discussion of baptism in his autobiography. "Baptism, Coan felt, was an outward sign of faith in Christ, but not essential to salvation."¹¹⁴ She next uncritically passes along Coan's view on the mode of baptism. "The mode of baptism, by immersion, pouring, or sprinkling, did not matter to Coan. Being asked to baptize people when no body of water was available made him an advocate of sprinkling." Coan arrived in the Sandwich Islands as a Presbyterian serving in a primarily Congregational mission organization. Both denominations practiced "sprinkling" of babies, so it followed to do the same with adults who came to faith.

A day or two after baptizing 1,705 adults, Coan baptized hundreds of the children of those adults. He does not provide the age range of the children. In addition to his Presbyterian view on baptism, it would probably be physically impossible without extensive assistance to have baptized so many adults in the ocean or a body of water. The claim of water not being nearby is rather specious. Hilo harbor was a short walk from the church building. And in the water-rich windward side of the Big Island, there are many pools where baptism could have taken place by immersion.¹¹⁵

When it comes to the Lord's Supper, "Coan said he had been 'in situations where it seemed a duty and a privilege to administer this sacrament, but could get neither bread nor wine.'¹¹⁶ This took place decades before the move to using grape juice for Communion in American Protestant churches due to concern over alcoholism.¹¹⁷

---

110. Coan, *Life*, 49, in Ehlke, "Enthusiastic Religion," 128.

111. Coan, *Memorial Volume*, 44, in Ehlke, "Enthusiastic Religion," 128.

112. Coan, *Life*, 50, in Ehlke, "Enthusiastic Religion," 128.

113. Emens, *Descendants of Captain Samuel Church*, 28, 32, in Ehlke, "Enthusiastic Religion," 129. Entire Ehlke quotation, 128–29.

114. That is the view of virtually all Protestants.

115. Coan, *Life*, 90–91, in Ehlke, "Enthusiastic Religion," 129.

116. While Coan was a temperance leader in Hawai'i, he does not address himself to such a concern over Communion but rather is focused on practical matters related to the sacrament/ordinance.

117. In his "Changing Wine into Grape Juice," Daniel Benedict writes, "Most United Methodists are aware that one of our practices is the use of unfermented juice of the grape for Holy Communion. While some other Protestant bodies share this practice, the possibility of the practice goes back to the late nineteenth century and a Methodist dentist named Thomas Bramwell Welch. Apparently, Welch had scruples about the use of wine and had heard of Louis Pasteur's process of pasteurization of milk. Welch was successful in applying the process to grape juice, and he began to use it in his church, where he was a Communion steward.

"Coan felt that the food people ate and the water they drank to sustain their bodies would do to con[s]ecreate the Lord's Supper. In Hilo, bread was used with a non-alcoholic beverage for the cup; while in the field, breadfruit, taro, or potato and water sufficed."[118]

COMING ABOUT: THE *VINCENNES* AND THE CONCLUSION OF THE GREAT AWAKENING IN THE HILO AREA

The Lord's Supper continued to be celebrated during the Great Awakening, as did the coming and going of ships in Hilo harbor. While the number of ships was low in the 1830s,[119] a significant visit took place when the *Vincennes* arrived as part of its Exploring Expedition. Titus Coan would identify the events surrounding the "Ex Ex" involvement in the Hilo and volcano areas.

With his love of science and passion to reach all people for Christ, Coan was torn. His ambivalence is evident in his discussion of the Expedition: providing an objective summary; lamenting the treatment of the Hawaiian men; the ending of the revival; and his developing friendships with those involved in the effort.

"The *Vincennes* arrived on Wedns. the ninth inst[an]t. On Mond. the fourteenth the caravan starts for the mountain."[120]

"In 1840, Charles Wilkes, commander of the United States Exploring Expedition, arrived in Hilo bay in the flag-ship *Vincennes*. Here with an admirable corps of scientists he spent three months in explorations, measurements, etc. Parties of officers and scientific gentlemen were detailed to visit different parts of the island, some to ascend the mountains, and some to survey the shore, making collections, drawings, and observations in all the branches of the natural history of the Islands. The commander called for three hundred young and vigorous men to take him, with the materials of a wooden house and all the apparatus of a large observatory, with food, fuel, water, beds, etc., to the summit of Mauna Loa, where he and his attendants were to spend twenty or thirty days in taking observations.

"His son, Dr. Charles Welch, was an enterprising Methodist layman (a dentist, like his father) from southern New Jersey. He marketed the pasteurized grape juice to temperance-minded evangelical Protestants as authentic biblical 'wine.' As word spread and as the temperance movement grew among evangelical Protestant churches, Welch left dentistry and produced Welch's Grape Juice commercially.

"The impact of the temperance movement and the availability of the 'unfermented juice of the grape' can be traced in the *Book of Discipline* and actions of the General Conference of the Methodist Episcopal Church and the Church of the United Brethren." United Methodist Church Disciple Ministries, "Turning Wine into Grape Juice."

118. Coan, *Life*, 120, in Ehlke, "Enthusiastic Religion," 129.

119. The number would greatly increase in 1849 because of the California Gold Rush.

120. Titus Coan to Edwin Hall, December 12 and 14, 1840, HMCS. Sarah and Edwin Hall arrived with the Coans as part of the Seventh Company. They remained in Honolulu. Judd, *Missionary Album*, 112–13. See also Forbes et al., *Partners in Change*, 298–303.

"Other parties required large numbers of men to carry baggage, instruments, etc., and to act as guides and assistants in making surveys and collecting a large amount of specimens."[121] In a letter to Edwin Hall, Coan writes of the arduousness of the trip up the mountain. "Capt. Wilkes and party are on the mountain. A difficult journey thither. Five hundred men were employed to get up the baggage with food, fuel, water, etc. They will spend two or three weeks on the summit." To keep that part of the letter as short as possible, Coan asks Hall to grill Mr. Brinsmade upon his return to Honolulu. "Mr. Brinsmade returns in the [ship] *Kahalai* and you must tax him for information on all points connected with the expedition etc."[122]

"Parties of natives thus employed needed to be recruited often on account of fatigue and exhaustion, and for the lack of shoes and warm clothing to endure the hard travel and the rains, cold, and snows of the mountains. Some died of cold. It is supposed that about one thousand of our strongest men were brought into this service, and with small pay, during these three months. Some parties of men were required to travel and work on Sunday as on other days. All this had a demoralizing effect upon the poor natives. They had been accustomed to rest from all physical toil, and to worship on the Lord's Day. Our congregations were much reduced in numbers. There was no little murmuring among the people at this new state of things, and for years the moral tone of the church and community could not by fully restored to its cheerful and normal state.

"This was a trial of faith, and a fan to winnow the church, but most of our Christians stood fast, and although it checked the progress of the revival, the loss to the church was less than might have been feared.

"The visit of the expedition to Hilo afforded us an opportunity to form an acquaintance with many worthy gentlemen, several of whom we met again in the United States in 1870–71. Among these we met and received as a very welcome guest the then youthful James D. Dana,[123] one of the scientific corps, now so distinguished in various departments of natural science, and honored as a Christian philosopher. The friendship then formed has been increased by years and can never wane."[124]

In the *Memorial Volume*, Lydia Bingham complements what Titus writes in his autobiography. In a portion of an early 1841 letter, Titus writes his brother Ezra about "adverse influences" against the revival. The two such influences were "Romanism"

---

121. Coan, *Life*, 66–67.

122. Titus Coan to Edwin Hall, December 30, 1840, HMH.

123. Dana was twenty-seven when the *Vincennes* arrived in Hilo. "He would go and [explore the] structure of continents and oceans around the world." His two books tying together science and the Bible are: *Science and the Bible: A Review of the Six Days of Creation* (1856), and *Creation, Or, The Biblical Cosmogony in the Light of Modern Science* (1885). He went on to become a geologist, mineralogist, volcanologist, and zoologist. "He made pioneering studies of mountain-building, volcanic activity, [and other matters.]" Wikipedia, "James Dwight Dana."

124. Coan, *Life*, 67–68. With regard to Coan's extensive correspondence with Dana, see Coan, *Memorial Volume*, and the LOC "Titus Coan Papers."

and the *Vincennes*. He discusses the cost of such an expedition. He writes contemporaneously about the visit and the contrast between the resources expended on an earthly endeavor and on matters of eternity. "The *Vincennes*, with the commander of the squadron, is now here, and has been lying at anchor for fifty days directly in front of our house. I suppose the expenses of this single ship, in full view from my study window, have been more during her stay at these islands, than those of this mission with all its operations for a year, and I have no doubt that more is annually expended by this little exploring squadron, than by the whole American church is in the propagation of the gospel among the heathen. When will as much zeal be displayed in exploring and subduing the world to Jesus, as in subduing and subjugating its resources and its glories to earthly princes?"[125]

Lydia provides a brief comment after this letter, concluding with a quotation from the autobiography.[126] "The influences of this expedition were such upon the natives, that for years, as Mr. Coan says in his book, 'the moral tone of the church and community could not be fully restored to its cheerful and normal state.'"[127]

Sarah Lyman writes of the mixed value of the Ex Ex. "The US Ship *Vincennes* arrived here on the ninth of December 1840 and this morning took her anchor and stood away for Lahaina via Kau and Kona. During her protracted stay here Commodore Wilkes, the scientific gentlemen, and the officers have been indefatigable in their labours and we are pleased to know they are highly gratified with the results. There is no doubt but the cause of science will be promoted by their visit to this place, but it is a matter of no small regret that the moral influence which they have exerted on these poor people has been deleterious in the extreme. Silly women have been led captive by the officers, ensnared and I fear are lost eternally."[128]

Stanton notes that the "randy sailors were doubtless a sore trial to the missionaries."[129]

With regard to the establishment and implementing of the Ex Ex, President John Quincy Adams requested funding from Congress in 1828. Congress did not authorize funding for the oceanic expedition until 1836. The implementation came under the auspices of President Andrew Jackson. It took place between 1838 and 1842, so the visit to Hilo came more than halfway through the journey.[130]

---

125. Titus Coan to Ezra Coan, January 29, 1841, in Coan, *Memorial Volume*, 62. The entire cost of the Ex Ex was $928,000. In early 2016 dollars that amount would be between 27 and 28 million dollars.

126. See above.

127. Coan, *Memorial Volume*, 62.

128. Lyman, *Lymans of Hilo*, 106.

129 Stanton, *First Great United States Exploring Expedition*. "For anyone wanting to know more about the US Exploring Expedition, the place to start" is Stanton's book. "Wonderfully written and researched, Stanton's book approaches the Expedition in terms of its contribution to the rise of science in America." Philbrick, *Scientific Legacy*, np.

130. Wikipedia, "United States Exploring Expedition."

Titus Coan: "Apostle to the Sandwich Islands"

The Library of Congress has an extensive collection—both hard copy and digital—on the Exploring Expedition.[131] Primary sources included Commander Charles Wilkes's *Narrative of the United States Exploring Expedition*, in five volumes. Volume IV, chapters I through VII, focus on Hawai'i.[132] A young Charles Erskine participated in the voyage and years later would pen *Twenty Years before the Mast: With the more thrilling scenes and incidents while circumnavigating the globe under the command of the late Admiral Charles Wilkes 1838–1842*.[133] Chapter XV covers his time in the Hilo and volcano area.[134] Almost 150[135] years after the Expedition, the letters of Lieutenant William Reynolds were published.[136] Sixteen years later Nathaniel and Thomas Philbrick edited and published *William Reynolds: The Private Journal of William Reynolds. United States Exploring Expedition, 1838–1842*.[137]

Another group of sources are the reports from the investigation of Wilkes that occurred after the Expedition was completed.[138] More on that subject is discussed later in this chapter.

---

131. Philbrick writes about the various locations of the Expedition and related matters in *Scientific Legacy*, np. "Anyone interested in braving the massive amount of unpublished material connected with the Expedition should consult Daniel C. Haskell's indispensable *The United States Exploring Expedition, 1838–1842 and Its Publications 1844–1874* published by the New York Public Library in 1942. Most of the existing officers' logs, letters, and courts-martial records are at the National Archives in Washington, DC, although the Library of Congress and the Smithsonian Institution also have much Ex Ex Material. The twenty-three journals at the National Archives are available on microfilm as "Records Relating to the United States Exploring Expedition under the Command of Lt. Charles Wilkes, 1836–1842" (Microcopy 75). A good number of the officers retrieved their journals at some point after the Expedition; as a result, many of the journals are now scattered among various repositories; these journals are also available on microfilm. The courts-martial records related to the Expedition are available on microfilm from the National Archives, Microcopy 75, Rolls 26 and 27. In 1978 an important cache of Wilkes material was donated to Duke University." Philbrick was the first to incorporate the Duke Papers in a published book. The "Wilkes Family Papers at Duke contain dozens of letters Wilkes wrote to his wife Jane during the Expedition, as well as letters from Jane, their children, Wilkes's brother Henry, his brother-in-law James Renwick, and others. Other important collections of Wilkes papers are at the Kansas State Historical Society, the Library of Congress, and the Wisconsin Historical Society."

132. Wilkes, *Voyage Round the World*. While praising Wilkes's description of the assault on Antarctica as "exhilarating," Philbrick characterizes the work as a "padded" and an "uneven read." Philbrick also observes that "Wilkes's personality is best revealed in his not always reliable, but always self-serving *Autobiography*."

133. Erskine, *Twenty Years*. Wilkes died in 1877 and Erskine published the book in 1896.

134. Erskine, *Twenty Years*, 212–226.

135. 1988.

136. Reynolds et al., *Voyage to the Southern Ocean*. Philbrick notes that "William Reynolds is well served by *Voyage to the Southern Ocean*, a collection of the letters he wrote home during the Expedition edited by Anne Hoffman Cleaver, a Reynolds descendant, and E. Jeffry Stann." Philbrick writes about some other primary sources. "The scientist and artist Titian Peale's journal has been published in a magnificently illustrated volume edited by Jessie Poesch, while the officer George Colvocoresses and the sailors Joseph Clark and Charles Erskine each published accounts during their lifetimes."

137. Philbrick, *Private Journal*.

138. Hibler, *Publication of the Wilkes Reports*.

The Great Awakening, Part 2

Secondary sources shed light on the Ex Ex. The most recent one is Nathaniel Philbrick's 2003 *Sea of Glory: America's Voyage of Discovery, the US Exploring Expedition, 1838–1842*.[139] *Magnificent Voyagers*, an illustrated catalogue of a 1985 exhibition at the Smithsonian Institution edited by Herman J. Viola and Carolyn Margolis, is much more than a catalogue, containing articles that analyze the Expedition from a multitude of perspectives.

An earlier book, David B. Tyler's *The Wilkes Expedition* is also useful, as is the important group of essays about the Expedition published by the American Philosophical Society in Centenary Celebration: *The Wilkes Exploring Expedition of the United States Navy, 1838–1842*. David Henderson's biography of Wilkes, *The Hidden Coasts*, make good use of Wilkes's own writing but seems reluctant to criticize or evaluate its subject. William H. Goetzmann's *New Lands, New Men: America and the Second Great Age of Discovery* investigates the impulse to explore by sea and land that culminated in the Expedition and the many US expeditions to the west that followed.[140]

Stanton answers the question of "Why Hilo?" "The *Vincennes* found herself at Hilo because, despite the fact that the Sandwich Islands were a good deal more familiar to the world than Samoa or the Fijis, Wilkes felt that the survey work had to be carried on." Wilkes "chose to lead the most spectacular of the excursions—the ascent of Mauna Loa, at nearly fourteen thousand feet[141] the largest[142] of active volcanoes."[143]

Before relating Erskine's account of his arrival in Hilo harbor, it is notable that he gives evidence of Christian faith in his Preface: "As you peruse these pages I trust that they will awaken in your heart an endearing love for the sublime and beautiful in God's wonderful creation." A little further on he writes, "to obey the first and last command of Almighty God, who has decreed that this earth shall be subdued [Gen 1:28], and the gospel preached to every creature" [Mark 16:15].[144]

Erskine describes the *Vincennes's* arrival in Hilo. "On the ninth [of December, 1840], we made Hilo Bay, and took a pilot, who proved to be John Ely." As it turns out, Ely "had been a shipmate of the commodore when he was a midshipman in the *Guierrere*[145] frigate in 1820." Both Ely and Wilkes had "grown into manhood and forgotten each other. Ely said that he had been living among" the Hawaiians ever since. Perhaps

---

139. Philbrick, *Sea of Glory*. See footnote, above.

140. Philbirck, *Scientific Legacy*, np.

141. The actual measured elevation of Mauna Loa is 16,020 feet (4883 meters). US Geological Survey Volcano Warch.

142. Mauna Loa is the "largest subaerial volcano in both mass and volume." Wikipedia, "Mauna Loa."

143. Stanton, *First Great United States Exploring Expedition*, 224.

144. Erskine, *Twenty Years*, vii.

145 The *Gueirrere* "was the first frigate built in the United States since 1801. The name came from a fast 38-gun British frigate captured and destroyed in a half-hour battle by" the USS *Constitution*. Wikipedia, "USS *Geurriere*."

due to lack of space, Erskine does not indicate whether Ely knew any ABCFM missionaries or attended the Coan church.

Erskine continues to show his attention to detail by describing specifics relating to dropping anchor in Hilo Bay: "At 5 o'clock we dropped anchor in six fathoms of water with muddy water."[146]

While the ninth was a Wednesday, Erskine notes that after the ship's arrival, nearly "all hands went to [Coan's] church on Sunday.[147] It was a very large building, seating nearly seven thousand people."

Kuykendall provides another perspective. "The long-awaited explorers were given a friendly welcome by respectable Honolulu." However, Kuykendall avers that "the squadron had come at a bad time, for there had just been a religious revival touched off at Hilo in 1837 by the missionary Titus Coan. Early in the squadron's visit laws were decreed 'for the protection of the Sabbath' which stopped Sunday riding, milk delivery, and work aboard ships in the harbor. What lay in store for seamen in the future was suggested in a provision of the new constitution that decreed 'That no law shall be enacted which is at variance with the word of the Lord Jehovah, or at variance with the general spirit of his word.' The men on liberty found that they were everywhere followed by armed police, who were quick to seize a man for unseemly conduct and lodge him in the fort."[148]

Kuykendall notes that restriction "was the harder to bear because of the elysian reputation these islands had enjoyed in the maritime world of the west before" the arrival of the Pioneer Company. "But all that was past. Honolulu now bore a good many resemblances to a New England village."[149] On the other hand, Wilkes and some of his officers approved of the "Protestant efforts in the Sandwich Islands."[150]

From Honolulu the Ex Ex continued on to Hilo. "From Byron's Bay at Hilo the men of the *Vincennes* could see their objective clearly, a great stone dome sixty miles away."[151]

The Ex Ex personnel established an "observatory" on the coast and prepared and followed through on the ascent up the volcano. "On arrival, our observatory was established at Point Waikaea.[152] An expedition to the mountains was fitted out, consisting of the commodore, ten officers, Mr. Brinsmade, Dr. Judd, a number of seamen, and two hundred natives." These "natives" were "to carry the portable houses, instruments, tents, and provisions. The natives were separated into parties, numbered,

---

146. Erskine, *Twenty Years*, 212.
147. December 12?
148. Kuykendall, *Hawaiian Kingdom*, 221.
149. Kuykendall, *Hawaiian Kingdom*, 221–22.
150. Kuykendall, *Hawaiian Kingdom*, 223.
151. Kuykendall, *Hawaiian Kingdom*, 224.
152. The low-lying bayfront areas of Hilo are on Waiākea peninsula and along Hilo. Wikipedia, "Hilo, Hawaii."

and loaded . . . It was 3 o'clock when we started with our two hundred bearers of burdens, forty hogs, a bullock, and a bullock hunter, fifty bearers of poe, twenty-five with calabashes, large and small, others with iron pots, kettles, frying-pans, etc." Some of the laborers were lightly and others heavily loaded, their burden being lashed to their backs, or carried on each end of sticks balanced across their shoulders, which is their usual mode of carrying burdens."[153]

Erskine describes what in later years would be called "altitude sickness." "One of our shipmates, William Longley, was missing for several days. When last seen he complained of being sick. Many of us had mountain fever—that is, a shortness of breath, sore eyes, with much headache, and a dryness of the skin." Erskine also has an eye for the aesthetic. He describes the view of looking from Mauna Loa down to Hilo. "We could not but admire the wonderful contrast."[154]

Erskine writes about establishing camps on the volcano[155] and the difficulty in building the pendulum/shelter due to the wind.[156] He also discusses from his perspective what Coan writes about, namely the poor working conditions for the Hawaiian men. Erskine writes about the complaints of the Hawaiian laborers, who were all "grumbling and complaining about their burdens. Shaking their heads, they pointed to their loads, and growled out, 'Oury miti'[157] and, to cap the climax, they even struck for higher wages."

Erskine seems to take Wilkes's position on this subject when he writes that the "commodore acceded to their demand, and seeing that they were all tired out, and the shoulders of many were sore, sent down for fifty more natives without their 'fraus,'[158] and concluded to lay to until the next day in order to give the natives rest."

Alluding to what Coan writes about more strongly above, Erskine writes about the challenges of snow and cold. One morning "after we had got fairly under way, we were overtaken and enveloped in a snow-cloud. The natives became much frightened, and shouted out, 'Oury miti': 'No good,' and nearly all of them left and ran down the mountain." Erskine puts it down to the difference in temperatures that the Hawaiians were used to—which is partly true, yet the differential could be deadly, as Coan indicates. "The thermometer was at thirty degrees, and they had been accustomed from childhood to a temperature of seventy to eighty degrees. Fortunately the commodore had previously sent down to the ship for a hundred or more men."[159]

Stanton does not seem to be aware of the hardship brought upon the Hawaiians, though reference is made to two hundred "bearers" carrying fifty pounds each.

153. Erskine, *Twenty Years*, 212–13.
154. Erskine, *Twenty Years*, 217.
155. Erskine, *Twenty Years*, 219.
156. Erskine, *Twenty Years*, 221.
157. "No good." See Erskine, *Twenty Years*, 217.
158. German for "wives."
159. Erskine, *Twenty Years*, 217.

Stanton notes the "provisions stowed in the great island calabashes."[160] Erskine by contrast specifies varying weights carried by different men and various sizes of calabashes as well.

Stanton also writes about the bearers tramping "through canefields (including missionary Titus Coan's)." When it comes to the trampling of Coan's canefield's, Stanton might provide a clue. "Peter A. Brinsmade, a Honolulu businessman, Bible teacher, and US Consul who had come along 'to share our troubles and fatigues.'"[161] Brinsmade "graduated from Bowdoin College in 1826 and attended Andover Seminary 1826–28 and Yale Theological Seminary 1828–29."

In Hawai'i Peter Brinsmade[162] participated in Ladd and Co., "an early business partnership" in the island kingdom. "The company was behind the first commercial sugar cane plantation and first international land speculation in the Hawaiian Islands . . . Joseph Goodrich of the Hilo mission and Samuel Ruggles[163] of the Kona Mission had experimented with using agriculture to support their missions as well as give employment to their students . . . After trying to get Rev. Goodrich to run the operation, [William Northey] Hooper[164] [became the] land manager, despite having no training in engineering nor agriculture."[165]

Goodrich left not long after Hooper took up his position in Hilo. Therefore, the sugar cane fields identified as being Coan's may have originally belonged to Goodrich. Another theory is that Brinsmade indicated they were Coan's fields because he assumed Coan had taken over the fields, if they were near the former Goodrich home in which the Coans now lived.

Pastor Brian Welsh of the Haili church in Hilo provided the author with the following information: "I found this in our Conference records about TC lands. 'These two parcels are located south of the town of Hilo and they are separated by the Old Saddle Road which runs between them. The area is zoned as conservation land because part of it forms a watershed, and there is income of almost thirty thousand dollars per year from the sale of water on Parcel 12.[166] These forested lands are still in a pristine state.

---

160. Stanton, *First Great United States Exploring Expedition*, 225.

161. Stanton, *First Great United States Exploring Expedition*, 225. Stanton provides no citation for this quotation.

162. Brinsmade also held diplomatic positions during the late 1830s and 1840s. "On April 13, 1839, Peter Brinsmade was appointed American consular agent after John Coffin Jones. This was originally an unpaid position of the lowest rank in the United States Department of State." That would have been his position during the Expedition's time in the Hilo area. "In July 1844 he was promoted to the rank of consul." Wikipedia, "Ladd & Co."

163. Samuel Ruggles returned for the United States in early 1834 because of poor health and was released from the ABCFM in 1836, Judd, *Missionary Album*, 168.

164. Another founding partner of Ladd and Co.

165. Wikipedia, "Ladd & Co."

166. This land might have been sold after this email. See the legacy chapter.

"'This land at Punahoa II was a part of larger area of land owned by the American Board of Commissioners for Foreign Missions (ABCFM). A subdivision of the ABCFM lands was made long ago under which 1/3 each set aside to COAN, [David] Lyman, and [Dr. Charles] Wetmore."[167]

C. S. Lyman addresses himself to the follow up to the *Vincennes* visit, including the treatment of Hawaiians and harming of Coan land. He provides further perspective a few years after the events breaking the momentum of the Awakening and harming many Hawaiian people. From his journal: "Mon. June 29. Eve [of leaving for trip to Kilauea][168] at Mr. Coan's. In speaking of Wilkes's Ex[ploring] Ex[pedition] Mr. Coan mentioned the facts in reference to certain matters where Wilkes does him gross injury and injustice." Coan is understated in his writings on his being "despitefully used" [Luke 6:28].[169]

Lyman then quotes from *Wilkes's Narrative*. "Mr. Goodrich, the missionary who preceded Mr. Coan, was very desirous of introducing the culture of sugar-cane and coffee, and became very active in promoting it. With the assistance of the natives he planted a large number of coffee trees, and was bent upon instructing them in the mode of cultivating both. He also erected a small sugar-mill. I regretted much to hear that his successor viewed all these improvements in a far different light, and, not content to allow the trees to fall into neglect, he actually took the trouble to root them up, in order to arrest the progress of the improvement of the natives in their culture.

"I walked around the garden with the missionary, and saw all the vines, fruit, and ornamental trees, to which his predecessor had paid so much attention, and in which he had taken such pride, going to waste. One would have thought that the spirit of his calling would have dictated a more worthy and enlightened course. I never was more satisfied with the folly of such a step, than when the question was asked me by an intelligent native, 'Why the missionaries no like grow sugar-cane and coffee?' . . .

"Being much engaged with the natives, I had a fair opportunity of observing their improvement in religious knowledge; and I regret to say, that it is not such as I anticipated from the accounts that were given me, or equal to what it ought to be from the exertions of their pastor; for, while I cannot but condemn the course he has pursued in rooting up the coffee plantations, and overturning the good works of his predecessor, I must do him the justice to say, he is untiring in his clerical duties, and his field is one of constant labour, both of mind and body."[170]

Wilkes claims that Coan had a different view than Goodrich on developing coffee and sugar cane. With regard to coffee, Lyman avers that "Wilkes's whole statement is grossly false and his insinuations unmanly and unjust . . . In reference to the sugar

---

167. Unspecified Hawaiian Conference of the United Church of Christ document, in Brian Walsh May 6, 2013, email to author, May 6, 2013.

168. Brackets added. Further brackets by Lyman unless otherwise noted.

169. Lyman, *Around the Horn*, np.

170. Wilkes, *Voyage Round the World*, 209–10, in Lyman, *Around the Horn*, 85–86.

cane Mr. Coan was urged by the complaints of the natives [to] drop a line to Capt. W[ilkes] stating the facts. At Wilkes's request [Coan] undertook to investigate the matter and distributed the $10 remuneration to the best of his judgment, thus spending a solid day in doing Capt. [Wilkes]'s own work, and for which Capt. [Wilkes] sent him a note of thanks and afterwards sent out the false insinuations contained in his book."[171]

Stanton appears to uncritically pass along Wilkes's perspective. Upon the Expedition members returning from "Pendulum Peak,"[172] "Titus Coan was waiting to show the commander around the Hilo mission, where he set the pupils to reciting, and then presented Wilkes with a bill for damage done to his sugar cane. Ten dollars. Wilkes regarded it as a piece of extortion but paid up. Whether he ever knew that his ship had been full of 'yellow hores' [sic] during his absence there is no knowing. But as shortly before departure he received from Coan a complimentary note on the 'exemplary conduct'[173] of the crew during their stay at Hilo, he[174] at least knew to leave well enough alone."[175]

Returning to Lyman's journal, C. S. talks about the Hawaiians and working on Sundays. "As to the men going up the Mt. on the Sabbath,[176] the people had too much conscience to hire themselves at all till Mr. Coan ascertained that it was professedly a case of necessity and gave them to understand that it was proper for them to go [up the mountain]. Instead of his hindering the party, they could have done nothing without his assistance. He afterwards found he had been imposed upon. Instead of ten or twelve as requested they took fifty men, and there was no necessity in this case. The mountain party was in want of nothing but tea, sugar, and such like articles."[177]

Whatever the details of the Ex Ex visit, the momentum of the Great Awakening gradually came to an end because of that period. The denouement of the Great Revival occurred in 1841.

Coan then seeks to make the best of the situation. "This was a trial of faith, and a fan to winnow the church, but most of our Christians stood fast, and although it checked the progress of the revival, for the loss to the church was less than might have been feared."[178]

Daws notes that as the years and decades passed, "it seemed the reputation of the revivalist wing of the Sandwich Islands mission stood higher than it had done during

---

171. Lyman, *Around the Horn*, 86.

172. The name given to the camp near the top of Mauna Loa.

173. Cf. Sarah Lyman comments above.

174. Wilkes?

175. Stanton, *First Great United States Exploring Expedition*, 225. NB: Online endnote has many citations making it difficult to know for certain what the Wilkes page number(s) is/are.

176. For Coan's views on whalers and Sunday in particular, see in later chapter, his *Sailor's Sabbath*.

177. Lyman, *Around the Horn*, 87–88.

178. Coan, *Life*, 67.

TITUS COAN AS A PASSIONATE REVIVAL LEADER

Daws writes that by "nature Coan was an extremely ardent man. Love was a driving force in his life: he loved his wife, he loved Christ, and he loved his work. Sometimes those affections were mingled in his thinking. On his second wedding anniversary he wrote to his wife of their joint marriage to 'him whom our souls love.' Jesus was their 'eternal husband,' and Coan looked forward to the time when 'we shall feel our union to him consummated and changeless.'"[180] Late in life, Coan wrote to a fellow-clergyman about the overwhelming passion of his early Christian love:

"'When I came to these Islands, and before I could use the Hawaiian language, I often felt as if I should burst with strong desires to speak the word to the natives around me. And when my mouth was opened to speak of the love of God in Christ, I felt that the very chords of my heart were wrapped around my hearers, and that some inward power was helping me to draw them in, as the fisherman feels when drawing in his net filled with fishes.'"[181]

"This 'personal magnetism of love' was what endeared him to his hearers. Looking back, S. E. Bishop . . . wrote of Coan 'wrapping his heart around his young listeners, and [drawing] us, sweetly and irresistibly, to the love of God in Christ. I, later, came under the stringent intellectual and spiritual force of Finney, and felt the piercing power of the Spirit's sword, in his hands, but have never known a winning power of love in any preacher like that of the spiritual father of our childhood.'"[182]

Daws continues. "Coan was able to translate his spiritual ardency into physical energy. His parish was difficult and dangerous to traverse, but he itinerated endlessly. He had a boundless enthusiasm for the practical work of evangelization. At the height of the Revival he wrote to his brother: 'I am pressed above measure with watchings and preachings, and with cares and toil which cannot be told. But the grace of God is sufficient and he sustains me wonderfully. I am preaching almost incessantly, and in my narrow sphere I am determined, through the grace of God, fully to preach the gospel of Christ . . . I am often unavoidably exposed by rains, wet garments, &c. But I am sure that labor, and sometimes hardship even, is the best physic for man. I need not tell you that I am exceedingly joyful in all these labors.'"

---

179. Daws, "Evangelism," 32–33.

180. Titus to Fidelia Coan, November 3, 1838, in Coan Letters, NYHS at HMCS, in Daws, "Evangelism," 24.

181. Coan to Bishop, December 24, 1881, in Coan, *Memorial Volume*, 223, in Daws, "Evangelism," 24–25.

182. Bishop, in Coan, *Memorial Volume*, 222–23, in Daws, "Evangelism," 25.

Daws sums up Coan's ardent nature by describing him as both mystical and practical. "Coan's almost mystical conception of love, then, was capable of transformation into a sturdy practicality. His New Testament gentleness and spirituality were also balanced by an Old Testament sense of the power and harshness of a wrathful God. His own writing was full of this classic evangelistic tension, and his greatest triumphs came at a time when God appeared to have acted to force his parishioners to make an immediate choice between suffering the punishments of the law and grasping the sweet rewards of the gospel."[183]

In his Doctor of Ministry dissertation, Tamashiro writes about "Titus Coan as Revival Leader."[184] He notes that he "was increasingly fulfilling his role as an evangelist." Reminding the reader of Coan's relation to the evangelist Asahel Nettleton and Coan's being "stirred by the explosive revival of Charles Finney," Tamshiro notes that Coan has the revival characteristic "of diligence and sacrifice in doing whatever it took to reach people for Christ. He was not lazy but worked hard to evangelize his mission field."[185]

The next revival characteristic Coan exhibits is "his conservative stance on doctrinal issues." This characteristic is fascinating, given the criticisms Coan received from traditionalists who might have well viewed themselves as traditionalists and conservatives upset with Coan's application of New Measures. Another way of putting it might be "revival results from sound doctrine" or "one of the side benefits of sound doctrine is revival." Tamashiro also rightly notes that "Coan had a systematic plan to assimilate converts into the church,"[186] to an extent that his critics refused to recognize.

The first revivalist trait Coan showed, according to Tamashiro, "was his love for the Hawaiian people . . . Coan was effective as a revival leader because people felt loved by him."[187]

Coan was not only a loving revivalist. He was also an observant Renaissance man.

---

183. Daws, "Evangelism," 24–25.

184. Tamashiro, "Original Monotheism."

185. Tamashiro, "Original Monotheism," 200–01.

186. Tamashiro, "Original Monotheism," 202.

187. Tamashiro, "Original Monotheism," 200. NB: This was written by someone who serves and loves his flock at Puna Baptist Church in Pahoa.

RENAISSANCE MAN

7

Scientist

"This is an age when enlightened skepticism makes gigantic strides, and with the weapons of false philosophy and perverted science strikes hard blows at simple faith and evangelical truth. It is, therefore, a great blessing to Zion that Christian savants are stationed over all the earth, able and willing to defend moral truth."[1]

"How surely discoveries and all true science go to confirm and elucidate the truths of our precious Bible!"[2]

"I do bless the Lord that your precious life is spared and that so much strength is given you to attend to the important duties of your profession, the illustration and defence of Christian science. I regard all Scripture as divine, and all true science none the less so; and the student and teacher of the one should ever be the student and teacher of the other. Both are filled with lofty and profound mysteries, and both proclaim the Infinite, Eternal, and All-wise God. Both are and must be reconcilable, and it has always been a joy to me that, in all your multiplied and varied labors in the department of natural science, you have recognized the divine hand."[3]

"Hands full of labor. Pressed, pressed, pressed. Must be doctor, school master, lawyer, minister, carpenter, mason, and a few other things in the same day."[4]

INTRODUCTION

Titus Coan was a revivalist. He was also a Renaissance man. As a part-time scientist, he is best known for his observations of and writing about volcanic activities. Those efforts will be examined in the following two chapters. Recognized as a scientist, he interacted with full-time scientists. Additionally, he was part of a cohort of missionaries

---

1. Coan to Dana, August 31, 1866, in Coan, *Memorial Volume*, 98.
2. Coan to DuPont, June 7, 1850, in Coan, *Memorial Volume*, 62.
3. Coan to Dana, October 6, 1874, in Coan, *Memorial Volume*, 137.
4. Coan to Edwin Hall, November 1, 1841, HMCS. The above words constitute the entire letter.

to Hawaii who followed various scientific pursuits. Coan kept climatological records. He served as a medical provider for fourteen years until a physician arrived. He experienced and wrote about the devastations of tsunamis and earthquakes. Some of the former and all of the latter were related to volcanoes. Those two scientific categories will provide the transition to the next two chapters.

COAN AND SCIENTISTS

Coan interacted through various writings, mostly letters, with various scientists. He wrote about Charles Darwin in his two books. In chapter XIV of *Patagonia*, he focuses on "Mr. Darwin's Explorations and Experiences."[5] The chapter opens with a date[6]: "*Hilo, Hawaii, December 1, 1876* . . . Since our visit to Patagonia I have much interested in several recent accounts of visitors to that savage land, as also to Tierra del Fuego and the Falkland Islands."

"From the published journals of some of these intelligent and observant travelers I take the liberty to make some extracts which will be of interest to readers." While Coan does not provide page numbers, he does cite a work by Darwin in the next paragraph. Therefore, quotation marks in the rest of the chapter can with some certainty be viewed as being from Darwin's book.

"The distinguished naturalist Charles Darwin, in his 'Voyage Round the World' in HMS *Beagle*, under the command of Captain Fitz Roy, RN, during the years 1832–36, visited the Falkland Islands, North and Eastern Patagonia, the Strait of Magellan, Tierra del Fuego, and the western shores of Patagonia. (See new edition, D. Appleton & Co., New York, 1873)."[7]

The above paragraph has fascinating items to draw out. First, this second journey of the *Beagle* overlapped in time and place with Coan's time in Patagonia. Second, Coan characterizes Darwin as the "distinguished naturalist Charles Darwin." By 1876, Darwin was a controversial figure in many Christian circles. As he often did, Coan stayed away from controversial matters that did not have direct bearing on his immediate ministry. It could also tie in with his above quotation on the validity of both the Bible and "true science."[8] Both men lived a similar life span—both died in 1882. Both secularists and Christians can be guilty of Darwin caricatures.

Perhaps Coan admires Darwin's Christian sympathies. Near the end of the Darwin chapter, Coan quotes Darwin's journal from the book commenting on the efforts of Captain Fitz Roy. Coan summarizes these writings with his own: "Who will not admire the generous, patient, and persistent efforts of Captain Fitz Roy in trying to plant the germs of Christianity and civilization in the heart of the wild, dreary, and

---

5. Coan, *Patagonia*, 269–86.
6. Journal entry?
7. Coan, *Patagonia*, 269.
8. Coan to Dana, October 6, 1874, in Coan, *Memorial Volume*, 137.

savage land of Tierra del Fuego? And who will not mourn that he felt compelled by the feelings of humanity to remove the missionary Matthews from scenes so sickening and dangerous so appalling as were met among these wretched savages?"[9]

For a little more than two pages Coan summarizes the pertinent part of the *Beagle*'s journey, and updates the population growth over a forty-year period. Coan characterizes Darwin as "our then young and enthusiastic scientist" who "had great opportunities to examine the flora, the fauna, and the geology of that wild country."[10] Coan's sojourn in Patagonia is limited in its scientific observations. While there are passing references to geography, any scientific descriptions appear to be primarily anthropological in nature.

In later years, Darwin asks Coan a question through his son Munson. Perhaps hoping to garner information confirming his theory of survival of the fittest, Darwin asks about infanticide in the Islands. "Darwin's queries about the practice of infanticide reached Coan in Hawaii . . . Through his son, he told Darwin that although infanticide was sometimes practiced, it was not prevalent in Hawaii, and moreover didn't favour the survival of one sex over the other as Darwin had suspected it might."[11]

Coan refers to Charles Darwin once in his autobiography. While visiting the Marquesas Islands, he ascends to a mountain ridge. "I measured the breadth of the spur or rib on which we ascended; it was two feet and four inches wide in one part of the way; in another it was only one foot in width, with awful gorges on either side. Mr. Darwin, describing a similar climb which he took in the island of Tahiti, says: 'I did not cease to wonder at these ravines and precipices; when viewing the country from one of the knife-edged ridges, the point of support was so small that the effect was nearly the same as it must be from a balloon.'"[12]

Coan was a lifelong friend of the American Christian C. S. Lyman from the time of the latter's visit to the Big Island of Hawai'i. Lyman was discussed in one of the revival chapters and will be found in the volcano chapters, as well as the "Ministry to Expatriates" chapter. A Yale professor of industrial mechanics and physics,[13] he visited the Coans for three months[14] and continued in correspondence with Coan until Coan's death in 1882.

While a naval officer, Samuel F. DuPont was scientifically curious. After he and Coan first met, they maintained a correspondence until DuPont's death in 1870.

Coan and James D. Dana met after the Exploratory Expedition arrived at Hilo in late 1840. Fidelia and Titus "received as a very welcome guest then youthful James D. Dana, one of the scientific corps, now so distinguished in various departments of

---

9. Coan, *Patagonia*, 286.
10. Coan, *Patagonia*, 270.
11. Charles Darwin Correspondence Project. No letter reference.
12. Coan, *Life*, 183–84. Coan does not cite the document of Darwin that Coan quotes.
13. Wikipedia, "Chester Lyman."
14. Coan, *Life*, 144.

natural science, and honored as a Christian philosopher. The friendship then formed has been increased by years and can never wane."[15]

In a letter to Dana, Coan links the two of them with C. S. Lyman. "Is it not a great blessing that you have a son to take your place in dear old Yale when you shall have gone up to the high school of heaven to explore and expatiate in the boundless realms of glory? I notice with interest 'Meeting of the American Association'[16] at Hartford, and that your son, as I suppose, took an active part in the exercises, and that our honored friend, C. S. Lyman, was vice president."[17]

After thanking Dana for his congratulations on his marriage to Lydia, Coan turns to a scientific discussion of coral reef-rock. Here Coan the scientist emerges. "You ask if there is any elevated coral reef-rock around the shores of Hawaii. I think not. I have traveled the whole circuit of this island by land, and in boats, canoes, and larger vessels, and there is hardly a point along the shores which I have not noticed carefully. Honolulu is built, much of it, upon elevated coral, and there are large areas of it in other portions of the Oahu shores. But I find nothing like it on Hawaii *nei*. You are aware that corals, even under the water, are not abundant on the 'weather side' of our islands, and all the good specimens we have are obtained by diving. Should I hereafter find that I am mistaken[18] in these statements, I will with great pleasure inform you."[19]

Coan appears to hold to a version of the "gap theory," in other words a gap of a great deal of time between Genesis chapter 1 verse 1 and verse 2. Further, he probably did not take the "days" of Genesis 1 to represent literal twenty-four hour days. Referring to Coan's letter on coral reefs, E. Alison Kay observes the following: "[N]either E. O. Hall, who had seen the Kahuku cliffs, nor Titus Coan, who had discussed coral reefs with James Dwight Dana, had problems with the earth's chronology."[20] Kay notes that, "describing his volcanoes, [Coan] frequently wrote of 'time immemorial.'"[21]

Dana worked with his father-in-law Professor Benjamin Silliman of Yale and brother-in-law Benjamin Silliman Jr. as co-editor of the *Silliman Journal*, which would

---

15. Coan, *Life*, 67–68.

16. Of science?

17. Coan to Dana, October 6, 1874, in Coan, *Memorial Volume*, 137–38.

18. One twenty-first-century scientist suggested that science has to do with correcting its most recent mistake. Coan's humility and openness to change his theory based on observation are praiseworthy.

19. Coan to Dana, October 6, 1874, in Coan, *Memorial Volume*, 138.

20. Kay, "Missionary Contributions" 45.

21. Kay, "Missionary Contributions," 45. In 52n103, Kay quotes Coan, *Life*, 313: "From time immemorial earthquakes have been common on Hawaii." In the main text, Kay continues with observing that Coan "would have been pleased by A. B. Lyons's description of occasional changes in sea level when coral reefs would be added to dry land, of the lowland regions of the older islands with strata of fossiliferous limestone, and conclusion that 'elevation of the land (or recession of the ocean) had taken place at a very recent period in geological time," 52n104.

become *The American Journal of Science*.[22] Numerous letter-articles would appear by Coan in that publication, mostly about volcanoes.

MISSIONARIES TO HAWAI'I AND THEIR SCIENTIFIC PURSUITS

Coan appears in an article with other missionaries to Hawai'i and their relatives. In her "Missionary Contributions to Hawaiian Natural History: What Darwin Didn't Know," E. Alison Kay[23] opens with a quotation by the young Benjamin Silliman:

> It is with great pleasure that we add our warm commendation of the late effort of the missionaries. Situated in a remote island, in the vast expanse of the Pacific intensely and ardently occupied in their great object, the moral improvement and civilization of the natives; remote from the lights of science, and subjected to the physical privations both frequent and severe, we certainly owe them many thanks for the great amount of valuable information which they have, incidentally, contributed, on the subject of the natural history of one of the most remarkable volcanic regions in the world.[24]

Kay notes the gap in the scholarship on this subject. "The role of the American missionaries and their descendants in the history of the Hawaiian Islands has been told in many different ways: in their own journals, letters, and autobiographies, and in biographies and analyses of their educational motives, churchly objectives, and family life. One role has received virtually no attention, their contributions to knowledge of Hawaiian natural history."[25]

Kay discusses Darwin's passion for the flora of Hawai'i. "Charles Darwin's comment to Joseph Dalton Hooker in 1850, 'Of all places in the world I would like to see a good flora of the Sandwich Islands. I would subscribe fifty pounds[26] to any collector to go there and work at these islands.'[27] This suggests that even Darwin, who had read

---

22. Wikipedia, "American Journal of Science." For Coan Letters/Articles, see LOC Boxes 19 and 20.

23. Professor of zoology at the University of Hawai'i at Manoa and co-editor of *The Hawaiian Journal of History*.

24. Benjamin Silliman, 1826 quotation, in Kay, "Missionary Contributions," 27.

25. Kay, "Missionary Contributions," 26.

26. In 1850 the exchange rate of one pound sterling was five dollars, while the 1850 dollar was worth at least $27 in 2007. 50 times 5 times 27 equals $6,750.

27. Kay, "Missionary Contributions," 26. 46n1: "Frederick Burkhardt and Sydney Smith, The Correspondence of Charles Darwin (Cambridge: Cambridge UP, 1984) 7:454. 'The Cambridge ornithologist Alfred Newton was even more blunt than Darwin—"The Sandwich Isles have not been fortunate in their Natural Historians"—although Newton did notice S. B. Dole's "Synopsis of the Birds . . ." As a 'serviceable foundation for future work' and 'an honest piece of work, doing credit to its compiler.' 'Ornithology of the Sandwich Isles,' *Nature* (March 17, 1892): 465, 467."

everything there was to read about the Pacific,[28] failed to recognize that the missionaries had arrived in Hawai'i a decade before Darwin's own voyage to the Pacific."[29]

Kay avers that "Darwin's challenge" for people to collect flora "was unnecessary. The missionaries not only Christianized and educated but were themselves collectors in the Darwinian sense: volcano watchers, geologists, botanists, zoologists, geographers, climatologists, and mapmakers.[30] Thirty of the pioneer missionaries recorded their observations of nature under some ninety-four published titles; another 170 titles were penned by twenty-four members of the second generation."

She provides specifics on the publications in which the missionary contributions were found. "These publications are found in nineteenth- and early twentieth-century scientific journals such as *The American Journal of Science, Edinburgh New Philosophical Journal, Nature,* and *Science,* as well as national and local media, *The Friend, The Hawaiian Gazette, The Hawaiian Spectator, Maile Quarterly, Royal Hawaiian Agricultural Society Transactions, The Missionary Herald,* and *Scribners.* Articles published locally gained national and international attention when they were excerpted in newspapers and journals from San Francisco to Edinburgh."[31]

Kay describes the purpose of her article. "This study summarizes the contributions of the first and second generations of missionaries sponsored by the American Board of Commissioners of Foreign Missions and examines the background and significance of their work." While her article uses mostly published material, she recognizes the value of examining handwritten letters and journals. "Except in two or three instances, published sources only are utilized; consideration of holograph letters and journals will undoubtedly add more to the story."[32]

Kay turns to a discussion of the "volcano." See the next chapter for that section of the article. She also examines Sarah Joiner Lyman's earthquake diary. That material will be examined later in this chapter, as will be the tsunami observations by Wilkes and others.

Kay lists several areas of scientific endeavor. "In the period 1826–1916, there are also eighty-one titles on botany, land snails, birds, climate, and geology, eleven by the

---

28. Kay, "Missionary Contributions," 27. 46n2: "E. Alison Kay, 'Darwin's Biogeography and the Oceanic Islands of the Central Pacific, 1859–1909,' In *Darwin's Laboratory: Evolutionary Theory and Natural History in the Pacific,* edited by Roy M. MacLeod and Philip F. Rehbock. Honolulu: University of Hawai'i Press, 1995. 49–69."

29. Kay, "Missionary Contributions," 27.

30. One needs only peruse the pages of Judd, *Missionary Album,* to see examples of most of the scientific categories listed in this quotation.

31. Kay, "Missionary Contributions," 28. Footnote 3, 46, Kay notes that the "missionaries included here are those listed in the 1969 *Missionary Album* [Judd] and, in addition, Chester S. Lyman and Rufus Anderson," the leader of the ABCFM.

32. Kay, "Missionary Contributions," 28.

missionary fathers, seventy by their sons.³³ The Rev. Edward Bailer and Dr. Charles Wetmore compiled the first lists of Hawaiian ferns and fishes respectively."³⁴

Kay explains sketches of native birds by Harriet Fidelia Coan. "The second-generation missionaries also engaged in the study of birds, botany, climate geology, and soils. Eleven species of native birds painted from life by [one of] Titus Coan's daughter[s], Harriet Fidelia Coan, about 1860³⁵ now grace the collections of the Lyman House Memorial Museum in Hilo."

Hattie exhibits an artistic gift with her attention to detail and beautiful sketches of the two birds portrayed in Figure 3 of the article. "Two of eight species of birds painted by Harriet Coan (1839–1906) in Hilo, probably about 1860. Top: Moho, the Hawaiian Rail, Porzana sand tvichensis, a small (5.5 inches in length) flightless bird known only from the island of Hawai'i on the grassy uplands adjacent to forests. It was last seen alive about 1894. Bottom: Kolea, the Pacific Golden Plover, Pluvialis fulva, which journeys more than two thousand miles each August from its breeding grounds in Siberia and Alaska to Hawai'i and returns to its nesting grounds in April."³⁶

Kay explains that the missionaries and their children were such keen scientific observers because of their New England heritage. "Answers to why and how the missionaries, parents and children, assembled such a remarkable record of information about Hawaiian natural history lie in their New England heritage, their education, their continuing bond with New England, and in an innate love of nature associated with the natural theology embraced by Congregationalists of the day. The study of God's creations was another route to the understanding of God."³⁷

She notes that Dana stayed with the Coans during the visit of the Exploring Expedition and suggests that most members of the Expedition stayed with someone in Hilo. "Most members of the US Exploring Expedition of 1840–41 found someone with whom to stay; and, indeed, it was on that visit that the lifelong friendship of one of the world's greatest geologists, James Dana, and the volcano-watching preacher, Titus Coan, was established."³⁸

She relates that the missionary doctor, Gerrit Judd,³⁹ "was entrusted with the execution of the Exploring Expedition ascent of Mauna Loa; he organized food and

---

33. Kay, "Missionary Contributions," 47n13. "Lists of the authors and their publications are deposited in the Hawaiian Historical Society Library, Hawaiian Mission Children's Society Library, and the University of Hawai'i Library."

34. Kay, "Missionary Contributions," 28–29. 47n16. "Edward Bailey, 'Hawaiian Ferns: A Synopsis,' HAA (1882) 5–62; Charles H. Wetmore, 'Concerning Hawaiian Fishes,' HAA (1889) 90–97."

35. When Harriet was in her early twenties.

36. Kay, "Missionary Contributions," 31, 33. "Photos courtesy of the Lyman House Memorial Museum."

37. Kay, "Missionary Contributions," 21.

38. Kay, Missionary Contributions,"35.

39. Though Gerrit and Laura "were stationed in Honolulu, Dr. Judd made frequent professional visits to other stations." Judd, *Missionary Album*, 128.

COAN THE SCIENTIST

In his lectures on the Bible and other subjects, he was open and made use of the most recent works, such as archaeology. In a June 7, 1850, letter to Captain Samuel F. DuPont, Coan thanks him for a box of books, and one in particular that tied in perfectly with his Bible lecture series. "The box also came in perfect order and is received with great gratitude. Like all tokens of true love it is *priceless*. The books, especially *Nineveh*, are what we longed to get hold of. Nothing could have been more opportune or acceptable. A short time ago I lectured to my people on the ancient history, the fall, and the recent disentombing of that vast Assyrian city. The facts stated were fresh in the recollection of many when your books came. The volumes were taken into our monthly lectures and the plates exhibited, illustrating and corroborating what the natives had before heard. I need not say that they excited enthusiastic interest. We anticipate a treat in reading the works you sent."[41]

Excavations of Nineveh took place not long before Coan received the volumes on the subject. "In 1847, the young British adventurer Sir Austen Henry Layard explored the ruins. In the Kuyunjik mound in 1849, Layard discovered the glorious edifice of Sennacherib, the 'Palace without Rival,' with many rooms and colossal bas-reliefs. He also unearthed the famous library of Ashurbanipal with twenty-two thousand cuneiform clay tablets."[42] Timothy Larsen further explains Layard and relates the adventurer's first two volumes on the subject. "In the middle of the nineteenth century, the English adventurer Austen Henry Layard (1817–94) uncovered several ancient, buried cities, including the capital Nineveh, and dragged sizeable bits of them back to the British Museum. His first book on his travels and discoveries, *Nineveh and Its Remains: With an Account of a Visit to the Chaldean Christians of Kurdistan, and the Yezidis; and an Inquiry into the Manner and Arts of the Ancient Assyrians*, published in two volumes in 1849, was a Victorian sensation and triumphant bestseller for many years."[43] Some of the plates found in the 1849 volumes might have also been found in Layard's 1854 *Discoveries at Nineveh*.[44]

---

40. Kay, "Missionary Contributions," 35. 49n54, "Judd, 'Dr. Judd,' 101, in Porteus, *Century of Social Thinking*, 353. Judd nearly lost his life on the expedition. While collecting gases in Kilauea crater, he was pinned under an over-hanging ledge by a sudden explosion just as a river of lava was rolling toward him. He was rescued by his Hawaiian guide, Kalama, with only a burned shirt and wrist."

41. Coan to DuPont, June 7, 1850, in Coan, *Memorial Volume*, 63. The next sentence in the letter is the second quotation at the beginning of this chapter.

42. New World Encyclopedia, "Nineveh."

43. Larsen, "Austin Henry Layard's Nineveh."

44. Bible History, "Discoveries at Nineveh."

SCIENTIST

Coan made geographic and geological observations. Humphrey introduces Coan via geography: "To this parish, occupying the eastern third of the island of Hawaii, a strange mingling of crags and valleys, of torrents and volcanoes, of beauty and barrenness, and to this interesting people, was called the young missionary Titus Coan."[45]

Coan made climatological observations. He kept regular records of rainfall in Hilo. He provides a "Daily Journal of Rain at Hilo, Hawaii, From August 1, 1847, to July 31, 1847." At the top of the introductory note is "From *The Polynesian*"[46] and at the bottom is "J. J. Jarves, Esp. Editor of *The Polynesian*."

The note Coan wrote to *The Polynesian* on August 18, 1847, is in between those two lines. It indicates scientific thoroughness and precision. "My dear Sir:—On this sheet I have provided an abstract from my Journal of Rain at Hilo, from August 1, 1846, to July 31, 1847. The amount of rain for each day is recorded in inches and thousandths[47] of an inch. The total amount which fell during the year, you will see to be 132 and 7 thousandths cubic inches. Of this, 90,730[48] fell in the night. The greatest amount which fell in a day is 10,466 inches. This was on the twenty-first of March. The greatest quantity which fell in any one month was 38,156 inches. This was in March. Taking the year together, it has been the most rainy of any we have experienced since our residence at the Islands.[49] Most truly yours. TITUS COAN."[50]

Another (by then) former ABCFM missionary solved a weather phenomenon mystery. "As an amateur scientist, [Sereno Edwards] Bishop gained some renown. Beginning in September 1883, a series of rings around the sun became apparent at sunset across the Pacific and in Hawai'i. This phenomenon, which puzzled the world, Bishop determined, was the result of the massive eruption and virtual destruction of Krakatoa Island, off the coast of Java on August 26, 1883. Bishop published his findings in an article titled 'The Equatorial Smoke-Stream from Krakatoa' in the *Hawaiian*

---

45. Humphrey, "VI. Titus Coan," 3–4.

46. "The four-to-eight page *Polynesian* was published weekly in Honolulu in English and some Hawaiian from June 6, 1840 to December 11, 1841 (first series), and again from May 18, 1844 to February 6, 1864 (second series). James Jackson Jarves ran the first series with a combination of mission support, advertising, and subscriptions. However, the paper was not profitable, and he shut it down after only two and a half years. Jarves reestablished the paper under the same title in May 1844. Two months later, the *Polynesian* became the "Official Journal of the Hawaiian Government" and remained so until 1861, with Charles E. Hitchcock, Edwin O. Hall, Charles G. Hopkins, and Abraham Fornander as subsequent editors. The *Polynesian* was the leading paper on O'ahu in the mid-1800s." LOC, "About the Polynesian."

47. Coan had a precise rain gauge. During the late twentieth century and early twenty-first century, rain inches were measured to the nearest hundredth.

48. Note that when Coan uses a comma, today a period would be used.

49. As of 2014, the average annual precipitation in Hilo was 126.69 inches. US Climate Data, "Climate Hilo–Hawaii."

50 Coan, "Daily Journal of Rain in Hilo, Hawaii," *The Friend* 5.17 (1847) 133.

Monthly of May 1884. Bishop's observations were accepted by the scientific world and in his honor the 'circles' were designated as 'Bishop's Rings.'"[51]

COAN THE MEDICAL CARE GIVER

Titus Coan's scientific efforts took an even more practical turn when he served as the sole provider of medical care to Hawaiians in the Hilo, Puna and Kau districts between 1835 and 1849, when Dr. Charles Wetmore arrived. As soon as he was sharing about the Great Physician, Coan provided medical help to Hawaiians. In his autobiography he writes about diseases and epidemics. As to the care of Hawaiians, he writes: "At the central station and on all my tours I was thronged with the sick and afflicted multitudes, or their friends, begging for remedies for almost all kinds of diseases. So numerous were the applications for medicines, and so varied and sad were the spectacles of disease, that it became a task for the skill and the whole time of a well-read and experienced physician. I had a fair collection of medical books, and these were consulted as much as was possible in connection with my other labors, but my regret was that I could not visit them as I wished, or pay them the attention that they needed."[52]

Coan writes about "the scourge" of small pox that would hit the Hawaiians in 1853.[53] In *Guns, Germs, and Steel: The Fates of Human Societies*, Jared Diamond writes about Europeans bringing illnesses to indigenous peoples, as well as Europeans falling to indigenous diseases, such as malaria.[54] About Hawai'i and epidemic illnesses, Diamond writes, "Syphilis, gonorrhea, tuberculosis, and influenza arriving with Captain Cook in 1779, followed by a big typhoid epidemic in 1804 and numerous 'minor' epidemics, reduced Hawaii's population from around half a million in 1779 to 84,000 in 1853, the year when smallpox finally reached Hawaii and killed around ten thousand of the survivors."[55]

"Since there was no resident doctor in Hilo until 1849, Native Hawaiians came to Coans' house at all hours for 'such simple medical treatment as a missionary must give where there is no doctor.'"[56]

---

51. *Hawaiian Monthly*, May 1884: 106–10, in Forbes et al., *Partners in Change*, 135.

52. Coan, *Life*, 63.

53. Coan, *Life*, 81; and in the Marquesas Islands, 198 and 202.

54. Diamond, *Guns, Germs, and Steel*, 214: Germs "did not act solely to Europeans' advantage. While the New World and Australia did not harbor native epidemic diseases awaiting Europeans, tropical Asia, Africa, Indonesia, and New Guinea certainly did." Additionally, Hawai'i's low-elevation tropical climate was salubrious to some missionaries and unhealthy for others. For specific care in the Hilo area, see Dr. Wetmore entry in Forbes et al., *Partners in Change*, 627.

55. Diamond, *Guns, Germs, and Steel*, 214.

56. Forbes et al., *Partners in Change*, 186. Unclear whether quotation is from daughter Hattie Coan, cited on 187.

Fourteen years after Titus Coan's arrival in Hilo, "a well-read and experienced physician" arrived in the person of Dr. Charles Wetmore. Coan notes the following with regard to Wetmore's arrival and the relief he brought to him. Showing something of his sense of humor Coan writes, "When at last, in 1849, a good physician, Charles H. Wetmore, was sent to our relief, my heart rejoiced. I immediately resigned my medical functions, turned over my medicine-chest and drugs to him, and blessed the Lord that I was not doomed to wander 'forty years in the wilderness [Deut 29:5] of powders and pills.' This kind and faithful doctor with his excellent wife[57] have been our nearest neighbors ever since their arrival."[58]

In his remembrance of Coan, Dr. Wetmore[59] noted in 1883, "Up to the time of my arrival at the Islands, Mr. Coan had labored assiduously both for the souls and bodies of his parishioners. As soon as my acquaintance with the Hawaiian language allowed me to take up the work of the physician he gave it into my hands cheerfully, that he might devote himself more efficiently 'to the ministry of the work.' I was often obliged to ask him to interpret for me, as new cases presented themselves and new language was required. How patiently he rendered the needed aid, and how gladly he helped me in acquiring a knowledge of the new tongue, I need only to allude to; these were prominent features of his character to the very last hours of his life."[60]

"VOLCANIC WAVES": TSUNAMIS

In addition to observing and treating sick and injured Hawaiians, Coan observed several tsunamis[61] and assisted in the rescue and recovery after each one. That name and scientific event was not in his lexicon. Called "a gigantic wave" in 1837,[62] "volcanic waves" in 1868, and a "tidal wave" in 1877,[63] Coan sometimes knew the proximate cause of the wave, but usually not. Using the modern tool of the internet, it is possible to know when a distant earthquake the day before probably caused the destructive and deadly wave.

An 1878 visitor to Hilo writes of how the calm presentation of the Hilo area makes it difficult to believe that violent natural events can occur. "Now we round the

---

57. Judd, *Missionary Album*, 196–97, and Forbes et al., *Partners in Change*, 629–30.

58. Coan, *Life*, 63–64. The Wetmore Papers reside at the Lyman House Museum in Hilo.

59. For short Dr. Wetmore biography, see Forbes et al., *Partners in Change*, 625–28.

60. Coan, *Memorial Volume*, 229–30.

61. "There are two words used to describe tsunamis. 'Kaieʻe' is a general word for tsunami waves, and 'Kai mimiki' is used to describe the withdraw[al?] of the water before the Kai e ʻe arrives. The withdrawal of the water is actually the trough of the tsunami reaching shore." http://tsunami.org/7science/10_faqs.html#Hawaiian. Because Hilo's location causes it to be "the tsunami capital of the world" (Wikipedia, "Hilo Bay"), it is home to the Pacific Tsunami Museum.

62. Coan, *Life*, 51. Fidelia calls it a "tidal wave" in a December 1, 1837, letter to Esther Nettleton, HMCS, in Ehlke, "Enthusiastic Religion," 111.

63. Coan, *Life*, 316 and 320; Coan, *Memorial Volume*, 158.

last point and behold that semi-circle of beauty, the cocoanut-fringed Bay of Hilo, never to be forgotten for its charm, and not less for the tales told by Father Coan of what happened on its sloping shores under his own eye. Successive tidal waves have come unheralded and devastated that fair city front. One occasion the sea rose fifteen feet above high water mark in an instant, and carried houses, stores and struggling victims out to sea, in its reflux, to the great loss of lives and property. And yet the hazy atmosphere is so soft, the eternal summer sea so peaceful in its ripple on the smooth sand, that one could listen to any tale of disaster by ocean or earthquake or volcano and lie down on the soft grass in perfect peace, and feel 'Oh! It cannot be here!'"[64]

The first instanced wave to arrive after Coan's arrival has already been related as part of a spur to the early part of the Great Awakening. After talking about spiritual manifestations and Coan admonishing the people about the need for repentance, "God visited the people in judgment as well as in mercy. On the seventh of November, 1837, at the hour of evening prayers, we were startled by a heavy thud, and a sudden jar of the earth. The sound was like the fall of some vast body upon the beach, and in a few seconds a noise of mingled voices rising for a mile along the shore thrilled us like the wall of doom."

Immediately the family heard cries. Papa Coan ran outside to observe. "Instantly this was followed by a like wail from all the native houses around us. I immediately ran down to the sea, where a scene of wild ruin was spread out before me. The sea, moved by an unseen hand, had all on a sudden risen in a gigantic wave, and this wave, rushing in with the speed of a race-horse, had fallen upon the shore, sweeping everything not more than fifteen or twenty feet above high-water mark into indiscriminate ruin. Houses, furniture, calabashes, fuel, timber, canoes, food, clothing, everything floated wild upon the flood. About two hundred people, from the old man and woman of three-score years and ten [Ps 90:10], to the new-born infant, stripped of their earthly all, were struggling in the tumultuous waves. So sudden and unexpected was the catastrophe, that the people along the shore were literally 'eating and drinking,' and they 'knew not, until the flood came and swept them all away'" [Matt 24:39].

Coan continues to relate the oceanic event and describe the human tragedy unfolding before him. "The harbor was full of strugglers calling for help, while frantic parents and children, wives and husbands ran to and fro along the beach, calling for their lost ones. As wave after wave came in and retired, the strugglers were brought near the shore, where the more vigorous landed with desperate efforts and the weaker and exhausted were carried back upon the retreating wave, some to sink and rise no more till the noise of judgment wakes them."

He writes about the efforts of the crew of an English whaler to save those whom they could. "Twelve individuals were picked up while drifting out of the bay by the boats of *Admiral Cockburn*, an English whaler then in port. For a time the captain of the ship feared the loss of his vessel, but as the oscillating waves grew weaker and

---

64. Hallock, *Hawaii under King Kalakaua*, 58–59.

weaker, he lowered all his boats and went in search of those who were floating upon the current. Had this catastrophe occurred at midnight when all were asleep, hundreds of lives would undoubtedly have been lost. Through the great mercy of God, only thirteen were drowned."[65]

Ehlke gives input from Hiram Bingham, Titus, and Fidelia Coan. "At seven in the evening on November 7, the third day of the protracted meeting in Hilo, the deafening sound of rushing water, followed by loud wailing and cries of terror, struck the ears of the Coan family, just gathering for evening prayer with their household."[66] Ehlke then quotes Titus from a letter that appeared in *The Missionary Herald*.[67] It is virtually identical to part of the *Life* quotation provided above. Fidelia writes that the "Hawaiians all said it was the voice of God, that Christ had come upon them like a thief in the night for their rejection of him."[68]

From the perspective of four decades, Leavitt Hallock, writing about a visit to Coan in 1878, shares what Coan shared with him about this tidal wave. From the perspective of another thirty-plus years, he laments that, in his opinion Coan left Earth too soon. Transitioning from a discussion of Mauna Loa and how Coan knew more secrets about volcanoes than any man living, Hallock writes of the scientific knowledge Coan took with him when he died in late 1881. "Alas! That he so early left us, carrying many secrets with him into the beyond! In 1837, November 7, the crescent sand beach bounding Hilo harbor, 'with its fringe of palms and groves, and the great ocean slept in summer calm.' Four sermons had been preached that day, one on the text, 'Be ye also ready' [Matt 24:44]. The natives were singing hymns out of doors and Mr. Coan had gathered his family for evening worship, when suddenly there came a sound as of some enormous body striking the shore with tremendous force."[69] Hallock continues to paraphrase and quote Coan on the event.

Sarah Lyman provides this perspective on the same event: "As we were about to kneel for prayers in the evening we heard a great outcry among the natives on the beach." She and her husband "concluded that there was trouble among the sailors of an English ship now in port."

The Lymans concluded their prayers. "As soon as the prayer was over Mr. L. went out to ascertain the cause of such confusion when to our great surprise we found that the water in the bay had risen so as to go many rods[70] beyond its usual bonds. A number of houses had been in an instant swept away and the inmates carried no one knew where. In a little time however they began to swim out of the water. Some had been

---

65. Hallock, *Hawaii under King Kalakaua*, 51–52.

66. Bingham, *Residence*, 517, in Ehlke, "Enthusiastic Religion," 111. Did the Coans relate the story to Bingham?

67. Coan letter, *Missionary Herald* 34 (December 1838) 477, in Ehlke, "Enthusiastic Religion," 111.

68. Fidelia Coan to Esther Nettleton, December 1, 1837, in Ehlke, "Enthusiastic Religion," 111.

69. Hallock, *Hawaii under King Kalakaua*, 67–68.

70. A rod is sixteen and a half feet. Wikipedia, "Rod (unit)."

carried a considerable distance from their home, but owing to their skill in swimming had escaped a watery grave. The father came out of the water not knowing but the other members of the family were all drowned and so with the mother and children. Some members of a family were carried in one direction and some in another. Some individuals were carried out so far in to the bay that they must have drowned, but for the aid of the ship's crew now in port. They took thirteen out of the water some of whom were much exhausted. Eight dead bodies have been found and others are missing. One of the men from Laupahoehoe,[71] received to the church last Sabbath, was drowned. In a canoe house was a large company of people from abroad to attend our meeting. The house was swept away and the people escaped with the skin of their teeth. In another large house was a company from Puna. The house was destroyed and the people were scattered hither and thither. Only two however were drowned. Most of the people came out of the water as naked and destitute as they came in to the world, without a bit of kappa to cover them or a place to lay their heads."[72]

What caused this tsunami? More than likely an 8.0-magnitude earthquake that occurred off the coast of Concepcion, Chile, at 8 a.m. local time.[73] Charles Wilkes, the Commodore of the Exploring Expedition, relays information from Coan more than two years later, material from the Lyman "Record" of earthquakes, and other information, including from the Samoan Islands. Coan is able to be objectively scientific in his conversation with Wilkes. "Mr. Coan obliged me with the following account of the influx of the sea at Hilo, on the seventh of November, 1837. A similar occurrence, it will be recollected, took place at the island of Tutuila, in the Samoan Group."[74]

Wilkes describes the Hilo wave(s) as related by Coan. Then Wilkes broadens the lens to include Honolulu and Tutuila in Samoa. "It appears from the facts that have been stated relative to a like phenomenon at Tutuila, that although the two were not coincident, yet they were so closely allied in point of time, as to leave no doubt of the same cause having produced both."

Tying the event in with the "almost coincident earthquake of Chili [sic] that happened on the seventh of November, 1837," Wilkes writes, "It is certain that the phenomenon took place first at the Samoan Group, and supposing that the two watches by which it was noted were both correct, as the difference of longitude is thirteen degrees, the elapsed time from the first wave at Tutuila to that of the observations at Oahu, allowing for the difference of longitude, was two hours, thirty minutes."[75]

Wilkes cites a writer in the *Hawaiian Spectator* with providing information concerning the wave's affect on Oahu and on to Hilo. "At Oahu this phenomenon was likewise noted by Dr. Rooke, who has given an account of it in the *Hawaiian Spectator*,

---

71. Laupahoehoe is on the coast twenty-five and a half miles north of Hilo.
72. Martin, *Sarah Joiner Lyman*, 97–98.
73. Wikipedia, "List of Earthquakes in Chile."
74. Wilkes, *Voyage Round the World*, 226.
75. Wilkes, *Voyage Round the World*, 228.

Vol. I., January, 1838. The time of its occurrence, as given by him, was 6 o'clock, p.m., and the sea continued to vibrate until the next day at noon. The time of commencement at Oahu preceded that at Hilo by half an hour."[76]

Writing of the distance from Samoa to Honolulu, Wilkes writes that the "actual distance [from Samoa to Honolulu] is two thousand two hundred and fifty miles, on a course N. 50*E.,[77] which would prove that the wave must have proceeded from south to north at the rate of nine hundred miles."[78]

In 1841, Sarah Lyman reports a tsunami that is found neither in *Life* or the *Memorial Volume*. "May 18, 1841. Last night I witnessed a wonderful display of the mighty power of him who holds the sea as in the hollow his hand. About half past 5 o'clock p.m. it was discovered that the water in the bay had receded several rods below low water mark, but it soon returned and continued to rise till twelve or fifteen feet above high water mark, and this in about ten minutes was followed by a reflux and then an influx . . . and thus it continued to do till dark closed upon us, though not rising so high as during the first six or seven times. This morning the tide was lower than usual till about 8 a.m. Then it came in as usual to high water mark. There was no noise accompanied the rising last night and the water flowed in so gently that no injury was done to the houses which it entered. It approached to within a few feet of our canoe house and flowed into the house at Hilo, occupied by Commodore Wilkes. The people were terrified and those living near the beach gathered up their earthly all and fled for safety to the houses on more elevated ground, where they remained during the night. It is very difficult to account for such a singular phenomenon."[79]

The phenomenon could well be explained by an earthquake occurring May 17, 1841, that led to a tsunami at Hilo of less than five meters in height. Geocases UK indicates that an 8.0 earthquake generates a tsunami between four and six meters in height.[80]

Before examining the 1868 "volcanic wave," for which the source is very well known, attention will first be given to the "tidal wave" of 1877. Titus Coan writes "his son,"[81] "On the tenth inst[ant] a great tidal wave swept our shores, destroying buildings along the beach, removing Waikea bridge, wharf, and warehouse, and destroying the buildings along the banks of the Wailoa, laying that pretty and thriving suburb of Hilo in utter ruin. Trees are torn up by the roots, and the debris of walls, gardens, bridge, abutments and all, is scattered in wild confusion over scores of acres. The wave was twelve to fourteen feet high, and the oscillations of the sea continued for three days. Five persons were drowned, many more bruised and maimed. The picture of

---

76. Wilkes, *Voyage Round the World*, 227.
77. Perhaps that is the direction from Chile?
78. Wilkes, *Voyage Round the World*, 227–28.
79. Martin, *Sarah Joiner Lyman*, 109.
80. http://www.geocases1.co.uk/printable/Tsunamis.htm.
81. It is not known whether this refers to Munson or Latimer.

loss and of suffering is sad. Bitter experience teaches what men are slow to believe, not to build houses on the sand [Matt 7:26] nor lay up treasures where destroyers are abroad" [Matt 6:19–20].[82]

Titus writes that a "volcanic wave fell upon Hilo on the morning of the tenth of May, 1877."[83] Dana notes that "it was of South American origin, where there were heavy earth-shocks, and not of Hawaiian." He characterizes it as a "destructive earthquake wave . . . felt at the Hawaiian Islands on May 10, 1877, which rose at Hilo to a height of thirty-six feet."[84]

In his autobiography, Coan quotes a letter by Lydia relating the description of the affects of the 1877 tsunami. She provides the most thorough description of the aftermath of a tsunami during the years of Coan's residence in Hilo. "A chilly, cheerless night shuts down upon a day that has had no parallel in kind in my previous experiences. I was just rousing from quiet slumbers this morning, not long after five, when heavy knocking at our door hastened me to it. There stood Kanuku, almost wild with excitement, and so breathless she could hardly give form to the words she poured forth; but I gathered their substance. A volcanic wave had swept in upon the shore; houses were going down, and people were hurrying *mauka* (inland) with what of earthly goods they could carry.'"

She writes how she and Titus hastened to the shore and describes what they saw. "We hastened to the beach. People on foot and on horseback were hurrying in all directions; men with chests and trunks on their backs, women with bundles of bedding and clothing under which they staggered, grandmothers with three- or four-year-old children on their shoulders, and mothers with little babes, all in quest of safety and a place to lodge their burdens. Arrived at the foot of our street what a sight we beheld! Houses were lifted off their underpinning and removed a fathom[85] or more—some had tumbled in sad confusion and lay prone in the little ponds that remained of the sea in various depressed places. Riders at breakneck speed from Waiekea brought word of still more complete ruin there; the bridge, they said, was gone.'"

Lydia and Titus continue to survey the devastation. They witness the arrival of more waves. "'We walked on toward the Wailama. Then a shout, and we looked back to see the waves rising and surging landward, so we dared not linger, but turned on our track, for a better chance of escape should the sea again overpass its bounds.'"

She observes people "wading in water where their homes had stood half an hour before, gathering up goods soaked by the brine, and begrimed with mud, men in wet garments who had had to swim for their lives, and women with terror in their faces caught up the refrain of a death-wail that reached our ears from the region of

---

82. Titus Coan, May 22, 1877, in Coan, *Memorial Volume*, 158–59.

83. Coan, *Life*, 320.

84. Dana, quoted on "sacred text." For earthquake information, see Zamudio et al.,"Seismic hazard assessment."

85. A fathom is six feet.

Kanae's place, and the word flew from lip to lip that old Kaipo was missing. Asleep, with Kanae's babe pillowed near her when the wave came upon them, she had wakened, and hastening out of the house found herself in deep water. Holding the little one above her head, she had courage and strength to keep it safe till the mother swam for it, and then, no one knows how, the old woman was swept out to sea, and hours after, the body was found at Honori."

Lydia notes how a rainstorm added insult to injury. "About 9 o'clock, the rain which had come infrequent light flurries before, began to pour in earnest, and has fallen in such pitiless inclemency through the day, that it has added to the discomforts of the poor homeless wanders, and to the general gloom that hangs over our little town."

She relates Titus's assistance to others and the calmness he brought to others. "Mr. Coan has been out much of the time here and there with words of sympathy and comfort. Rebecca Nakuina told me the natives said they were safe wherever he was. One poor old man came to our door and asked in most pathetic tones if it was true that Mr. Coan had said that at noon there would be another and heavier wave, and went away comforted when assured that he had not."

She tells of a ship in the harbor affected by the wave. "A large barque at anchor in our harbor was tossed about most marvelously at the very mercy of every efflux and reflux wave. For hours she writhed under this restless tossing, one moment pointing her prow toward Puna, and the next in the opposite direction, running back and forth the full length of her cable, like a weaver's shuttle, sometimes careening so far that we feared the next moment to see her on her beam ends, and then struggling to right herself, and for a little recovering her usual position, only to repeat these movements."

On the next day, Lydia describes the weather and is affected by the deepening understanding of the affects of the devastation. "The birds sang and the sun shone this morning, as if there were no sorrow here. But it was a great blessing that the day was fair; the sunshine was needed for heart-warmth and for drying what of clothing and household effects had been collected from the mud and slime in which they were found.

"We went over the same ground on the nearest beach that we visited yesterday, only to realize more fully the wild havoc that had been made.

"What shall I say of what we saw on the other side of the bay! If I tell you that Mr. Coan was bewildered, seeing no familiar object by which to get his bearings, so that he exclaimed 'Where are we!' you will understand something of what destruction must have gone there. But unseen it can not be realized, the dreariness and desolation of a little region that was so late one of Hilo's prettiest suburbs. Not a house standing on all that frontage. Waiakea bridge had been carried a hundred rods or more from its abutments. Even the little church had been set back some two hundred feet, tolling its bell as it went, while the *lunnas* that before nestled under the shade of the pride of

India trees on the grassy bank had borne it company, and fallen into shapeless ruin at the very side of the almost uninjured church."

With compassion she relates the situation of those made homeless by the wave. "At this spot the people began to gather about us, so sorrowful in their homelessness, that their voices and ours choked as we exchanged 'alohas.' Some of them led the way to a hut, too small to be a shelter, but under whose low roof we found a mother sitting by the corpse of her little one that the waters had not spared to her. Close on one side, an old man lay groaning with the pain of fractured ribs and a broken leg, and on the other side, a heap of something, I could hardly tell what at first, lifted a battered head to tell us how he had been thrown upon the rocks and they had bruised his skull."

She relates an Englishman's "wonderful" escape from death. He had difficulties with the wave because he went back for six hundred dollars, which was lost. "Kneeling by the poor man Mr. Coan offered an earnest prayer. We left him, feeling that he was very likely past working much longer."

Lydia gives human and structural data, noting that five "lives have been lost; twenty persons are more or less injured. Forty-four dwellings are demolished, and one hundred and sixty-three people left homeless, their means of procuring sustenance snatched from them.'" As Titus had in 1837, Lydia notes that had "the wave fallen in the darkness of the night, many more must have perished."

She expresses thankfulness for it to have happened "before our going down to Honolulu" for the annual General Meeting, "so that Mr. Coan is among his people to comfort and direct them. Only a few Sabbaths ago he preached a sermon on laying up treasure where thieves could not break through and steal. Who thought then of *this thief*?'" [Matt 6:19–21].

Titus wraps up the chapter with two paragraphs about the longer-term aftermath of the tsunami. "Deep sympathy was awakened in our whole community for those who suffered by this calamity. Food, clothing, blankets, were given in abundance. The report of the disaster spread over the islands, and help came from every quarter. His Excellency John Dominis, Governor of Oahu, and Her Royal Highness Lydia Dominis, the king's sister, were commissioned to come to our aid with the donations from Honolulu. A judicious distribution of money, clothing, lumber, etc., was made among the people, and thus encouraged they went cheerfully to work, and in a few months most of the losses were repaired; better houses were built, and the sufferers seemed more prosperous than before.

"Then now annually commemorate the tenth of May to be a religious festival and a thanksgiving offering to the treasury of the Lord."[86]

Everyone in Hilo and on the coast of much of the Big Island knew whence came the wave of 1868. It is called a "volcanic wave" because of the 6.8 earthquake associated with the great eruption of Kilauea. While earthquake, tsunami, and volcanic activity are related, the three will be separated out in order to examine them individually.

---

86. Coan, *Life*, 320–26.

Coan writes that on April seventh an earthquake led to the sea rising "twenty feet along the southern shore of the island, and in Kau 108 houses were destroyed and forty-six people drowned, making a loss of 118 houses and seventy-seven lives in that district, during this one hour."[87] He continues by noting that many "houses were also destroyed in Puna, but no lives were lost. During this awful hour the coast of Puna and Kau, for the distance of seventy-five miles, subsided seven feet on the average, submerging a line of small villages all along the shore. One of my rough stone meeting-houses in Puna, where we once had a congregation of five hundred to one thousand, was swept away with the influx of the sea, and its walls are now under water. Fortunately there was but one stone building in Hilo, our prison; that fell immediately. Had our coast been studded with cities built of stone and brick, the destruction of life and property would have been terrific."[88]

Coan writes these specifics in a letter to missionary John Paris, living and serving on the other side of the Big Island. "The sea came in up to Front Street, and threatened to overwhelm all along the shore."[89]

Frederick Lyman, son of David and Sarah Lyman, writes at the age of twenty-one[90] about the April 7, 1868, tsunami. "Just after the hard shaking had ceased at home someone called out, 'look at the sea'—all along the coast it was surging and boiling furiously. Tidal waves, which wiped out the villages along the coast; seventy-five people swallowed up in it, all who fled quickly escaped—a few turned back for their money, or something, and were taken by the sea and perished; with one exception, a man was carried by the waves a mile and thrown on the ragged lava [*aa*] coast, and escaped to tell his tale."[91]

Another tsunami hit Hilo on August 14, 1868. The source of this wave was an earthquake epicentered in Arica, Peru.[92] "On August 13, 1868, at 21:30 UTI a 9.0 . . . that affected locations throughout the Pacific basin."[93] Coan reports what the USGS characterizes as a catastrophic tsunami generated over a broad area[94] that on "the fourteenth of August, 1868, a remarkable rise and fall of the sea commenced in

---

87. Coan, *Life*, 316.
88. Coan, *Life*, 316.
89. Coan to Paris, April 11, 1868, in Coan, *Memorial Volume*, 117.
90. Judd, *Missionary Album*, 143.
91. Martin, *Sarah Joiner Lyman*, "Appendix C."
92. Now Chile. See above.
93. "Two great earthquakes occurred at Arica, Peru (now Chile) that generated catastrophic tsunamis that affected locations throughout the Pacific Basin. The towns of Arica, Arequipa, Moquegua, Mollendo, and Ilo were largely destroyed by the earthquake. In South America, more than 25,000 people were killed from the earthquake and tsunami." http://earthquake.usgs.gov/earthquakes/world/events/1868_08_13.php.
94. "The agitation of the ocean reached as far as California, Hawaii, Yokohama, the Philippines, Sydney, and New Zealand. It is reported that the earth opened up in various places, spewing out muddy water," http://earthquake.usgs.gov/earthquakes/world/events/1868_08_13.php.

our harbor, and continued for three days. The oscillation, or the influx and efflux of the waves, occupied only ten minutes, and the rise and fall of the water was only three to four feet. What rendered this motion of the water remarkable was its long continuance, and the short intervals of the rise and fall with no apparent cause."[95]

EARTHQUAKES

While this section relates many earthquakes, it will build to "the great Kaʻu Earthquake of 1868." Three Lymans were the best chroniclers. They are cited in Kay's "Contributions to Hawaiian Natural History," Max Wyss, Robert Y. Koyanagi, and Doak C. Cox published "The Lyman Hawaiian Earthquake Diary, 1833–1917."[96] Before the title page, the USGS article notes that theirs is an "amazing accomplishment of record-keeping covering the significant years before, during, and after the strongest earthquake in the [recorded] history of Hawaii. The eighty-four-year collection of earthquake information credits the perseverance and foresight of Sarah, Isabella,[97] and Frederick Lyman."[98]

After arriving in Hilo in 1832, Sarah noted earthquakes in her diary when she "felt them and found that visiting sea captains and naturalists were very interested in her observations."[99] "This encouraged her to start a separate diary where she primarily described earthquakes that she felt and volcanic eruptions reported in Hawaii. She kept up this special diary for five decades, essentially until her death in December of 1885. Following her death, her son Frederick and particularly Frederick's wife Isabella continued the diary faithfully for another three decades until 1917. This succession of efforts produced a list of earthquakes felt in Hilo spanning a period of eight decades."[100]

---

95. Coan, *Life*, 320.

96. Wyss et al., "Lyman Hawaiian Earthquake Diary," US Geological Survey 2027 (1992) 1–12, in Kay, "Missionary Contributions," 47n12.

97. Sarah was Frederick's wife and the daughter of Levi Chamberlain, member of the "Second Company" of missionaries. Maria Patton Chamberlain arrived unmarried "as a teacher with the Third Company," Judd, *Missionary Album*, 64–65. Picture of Maria and Isabella, Judd, *Missionary Album*, 64. For more on Sarah Joiner Lyman, the wife of David Lyman, see Forbes et al., *Partners in Change*, 451–54.

98. Wyss et al., "Lyman Hawaiian earthquake Diary," inside cover.

99. See Wyss et al., "Lyman Hawaiian Earthquake Diary," 1. Wilkes was one of the first to use the journal, as well as comment on the sound of earthquakes. "Earthquakes are quite common on [the Big Island of] Hawaii: they appear to be for the most part local; thus they are occasionally felt at Maui, but I heard of none at Oahu or Kauai . . . The following are those observed at Hilo since July 1832, which the Rev. Lyman furnished me from his [sic] memorandum [sic?], viz: June 1833 through March 18, 1841 . . . Making in all fifty shocks in eight years . . . The usual motion or jar is like that produced by the firing of distant artillery, or the falling of a heavy body on the ground; to this is added a tremulous motion when the earthquake is slight. [A] journal recording earthquakes felt in Hilo and volcanic eruptions on Hawaiʻi, has attracted attention worldwide as an informative record on the frequency and strength of tremors and of volcanic activity," Wilkes, *Voyage Round the World*, 228–29.

100. Wyss et al., "Lyman Hawaiian Earthquake Diary," 1.

SCIENTIST

"The original earthquake diary was initiated by Mrs. S. J. Lyman several years after her arrival in Hilo. She copied into it a note concerning each of the earthquakes that she had noted in her regular diary between the beginning of her residence in Hilo and the start of her purposeful earthquake record. The principal document [is] preserved at the Lyman House Memorial Museum is entitled 'A Copy, Mrs. Sarah Joiner Lyman's Earthquake Records, 1883–1887.'"[101]

Sarah Lyman faithfully recorded earthquakes until almost her death in 1885. Following her death Frederick's wife Isabella primarily continued to record the earthquakes in 1912. Frederick recorded it less so until his death in 1918.[102]

Wyss, etc. provide a faithful copying of the diary. The only change is to put the date of each earthquake first. A few corrections were placed in brackets.[103] Beginning in the second half of 1835, Titus Coan felt the same earthquakes Sarah Lyman did until his death in 1882. Sarah Lyman "reported three to four earthquakes a year consistently until the great Kau earthquake in 1868, after which the count increased to double-digit numbers for about a decade."[104]

"Surprisingly constant rates were reported by Sarah and Isabella over the decades of note-keeping. Both Lyman families lived at several residences in Hilo during their years of record-keeping. Recent compilations of intensity information indicate earthquakes are felt at varying intensities in different parts of Hilo.[105] Thus, when the families changed residences, the physical difference in locality and building type may have caused some variance in the number and strength of the earthquakes they reported."[106]

Wyss, etc. have an "Appendix A: Earthquakes not listed by Mrs. S. J. Lyman but reported by Wilkes (1845) who gave Mr. D. B. Lyman as his source." Wilkes lists four specific events. Also, in February and in March of 1841 one event each is listed by Wilkes that does not appear in the Lyman catalogue. It is not known whether these differences in reporting were due to differences in location of the reporters or were due to errors and omissions. The inconsistencies are minor in view of the many years of record-keeping. "It is truly fortunate that the remarkable document initiated by Sarah Lyman was continued and preserved, giving us a record of the seismic activity for eighty-four years during the early history of Hawaii. This outstanding accomplishment reflects the exceptional interest and perseverance of Sarah, Frederick, and Isabella Lyman."[107]

---

101. Wyss et al., "Lyman Hawaiian Earthquake Diary," 1–2.
102. Wyss et al., "Lyman Hawaiian Earthquake Diary," 2.
103. Wyss et al., "Lyman Hawaiian Earthquake Diary," 2.
104. Wyss et al., "Lyman Hawaiian Earthquake Diary," 2.
105. Wyss et al., "Lyman Hawaiian Earthquake Diary," 2.
106. Wyss et al., "Lyman Hawaiian Earthquake Diary," 2.
107. Wyss et al., "Lyman Hawaiian Earthquake Diary," 6.

"The awesome shaking experienced by Frederick and Isabella in the epicentral area of the 1868 Kau earthquake, the strongest historic earthquake in Hawaii, undoubtedly left a profound impression in their lives and, very likely, enhanced their concern and determination in maintaining the earthquake record."[108]

"April 2 marks the anniversary of the largest earthquake to occur in the Hawaiian Islands in historic time. This great earthquake occurred in 1868 and had an estimated magnitude of 7.9. The magnitude and epicentral location of the earthquake are constrained by the distribution and severity of the damage. However, due to the sparse population of the region at that time, neither the magnitude nor the location is precisely known. The epicenter was located about five miles north or northeast of Pahala. Like most of the larger earthquakes in Hawaii, it was probably caused by a slip on a near-horizontal plane about six miles (9.5 km) beneath the surface. Many of the thousands of earthquakes in Hawaii, including these larger events, are caused by seaward movement of the south flank of the island. The eyewitness accounts of this great earthquake are a worst-case scenario for earthquakes in Hawaii."[109]

While the author of the above paragraph knows about Frederick Lyman (see below), the author does acknowledge Coan, but not John Paris and others. The first major earthquake was on March 27. The above author writes that the "best account comes from a letter by Frederick Lyman. He wrote on Friday morning, March 27, 1868: 'Between 9 and 10 o'clock, a slight tremble, soon another, and another, at short intervals. Bella tried to keep a record of them, but soon gave it up, when they went into the hundreds during the day—some of the harder, and continued thro the night . . . with more earthquakes, increasing in violence. On Saturday, just after lunch, there was a hard one, peculiar, it seemed as if we moved backwards and forwards, two or three feet each time, for several seconds—it made the small children seasick—and it threw down some of our stone walls . . . but the earthquakes kept on too—every few minutes, often we could hear it coming from the south, then give us a good smart shake and pass on towards Kilauea, northeast from us—at night it made the house rock and creak like a ship in a heavy sea, and we could not sleep.' The large event early Saturday afternoon had an estimated magnitude of 7.1, and the epicenter was located near Waiohinu. It may have been this near Waiohinu by more than the width of the road."[110]

Forty-four years after the 1868 earthquake, Frederick Lyman writes his cousin Josie Lyman about his reflections on that event, beginning with where he was living and how far it was from the volcano. He was some distance from Hilo in Kau, where the earthquake was centered. "You ask where we were living at the time of the great earthquake in 1868? We were living on our Stock Farm, in Kau thirty miles south west of the Volcano, at the foot of Mauna Loa (long mountain) some four or five miles from

---

108. Wyss et al., "Lyman Hawaiian Earthquake Diary," 6.
109. USGS Volcano Watch.
110. Wyss et al., "Lyman Hawaiian Earthquake Diary," 6.

the sea shore. About su rise Friday morning, March 26 [sic? 27?] the boys who were milking the cows called out 'see the fire on the mountain'—we saw a column of thick smoke rising rapidly on the top of the mountain . . . Between 9 and 10 o'clock, a slight tremble, soon another, at short intervals. [Frederick's wife] Bella tried to keep a record of them, but soon gave it up, when they went into the hundreds during the day—some of them harder, and continued thro the night."[111]

In conversation with Titus Coan approximately ten years after the Great Quake, Leavitt Hallock writes the following. "The motion grew daily more intense and violent. 'The crust of the earth rose and sank like the sea in a gale.'[112] He showed me where the earth opened, huge seams gaped in the very streets of the city, rocks were rent, buildings shattered, animals thrown to the ground, and earthquakes followed one another in unbroken succession. A person lying on the ground would be rolled over and over; trees thrashed about as in a strong wind. The south shore settled from four to six feet and villages are swallowed up."[113]

Coan notes that from "time immemorial earthquakes have been common on Hawaii. We have felt the jar of thousands. Most of these shocks have been harmless. A few have broken a little crockery, cracked plastering, and thrown down stone walls."

He turns to the one period when earthquakes were qualitatively different from anything experienced before. "But on the twenty-seventh of March, 1868, a series of remarkable earthquakes commenced." He recognizes the connection with the volcanic activity of Kilauea. "Kilauea was unusually full and in vehement action. Day after day from March 27 and onward, shocks were frequent, and growing more and more earnest." He would write more about the larger earthquake of April second.

"At 4 p.m., April 2, a terrific shock rent the ground, sending consternation through all Hilo, Puna, and Kau. In some places fissures of great length, breadth, and depth were opened. Rocks of twenty to fifty tons were sent thundering down from the walls of Kilauea, and massive boulders were torn from hill-sides and crashing down upon the plains and valleys below. Stone houses were rent and ruined, and stone walls sent flying in every direction. Horses and men were thrown to the ground; houses tilted from their foundations; furniture, hardware, crockery, books and bottles, and all things movable in houses were dashed hither and thither, as of no account. It seemed as if the ribs and the pillars of the earth were being shattered."

He relays where he was when the earthquake occurred. "I was sitting, as at the present moment, at my study-table, when a fearful jerk startled me, and before I could arise, a jar still more terrible caused me to rush for the stairs, and while going down, such a crash shook the house that I supposed the roof had fallen."

---

111. Martin, *Sarah Joiner Lyman*, "Appendix C: The Great Earthquake of 1868, by Frederick S. Lyman, a son. Reminiscences of Frederick S. Lyman to his cousin, Josie Sperry Lyman, March 31, 1912."

112. See Coan *Scribner's Weekly* article, below.

113. Hallock, *Hawaii under King Kalakaua*, 70.

Continuing to go against more recent recommendations, he goes outside. "Going out of doors, I found my wife standing at a distance from the house, watching with an intense gaze its swaying and trembling, while the ground rose and sank like waves, and there was no place stable where hand or foot could rest."

As the worst shock receded, Coan observed the aftermath. "When the shocks intermitted a little, I went upstairs to witness a scene of wild confusion. A large bookcase, seven feet high by four wide, with glass doors, and filled with books, lay prostrate on the floor near where I had been sitting, with the glass broken into a thousand pieces.

"My study-table, eight feet long, and loaded with large volumes, was thrown out from the wall into the center of the room, with one leg broken square off, and the books and papers scattered on the floor. Another bookcase, fastened to the wall, was rent from its fastenings and thrown out near the table, and three of the sleepers which supported the floor were broken by the fall of the case."

He relates how the shaking continued throughout the evening hours. "The shaking continued all night, and most or all of the Hilo people spent the night out of doors, fearing to remain in their houses. Some said they counted a thousand shocks before morning, and so rapid were these shocks, that the earth seemed to be in a continuous quiver, like a ship in a battle."

His attention turns to the region most affected by the earthquake. "But the heaviest blows fell on Kau, the district lying south of us on the other side of Kilauea. There the earth was rent in a thousand places, and along the foot-hills of Mauna Loa a number of land-slips were shaken off from steep places, and thrown down with soil, boulders, and trees. In one place a slide of half a mile in width was started on a steep inclined plane, till, coming to a precipice of some seven hundred feet, on an angle of about seventy degrees, the vast avalanche, mixing with the waters of a running stream and several springs, was pitched down this precipice, receiving such fearful momentum as to carry it three miles in as many minutes. Ten houses, with thirty-one souls and five hundred head of cattle were buried instantly, and not one of them has been recovered."

His scientific inclinations show as he talks about measuring "this avalanche and found it just three miles long, one half a mile wide at the head, and of a supposed average depth of twenty feet."[114] Continuing his scientific tendency, he discusses his theory for the cause of the earthquake.[115] "This terrible earthquake was evidently caused by the subterraneous flow of the lavas from Kilauea, for the bottom of the crater sank rapidly hundreds of feet, as ice goes down when the water beneath it is drawn off. The course and terminus of this flow were indicated by fissures, steam, and spouting of lava-jets along the whole line from Kilauea to Kahuku in Western Kau, a distance of forty miles, and I have found folding and faults in several places.

114. Coan, *Life*, 313–16.

115. Cf the two models discussed in the 1994 USGS article below.

"During these days of subterranean passage, the earth was in a remarkable state of unrest; shocks were frequent, and it was asserted by trustworthy witnesses that, in several places, the ragings of the subterranean river were heard by listeners who put their ears to the ground."[116]

Compare his writing in his autobiography with his article "for *Scribner's Weekly* in 1871" that for "four days this state of things continued, until at 4 p.m. on the second of April, 1868, an event occurred which defies description. Such a convulsion has no parallel in the memory, the history, or the traditions of the Hawaiian Islands. The shock was awful. The crust of the earth rose and sunk like the sea in a storm. The rending of rocks, the shattering of buildings, the crash of furniture, glass, and earthenware, the falling of walls and chimneys, the swaying of trees, the trembling of shrubs, the fright of men and animals, made throughout the southern half of Hawaii such scenes of terror as had never been witnessed before. The streams ran mud, the earth was rent in thousands of places; and the very streets of Hilo cracked open. Horses and their riders were thrown to the ground; and multitudes of people were prostrated by the shocks. In the district of Ka'u more than three hundred shocks were counted[117] upon this terrible day; people were made seasick by their frequency. By the culminating shock, nearly every stone wall and house in Ka'u was demolished in an instant."[118]

Frederick Lyman wrote, "About 4 o'clock it shook as usual, but did not stop—shook east and west, north and south, round and round, and up and down—lessen, then increase in violence. It was impossible to stand; we had to sit on the ground, bracing with hands and feet to keep from rolling over."[119]

The USGS article presents two possible models for the two major earthquakes. One geological model is "simply that the entire southern side of the island . . . slid seaward on April 2. The seaward extent of the sliding block in this model is located near the southern shoreline of the island and extends from near South Point to Kapoho."

The second model is "more complex" and is "based on the sequence of events between March 27 and April 2, and on newly-acquired bathymetric data offshore that suggests that there are two separate landslide structures on the south flank of the island, and that each moved during this sequence of events. In this model, the magnitude 7.1 earthquake on March 28 was triggered by movement of a landslide . . . On April 2, a different, and much larger, landslide block, consisting entirely of the south flank of Kilauea Volcano, moved seaward and caused the magnitude-7.9 earthquake."[120]

Coan writes of his gratefulness for the solid building of the Hilo meeting house/church completed in 1859 and how that strong construction enabled it to survive the 1868 earthquake. "In 1868 an awful earthquake tore in pieces stone walls and stone

---

116. Coan, *Life*, 316–17.
117. By Bella Lyman?
118. Coan, *Scribner's Weekly*, 1871 np, in USGS Volcano Watch.
119. Lyman letter, US Geological Survey Volcano Watch.
120. US Geological Survey Volcano Watch.

houses, and rent the earth in various parts of Hilo, Puna, and Kau. Had we built according to our original plan and agreement with the mason, 'our holy and beautiful house' [Is 64:11] would have become a heap of rubbish, and our hearts would have sunk within us with sorrow. How true that 'a man's heart deviseth his way, but the Lord directeth his steps'" [Prov 16:9].[121]

Coan's heart would sink over the loss of so many stone worship centers throughout the three districts under his care: Hilo, Puna, and Kau. Days after the April earthquake, Coan writes fellow missionary John D. Paris in Kealakekua, South Kona,[122] northwest of Kau. Paris had written Coan a few days after the first earthquake.[123] "Yours of the thirty-first ult. found us as it left you, in fear and trembling [Phil 2:12]. Your experiences and ours were alike. 'The whole land trembled, the earth reeled to and fro' [Jer 8:16]. I would have answered your letter in an hour had it been possible, but I have been obliged to wait the tardy heels of our post-boy. Of the horrors of Kau I need not write, for you must have heard all. The scenes and the sufferings there were awful. Nearly all the foreigners of Eastern Kau fled this way after the terrific shock and eruption of Thursday the second inst. That shock filled all Kau, Hilo, and Puna with awe and consternation. It seemed as if the very pillars and framework of creation would break. For three minutes while it continued, I had scarcely a hope for our house or for our town."

He continues with some Hilo specifics, that he put neither in the *Scribner's Weekly* article nor even his autobiography. "One woman was killed near us by a falling bank that buried her, and her husband received, as we suppose, a mortal wound. Scores of people escaped as by a miracle while the rocks were falling around them."

After relating eight days of daily prayer and the flock of the people at the church, Coan notes that earthquakes are more frightening to him than volcanic eruptions. "Earthquakes are to me more terrific than volcanic eruptions, because they come so *suddenly*, giving no warning and no time to escape, while men may usually walk deliberately away from a lava stream, taking many of their precious things with them. How blessed to feel that 'God is a Refuge and Strength'" [Ps 46:1].[124]

The USGS article concludes that scientists "will probably never be able to completely reconstruct the events of 1868, and some controversy and difference of opinion about what happened will certainly continue. However, the Hawaiian Volcano Observatory's seismic and deformation monitoring programs are working to define the boundaries of the mobile flanks of the volcanoes and will work towards determining the conditions that lead to such large events."[125]

---

121. Coan, *Life*, 86–87.
122. Judd, *Missionary Album*, 152.
123. Coan letter to Paris, April 11, 1868, in Coan, *Memorial Volume*, 116–19.
124. Coan to John Paris, April 11, 1868, in Coan, *Memorial Volume*, 116–17.
125. USGS Volcano Watch.

SCIENTIST

Leavitt H. Hallock writes of how Coan was introduced once in Boston during his visit to the United States. "On one occasion . . . he was introduced at a Boston dinner as 'The king of the volcanoes and manager of earthquakes at the Sandwich Islands!'"[126]

One scientific certainty agreed on by all is that the earthquakes of 1868 were related to major volcanic activity. It is that aspect of the Big Island that the next two chapters address.

---

126. Hallock, *Hawaii under King Kalakaua*, 57.

8

Vulcanologist

"No narrow bounds confined his work, and while acting as a true bishop to his flock, and a wise citizen and friend, he yet found time to do more for science in watching and recording the wonderful fiery work of Kilauea and Makuaweweo [sic][1], than all other men united."[2]

"I must tell you of some scenes witnessed in Hilo by Father Coan touching the giant volcano, Mauna Loa, as related to me in his summer parlor[3] by that venerable man who probably knew more about volcanoes and their secrets than any man then living."[4]

INTRODUCTION

Before Titus Coan, there was Pele: goddess of the volcanoes. During the Great Awakening, first the priest of Pele and then his sister the priestess became Christians. The sister was especially adamant that the Christian God was the true God. During Coan's decades of observation he would refer to Pele, but not as a deity. Rather he refers to her as a descriptor, using such anthropomorphisms as "Pele's hair,"[5] "the domains of Pele,"[6] and "the house of Pele."[7]

Pele migrated from a goddess worshipped, feared, and propitiated, to a being in the pantheon of Hawaiian mythology, to an anthropomorphic reference. While some

---

1. Coan, *Life*, Index, 339, "Moku'āweoweo."
2. William T. Brigham to Rev. E. P. Baker, January 1, 1883, in Coan, *Memorial Volume*. 207.
3. In 1878.
4. Hallock, *Hawaii under King Kalakaua*, 98.
5. Coan, *Life*, 267.
6. Coan, *Life*, 262.
7. Coan, *Life*, 267.

continue to "worship" Pele, it seems to be more symbolic[8] than a return to the fear of the volcano's rumblings and fire. An online article indicates that the "Earth has been a source of constant inspiration and awe for humanity and has motivated a range of creative endeavors." The article cites worship of various god and goddesses of volcanoes. It writes of an 1824 Chiefess Kapiolani who "traveled to the rim of Halemaumau[9] Crater, where she prayed to the Christian god [sic], in defiance of the Pele beliefs of her followers, to demonstrate the power of Christianity over traditional beliefs."[10]

In an 1866 letter to James Dana, Coan expresses his hope that Dana will again visit Hawai'i. "Who can tell that you will not see Hawai'i again and renew your acquaintance with Mother Pele and her numerous daughters?"[11]

Titus Coan, sometimes at great risk to himself, brought scientific rigor to his volcano observations and writings. At times, Hilo was threatened by lava flows. After his preaching and being a pastor, Coan is perhaps best known for his work in the area of volcanoes.

In this chapter and the next, sources will be introduced and interacted with; the volcanoes and their subsections will be described both scientifically and by Coan; and each year of an eruption presented in his autobiography will be analyzed, including comparing one such chapter with an extensive *Missionary Herald* report by Coan on the same eruption.

The authors of *Partners in Change* summarize his activities with these words: "During his long residence in Hilo, Coan became an ardent volcanologist, and undertook exploratory trips to Kilauea, Mauna Loa, and Mauna Kea, as often as time permitted. His reports on the same appeared in both the Honolulu press and in Benjamin Silliman's periodical . . . *The Friend* published an interesting summary of his volcanic observations, titled 'Volcanic Phenomena of the Island of Hawaii' on February 1,

---

8. In an ironic twist, US National Park rangers speak of the negative environmental impact of people tossing floral and other offerings into the Haleakala dormant volcano on Maui. An April 21, 2007, Associated Press article entitled "Hawaii Park Rangers Trying to Stop Offerings at Volcano," notes that rangers "at Hawaii Volcanoes National Park are launching a program to stop people from littering the summit of Kilauea with 'offerings' like incense, candles, and food that attracts rats and cockroaches.

"Some park visitors appear to be under the impression that the items are a suitable offering to Pele, the Hawaiian fire goddess. But park service officials say the objects actually desecrate a site that is sacred to many Native Hawaiians.

"'Many of these items are being lifted by people who are not from here' . . . Rangers say they remove some forty-five pounds of such offerings from Halemaumau Crater each week . . .

"Native Hawaiians are guaranteed access to Kilauea for traditional religious ceremonies in which offerings can be made. Some Hawaiians believe lava is the physical representation of the fire goddess Pele, making the volcano summit sacred." AP, "At Sacred Hawaiian Site," in "Coan Chronicles," 126–27.

9. Halemaʻumaʻu is a pit crater within Kilauea which is part of Mauna Loa. See below.

10. USGS, "Volcano Watch: Strong ties between volcanoes and religion."

11. Coan to Dana, August 31, 1866, in Coan, *Memorial Volume*, 98.

1866. In an introduction to Coan's essay, S. C. Damon, editor of the *Friend*, notes that the essay was originally 'written for a Scientific Society in Paris.'"[12]

SOURCES

Scholars from parts or all of three centuries have based their writings about the volcanic eruptions[13] of the Big Island on the foundation of Coan's first-person narratives of volcanic eruptions and related matters. In 1987, John P. Lockwood and Peter W. Lipman credited Coan with: making the first real scientific on-site observations of volcanoes[14] on the Big Island; making significant observations on various eruptions; and being the most significant Big Island volcano observer of the nineteenth century, which designation would be recognized by at least three scientific authors in the subsequent decades into the twentieth century.[15] They note that "Coan sent many eruption descriptions to his friend James Dana, editor of the *Silliman Journal* (later the *American Journal of Science*)"[16] over a forty-year period.[17] They further explain that Coan's letters to Dana "form much of the basis for the excellent accounts of nineteenth-century eruptive activity later summarized by Dana (1890) and Brigham (1909)."[18]

James Dwight Dana[19] wrote in 1888 his "History of Changes in the M. Loa Craters, Pt. 2 on Mokuaweoweo."[20] In 1890 he published his 339-page *Characteristics of Volcanoes, with Contributions of Facts and Principles from the Hawaiian Islands, Including a Historical Review of Hawaiian Volcanic Action for the Past Sixty-Seven Years, a Discussion of the Relations of Volcanic Islands to Deep-Sea Topography, and a Chapter on Volcanic Denudation*.[21] The full title reflects the four parts of the book.

In 1906, Charles Henry Hitchcock[22] wrote an article, "Mohokea Caldera,"[23] followed in 1909 by *Hawaii and Its Volcanoes, with Contributions of Facts and Principles*

12. Forbes et al., *Partners in Change*, 187. *The Friend* article cited as February 1, 1866,: 9–11, 14.

13. Hawaiian volcanic eruptions are distinctive enough to have their own designation. "A Hawaiian eruption is a type of volcanic eruption where lava flows from the vent in a relatively gentle, low level eruption; it is so named because it is characteristic of Hawaiian volcanoes. Typically they are effusive eruptions, with basaltic magmas of low viscosity, low content of gases, and high temperature at the vent. Wikipedia, "Hawaiian Eruption."

14. Such as lava tubes.

15. Lockwood and Lipman, "Holocene Eruptive History."

16. See LOC Boxes 19–21 for his published writings in *The American Journal of Science*, 1858 and 1880.

17. Lockwood and Lipman, "Holocene Eruptive History," 511.

18. Lockwood and Lipman, "Holocene Eruptive History," 511.

19. 1813–95. For Coan's friendship with Dana, see the *Vincennes* section in the first Great Awakening chapter.

20. Dana, "History of Changes," *American Journal of Science* 93:36:212, 81–112.

21. Dana, *Characteristics of Volcanoes*.

22. 1836–1919.

23. Hitchcock, "Mohokea caldera."

from the Hawaiian Islands.[24] Coan is listed with many pages in the index of Hitchcock's work, most of which are quotations and summaries from Coan's writings. The same year saw the publication of William Tufts Brigham's[25] 222-page *The Volcanoes of Kiluea and Mauna Loa on the Island of Hawaii.*[26]

Hitchcock includes a biographical sketch of Coan. He notes the "conspicuous" nature of the volcano observers Titus Coan, Sereno E. Bishop, W. T. Brigham, and C[larence]. E. Dutton."[27]

Lockwood and Lipman have already been introduced as scholars later in the twentieth and early twenty-first centuries. In 1970, Coan descendant Sarah Acheson[28] would witness firsthand the enduring respect for Titus Coan and volcano research. During the 2018 Kīlauea outbreak she writes, "Watching coverage of recent lava flows on the Big Island, I have been wondering how much has changed since I last saw Hilo. I didn't even know there was a Volcano Museum. When I was there in 1970 there was only the Volcano Observatory near the summit—a small, temporary-looking structure crammed with scientists pouring over seismographs, the machines humming like a swarm of bees. When I was introduced as 'Titus Coan's great-granddaughter' (erroneously skipping a generation), every head turned and stared as maps snapped into resting positions. Nearly a century and a half later, Titus Coan's contribution to early volcano observation was still known and respected!"[29]

During the 1990s, Edward J. Coan[30] and Ken Rubin[31] teamed up to digitize Coan's autobiography,[32] primarily to bring to the public Coan's writings on volcanoes.[33] They corrected minor errors and statistics of a scientific nature, especially distances and elevations.[34] In 2014, Paul Rapoza, with permission, made the Coan/Rubin version available on another online platform.[35]

---

24. Hitchcock, *Hawaii and Its Volcanoes.*
25. 1841–1926.
26. Brigham, *Volcanoes of Kiluea.*
27. Hitchcock, *Hawaii and Its Volcanoes,* 302.
28. Married name, Stephens.
29. Sarah Stephens email to author, September 21, 2018.
30. A direct descendant of Titus Coan.
31. Of the Hawaiian USGS.
32. http://www.soest.hawaii.edu/GG/HCV/COAN/coan.
33. Ed Coan told the author that until he contacted him in 2009, all previous contacts and usage of the digitized autobiography had been with regard to volcanoes.
34. From cover page of Ed Coan's digitized version of Coan, *Life*: "Dates and other numerical data have been carefully checked against the original book for accuracy. However, several of his measurements are known to be inaccurate (e.g., the distance from Oahu to Kauai is given as seventy-five miles, which distance is nearer ninety-nine miles; and the highest peak on Kauai is given as 8,000 feet, which height is nearer 5,200 feet). The accuracy of other reported measurements may therefore be suspect."
35. Available at the Titus Coan Memorial Library: https://www.tc-lib.org/.

Titus Coan: "Apostle to the Sandwich Islands"

In 1992, Thomas L. Wright, Taeko Jane Takahashi, and J. D. Griggs wrote *Hawai'i: A Pictorial History, 1779–1991*. The work includes images and maps from the Coan period, as well as this description: "A few years before Wilkes's visit, the Reverend Titus Coan (fig. 39) had arrived to take over [sic][36] the Hilo mission, which he was to serve for over forty years. Coan was an avid and astute observer of volcanic activity."[37]

E. Alison Kay indicates that the "volcano, in Joseph Goodrich's words, was 'by far the greatest curiosity in the Islands.'"[38] Kay brings together the names of many ABCFM and related missionaries in their volcano observations and reportings. The "records of earthquakes, eruptions, fire fountains, and the like are the most numerous of the missionary publications. Of seven hundred annotated bibliographic records from the period 1826–1916 on the volcano,[39] 25 percent are those of the pioneer missionaries and their immediate descendants. The authors' names read like [a] roll call at the annual meetings of the Mission Children's Society: Alexander, Bailey, Baldwin, Bond, Bingham, Bishop, Coan, Ellis, Emerson, Forbes, Goodrich, Judd, Lyman, and so on. Ninety-one of the contributions are by first-generation missionaries, and seventy-seven are by their sons. Twenty-two of the missionary fathers wrote of their excursions to Kilauea, Mauna Kea, and Mauna Loa, describing landscapes of lava, bubbling craters, bottomless crevices, fire fountains, and, incidentally, retrieving molten lava in a frying pan."[40]

She writes about the first recorded visit to a Hawaiian volcano by Westerners. "The Rev. William Ellis of the London Missionary Society and three members of the pioneer mission company, Asa Thurston, Artemis Bishop, and Goodrich were the first Westerners to record a visit to Kilauea.[41] In 1823, Goodrich also ascended Mauna Kea. He apparently left other members of the mission party on the lower slopes of the mountain and reached the summit on his own, the first Westerner to have achieved that goal."[42]

Kay avers that one "of the missionary fathers outdid all the others as volcano reporter: The Rev. Titus Coan, 'who observed nearly every eruption of Mauna Loa

---

36. The Goodriches left a few months after the Coans arrived to work with the Lymans who were assigned to continue at Hilo.

37. Wright, *Hawaii Volcano Watch*, 27. See also Doughty, *Hawai'i*, 85–105, *passim*.

38. Joseph Goodrich, "Letter": "Notice of the volcanic character of the Island of Hawaii, in a letter to the Editor, and of various facts connected with late observations of the Christian Missionaries in that country, abstracted from a Journal of a Tour around Hawaii, the largest of the Sandwich Islands." Silliman, *American Journal of Science* 1.11 (1826) 5, in Kay, "Missionary Contributions," 28.

39. Kay, "Missionary Contributions," 28.

40. Judd II, "Dr. Judd," in Kay, "Missionary Contributions," 28.

41. Kay, "Missionary Contributions," 28.

42. Goodrich, "Letter," in Silliman, "Notice," 4; Walther M. Barnard, "Earliest Ascents of Mauna Loa Volcano, Hawai'i," HJH 25 (1991): 68, in Kay, "Missionary Contributions," 28.

and Kilauea between 1835 and 1882,' was author of more than one-third of the 168 citations on volcanoes."[43]

Kay continues: "Coan was familiarly known as 'the bishop of Kilauea,' and it was said that he 'cared for it as he did for all his parishioners.'"[44] Mention has already been made of the 2010 USGS "Volcano Watch" blog post. Also in 2010, John P. Lockwood[45] and Richard W. Hazlett[46] published *Volcanoes: A Global Perspective*. While primarily rehabilitating Coan's use of the word "pyroduct," Lockwood and Hazlett review Coan's life and observations. This "well-illustrated [and] broad treatment of modern volcanology . . . provides the reader with a good understanding of how volcanoes work. Of special interest are stories with Hawai'i ties, like the origin of the term 'pyroduct.' The first person to theorize how lava is able to travel so far from its vent was not a geologist but a Christian missionary—the Reverend Titus Coan—who was very interested in the workings of active volcanoes. Reverend Coan was stationed in Hilo between 1835 and his death in 1882, and witnessed every eruption of Mauna Loa during that time."[47]

More than ten years before Titus Coan arrived in Hilo, the English missionary William Ellis toured the Big Island and made observations about many subjects, including volcanoes. Chapters IV, V, and VI look at volcanic activity and descriptions. Among other matters, he discusses leaving "Kapapala for the volcano lodge in a cavern" and "Great Crater of Kilauea." The full title of the book is *Journal of a Tour Around Hawaii, the Largest of the Sandwich Islands. By a Deputation from the Mission of the Sandwich Islands*.[48] References to volcanic activity are found in chapters VI, VII, VIII, IX, and XI. Though a member of the London Missionary Society, the *Missionary Album* includes him on its pages.[49]

Numerous people reported on volcanic activity on the Big Island during Coan's many years there. Other missionaries, including missionary wives, wrote about volcanic activity. Hiram Bingham refers to volcanoes on seventeen pages of his autobiography, *A Residence of Twenty-One Years in the Sandwich Islands*.[50] Fidelia Coan and Lydia Coan did so.[51] Kay writes that Coan's "first wife, Fidelia, and his second wife, Lydia, each wrote a piece about the volcano, as did his two sons, Titus M[unson] and

---

43. Kay, "Missionary Contributions," 28n9.

44. Brigham, "The Volcanoes of Kilauea and Mauna Loa" Memoirs Bishop Museum 2.4 (1909), 302, in Kay, "Missionary Contributions," np.

45. "Jack" Lockwood "retired after a long career with [the Hawaiian Volcano Observatory] and is now an internationally known consulting volcanologist." No citation.

46. "Rick" Hazlett "wrote and illustrated several field guides about Hawai'i and has been a long-time geology professor at Pomona College, California." Sterman, "Retiring But Not Shy."

47. USGS, "Volcano Watch: New Book Reintroduces Old Terminology."

48. Ellis, *Journal*.

49. Judd, *Missionary Album*, 88–89. For expanded material on William Ellis—including primary sources—see Forbes et al., *Partners in Change*, 236–45.

50. Bingham, *Residence*.

51. Corr, "Titus Coan," 252.

Samuel L[atimer] Munson."[52] Sarah Lyman also wrote about volcanic activity.[53] Both Charles Erskine[54] and James Dana met Coan and wrote about their time on Mauna Loa during the *Vincennes* Exploratory Expedition during 1840. After the Ex Ex, many more people visited Mauna Loa with Coan, with one of the first people being C. S. Lyman.[55] Coan writes in his biography of the many numbers who visited Mauna Loa. "Our great volcano has attracted many hundreds of visitors, and they have come from nearly all the nations under heaven [Acts 2:5]. Many have been distinguished scientists. Statesmen and foreign officials of almost every rank have looked in upon us, and our intercourse has been most precious with the many Christians that we have been permitted to entertain."[56] In the subsequent pages, Coan writes about Chief Justice[57] William L. Lee,[58] William T. Brigham,[59] the "widowed Lady Franklin,"[60] and many more,[61] including Isabelle Bird in 1873.[62]

In 1846 a "Volcano House" was built. Doughty characterizes it as "a twelve-by-eighteen-foot hut without anyone hosting it."[63] Coan would make use of this for at least twenty years.

In the 1850s, at least two Mormons—George Q. Cannon and founder Joseph Smith's nephew Joseph F. Smith[64]—wrote about their visits to Mauna Loa. Cannon does so in *My First Mission*[65] and Smith does so in his journal.[66]

---

52. Wright and Takahashi, "Observations and Interpretation," 48–49, footnote in Kay, np. Only one article cited: Fidelia C. Coan, "Eruption from the summit."

53. Martin, *Sarah Joiner Lyman*.

54. Erskine, *Twenty Years*.

55. Lyman, *Around the Horn*. See also Coan, *Life*, 144–45.

56. Coan, *Life*, 143.

57. Of the Hawaiian kingdom.

58. Coan, *Life*, 143–44.

59. Coan, *Life*, 145–146. See above.

60. Coan, *Life*, 146. She spent all of her money looking for her husband John, who had died trying a second time to find a Northwest Passage.

61. Coan, *Life* 149–50.

62. Bird, *Six Months*. Characterized as "perhaps the most prolific and popular female traveller and writer of the nineteenth century," whose travel experiences "transformed a quiet English lady into the darling and dashing world traveler" as she eventually made "her way to the fiery volcano of Mauna Loa." https://books.google.com/books/about/Six_Months_in_Hawaii.html?id=0S0OAAAAQAAJ.

63. Doughty, *Hawai'i*, 306. Doughty further describes the Volcano House over the years. It was reopened "in 2013 after a three-year closure. Before that it was the longest 'continually running' hotel in the state . . . Over the years more buildings were added, eventually totaling one hundred rooms. Sadly, the hotel burned to the ground in 1940 (except the 1877 building). The 1940s building now has thirty-three rooms and is across the street from the location of the original Volcano House." Doughty says that rooms 11, 29 and 33 "have excellent crater views." Room 11 is said to be the favorite of a long-ago innkeeper.

64. See "Other Religions" chapter.

65. Cannon, *My First Mission*, 48–50. See also Cannon, *Journals*.

66. See Joseph F. Smith journal in Brigham Young University archives.

VULCANOLOGIST

In 1869, the thirty-four-year-old Lydia Bingham[67] "accompanied Mr. Coan[68] on an excursion to the volcano. Coan had continued on to Kalapana from the volcano and wrote his wife: 'By Lydia I sent you two "rough and ready" sheets; I trust she reached Hilo on Monday in good condition. She enjoyed the volcano trip greatly.'"[69]

From the secondary sources of scholars and primary sources of missionaries, scientists, and visitors, we turn to descriptions of volcanoes in Hawai'i, in particular the most active one on the Big Island; followed by the years of eruptions he discusses in his autobiography.

DESCRIPTION OF VOLCANOES

Titus Coan writes in his autobiography of the Hawaiian island chain and volcanoes in the opening paragraph of his first chapter on volcanic activity. "It is widely known that the Hawaiian Islands are all of volcanic origin. They are the summits of mountains whose bases are far down in the sea. Their structure is plutonic,[70] and the marks of fire are everywhere visible. They are scarred with hundreds and hundreds of pit and cone craters, most of which are extinct."[71] He makes a similar observation with regard to the Marquesas Islands. "The origin of that group, like that of the Hawaiian, is distinctly igneous.[72] All the islands give evidence of having been raised up from the depths of the ocean by volcanic fires."[73]

Kuykendall, MauiHawaii.org, and the USGS sound scholarly and secular yet similar to Coan. First Kuykendall: "the Hawaiian Islands, as a whole, consist of a chain of islands extending over a distance of nearly two thousand miles . . . The whole range is of volcanic origin, the separate islands having been built up by outpouring of lava from vents along a crack in the earth's crust. Raised up by volcanic

---

67. See "Final years" chapter.

68. Sixty-eight at the time.

69. Titus to Fidelia Coan, August 12, 1869, HMCS, in Ehlke, "Enthusiastic Religion," 258.

70. Definition: "formed by solidification of magma deep within the earth and crystalline throughout." Merriam Webster, "Plutonic." The root of the word is from the mythological underworld god, Pluto.

71. Coan, *Life*, 69.

72. "(Of rock) having solidified from lava or magma." Oxford Dictionaries, "Igneous."

73. Coan, *Life*, 160. On the same page, Coan appears to hold to what is called a "gap" theory of creation: ". . . and volcanic products testify to the terrific rage of Plutonic agencies in *unknown ages past*." [emphasis added] In *Hawai'i*, Doughty further explains the subterranean and transiting nature of the formation of the Hawaiian Islands: Many years ago a "hot spot of liquid rock blasted through the Pacific plate like a giant cutting torch, forcing magma to the surface off the coast of Russia, forming the Emperor Seamounts. As the tectonic plate moved slowly over this hot spot, this torch cut a long scar along the plate, piling up mountains of rock, producing island after island. The oldest of these islands to have survived is Kure. Once a massive island with its own unique eco-system, only its ghost remains in the form of a fringing coral reef, called an atoll." 11.

action, they have been sculptured by geological processes and modified by growth of coral into their present forms."[74]

MauiHawaii.org notes that all "of the Hawaiian islands were formed by volcanoes that began from the ocean floor, with eruptions over millions of years[75] growing each island up to and above the surface of the ocean."[76] Then the USGS: "The Hawaiian Islands are the tops of gigantic volcanic mountains formed by countless eruptions of fluid lava over several million years; some tower more than thirty thousand feet above the sea floor. The Islands are composed of linear chains of shield volcanoes including Kīlauea and Mauna Loa on the island of Hawaii—two of the world's most active volcanoes."[77]

On the subject of Coan's extensive correspondence, Lydia Coan notes that his "letters on volcanic phenomena have been widely circulated in scientific works."[78] Coan's writing about volcanoes and, indeed, almost any subject led the *American Journal of Science* to coin a new word: "penpainter." The word does an excellent job of describing Titus Coan's gift of vivid painting of pictures with his pen.

In an online article, Philip R. Devlin writes of "Titus Coan of Killingworth: 'The Prince of Penpainters.'" Devlin notes that Titus Coan was born "on land near a dormant volcano—the Killingworth Dome—[and] spent most of his adult life living in proximity to active volcanoes in Hawaii and, without intending to do so, made a huge impact on the course of geology in the nineteenth century."

Without citing the reference in the *Memorial Volume*, Devlin quotes William Alexander on geology's debt to Titus Coan: "Although he had not enjoyed any special scientific training and made no pretensions to the character of a professional geologist, he was a good observer. For physical endurance he had few equals. In addition, he had a natural gift of language and his descriptions are remarkably vivid and true to nature." Devlin continues, "Professor Alexander puts the importance of Titus Coan to the development of nineteenth-century geology this way: 'To him geology is indebted for a continuous record of the Hawaiian volcanoes for more than forty years . . . The near view which he had of the sublime lava fountain of 1852,[79] was an experience unparalleled by anything on record.'"[80]

See also Hiram Bingham II on 219 of the *Memorial Volume*: "To him Geology is indebted for a continuous record of the Hawaiian volcanoes for more than forty

---

74. Kuykendall, *Hawaiian Kingdom*, 1.

75. Remember Coan's holding to an apparent "Gap theory," relative to the early part of Genesis 1. See also Grudem, *Systematic Theology*.

76. MauiHawaii.org, "Loihi."

77. http://www.usgs.gov/faq/categories/10169/2719.

78. Lydia Bingham Coan bridge passage in Coan, *Memorial Volume*, 53.

79. See below.

80. Brown, "Titus Coan: The Prince of Penpainters."

years. With indefatigable energy he traced almost every eruption to its source on the mountain side, and observed it in all its various phases."[81]

On the subject of lava, Coan reflects on the distance it travels. He does so near the end of his discussion of the 1881 eruption. "I may add a word upon the curious process by which this lava flow, like others, has made its way over so great a distance from its source. The average slope of Mauna Loa is seven degrees; but this is made up of secondary slopes, varying from one to twenty degrees. As the lava first rushes down the steeper inclinations it flows uncovered; but its surface soon hardens, forming a firm, thick crust like ice on a river, and under this crust the torrent runs highly fluid, and retaining nearly all of its heat. In this pyroduct, if I may so call it,[82] the lava stream may pour down the mountainside for a year or more, flowing unseen, except where openings in the roof of its covered way reveal it.

"When the molten river reaches the more level highlands at the base of the mountain, it moves more slowly, and sometimes spreads out into lakes of miles in diameter. The surface of it soon hardens; the lavas below are sealed within a rigid crust that confines them on every side. Their upward progress is thus checked for hours or days. But as the tremendous pressure of the stream behind increases, the crust is rent, and the liquid lava bursts out and gushes forward or laterally for a hundred, five hundred, or a thousand feet or more, as the case may be. The surface of this extruded mass cools and stiffens in turn, again confining the living lava; then, with the pressure from behind, there is a fresh rupture in the confining shell. While the lava is held in check as I have described, the uninitiated visitor will pronounce the flow to have ceased. But it is only accumulating its forces. The lava presses down from the source, until suddenly the hardened crust is ruptured with a crash, the lava moves forward again, and a new joint is added to the covered way. Thus overcoming all obstacles, the fusion is kept under cover, and moves forward or laterally in its own ducts for an indefinite distance. It may flow at white heat in this way for thirty or forty miles and reach the sea at a distance of more than fifty miles from the mountain source.

"By virtue of this pressure from behind, and of its own viscosity, the lava may even be propelled *up-hill* for a certain distance, if the outbursting rush of lava be directed upon an upward slope. The lava thus grades its own path as it goes seaward."[83]

Before looking at the active volcanoes of the Big Island, we will first examine two dormant volcanoes:

---

81. William Alexander in Coan, *Memorial Volume*, 219, in Brown, "Titus Coan: The Prince of Penpainters."

82. Coan coined this word. See above for twenty-first-century discussion and affirmation by a scientist of Coan's word: USGS, "Volcano Watch: New Book Reintroduces Old Terminology."

83. Coan, *Life*, 332–34.

Titus Coan: "Apostle to the Sandwich Islands"

HALEAKALĀ AND MAUNA KEA

In his chapter[84] on visits to the stations of the Hawaiian Islands, Coan writes about his visit to the Haleakalā volcano. "During this visit at Makawao[85] we made up a party to ascend to the summit crater[86] of Haleakala—'House of the Sun,' the distance from this point being about thirteen miles, with a bridle-path for horses all the way. Notwithstanding many previous visits to Maui, I had never before indulged myself with a trip to this monster of craters. We had a delightful ride over hills and swales, and through fields of strawberries and ohelos.[87] About midway of the distance we rested for a short time under shade trees near a lovely rill of cool limpid water, a beautiful spot which has since been selected by the Alexanders, as an invigorating retreat from the heat and dust of Wailuku and Haiku, and which they have named Olinda.[88]

"We arrived at the summit about 3 p.m. We were now 10,217 feet[89] above sealevel, and yet the sun was hot and the mercury high. In eight hours the thermometer had fallen forty degrees, and the cold was intense. Our guide and some of the party had collected such scanty fuel as could be found, and we made ourselves as comfortable as was possible for the night, around the fire that was kindled, and under shelter of an overhanging rock. In the morning the ground was whitened with frost, and water was frozen.

"The view of this vast cauldron needs to be repeated and continued for a long time, in order to get a full and clear impression of its magnitude. It has been estimated that the circumference on the outer rim is thirty miles, and the depth 1,800 feet."[90] Coan's observant and descriptive nature kicks in as he begins to describe details. "The floor of this amphitheater is studded with sixteen cones, four to six hundred feet high, composed of scoria and cinders, appearing from the upper rim like small sand dunes dropped from a dumping-car."

---

84. Coan, *Life*, Chapter XVI.

85. On the western slope of Haleakalā. The town of Papa Jonathan Green's church and the location of a Female "Seminary" (meaning school, not a graduate-level school).

86. Coan is correct that it is not a caldera. Technically it is not a crater either. It is believed to have been "formed when the headwalls of two large erosional valleys merged at the summit of the volcano. These valleys formed the two large gaps—Koʻolau on the north side and Kaupō on the south—on either side of the depression." Wikipedia, "Haleakalā."

87. Hawaiian blueberries.

88. "Olinda is an agricultural and residential community on the island of Maui in the US state of Hawaii, located approximately two miles southeast of Makawao. It has an approximate elevation of 3573 ft. Mark Twain once lived on Olinda Road." Wikipedia, "Olinda, Hawaii."

89. 10,023 ft (3,055 m) according to Wikipedia, "Haleakalā."

90. In actuality, twenty-one miles and 4,500 feet deep.

Here is an image of a few of the cones to which Coan refers:[91]

"The eastern rim of the crater is broken down as low as its floor, furnishing a broad passage for the molten flood to the sea. This river of fire, some three miles wide, must have been a terrific spectacle, as it rushed in raging billows from the mouth of the crater and hurried down the mountain-side and into the ocean."

Wikipedia provides this "hazard map of Haleakalā":[92]

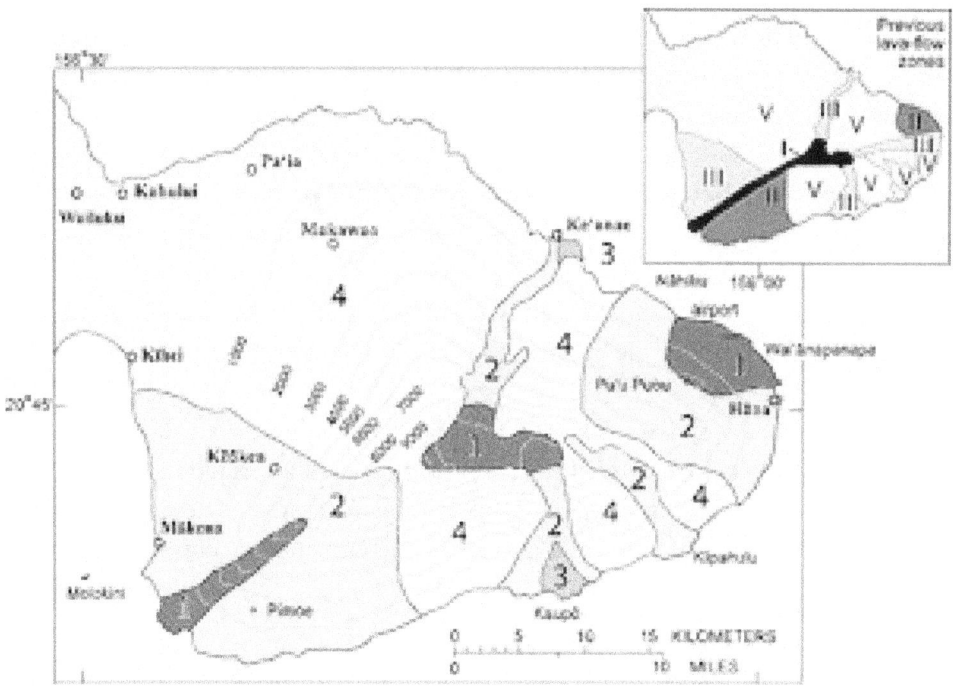

91. USGS, public domain.
92. USGS, public domain.

"The Maui Hazard Zone numbers are two less than the equivalent Hawai'i Hazard Zone numbers."[93]

Coan continues. "It is supposed that this crater is the largest and deepest on our planet,[94] and more nearly resembles some of the yawning craters of the moon.[95] Time was when the raging fires on this mountain must have surpassed in grandeur and brilliancy any that have been anywhere seen by later generations.[96] For ages these lurid fires have been extinct, and from time immemorial silence has reigned over the sleeping hill."

Coan next combines science and the Bible. "Can geology, can all human science tell us when these fires were kindled? How long they raged and roared? And when they were extinguished? Was it before or after the Prophet Isaiah uttered, in sublime language, a description of the Tophet near Jerusalem? 'For Tophet is ordained of old . . . He hath made it deep and large: the pile thereof is fire and much wood; the breath of the Lord like a stream of brimstone doth kindle it' [Isa 30:33].

"But another scene, if less grand, yet more beautiful, awaited us. As the sun descended lower and lower in the west, the fleecy clouds came drifting in from the sea, and, massing around the bases of East and West Maui, covered all the seas, and bays, and channels in every direction, leaving only the tops of Hawaii, Maui, and Lanai visible. The upper surface of these clouds was fleecy white, and appeared like a vast sea of eider-down. We stood above the clouds in bright sunshine, but we saw no water and no land in any direction, except the summits of the mountains gilded in the setting sun. We gazed upon the scene below us with intense interest. As the sun went lower and lower, his rays began to dance, and play, and sparkle upon this vast sea of snowy whiteness, in lambent beauty, and as he dipped into the fleecy bed a flood of glowing scintillations flashed over the whole surface, the prismatic tints twinkling, dancing, gleaming, and quivering in inimitable beauty. A scene unique indeed, and unexcelled by anything of the kind I had seen from the heights of Chili or of Hawaii.

"The night came on, and the clouds rested like a pall over land and sea, while in the clear heavens above us the bright constellations sparkled as on a winter's night in the far-away homeland."[97]

The USGS provides this summary of Haleakalā: "When asked about Hawaiian volcanoes, most people imagine the Island of Hawai'i and its eruptions at Kilauea or Mauna Loa volcanoes. But East Maui's volcano has witnessed at least ten eruptions in the past one thousand years, and numerous eruptions have occurred there in the

---

93. Wikipedia, "Haleakalā."

94. Mauna Loa is the largest volcano, though the Hawaiian chain of shield volcanoes are as a group the largest on earth. http://volcano.oregonstate.edu/book/export/html/111.

95. Coan knew more than he realized on this subject. In writing about the largest crater on the moon, a NASA article says it gives evidence of the early violent years on Earth. NASA, "Biggest, Deepest Crater Exposes Hidden, Ancient Moon."

96. That is striking, given Coan's vivid descriptions of volcanic activity on the Big Island.

97. Coan, *Life*, 235–38.

past ten thousand years. Thus, East Maui's long eruptive history and recent activity indicate that the volcano will erupt in the future."[98]

Haleakalā has a more recent active history than Mauna Kea. Nevertheless, it is dormant, not extinct. "Mauna Kea is presently a dormant volcano, having last erupted about 4,500 years ago. However, Mauna Kea is likely to erupt again. Its quiescent periods between eruptions are long compared to those of the active volcanoes Hualālai (which erupts every few hundred years), Mauna Loa (which erupts every few years to few tens of years) and Kīlauea (which erupts every few years). A swarm of earthquakes beneath Mauna Kea might signal that an eruption could occur within a short time, but such swarms do not always result in an eruption. Sensitive astronomical telescopes on top of Mauna Kea would, as a byproduct of their stargazing, detect minute ground tilts possibly foretelling a future eruption."[99]

Doughty notes that none of the Big Island hot spots are technically extinct. "The latest and newest star in this island chain is Hawai'i . . . [T]his youngster is still vigorously growing. Though none of its five volcano mountains is considered truly dead, these days Mauna Loa and Kilauea are doing most of the work of making the Big Island bigger. Mauna Loa, the most massive mountain on Earth, consists of ten thousand *cubic miles* of rock. Quieter of the two active volcanoes, it last erupted in 1984. Kilauea is the most boisterous of the volcanoes and is the most active volcano on the planet. Kilauea's most recent eruption began in 1983 and was still going strong as we went to press."[100]

The USGS map also provides a visual overview of the five "hotspots":[101]

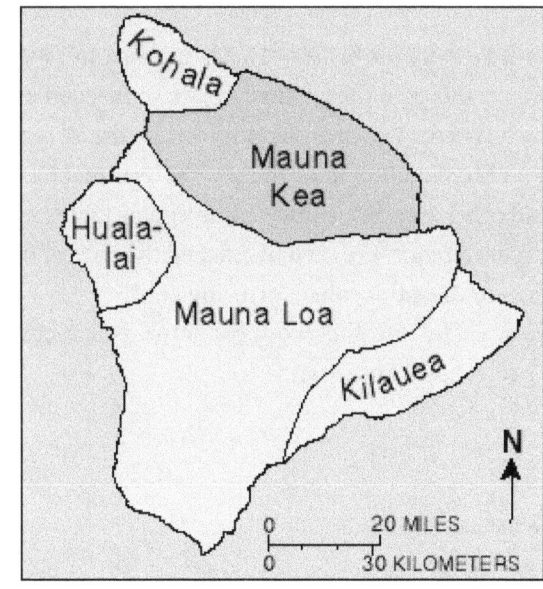

98. USGS Hawaiian Volcano Observatory.
99. USGS Hawaiian Volcano Observatory. For more information, see Wikipedia, "Mauna Kea."
100. 2018, but published before Kilauea's-months-long event in 2018. Doughty, *Hawai'i*, 13.
101. USGS, public domain.

"Mauna" means mountain. Kea means "White." "The Hawaiian name 'Mauna Kea' means 'White Mountain' but is also known in native traditions and prayers as 'Mauna a Wākea' or 'The mountain of Wākea.' Mauna a Wākea is the first-born mountain son of Wākea and Papa, the progenitors of the Hawaiian race."[102]

[103]

Coan provides a panoramic view from the perspective of the slope of Mauna Kea. "I have stood on the very summit of Mauna Kea, fourteen thousand[104] feet above my Hilo home, and looked down upon the three neighboring mountains, over the great valley of Waimea, upon the green fields and shining bay of Hilo, and right opposite upon the calm waters of Kawaihae, and over and beyond the thirty miles' channel upon the sleeping[105] mountain of Maui, and the quiet heights of Lanai and Kahoolawe."[106]

Hiram Bingham writes about his visit to Mauna Kea in 1830. "After refreshing and amusing ourselves at this cold mountain lake, we proceeded a little west of north, and soon reached the lofty area which is surmounted by the 'seven pillars' which wisdom had hewed out and based upon it, or the several terminal peaks near each other, resting on what would otherwise be a somewhat irregular table land, or some plain of some twelve miles circumference. Ere we had reached the base of the highest peak, the sun was fast declining and the atmosphere growing cold."[107]

From Mauna Kea, we turn to the two most active volcanoes, followed by visits and writings on the subject by Titus Coan.

---

102. USGS Hawaiian Volcano Observatory.

103. USGS, public domain.

104. Actual elevation 4,025 meters, or 13,205 feet.

105. Note that Coan calls Haleakalā "sleeping," not dead. It is the difference between dormant and extinct.

106. Coan, *Life*, 225.

107. Bingham, *Residence*, 378.

VULCANOLOGIST

MAUNA LOA AND KĪLAUEA

The USGS summarizes Mauna Loa as follows: "Rising gradually to more than four km above sea level, Mauna Loa is the largest volcano on our planet. Its long submarine flanks descend to the sea floor an additional five km, and the sea floor in turn is depressed by Mauna Loa's great mass another eight km. This makes the volcano's summit about seventeen km (fifty-six thousand feet) above its base! The enormous volcano covers half of the Island of Hawai'i and by itself amounts to about 85 percent of all the other Hawaiian Islands combined." With regard to recorded eruptions, the USGS provides the following: "Mauna Loa is among Earth's most active volcanoes, having erupted thirty-three times since its first well-documented historical eruption in 1843.[108] Its most recent eruption was in 1984."

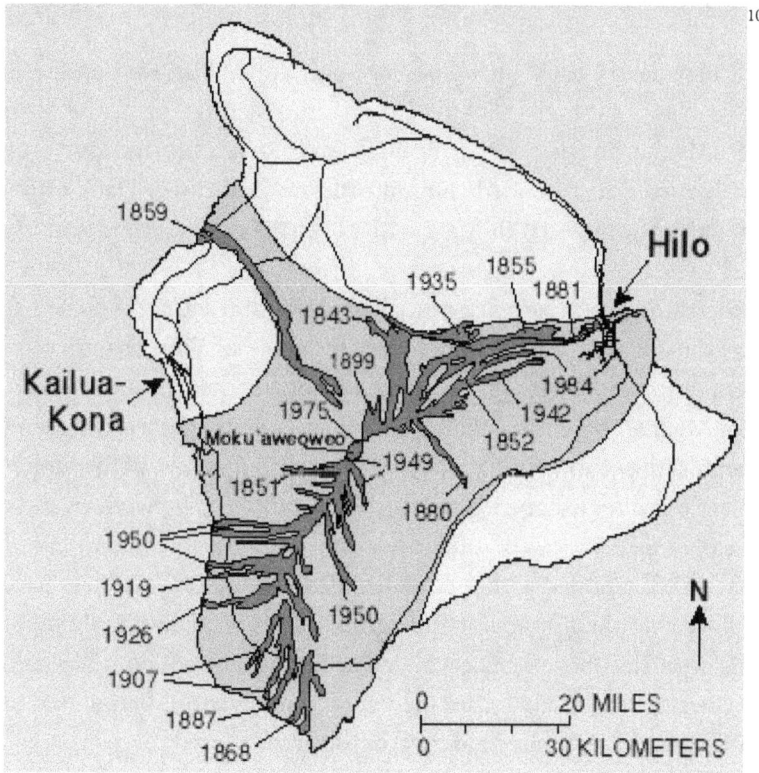

Mauna Loa means "Long Mountain," which is "apt, for the subaerial part of Mauna Loa extends for about 120 km from the southern tip of the island to the summit caldera and then east-northeast to the coastline near Hilo."

108. See Coan below under that year.
109. USGS, public domain.

Titus Coan: "Apostle to the Sandwich Islands"

Titus Coan describes Mauna Loa's average slope,[111] as well as the eruptions of 1843, 1852, 1855–56, and 1880–81. He presents Mauna Loa at the beginning of chapter VI. "Mauna Loa is a vast volcanic dome, subject to igneous eruptions at any time, either from its extended summit or sides. Prof[essor] Dana estimates that 'there is enough rock material in Mauna Loa to make one hundred and twenty-five Vesuviuses.'"[112]

In 1880, at the age of seventy-nine, he writes John Paris[113] on their exploring Mauna Loa years before. "Well, we are nearer the shore of Time than in our youthful days. Nearer than when we struggled and panted together for the first time up the rugged steeps of Mauna Loa; nearer than when in our nightly descent we stumbled and fell, often, amidst the scoriatic ridges and into the jagged valleys of the mountain, and when we felt in our utter exhaustion that there was but a step between us and death."[114]

Coan calls Moku'āweoweo "the great summit crater" of Mauna Loa. Its "deep cauldron has so often boiled with intense heat, and whose brilliant fires have thrown a sheen of glory over the firmament and lighted all eastern Hawaii. Mokuaweoweo is probably the great chimney or shaft which reaches the abyss of liquid lava below, and which furnishes the materials for all the lateral outbursts of Mauna Loa, except for those of Kilauea which are independent eruptions."[115]

---

110. USGS, public domain.

111. Coan, *Life*, 332.

112. Coan, *Life*, 69. After the period, Coan places an asterisk which leads to a footnote, "*Am[erican] Journal of Science*, May 1859, p. 415." Coan, *Life*, 69. Dana had a long-time interest in Mount Vesuvius [a significant and somewhat rare "five" on the Volcanic Explosivity Index] and comparing it with the volcanoes of Hawai'i. Also, during the last two years of Coan's life (1880–81), Dana led the first official geological study of volcanic of the Big Island. Wikipedia, "James Dwight Dana."

113. Seventy at the time he received the letter.

114. Coan to Paris, Honolulu, June 17, 1880, in Coan, *Memorial Volume*, 167. See Coan, *Life*, 270–78, for the Paris and Coan arduous Mauna Loa visit.

115. Coan, *Life*, 295. The USGS characterizes Mokuaweoweo as a "summit caldera." See image by

Hilo is at the northeastern edge of the Mauna Loa lava flow region. Coan seems to call Kīlauea a crater of Mauna Loa. "About mid-way from [Mauna Loa's] summit to the sea on the eastern flank of the mountain and on a nearly level plain is Kīlauea, the largest known active crater in the world. The brink of this crater is 4,440 feet above the sea level;[116] its depth varies from seven hundred to 1,200 feet, and its longer diameter is about three miles. Grand eruptions have issued from it in past ages, covering hundreds of square miles in different parts of Puna and Kau."[117]

Predating the arrival of the Hawaiian missionaries, indigenous people reported the massive 1790 Kīlauea eruption. The following account was provided by students at the Lahainaluna, Maui, school in the early 1830s who interviewed eyewitnesses who were still alive.

"Kaiana, Namakeha and some other chiefs in the train of Kamehameha went with soldiers to Kau to exterminate Keoua. But Keoua was at Hilo. He heard of the invasion of the enemy and hastened to the scene of action. His path led by the great volcano of Kilauea. There they encamped. In the night a terrific eruption took place, throwing out flame, cinders, and even heavy stones to a great distance, and accompanied from above with intense lightning and heavy thunder. In the morning Keoua and his companions were afraid to proceed and spent the day in trying to appease the goddess of the volcano, whom they supposed they had offended the day before by rolling stones into the crater. But on the second night and on the third night also there were similar eruptions. On the third day they ventured to proceed on their way, but had not advanced far before a more terrible and destructive eruption than any before took place; an account of which, taken from the lips of those who were part of the company and present in the scene, may not be an unwelcome digression.

"The army of Keoua set out on their way in three different companies. The company in advance had not proceeded far before the ground began to shake and rock beneath their feet and it became quite impossible to stand. Soon a dense cloud of darkness was seen to rise out of the crater, and almost at the same instant the electrical effect upon the air was so great that the thunder began to roar in the heavens and the lightning to flash. It continued to ascend and spread abroad until the whole region was enveloped and the light of day was entirely excluded. The darkness was the more

USGS, public domain:

116. Wikipedia, "Kilauea."
117. Coan, *Life*, 69–70.

terrific, being made visible by an awful glare from streams of red and blue light variously combined that issued from the pit below, and being lit up at intervals by the intense flashes of lightning from above. Soon followed an immense volume of sand and cinders which were thrown in high heaven and came down in a destructive shower for many miles around. Some few persons of the forward company were burned to death by the sand and cinders and others were seriously injured. All experienced a suffocating sensation upon the lungs and hastened on with all possible speed.

"The rear body, which was nearest the volcano at the time of the eruption, seemed to suffer the least injury, and after the earthquake and shower of sand had passed over, hastened forward to escape the dangers which threatened them, and rejoicing in mutual congratulations that they had been preserved in the midst of such imminent peril. But what was their surprise and consternation, when on coming up with their comrades of the center party, they discovered them all to have become corpses. Some were lying down, and others sitting upright clasping with dying grasp their wives and children and joining noses (their form of expressing affection) as in the act of taking a final leave. So much like life they looked that they at first supposed them merely at rest, and it was not until they had come up to them and handled them that they could detect their mistake. The whole party, including women and children, not one of them survived to relate the catastrophe that had befallen their comrades. The only living being they found was a solitary hog, in company with one of the families which had been so suddenly bereft of life. In those perilous circumstances, the surviving party did not even stay to bewail their fate, but leaving their deceased companions as they found them, hurried on and overtook the company in advance at the place of their encampment."[118]

Wikipedia indicates that Mauna Loa and Kīlauea are viewed as separate volcanoes. In his autobiography, Coan distinguishes between the eruptions of Mauna Loa and Kīlauea. Wikipedia notes that Mauna Loa "is the largest volcano on Earth in terms of volume and area covered, and one of five volcanoes that form the Island of Hawaii."[119] Wikipedia calls Kīlauea "a volcano in the Hawaiian Islands."[120]

Kīlauea is in the Puna district. Coan devotes most of a chapter to Kīlauea.[121] "The volcano of Kilauea is always in action. Its lake of lava and brimstone rolls and surges from age to age.

"Sometimes these fires are sluggish, and one might feel safe in pitching his tent upon the floor of the crater. Again the ponderous masses of hardened lava, in appearance like vast coal-beds, are broken up by the surging floods below, and tossed hither and thither, while the great bellows of Jehovah blows [Jer 6:26] upon these hills and

---

118. "Massive Eruption at Kilauea volcano (November 1790)," in 1909 edition of Dibble, *History*, 53–55. Discussed by Paul Rapoza, email to author, June 4, 2018.
119. Wikipedia, "Mauna Loa."
120. Wikipedia, "Kīlauea."
121. Coan, *Life*, 262–69.

cones and ridges of solidified rocks, and melts them down into seas and lakes and streams of liquid fire." He notes that Kilauea is part of his parish and the variety of its actions. "As the great volcano is within the limits of my parish, and as my missionary trail flanks on three sides, I may have observed it a hundred times; but never twice in the same state."[122]

An online article indicates that "Kīlauea has been the site of sixty-one separate eruptions since 1823, easily making it one of the most active volcanoes on Earth."[123] It shows up several times on the Volcanic Explosivity Index.[124]

Hiram Bingham writes about Kīlauea in his same 1830 chapter referenced above. "Then the angry abyss, the fabled habitation and throne of PELE, the great ex-goddess of the Hawaiians, opened before us.

"Coming near the rim, I fell upon my hands and knees, and crept cautiously to the rocky brink; for withal my natural and acquired courage, I was unwilling at once to walk up to the giddy verge and look down upon the noisy, fiery gulf beneath my feet. Shortly, however, I was able to stand very near and gaze upon this wonder of the world, which I wish I could set before my readers in all its mystery, magnitude, and grandeur."

Bingham tries to explain the magnitude of the volcanic gulf by comparing it to America's two greatest cities at the time he wrote his memoirs. "Such is the extent and depth of Kilauea, that it would take in entire, the city of Philadelphia or New York, and make their loftiest spires, viewed from the rim, appear small and low."[125]

George Q. Cannon—the leader of the first group of Mormon missionaries to the Sandwich Islands during the 1850s—writes about a visit to Kilauea in his book covering his time in the islands. Though based on Maui, he does relate a visit to the Big Island. He devotes several pages to volcanoes, with no reference to Coan.[126] "We traveled around the island, and visited the famous volcano, the largest[127] in the world. Its name is Kilauea." He complements Coan's descriptions using his own descriptive abilities and writing style.

He has a paragraph on the Pele myth that begins with this sentence: "The Sandwich Islanders entertained a singular [sic][128] idea about the manner in which their islands came into being."[129] He returns to more scientific observations: "The pit of the

---

122. Coan, *Life*, 262.

123. Wikipedia, "Kīlauea."

124. On a scale of one through eight, the 1790 eruption was a four. Kilauea has four at two. Somewhat surprisingly, the massive 1868 eruption (combined with a 6.8 earthquake) rates as a mere one on the scale, in Wikipedia, "Volcanic Explosivity Index." No Mauna Loa VEI was found.

125. Bingham, *Residence*, 387.

126. Cannon, *My First Mission*, 48–51.

127. Cannon appears to conflate Kilauea and Mauna Loa.

128. Cannon does not appear to be aware of the full-orbed Pele myth and her "journey" to the island chain.

129. Cannon, *My First Mission*, 48, 49. He also writes about Pele on 50.

volcano is probably three miles across. There have been times when the whole bottom of the pit was one mass of lurid, seething fire."[130]

He continues, "When we visited the pit, we found an immense field of lava which extended all around the pit, and which resembled, in many respects, the sea in its wave-like appearance."[131] The pit "might also have been compared to a field [of] shore-ice, from which the water had receded, leaving it shattered and cracked; in fact, it looked like a frozen sea, except that it was black coal. In cooling, it had cracked, leaving large seams, from which steam and heat had issued. We found the pit in which the fire was raging to be about fifty or sixty feet deep; it was nearly round, and about one hundred yards across."[132]

Cannon provides some descriptions—the sides are perpendicular—and descriptions—one side had two very large holes together. Here "the melted lava was in constant motion, surging and heaving like the waves of the sea." Cannon talks about the incredible sound that meets his ears. "The sound which it made was somewhat similar to the paddles of a steam vessel in the ocean, only it was far greater. We heard this sound before we reached the mouth of the volcano, and it resembled to our ears the booming of heavy artillery at a distance."[133]

On these pages, Cannon provides no biblical references or metaphors, as does Coan. He does provide his impression of what he saw. "The sight of this pit surpassed in sublimity and grandeur anything I had witnessed or imagined. It far exceeded what I had read in written descriptions, or even what I expected to see. Language fails to convey to the mind a correct idea of its appearance."

Cannon also writes about the effect on the surrounding water of the eruption. The "fire and smoke of which had been seen at a long distance, and ashes from which, it is said, had fallen on the decks of vessels hundreds of miles at sea. From these eruptions the lava had run down to the sea, sweeping everything before it, and heating the sea for several miles in such a manner as to kill large quantities of fish."[134]

Coan gives examples of the varied nature of Kīlauea's activity. "Its outer wall remains nearly the same from age to age, but all within the vast cauldron undergoes changes. I have visited it when there was but one small pool of fusion visible, and at another time I have counted eighty fires in the bottom of the crater. Sometimes I have seen what is called Halemaumau,[135] or South Lake, enlarged to a circuit of three miles,

---

130. Cf, Coan, *Life*, 293 and 195.
131. Cannon, *My First Mission*, 48–49.
132. Cannon, *My First Mission*, 49–50.
133. Cannon, *My First Mission*, 50.
134. Cannon, *My First Mission*, 50.
135. From a May 15, 2015, *Daily Mail* online article, "Breathtaking moment Hawaiian volcano explodes as crater wall collapses causing flaming lava lake blast . . . Video has captured the moment a wall of Hawaii's Halema'uma'u Crater in the Kilauea Volcano collapsed." Spargo, "Breathtaking Moment." When viewing the images in a large-enough manner, one can see the outer wall, to which Coan refers.

and raging as if filled with infernal demons, and again domed over with a solid roof, excepting a single aperture of about twenty feet in diameter at the apex, which served as a vent to the steam and gases. On my next visit I would find this dome broken in and the great sea of fiery billows, of near a mile in diameter, rolling below."[136]

Here is an image of the lava lake in Halemaʻumaʻu Crater:

[137]

Coan shares about two instances of visiting Kīlauea. "On one occasion, when there with a party of friends, we found the door of entrance to the floor of the crater closed against us. A flood of burning fusion, covering some fifty acres, had burst out at the lower end of the path, shutting out all visitors, so that we spent the day and night upon the upper rim of the abyss.

"On another occasion I found the great South Lake filled to the brim, and pouring out in two deep and broad canals at nearly opposite points of the lake. The lava followed these crescent fissures of fifty or more feet deep and wide until they came within half a mile of meeting under the northern wall of the crater, thus nearly enclosing an area of about two miles in length and a mile and a half in breadth."[138]

Coan next introduces a measuring instrument. "A pyrometer[139] sent out by Professor J. D. Dana was put into my hands to measure the heat of melted lava."[140] Coan

---

136. Coan, *Life*, 262–63.

137. USGS, public domain. Note the outer wall in the distance.

138. Coan, *Life*, 263.

139. First invented in the mid-seventeenth century, a pyrometer is "an apparatus for measuring high temperatures that uses the radiation emitted by a hot body as a basis for measurement." Dictionary.com, "Pyrometer."

140. Coan, *Life*, 264.

explains why the pyrometer could not be used in his context. "I had taken it with me twice to the crater unsuccessfully, the fusion being too deep in the lake to be reached. I had also sent it up by others, with instructions, hoping to get it inserted; but failing, I went up again with my friend, Dr. Lafon. We descended the crater and traveled south about two miles, when a vast mount like a truncated cone rose before us. Not recognizing this elevation, I said to my companion, 'This is a new feature in the crater; I have not seen it before. It is about where the lake used to be; but let us pass over it, and we shall probably find the lake on the other side.' With the instrument in hand, we began to ascend the elevation on angle of about twenty degrees. When half-way up, there came over a splash of burning fusion, which fell near our feet. Our hair was electrified, and we treated in haste." Time after time Coan relates in his writings such brushes with death in the volcanic context. "Going to a little distance, we mounted an extinct cone which overlooked the eminence we had left, when, lo! To our amazement, it was the great South Lake of fire, no longer, as often, one to two hundred feet below us, but risen to a level of about twenty-five feet above the surrounding plain, and contained by a circular dam of cooled lava some three miles in circumference. The scene was awful. Over all that high and extended surface the fiery billows were surging and dashing with infernal seething and mutterings and hissings. The whole surface was in ebullition,[141] and now and then large blisters, many feet in length, viscous films, of the consistency of glutinous matter, would rise in gigantic bubbles created by the lifting gases, and then burst and disappear."

Coan describes his feelings in witnessing this roiling vista and asks a question. "We were struck with amazement; and the question was, Shall we again venture near that awful furnace? We could frequently see the lava flood spilling over the rim like a boiling cauldron, and what if the encircling dam should burst and pour its deluge of fiery ruin over all the surrounding area! But unwilling to fail in our experiment we came down from the cone, and carefully, and with eyes agaze, began to ascend the wall; again and again we were driven back by the splashes of red-hot lava." He returns to the point of attempting to use the pyrometer. "We persevered, and watching and dodging the spittings, I was at last able to reach so near the top of the dam as to thrust the pyrometer through the thin part of the upper rim, when out burst a gory stream of lava, and we ran down to wait the time for withdrawing the instrument." He describes the instrument and an adaptation he had made to the length of the shaft. "The shaft of the pyrometer was about four feet long, with a socket into which I had firmly fastened a ten-foot pole. When at last we grasped the pole and pulled, the strength of four strong arms could not dislodge the pyrometer. We pulled and pulled until the pole was wrenched from the socket. The instrument was fast beyond recovery, and with keen regret we left it in the hardened lava."[142]

---

141. "The action of bubbling or boiling." Oxford Dictionaries, "Ebullition."
142. Coan, *Life*, 264–65.

Coan relates his retreat, the circular dam, avalanches of rocks, and lava waves. "We turned to retreat from the crater, and before we had reached the upper rim, we looked back and saw that awful lake emptying itself at two points, one of which appeared to be in the very place where we had stood only half an hour before. The whole southern portion of the crater was a sea of liquid fire, covering, as I estimated, about two square miles, with a probable depth of three feet.

"This circular dam which enclosed the elevated lava-lake was formed gradually by successive overflowing upon the rim, depositing stratum upon stratum, until the solidified layers had raised the dam some twenty-five feet; when the lateral pressure became so great as to burst the barrier and give vent to this terrific flood.

"I have heard great avalanches of rocks fall from the outer walls of the crater some eight hundred feet into the dread abyss below with thundering uproar. At the distance of two miles I have heard the soughing and sighing of the lava waves, and upon the surface of that awful lake I have seen as it were gory forms leaping up with shrieks, as if struggling to escape their doom, and again plunging and disappearing beneath the burning billows. To stand upon the margin of the lake of fire and brimstone, to listen to its infernal sounds, the rolling, surfing, tossing, dashing, and spouting of its furious waves; to witness its restless throbbing, its gyrations, its fierce ebullitions, its writhing, and its fearful throes as if in anguish, and to feel the hot flushes of its sulphurous breath, as to give one sensations which no human language can express."

Coan rightly expresses how it is impossible to understand the full experience of volcanic activity without being present; to feel with all the senses: sight, sound, touch, smell, and taste. He talks about a kind of film and Pele's hair. "Sometimes an indurated[143] film, two to four inches thick, will form over all the central part of the lake, while its periphery is a circle of boiling lava, spouting, leaping, and dancing as if in merry gambols. All at once the scene changes, the central portion begins like a gigantic bubble, and out rushes a sea of crimson fusion, which pours down to the surrounding wall with an awful seething and roaring, striking that its sanguinary jets are thrown back like a repulsed charge upon a battle-field, or tossed into the air fifty to a hundred feet high, to fall upon the upper rim of the pit in a hail-storm of fire.

"This makes the filamentous vitrification called 'Pele's hair.'[144] The sudden sundering of the fusion into thousands of particles, by the force that thus ejects the igneous masses upward, and their separation when in this fused state, spins out vitreous threads like spun glass. These threads are light, and when taken up by brisk winds, are often kept floating and gyrating in the atmosphere, until they come into a calmer stratum of air; when they fall over the surrounding regions, sometimes in masses in quiet and sheltered places. They are sometimes carried a hundred miles, as is proved

---

143. "To make hard; harden, as rock, tissue, etc." Dictionary.com, "Indurate."

144. For a modern video presentation on Pele's hair see the Weather Channel presentation, "Kilauea Volcano." This presentation notes that the phenomenon is found on only a few volcanoes around the globe.

by their dropping on ships at sea. This 'hair' takes the color of the lava of which it is formed. Some of it is a dark gray, some auburn, or it may be yellow, or red, or of a brick color."

Chester Smith Lyman writes the following about Pele's hair. "Passing around the lake to the leeward side we found the fibrous lava of Pele's hair everywhere collected in the holes and crevices. It appears to be formed by the stringing out and sudden cooling of the lava as it is thrown up in the process of boiling, like the threads of melted sealing wax. These fibers are borne by the wind and scattered all over the leeward side of the crater."[145]

Coan writes about other modes of action of the lava lake and the intensity of the heat, again returning to trying to describe the indescribable, unless one is at the location being written about. "Another mode of action in this lake is to encrust nearly all the surface with the hardened covering, while active boiling is kept up at the margin one side only. When this ebullition becomes intense, the fusion rises on that side, while the other side is quiet. After a little, this agitated lava will rise and fall over upon the crust, pressing or breaking it down, and rolling in a fiery wave across the lake, and thus covering its whole surface with an intense boiling and surging, so fierce and so hot that the spectator withdraws from the insufferable heat to a cooler and safer position.

"To be struck with this heat in its intensity, is to be death-struck, and to inhale a full draught of this sulphurous acid gas in its strength would be to extinguish life." He uses this dangerous situation to transition to visitors to the volcano. "All visitors must keep on the windward side of the lake and avoid all currents of hot steam gases.

"Some visitors are too daring. Others are too timid. I have known several gentlemen who have ventured into places of peril, and escaped death as by a miracle; and I have known one at least so timid as to turn back to Hilo as soon as he saw smoke and steam, and smelt sulphur, though he was still more than a mile distant from the volcano.

"And I have seen ladies tremble and almost faint on going down into the crater while yet a full mile from any visible fire. One who was in my charge was so terrified that no assurance of safety and no effort to persuade could move her. She sat down upon a rock a mile from Halemaumau, and would not move until we led her out of the crater. Others, though transfixed and awe-struck at first, become so fearless that they play with the pools and little rills of lava, dipping up specimens of it to take away. In order to carry it conveniently, one lady put a specimen which had hardened, but not yet cooled, into her handkerchief, when, instead of remaining, it burnt through and fell at her feet."[146]

Leavitt Hallock relates a trip with Titus Coan to Halema'uma'u in 1878. "We breakfast on meat, fried bananas, boiled taro root and luscious figs from the tree at the

---

145. Lyman, *Around the Horn*, 92.
146. Coan, *Life*, 266–69.

garden gate, mangoes for dessert and coffee from the plantation over the hill yonder." With "Father Coan's grey horse, newly shod, with saddle and spurs, rubber coat and saddle-bags and plenty of courage and curiosity, we started on the twenty-nine-mile climb to the crater of Kilauea. What we saw there of the bottomless pit, the lake which the natives call Halemaumau, or 'house of everlasting burning,' the molten lava, forests of ferns springing quick from the warm crevasse, herds of wild cattle often sighted afar, mountain goats aloft on the lava ridges, we have already described. It is a rare chamber of art in God's inimitable studio."[147]

In 1846 a twelve-by-eighteen hut was erected near Halema'uma'u. Coan would stay the night there on occasion.[148]

Further aspects of Kilauea and Mauna Loa will be related during the discussion of the years of major eruptions during Titus Coan's time on the Big Island.

MAJOR ERUPTIONS BY YEAR

In his autobiography, Titus Coan relates major eruptions, with one chapter for each. Years later, Coan relates an 1839 Mauna Loa eruption to James Dana. Coan provides observations, questions, and speculations. Note the mix of Hawaiian and Greco-Roman mythology, along with the ever-present biblical allusions. "In the spring of 1839, we had a beautiful eruption in the old crater on the summit of Mauna Loa at the very spot where Wilkes encamped. The crater is deep and ample, and the fusion exhausted itself without overflowing the rim. At the distance of Hilo it was a pretty, not a terrific sight. A beautiful cloud pillar [Exod 13:21; also "pillar of fire"] stood on the mountain summit by day, and this was converted into a pillar of fire by night. It was a beacon light. It was heaven's high monument, whose apex pierced the clouds, and whose pedestal was the everlasting hills. Thus it stood a lofty column shining in its solitary height for about two months, when the breath that kindled, extinguished it. I longed to visit it but could not. To have stood upon the verge of the deep caldron and looked down upon the fiery billows raging in the abyss below must have filled one with awe."

He focuses next on Kīlauea, bringing it to the present of Coan's writing the letter. "Old Kilauea has had no freaks of horrid sport since you were here. The great boiling lake which you saw is now dammed over with a solid roof of hot lava, the apex of which is some seven hundred or eight hundred feet higher than was the surface of the fire lake in 1840. Steam and gases are constantly issuing from a thousand holes and fissures over the crater, but scarcely a spark of fire is to be seen by day or night. In fact Mother Pele has buried her fires, stopped her forges, extinguished her lamps and retired within the deep recesses of her infernal caverns. Is she dead? Does she sleep? Or has she only closed her adamantine doors, and with Pluto and Vulcan descended to the fiery bowels of the earth to prepare with deeper secrecy her magazines of wrath

---

147. Hallock, *Hawaii under King Kalakaua*, 59.
148. For the development of places to stay, see previous discussion from Doughty's *Hawai'i*.

which shall one day burst forth with more desolating terror? To us it is a lonely idea that the volcano should become extinct; for we confess that her mutterings, her thundering, her flashings, the smoke of her nostrils and the shaking of her rocky ribs are music, beauty, sublimity, and grandeur to us. They seem so like the voice of Almighty God, so like the footsteps of Deity."[149]

1840

"VI.

Mauna Loa—Kilauea—The Eruption of 1840—The River of Fire—It reaches the Sea at Nanawale—Lava Chimneys—Destruction of a Village"[150]

Occurring during the denouement of the Great Awakening, Coan's vivid pen-painter portrayals of the 1840 eruption of Kilauea catapulted him to the position of Renaissance man, in addition to being a successful revivalist. To Coan's great disappointment, the eruption began while he was in Honolulu at the annual General Meeting of the mission. Upon his return, he interviewed eye witnesses and made his own visits to the area.

"The first eruption from Kilauea which occurred after my arrival in Hilo, began on the thirtieth of May, 1840. To my regret, I was then absent at the annual General Meeting of this mission in Honolulu, a meeting which I have always attended. I therefore record a portion of the facts as given by the natives and foreigners who saw the eruption, adding my own observations on a visit to the scene after my return from Honolulu."[151]

The Exploring Expedition was in the Hilo area during this time and established a location up on a volcano. In the previous chapter it was mentioned that Dr. Judd was the guide for the Ex Ex team.[152]

Coan wrote about the eruption almost contemporaneously, and much of their writings made their way into the July 1841 *Missionary Herald*. In his book on the Hawai'i volcanoes, Dana in chapter XIII relates an "Account by Rev. Titus Coan."[153] This section will examine the eruption from both his *Missionary Herald* report and his autobiography chapter written forty years later.

In *The Missionary Herald*, Coan transitions from the other matters he has written about. "Though my letter is already long, I cannot close it without saying a word

---

149. Coan to DuPont, June 7, 1850, in Coan, *Memorial Volume*, 66–67.

150. Coan, *Memorial Volume*, "Table of Contents," np; and restated on the first page of the chapter itself, 69.

151. Coan, *Life*, 70.

152. Kay, "Missionary Contributions," np.

153. Coan letter, September 1840, in *Missionary Herald* 38.7 (July 1841) 283, in Dana, *Characteristics of Volcanoes*, 427.

respecting the late volcanic eruption in Puna, on this island."[154] In his letter he also laments not being present for the beginning of the eruption.

He works to make up for lost time and presence. "Since our return from Oahu I have made a pretty thorough exploration of the tract of country where the eruption occurred, having found its source, and traced the stream through most of its windings, to the sea."[155] In his letter he writes, "I therefore record a portion of the facts as given by the natives and foreigners who saw the eruption, adding my own observations on a visit to the scene after my return from Honolulu."[156]

In both documents, Coan discusses the lead-up to the 1840 Kīlauea eruption. In his autobiography he writes, "There had been no grand eruption from this crater for the previous seventeen years, so that the lavas in the crater had risen several hundred feet, and the action had, at times, been terrific."[157] In *The Missionary Herald*, he writes, "For several years past the great crater of Kilauea has been rapidly filling up, by the rising of the superincumbent crust, and by the frequent gushing forth of the molten sea below. These silent eruptions continued to occur at intervals, until the black ledge was repeatedly overflowed."[158]

Coan writes about the sights of the 1840 eruption. In his autobiography Coan writes that the "volcano is thirty miles by road from Hilo, and under favorable conditions of the atmosphere we could see the splendid light by night, and the white cloudy pillar of steam by day. It was reported that, for several days before the outburst, the whole vast floor of the crater was in a state of intense ebullition."[159]

He puts it this way in *The Missionary Herald*: "[W]hen, as many natives testify, the whole area of the crater became one entire sea of ignifluous[160] matter, raging [missing word/s] old ocean when lashed into fury by a tempest. For several days the fires raged with fearful intensity, exhibiting a scene awfully terrific."[161] Back to his autobiography, Coan writes that the "eruption was first noticed by the people of Puna, who were living only twenty miles from it. The light appeared at first like a highland jumble on fire; and so it was."[162]

---

154. Coan letter, September 1840, in *Missionary Herald* 38.7 (July 1841) 283, in Dana, *Characteristics of Volcanoes*, 427.

155. Coan, *Life*, 70.

156. Coan letter, September 1840, in *Missionary Herald* 38.7 (July 1841) 283, in Dana, *Characteristics of Volcanoes*, 427.

157. Coan, *Life*, 70.

158. Coan letter, September 1840, in *Missionary Herald* 38.7 (July 1841) 283, in Dana, *Characteristics of Volcanoes*, 427.

159. Coan, *Life*, 70.

160. "Flowing with fire." Dictionary.com, "Ignifluous."

161. Coan letter, September 1840, in *Missionary Herald* 38.7 (July 1841) 283, in Dana, *Characteristics of Volcanoes*, 427.

162. Coan, *Life*, 71.

When it comes to sound, Coan writes the following: "The infuriated waves sent up infernal sounds, and dashed with such maddening energy against the sides of the awful caldron, as to shake the solid earth above, and to detach huge masses of overhanging rocks, which, leaving their ancient beds, plunged into the fiery gulf below."[163]

In both *Life* and the *Missionary Herald* letter, Coan talks about how the heat of the eruption affected travelers on the road. "It was even stated that the heat was so intense, and the surges so infernal, that travelers near the upper rim of the crater left the path on account of the heat, and for fear of the falling of the precipice over which the trail lay and passed at a considerable distance from the crater." Coan then notes the proximity of the overland road. "Kilauea is about half in Puna and half in Kau, and all travelers going from Kau to Hilo by the inland road pass the very brink of this crater."[164] "So terrific was the scene that no one dared to approach near it, and travelers on the main road, which lay along the verge of the crater, feeling the ground tremble beneath their feet, fled and passed by at a distance."[165]

Coan indicates in *The Missionary Herald* that he would have doubted the islanders'[166] reports of the immensity of the eruption had he not seen the results with his own eyes and compared it with his memories of the pre-eruption status. "I should be inclined to discredit these statements of the natives, had I not since been to Kilauea and examined it minutely with these reports in view." Coan then provides his eyewitness account. "Every appearance, however, of the crater confirms these reports. Everything within the caldron is new. Not a particle of lava remains as it was when I last visited it." He again emphasizes the newness caused by the eruption. "All has been melted down and re-cast. All is new. The whole appears like a raging sea, whose waves had been suddenly solidified while in the most violent agitation."[167]

By contrast, with the perspective provided by forty years of reflection in *Life*, Coan presents the reports of the Hawaiians in Puna as a matter of course. Coan builds on the reports with specific measurements, observations, and descriptions. "The eruption was first noticed by the people of Puna, who were living only twenty miles from it." The "fiery river found vent some 1,200 to 1,500 feet below the rim of Kilauea, and flowing subterraneous in a N. E. direction, for about four miles, marking its course by rending the superincumbent[168] strata and throwing up light puffs of sumptuous

---

163. Coan letter, September 1840, in *Missionary Herald* 38.7 (July 1841) 283, in Dana, *Characteristics of Volcanoes*, 427.

164. Coan, *Life*, 70–71.

165. Coan letter, September 1840, in *Missionary Herald* 38.7 (July 1841) 283, in Dana, *Characteristics of Volcanoes*, 427.

166. And anyone?

167. Coan letter, September 1840, in *Missionary Herald* 38.7 (July 1841) 283, in Dana, *Characteristics of Volcanoes*, 427.

168. "Lying or resting and usually exerting pressure on something else." Merriam Webster, "Superincumbent."

steam, it broke ground in the bottom of a wooded crater about five hundred feet deep, consuming the shrubs, vines, and grasses, and leaving a smouldering mass instead."[169]

Returning to *The Missionary Herald*, Coan concludes his description of the appearance of the crater and transitions to the history of the eruption. "Having stated something of the appearance of the great crater, for several days previous to the disgorgement of its fiery contents, I will now give a short history of the eruption itself." He makes a comment about the "shortness" of the description. "I say short, because it would require a volume to give a full and minute detail of all the facts of the case."[170] An entire volume could well be written on this eruption alone, as well as the other five that took place while Coan was in Hilo.

Coan begins his specific history of the 1840 eruption of Kīlauea: "On the thirtieth of May the people of Puna observed the appearance of smoke and fire in the interior, a mountainous and desolate region of that distinct [sic. read "district."]. Thinking that the fire might be the burning of some jungle, they took little notice of it until the next day, Sabbath, when the meetings in the different villages were thrown into confusion by sudden and grand exhibitions of fire, on a scale so large and fearful as to leave them no room to doubt the cause of the phenomenon."[171] The eruption affected the Hawaiian Christians' day of worship.

In *The Missionary Herald*, Coan describes the path of the lava.[172] Again from the perspective of forty years, Coan notes the following effects. "The great stream forced its way underground in a wild and wooded region for two miles more, when it again threw up a jet of fire and sulphur, covering about an acre. At this point, a large amount of brilliant sulphur crystals continued to be formed for several years." There is an even longer effect: "Only a little further on, and an old wooded cone was rent with fissures several feet wide, and about half an acre of burning lava spouted up, consuming the trees and jungle. This crevasse emitted scalding vapor for twenty-five years." He describes the path of the lava through June 3.[173]

In both publications, Coan writes about the subterranean lava flow followed by the effect on the coast and in the ocean. He notes the difficulty in keeping track of the subterranean flows. Once more the lava "disappears, and flowing in a subterranean channel, cracks and breaks the earth, opening fissures from six inches to twelve feet in width, and sometimes splitting the trunk of a tree so exactly that its legs stand astride

---

169. Coan, *Life*, 71.

170. Coan letter, September 1840, in *Missionary Herald* 38.7 (July 1841) 283, in Dana, *Characteristics of Volcanoes*, 427.

171. Coan letter, September 1840, in *Missionary Herald* 38.7 (July 1841) 283, in Dana, *Characteristics of Volcanoes*, 427.

172. Coan letter, September 1840, in *Missionary Herald* 38.7 (July 1841) 283.

173. Coan, *Life*, 71–72. Coan letter, September 1840, in *Missionary Herald* 38.7 (July 1841) 283, complements that discussion.

at the fissure. At some places it is impossible to trace the subterranean stream, on account of the impenetrable thicket under which it passes."[174]

Coan continues his description of the lava flow. "onward went the burning river, deep underground some six miles more, when the earth was rent again with an enormous fissure, and floods of devouring fire were poured out, consuming the forest and spreading over perhaps fifty acres. And still the passage seaward was underground for about another six miles, when it broke out in a terrific flood and rolled and surged along henceforth upon the surface, contracting to a half a mile, or expanding to two miles in width, and moving from half a mile, to five miles an hour, according to the angle of descent and the inequalities and obstructions of the surface, until it poured over the perpendicular sea-wall about thirty feet high, in a sheet of burning fusion only a little more than a mile wide."[175]

He writes of the lava and the ocean. "After flowing under ground several miles, perhaps six or eight, it again broke out like overwhelming flood, and sweeping forest, hamlet, plantation, and everything before it rolled down with resistless energy to the sea, where leaping a precipice of forty or fifty feet, it poured itself in one vast cataract of fire into the deep below, with loud detonations, fearful hissings, and a thousand unearthly and indescribable sounds."[176]

Coan compares the sound of the lava with the best known waterfall in the United States: "Imagine to yourself a river of fused minerals, of the breadth and depth of Niagra, and of a deep gory red, falling in one emblazoned sheet, one raging torrent into the ocean!" He describes the collision of lava and ocean: "The scene, as described by eyewitnesses, was terribly sublime. Two mighty agencies in collision! Two antagonist and giant forces in contact, and producing effects on a scale inconceivably grand!"[177]

And this from the autobiography: "As this grand cataract of fire poured over the basaltic sea-wall, the sights and sounds were said to be indescribable. Two mighty antagonistic forces were in conflict. The sea boiled and raged as with infernal fury, while the burning flood continued to pour into the troubled waves by night and by day for three weeks."[178] He writes about lava going into the ocean in *The Missionary Herald*. "For three weeks this terrific river disgorged itself into the sea with little abatement. Dense clouds of steam rolled up heavenward, veiling sun and stars, and so covering the lava flow the objects could not be seen from one margin to the other."[179]

He describes the growth of the coastal area[180] thanks to the lava: "The coast was extended into the sea for a quarter of a mile, and a pretty sand-beach and a new

---

174. Coan letter, September 1840, in *Missionary Herald* 38.7 (July 1841) 283.
175. Coan, *Life*, 72.
176. Coan letter, September 1840, in *Missionary Herald* 38.7 (July 1841) 283.
177. Coan letter, September 1840, in *Missionary Herald* 38.7 (July 1841) 284.
178. Coan, *Life*, 72.
179. Coan letter, September 1840, in *Missionary Herald* 38.7 (July 1841) 284.
180. And, therefore, the island.

cape were formed."[181] During "this flow, the sea-line along the whole breadth of the fire-stream was pushed out many yards by the solidified lavas."[182] He writes about the underwater growths. Three "tufaceous[183] cones were raised in the water where ships could once sail. They were formed of lava-sand made by the shivering of the mineral flood coming in contact with the sea, and standing in a line two hundred, three hundred, and four hundred feet above the water, with their bases deep down in the sea."[184] "Three hills of scoria[185] and sand were also formed in the sea, the lowest about two hundred and the highest about three hundred feet."[186] From the perspective of several decades Coan writes, "These dunes have been greatly reduced by the waves thundering at their bases and the winds and storms beating upon their summits. One of them, indeed, is now entirely obliterated."[187]

In both his autobiography and the *Missionary Herald*, Coan makes another comparison to a well-known American body of water: the Mississippi River. He is briefer on this matter in the autobiography. "Imagine the Mississippi converted into liquid fire of the consistency of fused iron, and moving onward sometimes rapidly, sometimes sluggishly; now widening into a lake, and anon rushing through a narrow gorge, breaking its way through mighty forests and ancient solitudes, and you will get some idea of the spectacle here exhibited."[188]

Compare the above with this from *The Missionary Herald*: "The breadth of the stream, where it fell into the sea, is about half a mile, but inland it varies from one to four or five miles in width, conforming itself, like a river, to the face of the country over which it flowed. Indeed, if you can imagine the Mississippi, converted into liquid fire, of the consistency of fused iron, and moving onward, sometimes rapidly, sometimes sluggishly, now widening into a sea, and anon rushing through a narrow defile, winding its way through mighty forests and ancient solitudes, you will get some idea of the spectacle here exhibited."

Coan then notes the depth of the lava stream. "The depth of the stream will probably vary from ten to two hundred feet, according to the inequalities of the surface over which it passed."[189] In his autobiography, Coan writes on the depth of the lava. "Along

---

181. Coan letter, September 1840, in *Missionary Herald* 38.7 (July 1841) 284.

182. Coan, *Life*, 73.

183. Noun, "tufa." "Also called calcareous tufa, calc-tufa, calc-tuff, a porous limestone formed from calcium carbonate deposited by springs or the like. Compare travertine . . . a porous rock composed of calcium carbonate and formed by precipitation from water, e.g., around mineral springs" Oxford Dictionaries, "Tufa."

184. Coan, *Life*, 73.

185. "Porous cinder-like fragments of dark lava. A cindery, vesicular basaltic lava, typically having a frothy texture." Oxford Dictionaries., "Scoria."

186. Coan letter, September 1840, in *Missionary Herald* 38.7 (July 1841) 284.

187. Coan, *Life*, 73.

188. Coan, *Life*, 73–74.

189. Coan letter, September 1840, in *Missionary Herald* 38.7 (July 1841) 284.

the central line of the stream its depth could not be measured accurately, for there was no trace of tree or ancient rock or floor. All was a vast bed of fresh, smouldering lava. On the margins, however, where the strata were thinner, I was able to measure with great accuracy... The numerous holes left in the hot lava bed by the gradual reduction of the trunks to ashes afforded the means of measuring the depth of the flow. With a long pole I was enabled to measure from a depth of five to twenty-five feet."[190]

He writes about the light provided by the lava. "During the flow, night was converted into day on all eastern Hawaii. The light rose and spread like the morning upon the mountains, and its glare was seen on the opposite side of the island. It "was also distinctly visible for more than one hundred miles at sea; and at the distance of forty miles fine print could be read at midnight. The brilliancy of the light was like a blazing firmament, and the scene is said to be one of sublimity."[191]

When it comes to the course[192] of the lava flow, Coan gives an estimate in *The Missionary Herald* that he would correct in his autobiography four decades later. "The whole course of the stream from Kilauea to the sea is about forty miles. Its mouth is about twenty-five miles from Hilo station."[193] In his autobiography, he notes the *Missionary Herald* article and gives his correction. "I went up the flow to where it burst out in volume and breadth from its subterranean chambers and continued on the surface to the sea, a distance of about twelve miles, making the entire length of the stream about thirty miles. In a letter published in *The Missionary Herald* of July 1841, I called it forty miles, but later measurements have led me to correct this and some other statements made on first sight." He does not directly indicate what the "other statements" were that he corrected.

Coan notes in both writings the cooling of the crust. "The crust is now cooled, and may be traversed with care, though scalding steam, pungent gases, and smoke are still emitted in many places."[194] In his autobiography he writes about the cooling and his spending two days examining the lava. "I spent nearly two days on the stream. It was solidified and mostly cooled, yet hot and steaming in places."[195]

In *The Missionary Herald* he transitions from the two days of observation to the wonder of what he beheld. "In pursuing my way for nearly two days over this mighty smouldering mass, I was more and more impressed at every step with the wonderful scene."[196] From here on out the two narratives diverge like two lava streams moving out from the same point. First, the rest of the *Missionary Herald* material. This

---

190. Coan, *Life*, 77.
191. Coan letter, September 1840, in *Missionary Herald* 38.7 (July 1841) 284.
192. Length.
193. Coan letter, September 1840, in *Missionary Herald* 38.7 (July 1841) 284.
194. Coan letter, September 1840, in *Missionary Herald* 38.7 (July 1841) 284.
195. Coan, *Life*, 76.
196. Coan letter, September 1840, in *Missionary Herald* 38.7 (July 1841) 284.

will be followed by the rest of Coan's wrap up on the 1840 eruption as related in his autobiography.

In *The Missionary Herald*, Coan expands on what he means by the wonder of the scene. "[H]ills had been melted down like wax; ravines and deep valleys had been filled; and majestic forests had disappeared like a feather in the flames. In some places the molten stream parted and flowed in separate channels for a considerable distance, and then reuniting, formed islands of various sizes from one to fifty acres, with trees still standing, but seared and blighted by the intense heat. On the outer edges of the lava, where the stream was more shallow and the heat less vehement, and where of course the liquid mass cooled soonest, the trees were mowed down like grass before the scythe, and left charred, crisped, smouldering, and only half-consumed. As the lava flowed around the trunks of large trees on the outskirts of the stream, the melted mass stiffened and consolidated before the trunk was consumed, and when this was effected, the top of the tree fell, and lay unconsumed on the crust, while the hole which marked the place of the trunk remains almost as smooth and perfect as the caliber of a cannon. These holes are innumerable, and I found them to measure from ten to forty feet deep, but as I remarked before, they are in the more shallow parts of the lava, the trees being entirely consumed where it was deeper. During the flow of this eruption, the great crater of Kilauea sunk about three hundred feet, and her fires became nearly extinct, one lake only out of many being left active in this mighty caldron. This, with other facts which have been named, demonstrates that the eruption was the disgorgement of the fires of Kilauea. The open lake in the old crater is at present intensely active, and the fires are increasing, as is evident from the glare visible at our station and from the testimony of visitors."[197]

Coan reflects on how humans were affected by the eruption and its aftermath by first reflecting on God's providential care. "Through the directing hands of a kind Providence no lives were lost, and but little property was consumed during this amazing flood of fiery ruin. The stream passed over an almost uninhabited desert. A few little hamlets were consumed, and a few plantations were destroyed, but the inhabitants, forewarned, fled and escaped. During the progress of the eruption some of the people in Puna spent most of their time in prayer and religious meetings, some flew in consternation from the face of the all-devouring element, others wandered along its margin, marking with idle curiosity its daily progress, while another class still coolly pursued their usual vocations, unawed by the burning fury as it rolled along within a mile of their doors. It was literally true that they ate, drank, bought, sold, planted, built, apparently indifferent [Luke 17:26–27] to the roar of consuming forests, the sight of devouring fire, the startling detonations, the hissing of escaping steam, the rending of the earth, the shivering and melting of gigantic rocks, the raging and dashing of fiery waves, the bellowings, the murmurings, the unearthly mutterings coming up from a burning deep. They went carelessly on amid the rain of ashes, sand, and

---

197. Coan letter, September 1840, in *Missionary Herald* 38.7 (July 1841) 284.

fiery scintillations, gazing vacantly on the fearful and ever-varying appearance of the atmosphere, murky, black, livid, blazing, the sudden rising of lofty pillars of flame, the upward curling of ten thousand columns of smoke, and their majestic roll in dense, dingy, lurid, or partly coloured clouds. All these moving phenomena were regarded by them as the fall of a shower, or the running of a brook; while to others they were as the tokens of a burning world, the departing heavens, and a coming Judge."

Coan continues his vivid descriptions and observations. "I will just remark here, that while the stream was flowing, it might be approached within a few yards on the windward side, while at the leeward no one could live within the distance of many miles, on account of the smoke, the impregnation of the atmosphere with pungent and deadly gases, and the fiery showers which were constantly descending, and destroying all vegetable life. During the progress of the descending stream, it would often fall into some fissure, and forcing itself into apertures and under massive rocks, and even hillocks and extended plats [plots] of ground, and lifting them from their ancient ground, bear them with all their superincumbent mass of soil, trees, etc., on its viscous and livid bosom, like a raft on the water. When the fused mass was sluggish, it had a gory appearance like clotted blood, mingled and thrown into violent agitation. Sometimes the flowing lava would find a subterranean gallery, diverging at right angles from the main channel, and pressing into it would flow off unobserved, till meeting with some obstruction in its dark passage, when, by its expansive force, it would raise the crust of the earth into a dome-like hill of fifteen or twenty feet in height, and then bursting this shell, pour itself out in a fiery torrent around. A man who was standing at a considerable distance from the main stream, and intensely gazing at the absorbing scene before him found himself suddenly raised to the height of ten or fifteen feet above the common level around him, and he had but just time to escape from his dangerous position, when the earth opened where he had stood, and a stream of fire gushed out."[198]

In his autobiography, Coan wraps up his discussion of before, during, and after the 1840 Kīlauea eruption with the following observations and reflections from the perspective of forty years. "I had seen fearful ragings and heard what seemed the wails of infernal beings in the great crater of Kilauea, but I had never before seen the amazing effects of a great exterior eruption of lava, and I returned from this weary exploration, after a missionary tour through Puna, with a deepened sense of the terrible dynamics of the fiery abyss [Rev 9:2 and elsewhere in the Book of Revelation] over which we tread.

"Since then, in crossing and re-crossing the wild highlands of my parish I have found in the consumed openings of forests a new class of volcanic monuments, consisting in numerous stacks of lava chimneys standing apart on the floor of an ancient flow. These chimneys measure from five to twenty-five feet in height, and five to ten

---

198. Coan letter, September 1840, in *Missionary Herald* 38.7 (July 1841) 284.

feet in diameter. I gazed at them at first sight as the work of human art, not knowing that they were cylindrical.

"Then came the question, how were they formed? The solution soon came—that an ancient eruption had passed through this forest at the height of many feet above the present surface, the fiery river surrounding large trees, but while it consumed all smaller growths, the waves subsided to their present level before these trunks were fully consumed, thus leaving partially cooled envelopes of lava adhering to them. These moulds or chimneys now stand as monuments of the volcanic action of an unknown age. Here I leave this subject for a while, purposing to return to it."[199]

In an 1884 report quoted in *Hawaiian Volcanoes*, Clarence E. Dutton writes about "Kīlauea-iki[200] and Poli-okeawe. The natives residing in the Puna district have always averred that eruptions have taken place along this line with considerable frequency, and within the reign of every king of that district from time immemorial." The last eruption "occurred in the year 1840, and was of very great magnitude. It has been described in considerable detail by Dr. Coan."[201]

Coan also writes in his autobiography of Chester Smith Lyman's visit to the Hilo area in 1846. After writing of the amazing items he made for Coan,[202] Titus avers, "*He made, also, one of the best surveys of Kīlauea crater that I have ever seen.*"[203] Those surveys would have been after the 1840 Kīlauea eruption.

C. S. Lyman notes that the trip to and up Kīlauea began on "thirtieth June 1846." He rather thoroughly describes the trip to Kīlauea. A rain storm hits and difficulties arise. "The way becomes difficult for the explorers. After searching for some time in rain and finding ourselves in the midst of crevices and chasms into which it w[oul]d be fatal to fall we began to despair of success and began to think of spending the night supperless and in the rain among these chasms and pitfalls. We shouted and screamed at the top of our voices to rouse our friends at the house which was almost directly above us, but owing to the noise of the wind, without success. At length, after groping our way in some places over passages not more than a foot wide with deep chasms on each side Mr. Douglass thought he had hit on the path. On examination it proved to be true, and with thankfulness for our deliverance we continued our ascent, and about 8 o'clock arrived at the house weary, wet, and hungry. Our friends had become anxious for our safety and were just preparing to hang out a lamp on the cliff for our guidance. Mr. Coan has visited the volcano several times a year for a number of years and is familiar with every part of it, yet on this occasion he was utterly unable to find the way. A stranger or one but little acquainted with the place would not have succeeded

---

199. Coan, *Life*, 78–79. He does not return to that subject.

200. A collapsed crater which is next to the main summit caldera of Kīlauea. http://dictionary.sensagent.com/kilauea%20iki/en-en/.

201. Dutton, *Hawaiian Volcanoes*, 125.

202. Sun dial and book case.

203. Coan, *Life*, 144. Emphasis added.

in reaching the top at all in such circumstances."[204] Lyman leaves unstated the obvious that Coan and others could have been lost to the world by an accident during the above-described difficulty.

Such high adventure for Titus Coan and colleagues continues with an examination of the major eruptions between 1843 and 1882.

---

204. Lyman, *Around the Horn*, 91–92.

9

Vulcanologist, Part Two

Major Eruptions, from 1843 through 1881.

INTRODUCTION

IN HIS AUTOBIOGRAPHY, TITUS Coan wrote one chapter on the Great Awakening. He devoted seven chapters to volcanoes. While he wrote other pages about being a missionary and pastor, he probably devoted more than one third of the pages to volcanic activity because his directly Christian labors were well known and he wanted to provide information to those interested in the volcanic activity. He also would weave together biblical references to the stunning aspects of the volcanoes.

This chapter examines the remaining five major eruptions during Coan's Hilo tenure. Most of the material is drawn from his autobiography.

1843: MAUNA LOA

"XIX

Eruptions from Mauna Loa—The Eruption of 1843—A Visit to it—Danger on the Mountain—
A Perilous Journey and a Narrow Escape"[1]

Coan begins this chapter with the first awareness of an eruption taking place. "During the night of January 10, 1843, a brilliant light was seen near the summit of Mauna Loa. In a short time a fiery stream was rushing down the mountain in a northerly direction toward Mauna Kea."

The light of day provides more information. "On the eleventh, vast columns of steam and smoke arose from the crater. After a few days the orifice on the top of

---

1. Coan, *Life*, Table of Contents, np; beginning of chapter, 270.

the mountain ceased to eject its burning masses, and the action appeared more vivid upon the slope of the mountain, until the lava reached the valley below, and struck the foot-hills of Mauna Kea."

The Paris family was visiting the Coans at the time. The two couples agree that John and Titus could visit the erupting mountain. It would be a sojourn fraught with peril. The rest of the chapter relates their visit to Mauna Loa.[2]

"The Rev. J. D. Paris and his family were our guests at the time, and, our good wives consenting, we prepared to go up to the flow, which shone with a strong glare in the valley between the mountains, and had the appearance of turning toward Hilo. Neither of us had ascended Mauna Loa before, and we started with great enthusiasm. Taking a guide and men to carry our food and sleeping-cloaks, we followed the bay of Hilo." He relates their first two and a half days of walking in a perilous region. "The pathway was rocky and full of cascades from ten to 150 feet in height; but the water was low at this time, and by wading, leaping from rock to rock, and crossing and recrossing the stream from ten to twenty times in a mile, and taking advantage of parts of its margins which were dry we made good progress, sleeping two nights in the forests on its banks and coming out of the woods into an open rolling country on the third day. This is a region where thousands of wild cattle roam."

Coan continues, relating the nature of the lava flow. "A little before night of this day, we came directly abreast of a stream of liquid fire half a mile wide, and bending its course toward Hilo. Passing along the front of this slowly-moving flood, we flanked another of about the same width, flowing quietly to the west toward Waimea; while far up on the side of the mountain we saw another stream moving toward Kona. This higher stream was a lateral branch of the main trunk, and this trunk was again divided at the base of Mauna Kea. As these lower branches were pushing slowly along upon level ground, and as the feeding flood had ceased to come down upon the surface from the terminal vent, but flowed in a subterranean duct or ducts, most of the flow was solidified above, and we could see the flowing lava only in a belt of a few rods wide across the ends of the streams, and at several points upon the side of the mountain."[3]

He next relates what happened that evening. "Having satisfied ourselves with the day's labors, we set about preparing our camp for the night. Besides our guide and burden-bearers, a number of natives had begged the privilege of going with us. Selecting an old wooded crater, about two hundred yards from the lava stream, and elevated some sixty feet above it, we prepared a booth of shrubs and leaves, collected fuel, made a rousing fire, ate our supper, made arrangements for the morrow, and lay down for the night.

"But before our eyes were closed by sleep, a dense cloud settled down upon us, covering all the wide uplands between Mauna Kea and Mauna Loa. We were now at an

---

2. See Coan to Paris, Honolulu June 17, 1880, in Coan, *Memorial Volume*, 167, for Coan reminiscing with Paris about this trip. See previous chapter for relevant quotation.

3. Coan, *Life*, 270–72.

elevation of about eight thousand feet above the ocean level, and the air was cold. Soon the vivid lightning began to flash from the clouds that covered us, instantly followed by crashing peals of rattling thunder. We found that we were in a sea of electricity, and the full-charged clouds rested on the ground. It was a flash and a crash simultaneously; the blaze and the roar were nearly coincident. The very heavens seemed ablaze; the hills and trees dropping their veil of darkness as if engaged in a fairy dance, while the thunder roared and reverberated among the mountains."

Coan writes of both the grandeur and the danger. "I had never before seen a tempest of equal grandeur. But the danger was imminent. The storm continued without intermission until near morning, and a great rain fell. The sun rose, and the mountains on both sides of us were crowned with glory. A heavy fall of pure snow covered their summits. Looking down from our lofty watch toward Hilo, we saw the clouds that had blazed around us during the night rolled down and massed along the shore, hiding the sea from our sight, the upper surface shining with light, and alive with dancing and quivering rays. We could also see the flashes of lightning dart among the clouds, followed in measured time by the booming thunder. The scene was of equal grandeur with that of the past night, but without its danger. We were in bright sunshine, thousands of feet above the clouds, while the coast and bay of Hilo were shrouded; and, for the first time in years, a great storm of hail fell upon the northern part of the district."[4]

He relates climbing as high as possible. "But to the hills! To the hills! Was the summons of the morning. Onward and upward was our motto. We each selected a man who volunteered to go with us to the summit. From our point of view we could trace the stream in all its windings from its source to its fiery terminus before us. The surface was all hardened except the fused belt of some two hundred feet wide at the lower end of the flow, pushing slowly out from under its indurated cover. Above this the whole flow was a shining *pahoehoe*, or field lava, steaming in light puffs from a thousand cracks and holes.

"We set out at sunrise with our two native guides, carrying a little food, a small supply of water in a gourd, and our camp-cloaks. We flanked the fresh lava stream some part of the way; crossed it occasionally, and walked directly upon it for many miles, making as straight a course as possible. Much of the way we were obliged to walk over fields and ridges, and down into gorges of *aa*, or clinker lava,[5] as sharp and jagged as slag around an iron furnace.

"The work was so severe that our men fell behind, and we were forced to halt often and encourage them to hasten up. At length, weary of this lingering pace, we hurried on, leaving them to follow as well as they could, but before noon we lost sight of them, and saw them no more until our return to camp. Taking with them all our

---

4. Coan, *Life*, 271–73. Note the volcano-related weather.

5. "Very irregular fragments [of lava] commonly called clinkers." Encyclopedia Britannica, "Clinker | lava fragments."

supplies, they had turned back to enjoy rest and shelter with their companions who remained behind.

"We passed over hills and through valleys; saw steaming cones and heard their hissings. We came to openings through the crust of twenty to fifty feet in diameter, out of which issued scalding gases, and in looking down these steaming vents, we saw the stream of incandescent lava rushing along a vitrified duct with awful speed, some fifty feet below us. Still pressing up the mountain, we saw through other openings this rushing stream as it hurried down its covered channel to spread itself out on the plains below. We threw large stones into these openings, and saw them strike the lava river, on whose burning bosom they passed out of sight instantly, before sinking into the flood. Far off to the right we heard the crashing and roaring of the lava-roof as it fell into the channel below made by the draining of the stream."[6]

The two men still had not reached the summit, meaning that decision time was approaching. "Noon passed, and the summit was not reached. 'Hills peeped o'er hills,'[7] and we were weary. We came to the snow. One, 2, and 3 p.m. made us anxious. We counted the hours, half hours, and minutes, while we plodded some five miles in the snow. We had no food, no wrappers for the night, and no shelter. Our condition was now not only one of suffering, but one of peril. Our strength began to fail. But to fail of the object before us when just within our grasp! Could we bear the disappointment?

"We fixed 3:30 p.m. as the latest moment before we must turn our faces down the mountain. To remain later where we were was death. At the last moment we came to the yawning fissures where the crimson flood had first poured out. The rents were terribly jagged, showing the fearful rage of the fires as they burst forth from their caverns into the midnight darkness.

"We had seen the object of our quest, and now life depended on our speedy return.

"Full twenty-five miles of rugged lava, without guide or trail, lay before us. We had tasted no food nor a drop of water since daylight."[8]

The two men offer a brief prayer, then continue down the mountain. "We knelt a moment, and 'looked to the hills whence cometh help,' and then began the descent. We ran, we stumbled and fell; we rose and ran again amidst scoria rocks, up and down, until at sunset we reached the point where we had stood at noon. Far off among the foot-hills of Mauna Kea, in the north, we could descry the green cone where our camp was pitched.

"Night came on apace. The moon was a little past her first quarter, and her mild light never appeared so precious to us as now. Down, down, we ran, falling amidst the scoriaceous masses, scaling ridges and plunging into rugged ravines, tearing our shoes and garments, and drawing blood from our hands, faces, and feet. Once in about

---

6. Coan, *Life*, 273–75.
7. Pope, "Essay on Criticism," Part 2, Line 32: "Hills peep o'er hills, and Alps on Alps arise."
8. Coan, *Life*, 275–76.

a mile we allowed ourselves a few seconds only to rest. To sit down fifteen minutes would stiffen us with cold, and to fall asleep in our exhausted condition would be to wake no more on earth."

The danger grew in their ability to continue on. "As we grew weaker and weaker, our falls were more frequent, until we could hardly rise or lift a foot from the ground. More than once, when one of us fell he would say to his companion, 'I can not rise again but must give up.' The other would reply, 'Brother, you *must* get up,' and extending his weary hand, and with encouraging voice he would aid the fallen one to rise. Thus we alternated in falling and rising; while our progress became slower and slower. When about half-way down the descent, we saw clouds rolling up from the sea, and our anxiety was intense lest such a storm as we had felt the preceding night should fall upon us. The clouds covered the moon and stars, and darkened all the volcanic lights of those breathing-holes, which by night shone like lamps on a hill-side. Our camp-hill, and the flood of lava near it, were covered with the cloud, and 'darkness which was felt' [Exod 10:21] came over us. It now seemed as if all was over. But thanks to God the veil was removed, the stars reappeared, and we ceased to wander as we had done under the shadow of the cloud. We had left the snow and the colder heights far behind, and now we felt that we were saved. When within half a mile of camp our natives heard our call, and two came out with torches to meet us. We came in like wounded soldiers who had been battling above the clouds, limping and bleeding. We threw ourselves prostrate upon the ground, and called for water and food, and did not rise until near noon of the next day."9

Coan shares how the narrowness of their escape put into perspective their view of the returning assistants. "Our providential escape filled us with too much gratitude to allow us to chide severely the guides who had deserted us, and whom we found with the rest of the party, full-fed and happy.

"This expedition taught us useful lessons. One of them was never to attempt another enterprise of this kind without completer arrangements for its success. We learned practically the truth, that 'Two are better than one, for if they fall, the one will lift up his fellow, but woe to him who is alone when he falleth' [Eccl 4:9].

"When about to leave our mountain camp, our chief guide, a wild-bird catcher and bullock hunter of the highlands, came to me with a sober and thoughtful countenance, and after a little hesitation said: 'Mr. Coan, we have guided you up the mountain for so much, and now how much will you give us to guide you back?' Looking him square in the face, I replied, 'You need not go down, you can stay up here if you like.' The fellow was dumfounded and stood speechless. His companions, who had gathered around him hoping to share in the double price for services, burst out into a laugh, and called him an ass. He submitted, took up his burden, and gave me no more trouble. But all the way down his comrades kept up the joke until he accepted the title and said: 'Yes, I am a jackass.'

9. Coan, *Life*, 276–77.

"We reached home after three days of hobbling on lame feet, but thankful to him who guides the wanderer."[10]

1852

"XX.

Eruptions of Mauna Loa—The Eruption of 1852—The Fire-Fountain—A Visit to it—Alone on the Mountain—Sights—on Mauna Loa"[11]

Chapters 19 and 20 have Mauna Loa eruptions in common. But there the similarities end. He partially learned the lesson of going with someone else by having Dr. Wetmore join with him.[12] He also waited almost six days before heading toward the mountain. Instead of providing a narrative looking back over the decades, he relates this eruption nine years later by revising an article of his that appeared in *The American Journal of Science and Arts*.[13] Because he was writing for a scientific journal, he provides some measurements and other specifics.

"My account of the eruption of Mauna Loa in February 1852 was originally published in *The American Journal of Science and Arts*[14] . . . It is here reproduced with slight corrections from later observations. I visited the locality three times; first while the lava fountain was playing a thousand feet high, and twice since the crater had cooled.

"It was a little before daybreak on the seventeenth of February 1852 that we saw through our window a beacon light resting on the apex of Mauna Loa. At first we supposed it to be a planet just setting. In a few minutes we were undeceived by the increasing brilliancy of the light, and by a grand outburst of a fiery column which shot high into the air, sending down a wonderful sheen of light, which illuminated our fields and flashed through our windows. Immediately a burning river came rushing down the side of the mountain at the apparent rate of fifteen to twenty miles an hour. This summit eruption was vivid and vigorous for forty hours, and I was preparing to visit the scene, when all at once the valves closed, and all signs of the eruption disappeared; accordingly I ceased my preparations to ascend the mountain.

"On the twentieth, the eruption broke out laterally, about four thousand feet below the summit, and at a point facing Hilo; from this aperture a brilliant column of fire shot up to a height of seven hundred feet, by angular measurement, with a diameter of from one hundred to three hundred feet. This lava fountain was sustained without

---

10. Coan, *Life*, 277–78.
11. Coan, *Life*, Table of Contents, np; 279.
12. Though he would go only part way with Coan.
13. Coan, "Eruption from the summit," 106–07. Fidelia Coan, 107, "adds a line," actually ten lines.
14. Coan, *Life*, 279; Coan, "Eruption from the summit," 106–07; letters dated February 21 and 24, 1852. 106–07.

intermission for twenty days and nights, during which time it built up a crater one mile in circumference, lacking one chain, and four hundred feet high. It also sent down a river of liquid fire more than forty miles long, which came within ten miles of Hilo."

Coan writes about the long distance the sound traveled; the quivering of the earth; and the light show, along with smoke, and steam. "The roar of this great furnace was heard along the shores of Hilo, and the earth quivered with its rage, while all the district was so lighted up that we could see to read at any hour of the night when the sky was not clouded. The smoke and steam rose in a vast column like a pillar of cloud by day, and at night it was illuminated with glowing brilliants, raising the pillar of fire thousands of feet in appearance. When it reached a stratum of atmosphere of its own specific gravity, it moved off like the tail of a comet, or spread out laterally, a vast canopy of illu[mi?]nated gases. The winds from the mountain brought down smoke, cinders, 'Pele's hair,' and gases, scattering the light products over houses and gardens, streets and fields, or bearing them far out to sea, dropped them upon the decks of vessels approaching our coast.

"The light of the eruption was seen more than one hundred miles at sea, and sailors told us that when they first saw the light flaming on the mountain they exclaimed, 'Look there, the moon is rising in the west!' Much of the time our atmosphere was murky, and the veiled sun looked as if in an eclipse."[15]

Coan gets ready to visit the mountain with his friend Dr. Charles Wetmore. He also writes extensively of others who accompany them. "On Monday, the twenty-third of February, Dr. Wetmore and myself, taking with us four natives as assistants, set out for the mountain. One of these natives was familiar with the woods and wilds, having been a bird-catcher, a canoe-digger, and a wild-cattle hunter in those high regions. His name was Kekai, 'Salt Sea.'

"We passed our first night in the skirt of the forest, having taken with us long knives, an old sword, clubs, and hatchets, purposing to cut and beat our way through the jungle in as straight a line as possible toward the fiery pillar[Exod 13:21]. On Tuesday we rose fresh and earnest, and pressed through the ferns and vines and through the tangled thicket, and over, under, and around gigantic trees, which lay thick in some places, cutting and beating as we went, our progress being sometimes half a mile, sometimes one, and again two miles an hour. At night we bivouacked in the ancient forest, hearing the distant roar of the volcano and seeing the glare of the igneous river, which had already passed us, cutting its way through the wood a few miles distant on our left."[16]

Dr. Wetmore decides to turn back. "On Wednesday Dr. Wetmore decided to return to Hilo, apprehensive that the stream might reach the sea before we could return

---

15. Coan, *Life*, 279–81.
16. Coan, *Life*, 281–82.

from the crater, and that our families might need his presence. Taking one of the men, he hastened back to the village, while I pressed on."

Dangerous fog or vog[17] develops. "Sleeping once more in the forest, we emerged on Thursday upon the high, open lava fields, but plunged into a dense fog darker and more dreary than the thicket itself. We were admonished not to journey far, as more than one man had been lost in these bewildering fogs, and wandering farther and farther from the way had left his bones to bleach in the desert; we therefore encamped for the fourth time. A little before sunset the fog rolled off, and Mauna Kea and Mauna Loa both stood out in grand relief; the former robed in a fleecy mantle almost to its base, and the latter belching out floods of fire. All night long we could see the glowing fires and listen to the awful roar twenty miles away.

"We left our mountain eyrie on the twenty-seventh, determined, if possible, to reach the seat of action that day. The scoriaceous hills and ridges, the plains and gorges bristled with the sharp and jagged *aa*, and our ascent was rough and difficult. We mounted ridges where the pillar of fire shone strongly upon us, and we plunged down deep dells and steep ravines where our horizon was only a few feet distant, the attraction increasing as the square of the distance decreased.

"At noon we came upon the confines of a tract of naked scoriae so intolerably sharp and jagged that our baggage-men could not pass it. Here I ordered a halt; stationed the two carriers, gave an extra pair of strong shoes to the guide, gave him my wrapper and blanket, put a few crackers and boiled eggs into my pocket, took my compass and staff, and said to Mr. Salt Sea, 'Now go ahead, and let us warm ourselves to-night by that fire yonder.'" Coan experiences the situation similar to the 1843 eruption of having the helper lag behind. "But I soon found that my guide needed a leader; he lagged behind, and I waited for him to come up, but fearing we should not reach the point before night I pressed forward alone, with an interest that mocked all obstacles."

"At half-past 3 p.m. I reached the awful crater, and stood alone in the light of its fires. It was a moment of unutterable interest. I was ten thousand feet above the sea, in a vast solitude untrodden by the foot of man or beast, amidst a silence unbroken by any living voice. The Eternal God alone spoke. His presence was attested as in the 'devouring fire on the top of Sinai' [Exod 24:17]. I was blinded by the insufferable brightness, almost petrified by the sublimity of the scene."[18]

Coan comments on the strong heat and relates the sound of the eruption. "The heat was so intense that I could not approach the pillar within forty or fifty yards, even on the windward side, and in the snowy breezes coming down from the mountain near four thousand feet above. On the leeward side the steam, the hot cinders, ashes, and burning pumice forbade approach within a mile or more.

---

17. Vog is a form of air pollution that results when sulfur dioxide and other gases. Vog and particles emitted by an erupting volcano react with oxygen and moisture in the presence of sunlight.

18. Coan, *Life*, 282–84.

"I stood amazed before this roaring furnace. I felt the flashing heat and the jar of the earth; I heard the subterranean thunders, and the poetry of the sacred Word came into my thoughts: 'He looketh on the earth, and it trembleth; he toucheth the hills, and they smoke; the mountains quake at him, and the hills melt; he uttered his voice, the earth melted; the hills melted like wax at the presence of the Lord'" [Ps 97:5].

Coan followed up the Bible verse with a little application to what he witnessed at the summit. "Here indeed the hills smoked and the earth melted, and I saw its gushings from the awful throat of the crater burning with intense white heat. I saw the vast column of melted rocks mounting higher and still higher, while dazzling volleys and coruscations shot out like flaming meteors in every direction, exploding all the way up the ascending column of a thousand feet with the sharp rattle of infantry fire in battle. There were unutterable sounds as the fierce fountain sent up the seething fusion to its utmost height; it came down in parabolic curves, crashing like a storm of fiery hail in conflict with the continuous ascending volume, a thousand tons of the descending mass falling back into the burning throat of the crater, where another thousand were struggling for vent."

While enraptured by the scene, Coan realizes he is alone and feels some concern on that matter. "For an hour I stood entranced; then there came to me the startling thought that I was *alone*. Where was my companion? I looked down the mountain, by there was no motion and no voice. The vast fields and valleys of dreary scoria lay slumbering before me; the sun was about to disappear behind the lofty snow-robed mountain in the rear. What if my guide had gone back! Remembering my former experience in 1843, only about five miles from this place, I could not be otherwise than anxious. Minutes seemed as hours while I watched for his coming, when lo! There is motion upon the rough *aa* about a mile below me: a straw hat peers up on a ridge and again disappears in a gorge, like a boat in the trough of the sea. Then at length 'Salt Sea' stood forth a life-sized figure in full view. Weary but faithful he was toiling upward. If ever my heart leaped for joy, it was then. As he came within speaking distance, he raised both his hands high above his head and shouted: 'Kupainaha! Kupaiahanah i keia hana mana a ke Akua mana loa!'—Wonderful, wonderful, is this mighty work of Almighty God.

"Could I help embracing the old man and praising the Lord?"[19]

The two spend the night, say prayers, and eventually return to Hilo. "We chose our station for the night within about two hundred feet of the crater and watched its pyrotechnics, and heard its mutterings, its detonations, and its crashing thunder until morning. Occasionally our eyelids became heavy, but before we were fairly asleep some new and rousing demonstration would bring us to our feet and excite the most intense interest. In addition to the marvelous sounds, the kaleidoscopic views of the playing column were so rapid and so brilliant that we could hardly turn our eyes for a moment from it. The fusion when issuing from the mouth of the crater was white-hot,

---

19. Coan, *Life*, 284–86.

but as it rose through the air its tints underwent continuous changes: it became a light red, then a deeper shade, then a glossy gray, and in patches a shining black, but these tints and shades with many others were intermingled, and as every particle was in motion the picture was splendid beyond the power of description. Thousands and millions of tons of sparkling lava were pouring from the rim of the crater, while the cone was rising rapidly, and spreading out at the base. From the lower side of this cone a large fissure opened, through which the molten flood was issuing and rushing down the mountain, burning its way through the forest. No tongue, no pen, no pencil can portray the beauty, the grandeur, the terrible sublimity of the scenes of this memorable night.

"Morning came, we offered our prayers, ate our breakfast, and descended the mountain with regrets. Rejoining the men whom we had left the preceding day, we retraced our steps to Hilo, and reached home in health and safety, though not without an experience it may be interesting to relate." The returning party comes up against an unexpected obstacle. "In the upper skirts of the forest in a narrow pass we were confronted by a magnificent wild bull. Coming suddenly upon a small herd in this defile, the cows and smaller cattle fled and were soon out of sight; not so the bull; he wheeled and faced us boldly, covering the retreat of the cows and calves, and bidding us defiance. As he stood with head proudly erect, we estimated the tips of his splendid horns to be eight feet from the ground.

"We were challenged by this mountain sentinel to stand, and stand we did. We were unwilling to retreat; to deploy to the right or left seemed impossible. We held a council, feeling that 'discretion was the better part of valor.' The bull was armed with ugly horns; we were unarmed. He stood and we stood. Our guide, an old mountaineer, advised us to arm ourselves with stones, and directed that when he hurled his missile and shouted, we should do the same. We all hurled and yelled at once. The proud monarch snorted, shook his head, turned slowly on his heels, retreated a few paces, and then suddenly wheeled right-about and again held the passage. We hurled another volley and shouted. The Bashan bull [Ps 22:12] wheeled slowly round, walked about a rod, and a second time turned and faced us, bidding defiance. We feared a charge, but as we had pushed our Goliath back some feet, we let go a third volley, and this decided the conflict. He turned, but he neither ran nor trotted; he maintained his dignity and retreated deliberately, while we waited for his highness to disappear, without attempting to disarm him or make him a prisoner. It was a compromise which we accepted thankfully. We breathed easier and moved on with lighter steps.

"This splendid eruption of 1852 was in blast only twenty days."[20]

Returning to the *American Journal of Science*, Titus writes the eruption of Mauna Loa as an "old lion [who] is again out of his den, his eyes flash fire and his roar is awful... Another correspondent"—Fidelia Coan—also describes the eruption of Mauna Loa. She had two letters published in the AJSA: one on February twenty-third, the

---

20. Coan, *Life*, 286–88.

other on the twenty-sixth. "Her first letter begins by saying that a new "eruption is now taking place on Mauna Loa. It presents a scene of sublimity unsurpassed." In the February twenty-sixth letter she combined her own observations with what she had heard from her husband. "DEAR SIR—I add a line to the above to inform you that up to this date the action of the late eruption is undiminished. Truly our island is on fire. A line from Mr. Coan informs me that he passed within five or six miles of a stream of lava, yesterday, which was burning its path through the woods, in the direction of Puna. The action on the mountains was more intense last night than it has been since the morning of the seventeenth. I need not add that we are all deeply interested in knowing when, and where, and how, this fiery flood is to reach the sea. The locality of its source almost precludes the hope that its progress can be as harmless as on a former occasion ... Yours Truly, F. COAN."

In the second letter her material on this eruption continues, "By advices to Hilo the second inst.,[21] we further learn that the stream of lava had burned through the woods to within fifteen miles of Hilo, and that it was still progressing. The current was not so rapid as at first, but it is gradually filling up all the inequalities of the ground, and it was supposed at that date it would ultimately reach the sea, and discharge itself into the bay of Hilo.

"The light at night was very brilliant, and at Hilo it was almost as bright as day. Persons who left this city last week on a visit to Hilo will arrive at a seasonable moment to witness one of the most sublime phenomena of nature, and one of so rare occurrence that few are fortunate enough to witness it.—*Alta California.*"[22]

The discussion concludes with a bracketed sentence. "[According to later accounts the eruption ceased when the stream reached within seven miles of Hilo.]"[23]

1855-56

"XXI.

The Eruption of 1855—A Climb to the Source—Mountain Hardships—Visits to Lower Parts of the Lava Stream—Hilo threatened with Destruction—Liquidity of the Hawaiian Lavas— Are the Lava-Streams fed from their Sources only?"[24]

In his 1855 [56?] Hilo station report, Coan combines volcanic activity with the work of God. "As when Jehovah gave the law on Sinai 'the mountain was altogether on a smoke' [Exod 19:18], and as 'the sight of the glory of the Lord was like devouring

---

21. March 2.

22. Perhaps Alta California is where the letter was first received (and sent along) on the American mainland. Merriam Webster online defines "Alta California" as a former Spanish and Mexican province (1772–1848). Today it comprises the present state of California. This is a term chiefly used to differentiate it from Baja California. Merriam Webster, "Alta California."

23. Coan, "Eruption from the summit," 106–07.

24. Coan, *Life*, Table of Contents, np. chapter XXI, 289.

fire on the top of the mount' [Exod 24:17] so it has been with us. His drapery of smoke and sulpher [sic][25] has hung around our horizon. His pavilion of clouds and darkness has been spread upon our mountains—His thunders have rolled along our hills."

"His lightening[s?] flashed in our land and for more than nine months a deluge of liquid fire has rolled down from the summit Mauna Loa, rending, melting, and consuming all in its way until it had approached within five or six miles of town."[26]

Leavitt Hallock summarizes the physical and spiritual realities of this eruption. In "1855, Mauna Loa evolved a mighty eruption, and 'mid glare, and subterranean thunders, poured volumes of molten lava from its summit crater. This time it moved straight toward the city of Hilo. Seven months it flowed, now swiftly, now halting to fill up some low level of outlying plain. From five to five hundred feet deep, from a half mile to three miles wide, the nearing, devastating deadly torrent of fire crept steadily on toward the doomed city.

"It would flow through a great forest, and presently one by one the giant trees would fall, eaten off by the devouring lava, and in a few hours not a trace of the forest would remain above the seething surface. The flow was within two weeks of their homes. A day of fasting and prayer was set apart throughout the realm and vessels were in the offing to convey people to a place of safety when the crisis came. Father Coan preached a fast day sermon, and led the prayers of a vast terror-stricken assembly of six thousand people; an honest, hearty 'Amen!' sixty hundred strong endorsed his petition. With a small party he then visited the on-coming stream and camped that night upon its margin. Slowly, in terrible march it came, and at daybreak next morning he left it pouring over a precipice into a deep pool of water boiling and licked up by its tongue of flame. It filled that pool but it never overflowed, and you cannot find a native old enough to remember, who does not know that Father Coan's prayers checked the flow, extinguished the fires of Mauna Loa and saved the city of Hilo!"[27]

In his autobiography, Coan does not cite a journal article with regard to this eruption. In contrast to the relatively short duration of the previous eruptions, he opens the *Life* chapter by indicating that it lasted for fifteen months and stretched across parts of two years. "The great eruption of 1855–56 continued fifteen months and the disgorgement of lava exceeded by millions of tons that of any other eruption we have seen.

"It was first observed on the evening of the eleventh of August 1855 shining like Sirius at a small point near the summit of Mauna Loa. This radiant point expanded rapidly, and in a short time the glow was like that of the rising sun. Soon a deluge of liquid fire rushed down the mountain-side in the direction of our town."

Coan expresses the concern about the threat the lava flow poses to Hilo while tracking its progress. "Day after day, and night after night, we could trace this stream

---

25. A later typewriter typo?
26. Coan, Hilo station report, 1885 [56?], 2/64–65, HMH online.
27. Hallock, *Hawaii under King Kalakaua*, 69, 70.

until it entered the deep forest, when the scene by day would often be made beautiful by the vast clouds of white vapor rolling up in wreaths from the boiling streams and water-basins below. In the night-time the spectacle was one of unrivaled sublimity. The broad and deep river of lava, moving resistlessly on through the festooned forest trees, would first scorch the low plants and fallen timber of the jungle, until they took fire, when suddenly a roaring flame would burst forth, covering perhaps a square mile, and surging up the hanging vines to the tree tops, leaping in lambent flashes from tree to tree, would make the light so gorgeous that for the time being night was turned into day.

"These brilliant scenes were long continued, and all Hilo watched the progress of the stream with increasing interest."[28] A little less than two months after the beginning of the eruption, Coan sets out with an unnamed friend and several Hawaiians. He refers to the 1843 visit to an eruption with Mr. Paris.

"On the second of October, in company with a friend and several natives, I set off to visit this approaching torrent of lava. As the jungle through which it was burning its pathway was too dense to be penetrated, we chose for our track the bed of the Wailuku river, the channel in which Mr. Paris and I went up to the eruption of 1843. We slept three nights in the great forest on the banks of the river, and the fourth night in a cave on the outskirts of the forest. Early in the morning of October sixth we emerged and came to the margin of the lava stream in the open plain. We had flanked it at the distance of some two miles on our left, and its terminus was about ten miles below us on its way to Hilo. Where we first struck it, we estimated the breadth to be about three miles, but twice that width in places where the country was level, and where it could easily expand. The surface was solidified, and so nearly cool that we took it for our highway. And highway indeed it was, for it was raised in some places twenty, fifty, and a hundred feet above the old floor on which it came down. In some places the walking was comfortable, and in others all was confusion thrice confounded. Ridges, cones, bluffs, hills, crevasses, *aa*, swirls, twisting precipices, and all shapes congealed, were there. No fire yet. Little puffs of white steam were coming up from unknown depths below. Far down the mountain terrible fires were gleaming, cutting down a mighty forest and licking up rivers of water. High above us raged a glowing furnace, and under our very feet a burning flood was rushing with an unknown commission, perhaps to consume all Hilo, to choke our beautiful harbor, to drive out our people, and leave this gem of the Pacific a heap of ruin. Thoughts of what might be could not be silenced; like ghosts from the buried cities of Pompeii and Herculaneum, they haunted our path."[29]

Coan and his unnamed companion approach the harder part of the journey. "Onward we went; the ascent grew steeper. We were startled; a yawning fissure was

---

28. Coan, *Life*, 289–90.
29. Coan, *Life*, 290–91.

before us—hot, sulphurous gases were rushing up—the sullen swash[30] of liquid lava was heard. We took the windward side of the opening, approached carefully, and with awe we saw the swift river of fire some fifty feet below us, rushing at white heat, and with such fearful speed that we stood amazed. The great tunnel in which this fiery flow swept down was a vitrified duct apparently as smooth as glass, and the speed, though it could not be measured, I estimated to be forty miles an hour. Leaving this opening, we pressed forward, and once in about one or two miles we found other rents from thirty to two hundred feet in length, down which we looked, and saw the lava-torrent hurrying toward the sea."

He provides a paragraph with some specific descriptions, as well as dangers. "These openings in the mountain were vents, or breathing holes for the discharge of the burning gases, and thus perhaps prevented earthquakes and terrific explosions. They were longitudinal, revealing the fiery channel at the depth of fifty to a hundred feet below, and exposing a sight to appall the stoutest heart. To fall into one of these orifices would be instant death. From 10 a.m. we were walking in the midst of steam and smoke and heat which were almost stifling. Valve after valve opened as we ascended, out of which issued fire, smoke, and brimstone, and to avoid suffocation, we were obliged to keep on the windward side, watching every change of the wind. Sometimes hot whirlwinds would sweep along loaded with deadly gases, and threatening the unwary traveler."

Coan continues with further observations. "In one place we saw the burning river uncovered for nearly five hundred feet, and dashing down a declivity of about twenty degrees, leaping precipices in a mad rage which was indescribable. Standing at the lower end of this opening we could look up, not only along the line of fire, but also thirty feet or more into the mouth of the tunnel out of which it issued, and see the fiery cataract leaping over a cliff some fifteen feet high, with a sullen roar which was terrific, while the arched roof of this tunnel, some forty feet above the stream, and the walls on each side of the open space were hung with glowing stalactites, tinged with fiery sulphates and festooned with immense quantities of filamentous glass. At the upper end of this opening we cast in stones of considerable size, and when they struck the surface of the rushing current, they were swept from our sight with a speed that blurred their form, and with a force that was amazing."[31]

He relates his continued trek while describing the environment. "Amidst clouds of steam and the smell of gases, jagged fissures opening all along the track and wonders of force arresting our attention, we still ascended, until at 1 p.m., October sixth, we reached the terminal crater. This was Saturday and the fifth day of our journey, and we were a little weary, but we set ourselves at once to examine this point where the first red light of August eleventh had been seen, and whence the amazing flood of melted minerals had been poured out to startle all eastern Hawaii. From this summit

30. Move with a splashing sound.
31. Coan, *Life*, 291–93.

elevation, for six miles down the side of the mountain we found a series of crevasses of a similar character, but no rounded or well-defined crater. This upper cleft was wide, some five hundred feet long, and indescribably jagged. It had vomited out floods of lava which now lay in bristling heaps forming a scoriaceous wall one hundred feet high on each side of the opening. These walls were so rough, so steep, and in such a shattered state, that it was very difficult to surmount them, but by care and effort we gained the giddy crest of the one on the windward side and gazed down into the Plutonic throat of the mountain. No fire could be seen. Blue and white steam with the smell of sulphur came curling up from unknown depths below, while the fearful throat that had so lately belched out such floods of fiery ruin was nearly choked with its own *debris*. The action had ceased; the fountain, no long able to throw out its burning steam from this high orifice, had subsided, probably a thousand feet, and found vent at the lower point where we had seen the flow in our ascent."

Coan explains the situation at the summit. "We were now more than twelve thousand feet above our home, and sitting on the lip of this mountain mortar, we could meditate on its recent thunder, and seem to see the belching of its fire and smoke and brimstone, while its stony hail lay heaped around us. What a battle-field of infinite forces in these realms of thunder and lightning, of stormy winds and hail and snow, of rending earthquakes and devouring fires."

He locates where the eruption occurred in relation to the 1843 and 1852 eruptions. "The source of this eruption is about midway between those of 1843 and 1852, and these three igneous rivers ran in parallel lines about five miles apart. This eruption was also only a few miles north of Mokuaweoweo, the great summit crater, whose deep cauldron has so often boiled with intense heat, and whose brilliant fires have thrown a sheen of glory over the firmament and lighted all eastern Hawaii. Mokuaweoweo is probably the great chimney or shaft which reaches the abyss of liquid lava below, and which furnishes the materials for all the lateral outbursts of Mauna Loa, except for those of Kilauea, which are independent eruptions."[32]

Coan explains adaptations to observe the Sabbath on a Sunday.[33] "It was evening before our explorations of the surrounding scenery closed, and the next day was Sunday. Unfortunately our guides had failed to supply our gourds with water. We had passed pool after pool, and had charged our natives to be sure and fill the gourds in time, but they as often answered that there was plenty of water further on. In this they were mistaken, and we reached our destination with only one quart of water for four persons. But we agreed to spend the Lord's Day and offer our sacrifices of prayer and praise on this high altar.

"It was cold and dreary, and our bed was hard and rough lava, but raising a low wall of lava blocks, as protection against the piercing night winds, we endured cold

---

32. Coan, *Life*, 293–95.
33. Had he already made arrangements with Lyman to take care of the service(s) in Hilo?

and thirst until Monday morning, having no fuel—we were above vegetation—and only one-half-pint of water each from Saturday until the afternoon of Monday.

"In itself we would not have deemed it wrong to go down the mountain on Sabbath, but as our natives are slow to discriminate and reason on points of religion, and as multitudes in all parts of the islands would be sure to hear that the teacher who had so often dissuaded them from unnecessary labor on the Lord's Day had himself been traveling on that day, it was prudent to give them no occasion to stumble on this point. I have never regretted the self-denial."[34]

Coan and the others headed down the mountain and found water. The party returns to Hilo and finds the people wondering what will happen next. "On our return we found all Hilo in a state of anxious suspense, and eager to hear what we had seen and what were the probabilities that the eruption would reach the town. The light of the blazing forest was evidently drawing nearer and nearer daily, but none of the fires had as yet penetrated the dense thicket of ferns and bramble and of tangle vines and fallen trees."

A few bird-hunters had checked the dense area. Coan resolves to check the area for himself. That evening someone who had climbed a tree cried out, "I see the fire! It is on our right, two miles distant." He encounters a two-mile-long lava flow. "The place where we stood commanded a scene of surpassing interest. We estimated the flow to be two miles wide, and our view of it to extend about ten miles, giving it some twenty square miles of area. Perhaps three-fourths of the surface was solidified, but hundreds or thousands of pools, and active fountains and streams of lava boiled and glittered and spouted, presenting a scene of marvelous brilliancy and beauty."

Coan describes the margin of the flow. Because it is nighttime and chilly he and the others warm themselves by standing as close to the lava flow "fire as near as we could bear it." They have supper and continue on in their exploration of the volcanic phenomena. "Two miles below us, along the whole front of the stream, a fiery edge, like the front of a war-column, was consuming the jungle, and leaving the giant trees standing in the burning flood to be brought down and consumed in their turn. All night long we watched this process." Coan vividly describes the igniting of tall trees.[35]

He and his party have difficulty crossing the lava flow to return to Hilo. He describes the advance of the lava and the alarm that develops in Hilo. "As the flood of consuming fire came nearer and nearer, the anxiety in Hilo became intense. Its approach was the great subject of conversation. In the streets, in the shops, and in our homes, the one question was, 'What of the volcano?' Watchers were out keeping vigils during the livelong night. Merchants began to pack their goods, and people looked out for boats and other conveyances, and for places of refuge to escape the impending ruin. Every house near the lower skirt of the forest was evacuated, and all the furniture and animals removed to places of safety. Our inland streams were choked, and the

---

34. Coan, *Life*, 295–96.
35. Coan, *Life*, 296–300.

river which waters our town and supplies ships was as black as ink, and emitted an offensive odor. The juices of vines, and the ashes of thousands of acres of burnt forests containing charred leaves and wood came into these streams, and the smell of pyroligneous acid was strong. By day the smoke went up like the smoke of Sodom [Gen 19:24]. By night the flames arose and spread out on high like a burning firmament. We thought we could calculate very nearly the day when Hilo would be on fire, when our beautiful harbor would be a pot of boiling fury, to be choked with volcanic products and abandoned forever. What could we do?"

Coan describes the approach of the lava flow. "The devouring enemy was within seven miles of us, his fiery lines extending two miles in width. Already had it descended on its devastated track fifty or sixty miles, persistently overcoming every obstacle; the little distance remaining was all open, and no human power could set up any barriers, or arrest the on-coming destroyer."

His focus turns to prayer. He recognizes how a crisis turns people to God, as the tsunami contributed to the depth of the Great Awakening. "All knew what we could *not* do. Someone said: 'We can pray'; and I have never seen more reverent audiences than those that assembled on our day of fasting and prayer. No vain mirth, no scoffing, no skepticism then. Native and foreigner alike felt it was well to pray to him who kindled the fire, that he would quench it."[36]

Joseph F. Smith[37] while a missionary on the Big Island "witnessed the 1856 volcanic eruption that threatened to destroy Hilo."[38] Similarly, Coan writes to his friend Professor Dana of the concern that Hilo might be overwhelmed by lava. "In a few days we may be called to announce the painful fact that our beauteous Hilo is no more—that our lovely, our inimitable landscape, our emerald bowers, our crescent strand, and our silver bay are blotted out. *A fiery sword hangs over us.*[39] A flood of burning ruin approaches us. Devouring fires are near us. With sure and solemn progress the glowing fusion advances through the dark forest and the dense jungle in our rear, cutting down ancient trees of enormous growth and sweeping away all vegetable life. For sixty-five days the great summit furnace on Mauna Loa has been in awful blast. Floods of burning destruction have swept wildly and widely over the top and down the sides of the mountain. The wrathful stream has overcome every obstacle, winding its fiery way from its high source to the bases of the everlasting hills, spreading in a molten sea over the plains, penetrating the ancient forests, driving the bellowing herds, the wild goats, and the affrighted birds before its lurid glare, leaving nothing but ebon blackness and smoldering ruin in its track."[40]

---

36. Coan, *Life*, 300–306.
37. A nephew of LDS founder Joseph Smith. See "Other Religions" chapter.
38. O'Driscoll, "Hyrum Smith."
39. Emphasis added.
40. Coan to Dana, October 15, 1855, in Coan, *Memorial Volume*, 75.

In *The Sailor's Magazine*, Coan writes of an answer to prayer, that our "volcano of August 11, 1855, still burns. A river of fire comes within five or six miles of us, and there is checked, spreads, and cooks. Our preservation is miraculous."[41]

Coan relates the story of "fifty or sixty foreigners" who decide "to visit the eruption." It turns from a party of pleasure to one of fear, though no one is harmed. Others join a ship-master who set up a "topsail canvas tent" to watch the lava enter a deep basin of water. The lava evaporates all the water. "By break of day there was not a drop of water left in this basin; the space was filled with smouldering lavas, and the precipice, which had reared itself at an angle of 80°, was converted into a gently sloping plane. A large slab of lava crust was tilted, and stood as a monument of the accomplished work; the flow ceased, a little red-hot lava was seen amidst the smouldering heaps of rocky coal, and from that day the fearful flood did not come another foot toward Hilo."

Coan notes that this development occurred six months after the eruption began. He continues to describe "what is most marvelous, confounding our geology, is the fact that for nine months longer, or until November 1856 after the arrest of the flow toward our town, the great terminal furnace on Mauna Loa was in full blast, sending down billions of cubic feet of molten rock in covered channels, and depositing it near the lower end of the stream, but without pushing beyond its breastworks."

Coan indicates what happened instead. "This lava gushed out laterally along the margins of the stream, or burst up vertically, rending the crust, throwing it about in wild confusion, or heaping it into cones and ridges a hundred feet high, as monuments of its fury. I have mounted some of these cones, finding them cracked from base to top in fissures six to eight feet apart, but so firm that I could walk to their summits and look down in the seams on the right and left, and see the red-hot lava glow like burning coals in a coal-pit, sending out deadly blasts of acid gases."

He writes of "immense fields of *pahoehoe*, boiling, seething, and flowing during the nine months that followed February thirteenth." He also notes that the water "of the Wailuku was so discolored, and so offensive in taste and smell, that ships refused it."[42]

Coan writes vividly in a letter published in *The Friend*. The headline is "New Eruption!—Hilo threatened—Imminent danger—Pele huhu loa!"[43] "The following extract from a letter from Rev. Mr. Coan, which we are permitted to use, will be read with interest. It is dated October 14, 1855 . . . The course is now down Piihouua and near the banks of the Wailuku. Progress slow but sure. We think this end of the stream is one [to?] two miles broad.

"I have just returned from Mauna Loa. Visited the great summit crater, which is in full blast—about ten days. The fusion is immense. It flows in a covered duct; stream some sixty miles in all its windings. It is now eating through the woods, and is near the old saw mill place, about ten miles from Hilo.

41. Coan, October 6, 1856, in *Sailor's Magazine*, 29, 1857, 184.
42. HMH 33.06–09.
43. A Hawaiian expression meaning greatly angered.

"Fifteenth. A native visited the lava stream yesterday. It is cutting through the forest and making resistless progress towards us. All Hilo is solemn. Many are planning—some are packing. There is little hope for our beauteous Hilo. Probably you will see our houses and emerald bower no more . . . We are now thinking it may sweep from Wailuku to the Waiakea stream."[44]

In the 1856 station report, Coan writes about the stopping of the lava. "And here the fiat went forth, 'No further' [Job 38:11] and here the fiery waves were stayed—This was on the morning of February [of 1856] since which time no progress has been made by the lava towards Hilo." As he so often does, Coan puts a Christian cast on the volcanic activity. "The great mountain furnace remains, however, in full blast, and immense quantities of incandescent materials are being sent to form hills, and cones and ridges near the terminus of the stream. Thus the Lord preserves us [Ps 31:23], and to him we [give] our unmeasured praise."[45]

He next provides statistics on the volcanic events. "The length of the stream is supposed to be from sixty to seventy-five miles, its breadth varying from one to five miles and its depth very unequal—In some places it may be two hundred or three hundred feet." Returning to Christian themes, Coan next writes of deliverance and prayer. "That this fiery flood should approach so near without coming down upon us seems marvelous—While our danger appeared eminent [sic], and while many were devising plans and making arrangements for removal, others were earnest in prayer . . . A day of fasting was also observed by natives and foreigners, and we ought to believe that the Lord heard the prayers of his people—and although there is much sin in Hilo yet we do believe that the place contains more than ten righteous men[Gen 18:25] . . . However this may be we pray God that we may never be left to forget his mercies in sparing us, and in not blotting from the book of nature so fair a landscape as Hilo."[46]

During this period, his friend Professor James Dana writes Coan, asking him to "ascertain on how great an angle of descent lavas would flow without breaking," since there was some disagreement about this in the scientific community. So Coan "took pains to measure accurately on one of my excursions, and found lava flowing continuously on declivities of from one to ninety degrees. I also noted that our Hawaiian volcanoes send out streams of such perfect fusion that they will run like oil down any angle, and even cleave like paste to an inward curve of the rock and form a thin veneering upon it."

Coan writes that "Another question arose." It appears that Coan developed this question rather than Dana having written him about it. "Can a lava stream flow for many miles longitudinally upon the surface, without being fed by vents or fissures from below?" Can "it push forward over broad files of almost level surface."

---

44. *The Friend*, 12.10, 250.
45. Coan, 1856 station report, 2/65. HMH.
46. Coan, *Life*, 265.

Coan answers with three responses. "First. On ascending the mountain to view an eruption I see no evidence of deep fractures until we are more than two-thirds the way to the summit.

"Second. Where there is an opening extending down to the fiery abyss below, there will, I think, always be a column of mineral smoke ascending to mark the spot, so long as action continues."

After further explaining his second point and relating it to Kīlauea, he writes, "Third. I have often surveyed, for distances of five to twenty miles, the ground upon which eruptions were approaching, and have seen the burning floods come on, covering to-day the ground on which I traveled yesterday, and consuming the hut where I slept."

Coan concludes the chapter on the eruption of 1855–56 with two scientific observations. This first is that this eruption "gave us an example of the law of compensation." The second is the process of refrigeration. "As before mentioned, surface lava exposed to the atmosphere crusts over before running very far, unless it is moving with great velocity, as down steep descents. This process of refrigeration so protects the liquid below that it flows onward at white-heat, it may be, until obstructed, when it gushes out on the margins, or bursts up vertically."[47]

In the next chapter, Coan turns from the 1855–56 eruption to that of 1868.

1868

"XXII.

The Eruption of 1868 from Kīlauea—The March and April Earthquakes—Land-Slips—Destruction of Life and Property—The Lava-Stream Bursts from Underground—The Volcanic Waves of August 1868, and of May 1877."[48]

Coan writes James Dana in 1866 about Kīlauea in a way that indicates a building toward the 1868 eruption. "There has been a vast filling up and an upraising in Kilauea since 1840. Should you now visit it you would recognize nothing except the outer walls and the surrounding regions. Internally *all* is changed and all is new. In May, June, and July the action in the crater was often vehement. The old South Lake overflowed several times, and a chain of lakes, three, four, and sometimes five or six, opened on a curved line from northwest to north and northeast from the old lake. The action in these was often intense. Jets of fusion were thrown fifty to two hundred feet high; the lakes overflowed, and fiery rivers seethed along the northern and eastern walls of the crater, the stream in some places half a mile wide. Cones and domes of lava were also raised, and yawning fissures opened, interrupting the traveler in crossing the bottom of the crater and cut off all ingress by the usual route, and many parties were obliged to view the surging waves from above."[49]

47. Coan, *Life*, 309–12.
48. Coan, *Life*, Table of Contents, np; and chapter XXI, 313.
49. Coan to Dana, August 31, 1866, in Coan, *Memorial Volume*, 99.

Near the end of the science chapter, the earthquakes and "volcanic wave"[50] of 1868 were discussed. The earthquake is difficult to separate from the eruption. Coan begins the 1868 eruption chapter by discussing the 1868 earthquake and the resulting onset of the eruption. The 6.8 earthquake occurred on "the twenty-seventh of March, 1868."[51]

Similarly, Hallock weaves together the earthquakes and eruptions of 1868. "The most fearful eruption was in 1868. On the twenty-seventh of March began an unprecedented series of earthquakes; then the terminal crater of Mo-kua-weo-weo blazed red into the heavens, and steam, smoke, and ashes issued in gigantic columns; four lava streams began to flow. Intense interest attended these phenomena. Suddenly the rivers congealed, the summit fires died away, and the blue outline of the giant cone stood cold and clear again against the sky. Ah! But it was not sleeping. Such a quivering, trembling, throbbing of the earth began as seems almost incredible. It continued five days and nights unabated."[52]

After all these earthquakes, Mauna Loa developed more lava flow. "At last, on the second day of April, it ended by the bursting out of a stream of lava through a new fissure two miles long in one of the old, settled, and populated districts forty miles away from the mountain, and flowed into the sea. This unparalleled disturbance had been caused by the mighty stream of lava ploughing its way for twenty-five miles underground until it found vent. Four thousand acres of valuable land was buried and a half-mile added to the contour of the island, built out into the deep sea. There seems little regularity to the eruptions, though approximating one in about eleven years."[53]

While this eruption would eventually affect the districts of Hilo and Puna, Ka'u was most affected by an earthquake and lava flow on April second.[54] "Nearly all the foreigners of Eastern Kau fled this way[55] after the terrific shock and eruption of Thurs the second inst[ant]."[56]

Ten days after the earthquake, the lava flow becomes visible above ground. The "ragings of the subterranean river [of lava] were heard by listeners who put their ears to the ground." On April seventh, more Kilauea lava became visible above ground. "On the seventh of April the lava burst out from the ground in Kahuku, nine miles from the sea, and flowed rapidly down to the shore."

In relating this lava outbreak, Coan appears to view Kīlauea as part of Mauna Loa. "The place of outbreak was in a wood on one of the foot-hills of Mauna Loa." He relates that people traveling to Hilo via Kona had to go back and travel "*via* Waimea, a circuit of one hundred and seventy miles." He writes about a massive fissure, what

---

50. Also known as a tidal wave and tsunami.
51. Coan, *Life*, 313.
52. Hallock, *Hawaii under King Kalakaua*, 70.
53. Hallock, *Hawaii under King Kalakaua*, 70.
54. Southeast of Puna.
55. Toward Hilo.
56. Coan to Rev. J. D. Paris, April 11, 1868.

issues from it, and the amazement felt by those viewing it. "A fissure of a mile long was opened for the disgorgement of this igneous river, and from the whole length of this orifice the lava rushed up with intense vehemence, spouting jets one hundred to two hundred feet high, burning the forest and spreading out a mile wide. The rending, the raging, the swirling of this stream were terrific, awakening awe in all the beholders."[57]

Coan describes this lava flow as it heads toward the ocean. He relates in detail how a rancher and his family have to flee the lava flow, with cattle rescued from their lava "prison" after ten days. Eventually the entire property is destroyed. "Their escape was marvelous. In a few minutes the house was wrapped in flames, the garden was consumed, and all the premises were covered with a burning sea."[58]

He next relates how the hut of two Hawaiians was surrounded by lava. Coan eventually visited them, finding "its inmates alive and rejoicing in their deliverance."[59] He explains how the lava came near a church, whose structure had been destroyed by the April second aftershock.

A few years after this eruption, Isabella Bird was "given a thrilling account of the great eruption in 1868, when beautiful Hilo was threatened with destruction."[60]

Isabella Bird writes about her visit to Kilauea in 1873 in "Letter VII."[61] She writes of the "volcano book" at the lodge at "the glorious Hale-mau-mau, the grandest type of force that the earth holds!"[62]

Coan concludes the chapter by discussing the "volcanic wave" of May 1877. Most of the material is from a letter written by Lydia Coan.[63] Coan writes the next chapter about the last volcanic eruption that he witnessed.

1880–81

"XXIII.

The Eruption of 1880–1881—Hilo Threatened as Never Before—A Day of Public Prayer—Visitors to the Lava-Flow—It Approaches within a Mile of the Shore—Hope Abandoned—After Nine Months the Action Suddenly Abates—The Deliverance—The Mechanism of a Great Lava-Flow—An Idolater Dislodged—Conclusion"[64]

It has been written that both Fidelia and Lydia Coan wrote about volcanic activity. Fidelia's discussion of the 1852 eruption is found above. All that can be found in print

---

57. Coan, *Life*, 317.
58. Coan, *Life*, 317–19.
59. Coan, *Life*, 319–20.
60. Bird, *Six Months*, 92.
61. Bird, *Six Months*, 69–92.
62. Bird, *Six Months*, 88.
63. Coan, *Life*, 320–26. See Scientist chapter.
64. Coan, *Life*, Table of Contents, np; chapter XXIII, 327.

by Lydia is in a bridge passage regarding the 1880–81 eruption. After noting Titus's continued vitality and writing of his manuscript autobiography, she writes, "For seven months of this year [of his life] he watched with others, sharing in their anxiety, that threatening lava flow from Mauna Loa, which, beginning on the fifth of November, 1880, continued until the tenth of August, 1881, without any abatement of action."[65]

Titus Coan concludes his autobiography with a chapter mostly about the last volcanic eruption he would ever witness. He introduces it by relating particulars of date, location, lava, and so on. "On the fifth of November, 1880, our latest eruption from Mauna Loa broke out at a point some twelve thousand feet above sea-level, and a few miles north of the great terminal crater, Mokua-weo-weo. The glare was intense, and was seen at great distances. Brilliant jets of lava were thrown high in the air, and a pillar of blazing gases mounted thousands of feet skyward, spreading out into a canopy of sanguinary light which resembled, though upon a larger scale, the so-called 'pine-tree appendage' formed over Vesuvius during its eruptions by the vertical column of vapors with its great horizontal cloud."[66]

He deepens his description of the lava flow. "Meanwhile a raging river of lava, about three-fourths of a mile wide and from fifteen to thirty feet deep, rushed down the north-east flank of the great dome, and ran some thirty miles to the base of Mauna Kea. This stream was composed mostly of *aa* or scoria."

Because Coan was approaching the age of eighty, he relates[67] observations made by the attorney David Hitchcock[68] of Hilo. "Its terminus was visited and well described by our townsman, David Hitchcock, Esq."[69]

65. Coan, *Memorial Volume*, 169.

66. Coan, *Life*, 327.

67. Without quotation marks.

68. This was probably David Howard Hitchcock Senior, 1831–1899. His son went by D. Howard Hitchcock and painted this observation of an 1888 eruption, entitled "Halemaumau Lake of Fire":

69. Coan, *Life*, 328. David Howard Hitchcock, "Halemaumau, Lake of Fire." Image is in the public domain.

Coan relates that there were many visitors to the lava stream. The Reverend Mr. Baker reached the crater on Mauna Loa on his third attempt. Coan indicates that were he SIXTY, he would have done so. "Were I twenty years younger, I should have been on the mountaintop also, but my time to climb such rugged heights is past."[70] Coan recognizes the limitations of the aging process without undue grief being expressed.

As with some previous eruption lava flows, Hilo is threatened. One lava stream threatened Hilo but then was checked. "But this check gave additional power to the south-east wing, so that on the twenty-sixth of June, a fierce stream broke out from the great lava pond and came rushing down the rocky channel of a stream with terrific force and uproar, exploding rocks and driving off the waters. Hilo was in trouble. We were now in immediate danger. The lava, confined in the water-channel of from fifty to a hundred feet wide, advanced so rapidly that by the thirtieth of June it was not more than two and a half miles from us, threatening to strike Volcano Street about a quarter of a mile from Church Street, on which I live and to fall into our harbor about midway of the beach. The stream was fearfully active, and the danger was now close upon us. From the town we could walk up to the living lava in forty minutes, and back again in thirty. A hundred people would sometimes visit it in a day. Its roar, on coming down the rough and rocky bed of the ravine, was like that of our Wailuku River during a freshet, but a deeper and grander sound. Explosions and detonations were frequent; I counted ten in a minute. The glare of it by night was terrific. The daily progress of the flow was now from one hundred to five hundred feet."

Coan relates the people he saw when he visited the stream of lava on July eighteenth. He explains that the flow came within one foot of the Waikea sugar-mill. Judge Severance attempted to save the Hilo prison, "with an embankment seven or eight feet high, hoping to avert the necessity of a general jail-delivery; but any considerable body of lava of course defies every obstruction. We made no preparations, however, for quitting our house."[71]

Worry grew about the lava reaching Hilo Bay in a brief time. "The flood came on until all agreed that in two or three days more it would be pouring into our beautiful bay. On the tenth of August it was but one mile from the sea, and half a mile from Hilo town." He writes of the relief that occurred in the nick of time and place. "On that day, nine months and five days from the outbursting of the great eruption, when hope had perished in nearly every heart, the action began to abate. The raging flood, the steam, the smoke, the noise of the flow were checked; and in a day or two the great red dragon lay stiffened and harmless upon the borders of our village. The relief was unspeakable."

Three days later, Coan visits the flow for the fifth time since it began approaching Hilo. I "felt the radiating heat, but saw no more liquid lava. But the great pall of the eruption lay upon the land for fifty miles. I estimate that the lava-stream covered a

70. Coan, *Life*, 329.
71. Coan, *Life*, 329–31.

hundred miles of mountain, forest, and farm land, to an average depth of twenty-five feet—enough to cover the State of Connecticut to a depth of six inches. No exact measurements, however, have yet been made."[72]

Coan concludes his discussion of the eruption and lava flow[73] by relating the defeat of a pre-Christian medicine man and his unsuccessful battle against Pele. "Five or six miles inland from our town there nestled, some twenty years ago, a quiet hamlet. There was a school-house in the place; and the land produced taro, potatoes, bananas, and other fruit-trees. The scenery was of enchanting beauty. But the population passed away; and of late years only one house remained on this lovely spot. Its occupant was reputed [to be] an inveterate heathen. He belonged to the ancient class of native physicians or medicine-men. When the burning flood struck the forest behind his house, he is said to have hoisted his flag in front of the slowly advancing lava, and to have forbidden it, in the name of the ancient gods of his race, to pass that flag. But onward came the flood, regardless of the edict. From time to time the heathen doctor was compelled to remove his flag to the rear, planting it nearer and nearer to his house; and at last the lava expelled him and his friends, and rolled over house, garden, and field, leaving a grisly pile of black lava over all."

One unusual development is reported in this matter. "One circumstance in the case was curious. The lava stream surrounded a single kalo-plant, growing on an islet of eighteen inches in diameter, and on another one twice as broad, a single banana plant. They have survived the heat and are growing finely, the only green things left in the garden from which the idolater was driven."[74]

Though the date of the book is 1911, Hallock does not write about the last eruption that occurred during Coan's life. After Coan writes about the 1880–81 eruption, he puts things into perspective with an indirect question. "When the next disaster shall occur, no man dare predict. Fair Hilo may some day be classed with Herculaneum and Pompeii among the buried cities of the world. We have only the story of a century, an hour of God's time! 'O, thou who taketh up the isles as a very little thing' [Isa 40:15]. 'What is man that thou art mindful of him!'"[Ps 8:4].[75]

During his decades in the Sandwich Islands, Coan passionately observed and wrote about volcanic activity. Throughout that time as well, he put great energy into advancing the missionary endeavor. The next two chapters present something of that involvement.

---

72. Coan, *Life*, 331–32.

73. See previous chapter for Coan's discussion of the characteristics of how lava makes its way over so long a distance. Coan, *Life*, 332–34.

74. Coan, *Life*, 334–35.

75. Hallock, *Hawaii under King Kalakaua*, 71.

10

Missions, Part 1

Morning Star(s) and Other

"Recent indications of Providence lead us to believe that a wide door is being opened for the enlargement of our operations in Micronesia."¹

"I usually preach a missionary sermon, or something connected with generosity, on the first Sabbath of every month, giving my people such facts as keep them informed on what God and his children are doing to evangelize the nations.

"Three words embrace our whole commission to the heathen, viz: *Pray! Give! Go!* And how can a man pray 'Thy kingdom come,' while he gives nothing, or nothing worthy of a man, to help the conquests and enlargements of this kingdom? How can the ambassadors of the Lord go without means of support? Or preach to the heathen unless they be sent? What must we think of pastors and churches who are often chanting 'The Lord's Prayer' [Matt 6:9–13] without giving or going? Will not their very prayers condemn them before the final judge?²

"And now I congratulate you again, and rejoice with you in the great work in which you have enlisted. To Christianize China, *in* China, and *out of* China, is, I apprehend, the greatest specific missionary enterprise of the age and of the world."³

INTRODUCTION

In the area of missions, Titus Coan worked with two organizations and served two people groups. The organizations were the American Board of Commissioners for Foreign Missions and the Hawaiian Evangelical Association. The people groups were the Patagonians and Polynesians. Within the Polynesians group were two subgroups:

1. Coan to the Secretaries of the ABCFM, spring of 1855, in Coan, *Memorial Volume*, 71.
2. Coan to Goodwin, August 14, 1882, in Coan, *Memorial Volume*, 196, 197.
3. Titus Coan to Mr. F. W. Damon, November 17, 1881, in Coan, *Memorial Volume*, 179.

Hawaiians and Micronesians. Coan's connection with the American Board began when he was at Auburn Seminary. Flowing out of his heart for reaching souls, he got involved with the Society of Inquiry. This eventually led to his responding to an appeal from the Board for fifty more missionaries. Even though he and Fidelia were leaning toward the Sandwich Islands, the Board asked him to go with Mr. Arms to Patagonia. Upon his return the Board asked them to go to the Sandwich Islands. While there he served as a missionary to the Hawaiian people. Because of the success in Hawai'i, the American Board concluded its connection, with the Hawaiian Missionary Society and the Hawaiian Evangelical Association being formed. Titus served as the first and longest president of the latter group. As a pastor and leader he mentored many Hawaiians who became lay leaders and pastors in the Sandwich Islands. He also mentored a few Hawaiians who became missionaries to the Marquesas Islands, Gilbert Islands, and Micronesia. As a member of the Micronesia Mission Committee and the head of the Hawaiian Evangelical Association, Titus would take the lead in raising funds for a missionary vessel called the *Morning Star*. There would eventually be three such ships, one of which Titus took for two trips to the Marquesas Islands. The latter trips will be discussed in the next chapter.

Coan wrote about his above involvements in letters, journals, and other venues. Others would write about the various aspects of his missionary involvement—both contemporaneously and retrospectively, primary and secondary. Through it all, Coan's heartbeat for missions is seen.

All of these matters weave in with developments small and large in the United States, the Hawaiian Islands, and elsewhere. Most especially would Coan be involved in transitions in Hawai'i that would affect him and Hawaiian missionaries alike.

AMERICAN BOARD

Established in 1810, the American Board sent forth its first missionaries in 1812. The Pioneer Company to Hawai'i arrived in 1820. Titus Coan became involved with the American Board in the early 1830s. With the American Board, Hawaiian organizations, and with various people groups, Coan was a leader.

Auburn and Patagonia

While at Auburn, Coan took the initiative in praying for other students. He walked through the door of opportunity to serve adult prisoners as their Sunday School leader. He responded to the revivals and led as he was able. He became involved in the leadership of the mission-oriented Society of Inquiry. He presented himself to the Board and accepted the leadership assignment with William Arms to go to Patagonia. In another chapter, Coan's preparation for, journey to presence in, return from, and recommendation regarding Patagonia were examined.

Titus Coan: "Apostle to the Sandwich Islands"

Hawai'i

Once in Hawai'i, thanks to his experience, training, and personality, Titus Coan served as a missionary leader for the rest of his life. His ministry would include expatriates and others, but his focus was always on the Hawaiians. He led with regard to the American Board. After joining the rest of the Seventh Company in a letter to General Secretary Rufus Anderson, Titus wrote his own separate letter with various suggestions.[4] During the controversy of the Hawaiian Great Awakening, Coan wrote a scathing private letter to Anderson along with the public letter that was published in *The Missionary Herald*.[5]

He provided leadership and input on various matters over the years, including the transition from being under the umbrella of the American Board to the development of the Hawaiian Evangelical Association. In 1848, the ABCFM Prudential Board decided that the mission to Hawai'i was completed. "The great foreign missionary experiment at the Islands, as such, is now nearly completed; and the Board stands ready, at the earliest day which will be agreeable to their beloved missionary brethren, to give them such a settlement as shall be in their power, and, with thanks to God for what he hath wrought, to acknowledge, before his church and the world, their *Independence*."[6]

Ehlke points out the basis for the success of the mission. "The success of the Sandwich Islands Mission rested on the results of the Great Awakening in the 1830s. Titus Coan's church was probably the largest in the world! Using the practices and doctrines of enthusiastic religion to bring a 'heathen' people to Christ, the pastors at Hilo and Waimea had succeeded beyond their wildest dreams."[7]

Even though the Mission did not receive this letter until after its General Meeting in 1848, it had taken up many of the issues "covered in it." Showing the regard with which the other missionaries held Titus Coan, he "was named moderator for the meeting which considered such cases as 'missionaries taking civil office' and 'missionaries' children,'[8] in particular their educational needs.

With regard to the former, the "Hawaiian government had asked the Rev. Richard Armstrong to leave the Mission to become the Minister of Public Instruction, filling the place left vacant by the death of the Rev. William Richards. Coan felt that unless Armstrong took the post, it would probably be abolished and the educational system which the Mission had established would be undermined.[9] The Hilo pastor could have been charged with self-interest, as the Mission had been told that if either

---

4. See "Early Years" chapter.

5. See second Great Awakening chapter.

6. Prudential Committee of the American Board of Commissioners for Foreign Missions to the Sandwich Mission, July 19, 1848, ABCFM at HMH, in Ehlke, "Enthusiastic Religion," 234.

7. Paraphrase of Titus Coan to Artemis Bishop, December 24, 1881, in Coan, *Memorial Volume*, 224.

8. Titus to Fidelia Coan, May 20, 1848, HMH, in Ehlke, "Enthusiastic Religion," 234.

9. Titus to Fidelia Coan, May 18, 1848, HMH, in Ehlke, "Enthusiastic Religion," 234.

Coan or [Lorenzo] Lyons [of Waiemea] was appointed to the Honolulu pulpit that the congregation would raise the money to support them.[10] Coan said, 'It is true that the king and chiefs and the great body of the church have expressed strong preference that we should come to Honolulu . . . But I give them no encouragement, nor would I feel flattered. The praise of man is wind. I would stand in my lot and do the work which God has given me to do.'[11] But it was not to be. After some debate, the post went to the Rev. Ephraim W. Clark. 'Brother Chamberlain and others said they must not think of removing us from Hilo; that no man would fill my place there etc. etc.,'[12] Coan told his wife."[13]

Five years later, the Hawaiian Evangelical Association was established. It would completely become the governing organization ten years later. The HEA Archives begin in 1853.[14]

A 1916 article in *The Friend* about "The Story of the Hawaiian Board" also includes a reference to the Hawaiian Evangelical Association. "In May 1854, 'it was thought best to discontinue the old organization known as the "General Meeting" and revise and enlarge the constitution of the Hawaiian Association,[15] adopting the name 'Hawaiian Evangelical Association.'" Westervelt further notes that "the Hawaiian Board at once assumed the close relation with the Hawaiian Churches, which it has continued to hold to the present day."[16]

A book published by the State Council of Hawaiian Congregational Churches states that the "Hawaiian mission was formally concluded in 1863 with the reorganization of the Hawaiian Evangelical Association as a freestanding church in the Congregationalist tradition."[17] That volume notes that Rufus Anderson "supervised the termination of the mission and the organization of a new, independent church in Hawai'i. It included twenty-five churches and 19,725 members, virtually all of whom were Hawaiian. Of its twenty pastors, four were Hawaiian. The HEA moved rapidly to ordain a Hawaiian clergy. By 1868 there were fifty churches with twelve Hawaiian-American (persons of white blood born in Hawai'i) and thirty Hawaiian pastors; by 1888 only one Hawaiian-American pastor remained."[18]

---

10. Titus to Fidelia Coan, May 20, 1848, HMH, in Ehlke, "Enthusiastic Religion," 235.

11. Titus to Fidelia Coan, May 9, 1848, HMH, in Ehlke, "Enthusiastic Religion," 235.

12. Titus to Fidelia Coan, May 20, 1848, in Ehlke, "Enthusiastic Religion," 234.

13. Ehlke, "Enthusiastic Religion," 235.

14. HEA archives give following dates: 1853–1947. Manuscript Finding Aids, "HEA."

15. Earlier in the article we read that the Hawaiian Association was begun on February 28, 1823 and linked with a "General Meeting" by September, 1826.

16. Westervelt, "Story of the Hawaiian Board," 84.

17. Kaohi et al., *Celebrating Advocacy*, 5.

18. Kaohi et al., *Celebrating Advocacy*, 5.

Titus Coan: "Apostle to the Sandwich Islands"

In 1863, Titus Coan was elected the first president of the Hawaiian Evangelical Association/Hawaiian Board and continued as such until his death in early December of 1882.[19] At one point Coan submitted a resignation letter, but it was withdrawn.[20]

MENTOR

As a missionary and a pastor, Titus Coan mentored many Hawaiians. Some became pastors; more, lay leaders. A few also became missionaries to the Micronesian and Marquesan Islands.

While he had lay leaders prior to the formal establishment of the Hawaiian Evangelical Association, Coan became even more intentional after that time. "During the year 1863 the Rev. Dr. Anderson, then corresponding secretary of the ABCFM, visited the Hawaiian Islands with a view of conferring with the missionaries on the subject of putting most of the churches under the care of native pastors.[21] He urged the plan earnestly, and a full discussion followed. Some of the missionaries favored the new departure at once, others doubted its wisdom, and others still were willing to see the plan commenced on a small scale, and to watch its operations. Each pastor and church determined the time and manner for themselves. And so the experiment began."

Coan threw himself into this project with his usual verve. "At length I began a movement in that direction, and on the sixteenth of October, 1864, the first church was set off from the mother church, and a native was ordained and installed over it. Not long after, on October 14, 1866, I organized another church in the district of Hilo, and a third in 1868; and pastors were ordained over them."

He continues to explain his church planting with Hawaiian pastors. The people were already there, it was a matter of raising up and placing a Hawaiian Christian leader as the pastor. "One was organized in Puna in 1868, and two more in 1869, so that there were now six churches set off from the old one . . . The number of church members dismissed to organize the six new churches was in all 2,604."[22]

Throughout out most of his ministry in and through Hilo, he engaged Hawaiian converts as leaders and preachers. "It was my habit to get all the help that could be obtained from converts, and this was much. As the company of disciples increased [Acts 6:1], 'they went everywhere preaching the word'"[Acts 8:4]. Coan sounds very much like Finney on ordination, the power of the Holy Spirit, and so forth. "The Lord ordained them, not man. In every hamlet and village there found some who were moved by the Holy Ghost, and to whom the spirit gave utterance [2 Pet 1:21]; and it

---

19. Westervelt, "Story of the Hawaiian Board," 84. Technically, Westervelt shows Coan serving until 1883, meaning that the position was vacant until the 1888 meeting of the group. Judd, *Missionary Album*, 129, begins the position in 1888 and serves until his death in 1900.

20. HMH hard copy file.

21. See discussion of Anderson's "Three-Self Principle" in Dorn, "Three-Self Principle," esp. 9–25.

22. Coan, *Life*, 136–37.

was joyfully true that 'where the Spirit of the Lord was, there was liberty' [2 Cor 3:17], not to dispute [1 Cor 6:1] and wrangle [2 Tim 2:14], not to speak vain and foolish things [Eph 5:4], not to lie and deceive [Lev 19:11], but to utter the truth in love [Eph 4:15], without the shackles of form and superstition, but with the freedom granted by Christ" [Rom 6:22, 23].[23]

In his 1862 Hilo station report, Coan writes about the renewal of licensure[24] for three Hawaiians. "The Hawaiian Association met at Hilo in October but several of our ministerial brethren were providentially prevented from attending. At this Meeting the licenses of Pilipo,[25] Kauhane,[26] and Pehe,[27] our three licentiates, were renewed."[28]

In the lead up to his and Fidelia's 1870 trip to the United States, Titus writes the wife of his brother George concerning Hawaiian church leadership. He expresses his concerns about their being left in charge during his absence. He also explains the process of ordination. It provides a window into what and how he taught candidates for the ministry. "Candidates for the ministry must be first selected, then taught theology, then tried for some time in the field, and when accepted, ordained and installed. Some of [t]hem die, some prove incompetent or unworthy, some forsake for other work, and some are not acceptable to the people. It often seems as if our earthly pilgrimage would close ere this work of reconstruction and re-organization[29] is done. I have given a vacation to a class of fifteen in theology, which I taught five days in a week besides spending two hours daily in revising and correcting a commentary on Matthew in the Hawaiian language.[30] And now our anniversaries are coming on; a great Sabbath School celebration on the first of January, then the week of prayer and then touring... Our work never seemed heavier or more responsible and absorbing than now. Do not think that our Hawaiian Christians are full grown and mature. They are all children and need paternal care. I doubt whether our American friends[31] realize this fact. If it is hard for parents to leave a family of five or ten small children how much more so for us to leave our five thousand?"[32]

Coan provides an 1880 update. "They have had ten pastors. Of these, five are dead, two have been called to other places, one has resigned on account of age and infirmities, and two only remain at their posts." He indicates that this variety resembles

---

23. Coan, *Life*, 87.
24. One step below ordination?
25. For George Washington Pilipo, see Benedetto and Morris, *Nā Kahu*, 235–37.
26. See James W. "John" Kauhane, in Benedetto and Morris, *Nā Kahu*, 138–40.
27. See Pihe, in Benedetto and Morris, *Nā Kahu*, 235.
28. Hilo station report, 1862, 3/135.
29. I.e., transition from American Board to HEA and Anderson Three-Self Principle.
30. While he arrived too late to do any Bible translation, here Coan in his spare time translates a lengthy commentary into Hawaiian.
31. Including Rufus Anderson.
32. Titus Coan to Mrs. George Coan, December 18, 1867, Coan, *Memorial Volume*, 116.

the entire island chain writ large. "This would be nearly the record of our Hawaiian pastors over the whole group. They waste away rapidly by disease and death, and they change places often. Some wear out; some fall into sin; and some engage in other callings. A goodly number run well, being steadfast in the faith, diligent workers, and patient withal."

Whereas the accusation of "hasty admission" had occurred during the Great Awakening, Coan now answers the indirect question as to whether there were "hasty ordinations"! "We are often asked how our native preachers wear, and whether we were not hasty in making them coordinate pastors with the missionaries. These questions may be answered differently by different observers."[33]

HAWAIIAN EVANGELICAL ASSOCIATION/HAWAIIAN MISSIONARY SOCIETY

Hawaiian churches and transitioning American Board missionaries would not wait for the beginnings of the Hawaiian Evangelical Association in 1853 and fully transitioning from the American Board to look beyond those to other islands. Three years after the transitional year of 1848, the "1851 General Meeting explored the idea of a Micronesian missionary effort. It was felt that before the new Hawaiian church could come of age, there had to be an emphasis on foreign missionary service. The Hawaiian Missionary Society, an auxiliary of the American Board, was formed for the purpose of 'propagating evangelical Christianity in the islands of the Pacific Ocean, or in other parts of the world.'"[34]

Coan, as a member of the Micronesian mission committee, both researched the practical feasibility of such a venture and counseled caution. He checked "with sea captains who had been in the area about the feasibility of such a venture. 'We shall recommend to send out a deputation one year from this. The committee feels we shall not be precipitate in this matter. The expedition to explore will occupy six months and cost five thousand dollars.'"[35]

Fundraising would exceed the goal and the Hawaiian church members enthusiastically endorsed and supported the endeavor. "In July 1852 Mr. Coan wrote his friend, the Rev. Chester S. Lyman, that over six thousand dollars had been raised in the islands for the Micronesian mission and that a vessel had sailed for the Carolines carrying three missionary couples from the United States and five Hawaiian missionaries. 'Our native churches,' he writes, 'are greatly interested in this expedition, and

---

33. Coan, *Life*, 137–38. Nancy Morris has written both about Hawaiian pastors and Hawaiian missionaries. Morris dissertation, "Hawaiian Missionaries Abroad, 1852–1909"; and Benedetto and Morris, *Nā Kahu: Portraits: Portraits of Native Hawaiian Pastors at Home and Abroad, 1820–1900*.

34. Prudential Committee of the American Board of Commissioners for Foreign Missions to the Sandwich Islands Mission, July 19, 1848, ABCFM Papers at HMH, in Ehlke, "Enthusiastic Religion," 235.

35. Titus Fidelia Coan to Fidelia, May 26, 1851, in Ehlke, "Enthusiastic Religion," 235–36.

should God plant a Christian mission in Micronesia it will be [word missing] and sustained, chiefly by the Hawaiian churches.' Coan had been elected to accompany the group, but declined the honor because there was no one to administer his large flock in Hilo."[36]

While in Honolulu in 1855, he wrote on behalf of the Hawaiian Evangelical Association to the Secretaries of the ABCFM: "Recent indications of Providence lead us to believe that a wide door is being opened for the enlargement of our operations in Micronesia."[37]

MORNING STAR(S)

During Titus Coan's life, three vessels played a key role in the outreach to other islands. Each bore the name *Morning Star*, which is drawn from Revelation 2:28, 22:16, and Isaiah 22:16, where Christ is referred to as "the morning star."[38] The voyages are related in primary sources by Titus Coan and Fidelia Coan, as well as in *The Friend*, *Missionary Herald*, and other sources.

Coan notes that a missionary spirit growing among a people that has received the gospel is an expected and welcome result of the gospel being faithfully preached. "In the prosecution of our work on the Hawaiian Islands, an active missionary spirit was developed in great strength. This was of course one of the legitimate fruits of a faithfully preached and truly accepted gospel."[39]

Nancy Morris notes that Coan had an informal pastoral school that prepared Hawaiians for both pastoral positions in Hawai'i and missionaries who would go to Micronesia and the Marquesas Islands. "The records pertaining to the preparatory years of the Hawaiian missionaries contain revealing conversion experiences of the newly-Christianized islanders and also support a contention that the Hawaiians were an articulate, well-trained group[40] deeply committed to mission endeavor. Hawaiian churches contributed heavily to financing the missions and the enterprise became a source of pride to a Hawaiian Christian community which regarded itself as the 'Light of the Pacific.' At work in the field the Hawaiians sometimes distinguished themselves as heroes who worked for peace and educational improvements, [but] at other times brought disgrace to the mission through involvement with holy wars and self-serving commercial ventures."[41]

---

36. Titus Coan to Chester S. Lyman, July 31, 1852, LOC, Ehlke, "Enthusiastic Religion," 236.
37. Titus Coan letter to ABCFM, in Coan, *Memorial Volume*, 73.
38. http://biblehub.com/commentaries/revelation/2-28.htm.
39. Coan, *Life*, 154.
40. Hallock, *Hawaii under King Kalakaua*, 60, avers that the Hilo church "sent twelve of its members as foreign missionaries to the South Sea Islands."
41. Morris, *Hawaiian Missionaries Abroad*, iv, v.

Titus Coan: "Apostle to the Sandwich Islands"

Coan writes of the drawbacks of the first effort at missions because of the lack of a vessel.[42] "We sent a mission to the Marquesas Islands, which for years we conducted under great disadvantages. We had no packet to communicate with that group, vessels, at high prices, to carry out our missionaries with their supplies and to send out our annual delegates to look after and encourage them."

He discusses moving beyond the mission field of the Marquesas. "Then as our funds and men increased we thought that the Marquesan field was too small for our energies, and the idea sprang up in the minds of some of our brethren that we might 'lengthen our cords' [Isa 54:2] by exploring among the numerous islands to the west, and establishing a mission in Micronesia in conjunction with the American Board."

The plans develop but the lack of a vessel is still felt. "This thought ripened into action, and American and Hawaiian missionaries were sent out. Still we had no vessel at command and were obliged to look to others to supply this want. Hence arose the thought of securing the needed packet."[43]

Titus comes up with the idea of having the children of America "invest" in such a ship. Writing about Coan's special relationship with children, Lydia writes that it "was not strange that with this children's friend should originate the plan of enlisting them to build 'a little ship' to wait upon the master."[44] She writes of a letter Coan wrote "in the spring of 1855" from Honolulu "on behalf of the Hawaiian Evangelical Association to the Secretaries of the ABCFM."

He relates the opportunity of an open door to expand the ministry in Micronesia. He mentions two "promising native helpers" who departed on another boat. He writes about gathering information concerning "regions hitherto unexplored by scientific expeditions, and nearly unknown to the scientific world."

He reaches his point of presentation and request. "We desire that you will purchase, or procure built, a clipper schooner of 150 or two hundred tons, of substantial materials and faithful workmanship, well coppered high above water, and thoroughly protected from the insects which so abound in these seas, and which are so destructive to all wood exposed to their ravages."

He provides the "details of construction and equipment." He gives two reasons.

"1. We desire to furnish our brethren and sisters now in Micronesia an opportunity for a general meeting of consultation and social and spiritual intercourse . . .

"2. Every indication of divine Providence urges to immediate preparation for enlargement. Many voices speak to us. The cloud is being lifted up and a sound from the fiery pillar [Exod 13:21] commands us to *go forward*" [Exod 14:15].

---

42. A very small vessel was used for a short-lived missionary outreach to the Marquesas and Society Islands in 1832. Called "The Missionary Packet" and "The Ten Commandments," its use by the ABCFM missionaries was relatively short-lived. Baker, *Morning Stars and Missionary Packet*.

43. Coan, *Life*, 154–55.

44. Coan, *Memorial Volume*, 70–71.

"Spare not," cries the note of inspiration, "'lengthen thy cords and strengthen thy stakes' [Isa 54:2]. We must go up and possess the land [Josh 1:11], and under Christ we will do it . . ."⁴⁵

Coan presents the way to raise the funds for the vessel. "As to the means and agencies, they are ample, exhaustless, infinite . . . As to funds, we have no fear on that score. Men will act when under the influence of a controlling motive." He writes specifically of children providing funds. "Even the Sabbath schools, the precious sons and daughters of our Zion, will, if properly led, purchase the vessel we need, and perhaps furnish funds to bring her to our shores. And why shall they not be allowed the joyous privilege? How many young eyes would glow, how many bright faces brighten, and how many youthful hearts beat with sacred pleasure to behold their own *Day Star* unfurling her signals and spreading her white wings to the winds of heaven, freighted with the priceless treasures of salvation!"⁴⁶

Coan notes in his autobiography that the only change the Board made to his proposal was the name of the vessel. "The proposal met with favor, with only one amendment, viz., that the name should be the *Morning Star*." He writes of the overwhelmingly positive response of the children to fund the ship. "The call on the children to take shares in this enterprise was popular, and it spread over many States. The needed sum was raised, and the *Morning Star* (**No. I**) was built, manned, and provided." He relates the sending forth of that vessel. "In due time she sailed from Boston with the prayers and benedictions of a multitude and with the old song,

> Waft, waft, ye winds, his story,
> And you, ye waters, roll."⁴⁷

The brig had cost $18,351⁴⁸ and weighed 156 tons. During its years of service to the Board, it would have three captains: Samuel G. Moore (1856), John W. Brown (1858), and Charles W. Gelett.⁴⁹

Hiram Bingham II writes about the "hopeful conversions" of crew members after they rounded Cape Horn. "Soon after entering the Pacific, we felt that the Holy Spirit was with us; and ere we reached the Sandwich Islands, we hoped that some of our company had given their hearts to the Saviour. Our carpenter had been very profane

---

45. Coan, *Memorial Volume*, 72.

46. Coan, *Memorial Volume*, 72–73.

47. Coan, *Life*, 155. The quotation is from Bishop Regina Heber's hymn "From Greenland's Icy Mountains." The entire verse is:

> "Waft, waft, ye winds, his story,
> And you, ye waters, roll,
> Till like a sea of glory
> It spreads from pole to pole!

48. Approximately $500,000 in 2015 dollars.

49. Baker, *Morning Stars and Missionary Packet*, np.

during the early part of the voyage, and, when reasoned with, he thought he could not help swearing. But when he determined to become a Christian, be strove hard and successfully against this great sin. Sometimes he would haul in a rope that might be accidentally dragging in the sea, without being told to do it. And when some of his companions wondered at this, he replied that the vessel belonged to Jesus, and he wished to help take care of it, even if he was not commanded by the officer to do what he knew be ought to do. It made us happy to think that God had blessed the little vessel on her first voyage."

He writes of his first view of Hawai'i and seeing the place of his birth from a distance: "On the twentieth of April, 1857, we had our first view of the snow-capped mountains of Hawaii, distant more than a hundred miles. The sunrise was beautiful, the clouds being tinged with a gorgeous crimson, and everything seemed to be in harmony with the feelings of joy which we experienced, when, at about 6 o'clock, as I was sweeping the western horizon with my glass, the majestic Mauna Kea was distinctly seen! Many hours did we spend that day on deck, awed by the stupendous pile which, so far away from us, was piercing the clouds.

"We passed Hawaii on our left; and the next morning had Maui and Molokai in full view. As we coasted along the shore of the latter, we were charmed with the numerous cascades which rushed down the rocky precipices near the sea.

"I shall not soon forget the first sight of Oahu, the island of my birth, with its rugged mountains, cocoa-nut groves, little villages, and, last of all, the beautiful harbor of Honolulu. Many years had rolled away since I had left it, then a mere boy. As we neared the land, a small schooner passed us, and her captain, standing upon her rail, shouted, 'Welcome to the *Morning Star*!' And then from the crowd of natives on her deck there went up a round of cheers, which seemed to come from full hearts. These people were very glad to see the *Morning Star*, of which they had heard so much, and toward the building of which many of their children had given their money. The captain who welcomed us was a brother of Dr. Gulick, of Micronesia; and he is now the principal of a Girls' Boarding School at Waialua, Oahu. He came on board with Mr. Bond, and the watermelon, cocoa-nuts, potatoes, sweet and Irish, which they gave us, were a great luxury, after we had been so many months upon the deep."[50]

The schooner arrived in Honolulu on April 24, 1857. "Thence she sailed for the Marquesas Islands with supplies; and on her return, early in July, she appeared off the entrance of Hilo harbor, dressed in all her white sails with her flag fluttering in the breeze and with her star shining in the center."[51]

---

50. Bingham, *The Story of the Morning Star*, np.
51. Coan, *Life*, 155–56.

Lydia writes, "How heartily the little brig was hailed at Hilo on her return from her first missionary cruise let Mr. Coan's pen relate:

"'The morning of the seventh of July, 1857, dawned gloriously on Hawaii. The mountains were throwing off their night robes, and adorning themselves in the light drapery of dawn; the fields were slowly unveiling their peerless beauty; the ocean began to reflect the first tinges of morning light, when suddenly the sound, "Hokuao!" (*Morning Star*) "Hokuao!" broke our slumbers. "Hokuao! Hokuao!" echoed and re-echoed from every headland and hill, and rolled back from every valley along our coast; and multitudes of children waked, and ran, and shouted, and caught the "flying joy." All Hilo was awake. Away in the eastern horizon floated that beauteous star of Hope, while Venus, like an angel's eye, looked down upon her from the vault of heaven. Then we felt that our prayers had been heard, and realized that the sleepless eye of him who proclaims himself "the Bright and Morning Star" [Rev 22:16] was also looking down upon that consecrated bark.'"[53]

Coan continues the narrative in his autobiography. "Hilo was jubilant. We had heard of her sailing, had counted on her time, and had been watching for her arrival. Arrangements had been made to give her a hearty welcome. Parents and children came hasting in from all quarters, winding over the hills and along their footpaths and filling our streets."

He relates the arrival of Captain Moore and the subsequent solemn celebration. "Captain Moore came on shore with his officers and passengers, and was met by the well-dressed and decorated children in double file, bearing a flag prepared for the occasion. With songs of welcome they were waited upon to the great church, which was soon filled to its entire capacity. Prayers were offered, hymns and an original ode to

52. *Morning Star I*, in Baker, *Morning Stars and Missionary Packet*. Image is in the public domain.
53. Coan, *Memorial Volume*, 73–74.

the *Star* were sung, addresses made, and all went off with a hearty goodwill. We were happy on this occasion to welcome the Rev. Hiram Bingham, Jr., with his young wife, bound to Micronesia, and little knowing what sufferings awaited them in those dark and distant islands."[54]

Along with his wife Clara, Hiram Bingham II, or Jr., became good friends of Titus. The brother of the woman who would become Titus's second wife (who assisted him in the production of the autobiography), Hiram carried the weight of the Bingham name. Born August 16, 1831, a scion of and with the name of the leader of the Pioneer Company and of the entire Hawaiian Mission until his departure in 1840,[55] Hiram Bingham II[56] figured significantly in Hawaiian missions and the *Morning Star* voyages.

Less than a month after being ordained, he and his new wife, Minerva Clarissa[57] Brewster Bingham, departed Boston on December 2, 1856, on the first *Morning Star*. When they arrived in Honolulu on April 24, 1857,[58] great pressure was brought upon the heir of the mission leader. Leaders and people wanted him to stay. Char Miller writes about this in his "Text in Context: The Journal of an Early Nineteenth-Century American Missionary."[59] Miller writes about the journal of Hiram Bingham. It sheds helpful light on the genre in general and Coan's journal-keeping in particular.

Miller discusses the nature and extent of the journal upon which this article is written. It was "a journal of more than two hundred pages in which Bingham chronicled his voyage from Boston to the Gilberts (now a part of Kiribati) in 1856 and 1857 . . . As the journal reveals (in what is itself a Western mode of discourse), this was more than just a voyage between designated points on a map. It was a psychological journey as well, a narrative in which Hiram Bingham Jr. marked his course from student to pioneer missionary, from youth to manhood."[60]

Coan wrote in his journal on the way to the Sandwich Islands in 1834 and 1835. He would continue to keep a journal (using this Western form of discourse) for the rest of his life. Lydia Bingham Coan quoted copiously from her husband's journal for his two trips to the Marquesas Islands. Those quotations complemented what Titus Coan wrote in his autobiography.

Hiram Bingham II lived all but the first four years of his life while Titus Coan lived in Hawai'i. Hiram would live twenty years after Coan's death. Unlike the namesake of the leader of the Pioneer Company, Titus had no missionary pressure upon

---

54. Coan, *Life*, 156.

55. And, some would argue, he continued as a very influential presence *in absentia* until his death in 1869 and beyond.

56. See Forbes et al., *Partners in Change*, 12–25.

57. Called "Clara."

58. Judd, *Missionary Album*, 44–45; and Forbes et al., *Partners in Change*, 120–25.

59. Miller, "Text in Context." Miller wrote about five generations of men with the name "Hiram Bingham" in his *Fathers and Sons*. He compiled the writings of Hiram Bingham in *Selected Writings* and spun off other articles in his early scholarly years.

60. Miller, "Text in Context," 49.

him. Apart from wanting him to know the Lord Jesus in a personal way, Titus Munson Coan's parents do not appear to have pressured him to serve as a missionary.

By contrast, Hiram Bingham II experienced intense pressure to be a missionary or serve as a pastor from his earliest years. "Bingham's youth was unlike that of others. When he was born on August 15, 1831, in Honolulu, the third surviving child of Hiram and Sybil Bingham, missionaries to Hawaii since 1820, he incurred a precise set of obligations. As the first (and only) son[61] he achieved a special status, one his father was at pains to make known within and without the family. He immediately urged his daughters, for instance, to pray for the preservation of their new brother's life so that he might become 'a good missionary . . . [and teach] others to know and love and worship the true God.'"[62]

Miller notes that the "first volume of" Hiram Bingham II's journal "covers the voyage of nearly five months from Boston to Hawaii" and reflects the perspective that for him, 'genealogy was destiny.'"[63]

This destiny is reflected in the minutest detail. One such example is the rounding of Cape Horn—which Fidelia and Titus Coan experienced as well (fifteen years after Hiram Bingham I and a little over twenty years before Hiram Bingham II). "For instance, during the most dangerous part of the voyage, rounding Cape Horn, Hiram Bingham kept a close record of the many difficulties and frustrations that arose during the passage of the *Morning Star* from the Atlantic to the Pacific. But when it came time to mark the event in a ceremonial manner he drew on his father's words: the couple sang 'Ebenezer,' which is the name of the hymn Hiram Bingham, Sr., had composed to commemorate his experience of a rough transit around the cape."[64]

Ebenezer in the Bible refers to 1 Samuel 7:2, when Samuel erected a stone and said, "Thus far the Lord has helped us." Ebenezer means "stone of help."[65] Among other books read during the long oceanic voyage read by Hiram Bingham II and his wife was Bingham Sr.'s "monumental *Twenty-One Year Residence in the Sandwich Islands* . . . using it as if it were a Baedeker[66] by which to confirm their sense of the importance of things."[67]

In his memoirs, Hiram Bingham writes of a special Sabbath while journeying to the Sandwich Islands. "One of the happiest Sabbaths of the voyage was the thirtieth of January, when we passed the Cape, and we found the region of terror and danger

---

61. Hiram and Sybil had previously had two sons who did not live beyond two years: Levi Parsons and Samuel Evarts, Judd, *Missionary Album*, 43; and Forbes et al., *Partners in Change*, 118.
62. Miller, "Text in Context," 49.
63. Miller, "Text in Context," 53.
64. Miller, "Text in Context," 53.
65. Dictionary.com, "Ebenezer."
66. A German travel guidebook.
67. Miller, "Text in Context," 53.

to the place of our special rejoicing, and we united in a special song, which was composed at the time,[68] to celebrate the event, and denominated our

EBENEZER.

With joyful hearts and grateful praise,

Our Helper God thy name we hail,

Our EBENEZER here we raise,

While round the stormy cape we sail."[69]

Miller indicates that what "is particularly striking in this regard is the way Bingham fashioned his experience in light of that of his parents; at the very least, their voyage to the Pacific in 1820 was the touchstone by which he gauged his own, indicating that the young man had not established his own sensibility, his own career."[70]

Miller describes the intense pressure upon Hiram Bingham II when he arrived in Honolulu. He experienced great turmoil upon his arrival. The Hawaiians wanted him to stay as pastor of his father's Kawaiahaʻo Church. Ultimately the decision rested with the Hawaiian Evangelical Association, of which Titus Coan was president at the time. "Bingham received his first taste of just how complicated religious life in the Pacific could be when he arrived in Honolulu, the city of his birth, in late April 1857."[71]

The following is a picture of "Gilbertina," where Hiram Bingham II and III grew up:

[72]

68. Bingham Sr. is modest in not naming himself, but apparently it became known he had written the verse.

69. Bingham, *Residence*, 66. See 66–67 for the remaining five verses, including the concluding:

> "So shall our grateful record stand,
> 'THUS FAR BY THY KIND AID WE'VE COME,
> So will we trust thy constant hand
> To bring our souls in safety home.'"

70. Miller, "Text in Context," 53.

71. Miller, "Text in Context," 53.

72. Wikimedia Commons, public domain.

The July 1, 1942, issue of *The Friend* relates a first-person description of the festivities surrounding the arrival of the *Morning Star* and its passengers.[73] But on "landing he was overwhelmed by the Hawaiians' acute memory of the man for whom he was named.[74] The Hawaiian Christians remembered especially the father's promise to Kaahuman[75] that Hiram Jr. would one day assume his father's former post at Kawaiaha'o Church, and they urged to the son to fulfill that promise, a plea that posed a dilemma for the new missionary if not a psychological crisis."[76]

Hiram Sr.[77] then encouraged his son to go to China. They ultimately agreed on Micronesia. But the pull was strong. "The pressure was intense. Hawaiian Christians approached Hiram and Clara at every opportunity to press their claims, the affective and historical bases of which were strikingly similar to those advanced by Hiram's father and others at his departure from New England several months earlier. But the expression of these concerns was different, and consistent with Hawaiian culture."[78]

This situation bears a tenuous connection with Titus Coan and his time in Patagonia. A difference is that he was not yet married to Fidelia Church, though they were already leaning toward the Sandwich Islands before they left and Fidelia urged him to go to the Sandwich Islands after he returned. Another difference is that Coan was still in seminary. But there is a similarity in that Coan ultimately recommended against establishing a mission in Patagonia and was sent to the Sandwich Islands instead. Hiram Bingham II was already headed to Micronesia, but he felt the tug of promises made and loyalty felt.

"Hiram's decision was, however, neither easy nor his alone to make. The Hawaiian Evangelical Association, which had jurisdiction over the Kawaiaha'o Church and was one of the sponsoring agencies of the Micronesian mission, sought to mediate the issue and hastily established a committee to assess it."[79]

Miller presents a trenchant analysis of the triangulation between the memory of Hiram Bingham I, his son Hiram Bingham II, and the Hawaiian Christians. He relates an address he gave to Kawaiaha'o church in which the members of the congregation could tell that he was of two minds of the situation. He was clearly leaning heavily toward going to Micronesia where people "were without a knowledge of Christ." He also pointed out that by going he could someday return with more experience to be a better pastor.

---

73. *The Friend* 112.7 (July 1, 1942), np.

74. Hiram Bingham had left Honolulu more than twenty-five years before.

75. "The Sandwich Island Mission in Hawai'i owes its successful operation more to the assistance of the great chiefess Ka'ahumanu than to any other person." Forbes et al., *Partners in Change*, 373.

76. Miller, "Text in Context," 54.

77. Hiram Bingham I died in 1869, the year before Fidelia and Titus traveled to the United States of America. Wikipedia, "Hiram Bingham I."

78. Miller, "Text in Context," 54.

79. Miller, "Text in Context," 55, 56.

Miller provides further analysis. "That it was finally a matter of choice is important, for this complicated and emotional experience enabled Bingham to breach a crucial psychological barrier, with the aid of the Hawaiian Christians who helped set the context. No more was he simply following in his father's footsteps. Micronesia was no longer simply a compromise worked out between father and son, but a field to which the son was publicly committed."[80]

When the Reverend Ephraim Weston Clark[81] did not become the Recording Secretary of the American Board, it fell to him to continue as the pastor of the church. Clark had gone to Micronesia in 1852 "to aid in establishing a mission and he made two visits to the United States, one in 1856 to superintend printing of the New Testament,[82] and one in 1859 for his second marriage." He served as pastor of Kawaiaha'o Church from 1848 until 1863.[83]

The Binghams debarked for the Gilbert Islands. They were stationed in Apaiang, Gilbert Islands, from November 19, 1857, until September 8, 1865. Clarissa "became expert in the Gilbertese language. She was a helper and co-worker with Mr. Bingham under the primitive conditions of those intensely tropical[84] islands."[85]

In 1866, he was asked to write *The Story of the Morning Star: The Children's Mission Vessel*. A short book with eighteen chapters averaging three to five pages, Bingham addresses the book to children and youth. It is very readable for adults as well. "MY DEAR YOUNG FRIENDS,—You have all heard of the missionary vessel that was sent to the Pacific Ocean in 1856; not a few of you took stock in her."

Bingham writes of the previous works on the *Morning Star*. "Perhaps you have read about her in *The Missionary Herald, The Journal of Missions, The Youth's Dayspring, The Friend*, or in a book written by Mrs. Warren."[86] He is referring to the 1860 American Tract Society printing of Jane S. Warren's *Morning Star: History of the Children's Missionary Vessel, and of the Marquesan and Micronisian [sic] Missions*.[87]

Warren writes of her "little book." While the pages are somewhat small, there are eighteen chapters with a little over three hundred pages. Chapter 1 examines "Why the *Morning Star* was built." She begins with "Henry Obookiah's" arrival at Yale. She continues on to the early Board missionaries to the Sandwich Islands. She writes about the revival of 1838. By 1839, the "people of Hawaii now felt that they had received great blessings, and they began to think that they ought to do something to give the gospel to others who still remained as degraded as they once were. We see that the love

---

80. Miller, "Text in Context," 56.
81. Judd, *Missionary Album*, 68; and Forbes et al., *Partners in Change*, 179–81.
82. And to be considered for the position of Recording Secretary?
83. Judd, *Missionary Album*, 68.
84. Hot and humid?
85. Judd, *Missionary Album*, 45.
86. Bingham II, *Story of the Morning Star*, np.
87. Warren, *Morning Star*.

of Christ enlarges the heart and makes it unselfish. The earnest desire, 'Lord, what wilt thou have me do?' [Acts 9:6] takes possession of the soul, and prompts to labor of love for others; and it was so with these Christians."[88]

Warren next explains why the Micronesian Islands became the focus of the missionaries. Two thousand miles from the Hawaiian Islands, Christianity had been made known to the Micronesians through the prism of trading vessels and whaling ships. She then relates the specific organizational efforts needed to send missionaries to those islands. "So the Hawaiian Christians thought they would undertake to send a mission to these islands, and for this purpose they formed a society at Honolulu, called 'The Hawaiian Mission Society.' The American Board at the same time determined to cooperate with the Hawaiian Christians, and send missionaries from this country to aid them in their enterprise. The people were delighted with the undertaking, and went to work in good earnest to raise the money with which to carry on the work."

Warren reports that in July of 1850 the chartered vessel *Caroline* carried the couples Snow, Sturges, and Gulick, "along with two Hawaiian assistants and their wives."[89] In response to mission interest by the Micronesians, two more Hawaiian missionaries were eventually sent.[90] But it was realized that the group needed a vessel of its own. "So, then, it was concluded by the Board that a little vessel must be provided for the purpose, and sent out for the use of the Micronesian mission. And this was why the *Morning Star* was built."[91]

Chapter 2 examines "How They Got the Money." The American Board could not spare the money. Neither could the Hawaiian Mission Society nor the churches of Hawai'i. Warren explains the subscription by children to pay for the vessel. "In Wisconsin, one Sabbath school formed a '*Morning Star* Association.'" Warren relates poignant stories that inspired further giving.[92] Students from various parts of the world donated, as did the Hawaiian Sabbath Schools. "In Hilo, the children gave liberally, and sent a request that the vessel might stop at their island. They were very anxious to see the object so often described to them [by Titus Coan], and on which their minds were set."[93]

Chapter 3 tells about "The Launch," while 4 presents "Voyage to the Sandwich Islands," and 5 "Arrival at Honolulu—The Marquesas." Chapter 3 includes a hymn that was sung, reflecting the "investment" by the children in the gospel which lasts as opposed to return on monetary investment. Entitled "The *Morning Star*,"[94] the verse reflects this outlook:

88. Warren, *Morning Star*, 7–17.
89. Warren, *Morning Star*, 17.
90. Warren, *Morning Star*, 20.
91. Warren, *Morning Star*, 21.
92. Warren, *Morning Star*, 28–33.
93. Warren, *Morning Star*, 33–34.
94. Warren, *Morning Star*, 45. "From the Hammond Baptist Church," Bangor, Maine.

> "Our silver and gold in the *Morning Star*
> We've invested, expecting our return from afar;
> The good ship is chartered for a very long run;
> Her cargo's insured till her haven is won.
> Rich, rich freight from far
> She will bring back again, the *Morning Star*."[95]

Upon arrival in Honolulu, five addresses were given and three hymns were sung, two of which are shared in their entirety: "The *Morning Star*" and "The Missionary Packet." The first one is in both Hawaiian and English, with the verses presented side by side. Here is verse one:

Ka Hokuao,	The *Morning Star*,
Ke Kamahao,	The beautiful,
He nanni maoli no,	The truly splendid *Star*,
Hei lama no na aina a pau,	A light to shine on every land,
E pau ka hewa, pau ka po	To banish sin and woe from man,
O Jesu no,	Our Jesus is—
Ka Hokuao,	The Morning Star,—
Ka haku wanaao.	The Star of early dawn.[96]

Here is the first verse of the second hymn, "written by Mrs. M. D. Strong, and sung by the children at the presentation of the banner:—

> We hail the bright sails gleaming
> On this far distant strand.
> Thou, *Star*, whose welcome beaming
> Shall lighten every land.
> We hail thee, gladly sharing
> In this blest work of love,
> Our bannered offering bearing,
> The *Star* and peaceful Dove."[97]

After the relating of the hymn, Warren provides a portion "of a letter from Mr. Coan, another missionary at the Sandwich Islands, which my young readers will like to see.

---

95. Warren, *Morning Star*, 57. The last verse is:
   > "God speed thee, God help thee, we earnestly pray,
   > Safe on the wild ocean, by night and by day;
   > Oh, ne'er was a ship so wafted by prayer;
   > Our young, loving hearts for thy safety shall care.
   > Speed, speed on thy way,
   > Till the Morning-Star pales in the Sun's golden ray."

96. Warren, *Morning Star*, 70. No author indicated for this hymn.

97. Warren, *Morning Star*, 70–71. The third refers to "Micronesian skies" and "Marquesan shores."

"'What an impulse the building and sailing of that little sea-bird produced! The action touched a chord which vibrates through the land. What gives such moral power and sublimity to that little vessel? Her name is a charm, but it is *derived*. It suggests the dawn of creation, when the morning stars sang together, and all the sons of God shouted for joy [Job 38:7]. It calls to memory the music of that voice which said, "I am the Bright and Morning Star." But the *object*, the *errand*, of that little bark is its glory. Our western waters are plowed by the ships of the greatest monarchs; in our harbors float the flags of the most renowned nations; but to those who love the Redeemer's cause, this little vessel, bearing the banner of our Eternal King, and waving the emblems of the Prince of Peace, has more significance than all the commercial, scientific, and warlike marines on earth.

"'How delightful to the think of the multitudes of young hearts which beat high in hopes for that missionary packet.'"[98]

Warren relates the names and nature of the islands that make up the "Marquesas: Fatuhiva, Hivaoa, Nukahiva, Hiaou, and Fetouhouhou. These are not coral islands— built on coral rocks— but, like the Hawaiian, rise in peaks two or three thousand feet above the ocean."[99]

Chapters 6 and 7 of Warren relate the first visit of the first *Morning Star* to the Marquesas.[100] Chapter 8 covers the first of Hiram Bingham Jr.'s visits to Honolulu. Chapters 9 through 11 examine the first visit to Micronesia. Warren provides the definition of the word and description of the islands of Micronesia. "Micronesia is a word signifying the *small islands*. It embraces the islands of the Pacific lying between 3 degrees south and 20 degrees north latitude, and between 130 and 178 degrees longitude. In the body of islands contained within this boundary perhaps more than two islands grouped together, go by different names, [such] as [the] Carolines, Mulgraves, &c., with many [sub?]groups."[101]

Chapters 12 through 14 portray the second voyage to Micronesia,[102] chapters 15 and 16 the third voyage,[103] and chapter 17 the fourth voyage.[104] The last chapter in Warren's book examines "Missionary Life at Apaiang," which brings us back to Hiram Bingham II. Warren is regrettably overly glowing in her description of the Binghams' life at the location, while the couple would describe in an understated way

---

98. Uncited Coan letter in Warren, *Morning Star*, 72.
99. Warren, *Morning Star*, 73.
100. Warren, *Morning Star*, 77–108.
101. Warren, *Morning Star*, 125.
102. Warren, *Morning Star*, 202–53.
103. Warren, *Morning Star*, 245–68.
104. Warren, *Morning Star*, 269–82.

as challenging. In Hiram's letters to Titus Coan[105] and Clara[106] in her letters to Lydia, significant ordeals would be shared.

Warren presents an idyllic life that Char Miller debunks in an article about Hiram Bingham III. "In 1856 the Binghams had begun a Christian mission in the Islands, but in less than a decade of labor had fled the Islands, suffering from numerous maladies; the intervening years [1865–75] had not fortified them against the hardships there."[107]

Instead of relating the hardships, Warren presents the following picture to the children. "Some of our readers will be pleased to learn of the particulars of the missionary's life and labors on the beautiful islands of Micronesia.[108] We propose, therefore, in our closing chapter, to introduce them to 'Happy Home,' Apaiang, where dwell our friends Mr. and Mrs. Bingham. We have before described the building of the house, and its pleasant situation, facing the still water—the lagoon—and standing in a grove of coconut trees. Some of these are very tall, especially one upon which steps have been nailed, and which is used by Mr. Bingham for a lookout.[109] On the top of which is a flag-staff, from which a flag floats upon the ocean breeze."[110]

Warren does admit to the Binghams at times being challenged in the area of food to which they are accustomed. "When the *Morning Star* reached Apaiang, on her third voyage, the families were destitute of almost all provisions except flour; but by Mrs. Bingham's good management, they had not suffered."

Warren also relates the enervating effect of Hiram Bingham Jr. as a result of his preaching tours. "Owing to the fatigue attendant these labors, which unfits him entirely for mental labor, Mr. Bingham more generally leaves them to Kanoa and Mahoe,[111] whose constitutions are better adapted to the climate."[112]

She indicates the difficulties, what she calls "annoyances," the rest of the family members experienced while the husbands were away from home. "While the missionaries are absent on these journeys, their families are left comparatively unprotected, and sometimes are subject to disagreeable annoyances."[113]

While the Binghams were in Apaiang, they exchanged correspondence with the Coans as they were able, whether with the all-too-rare visits from the *Morning Star* or

---

105. See miscellaneous letters of Hiram to Titus.
106. See letters from Clara to Lydia in the Bingham collection in Connecticut.
107. Char Miller, "The World Creeps In," 81.
108. While the islands certainly are beautiful to the eye, the unremitting high temperatures and humidity took their toll on the Binghams and other missionaries, as did a loneliness similar to what the Coans experienced in their early months in Hilo. Unlike the Coans, more civilization was not as close as Lahaina or Honolulu.
109. Hoping for the all too infrequent visit of a vessel.
110. Warren, *Morning Star,* 283.
111. For Joel Hulu Mahoe, see Morris and Benedetto, *Nā Kahu,* 194–99.
112. Warren, *Morning Star,* 287–88.
113. Warren, *Morning Star,* 288.

via other vessels. The first such letter from Titus to Hiram is upbeat[114]—even with the recognition of missionary sacrifice—as Titus awaits the return voyage of the *Morning Star*. "We now await the return of the *Morning Star* with deep interest. By her we expect to hear good tidings from you and your dear companion, and from the precious cause in which you have embarked. Long ago we trust you have met your fellow-laborers in the Micronesian field. I can imagine the bounding joy with which your arrival was hailed in those lonely isles. How my soul would have rejoiced to have been one of your number, and to have mingled its sympathies in the scenes through which you have passed. Do we not in the service of our Lord often 'drink of the brook in the way' [Ps 110:7], and 'with joy draw water from the wells of salvation' [Isa 12:3]? Is there not sometimes an unuttered pleasure, a holy triumph of soul, in denying ourselves, in taking the cross and in following [Matt 16:24] our Redeemer in his works of mercy on earth? Do we not find purer and more purifying pleasure in *forsaking* all for Christ than in grasping all for ourselves? Beloved Brother and Sister, only see that your consecration to your work is entire and irreversible, and you will realize in your own souls the fulfillment of the promise of an hundredfold more in this present time."[115]

Two and a half years later, Titus encourages Hiram when he is discouraged by the apathetic response to the preached Good News. "You are still pained at the indifference of your people to the gospel messages. So it will be for a time. They know not the import and cannot appreciate the treasures of the gospel. But you will reap in due season if you faint not [Gal 6:9]. Passion and animal instincts sway the heathen; and the missionary is to meet and measure a hundred ebbings and fluxes of animal passion before enlightened piety and settled principles gain a full ascendancy, before the great deep of human depravity ceases to rise and fall and surge like the ocean under temperature and tempest, and all becomes so placid and reliable that you can say, 'There is no more sea' [Rev 21:1]. Christ has determined to convert all nations, and he will not fail or be discouraged in the work. The isles and peoples shall wait for his law and welcome it; and he is with his believing laborers *always* [Matt 28:20] not occasionally, not in peace and sunshine only, but in war and tempest."[116]

Bingham Jr. explains why he came to write the book and why it was important to write. "As I was the first missionary that went to sea in her, and have known her ever since, the Secretaries of the American Board a few weeks ago requested me to write a short story about her, in order that you may see how much good she has done, and so be all the more glad to aid in building another *Morning Star* to take her place."[117]

Three years later Titus writes Hiram with condolences concerning the death of Minerva's father, as well as a discussion of a southern Catholic's opponent to Hiram's

---

114. Remember that this is at the beginning of the Binghams' service and with letters chosen through Lydia's filter, as well as that Lydia is the youngest sister to Hiram.

115. Titus Coan to Rev. H. Bingham, Jr., November 3, 1857, in Coan, *Memorial Volume*, 82–83.

116. Coan to Bingham II, March 14, 1860, in Coan, *Memorial Volume*, 85–86.

117. Bingham II, *Story of the Morning Star*, np.

speech in Honolulu on the Fourth of July in 1862. He concludes the letter by writing of the challenges of the climate and monotony.[118] To those he provides advice and the desire that the Binghams' lives be preserved for fruitful labor. "We have felt a constant desire that your lives, health, and happiness might be preserved to labor in the vineyard of our Lord. But *we apprehend that you suffer from climate and from monotony of life.*[119] To keep the heart happy, the mind buoyant, and the spirits elastic, physical health must be secured; and a wise care of our earthly tabernacles is important to a vigorous, cheerful, and successful prosecution of our spiritual labors."[120]

After 1865, Hiram Bingham II would be based in Honolulu. Between that year and 1875, he and his wife "made several annual and two stopover visits from Honolulu to the Gilbert Islands. Char Miller relates the challenging medical situations for both husband and wife, as well as the challenges in getting transportation from the Gilberts back to Honolulu. It became a very indirect route. "The circumstances surrounding Hiram III's birth on November 19, 1875, were traumatic as well as symbolic of his impending break with family [missionary] tradition. A year and a half before their son was born, Hiram Jr. and Clara Bingham had returned to the Gilbert Islands to resume briefly their mission station there."

Not long after their return, Hiram experiences the return of symptoms he had had during their previous permanent stay. Clara compares his struggles with those of eleven years before, but with a significant difference. Soon after landing on Abaiang Island for this second time, Bingham, Jr.'s intestinal problems recurred; he again begins to lose weight, strength, and composure. As his wife noted in her diary, "weakness and often pain and depression are my loved one's portion. How like 1864."[121]

Miller notes the difference accompanying Hiram's maladies this time. Unlike that earlier year, however, Clara was now pregnant. As the pregnancy proceeded, her husband's health withered; he was largely confined to bed. Miller relates the ordeal of their return itinerary to Honolulu. "On May 16, 1875, the Binghams once again departed from the Gilberts, taking a circuitous route to Honolulu. From Abaiang, they sailed to Samoa. From there to Fiji, and then to Auckland, New Zealand; at each port Bingham had to be carried ashore and nursed back to health. And each port was successively further from Honolulu and the medical care both Binghams required. Finally, they were able to gain passage on a steamer sailing for Hawaii, arriving but six days before Hiram III was born."[122]

Returning to Hiram Bingham II's discussion of the first *Morning Star*, his first chapter is entitled "The Lands She Was to Visit." Other chapter titles include: "Around the Horn"; "She Visits the Marquesas Islands"; "She Sets Out for Micronesia"; "Her

---

118. Loneliness?
119. Emphasis added.
120. Coan to Bingham II, April 7, 1863, in Coan, *Memorial Volume*, 93–94.
121. Miller, "The World Creeps In," 81.
122. Miller, "The World Creeps In," 81.

MISSIONS, PART 1

Visit to Kusaie"; "Her Visit to Ponape"; "Her Visit to Apaiang:" "Her Visit to Ebon"; "Waiting for the *Morning Star*"[123]; "Her Early Visits"; "Some things She Brought and How We Used Them"; "Micronesians Who Sailed in Her"; "Her Last Visit to the Marquesas Islands"; and "Conclusion."[124]

In an appendix, Bingham Jr. provides several examples of varioius languages, including the Gilbertese into which he translated the entire Bible and other items. Here is the Lord's Prayer in Gilbertese:

"*Tamara are i karawa, a na tabuaki aram. E na roko ueam: E na tauaki am taeka i aon te aba n ai aron tauana i karawa. Ko na añanira karara ae ti a tau iai n te boñ aei. Ao ko na kabara ara buakaka mairoura n ai arora ñkai ti kabara te buakaka mairouia akana ioawa nako ira. Ao tai kairira nakon to karíriaki, ma ko na kamaiuira man to buakaka; ba ambai te uea, ao te maka, ae to neboaki, n aki toki. Amene.*"[125]

At the end of his discussion of the first *Morning Star*, Albert S. Baker explains why there was a need for a second vessel. "She had finally become so worn that it seemed best to sell her when she had ended her return to Honolulu on December 12, 1865, and build another vessel."[126]

In his autobiography, Coan notes that the *Morning Star II* was built by the funds "received from the sale of the old one, supplemented by further gifts from the children. She was a larger, better-built, and more convenient boat than the first and did good service."[127] The *Morning Star* brig was 181 tons in size and cost $23,406.[128]

123. Where he and Clara had debarked from the *Morning Star*.
124. Bingham II, *Story of the Morning Star*, np.
125. Bingham II, *Story of the Morning Star*, np.
126. Baker, *Morning Stars and Missionary Packet*, np.
127. Coan, *Life*, 157.
128. Baker, *Morning Stars and Missionary Packet*, np.
129. *Morning Star II*, in Baker, *Morning Stars and Missionary Packet*. Image is in the public domain.

Hiram II would become "the first captain[130] to sail the second *Morning Star* and commanded her voyage through the islands of Micronesia for one year, 1867, before deciding to remain in Honolulu and serve the Gilbert Islands from there. This *Morning Star* was one of a series of brigs which served the missionary stations in the South Seas proudly financed by Sunday School children in the Hawaiian Islands and all over the United States."[131]

Coan notes that the second *Morning Star*'s "end came all too soon. After a successful cruise among the Islands of Micronesia, and on leaving the little islet of Kussuaie, or Strong's Island, when all seemed propitious, she drifted upon the rocks and was broken in pieces. All on board escaped to the land to wait an opportunity to return to their homes."[132]

A few days before Hiram Bingham III was born, the Binghams arrived in Honolulu after taking a circuitous route there from the Gilbert Islands. From then on they would live in Honolulu. Hiram Bingham II would die in Baltimore, Maryland, in October 25, 1908, while Clarissa had died seven years before in Honolulu.

"After 1875 they labored in Honolulu for the Gilbertese nation and the colony in Hawaii. Mr. Bingham was Secretary of the Hawaiian Board 1877–80." As his father had been deeply involved in the first Hawaiian Bible translation, hymns, and other books, Hiram II singlehandedly worked on such matters in his missionary endeavors. "He finished translation of the New Testament into Gilbertese, April 11, 1873; the Old Testament, April 11, 1890; revised and printed the complete Bible, which he finished April 11, 1893. He also translated numerous other books including a Gilbertese dictionary."[133]

Coan writes about the *Morning Star III* and expresses his hope for a steamer *Morning Star*. "Two *Stars* have set in the west, and here comes the *Morning Star No. 3*, fairer and brighter than those which have disappeared, well built, larger and better than the other two.

"The insurance money on No. 2, with another lift from the children, had soon brought her keel into the waters, raised her well-shaped spars, set up her standing, and arrayed her running rigging, clothed her with a white cloud of canvas, and run up her beautiful flag to wave in the breezes of heaven. Well furnished, with a well-appointed crew, with an excellent captain and good officers, she is now [1880] on her tenth voyage to Micronesia, taking out supplies to the laborers in that widening field, and a reinforcement, long waited for, for the Gilbert Islands."[134] Also 181 tons, it cost $28,462

---

130. Tengstrom was the second captain beginning in 1868. Baker, *Morning Stars and Missionary Packet*, np.

131. Judd, *Missionary Album*, 44.

132. Coan, *Life*, 156.

133. Judd, *Missionary Album*, 45.

134. Coan, *Life*, 158.

and had six captains: Nathaniel Matthews (1871), William B. Hallett (1872), Charles W. Gelett (1874), Isaiah Bray (1878), and George F. Garland with Bray on "leave."[135]

[136]

What Coan did not know was that the third *Morning Star* would go the way of the second. "On the annual voyage from Honolulu leaving June 22, 1883, having nearly finished her work in all the groups, she was off the harbor of Kusaie on February 22, 1884. She was under the temporary command of Capt. George F. Garland, in the absence of Capt. Bray, with whom he had been mate. Here she was wrecked, only about six miles from where the second *Star* had been wrecked. The wind was not favorable for sailing through the entrance into the harbor, but four buoys were kept there by means of which, with ropes, a vessel could be hauled through to an anchorage. They had made fast to a buoy, but there was a heavy swell that morning, and then the wind began to increase. Suddenly they began to go astern, for the buoy had pulled loose. It was too deep to anchor, for enough chain to hold would have put them on the rocks. They cast off and tried to sail free, but before they could come around they were on the rocks, each wave carrying them farther up the reef. It was all over in less than five minutes, but almost everything on board was saved. After six weeks they decked over one of their boats, and, with two months' provisions, sailed for Ponape. From there Capt. Garland got passage to Hong-Kong, and so to the United States, with news

---

135. Baker, *Morning Stars and Missionary Packet*.

136. *Morning Star III*, Baker, *Morning Stars and Missionary Packet*, np. Baker provides only five names. Image is in the public domain.

of the wreck. Fortunately, some months before this second wreck of a *Star*, plans had been made to build another vessel, in regard to which Capt. Bray had gone east. It was to be larger for the growing work and with auxiliary steam-power to guard against the calms and currents prevailing among the islands and the special danger always encountered in entering lagoons."[137]

Writing of all the military steamers, Coan expresses the hope that there will eventually be a *Morning Star* that is a steamer to reach "the lost tribes of men. If the Lord will, I hope to hear the whistle of a missionary steamer in our waters before I go hence."[138] It was not to be. Many hoped that the fourth *Morning Star* would be a steamer. They were disappointed. "In 1883 Capt. Isaiah Bray of the third *Star* had gone east to present to the Prudential Committee's sub-committee of the American Board on the *Morning Star*, drawings for a steamer of a little over six hundred tons, as the hearts of friends in Hawaii and the missionaries in Micronesia were fixed on this idea. The Prudential Committee, however, felt that the cost of building and maintaining such a boat was too great."[139]

In late 1883, an appeal went out to children to "buy stock" in the *Morning Star IV*. The cost jumped from the first one at ten cents to twenty-five cents a share. Nevertheless, within a few months the full amount needed was raised. "In December 1883, an appeal was made to the children and youth of our country to take stock in a new "\ *Morning Star* at twenty-five cents a share, to the total amount of $45,000. Such was the response that by February 1884 the Board felt justified in building at once, and the contract was made at Bath, Maine. Thus they began to build the same month that the third *Morning Star* was wrecked."[140]

Though the Hawaiian Board was no longer involved in the process, there was a fifth *Morning Star* and it was a steamer. "Since the Hawaiian Board no longer shared in this particular mission work, it was very difficult to find details of the fifth *Morning Star* in Honolulu." Baker engaged in extensive research and found out a great deal of material on number five, as well as the two vessels that were already in service.

"Between the sale of the fourth *Star* in 1900 and the fifth *Morning Star* of 1904, other vessels were employed to tour the island groups, but all were unsatisfactory and considered only temporary. It is interesting to note that while the fourth *Star* was still active, a schooner of about fifty tons, the *Robert W. Logan* was in use for local work for the western section of the Caroline Islands, and a gasoline launch, the *Hiram Bingham*, was touring for most of the time among the Gilbert Islands. The former was lost in three years, but the latter long continued its usefulness."[141]

137. Baker, *Morning Stars and Missionary Packet,* np.
138. Coan, *Life,* 158.
139. Baker, *Morning Stars and Missionary Packet,* np.
140. Baker, *Morning Stars and Missionary Packet,* np.
141. Baker, *Morning Stars and Missionary Packet,* np.

A slightly used combined sail and steam vessel was purchased. "She was described as 'about four years old, of wood, coppered, well-built, and thoroughly furnished.' Her length was 140 feet, over all, and thirty feet beam; her draft was nine and a half feet, and her tonnage 403. She was smaller than the fourth *Star* of 430 tons, or the steamer *Mikahala* of 444 tons, which many readers will remember in Hawaii. She had two masts, fitted with sails, for aid when winds favored, and she could readily steam ten or eleven knots an hour."[142]

A goal was set for two hundred thousand children to invest a dime each. It took longer to raise the money. Nevertheless, the *Morning Star* stayed in the Micronesian area and was supplied by ships from Hong Kong. But it only lasted one year. It was sold after some difficulty. "The *Star* was finally taken to the Coast and sold in 1908, although it was not officially voted to authorize the signing of the bill of sale to Hind, Rolph, and Co., Inc., until January 19, 1909. In 1910 she was seen in service between various ports in Puget Sound.

"Thus ended a half-entury of missionary *Stars*, 1856 to 1905. It does not seem possible that mission work in the Marquesas Islands and Micronesia could have survived without them. These *Morning Stars* have passed, but the influence of their service continues, not only in those distant islands but throughout the United States and Hawaii, where many a person today says proudly, as a result of lifelong missionary interest and enthusiasm, 'I owned shares in a *Morning Star.*'"[143]

"The *Stars* have passed, but the work goes on to this day, although we know nothing about it since the war. Articles by Willard Price, well illustrated and with unusually full maps, in *The Saturday Evening Post* of April 25, 1942, and in *The National Geographic Magazine* for June 1942 give an excellent idea of Micronesia. The latter magazine mentions our ABCFM work, with pictures of a native Christian minister of Truk and of the Baldwin sisters, who at that time had worked for forty years on Kusaie and 'were both over seventy years of age. Some of us had the pleasure of meeting the younger sister on her return home in March 1941, then over eighty. The older sister, who continued her work though blind, had died. The results of their work will endure."[144]

Baker wrote his article on all the *Morning Stars* while the Pacific War of World War 2 was still taking place.[145] "Printed in *The Friend* during its One Hundredth Year of Publication, 1942–43, by the Board of the Hawaiian Evangelical Association, Honolulu, Hawaii." Thus, it first appeared in the midst of the war.

---

142. Baker, *Morning Stars and Missionary Packet,* np.

143. Baker, *Morning Stars and Missionary Packet,* np.

144. Baker, *Morning Stars and Missionary Packet,* np.

145. The first printing was in February of 1945. A second printing was in 1945. Printed in Honolulu by the Honolulu-Star Bulletin, Ltd., 38 pages.

Admiral Chester W. Nimitz[146] wrote the Foreword to Baker's work. He notes that "Albert S. Baker has written an interesting account of the *Morning Stars* and of the men who 'combined theology with navigation.'

"Those *Morning Stars*, all five of them, were on missions of conquest even as we are today. The task of those men was outlined in Honolulu in 1870 at the Hawaiian Evangelical Association, where it was said, as reported by Secretary Clark of the American Board, 'Not with powder and balls and swords and cannons, but with the loving word of God and with his spirit do we go forth to conquer the islands for Christ.'" He relates the bittersweet nature of militarily liberating the islands the *Morning Stars* visited in peace. "Our duty in sailing on a mission of conquest is both fortunate and unfortunate. Fortunate because we know by taking those islands we are liberating a people who again will be able to practice the Christian virtues brought to them by those early missionaries. Unfortunate because we do this work with sword and gun, and swords and guns must bring death for some who go with us on this mission."

Earlier Nimitz had written: "Today it is our duty to follow the sea-trails of those *Morning Stars*, the trails left by those small brigs, barkentines, and steamers." He concludes with: "The days of those *Morning Star* missionaries were hard. They fought their tiny ships through heavy storms and heavy seas—and they had to fight the lassitude of nations governing Micronesian lands to do their work.

"But on Micronesian islands we have occupied we have seen the enduring evidence of that work. The men who sailed on those *Morning Stars* planted a seed of faith which the years and the cruel strain of Japanese conquest could not wither. We are proud to follow their trails."[147]

The legacy continues into the early twenty-first century, with the Conservative Congregational Christian Conference serving Micronesians on the Islands and beyond. Since the 1980s, there has been a Micronesia Committee. There is also a pastor teaching and training program appropriately named the "Morning Star Institute."[148]

These contemporary efforts overlap Coan's visits to the Marquesas Islands, as the next chapter will examine.

---

146. At the time, Commander in Chief for the US Pacific Fleet and Pacific Ocean Areas.
147. Nimitz, in Baker, *Morning Stars and Missionary Packets*, np.
148. Conservative Congregational Christian Conference, Micronesia.

11

Missions, Part 2

Two Trips to the Marquesas Islands

REMINISCENCES OF THE TWO visits made by Mr. Coan to the Marquesans, as delegate of the Hawaiian Board, are given in his *Life in Hawaii*. Extracts from the journal of his second voyage to that mission present vivid pictures of the scenes as witnessed.[1]

In 1860 Coan was one of a deputation of the Hawaiian Evangelical Association to visit the Marquesas Islands. The company departed aboard the *Morning Star*[2] on March 17 and returned to Honolulu on May 16, 1860.

In 1867 Coan made a second trip to the Marquesas on the *Morning Star*,[3] departing on April 3, 1867, and returning on June 10, 1867. The group also brought back the body of Joseph Tiiekai, a Marquesan chief, "and one of the first converts to Christianity on the islands" who had died in Honolulu, and was being returned for burial in "his native Fatuhiva."[4]

INTRODUCTION

As mentioned above, Titus Coan participated in two visits to the Marquesas Islands. As a delegate both times, he represented the Hawaiian Board of Missions.[5] Chapter XIII of his autobiography introduces the islands and discusses his first visit there in 1860. Chapter XIV of *Life* and VIII of the *Memorial Volume* cover the second visit. The

---

1. Coan, *Memorial Volume*, 103.
2. *Morning Star I*. See previous chapter.
3. *Morning Star II*. See previous chapter and citation/source below.
4. Forbes et al., *Partners in Change*, 186. Quotations under sources, *Partners in Change*, 187: Titus Coan, "The Marquesas Mission Report," *Supplement to The Friend*, June 1, 1860: 1–7; and "The first Missionary Trip of the New *Morning Star*," *Supplement to The Friend* (July 1, 1867): 57–64, quotation on 57.
5. Coan mentions the name in *Life*, 163.

autobiography provides the perspective of twenty years, while the *Memorial Volume* has contemporaneous writings of his visit.

Coan adds detail to Warren's description[6] of the Marquesas Islands. "The Marquesas Archipelago consists of thirteen islands, only six of which are inhabited." He lists the same ones that Warren does, then notes: "Seven are small islets or rocky piles of little importance."[7]

He also writes of the European discoveries of the islands. "The windward group was discovered in 1595 by Mendaña de Neyra, the commander of a Spanish squadron bound from Peru to colonize the Solomon Islands during the reign of Philip II of Spain, and was named Las Marquesas de Mendoza in honor of the Viceroy of Peru."

Despite their proximity, Coan relates how it was almost two hundred years before the rest of the islands were "discovered." "The leeward islands, though but a short distance off, were not discovered until 1791, nearly two hundred years later, when they were seen by Capt. Ingraham, of Boston, and named Washington Islands. But the term Marquesas now embraces both groups, as it properly should, the inhabitants being one in language, manners, and race."[8]

In the *Memorial Volume*, Lydia Bingham Coan writes in the Table of Contents at the beginning "Voyage to Micronesia" and near the end "General Meeting of Micronesian Mission,"[9] while the chapter title is "Voyage to the Marquesas" and the phrase "to the Marquesans" by Lydia is in the introductory paragraph.[10] Writing in Oma, Fatuiva,[11] Coan notes that the "general meeting of the mission was organized on the eleventh, and today the business of the meeting was taken up in earnest."[12]

Micronesia is southwest of the Hawaiian Islands, while the Marquesas are southeast. There are approximately 31 longitudinal degrees of difference and 10 latitudinal degrees of difference between one point of the Marquesas[13] and Pohnpei,[14] Micronesia. Therefore it appears that while the principals understood the distinction of the two island chains, there was some fluidity in reference.

He relates the geographical similarities between these islands and those of the Hawaiian Islands. "The origin of the group, like that of the Hawaiian, is distinctly igneous." The rest of the page provides more details on this matter.[15] He next turns to a description of the residents of the islands. "The inhabitants are of the Polynesian

6. See Warren, *Morning Star*.
7. Coan, *Life*, 159.
8. Coan, *Life*, 159–60.
9. Coan, *Memorial Volume*, ii.
10. Coan, *Memorial Volume*, 103.
11. A Marquesan island.
12. Coan journal entry, May 13, 1867, in Coan, *Memorial Volume*, 110.
13. Find Latitude and Longitude, "Marquesas Islands."
14. Maps of World, "Micronesia Lat-Long."
15. Coan, *Life*, 160.

race, and their language was originally the same as that of the Hawaiian and Society Islands, New Zealand, and other islands of the Polynesian archipelagoes.

"They are more bold, independent, fierce, and blood-thirsty than most of their neighbors, and they have always been cannibals of the most savage kind... They dress very little, and mostly in bark tapa,[16] like the ancient Hawaiians. They live in small thatched houses, and feed on cocoanuts, breadfruits, and fish." Coan notes that the people have been ravaged by western illnesses. "They were once numerous, but the introduction of foreigners and foreign diseases have wasted them so that they have been reduced more than two-thirds."[17]

Coan reports on the history of missionaries visiting this island chain. "In 1779 the English ship *Duff* took Messrs. Crook and Harris to the Marquesas as missionaries. The natives were fierce-looking and savage, and Mr. Harris preferred to return in the same vessel to Tahiti. Mr. Crook remained alone at the island of Tahuata about six months. He then went to Nuuhiva, where he lived six months more, and then returned in a whaleship to England, hoping to come back to the Marquesas with a reinforcement of missionaries. Eventually, however, he joined the mission at Tahiti."

He explains the brief tenure of the Society Island of Society Islands' indigenous Christians during the 1820s. "In 1821 two natives of the Society Islands were sent as missionaries to the Marquesas, but fearing the savages, they soon returned. In 1825 Mr. Crook revisited the Islands, leaving two Society Island Christians at Tahuata. These also soon returned, and were succeeded by others who remained but a short time."

An English missionary did not last long in the early 1830s. "In 1831 Mr. Darling, an English missionary of Tahiti, visited the group and left native teachers at Fatuiva and Tahuata. These, like their predecessors, had no success." The Hawaiian mission fared no better in the 1830s. "At length the Hawaiian mission took up the subject of evangelizing the cannibals of Marquesas. The first step was to send a delegation thither to examine the situation; and, in 1833, Messrs. [Richard] Armstrong,[18] [William] Alexander,[19] and [Benjamin] Parker,[20] with their wives, went to Taiohae, Nuuhiva, to labor for the good of the savages. But their situation was so uncomfortable, and the circumstances of the ladies and children so distressing, not to say dangerous, that

---

16. "Bark cloth, or tapa, is not a woven material, but made from bark that has been softened through a process of soaking and beating. The inner bark is taken from several types of trees or shrubs, often mulberry and fig, and designs are applied with paints and vegetable dyes of light brown, red, and black. Bark cloth is manufactured for everyday needs such as room dividers, clothing, and floor mats, as well as ceremonial uses in weddings and funerals." University of Oregon Museum of Natural and Cultural History, http://natural-history.uoregon.edu/collections/web-galleries/tapa-cloth.

17. Coan, *Life*, 161.

18. Forbes et al., *Partners in Change*, 72–80.

19. Forbes et al., *Partners in Change*, 51–56.

20. Forbes et al., *Partners in Change*, 499–504.

they all returned after eight months to the Hawaiian Islands, which were even then a paradise compared with the Marquesas."[21]

Coan relates the unsuccessful efforts of multiple missionaries being sent during the second half of the 1830s. Reviewing the entire mission outreach up to that time, Coan comments with regret that the "history of these efforts to tame the Marquesan cannibals is remarkable and the failure sad. For more than forty years company after company of devoted men and heroic women toiled and prayed for that stubborn race, and gave up in despair. And the history of these tribes is unique[22] among the Polynesian family."

Coan presents the arrival of Catholic missionaries, backed up by French naval efforts that "took forcible possession of the Islands" in 1842. He arrives at the efforts of the Hawaiian Mission Board, which in 1853 "sent out its first band of missionaries to those shores, and these have been reinforced from time to time, and have been visited and encouraged by delegates of our Board."

He indicates that the "first station was at Omoa, on the island of Fatuiva, the south-east island of the group. Afterward stations were taken on all the inhabited islands except Nuuhiva, where our American missionaries labored in 1833. As a delegate, I have been permitted to visit this Mission twice, and have seen every island and every station of the group."[23]

Having provided the background to the islands and the mission efforts, Coan arrives at a presentation of his first deputation to the Marquesas in 1860. His first visit was on *Morning Star I*; the second on *Morning Star II*.

1860

"My first visit was in 1860. We sailed from Hilo, March 17, in the *Morning Star No. I*, under command of Captain J. Brown, and anchored in Vaitahu, or Resolution Bay, Tahuata, April 11." Probably drawing from his journal and other sources, Coan writes that Resolution Bay "forms a quiet and safe harbor on the leeward side of the island. It is half a mile wide and half a mile deep, walled on the right and left by lofty and rugged precipices some two thousand feet high, with a beach of lava, sand, and shingle."[24]

He continues to describe the island and the people there: the "number of inhabitants upon Tahuata at the time of my visit was only 154, though it had once been several hundreds. We had one Hawaiian missionary with his wife in this valley, and they were laboring patiently in a small school, but with little encouragement. The people seemed hardened against Christianity, and no wonder, for in 1842 the French took possession of this bay, after having crushed the natives."

---

21. Coan, *Life*, 162.
22. Meaning the lack of response to Protestant missionary labors?
23. Con, *Life*, 163–64.
24. Coan, *Life*, 164.

Coan relates how the Marquesans bloodied the French before ultimately being subjugated. "The remains of the fallen sailors were carried up near the head of the valley and buried. With the Hawaiian missionary and Captain Brown, I visited the cemetery."[25] He writes rhetorical questions about missionaries and warfare. "Why should the professed disciples of the 'Prince of Peace' endeavor to propagate the Christian religion by the use of fire and sword? And why do men who call themselves 'priests of the Most High God' call in the aid of weapons, and go and come and live under the cover of cannon? Did the Captain of our salvation teach his disciples such doctrines?"[26]

Coan continues his narrative of travel by the delegation. From Vaitahu we went to Hivaoa[27] or La Dominica. The missionary at this station was the Rev. Samuel Kauwealoha,[28] a native of Hilo, and a member of the Hilo church."[29] Morris notes the high quality of missionaries of the Hawaiian Evangelical Society and the quality of Kauweahola as a person and his dedication to Christ. "When the Hawaiian Evangelical Society chose missionaries for the Marquesas, they took from the best of Hawaiʻi's new leaders. Samuel Kauwealoha had repeatedly turned down prestigious government offices in favor of ministerial work, and in refusing a district judgeship, he had written: 'In looking over the islands, I see many competent to fill the office you have offered me . . . There are not wanting those who, from my preference, are ready to fill all the offices in the gift . . . But I do not find those who are competent and willing to preach the gospel.'"[30]

Morris relates Robert Louis Stevenson's description of Kauweloha. In the late 1880s on Ua Poa, he used his "novelist's eye for style and detail." He "drew a portrait in words of the 'fine, rugged old[31] gentleman, of that leonine type so common in Hawaii.'[32] Stevenson also recorded a page of Kauwealoha's broken English ('One time a shippee he come from Pelu, he take away plenty Kanaka[33] . . . ')[34] but in doing so Stevenson perpetuated a false impression of Kauweahola. In his own language Kauweahola was a literate and eloquent observer of the Marquesan scene. Of

---

25. Coan, *Life*, 165–66.

26. Coan, *Life*, 166.

27. Hiva Oa is the second largest Marquesan island. Every Marquesan island reflects the early islanders' view that "the gods created Marquesas as their home. Therefore, all islands have names that are related with the building of a house; Hiva Oa means long ridgepole." Wikipedia, "Hiva Oa."

28. Forbes et al., *Partners in Change*, 399–401. See also Morris and Benedetto, *Nā Kahu*, 149–53 (including a full page image of a handwritten letter from Kauwealoha, as well as a photo on another page).

29. Coan, *Life*, 166.

30. Quoted in Loomis, *To All People*, 148, in Morris, "Hawaiian Missionaries Abroad," 341.

31. Born 1809, in Hilo, Morris, *Hawaiian Missionaries Abroad*, 341.

32. Stevenson, *In the South Seas*, 87; in Morris, *Hawaiian Missionaries Abroad*, 341.

33. People.

34. Stevenson, *In the South Seas*, 88–89, in Morris, *Hawaiian Missionaries Abroad*, 341.

the many reports he contributed over the years on the Marquesas of the last century several might be singled out as especially important for historians. One traces the introduction of Christianity to the Marquesas, and includes some unique insights of the Marquesans to the various missionaries.[35] Three others are valuable 1857 census reports[36] of three Marquesan Islands, Hiva Oa, Tahuata, and Ua Pou, including the name of chiefs in the various valleys of those three islands."[37]

Morris next shares about Kauwealoha's humility and Coan-like eloquence. His "congregations were not large, never over some twenty-five numbers, but he regarded them with a devotion rarely expressed by other missionaries. "'I was born in a *malo*,'[38] he wrote, 'and I may die in a *malo*. I was baptised in a *malo* and I can return to my *malo* and die in my *malo*, but I cannot abandon the people who I love more than my earthly kindred of my native land.'"[39]

Returning to Coan's narrative: "Kauwealoha came out in his boat, boarding us five or six miles from the shore, and gave us a most hearty welcome. We landed on a beautiful beach of white sand, and walked half a mile through a charming grove of tropical trees, along the margin of a crystal brook . . . It is a paradise of natural loveliness, charmed forever with the music of its rippling stream."[40]

Coan writes about Kauwealoha's home and ministry. "We found Mr. Kauwealoha living in a substantial stone house, twenty-five by forty-four feet, with walls ten feet high, a cellar, floor, glazed windows, and thatched roof, and all built by himself. He dived for the coral, burnt it into lime, hewed the blocks of basalt, made the mortar, and did all the work of the carpenter and mason. Here, amidst the shade of lofty trees, he was living with his devoted wife, teaching the children to read and write, and preaching 'Christ our Life' to 149[41] savages."

Coan shares about a joyful Sunday where he preaches and Kauwealoha translates. One can imagine his giving and receiving smiles that day. Here, "under the tree, with the bright-eyed little children in front, all seeming to love their teacher, and to welcome the stranger, to whom they listened, Kauwealoha interpreting. When service was over, they came forward with outstretched hands and glistening eyes and gave me their *Kaoha*, the same as the Hawaiian *Aloha*.[42]

---

35. Kaweaualoha to Oliver Pomeroy Emerson (Judd, *Missionary Album*, 94–95), February 18, 1891, Marquesan Mission Archives, HMCS, in Morris, *Hawaiian Missionaries Abroad*, 342.

36. "These documents are part of the Marquesan Archives, HMCS [HMH]," in Morris, *Hawaiian Missionaries Abroad*, 342.

37. Morris, *Hawaiian Missionaries Abroad*, 341–42.

38. Loincloth.

39. *The Friend*, Supplement to June 1860, 4, in Morris, *Hawaiian Missionaries Abroad*, 342.

40. Coan, *Life*, 166–67.

41. In 2012, the population of Hiva Oa was 2,190, of which 1,845 lived in the commune of Acounda and 345 in the village of Puama'u. Wikipedia, "Hiva Oa."

42. The Hawaiian and the South Marquesan languages both belong to the Polynesian family.

Coan describes three Marquesan worship services, one Sunday school and one English service. "One service was held at sunrise in the house; the next service under the tree, at 10 a.m., when sixty were present. We had also a Sunday-school, where the pupils recited the Lord's prayer and the ten commandments, with some other lessons, in tones and inflections of voice which were soft and melodious.

"At 11 a.m. Captain Brown and his mate, Captain Golett, a good Christian man, who had commanded many a ship, came on shore with the crew of the *Morning Star*, and we had service in English. At 4 p.m. another service was held with the natives, making four for the day, beside much time spent in conversation with those of the islanders who lingered around and seemed tame and docile."[43]

Coan describes the "wilder savages" who "would come up now and then to the outer side of our circle ... Some were armed." He relates that war "raged in this valley," with two fighting clans—one at each end of the valley. Despite the "Eden-like" beauty of the valley war did occur off and on. Coan relates that the coming of missionaries lessened the warfare, but that before 1867 "Kauwealoha's fine house was plundered and torn down, and he with his heroic wife fled the valley never to return. Thus the savages extinguished the rays of light which had begun to dawn upon them."[44]

Returning to 1860, Coan explains that on "Monday, April 16, we took our energetic friend, Kauwealoha, on board the *Star*, as my companion, guide, and interpreter, and sailed for the island of Fatuiva. At Omoa,[45] its largest and most populous valley, was the resident missionary, J. W. Kaivi."[46] Morris notes the tragic case of Isaiah W. Kaivi. "Despite a twenty-year sojourn in the Marquesas, little evidence of Isaiah Kaiwi's influence was apparent. When he wrote of the Marquesans to whom he ministered, it was with a note of bitterness and sense of futility ... [He] began to exhibit symptoms of a mental breakdown and fellow Hawaiian missionary Zachariah Hapuku brought Kaiwi to Hapuku's home at Atuona in order to care for him. His Hawaiian associates were sure that the cause of Kaiwi's insanity lay with the hostility of the Omo'a people toward Kaiwi. 'He is all right in a different place, but insane at Omo'a,' reported Samuel Kauwealoha[47]. There was a special cause for the coldness of the Omo'a people toward the missionaries. Seventeen of them had been transported to Hawai'i to be educated; most died. 'The people have not, and probably never will forget that painful

43. Coan, *Life*, 167–68.

44. Coan, *Life*, 168–69.

45. "The bay of Omo'a is the southernmost bay on the western coast of Fatu Hiva, and provides a good anchorage. The village of Omo'a was home to 247 inhabitants at the 2002 census. The village is home to the island's only Protestant church. The valley of Omo'a is well-watered, and curves in a half-moon shape, first to the southeast, and then to the northeast, terminating at the island's central plateau. This is where Thor Heyerdahl and his wife came ashore in 1937, an experience recorded in his book *Fatu Hiva*." Wikipedia, "Omo'a."

46. Coan, *Life*, 169. For Isaiah W. Kaiwi or J. W. Kaivi, see also Morris and Benedetto, *Nā Kahu*, 107–09.

47. Kauwealoha to Pogue, April 16, 1872, Marquesan Mission Archives, in Morris, *Hawaiian Missionaries Abroad*, 302.

circumstance,' reported the *Friend*, and they call the Hawaiian missionaries *he poe pepehe kanaka* (murderers of our people).[48]

"Insane and almost blind, Kaiwi continued to correspond with the Hawaiian Board in a pathetic, grossly-enlarged scrawl that at length forced the Board to dismiss him 'with aloha,' and to bring him home, where, it was hoped, his mental condition would improve. The 'cloud on his intellect' persisted and he was dead within a year after his return to Hawai'i. His widow Hana married a missionary to the Marquesas, Alexander Kaukau, after Kaukau's return to Hawai'i."[49]

Coan makes no mention of this Hawaiian missionary's struggle as he continues his narrative. "It was at this station that our pioneer missionaries were first landed, and here they labored together for a long time before they separated to occupy other islands. The fruits of these concentrated labors are seen in the greater tameness of the people, especially of the children."[50]

Coan next relates a touching scene with children.[51] This vignette is followed by adults joining in attending to the preaching of the gospel. "Not the children only, but many of the adults rallied around and filled the house, while scores remained outside for want of room within. My heart was touched by the scene, it was so different from that on Vaitahu, when powder and iron hail had driven the people of the valley to madness."

He describes the Omoa valley, followed by a trek up the valley. They are struck by the contrast of the beauty of the land with human idolatry and cannibalism. The "day after our arrival, Kaivi, Kauwealoha, Timothy,[52] one of my Hilo church members who accompanied me, took a stroll of four hours up the valley, and we were more and more delighted with its beauty and fertility. But we were everywhere pained with the marks of savage idolatry and cannibalism. The number and nature of the tabus were shocking. We saw tabu houses, tabu trees, tabu hogs, tabu tombs, tabu places for offering human sacrifices, and tabu theaters or places for lascivious dances, where with midnight drums and infernal howlings the most obscene orgies were performed." Coan goes into more detail about this matter. Kauwealoha relates to Coan his secret visits to these locations. "These and scores of other tabus have their histories of cruelty and horror which I can not here find time and space to explain. But what was uttered by a prophet of old is still true: 'The dark places of the earth are full of the habitations of cruelty'" [Ps 74:20].[53]

---

48. *The Friend*, July 1874, 64, in Morris, *Hawaiian Missionaries Abroad*, 302.

49. Morris, *Hawaiian Missionaries Abroad*, 302–03. See also Morris and Benedetto, *Nā Kahu*, 107–09.

50. Coan, *Life*, 169–70.

51. Coan, *Life*, 170.

52. For more on Enoch Semaia Timoteo, see Morris and Benedetto, *Nā Kahu*, 245–47.

53. Coan, *Life*, 171–72.

On a more positive note, Coan relates an examination at the Omoa mission school. "I spoke to parents and children on the salvation through Christ and on the value of education." He further passes along a communion service and the "first fruits" of the mission. "In the evening the little church of six members, together with the missionary Kaivi and his wife, and three from the *Morning Star*, partook of the Lord's Supper. "Here were some of the first-fruits of the gospel among the Marquesans. There sat the tall and dignified Natua, now baptized Abraham, with his quiet wife Rebecca. Abraham was a chief and a man of influence, and we hoped he might be the leader of many faithful disciples. The other members were Eve, a very aged woman, Joseph, Solomon, and his wife Elizabeth."

Coan contrasts the past life of these church members with their new life in Christ. "All these had eaten human flesh, and drank the blood of their enemies. They were now sitting at the feet of Jesus[Luke 10:39] and in their right minds [Mark 5:15], eating and drinking the emblems of that body which was broken, and that blood which was shed for man. It was a precious season, and one which may be remembered with joy during eternal ages."[54]

Coan provides a dialectic on the other hand when he writes about the gospel and war nature of "the large heathen party" of Omoa. "But notwithstanding the success which has attended the gospel and the school at Omoa, the large heathen party are still bloodthirsty cannibals, and always at war with the people in Hanavave, a valley five miles distant. The watchful belligerents kill and cook one another, whenever they can do it secretly."[55]

Coan boldly sails to "the hostile Hanavave in two of the ship's boats." Understandably, none of the residents of Omoa were willing to accompany him. He notes, however, that "our Hawaiian missionaries are safe and free to travel where they please, so Kaivi went with us." Coan relates conversations with bare-legged soldiers who were "strutting about with old muskets, rusty swords, and bayonets fastened on poles, and all seemed to feel as important as imperial guards." He returns to the *Morning Star* and sails "for Puamau, on the northern side of Hivaoa. This is the station of Rev. James Kekela and his good wife Naomi."[56]

Morris relates the prophetic chant sung at the time of Kekela's birth. "The chant composed to celebrate the impending birth of James Kekela prophesied that he 'would live in humbleness, walking quietly on a foreign shore to the south.' The foreign shore to the south is even specified: Nuuhiva. Fulfilling the prophecy, Kekela did visit and walk the sands of Nukuhiva (whose spelling is now rendered so), although he was stationed on the nearby islands of Fatuiva, and later, Hiva Oa."

---

54. Coan, *Life*, 172–73.

55. Coan, *Life*, 173.

56. Forbes et al., *Partners in Change*, 402–05. For more on James Hunnewell Kekela, see Morris and Benedetto, *Nā Kahu*, 158–66, including a family photograph in his later years.

Kekela would study at American Board schools sponsored by the first mate of the Pioneer company vessel, *Thaddeus*, James Hunnewell. Hunnewell, who had become a wealthy Boston merchant since 1820, continued to have a great interest in the Hawaiian mission. Out of gratitude for Hunnewell's support, Kekela—who had shortened his name from Kekelaokalani ("Kekela most high")—took Hunnewell's first and last name.

Kekela became a teacher. In 1852, he "accompanied a mission reconnaissance cruise to Micronesia. 'One of our most promising native preachers will accompany the expedition and bring back a report to the country of what he shall have seen and heard, that a deeper interest may be aroused in the native churches in this good work,' explained the *Friend*. Kekela wrote a long and perceptive letter about his Micronesian impressions, and clearly the seven-month trip shaped his decision to take up foreign mission work himself. What most impressed him were islanders long jaded by the debaucheries and greed of the Westerners but little exposed to schools and churches. White men enriched themselves by appropriating the only sources of wealth in the islands, coconut oil, but gave little back to the islands, Kekela noted."[57]

After returning from the scouting mission, Kekela lectured in all the churches on Oahu, Molaki, Maui, and Hawai'i. Drawing large crowds to his lectures, he "exhibited proof of the nakedness and wickedness' of the Micronesians," with physical examples of items he had brought back from his trip. "His preaching style was dramatic,[58] and embellished with such traditional Hawaiian gestures as the pulling back of one of his eyelids to denounce half-hearted Christians."[59]

Instead of Micronesia, Kekela would go as a missionary to the Marquesas Islands. "Within a month after the May 1853 appearance in Honolulu of the Marquesan chief Matuunui who visited Hawai'i's churches asking for missionaries, Kekela had joined the small group of Hawaiian volunteers destined for the Marquesan mission. The choice of Kekela was an indication that the Hawaiian churches were committed to sending their best ministers to the mission field, even if it meant depriving local congregations. As the first ordained Hawaiian minister, as delegate to Micronesia, and as a respected local minister, Kekela had earned considerable distinction. He and his wife made personal sacrifices for the mission, leaving behind aged parents and a young daughter, Maria."[60]

Coan describes Puamau as "a large valley with five hundred inhabitants. With Kekela and Kauwealoha, I went all over it to its head, two miles inland, where it terminates in an abrupt precipice two thousand feet high." He sees the great heiau, "or place of feasting, dancing, and of offering human sacrifices."[61] He notes that it "was to

57. Morris, *Hawaiian Missionaries Abroad*, 346–47.
58. Similar to Pua'iki and Coan?
59. *Missionary Herald*, 1852, 372, in Morris, *Hawaiian Missionaries Abroad*, 348.
60. Morris, *Hawaiian Missionaries Abroad*, 398.
61. See Coan journal entries in 1836 of a royal heiau where there is ample evidence of human

this place of infernal rites that Mr. Whalon, first officer of the American whale-ship *Congress*, was brought in 1864, bound hand and foot for slaughter, and to be devoured by savages."[62]

Whalon was tortured, but he was not murdered—after the intercession of the missionary Kekela. Finally an exchange was effected among the contending cannibals, and for a gun and various other articles Mr. Whalon was released. The missionary took him to his house, and with his intelligent wife showed him the greatest kindness and attention.

After President Lincoln heard about "this deed of Mr. Kekela and his helpers, he sent out the value of five hundred dollars, with a letter of congratulation, as a reward for the prompt and successful action which saved an American citizen from death at the hands of Marquesan cannibals."[63]

Morris calls Kekela's rescue of Whalon the psychological turning point of his missionary ministry. She also points out the role played by Marquesan leaders in effecting Whalon's release.[64]

Coan explains Kekela's ministry. "Kekela had only twenty-six pupils in all, and those were very irregular in their attendance. We spent a Sabbath at Puamau, and I preached to fifty people inside of the house, while numbers were standing or walking outside, some looking in at the windows, some pacing to and fro, talking, laughing," and so on.

Coan relates that he preached in the afternoon. "In the afternoon I preached to an assembly of one hundred, who sat quietly before me under a large tree." But there could be distractions, such as boys climbing trees and guns "often fired during the day, as well as the ring of the tapa-beater" and other pastimes.

In one sentence Coan writes something that grieved his heart: "There was no Sunday." He further indicates that the nearby Catholic priests "do little to create respect for the Lord's Day in the minds of the people."[65] Coan writes both of some encouragement and challenges. "Several individuals appeared interested in religious instructions, and we believe that faith and love and patient labor will not be lost upon this benighted people. But they are a hard race, bold, independent, and defiant."[66]

He describes indigenous government, as well as the customs of tattooing and shaving heads. "Their faces and bodies are so nearly covered with grotesque figures that they appear almost as black as Africans.

---

sacrifice.

62. Coan, *Life*, 173–77.
63. Coan, *Life*, 178–79.
64. Morris, *Hawaiian Missionaries Abroad*, 351–52.
65. Coan, *Life*, 179–80.
66. Coan, *Life*, 180.

Titus Coan: "Apostle to the Sandwich Islands"

"The shaving of their heads is equally grotesque and fantastic. Some shave only the crown, or one side; some leave a small tuft of hair on the apex only; others still shave several such belts."[67]

The next mission station Titus Coan visits is in the valley of Hanahi and is manned by Mr. James Bicknell.[68] He was a "son of one of the English missionaries of the Society Islands, [and] was stationed by his own request." Because there was no safe harbor there, Captain Brown sent Mr. Bicknell's supplies in a boat, in which Coan took passage. He notes that this "is a new station, with a population of only ninety souls, but there is a populous valley on each side of it. There was no school here, but Mr. Bicknell has one convert, whom he has baptized." Coan writes briefly of the Hawaiian missionary couple, the Reverend and Mrs. "A. Kaukau."

Coan relates a missionary and Marquesan convention that he attends. "All the missionaries of the three islands met in this place[69] to hold a convention. There were eight in all, with most of their wives and several delegates, representing three thousand Marquesans and reporting thirty-four church members, 221 pupils, seventy-six readers, forty writers, sixty-seven in the outlines of geography, and 104 in arithmetic. The chief woman of Kauwealoha's station labored over the lofty ridges on foot with her twenty-four girls to attend this convention and examination. As all canoes and boats are rigidly taboo to the women, they have no other way to leave their valley except to climb the rugged steeps, or swim around the cliffs and headlands, resting now and then by clinging to some jutting crag or rock along the sea-walls."

Coan writes about the girls who arrive for their school examinations. "These twenty-four bright-eyed girls were neatly robed in a profusion of thin white tapa, worn loosely and tied in a large knot on the shoulder. Their hair was gathered into a crown on the top of the head, and confined by bands and nets of tapa so thin and delicate as to resemble gauze. Many of them wore delicate ear and wrist ornaments made by the natives. This picture looked like the dawn of civilization, and was in delightful contrast with most of the scenes I had witnessed in the group."

After the completion of the school examination, the convention continued to meet. "After the examination of Kaukau's school of nine girls, we went on with the business of the convention, spending five days in deliberations and discussions on a great variety of practical questions, interspersed with frequent prayers. The meetings grew in interest from day to day, and the parting scene was touching. Every member of the convention offered prayer, and there was not a dry eye in the company."[70]

When the *Morning Star* party learned of a way to get supplies to a Hawaiian, Coan jumps at the opportunity. "Learning that a landing could be effected at Heteani,

---

67. Coan, *Life*, 180–81.

68. Forbes et al., *Partners in Change*, 103–04. For more on Kaukau, see Morris and Benedetto, *Nā Kahu*, 140–143.

69. The north side of Hivaoa, where the Kaukaus lived and served?

70. Coan, *Life*, 182–83.

on the south side of the island, where Paul Kapohaku, 'Paul the Rock,'[71] had been stationed, our captain agreed to return the missionaries to Fatuhiva, and then sail round the eastern end of Hivaoa, and lie off and on opposite Heteani, while I with Bicknell, Kapohaku, and his wife, should climb the heights of the mountain, some 3,500 feet, to visit that lone station where he would send in his boat to receive me on board."[72]

Coan details his climb and, as Renaissance man,[73] he compares a measurement of ridges with a writing by Charles Darwin. "Our path led up steep and sharp ridges, down which on either hand we looked into depths of five hundred or one thousand feet below. I measured the breadth of the spur or rib on which we ascended; it was two feet and four inches wide in one part of the way; in another it was only one foot in width, with awful gorges on either side. Mr. Darwin, describing a similar climb which he took in the island of Tahiti, says: 'I did not cease to wonder at these ravines and precipices; when viewing the country from one of the knife-edged ridges, the point of support was so small that the effect was nearly the same as it must be from a balloon.'[74] The extraordinary sharpness of these ridges and abruptness of these mountain slopes may be accounted for by the absence of violent storms in these groups, and more especially by the fact that there is never any frost to disintegrate these sharp ridges and fine-drawn peaks."[75]

Coan writes that the grueling climb is rewarded by a transfixing view. "The scene from this height was grand in the extreme. At our feet lay the broad Pacific, shining like molten silver, and from this elevation showing no ripple. Around us was a vast panorama of cones, ridges, spurs, and valleys . . . It was a wild assemblage of hills and ridges, of gulfs and chasms, of towers and precipices."

They descend and arrive at the shore, "safe and weary at 4 p.m." The people of Heteani welcome the small party enthusiastically. "Paul" shows proof of cannibalism on this side of the island as being "fearful." On May third, the *Morning Star* picks up Coan and the rest of the party. The next day they "were off the mouth of the spacious harbor Taiohai, the principal harbor of Nuuhiva."

Coan writes about how the French kept a fortified garrison for many years. They see the house where the three American Board missionaries lived for eight months in 1833. Coan explains that the tabu system of "the Marquesas Islands, as in other parts of Polynesia, is ancient, complex, and deeply rooted in the social and religious polity

---

71. See Morris, *Hawaiian Missionaries Abroad,* 328, where she lists his education as "not in any school, but by 'the word of God and the Holy Spirit.' Kapohaku's intellectual forte was knowledge of the Bible. He read carefully the Bible four times, and he committed to memory many passages, with which he embellished his simple sermons. His speaking style was legendary and charismatic." See also Morris and Benedetto, *Nā Kahu,* 130–31.

72. Coan, *Life,* 183.

73. See "Renaissance Man" section, including chapter on science.

74. Charles Darwin, no citation, in Coan, *Life,* 184.

75. Coan, *Life,* 183–84.

of the people." He provides a "few notes . . . on the subject."[76] He concludes with, "It will be seen from the above, that the subjection and servitude of women are a principal feature of the tabu."

"Returning on board the *Star*, we bore away around the western side of Nuuhiva, looking into all the valleys and dells as they opened one after another to our view." He shows that he is well-read when he refers to the location for a well-known American novel. "Among others, we passed the famed valley of Taipi (Typee), the scene of Herman Melville's narrative drawn from life."[77]

Coan relates his return to Hilo and provides some statistics, as he was wont to do. "Bearing away for Hawaii, we dropped anchor in Hilo on the sixteenth of May, having been absent just two months.

"On this visit to the Marquesas I gathered, from the reports of the missionaries at their general convention, the following statistics." The missionaries had access to 2,800 members of the population. The total number of church members was thirty-four. The whole number of pupils, "more or less," under missionary instruction, 221.

He puts these numbers in perspective. "These results, though on a small scale, seemed encouraging, compared with the long, repeated, and unfruitful efforts which had been made before, and there seemed hope that, by patience and perseverance, many of these savages might be tamed, and the diabolical and bloody rites which had been practiced from time immemorial be utterly abolished."

He gives the French some credit for the benefits of the rule of law, as well as "liberal" individual administrators. "The laws enacted and enforced by the French governors in the Marquesas have checked murders and cannibalism wherever they could be brought to bear upon the guilty. And some of the governors have been liberal in their sentiments, and willing that the savages should be tamed and Christianized by any who would undertake the self-denying task."[78]

Coan's respect for Catholics in the Marquesas will be evident during his next visit to that island group.

1867

Lydia Coan adds to Coan's autobiography account of his 1867 visit to the Marqueseas by publishing journal entries in the *Memorial Volume*. While Coan no doubt drew from his journal to write the chapter, the combination of contemporary and reflective observations provides another dimension of insight to this sojourn. The complementary nature of journal and autobiography are evident in the discussion of whom went on his journey. The journal entry is "*Morning Star, April 3, 1867.*—'We left Hilo this day on a missionary voyage to the Marquesas. On board, Rev. H. Bingham, Jr., master

---

76. Coan, *Life*, 153.
77. Melville's first published work, *Typee*, 1845.
78. Coan, *Life*, 190–91.

and wife ... Rev B[enjamin] W[yman] Parker and T. Coan, delegates of Hawaiian Board ... Twenty-six all told."[79]

Perhaps Lydia omits what Coan wrote in his autobiography, including complete sentences "On the third of April 1867 I embarked again, on board the *Morning Star No. 2*, [to] revisit our Marquesas mission. The *Star* was commanded by the Rev. Hiram Bingham, Jr., who had brought her out from Boston, and who was still [sic?] her captain."

In the autobiography, Coan also reports the sad duty being carried out by the *Morning Star*. "We also had on board the body of Joseph Tiietai, one of the first converts of Omoa, who had died at Honolulu while on a visit there."[80] Coan further explains Joseph's presence in Hawai'i and that of others. "In 1865 Mr. Bicknell left the Marquesas and returned to Oahu, bringing with him seventeen Marquesans, male and female, in order to train them on the Hawaiian Islands, and then return them to teach their people. Of these seventeen, nine died[81] within two years, and the eight who survived were anxious to return to their old homes. We therefore took them on board. They were all baptized before they left Oahu, Mr. Bicknell recommending them as converts to Christianity."

He relates the death of someone while on the voyage. "Meto, the wife of one of the returning Marquesans, died after a sickness of several weeks, professing her faith in Jesus." He explains the burial and sea, where "the remains of the poor woman were committed to the deep, to be seen no more until 'the sea shall give up her dead'" [Rev 20:13]. Coan writes how this was the first at-sea burial he had witnessed.[82] He concludes his discussion of Meto with his resurrection hope for her. "Thou wast once blind, and a savage, but 'the day-spring from on high' dawned upon thee ere thou wast called away and we have for thee that thou wilt appear a shining angel [sic?] among the joyous throng who have been redeemed from among all nations and kindreds and peoples and tongues."[83]

In his autobiography, he calmly writes, "On the twenty-first of April we made the Paumotu Archipelago."[84] He is more exuberant in his journal: "*April*, 21—'Land ho!' rang from our decks at dawn this morning. Light winds, calms, and a three-knot current have set us far west of our course, and we are among the Paumotu group, named by Bougainville, Dangerous Archipelago. Two beautiful islands are within two miles of us, called King George's Isles."

---

79. Coan journal entry, April 3, 1867, in Coan, *Memorial Volume*, 103.

80. Coan, *Life*, 192.

81. In the previous chapter, see the negative view of the missionaries held by the fellow islanders of those who died.

82. Coan, *Life*, 193.

83. Coan, *Life*, 194.

84. Coan, *Life*, 194.

Titus Coan: "Apostle to the Sandwich Islands"

Coan is the pen painter as he describes the Sabbath vista. "The sight of these on this bright Sabbath morning was truly charming. The shores are one continuous belt of white coral sand, kissed by the blue rippling wavelets. Within this encircling zone is a garland of evergreens, composed of the cocoanut, pandanus, kou, and various shrubs and grasses, so intertwined as to form a beautiful coronal of tropical green on the brow of Neptune.[85] Enclosed by this fadeless wreath is the quiet lagoon, bathed in silver sunbeams and rippling upon its shores. After an enchanting view of this gem of the Pacific, the *Star* went about and stood off from the land. We looked with a sigh for the dark dwellers on these bright islets."[86]

Coan is the Renaissance man as he lists every Western discoverer, with year, in the autobiography. After writing about "the beautiful islets resting like swans upon the smooth water," he notes that different "islands of this archipelago were discovered by different navigators and at various times: by Quinos, in 1606; Maire and Schouter, in 1616; Roggewein, in 1722; Byron, in 1765; Wallis and Carteret, in 1767; Cook, in 1769, 1773, and 1774; Bougainville, in 1763; Boenecheo, in 1772 and 1774; Edwards, in 1791; Bligh, in 1792; Wilson, in 1797; Turnbull, in 1803."

He next lists those who made later "and more careful observations . . . on this beautiful group" by the likes of "Kotzebue, in 1816; Bellingshausen, in 1819; Deuperry, in 1823; Beechey, in 1826; Fitzroy, in 1835; and Wilkes, in 1841." Referring to the leader of the US Exploring Expedition after it had visited Hilo, Coan objectively relates Wilkes's estimated population of ten thousand. "The people were represented as in a semi-savage state." In contrast to the volcanic islands observed in 1860, Coan says that these "islands are all of coral formation, and were built up by that silent and wonder-working architect, the so-called coral insect."[87]

He laments that the people of these islands do not have someone to share the gospel with them. He contrasts the beauty of the islands with the dark moral picture. "Our view of these islands, garlanded with green, and shining under a tropical sky, was enchanting, but the moral picture was dark. Why are these thousands of immortal beings left to perish in ignorance, poverty, and paganism?"[88]

On April 29, Coan describes the valley of Hakahekau. While describing the natural beauty of the valley, he laments the lack of people in this location. "It was mournful, as we strolled up this beautiful and rich vale, to mark the silence and desolation

---

85. Mythological god of the sea.

86. Coan journal entry, April 21, 1867, in Coan, *Memorial Volume*, 103–04.

87. Coan, *Life*, 194. Wikipedia writes the following about the coral polyp: "The name polyp was given by René Antoine Ferchault de Réaumur to these organisms from their superficial resemblance to an octopus (Fr. *poulpe*, ultimately from Greek adverb πολύ (poly, "much") + noun πούς (pous, "foot")), with its circle of writhing arms around the mouth. This comparison contrasts to the common name "coral-insects" applied to the polyps which form coral." Wikipedia, "Polyp."

88. Coan, *Life*, 195.

that reined there." Lydia places an asterisk at this point with the notation: "In 1863 about seven-tenths of the population died of smallpox."[89]

Lydia presents less than one page on Hakahekau, perhaps because in the autobiography Coan devotes three pages to the visit. He relates the Hawaiian missionary enthusiastically welcoming the deputation. Coan describes with great detail the challenges of safely mooring in the harbor. Once ashore a service is held at the missionary's house. He goes into great detail on the grandeur and beauty of the natural features of the area. He then goes into detail about the smallpox epidemic. After writing in detail about the empty heiaus, he again makes a lamentation, followed by prayerful hope. "Those baleful fires are extinguished, and the voice of revelry is hushed in death. But, alas! Darkness still broods over the few who remain on this island. We will, however, hope and pray for brighter days."[90]

On April 30 at "4 p.m., we were at the entrance of Taiohae, the principal harbor of Nuuhiva. A French pilot brought us to anchor at 5 p.m. Two English gentlemen came on board and spent the evening." Coan contrasts the cannon salute by a French bark with the absolute peace nature of the *Morning Star*. "A French bark, the *Tampico*, had come in the day before. The captain set his flag and fired us a salute of one gun. The latter compliment we were unable to return, as we have not seen fire-arms or smelt powder on board the *Morning Star*."[91]

In his autobiography, Coan writes more[92] about Herman Melville and his time in Taipi, which became the published work *Typee*. He also writes about his visit the Catholic bishop and the French nuns.[93] In his journal he again alludes to the depopulation through illness and the resulting sale of land to a company "to commence plantations of cotton and coffee," as well as the French forts being abandoned. The jetty and other improvements are being reclaimed by nature, "fast going to decay." He continues his inveterate scientific observations. "I measured a banyan [tree] and found its circumference to be eighty-five feet, while its umbrageous boughs covered a circle of some six hundred feet."[94]

On May 3, the Hawaiian "missionaries, Laioha and his wife,[95] welcomed us to their thatched cottage, and the people were called together by the sound of the horn. Donning their light tapas, they came streaming in from all the jungle trails of the valley, bringing their children for examination. Boys, girls, and adults gathered around

---

89. Coan journal entry, April 29, 1867, in Coan, *Memorial Volume*, 104.

90. Coan, *Life*, 195–98.

91. Coan journal entry, April 30, 1867, in Coan, *Memorial Volume*, 104–05. To have defensive weapons or not has been a long-time question for missionaries. It is the difference of Ezra (who did not accept an escort of armed king's soldiers) and Nehemiah (who did).

92. As he did in 1860.

93. Coan, *Life*, 200–01. This amicable visit is discussed in the "Other Religion" chapter.

94. Coan journal entry, April 30, 1867, in Coan, *Memorial Volume*, 105–06.

95. For more on J. W. and Hannah (Eva) Ihuanu Laioha, see Morris and Benedetto, *Nā Kahu*, 182.

us with beaming faces, grasping our hands and saluting us with their melodious 'Kaoha.' Thirty-two pupils were examined, after which we held religious services, and celebrated the Lord's Supper as was our habit at the various stations."[96]

Morris summarizes Laioha's life and labors. His was a troubled tenure. "Misfortune dogged Laihoa's mission. Soon after the arrival of the family, both Kekela and Kauwealoha[97] . . . reported to Honolulu that Eva Laioha was possessed by 'an evil spirit.' Laioha drew apart from his co-workers and made his own decisions as to the locations of his mission stations. He drew criticism from the home office for moving too often and for poor results.[98] Angered by the criticism, Laioha threatened to join the Catholic mission."[99]

Laioha agreed to resign under pressure from the visiting John Pogue in 1869. He became an overseer for a "cotton plantation at Taipi Valley." He bragged about his relative wealth to missionary acquaintances. Ultimately dismissed by his employer, American Board missionary William Alexander said that he was an "object lesson of the folly of vanity." His children would live as Marquesans, "tattooed, their bodies smeared with olena (turmeric), and dressed in bark cloth."[100]

Returning to his narrative, Con writes that we "then returned to the *Star*, taking with us Laioha, and Jose, a Peruvian whom I had baptized at Puamau in 1860, when he took the name of David."[101]

Coan provides background for the life and labors of David Jose between 1860 and 1867. "The history of this David Jose after his baptism was interesting. Desiring to labor for Christ, he went of his own accord in 1863 to Hooumi, a valley adjoining Taipi, on Nuuhiva, where he labored earnestly and without pay to convert the people to Christ, working with his own hands to supply his bodily wants. He collected thirty pupils, who were greatly attached to him, and for whom he had high hopes."

Then the scourge of illness hit. "Soon the small-pox struck the people with the blast of death. Consternation seized the multitude, and leaving friends and relatives to their fate, many fled to the mountains or wherever else they might hope for shelter. And faithful David had forty cases under his care with no one to help him. Of these, twenty died, and he buried them all with his own hands. He labored on until 1866, when the French sold the valleys of Hooumi, Taipi, and Hapa, adjoining one another, to a company who ordered David to leave."[102]

In his journal, Coan relates the 1867 visit at Hakatu. Laioha "has a school of thirty-two pupils; they were examined in reading, writing and in lessons committed to

---

96. Coan, *Life*, 201.
97. See above for descriptions of both missionaries.
98. The two are probably related.
99. Morris, *Hawaiian Missionaries Abroad*, 365.
100. Morris, *Hawaiian Missionaries Abroad*, 365.
101. Coan, *Life*, 201.
102. Coan, *Life*, 201–02.

memory. After examination we held a meeting with the people, when many addresses were made and Captain and Mrs. Bingham sang 'Happy Land,'[103] in the Gilbert Island language. This pleased the natives greatly."[104]

The May 6 journal entry relating the arrival in Hanamenu is the basis for the same event described in the autobiography. He vividly portrays the reuniting of the Marquesans with family and friends who had journeyed from Oahu. "On landing with six Marquesans . . . the whole valley was alive and the beach thronged with people. Fathers, mothers, grandparents, brothers, sisters, all the kith and kin of the exiles came down to the shore, and the weeping, wailing, rubbing of noses, kissing and embracing were affecting. Soon the breadfruit began to fall, the pigs to squeal, and the ovens to smoke. A feast was prepared with surprising rapidity, and it seemed joyful as at the return of the lost and dead prodigal" [Luke 15:11–32].[105]

The next day he relates the formation of a church. "This morning we organized a Christian church at Hanamenu, consisting of ten members. After this the Lord's Supper was administered for the first time in this place. At 11 a.m. we bade our six fellow-passengers from Hawaii, our ten Christian brethren and sisters in Christ, and the mixed multitude which gathered around, an affectionate and sincere farewell, and returned to the packet." In regards to the *Morning Star,* he writes, "How faithfully this dear vessel waits on our ministrations and administers to our wants."[106]

Arriving at Puamau on May 8, the Hawaiian missionary reports that the war is over and that it "had demoralized his people. He had no church, his school was broken up, his congregation dispersed, his pits and potatoes were stolen, his mules and donkey killed and eaten," and many more depredations.[107]

On May 9 they arrived at Auona. Coan wonders at the "massive piles of rock" and laments the limits of pen painting. "They are masses of confused harmony, defying all

---

103. The first verse of Andrew Young's "The Happy Land":

> There is a happy land,
> Far, far away,
> Where saints in glory stand,
> Bright, bright as day;
> O how they sweetly sing,
> Worthy is our Saviour King,
> Loud let His praises ring,
> Loud let His praises ring,
> Praise, praise for aye.

Hymnary.org, "The Happy Land."

104. Coan journal entry, May 3, 1867, in Coan, *Memorial Volume,* 106.
105. Coan journal entry, May 6, 1867, in Coan, *Memorial Volume,* 107.
106. Coan journal entry, May 6, 1867, in Coan, *Memorial Volume,* 107.
107. Coan, *Life,* 204–05.

the art of the limner,[108] the pen and ink painter, and the descriptive powers of man."[109] Because the waves were too strong to get on shore, David Jose, the Peruvian, swam ashore. He found the Hawaiian missionary Hapuku,[110] who "dove into the raging surf like a porpoise, and soon came dripping into our boat."

He guided them to a nearby bay where they landed. Coan observes that this "is, perhaps, the richest valley we have seen ... Our pathway from the beach to Hapuku's house was an avenue cut through the hibiscus, the cotton and other plants, and impervious to the sun. Seventeen scholars and about fifty people came out on short notice, and we examined the school. It was perfectly quiet and attentive, and appeared well. Several of the scholars sang hymns sweetly. We preached, then baptized three adults and three children, organized a church of five, and returned to the ship after three hours at the station."[111]

Morris indicates an at best checkered time of service by Zachariah Hapuku. He was stationed there all forty years of service from 1861 until his death in 1901. He claimed to have had about thirty church goers, all of which he had a negative view of. There were reports that he involved himself in the fighting that took place in the area where he lived. See the "Peace" chapter with input from Morris on this matter. He did not do much to open boarding schools.

Morris concludes her summary of the life and labors of Hapuku, who did live to assist Kaivi/Kaiwi during his difficult times[112] with this paragraph: "In 1894 the Hawaiian Board dismissed Hapuku from the mission, charging that Hapuku had sought the services of a Marquesan 'witch-doctor' to cure an illness of his daughter. Hapuku remained in the Marquesas, carrying on his work, and the Board reinstated him in 1897. Hapuku's associates in the Marquesas, James Kekela and Samuel Kauwealoha of the Marquesan mission, are well-remembered today in mission annals as missionary heroes, but probably because of the witch-doctor incident, Hapuku's forty-year career is largely neglected in church-sponsored literature."[113]

The *Morning Star* traveled on to Omoa, where it remained for five days. Sunday, May 12, passed much the same way as it would in Hilo or the Puna district. We "sat up until midnight to converse with the people who came in, to examine candidates for the church, and Mr. Hapuku for ordination. On the morrow the ordination took place; seventeen candidates were baptized and received to the church on profession of faith, and one by letter. Ten had been received before, making the whole number

---

108. "A limner is an illuminator of manuscripts, or more generally, a painter of ornamental decoration." Wikipedia, "Limner."
109. Coan journal entry, May 8, 1867, in Coan, *Memorial Volume*, 109.
110. For more on Zachariah Hapuku, see Morris and Benedetto, *Nā Kahu*, 73–74.
111. Coan journal entry, May 8, 1867, in Coan, *Memorial Volume*, 109–10.
112. See above.
113. Morris, *Hawaiian Missionaries Abroad*, 278–79.

gathered into this church twenty-eight. Of these four had died. The Lord's Supper was then administered to about forty communicants, representing seven nationalities."[114]

In his journal entry for Omoa, Coan focuses on the General Meeting of missionaries, about which he had also reported in 1860. "The general meeting of the mission was organized on the eleventh, and today the business of the meeting was taken up in earnest. All the brethren read written and full accounts of their stations and labors for the last two years. Some of these reports were deeply interesting. The subject of Boarding Schools engrossed much attention, and it was resolved to establish at once a school for girls at Puamau, and one for boys at Hakanahi. For the purpose the delegates placed two hundred dollars in the hands of the appointed teachers. It is hoped the schools will be in a great measure self-supporting."

Coan expresses confidence that the Christian Americans and others in Hawai'i will help support this endeavor. He writes about the positive nature of the Marquesan Christians. "We feel sure that the benevolent ladies and gentlemen of the Hawaiian Islands will rejoice to contribute enough to clothe these sons and daughters of the Marquesas, and to rescue them from the dreadful darkness of heathen cannibalism. I have rarely seen more perfect specimens of physical organization or brighter faces and more active minds than among these children. Many of them are beautiful, in spite of their . . . sad surroundings, and it is painful to leave them, bright and blithesome as they are, to the horrors that await them if they are not soon redeemed from the deep darkness which covers them."[115]

On May 16, Coan and Bingham II helped load the Hanave missionary's goods onto the *Morning Star* for his return to Hawai'i.[116] Returning to Puamau on May 19, they returned Kekela and his family to their station. "Brother Parker, the native missionaries, and myself came on shore to hold service. More than a hundred people collected under the trees, to whom we preached the gospel of the Kingdom."[117]

On May 21, with the vessel poised to leave the Marquesas and return to Hawai'i, Captain Bingham calls together everyone on the *Morning Star* for a celebratory service. "Having landed Kauwealoha at Hakatu, Capt. Bingham called all hands off, spoke of the mercy of God in thus bringing our work at the islands to a happy close, and proposed prayer and thanksgiving. This offered, we sung the stanza, 'Waft, waft, ye winds, his story,' etc., followed by three hearty cheers; when our sails were trimmed and the noble *Morning Star* turned her prow toward the Hawaiian Islands. Our vessel seems to feel the inspiration of heaven, and, like a fleet steed homeward bound, she makes through the water at the rate of ten knots, dashing the white foam from her head and sides."

---

114. Coan, *Life*, 205.
115. Coan journal entry, May 13, 1867, in Coan, *Memorial Volume*, 109–11.
116. Coan journal entry, May 16, 1867, in Coan, *Memorial Volume*, 111–12.
117. Coan journal entry, May 19, 1867, in Coan, *Memorial Volume*, 112–13.

Titus Coan: "Apostle to the Sandwich Islands"

Titus Coan concludes his journal entry on his second journey to the Marquesas Islands with praise for the ship, crew, and his Savior. "The *Morning Star* is a noble vessel, well-modeled, well-built, well-furnished and well-appointed. Altogether she is the neatest and most comfortable vessel of her size in which I have ever sailed . . . The officers and crew have treated us with uniform kindness, and in all things we have been blessed, greatly blessed of our divine Lord and Master, and to him be all glory and praise forever."[118]

Coan's missionary heart continues to beat in his autobiography. Looking back from the perspective of over ten years, he shares mixed results and hopes for more missionaries to go to the Marquesan mission field. "The commencement of our work there was auspicious, and its progress and fruits were encouraging, more so than of the mission to the Society Islands, or to China, or to many other parts of the world.

"But as it is said in Scripture, 'The destruction of the poor is his poverty' [Prov 10:15], so we must say of our work. And this is the wail over all the earth, want of laborers to gather the harvest [Matt 9:37], and want of material means to give strength, courage, and due success to the weary toilers in the field. Our three missionaries in the Marquesas are doing what they can, and there is still encouragement that war, idolatry, and cannibalism would soon cease, could we but continue the gospel work among that people."[119]

Titus Coan was passionate about bringing the gospel to Hawaiians, Marquesans, and Micronesians. The next chapter will exhibit a similar passion for those who come to Hawai'i's shores from throughout the world, those who are now called "expatriates."

---

118. Coan journal entry, May 21, 1867, in Coan, *Memorial Volume*, 113–14.
119. Coan, *Life*, 211–12.

12

Expatriate Ministry

"The grand business of Mr. Coan's life has been to preach the gospel among the Hawaiians, and right nobly has he performed his life-work. But he had broad sympathies, which led him to labor efficiently for his fellow-men of all races, so far as they were brought under his influence. For many years he has been a most efficient seamen's chaplain. Assisted by the Rev. Mr. Lyman, a chaplaincy was sustained at Hilo, by their voluntary, well-directed efforts, which for usefulness equaled almost any chaplaincy in any other part of the world.

"Upon this subject I can speak with great freedom and assurance, for during the past forty years I have been in the most intimate correspondence with Mr. Coan. I feel sure the spiritual interests of seamen attached to the whaling fleet and vessels of war could not have been more thoughtfully cared for if a chaplain had been sent out from America or England for this special field of labor; yet this extra service was discharged with the most hearty cheer and thoughtful consideration. Many masters, officers, and seamen must have good reason to bless God to all eternity that they touched at Hilo in their long voyages, and came under the happy influence of Mr. Coan and other resident missionaries at that port."[1]

"When ships were in port we often had a full house, and not a few hearers professed a determination to forsake all sin and live godly lives. Of some we afterward learned, either by their own letters or otherwise, that they had kept their vows and united with Christian churches, and that some had become ministers of the gospel."[2]

"But, my work is chiefly among the natives. All I can do for seamen is extra and incidental; robbed, as it were, from the people to whom we are consecrated. With a rough and toilsome parish of more than one hundred miles in length, and a multitude of people constantly on my heart, I can only labor for seamen under heavy

---

1. From Damon, "In Memoriam" chapter, in Coan, *Memorial Volume*, 215–16.
2. Coan, *Life*, 65.

pressure … After four services for the natives, I preach once a Sabbath to foreigners in English, including to sailors and officers."[3]

"We were at once ready to help in this important work. Masters, officers, and sailors were made welcome to our house; books and tracts were provided for them to take to sea, and a religious service was held for them every Sunday afternoon. For many years this service was held in one of the houses of the missionaries. Finally, we fitted up the old stone-building, our first home, for a Bethel, and added a library of about two hundred volumes, with periodicals."[4]

INTRODUCTION

Titus Coan had a passion to reach every person with the gospel of Christ. After his calling to serve the Hawaiian people, Coan stretched every nerve to minister to sailors, seamen, visitors, and, increasingly over the years, non-Hawaiians who came to live and work in the Hilo area.

Ehlke notes that he "knew the difficulties and hardship of their life aboard ship, the temptations and lack of Christian opportunities in the ports, and had great sympathy for the men as they risked life and limb to bring in the great whales, trade with distant lands, and conduct naval explorations in the Pacific. He prayed with them, counseled them and urged them to turn to Jesus Christ in their hour of peril."[5]

A Sunday afternoon service in English existed before his arrival during the second half of 1835. He preached there before he ventured to proclaim in Hawaiian. When he first arrived, Hilo was a backwater as is evident in the lack of correspondence the Coans felt. The number of visiting sailors and seamen increased, especially after the California Gold Rush began in 1849.

As a mentor and example in ministry to sailors, seamen, and nautical officers, Coan looked to the Reverend Samuel Chenery Damon,[6] who served them as the Chaplain of the American Seamen's Friend Society for a little over fifty years. While the primary title of the 1992 book about Damon is *Seamen's Chaplain*,[7] only one

---

3. Coan letter, October 6, 1857, in *Sailors Magazine* 29 (1857). 184.
4. Coan, *Life*, 64.
5. Ehlke, "Enthusiastic Religion," 144.
6. Forbes et al., *Partners in Change*, 206–210.
7. Damon, *Seamen's Chaplain*. On xii, Gavan Daws is identified as the co-author with the compiler. The volume also includes a Foreword by John Dominis Holt; a Preface by the four-member editorial committee, all Damon descendants; "Centennial Reflections" and "Damon [Family] Memorial" by Samuel C. Chenery. There is also a quaint period piece from the "Pacific Commercial Advertiser," October 13, 1866, nv, 122–24, entitled "A Silver Wedding," reporting on the celebration by many of the Chenery's twenty-fifth wedding anniversary. Money was raised and the couple was surprised with silver settings. "Beyond the congratulations of their friends during the day, we believe the worthy Seamen's Chaplain and his wife knew nothing of the singular proceedings on foot. About 6 ½ p.m., as they were seated quietly by their evening lamp, thinking, perhaps, that their friends *might* have done something had they only thought of it in time, two of their parishioners, a lady and gentleman,

chapter is entitled "Seamen." Nevertheless, Damon's passion to reach seamen is woven throughout the chapters of the book.

The editorial committee identifies the origin of the book as being based upon "a suggestion made in 1990 by Andrew M. Damon that an essay on Samuel C. Damon, his great-great-grandfather, be written for the celebration of the one hundred fiftieth anniversary of Samuel and Julia [Sherman Mills] Damon's[8] arrival in Hawaii on October 19, 1842."[9] The opening sentence of the Introduction's second paragraph explains what the book is *not*. "This book is not a biography in the conventional sense—no attempt has been made to detail the events of Damon's life as they unfolded."[10] The co-authors credit Ethel M. Damon's sixteen-years-prior biography for that form of biography. "Indeed a biography, *Samuel Chenery Damon*,[11] has already been written by Damon's granddaughter Ethel M. Damon."[12]

Instead, the 1992 "essay" with other material helps the reader see the forest for the trees. It "is a portrait in words, an analysis of the character of Samuel C. Damon. It seeks to illuminate some of the influences that created him and what he in turn tried to make of himself and the world as he found it." The authors indicate the depth of Damon's passion and ministry. "Although Damon spent most of his life as a chaplain in the distant kingdom of Hawaii, it would be a mistake to infer from this fact that his was therefore a placid pastoral existence. Damon was an extraordinarily active

---

dropped in, and after congratulating them on their twenty-fifth wedding anniversary, told them it would be well to prepare for their friends . . . and requested the privilege of taking possession of their dining room . . .

"At half-past seven the door of the *tabooed* apartment was thrown open, and the crowd, led by Rev. Mr. Corwin, pastor of the Fort Street Church, and Chief Justice Allen, entered the supper room. Here, on a table spread out alone, were the silver presents, consisting of knives, forks, spoons, cream and milk dishes, butter and cheese knives, napkin-rings, &c., &c., and in the center of the table a silver cake dish piled full with bright silver half-dollars, in all about six hundred pieces. The silverware is valued at about five hundred dollars, and the money three hundred more. On another long dining table was spread the generous repast prepared by unknown friends . . .

"We need hardly add that the whole affair was a most perfect 'surprise' to the worthy chaplain and his wife. And we have never seen a happier gathering than that afforded by the two hundred guests who assembled at the chaplaincy on Saturday. The ovation was by no means confined to his parishioners, although it originated among them; but it was a general and spontaneous testimonial to one who was [has?] spent a quarter of a century in Honolulu, and occupied during that period the same dwelling and the same pulpit. The effect will be to impart a happy and harmonious feeling among all who took part in it, and we trust Mr. D, and his wife may live to witness their golden wedding anniversary." NB: Samuel would die eighteen years later.

8. Married October 6, 1851, a little over five months before their March 10, 1842, from New York. Judd, *Missionary Album*, 76.

9. Damon, *Seamen's Chaplain*, xiii.

10. Damon, *Seamen's Chaplain*, xiii.

11. Damon, *Samuel Chenery Damon*.

12. Damon, *Seamen's Chaplain*, 1.

missionary, an evangelist, based in a port which by the 1840s was being visited by more American ships than any other foreign port in the world."[13]

Backing up to Damon's calling to serve overseas, the authors note that while "still a student, Samuel C. Damon once wrote an essay about missionaries in which he explored the low morals evinced by American sailors in foreign ports. The essay proposed that evangelical work be undertaken among those men."[14] While it is not known whether Damon saw himself as one to help implement the call in his essay, the paper would come to be seen as prescient. As with many other aspiring missionaries, Damon initially wanted to serve among people of another culture in a foreign land. Arguably, seamen could be viewed as being of another culture[15] and moving through the ports of many countries.

Damon's "initial step toward missionary work was to apply to the American Board of Commissioners for Foreign Missions for a position in India. Instead, another opportunity presented itself: the seamen's chaplain in Honolulu had died, and Damon was offered the job by the American Seamen's Society. It was apparently difficult for the society to find chaplains at the time. 'Most would-be missionaries dreamed of working with the natives in far, foreign lands; few felt called to work with young men from their own homeland in foreign harbors.'[16] Damon nevertheless accepted the position and was ordained a seamen's chaplain.[17] In 1842 he took up his post in Honolulu, where he soon found himself applying his great energy to transforming the spiritual and material conditions of the sailors who passed through the port of Honolulu."[18]

Cooper and Daws explain the whaling industry at the time before, during, and after Damon's arrival in Honolulu. They describe the "extremely difficult" life "of the ordinary sailor aboard an American whaler in the mid-nineteenth century." They mention conflict and mutinies on the ships. "All in all sailors endured a great deal in order to earn their livelihood... Damon had ample occasion to observe that the sailor 'often feels himself an outcast from society.'[19] The long months and years sailors spent away from home made them exceedingly lonely. But lonely also were the families left behind."[20]

After describing the many difficulties caused by sailors—including those who deserted or were left in Honolulu for insubordination—the authors note that it "was

---

13. Damon, *Seamen's Chaplain*, 1.
14. Damon, *Seamen's Chaplain*, 42.
15. What would come to be called a "people group."
16. Dabagh and Case, *Central Union Church*, 7, on 114 in *Seamen's Chaplain*.
17. September 15, 1841. Judd, *Missionary Album*, 76.
18. Damon, *Seamen's Chaplain*, 42.
19. *The Friend* 7.2 (October 28, 1843), in Damon, *Seamen's Chaplain*, 49.
20. Damon, *Seamen's Chaplain*, 49.

toward this human maelstrom that Samuel and Julia Damon sailed in 1842 on the *Victoria*."

The authors explain Damon's introduction and use of *The Friend*. "As a seamen's chaplain, Damon made his mission among men who were a generally rough and exploited and often drunken lot. One of his first ideas upon assuming his post in Honolulu was to start a newspaper for them, initially called *Temperance Advocate* and later *The Friend*; he was the paper's sole writer and editor. Typical editions contained world news gleaned from American and English papers, announcements of upcoming religious events, reprints of sermons given by Damon and other ministers, book reviews, editorials on temperance, extensive articles on Pacific maritime matters, local news, poetry, ship arrivals at and departures from Honolulu harbor, lists of passengers aboard these ships, and notices of marriages[21] and deaths. In his lifetime Damon published between a half million and a million copies of *The Friend*, most of which he personally distributed."[22]

Damon's establishing of *The Friend* was inspired by Dr. Spaulding of the American Seamen's Friend. In his charge to Damon, Spaulding exhorted Damon "to ensure that 'the special objects of your solicitude, prayers and efforts will be the sons of the ocean.'"[23] Damon took the injunction seriously, as he indicated when he began publishing *The Friend*: 'The great aim of the publisher will be to make the paper useful among seamen... The thousands of seamen of various nations annually visiting the shores of this archipelago claim, and shall have the first place in all our plans for doing good.'"[24]

While *The Friend* was the publishing heart of Damon's ministry, the Bethel Church was the physical location. "Damon's headquarters in Honolulu became the two-story Seamen's Bethel Church at the intersection of King and Bethel streets on the Honolulu waterfront. In its day this was a substantial building; a sailor who arrived in Honolulu in 1846, Henry Sheldon, wrote that 'the largest foreign-built structure at this date—with the exception of the King's palace—was the Bethel Church.'"[25]

Like Coan, Damon was non-stop in his ministry to others. Additionally, they both engaged in multiple kinds of service. "With such a large flock to attend to, the new seamen's chaplain became a man in perpetual motion from the moment he arrived... It is evident that Damon conceived of his charter broadly; he involved himself in all manner of things that pertained to seamen—medical, spiritual, political, literary, and so on."[26]

---

21. Though not, apparently, the marriage of Titus Coan and Lydia Bingham. See "Final Years" chapter.

22. Damon, *Seamen's Chaplain*, 2.

23. Damon, *Samuel Chenery Damon*, 87n 115 in *Seamen's Chaplain*.

24. *The Friend* 6.1 (December 18, 184) on 115 of notes in *Seamen's Chaplain*.

25. Bishop, *Reminiscences*, 116, in *Seamen's Chaplain*, 51.

26. Damon, *Seamen's Chaplain*, 51.

During his early years, Damon got off to a fast start by visiting sailors in every possible setting. He "was tireless in visiting the ships, wharves, boarding houses, prisons, and hospitals in and near Honolulu harbor. He would spread kind words, invite sailors to church or to his study for consultation, and hand out free copies of *The Friend*. According to one account, 'It was said of Damon in 1848[27] that he had met during that year not [less] than ten thousand seamen of at least ten nationalities either on shipboard or in his study.'"[28]

Damon also developed institutions that assisted sailors. He and his wife Julia founded in 1852 "the Stranger's Friend Society, for which, Damon wrote, 'perhaps a better name would be Society for aiding poor sailors whom neither British nor American Consuls would support.'"[29] He co-founded "the Honolulu Sailors' Home, which first opened its doors in 1856 . . . From the beginning, the Honolulu Sailors' Home was a well-run, clean, and inexpensive lodging facility for sailors and other voyagers from distant lands."[30]

The Sailors' Home was "far more than a well-furnished bed-and-breakfast for sailors. In his 1880–81 annual report on the home, Damon wrote: 'Scarcely a day passes that the keeper of the 'Home' is not assisting some stranger newly arrived, onward to his future home on other islands[31] or distant part of the world. Hence I am confident in asserting that the Honolulu Sailors' Home with its 'lodgings,' 'Reading Room,' 'Bible and Tract Depository' and other elements of moral good, is now accomplishing the grand object of its original desire under the reign of Kamehameha III, and which has been continued under his successors to the present time. The 'Home' has been a centre from whence has emanated good to both the bodies and souls of hundreds and thousands."[32]

The Bethel Seamen's Chapel became a spiritual home for sailors arriving in Honolulu. This was in large part because of Damon's winsome nature, wry sense of humor, service to sailors, and his faith in Christ. "Over the course of his ministry Damon won the affection of many seafaring men. The author of an account of Honolulu in the 1840s said that 'few men of that time were more respected by the seamen . . . than was the chaplain.' As a result, when 'the whale ships were in port the [Bethel] was generally well-filled with sailors from the ships.'"[33]

The Friend also became the unofficial journal first of the American Board missionaries and, in the 1850s, of the Hawaiian Evangelical Association. Titus Coan wrote

---

27. His fifth full year in Honolulu.

28. Dabagh and Case, *Central Union Church*, 131–133, in Damon, *Seamen's Chaplain*, 55n116.

29. Report to American Seamen's Friend Society, February 28, 1859, DPMCS, Box 10, in Damon, *Seamen's Chaplain*, 57.

30. Damon, *Seamen's Chaplain*, 57.

31. Including the Big Island and the harbor town of Hilo.

32. Quoted in Damon, *Samuel Chenery Damon*, 83, in Damon, *Seamen's Chaplain*, 58–59n117.

33. Damon, *Seamen's Chaplain*, 58n116.

in and was referred to numerous times in *The Friend*. In reading descriptions of Damon, one is reminded of Coan. This "missionary clad in the heavy, tight-fitting garb of a nineteenth-century Protestant evangelist was also a man who had a tremendous ebullience and a profound sense of good will. He put himself out to an amazing extent in the service of humanity, without restriction, and he moved through the world with great energy, joy, and kindness."[34]

Coan's efforts among seamen reflected Damon's work writ small, yet was no less significant. During Coan's forty-seven years, he would see hopeful conversions among expatriates passing through Hilo. Many who became Christians and those who were already Christians upon arrival in Hilo would maintain correspondence with Titus.

Coan's care for those who "went out on the sea in ships" [Ps 127:3] extended to the Sabbath-keeping commandment. In his printed pamphlet "Sailor's Sabbath," Coan writes about the biblically-based importance to civilization and value for the individual to have a day of worship, reflection and rest even while on the high seas. He distributed that pamphlet, along with Bibles, and material from virtually all of the Christian voluntary associations.

SUNDAY AFTERNOON CHURCH

After four services for Hawaiians on Sunday mornings, Coan held one in English in the afternoon for foreigners. "I preach one sermon in the Bethel at 3 1–2[35] on every Sabbath, after having had four exercises with the native people."[36]

Coan describes the first building dedicated to worship services for sailors. The building used was where the Coans had first lived in Hilo: in the Lyman home with the Lymans. Both couples had long since moved into their own dwellings—the Lymans' home built for them; the Coans the "Emerald Bower" of the Goodrich home, expanded and improved over the years. "For many years this service was held in one of the houses of the missionaries. Finally, we fitted up the old stone building, our first home, for a Bethel and added a library of about two hundred volumes."[37]

In a June 7, 1850, letter to S. F. DuPont, Coan rejoices that our "little Bethel or seaman's chapel is completed, and it is very useful. It is worth four times what it cost. We have English services in it most of the year. I have already obtained about two hundred volumes of good books for it, besides periodicals, Dr. Jewett's plates of the human stomach and some other paintings. We shall never forget the lift which the *Cayane* gave to the enterprise.[38] Since you left we have received $30.50 from the officers of the *Preble*, $104 from the *Independence*, and $119 from the *Ohio*." Coan notes the

34. Damon, *Seamen's Chaplain*, 3. NB: More on Damon will be presented later in the chapter.
35. 3:30.
36. Coan letters, June 11, 1856, in *Sailor's Magazine*, September 1856, 26.
37. Coan, *Life*, 65.
38. See below.

tension between various vessel members and others. "Forty or fifty of the *Preble's* men subscribed cheerfully but Commander G. would not authorize the purser to pay."[39]

Ministry to whalers, naval personnel, and visitors to Hilo eventually included residents of Hilo whose first language was English. It was resolved "to organize a church and seek a pastor for this class of our inhabitants; and on the ninth of February 1868, a church was organized with fourteen foreign members." Years later, the Reverend C. W. Hill noted that this formation took place as a result of the decline of whaling during and after the Civil War. In 1867 a minister was sought "to act *primarily as a Pastor* of the foreign community, and secondarily as Seaman's Chaplain."[40]

The first pastor of this church was the Reverend Frank Thompson, followed by the Reverend Anderson Oliver Forbes.[41] "At the end of 1874 [Forbes] was called to the pastorate of the First Foreign Church of Hilo. In June 1880, Mr. Forbes was elected Corresponding Secretary of the Hawaiian Board, a post in which he labored with the greatest efficiency until his death" in 1888 when he died suddenly at the age of 55 in Colorado Springs,[42] Colorado.[43]

Coan notes that Rev. Forbes was the "son of the late missionary, Cochran Forbes"[44] and that he labored faithfully until he resigned to accept the secretaryship of the Hawaiian Evangelical Association.[45] He goes on to write about the church as of August of 1881. "The foreign church, though small and not wealthy, is active and generous. They pay a salary of $1,200 or $1,400, furnishing a parsonage to the pastor, and they give generous sums for missionary purposes and for other Christian philanthropic objects."[46]

VISITS IN THE HOME

The Coans entertained individual travelers, whalers, and naval personnel. They welcomed scholars, explorers, and travelers. He writes about the broad spectrum of people welcomed to the Emerald Bower. "We have not only enjoyed the privilege of entertaining men of rank, but also men of low estate, for poor and friendless strangers came to our distant shores as well as the rich and the noble, and we feel it to be no less, and often a greater, privilege to care for the neglected and needy than for the honorable. The lessons of Christ are plain, practical, and personal. '*I was hungry* and ye

---

39. Coan to DuPont, June 7, 1850, in Coan, *Memorial Volume*, 63.
40. Hill, "Hilo's First Foreign Church," in *The Friend* 61.4 (April 1, 1904) 12.
41. Coan, *Life*, 135.
42. Where he was visiting for his health.
43. Judd, *Missionary Album*, 96–97; and Forbes et al., *Partners in Change*, 259–61.
44. Judd, *Missionary Album*, 98–99; and Forbes et al., *Partners in Change*, 262–65. Cochran Forbes died in 1880, less than a year after Coan completed his autobiography draft.
45. Coan, *Life*, 135.
46. Coan, *Life*, 135.

gave me meat' [Matt 25:35], 'When thou makest a feast—call the poor' [Luke 14:13], 'Remember the stranger' [Lev 19:34], and 'Be careful to remember the poor' [Gal 2:10]. And we have sometimes entertained angels unawares" [Heb 13:2].[47]

"Professor C. S. Lyman, of Yale College, was our guest for three months, and his scientific tastes and acquirements, and his mechanical skill, made his visit especially interesting."[48]

Long after Lyman's visit, William T. Brigham, "of Boston, spent a season with us, and went the same rounds [as Lyman] with me. On this occasion we visited a pulu[49] station upon the highlands, and in a deep forest. Here were about thirty or forty men and women employed in gathering this soft, silky fern-down for upholstery, and here, ten miles from Kilauea, we saw the natives cook their food over hot steam cracks without fuel. Near the volcano this is frequently done."[50]

While Isabella Bird did not stay at the Coans',[51] she did stay in Hilo and described the exterior of the homes of both Titus Coan and the Lymans. After explaining their New England Appearance, she characterizes them as "cool retreats, embowered among breadfruit, tamarind, and bamboo, through whose graceful leafage the blue waters of the bay are visible. Innumerable exotics are domesticated round these fair homesteads."[52]

One of Coan's most significant life trajectory influences he ever exercised was in the life of Hugo Stangenwald, who might have stayed at the Emerald Bower. Stangenwald arrived in Hilo perhaps in 1850 in his early thirties after being in California for the Gold Rush. Titus Coan first learned of him through poetry published in a San Jose newspaper in 1849. The two might have further connected because he had been a Presbyterian elder in the Oregon Territory. Stangenwald would become one of Hawai'i's most accomplished early daguerrian[53] artists.

In March of 1853 he displayed views "taken on the western coast of America."[54] Lynn Ann Davis notes that in "January 1853,[55] Stangenwald landed at Hilo, on the

47. Coan, *Life*, 149.

48. Coan, *Life*, 144.

49. "A soft, elastic vegetable fiber of yellow-brown hue obtained from the young fronds of Hawaiian tree ferns, used for mattress and pillow stuffing." "also called pulu fiber." Dictionary.com, "Pulu."

50. Coan, *Life*, 145–46.

51. It appears she visited Hilo just months before Titus and Lydia united in Holy Matrimony in 1873.

52. Bird, *Six Months*, 97.

53. Dagguerotypes are photographs that create "a positive image on a sheet of glass using the wet plate collodion process." The process was invented by Louis Daguerre in 1839. Wikipedia, "Daguerreotype." They predate the photographs that came into usage after the Civil War.

54. Lynn Ann Davis,"'From California Gold Fields: Daguerrotypists in Hawai'i" (typescript 1985), 9, 10, "Titus Coan to 'My Dear Bro. Armstrong,' Hilo February 10, 1853, Hawaii State Archives, quoted in Bruce T. Eris[?]kson, 'Early Hawaiian Photography,' unpublished essay, 1996, 3–4; Joan Abramson, *Photographers of Old Hawaii*, 3rd ed (Honolulu: Island Heritage, 1976)," 18.

55. 1850 is referenced a number of times elsewhere.

island of Hawaii, aboard a British brig. He was bound for Sydney, Australia, with his partner Stephen Goodfellow, recently a resident of San Francisco. Together, as Stangenwald and Goodfellow, they found a profitable field of enterprise taking portraits of American missionaries[56] and views of Hawaiian scenery during what was to have been a temporary stay. Missionary Titus Coan called Strangenwald 'the chief artist'[57] and a 'physician' (so reported)[58] and summed him up as 'a pleasant and pious young man.' On February 10, Coan wrote that Stangenwald and Goodfellow 'are now using up all the faces in Hilo, and they soon will be through.' Coan added that their prices were comparatively moderate: 'They charged 3$ [sic] for the smallest plates in a neat case, and a frame in proportion to the size, the amount[59] of gold in ornamentation.' This helpful missionary went so far as to enlist the help of his colleagues in Honolulu to assist Stangenwald and Goodfellow in establishing themselves in that town."[60]

Coan writes a paragraph listing many visitors to the Coan home. "But time would fail me to speak of the visits of the venerable Dr. Anderson and his wife, of Boston; the gifted Dr. Boyd and his estimable wife, of Geneva, with whom we held sweet converse; the 'Friends' Wheeler, of London; Joel and Hannah Bean,[61] of Iowa; President Moore, of Earlham College,[62] through whom we have been brought into Christian fellowship with many of his denomination; of Dr. Thompson, of Detroit, who in his advanced years came to look upon this distant missionary field, and was most enamored with the beauties of Hilo; of the Rev. Mr. Hallock, who with glowing heart went back to tell his people of what he had seen in these isles of the sea; and of many others whose visits of Christian love and fellowship were cheering and refreshing in this far-off land."[63]

Leavitt Horman Hallock[64] wrote about his visit to the Emerald Bower and related excursions during his 1878 visit to Hilo. He met Coan before ever reaching Hilo. "Leaving Maui we boarded the interisland steamer for Hilo, and found on deck the man I longed most of all to see, the Rev. Titus Coan, famous early missionary to Hawaii."

56. Many of the daguerreotypes in Judd, *Missionary Album*, are listed as taken "about 1850" and other early 1850 dates. The Titus and Fidelia Church Coan daguerreotype is indicated as "about 1850," [70] while the David and Sarah Joiner Lyman family daguerreotype is listed as "about 1853" [142] courtesy of the Lyman House Memorial Museum.

57. Written by the "pen painter."

58. Reports that he studied medicine in Pennsylvania.

59. From California?

60. Davis, above footnote, 17–19, Lynne Ann Davis *Na Pai'i i'i: The Photographers in the Hawaiian Islands, 1845–1900* (Honolulu: Bishop Museum Press, 1980), 14; Coan to Armstrong, Febru0ary 10, 1853.

61. Quaker Friends with whom Titus exchanged many letters on the subject of "peace." See the chapter by that name.

62. A Quaker college in Richmond, Indiana.

63. *Life*, 150.

64. A Congressman and then a federal judge, Leavitt lived from 1842 until 1921. Wikipedia, "Humphrey H. Leavitt."

EXPATRIATE MINISTRY

Once in Hilo, Hallock writes of his time at Lydia and Titus, home, including a far-ranging prayer of approximately sixty minutes. "I sat in Mr. Coan's cool parlor looking out on the sea, while bananas waved their broad leaves at his door, and the fragrant air played with the grand old man's white locks upon a head massive intellectual, like the classic outline of Daniel Webster's,[65] and fanned a face, fairly glowing with Christian peace and likeness to his divine Master. And then I heard him pray, as if the door were wide open into the kingdom and he were speaking into the ear of his heavenly Lover; the only prayer I ever heard that lasted a full hour and I sincerely wished might continue. He pleaded, O how tenderly! For his scattered people there, for his old New England friends, and for his transient guest, aye! And for all the round world, for, though secluded in that tiny isle, he was broad and cosmopolitan to a wonderful degree."

Next, Hallock compares Coan to Moses.[66] "And then he told of such scenes of apostolic benediction as had never been since Pentecost, and of such terrific tumblings of the earth crust, such tearing and bursting of the internal fires of Mauna Loa, that he held me spellbound far into the night, speaking in his quiet dignity of things which mortals seldom see and live. I could only think of Moses of old when he came down with shining face from the mountain where he had seen God"[67] [Exod 34:29–35].

Very "precious friendships were formed with many of these seamen, whose friendships continue to this day. We have found many noble specimens, not only of generosity and fine natural talent among this class of men, but also many choice Christians."[68] "The Coans enjoyed welcoming to the Emerald Bower both whalers and members of national navies. They had 'many friends among the men of the sea.' While they welcomed individuals from all nationalities, they had a special place in their hearts for Americans. Seeing the stars and stripes hanging from mastheads[69] made them feel closer to home, and the Coans looked forward to conversing with educated masters."[70] Coan continues by noting the rather startling fact of births in the Coan home. "Not a few sailors' boys and girls have been born in Hilo, and several have been born in our house."[71]

Visits in the home included extended stays for children and wives of masters of ships. "Some 'masters brought cultivated and pious wives, and from time to time they,

---

65. 1782 until 1852.

66. The stained-glass window of Moses carrying the Ten Commandments is said to show a striking likeness to Coan's visage.

67. Hallock, *Hawaii under King Kalakaua*, 54 and 61–62.

68. Lyman, *Around the Horn*, 65.

69. This is a paraphrase (page later cited as part of a quotation) of Coan, *Life*, 141: "The very sight of the stars and stripes at their masthead, the snowy canvas, or the weather-beaten and tempest-torn sails, was pleasant."

70. Coan, *Life*, 141, in Ehlke, "Enthusiastic Religion," 144, 45.

71. Coan, *Life*, 141.

with their little children, would be left with us for months while the ships were absent on their cruises.'"[72]

When a new church edifice was completed and dedicated, Coan "welcomed Commodore Ap Catesby Jones[73] of the frigate *United States*, with his officers and brass band. The courteous commodore and his chaplain consented to deliver each an address of congratulation and encouragement to the people for their ready acceptance of the gospel, and for their progress in Christian civilization. Jones also spoke of a previous visit to the islands when he had investigated and cleared missionaries of 'complaints made by a class of foreign residents against the American missionaries.'"[74]

Coan writes of another band and how impressed the Hawaiians were. "Perhaps the most perfect band we have heard in Hilo was that of the Duke of Edinburgh, who visited us in the steam frigate *Galatea* in 1869."[75]

In 1846, C. S. Lyman notes that "in conversation Mr. Coan mentioned several cases of ship masters who have been hopefully converted while stopping at his house. His kindness of manner is well fitted to touch the heart and prepare it to receive gospel truth."[76]

Coan's understanding and tenderness are evident in his ministering to two military leaders. The first took place after the 1837 "volcanic wave." The captain of the *Admiral Cockburn* and his clerk were affected by the event and its aftermath. "Even the English captain, who spent his nights in our family, and his intelligent and courteous clerk, professed to give themselves to the Lord while with us, and both kneeling with us at the family altar, silently united in our morning and evening devotions, or cheerfully led in prayer. The captain was a large and powerful man, bronzed by wind and wave and scorching sun. He had been long upon the deep, had suffered shipwreck, had been unable to reach his London home for more than three years, and had been given up as dead by all his friends. Under this belief his wife had married another, when he surprised her by his return, and she gave him joy by returning to him. He gave us an interesting account of his eventful life, and confessed that he had enjoyed very few religious privileges and had thought little of God or the salvation of his soul. He now accepted the offer of life through Christ, with the spirit of a little child."

The captain exhibited "fruits meet with repentance" [Matt 3:8]. "On returning to the ship he immediately told his officers and crew that he should drink no more

---

72. Coan, *Life*, 145.

73. Jones was the original choice for the Exploring expedition, but due to delays Wilkes became the leader. Wikipedia, "United States Exploring Expedition."
What might have happened with the Ex Ex in Hilo had Jones been the leader?

74. Coan, *Life*, 84.

75. Coan, *Life*, 85.

76. Lyman, *Around the Horn*, 85.

intoxicants, swear no more, and chase whales no more on the Lord's Day, but, on the contrary, observe the Sabbath and have religious services on that holy day."[77]

Coan also ministered to an "honored officer[78] of the British army in India" who "once spent a week with us. He came an entire stranger, but by his great intelligence, his urbanity, his noble figure, and his gentlemanly address, he made an indelible impression upon us. And this impression was deepened by such a frank and affecting tale of his life as filled us with interest in his behalf."

Coan relates how this officer's wrought emotions led to the confession of his having killed a fellow officer because of a "false sense of honor." Coan relates that the officer's "plaintive story struck us dumb for a while; our hearts were melted with sympathy; but presently we blessed the gracious Lord for this opportunity. We saw his difficulty, that he was filled with 'the sorrow of the world which worketh death.'[79] He had labored in agony to *save himself*, and the cloud of despair grew thicker and darker over him. I at once pointed him to 'the Lamb of God who taketh away the sins of the world' [John 1:29]. 'Yes,' said he, 'but can Jesus forgive *my* sin? It seems too great to be forgiven.' I assured him that 'the blood of Jesus Christ cleanses from *all sin*' [1 John 1:9] and that Isaiah had told us long ago that if we would but listen to our God, 'though our sins be as scarlet they should be white as snow, and though red as crimson they should be as wool' [Isa 1:18]. And that Jesus 'will in no wise cast out' [John 6:37] one penitent sinner that comes to him.'"

Coan explained to the officer that it "was his duty, and it was an infinite privilege to believe and accept pardon and peace as a free gift of God, while it was an insult to God to doubt his call and his promises; this 'treading underfoot the blood of the Son of God' [Heb 10:29] would be a greater and a more fatal sin than to have shed the blood of his friend. He accepted the offer of salvation, and rejoiced in hope. He found, to his joy, that there is 'a blood which speaketh better things than the blood of Abel' [Heb 12:24] or the blood of his murdered companion."

Coan writes about his follow-up with this officer, both in person and via correspondence. He also further describes his physical appearance and character. "We have heard from him several times since, and learned that he had been promoted in the army and in civil life, and that he was happy. He was, I think, six feet four inches tall, weighing some 225 pounds, well-formed, a man of great physical power, of superior strength of intellect, and excellent executive ability. With a heart and conscience of tender sensibilities, he was 'bold as a lion' [Prov 28:1] in all he felt to be right, but he quailed before what he believed to be wrong."[80]

---

77. Coan, *Life*, 53.
78. At no point does Coan provide a name.
79. 2 Cor 7:10, in contrast to "godly sorrow."
80. Coan, *Life*, 146–49.

He writes, "I should like to speak of many more of those whose acquaintance we have made, and who have been our guests in our Hilo home." He talks about "Admiral Pearson, who with his wife and daughter spent a season in our family."[81]

He characterizes Samuel DuPont as a "gallant officer, the accomplished gentleman and the sincere Christian, whose dearly-cherished friendship we enjoyed until the day of his death."[82] The members of his "naval vessel the *Cayane* donated $94 to help build the Seaman's Chapel in 1847."[83]

FOLLOW-UP CORRESPONDENCE

DuPont and Coan "sustained a correspondence of almost twenty years,[84] based on their mutual 'sympathies and moral affinities.'" Coan wrote DuPont, thanking him for the gift to the Seamen's chapel and commenting on DuPont's Christian demeanor. "But we are happy to learn that you, like Joshua, have resolved to 'serve the Lord' [Josh 24:15]—and that you feel strengthened and encouraged in this service. You have, doubtless, weighed the matter candidly and intelligently, and have come to the rational conclusion that a *new heart* [Ez 36:26], or *true religion* [James 1:27], is the 'one thing needful.' You have engaged your intellectual and moral powers—your *head* and *heart*—in believing, loving, aiding, and obeying the Lord Jesus" [Luke 10:42].[85]

Two letters from Coan to DuPont are found in the *Memorial Volume*. The first one is dated June 7, 1850. It covers four pages. In the first paragraph he thanks DuPont for his September 1, 1849, letter and indicates that "the box" of books arrived "in perfect order and is received with great gratitude." He refers to a volume discussing the late 1840s archaeological findings at Nineveh.

"Like all tokens of true love [the box's content] is *priceless*. The books, especially *Nineveh*, are what we longed to get hold of. Nothing could have been more opportune or acceptable." He indicates the books use in his lectures[86] on the Old Testament.

---

81. Coan, *Life*, 149–50.

82. Coan, *Life*, 149.

83. Ehlke, "Enthusiastic Religion," 145. "Du Pont was given command of the sloop *Cyane* in 1846," Wikipedia, "Francis DuPont."

84. Until DuPont's death in 1865.

85. Coan to DuPont, October 13, 1847, HMH, in Ehlke, "Enthusiastic Religion," 145. Ehlke further notes that "Mrs. Coan and Mrs. DuPont became correspondents and later friends with the Coans, who invited them to spend time with them at Hilo. Mrs. DuPont never visited Hilo, but when the Coans returned to the United States in 1870, they spent time with Mrs. DuPont, then a widow. And when the Coan's youngest daughter married in America, it was at the DuPont estate in Delaware." Coan notes visiting DuPonts widow and the Pearson family in the United States, Coan, *Life*, 149–50.

86. Coan's lectures through the Bible, on Catholicism, and other subjects are apparently lost to history. After mentioning his name in the next to the last Hilo station report synopsis, he writes that the "pastor has just [finished] his last lecture of a series embracing every chapter of the Bible." It is not yet known how many years it took to go through the 1,189 chapters of the combined Old and New Testaments. Perhaps more than twenty years.

"Nothing could have been more opportune or acceptable. A short time ago I lectured to my people on the ancient history, the fall, and the recent disentombing of that vast Assyrian city. The facts stated were fresh in the recollection of many when your books came. The volumes were taken into our monthly lectures and the plates exhibited, illustrating and corroborating what the natives had before heard. I need not say that they excited enthusiastic interest. We anticipate a treat in reading the works you sent."

Coan expresses his pleasure that DuPont has arrived safely home. Next he writes of DuPont's ecumenical Christian spirit. "And here, my beloved brother, let me from my very soul reciprocate the catholic, the truly Christian sentiment expressed in your letter 'without a shadow of sectarian feeling.' I love the image, the spirit of Christ wherever seen, and as to names and forms and organizations let these be left to the tastes, convictions, and circumstances of the different members of the household of faith. I love different members of the household of faith. I love the Episcopal church ardently, and I highly esteem and warmly love many of her clergy and her laity. I also love other evangelical denominations who hold the Head and feel the Love which unites all the saints on earth and in heaven in one body, in one holy brotherhood."[87]

The second *Memorial Volume* Coan-to-DuPont letter is dated September 20, 1862.[88] Lydia Coan characterizes DuPont as "Flag Officer" and in the letter Titus addresses him as "Admiral." The contents are found in the "Peace Man" chapter.

GROWTH OF SHIPS IN THE HARBOR

Coan writes about the various kinds of ships that visited and the nationalities represented by those ships. "Not a few national ships have visited Hilo, from the tender or schooner up to the sloop-of-war, the frigate and the great seventy-four-gun line-of-battle ship, as the *Collingwood* and *Ohio*.

"The largest of these ships represented the United States of America, the next Great Britain, then France, Russia, Germany, and Denmark. We have had more than seventy-five of these warships of different nationalities in our harbor, and of all classes of vessels about four thousand. The approximate number of seamen who have visited Hilo during our residence here we put at forty thousand."[89]

While Coan does not seem to count the intra-island vessels, the growth of ships in Hilo harbor began before the California Gold Rush. Coan wrote "his long-time friend, the Rev. Herman Halsey of Niagara, New York" in 1846 about "the problems posed by the expansion of shipping in the port of Hilo. 'Six ships are now at anchorage before my door, and we have had nearly one hundred arrivals during the past year; among wh[ich] were five large ships of war. This brings us constantly in contact with foreign sailors of almost all nations, the influence of many of whom is withering

---

87. Coan to DuPont, June 7, 1850, in Coan, *Memorial Volume*, 62–64.
88. Coan to DuPont, September 20, 1862, in Coan, *Memorial Volume*, 90–92.
89. Coan, *Life* 65–66.

upon our native population. Consequently our labor and anxiety is doubled from this source. In addition to four or five services for the natives I preach a sermon to seamen &c. every Lord's Day, and during the week our doors are open to this class of men. They must be noticed, cared for, loved, supplied with books, Bibles, tracts, &c. &c. or they will grow worse and worse."[90]

"Expecting the number of ships to double in the next year, Coan said that there were rumors that the United States [N]avy would be establishing a depot in Hilo. Hilo had the reputation of being 'the most temperate port in the Pacific, perhaps the world,' a label that Coan worked hard to maintain by discouraging the sale of liquor in Hilo."[91]

In 1904, the Reverend C. W. Hill wrote about the change wrought by vessels calling at Hilo during the 1849 California Gold Rush and the related greater need to minister to the officers and crews of the vessels. "In the days when the gold fever was raging in California, the whaling vessels of the North were wont to avoid San Francisco, partly because provisions were dear, but chiefly because sailors would desert their ships to join the quest for gold. As a result, the Hawaiian islands became the whalers' rendezvous for fresh water and supplies. Hilo Bay was often enlivened by large fleets, and numerous sailors visited its shores.

"Hitherto the missionary spirit had concerned itself with the Hawaiian race, but now a new problem was presented, that of preaching the gospel to sailors. Mr. [Rev. Sheldon] Dibble was then living in a long stone building, with partitions removed." It "was converted into a Seaman's Bethel. It also became the nucleus of 'The First Foreign Church.'"[92]

By 1853 the concerns of the pastor of Hilo and Puna coincided with those of the seaman's chaplain, as Coan reported that "a tenth to a twentieth of our able-bodied young men are employed on board these ships, and there taught, but by precept and example, the superiority of the whaleman's morality and religion over those of the missionary and of the Bible."[93]

Coan expresses his awareness of the "shipping season" in an 1856 letter to *The Sailor's Magazine*. "Our last shipping season at Hilo was one of unusual interest. I have never seen seamen more accessible. Large numbers [of seamen] called on us during the week and our Bethel was well filled on the Sabbath. From seven vessels all except three or four who kept ship came out to our Sabbath services, and many were deeply impressed with the truth. It is a rare thing that a ship master absents himself from our Bethel on the Lord's Day."[94]

---

90. Coan to Herman Halsey, January 20, 1846, HMH, in Ehlke, "Enthusiastic Religion," 144.
91. Coan to Halsey in Ehlke, "Enthusiastic Religion," 144.
92. Hill, "Hilo's First Foreign Church," in *The Friend* 61.4 (April 1, 1904) 12.
93. Coan, *Missionary Herald* 49 (December 1853) 374, in Ehlke, "Enthusiastic Religion," 144.
94. Coan letter, June 6, 1856, in *Sailor's Magazine*, September 1856, 26.

SAMUEL DAMON: "THE SAILOR'S FRIEND"

Though he arrived in Honolulu seven and a half years after Coan did, the Reverend Samuel Cheney Damon became an example and mentor to Titus Coan in the area of serving seamen who came to port in Hawai'i. Coan writes in 1880 of Honolulu having "a seamen's Bethel where many thousands of the sons of the deep have heard the sound of the gospel, first from the lips of the Rev. Mr. Diell,[96] and now for some forty years from Dr. Damon."[97]

The Reverend John Diell was "the first Chaplain of the American Seamen's Friend Society in the port of Honolulu. He organized the Oahu Bethel Church with eight members in 1837. He was given two plots of land by Kamehameha III, one for a chapel and one for a parsonage, and during his tenure the two-story chapel was built. Activities at the Bethel included the Sandwich Islands Institute, which studied all lands bordering the Pacific, an ambitious subject which was a forerunner of similar contributions to be made by Bishop Museum. Mr. Diell spent five years in this work. Several years later he took an extended sea voyage for his health; left for the United States December 2, 1840, on the ship *Lausanne*, Captain Spaulding, with Mrs. Diell and their four children,[98] but died before reaching the United States," at the age of thirty-two.[99]

Damon replaced Diell one year to the month of Diell's death. Born in 1815, he attended Princeton and Andover Theological seminaries. Ordained in 1841, "he arrived in Hawaii in [January of] 1842, accompanied by his wife, Julia Mills Damon, to take the post of Seamen's Chaplain in Honolulu for the American Seamen's Friend Society of New York . . . Damon made several trips to the US, Europe, Japan and China. He corresponded with relatives in New England. He was an avid collector of genealogical materials relating to both the Damon and Mills families and published a book[100] on the subject." He died in 1885.[101]

C. S. Lyman provides fascinating details of his meeting Damon, within two years of Damon's arrival. "Honolulu May 1846. Friday fifteenth. Came ashore after breakfast,

---

95. Hill, "Hilo's First Foreign Church," in *The Friend* 61.4 (April 1, 1904) 12.
96. For Diell, see Forbes et al., *Partners in Change*, 128–30.
97. Coan, *Life*, 241.
98. Ranging in age from three through seven.
99. Judd, *Missionary Album*, 80.
100. Damon, *Damon Memorial*.
101. Coan, *Memorial Volume*, 76–77.

called with Capt. S[palding][102] at Mr. Green's store, and under the guidance of a native lad proceeded to Rev. S[amuel] C[heney] Damon's, Seamen's Chap[lain], to whom I had a letter from Mr. Trumbull of Valp[arias]o. Found him just harnessing his horse to go to the General Meeting of the Missionaries at the large Church ¾ of a mile distant. He is a man prepossessing in appearance, apparently thirty or thirty-five[103] years of age, and received me with a cordial Xn [Christian] welcome and made me at once at home in his family; was introduced to his good lady and her sister and immediately rode with him to the Miss[ionar]y meeting."[104]

Lyman is referring to the annual meeting of the missionaries. On the evening of the fifteenth he dined "at Mr. Damon's. Stayed with him overnight, became acquainted with several of the Miss[ionarie]s." Two days later, Lyman describes a "delightful Sabbath, attended the Seamen's Chapel. Streets of the town as quiet as in a N. E. village. The Chapel is situated near the [ships'] landing. It is capable of seating 250 or three hundred and was well filled, mostly by foreign Am[erica]n and Eng[lis]h residents and the officers and seamen of the ships in the harbor. The preacher was Mr. [Daniel T.] Conde,[105] one of the missionaries. He gave a well-built practical sermon on the pearl of great price" [Matt 13:45–46].[106] That evening he attended another "service at the Seamen's Chapel and heard Rev. Mr. [John F.] Pogue[107] miss[ionar]y on Kauai, and one of the last reinforcements two years since. He gave a good sermon on taking up the Cross and following Xt. Chapel well filled."[108]

Lyman makes more references to Damon during Lyman's stay in Honolulu. On Thursday, May 21, in the "p.m. [I] attended communion service in connection with the Missionary meeting at the Church. After meeting rode with Mr. Damon and Miss Mills[109] on horseback to Mr. Adams's place three miles W. of Honolulu; the ride is a pleasant one."[110]

Lyman notes several sermons by Damon, that the sailors present would have heard. "Sun. May 24. At 11 attended service at Seamen's Chapel. Mr. D[amon] preached a sermon on behalf of the Hawaiian B[ible] Soc. from the text 'His word runneth very swiftly' [Ps 147:15], showing that more Bibles have been circulated since 1800 than in all previous time, and detailing his own labors in Bible distribution. The last year he

---

102. For the publication of his journal, Lyman fills out the abbreviations he first wrote down.

103. Thirty-one at the time of this meeting.

104. Lyman, *Around the Horn*, 61.

105. Conde was based at Hana, Maui, at the time, Judd, *Missionary Album*, 72–73; Forbes et al., *Partners in Change*, 190–95.

106. Lyman, *Around the Horn*, 63, 64.

107. Judd, *Missionary Album*, 158–59.; and Forbes et al., *Partners in Change*, 206–10.

108. Lyman, *Around the Horn*, 64.

109. Julia Sherman Mills Damon, who was "the first president of the Stranger's Friend Society," Judd, *Missionary Album*, 77.

110. Lyman, *Around the Horn*, 66.

had sold and given away 356 Bibles and about the same number of Test[ament]s.[111] Many seamen call for Bibles and papers every day, and seem to be very thankful that they have a true friend in the midst of the ocean."[112]

On February 7,[113] "Damon preached on the personality and divinity of the Holy Spirit."[114] One month later he preached from "'For if the righteous scarcely be saved, where &c &c' [1 Pet 4:18], a good sermon in which he took occasion to condemn Sunday whaling."[115]

Coan preached to sailors almost from the beginning of his arriving in Hilo. By 1850,[116] a Hilo Seamen's Bethel had been built. As was mentioned earlier in this chapter, Coan wrote to his friend of over ten years, Captain Samuel F. Dupont, about the establishment and efficacy of the Hilo Bethel.

Ehlke writes about the varied responsibilities Coan discharged on behalf of sailors. "The duties of the seamen's chaplain also called for nursing sick seamen, burying their remains when they did not recover, caring for their secular affairs, and writing their parents. But it was a post that Coan filled in addition to his ministry with the Hawaiian people of Hilo and Puna."[117]

"SAILOR'S SABBATH"

In or near 1849, Coan penned his "Sailor's Sabbath." The timing would track with the spike in nautical vessels visiting Hilo harbor with the beginning of the California Gold Rush. Coan worked closely with all of the American Christian voluntary associations. The Sabbath[118] was emphasized by one or more of those groups.[119] The February 1850 edition of *The Sailor's Magazine* cites and reviews the pamphlet as follows: "The Rev. Mr. Coan has in his excellent tract on the 'Sailor's Sabbath' written much of very great interest to the whaling fleet, to everyone, from the owner to the cabin boy. It would be well were it on board every ship and its precepts attended to; for although the owners of ships have done very much for the benefit of the sailor as a general thing, while

---

111. Meaning New Testaments.
112. Lyman, *Around the Horn*, 68.
113. 1847?
114. Lyman, *Around the Horn*, 165.
115. Lyman, *Around the Horn*, 167. Cf. below, Coan's "Sailor's Sabbath."
116. Just after the beginning of the Gold Rush surge.
117. Ehlke, "Enthusiastic Religion," 145.
118. While Seventh Day Adventists and Seventh Day Baptists observe their Sabbath on Saturday, most Christians moved the observance to Sunday or "Resurrection Day," commemorating the bodily resurrection of Jesus. In Romans 14, the Apostle Paul counsels Christians to not battle over which day the Sabbath should be celebrated. For Coan, it would be Sunday.
119. Including the temperance organizations.

away upon the ocean he has not his Sabbath. There is still too much truth in the assertion of Mr. Coan: 'there is no Sabbath for the sailor.'"[120]

Coan writes in the opening paragraph, "It is a bright feature of the present age that truth, philanthropy, and love are extending their influences to all classes of men. Among the many objects of benevolent interest the seaman is not forgotten. His temporal and eternal wants have found a place in the hearts for the good. An earnest desire is enkindled in the souls of Christians, to promote the happiness of his whole being—physical, civil, social, intellectual, and moral."[121]

He applies the first paragraph directly to those who are engaged in some form of water-borne enterprise, while focusing on the whaling business. "This is true of those who ride upon the mountain billow, and brave the loud tempest of mid-ocean; of those who plow the bosom of inland seas, or thread the sinuous coast; and also of those who glide along the more quiet waters of rivers and canals. To this class of men, and more especially to those connected with the *whaling service* and their friends, the writer would address a few remarks."

He relates his more than twenty years of interaction with individuals and understanding of the business by way of whaling ships in Hilo harbor and probably Honolulu as well. Ehlke notes that the twenty years began on his trip to Patagonia. "Coan knew sailors firsthand, having shipped out to Patagonia on his first missionary venture aboard a sealing schooner, been rescued by the clipper *Antarctica* on the shores of Gregory Bay to conclude the Patagonia exploration, spent a month in the harbor in the Falkland Islands awaiting passage to the United States, and preached to the seamen aboard the *Hellespont* on his voyage to the Islands."[122]

"Having been for more than twenty years, conversant with this vigorous and enterprising portion of our race, he is happy to say that, among the numerous sons of the deep, there are not a few of enlightened, elevated, noble, and generous minds, as well as many sincere Christians. Still, it is an undeniable and an affecting fact that the great mass of seafaring men, are very [far] from that high standard of excellence, both moral and intellectual, which they might attain. Such improvement and elevation of character as we desire would carry in it a *double blessing*; for while it inspired in the sailor self-respect, and clothed him with respectability—while it augmented his happiness in time, and prepared him for a bright immortality, it would also convert him into a friend, a benefactor, and an angel of light to the nations."[123]

Before posing eight questions, he provides a paragraph on the facts of how observing the Sabbath involves the highest state of civilization. "It were easy to show from all history, from observation, and from innumerable *facts*, that the highest state of civilization, refinement, enterprise, intelligence, and temporal prosperity can never

---

120. *Sailor's Magazine* 22.6 (February 1850) 162–63.
121. Coan, "Sailor's Sabbath."
122. Ehlke, "Enthusiastic Relgion," 143.
123. Coan, "Sailor's Sabbath," 1.

exist without the Sabbath. And the *world* may be challenged to produce a single instance of a nation, either ancient or modern, which has, without a Sabbath, maintained a pure and unsullied virtue, a sound and vigorous morality, and a spiritual and heavenly religion. Among all nations, and in all time, public and private virtue, and 'pure and undefiled religion' [James 1:27] have flourished or declined as the Sabbath has been sacredly kept or wantonly desecrated. Whoever, therefore, shall throw his whole influence on the side of a proper observance of this sacred day, will be a friend and a benefactor of mankind; and he who throws his influence into the opposite scale, is a practical enemy to his race."

He explains what he is going to do in most of the rest of the pamphlet. "We will now proceed to apply these remarks by an appeal to that class of men who are engaged or interested in a seafaring life, especially to those connected with the whaling service."[124]

Coan asks and answers eight questions. The questions themselves show Coan's views and the importance in which he holds the keeping of the Fourth Commandment [Exod 20:8] of all employments.

"I. Our first inquiry is, Why do ships so often leave port on the Lord's Day?" He answers in the first paragraph. "It has been said—and probably with truth—that more ships leave port on the Sabbath than on any other day of the week. Now why is this? Does it merely *happen*? Or is it done through carelessness and want of consideration? Is it done to pain the hearts of a Sabbath-keeping community, and to insult the 'Lord of the Sabbath?' [Matt 12:8]. Or do the breezes of heaven blow more favorably and more wooingly on that hallowed day? Are seamen in *haste* to leave parents, brothers, sisters, wives, children, and companions? Do they feel impatient of *one day's delay* amidst sanctuaries, and Christian privileges, and the cherished scenes of a loved land? Or do they esteem it an act of pious and exhilarating devotion, to spread their white canvas to the winds of heaven and to move forth upon the bosom of the *great deep* amidst the chime of church-going bells, the solemn peals of the organ, and the glad anthems of the saints?"

In the next part of the paragraph he suggests that an uncommonly high amount of disasters come the way of those who desecrate the Sabbath by heaving ho on a Sunday. "But how often have these slighted melodies been the *prelude* to the mariner's death knell! How often have they but a little preceded the funeral dirge which the howling winds have swept over the sailor's watery grave! And what assurance has the seaman who thus launches forth upon the stormy sea, to pursue his worldly schemes, in open disregard of the command, 'Remember the Sabbath day to keep it holy,' that he will ever again enter the hallowed precincts of the sanctuary, or hear any more the voice of the messenger of peace?"[125]

---

124. Coan, "Sailor's Sabbath," 2–3.
125. Coan, "Sailor's Sabbath," 3.

Coan comes to the second inquiry. "II. . . . Do owners of whale ships know that their vessels whale on the Lord's Day?" Here is the first paragraph of his response. He writes about different kinds of ship owners. "It has been said that they do; and not only so, but that they *approve* and *expect* it. And, furthermore, it is affirmed by many, that they absolutely *require* it as one of the conditions on which they give their ships to their commanders. It is also said that many of these ship owners are members of evangelical churches in Nantucket, New Bedford, Fair Haven, New London, Warren, Newport, and other places. Some owners, it is said, say nothing to their captains on the subject, and if their ships do but return *full* no inquiries are made how or on *what days* the oil was obtained. Now and then a shrewd Yankee Captain 'guesses that his pious owners have no objections to his taking oil *when he can get it.*'[126] A full ship fills the heart with joy, and lights up the countenance with an approving and benignant smile; while a half-filled ship often clouds the brow, excites the spleen, fills the biliary ducts, and disturbs the joyful and generous action of the heart. Especially would this be so, had the crew of the half-filled ship been permitted to rest one day in seven, 'according to the commandment'" [Luke 23:56].[127]

He poses the third inquiry in this way: "III. . . . Do professors of religion engage in Sabbath Whaling?" He writes positively about Christian captains of whaling and other ships who endeavor to keep the Sabbath while on the high seas. "It is truly gratifying to know that there are pious ship masters, both in the whaling and the merchant service, who make it a rule never to leave port or to do any unnecessary business on the Lord's Day. There are a few whale ships whose boats are never lowered to pursue the leviathans of the deep [Job 41:1] on the Sabbath. No '*look out*' is kept 'at masthead,' and no man on board is compelled to break the laws of his maker. These are bright spots upon a dark ocean. They are cheering stars in the seaman's lowering firmament. They are heralds and harbingers of day to the benighted and tempest-driven mariner. To such masters, and to all who co-operate with them, we would say:

> Launch thy bark, mariner—
> Christian, God speed thee—
> Let loose the rudder band—
> Good angels lead thee."[128]

Coan continues on for another four pages on this matter. He firmly responds to a complaint by some Christian whaling captains and tells an extended story about the hypocrisy of some others. "Lord's Day whalemen often complain that it is hard to maintain religion, and especially so, to keep up divine service at sea. No doubt it is hard and perhaps it is *impossible* to exercise *true religion* in connection with Sabbath

---

126. Coan provides no citation for these quotation marks. Are they what Coan heard? Read?
127. Coan, "Sailor's Sabbath," 5.
128. "Launch thy bark, mariner," by Caroline A. B. Southey, "The Mariner's Hymn" in Coan, "Sailor's Sabbath," 7.

breaking. The two cannot be reconciled. 'No man can serve two masters. *Ye cannot serve God and Mammon*"[129] [Matt 6:24].

Coan relates a multiple-paragraph story about a "clergyman [who] was once invited to preach on board a whale ship." Coan does not identify himself as that clergyman, but the story is told in such a detailed way that one wonders. It is the story of hypocrisy regarding the Sabbath by a Christian sailor. The punch line is spoken by a "Jack" who will not budge from the blubber room to attend the service. The old sailor "thundered out—'I don't want any of Captain ———'s religion! One Sunday it is all preach and pray, and the next Sunday it is *work! Work! Catch whales! Catch whales!* I tell you I don't want any *such* religion.' . . . and old Jack remained in the blubber room."[130]

Coan asks a fourth question. "IV. . . . Do clergymen in sea ports and seamen's chaplains preach against Sabbath Whaling?" At the end of the first paragraph he writes, "Probably many good ministers of the gospel are not at all aware how extensively—how nearly *universally* the Sabbath is desecrated by whalemen.

"But, we ask again, do ministers who are called to preach to ship owners and seafaring men labor to enlighten and reform them on this subject? Coan directly addresses such touchy subjects as Hawai'i being the first place sailors have heard about keeping the Sabbath on the high seas, as well as the employment challenge were coastal New England pastors to address this subject from their pulpits. "Very many masters, officers, and seamen assert that they never heard a minister preach against Sabbath whaling until they came to the Sandwich Islands; and some have even intimated that a clergyman who should be faithful in reproving for this sin, would not stop long in New Bedford, Nantucket, &c. Many seamen acknowledge the practice to be wrong, and express surprise that chaplains and other ministers in sea ports do not labor to break it up. Some who were members of evangelical churches in the United States have declared to the writer that their pastors, when questioned as to the morality of Sabbath whaling, have expressed the opinion that '*from the peculiarity of the circumstances*, it might be right for them to pursue this business on the Lord's Day!' This amounted to practical advice, and greatly soothed the troubled consciences of the pious sailors."[131]

Sounding as he does on the subject of preaching peace, Coan looks to the day when the preachers and newsmen will unite on the value of whalers keeping the Sabbath. "When the pulpit and the press in our sea ports shall become the trumpet of Jehovah, sounding forth the high sanctions of the Sabbath, and kindly calling on all the weary and storm-rocked sons of ocean, to *rest* from their toils on that holy day, and to worship and adore him who made the deep and the dry land, then may we hope that the time *hastens* when 'the abundance of the sea shall be converted to God.'

129. Coan, "Sailor's Sabbath," 9.
130. Coan, "Sailor's Sabbath," 9–10.
131. Coan, "Sailor's Sabbath," 11.

Then may we look for the day when the peaceful Sabbath sun, as it gilds with golden glory the ocean's horizon, shall be joyfully hailed by ten-thousands of happy seamen; and when the glad anthem of praise shall, like an incense cloud, roll upward from the bosom of every ocean and sea and navigable water of the world."[132]

Coan poses and answers the fifth question. "V. . . . Do churches discipline their members for whaling, &c, on the Sabbath?" Coan focuses directly on a matter of concern in those days. If discipline were exercised by the home churches, the situation could well change for the better. He looks at the bigger picture of church discipline before narrowing in on specifics. "By the arrangement of Christ, and by the common consent of Christendom, ministers of the gospel and Christian churches are the public and practical expounders of the Word of God. It follows, of course, that the doctrines and practices of the great mass of Christian professors will form the standard of morals and furnish the code of appeal among men. Consequently, if a mistake be made, an error propagated, or a vice practiced by Christians generally, this mistake, this error or this vice, will be viewed as harmless, adopted without scruple, and practiced without compunction by mankind. To a certain extent, therefore, ministers of the gospel are culpable by their silence of members engage in practices forbidden by the Bible.

Coan gives a few examples. One is mindful of his admonitions that the War of Rebellion took place in large part because the pastors of the South did not do their job by preaching and laboring against slavery. "For illustration of this statement we need only refer to the former views and practices of Christians in relation to spirituous liquors, slavery, war, etc."

He argues that pastors' slumbers on these and other subjects cause the world to be asleep to these wrongs as well. If the pastors do not do their job, how can the world be expected to respond in a godly manner? "The world will slumber over any cherished sin so long as ministers of the gospel and Christian churches slumber over it. The world will call darkness light, bitter sweet, and evil good, so long as ministers and churches do not, in doctrine, discipline, and life, contradict them."

"*Dare not* neglect to teach his flock the sin of engaging in a business in which they will be *driven* to desecrate God's holy day. 'Remember the Sabbath day to keep it holy' is just as clear and just as binding as any other law of the decalogue;[133] and its violation has called down as severe and terrible retribution on individuals and on nations as the violation of any other command of Jehovah."

He asks a rhetorical question and shows how ship captains who break the Sabbath are members in good standing of a church. "How then can a ship master, an officer or a common seaman, who has no more scruples to whale on the Lord's Day than to eat his daily food, be esteemed a member of an evangelical church, and receive a certificate to that effect from his pastor? If we are to take the *Bible*, and not the maxims and customs of men, for our rule of faith, and our standard of morality, we might as well

---

132. Coan, "Sailor's Sabbath," 11–12.
133. I.e., the Ten Commandments.

certify that the man who steals or commits adultery is in good and regular standing in the church of Christ, as the professor who thus willfully, deliberately, and constantly tramples on the Sabbath." Coan quotes the relevant commandments of what he has just written about. He concludes the paragraph by posing another rhetorical question. "What then is the difference in the morality of the thing, and what shields the professor from censure, when the same worldly, money-seeking passion is indulged on a *broader scale* upon the wide ocean?"

He turns to churches established by missionaries and the importance of keeping the Sabbath. "The missionary church, just gathered from heathenism, would be looked upon as a *burlesque* and a *scandal* upon the Christian name, were its members allowed, without rebuke, to sail their canoes, drag their nets, and ply their fishing tackle on the Lord's Day. And yet the plea of necessity, were it to be admitted at all, would be much more plausible here than in the case of the whalemen. No, every one knows that it *is not right* to pursue this business as it is pursued by most whalers, whether professors or non-professors."

Coan relates the deleterious consequences of not keeping the Sabbath upon the residents of the Hawaiian Islands. "And this evil is not confined, in its influences, to churches in Christian lands. Its unhappy effects are also felt on heathen shores. Take, for instance, the Hawaiian Islands. These are visited annually by two hundred or three hundred whale ships, most of whose masters wish to ship more or less natives in the service. Consequently, not a few of the church members are, by the hope of gain, lured to embark in an enterprise where the law of Jehovah has less practical influence over the mind than the love of money. This often brings the pastor[134] into painful collision with shipmasters and other interested persons, as, from a sense of duty he *cannot*, and *dare not* neglect to teach his flock the sin of engaging in a business in which they will be *driven* to desecrate God's holy day."

Coan next relates the evil of Hawaiians being excommunicated from their church while the Americans are not. "Nor does the evil stop here. Church members who are thus enticed to violate their solemn vows—by laboring on the Lord's Day—must be cut off from our fellowship, while many of their employers from enlightened and Christian lands are suffered to remain in regular standing, and, so far as we can learn, unrebuked in their respective churches."

In 1840 Coan showed flexibility on this subject by allowing Hawaiian men to assist the Exploratory Expedition going up the volcano on a Sabbath. He came to realize what a mistake that exception had been. Men were physically affected and the cumulative action led, in Coan's opinion, to braking and ending the Great Awakening.[135]

Coan concludes this section by expressing his wish for how the whaling business could be conducted, while closing with a warning. "Were the whaling business conducted on Christian and liberal principles, many of the best and most conscientious

---

134. Does Coan likely include himself in this observation?
135. Coan, *Life*, 67.

young men would be encouraged to ship in the service, thus gaining for themselves an honest and competent support, while they benefited their employers. But, as the enterprise is now conducted, sincere Christians, who have been faithfully instructed, and who duly regard their sacred vows to heaven, cannot engage in it with impunity."[136]

"VI. . . . Why do common seamen whale on the Lord's Day?" Coan relates a question he has probably heard numerous times, namely, the argument that everyone is doing it. Several other arguments are packed into the one statement. "One says, 'I know it is not right any more than it is right to plant potatoes on the Sabbath. But then it is *custom*. Every body does it, and it is of no use for one to stop if others don't. If all the rest would give it up *I* would.'"

Coan responds to what he considers to be weak arguments. "But you do not mean to say that you must do every thing that others do; or that you cannot refrain from following *every custom* around you. Suppose you lived in a community where it was the *custom* to lie, swear, fight, steal, and get drunk, would it not do for you to refrain from such customs till *all* did so?" Coan reminds the reader of God sending both watery and fiery ruin upon breakers of his law. "Scoffing was a custom in the time of Noah [Gen 6–9], and God poured a flood of wrath upon the custom. 'Filthy conversation' and 'unrighteous deeds' were the custom of the Sodomites [Gen 19 and Jude 7], and God rained a deluge of fiery ruin upon the people. But did Noah and Lot gain nothing by abjuring the customs of their time? No! No!"

Coan directly addresses the weakness of the argument. "This plea of custom is a weak one—it will not do. All that an independent, self-respecting, God-honoring man will do in such cases is, to determine whether a practice is *right*, and, if not, to abstain from it, *custom to the contrary notwithstanding*. There is honor, there is dignity, there is moral sublimity in this. What glory irradiates the brows, and what sacred veneration enshrines the memories of the *bold pioneers*—the *leaders of high resolve* in the cause of human freedom, of temperance and philanthropy."

He continues to address another "excuse." "But *custom* is not the only excuse. The master often says that his *officers* would be unwilling to abandon Sabbath whaling, and the officers, in their turn, think that the *captain* would not consent to such an arrangement. Now this is often so: neither master nor officers are willing to give up the practice. They understand each other, and, like Ananias and Sapphira [Acts 5:1–11], agree together to sin against the Lord. Let them look to that matter."

Coan brings up another objection. "Sometimes it is objected that the *crew* would not consent to renounce Sabbath whaling. They would murmur, mutinize, etc. As every one knows that the master commands and controls the ship, it is enough simply to *state* this excuse without comment."

Coan continues the colloquy with many objections and answers. No doubt these are all questions that Coan himself heard and endeavored to answer with a biblical basis. The final paragraph of this section sums up the matter powerfully. "It is a common

---

136 Coan, "Sailor's Sabbath," 12–14.

remark of masters and officers, 'If we should refuse to whale on the Sabbath we should never get another ship. We must please our owners or we are out of business.' Then it would be better to be out of business. Yea, it would be better to beg your bread from door to door, than to grow rich by doing wrong. '*Ye cannot serve two masters*' [Mat 6:24]. If ship owners are so illiberal and oppressive as not to allow a Sabbath to those in their employ, then it is time that all good and honest men seek business in which they may act up to the dictates of their consciences. Masters have been heard to say, 'Our owners are church members, but they would never give their ships to any who would not whale on Sunday.' For the honor of such men it is to be hoped that is a mistake. But, if it be true, it only furnishes an illustration of the assertions—'The love of money is the root of all evil' [1 Tim 6:10]. 'He that *maketh haste* to be rich shall not be innocent' [Prov 28:20]; and 'they that *will be rich* fall into temptation and a snare, and into many foolish and hurtful lusts which drown men in destruction, and perdition'"[137] [1 Tim 6:9].

"VII. We must next inquire why common seamen whale on the Lord's Day." Coan notes that it "is a question of deep interest, as it must effect the temporal and eternal wellbeing of many thousands of sailors." He suggests that the sailors have not thought through their situation. "Perhaps most whale men never stop to ask why they do it. It is a *custom* and they fall in with it. It is *commanded* and they do it. But why the custom and the command? 'The Sabbath was made for man' [Mark 2:27]—for man *generic*. i.e., for *all men*. Why, then, is there no Sabbath for the sailor? No day which he can call his own? No day on which he may not be required to perform the most arduous and perilous labors? No day on which he may rest his weary limbs? No day on which he may retire with his Bible and his God, and feel the calm consciousness of relaxation from toil, and the assurance that, during these peaceful hours, no mortal may control his muscles or his mind?"

He recognizes that some sailors do not care about observing the Sabbath, but also avers that some do. "It is true that many, and perhaps, *most* sailors, are willing to whale on the Sabbath. Of course such must bear their own responsibility. But it is also true that a goodly number would prefer *not to labor on that day*.—Hundreds of young men are annually shipped from the country. Among these are sometimes found sober, moral, and pious men, who have been taught by religious parents and Christian ministers to 'remember the Sabbath.'"

Coan makes recommendations for the pious sailor and concludes by writing: "This may be called 'preaching mutiny and encouraging insubordination among seamen.' Nothing, however, is farther from the heart of the writer, or from the true interpretation of these remarks. In fact, no true Sabbath-keeping seaman ever did or ever will engage in mutiny. This conduct may be expected only from those who do not fear God or regard his Sabbaths. But it will be sufficient to reply to such an ungenerous insinuation, that *if this be mutiny*, then Daniel, Shadrach, Paul, Peter, yea,

---

137 Coan, "Sailor's Sabbath," 14–17.

all the prophets and apostles, and even Christ himself preached and practiced the same doctrine."[138]

He turns to the final question. "VIII. . . . Have ship-masters a right to compel their crews to whale on the Sabbath?" He is direct in the first sentence. "The only legitimate answer to this question is *no*." He gives three reasons why. "First. Because the sailor has signed no papers, bonds, instruments, or anything else whatsoever, in which he promises to whale seven days in a week. And, moreover, as has been remarked, many do not know at the time of shipping, that such is the practice among whalemen.

"Second. Because the civil law does not grant this power to the master. The laws of most Christian states distinctly recognize the Lord's Day; and offer protection to all who wish to observe it. Nowhere, in a free and Christian community, are common laborers compelled by the civil power to toil on the Sabbath . . .

"Third. Because the Almighty never gave this power to the master.

"In the beginning God gave the Sabbath to man—*to all men* of *every class*. It is heaven's rich legacy to all—It is *inalienable*, and no man can take it from his fellow without entrenching on the prerogatives of Jehovah. How then shall the master of a ship have power to disannul, or to suspend at pleasure, this statute of heaven, by refusing those under his command, the enjoyment of that day of rest, which none but the eternal King, who first gave the boon, can, with impunity, take from them?"[139]

Coan deals with a few more objections near the end of the pamphlet. He eloquently and powerfully brings his argument home in the concluding two paragraphs. "The foregoing remarks have been written with great plainness and freedom, but with the utmost candor and good will, and with an earnest and sincere desire to promote the temporal and eternal honest lover of truth. None will be offended at their plainness, but those who are determined to resist the light 'because their deeds are evil' [John 3:19]. The sentiments herein expressed are those which the writer is willing to meet, and those which every whaleman, and all others concerned, will meet at the Judgment Day.

"May the time hasten when the Sabbath sun shall be hailed joyfully by every seaman—when the Bethel Flag shall wave aloft on every ship, and when every ocean and sea shall echo the glad anthem of the sailor, as his song of praise is borne on the breath of heaven into the ear of him 'who made the sea and the dry land'"[140] [Gen 1:9–10].

Once printed, the "Sailor's Sabbath" was one of the many items Coan distributed to sailors. "During the week I husband *minutes* and *seize* occasions to distribute Bibles, tracts, &c., and to converse with the wanderer of the deep." He writes *The Sailor's Magazine*, "Your cause is ever dear to us, and we shall never cease to pray and sympathize with you, and to cooperate so far as God gives us ability." As he would write to *The Advocate of Peace*, he cites the cost of building a church for the straightened

---

138. Coan, "Sailor's Sabbath," 17–20.
139. Coan, "Sailor's Sabbath," 20–21.
140. Coan, "Sailor's Sabbath," 24.

circumstances limiting the amount of donations. "We may not be able to send you a donation this year, as we wish to do. We are striving to collect eight thousand or ten thousand dollars to build a neat and substantial church edifice. More than four thousand dollars have been secured, but the rest must come hard and be heavy on our poor natives, unless we appropriate a part of their monthly contributions, which used to go to foreign objects to this purpose. This, we shall, I think, do for a year or two, until we see the temple of the Lord reared among us. My people built twenty-five meeting houses in the whole parish."[141]

CONVERSATIONS WITH AND DISTRIBUTION OF LITERATURE TO CREWS AND OFFICERS

Coan says, "I have conversed with scores of sailors during the past season, and have seen the tear tremble in many an eye, and have heard the expressed resolve to serve the Lord." Printed material assisted Coan in his evangelizing sailors of naval or commercial vessels. In addition to English, "I have also distributed many Bibles and testaments among the Americans, French, Germans, Spanish, and Portuguese. All the ships have been supplied with a large bundle of assorted tracts, papers, pamphlets, books, etc., and many books and tracts have been given to individuals."[142]

Coan was passionate about distributing Bibles and Testaments[143] in every language represented by the seafarers who touched land in Hilo. His dedication is seen in his unhesitating willingness to give away some of his own Bibles. In 1841, he asks Levi Chamberlain to send him the varieties of Holy Scripture that he needs. "I drop you this note in the greatest haste as I am now packing up for the tour of Hilo,[144] which I commence to-day . . . Supposing that an opportunity for Oahu may occur before my return, I leave this line to request you, if you have them on hand, to send me some of the Bibles and Test[ament]s of the A[merican] B[ible] S[ociety]. I would like twenty Eng. Bibles, as many Test[ament]s, ten French Bibles or Test[aments]s. And as many Spanish for distribution among seamen, etc. I do not know whether you have such books on hand for distribution, or whether you can procure them. Bro. [John] Diell

---

141. *Sailor's Magazine*, 184.
142. *Sailor's Magazine*, 184.
143. New Testaments; sometimes with the Psalms and Proverbs added from the Old Testament.
144. The Hilo district; outlying villages to the north, west, and east of the village of Hilo.

formerly supplied me with Bibles for seamen but I have given out the last of them this season[145] besides giving out some of my own family Bibles."[146]

In his 1860 station report, Coan writes about the challenges and rewards of his labors among seamen. "In this labor for seamen I have been led to correspond with the American Bible, Tract, Peace, Temperance, and Seamen's Friend Societies, and have obtained Bibles and tracts in the English, French, German Spanish, Portuguese, Swedish, Danish, and Chinese languages; which with many thousands of tracts have been distributed among these vessels. Some of this 'bread cast upon the waters' [Eccl 11:1] has been found again according to the promise."[147] Can one imagine the organization and storage required for this one aspect of Coan's varied ministries?

Coan did whatever necessary organization and logistics were required to minister to seamen. He plugged away and occasionally saw some encouraging results. "But we do not labor for seamen without hope. There are stars in the midnight sky—and there are some among the seamen who reflect a few rays of light, and who appear as harbingers of a future day yet to dawn upon the sea."[148]

Both Coan's future hope and his distribution of Peace Society material point to his being a "peace man."

---

145. From HawaiiHistory.org: "Whalers—primarily American vessels—began arriving in Hawai'i in the early nineteenth century. At this time, whale oil was used for heating, lamps and in industrial machinery; whale bone (actually the baleen strips suspended from the whale's upper jaw) was used in corsets, skirt hoops, umbrellas and buggy whips. Whaling ships visiting hunting grounds in the Japan Sea, the South Pacific and later the Arctic, usually punctuated their forays twice a year with stops to restock provisions, replenish their crews and transship their whale oil cargoes. For Hawaiian ports, especially Honolulu and Lahaina, the whaling fleet was the crux of the economy for twenty years or more. More than one hundred ships stopped in Hawaiian ports in 1824. Over the next two decades, the Pacific whaling fleet nearly quadrupled in size and in the record year of 1846, 736 whaling ships arrived in Hawai'i."

146. Titus Coan to Levi Chamberlin, November 23, 1841, Coan, *Memorial Volume*?, np.

147. Coan, 1860 station report.

148. Coan, HMH digitized 1860 Hilo station report, 118.

13

Peace Man

WAR AND PEACE: AN EXAMINATION OF TITUS COAN'S COMPLEX VIEW OF A PERENNIAL ISSUE

"If I ever became a disciple of Christ, I then became a *peace man*."[1]

"You allude to the subject of war and you say that all war is wrong. That is, I think, a true proposition. On the question whether it be lawful for a disciple of Christ to engage in it, much may be said on both sides. I prefer what I esteem the safer side, still there are many sincere Christians and men whom I ardently love who have been trained to the profession of arms. It is my opinion that if all professed Christians of every name would, both in doctrine and practice, decidedly discountenance war, the evil would soon cease in Christendom by a moral necessity. But the world is not yet prepared for such a new and strange doctrine. Nor has the church faith enough to try the experiment. But the good Lord will accomplish it in his time. It is a consummation of love such as I know your heart as well as mine devoutly desires. We will then pray that the 'Prince of Peace' [Isa 9:6] may reign from east to west and from pole to pole, and that there may be a truly and universally 'peace on earth and good will among men.'"[2]

Titus Coan's letters "were ever found" to be "very acceptable to the readers. The thoughts themselves are invariably good, but it is the spirit pervading and impregnating them that makes our friends like them so much."[3]

---

1 Titus Coan to J. B. Miles, *Advocate of Peace* 5 (January 1873).

2. Coan to DuPont, June 7, 1850, in Coan, *Memorial Volume*, 67.

3. Dr. Beckwith, Secretary of the Peace Society, in Coan, *Memorial Volume*, 52.

Titus Coan: "Apostle to the Sandwich Islands"

INTRODUCTION

Although it was a cause close to his heart throughout his ministry in Hawai'i, no scholar has examined Coan's focus on peace—in his life, with his pen, and as a pastor. This chapter examines Coan's development from involvement in the military to becoming a peace man who uses the power of his pen and his pastorate for the cause of the Prince of Peace.

SOJOURN TO BECOMING A "PEACE MAN"

Titus Coan did not begin as a peace man. As a preteen through young adulthood, he enthusiastically entered into militaristic activity—first in imitation, then as an armed soldier. In an 1873 "Letter to the Children" in the *Angel of Peace*, he confesses his militaristic involvement, shares his change of view, and calls all youth and children to enlist under the banner of "the God of Love and Peace."

He begins the letter by explaining that when "I was a school-boy, eleven years old," the War of 1812 took place. He writes of the ambivalence of the community. People grieved the death of loved ones. A peace celebration is held, but includes military aspects. Coan becomes involved in an imitation army in his home town of Killingworth.

"Then came the Jubilee.[4] Many good men had wept and prayed that the war might cease. Many fathers and mothers, and widows, and orphans, and many friends and lovers wept and mourned for dear ones smitten to the earth by the fiery hail of war.

"Now the country was ablaze with illuminations, jarring under the thunder of artillery, and shouting under the electricity of eloquence—some praying and praising the Lord, and others feasting, reveling, and dancing.

"My townsmen prepared for a grand peace celebration. The programme was published, which included religious exercises, a parade of infantry, cavalry, and artillery, firing, a big dinner, etc. I was a school-boy, and all the boys caught the spirit of the times." Coan's leadership abilities are seen in this ersatz gathering, even though he later laments his involvement. "We met in council, organized a company of Light Artillery, chose officers, prescribed an uniform and procured a small blunderbuss, mounted it on a carriage . . . The boys all chose me captain; but I declined . . . I nominated another boy, a year older than myself, and told them to elect him, and I would consent to be lieutenant."[5]

In his autobiography, Coan writes, "I had been dazzled, while a boy, with the tales of military and naval exploits, with the flashing of sabers, the waving of plumes, and with the beauty of uniforms. It had been my delight to watch the evolutions of

---

4. End of the war?
5. Coan to children by way of Brother Miles, *Angel of Peace*, January 1873.

cavalry, artillery, and militia regiments on days of drill and of general review. I had seen the proud war-ships of Britain driving the fishing-boats, the sloops, schooners, brigs, barks, ships, all the floating commerce of Long Island Sound, into our rivers, lagoons, bays, creeks, and harbors."

He continues with what he observed of the war and of the battles about which he heard. "I had seen the flashes and heard the thunder of their guns; had been wakened at midnight by the alarm-bells of the town, and the quick fire of the garrison. I had heard of Canada, of Buffalo, of the Northern and Southern Lakes, of the Potomac, of Washington, of New Orleans, and of the peace with its joyful celebrations, and its thunder-notes of gladness rolling over the land."[6]

Returning to his letter to children, Coan notes that the seeds sown in his youth germinated as an adult. "And what came of all this? Let me tell you:

"I grew up a youth fond of military display. The seeds planted in boyhood germinated. I became an officer in artillery, with a second lieutenant's, and soon after, a first lieutenant's commission, with the prospect of rising as high as the gas in the balloon would lift me . . . Had war come on then, I should doubtless have been in it, and perhaps in another world fifty years ago."[7]

Returning to his autobiography, Coan appears to at least partially blame the laws of his state as to why he served in the militia. "When the time came[8] for me to enter the militia ranks, according to the laws of the state, I enlisted in a company of light artillery whose regiment had been commanded by Col. Bray during the war of 1812–15,[9] and in which one of my brothers had served in the garrison of my native town during that war."

He notes that eventually all the military enthusiasm "died out, and a more rational, a calmer and purer peace spread over land and sea, there came a change in my military feelings and aspirations."[10] Returning to his letter Coan writes the children, "I went into the state of New York to visit. The Lord detained me. I was offered business. I remained a teacher and a student. I was I think *converted*."

He indicates that his position on war and peace changed after his conversion. "All my military ardor left me. I resigned my commission against the earnest remonstrances of my fellow-officers. I exchanged my sword for the 'sword of the Spirit' [Eph 6:16]; my foolish uniform for the 'robe of Righteousness' [Rev. 19:8], offered me by the Prince of Peace;[11] studied now to *save* men, and not to *kill*; became an humble Sabbath Superintendent, then an ordained minister of the gospel; then a missionary to Patagonia, and, finally, a missionary to the Hawaiian Islands, where, with the best

---

6. Coan, *Life*, 6–7.
7. Titus Coan to J. B. Miles, *Advocate of Peace* 5 (January 1873).
8. At the age of eighteen? Twenty-one?
9. Coan was fourteen when the war ended.
10. Coan, *Life*, 7.
11. This oft-repeated phrase is from Isaiah 9:6.

temporal gift God ever gave to man, precious wife, just gone to heaven, I have lived near thirty-eight years, with more happiness than any king upon an earthly throne."

Coan next tells of recently admitting some boys to church membership and calling the young readers to enlist as soldiers of Christ. "Last Sabbath I received a number of boys, about twelve years old, to the Hilo Church, making the whole number gathered to the church under my care twelve thousand.[12]

"And now, my young friends, let me ask you which course would have been the wiser in me—to have been a solder and to have killed twelve thousand men, or to be a soldier of Jesus Christ, [2 Tim 2:3] to bring a few thousands to lay down their arms, and submit to our good and glorious King?

"Let me persuade you all to *enlist now* under the banner of Jesus, and may the God of Love and of Peace make you useful and happy in life, peaceful and triumphant in death, and glorious in heaven."

In his final paragraph, addressed to Brother Miles, Coan apologizes for the length of the letter but also provides the quotation used at the beginning of the chapter. "If I ever became a disciple of Christ, I then became a *peace man*. God help the blessed cause [of peace], Yours, in the bands of peace, T. COAN."[13]

PEN WARRIOR FOR PEACE: *ADVOCATE OF PEACE*

Titus Coan used the power of his pen to further the cause of peace: with his Hawaiian congregation and to persuade people in America. The Library of Congress has a typed list with the title[14] "Letters from Titus Coan are in the *ADVOCATE OF PEACE* AS FOLLOWS."[15] The letters stretch from February of 1849 through April of 1882.
The typewritten page in the Library of Congress Coan collection lists page numbers (in most cases) and dates of publication in *The Advocate of Peace* journal of twenty-five letters from Titus Coan between February of 1849 and April of 1882. An entire set of *Advocate* editions resides at the Swarthmore College Peace Collection archives. Six of those letters (32 percent) were published during the Civil War. Rev. Samuel Hopkins Emery writes about Titus Coan in an unattributed article in the Library of Congress Coan papers. He imposes a pacifistic cast upon Coan, whom he heard "in

---

12. This number includes all who joined over the years. Some would have died, others fallen away, and perhaps moved during that period, meaning there were not twelve thousand members actively attending the First Hawaiian Church of Hilo at the time of writing this letter. Conversely, this number does not include the number of non-Hawaiians whom Coan brought to Christ and otherwise influence. The metaphor he is developing is an apt one.

13. Titus Coan to J. B. Miles, *Advocate of Peace* 5, January 1873.

14. LOC Box 17?

15. A review of microfilm covering the time window for all the Coan letters reveals the following information: twenty-five letters are listed; two were not found; and one was missing from a reel (Vol. 6 no. 1); two were found that were not listed—May 12, 1853, September 1853, April 1856, 56–57; two of the letters are to *The Advocate of Peace*'s short-lived *Angel of Peace* publication for children. This makes a net twenty-five letters, though with six different from the ones on the list.

the city of Providence,[16] and was greatly interested in his statements concerning his work in general, and especially the teachings of the mission from the beginning on the subject of war." Emery is impressed that Coan convinced the violent and cruel Hawaiians "in favor of peace. The mission appears to have adopted the principle of the early Christians, that it is unchristian to fight." Mr. Coan has "encouraged his church[17]—the largest probably, but by no means the wealthiest in the world—to contribute with exemplary liberality to the Treasury of the American Peace Society." Emery is gratuitously biased when he notes with disapproval that the Sumatra martyrs Lyman and Munson "were found with weapons of offence as well as defence in their hands."[18]

In 1862, he writes of squeezing in time to write on a subject close to his heart. "I am on the wing a large part of my time, and can only *snatch* a moment to write to my friends, to disburden my heart in the cause of peace, or to contemplate the great themes and the vast movements which mark the times, and shake the world."[19]

In the February 1849 issue of *The Advocate of Peace*,[20] the editor indicates that two or three years prior, every American Board missionary was given copies of *The Peace Book*.[21] Coan's first letter comes after this opportunity. It "will be remembered that some two or three years ago we began to furnish every American Missionary station among the heathen with a copy of our BOOK of PEACE, containing the full series of our tracts."[22]

The BYU library online indicates that the World Affairs Institute "is collaborating with JSTOR to digitize, preserve and extend access to *Advocate of Peace* (1847-1884)."[23] The September 1853 *Advocate of Peace*[24] is significant for at least three reasons. It includes: 1) A letter from Coan that the Library of Congress does not list; and, 2) It includes a letter from former American Board missionary Jonathan Green[25] and the circular[26] sent from the journal to missionaries.

The editor George Cone Beckwith introduces the letter responses by Coan and Green by explaining that near the end of 1852, *The Advocate of Peace* "sent to American Missionaries in foreign lands a Circular specifying a series of points on

16. Late 1870, early 1871?

17. First Hawaiian Church of Hilo.

18. S. Hopkins Emery, in undated, untitled article in Titus Coan Papers, LOC.

19. *Advocate of Peace* 22 (September 1862) 138.

20. American Peace Society published under the name of *The Advocate of Peace* from 1834 through 1932, at which time it changed the name to *World Affairs*.

21. See previous chapter.

22. *Advocate of Peace* 9 (February 1849) 22.

23. http://lib.byu.edu/.

24. *Advocate of Peace* 13 (September 1853) 340-48.

25. Judd, *Missionary Album*, provides the uncited reason for the Greens' departure: "'they were convinced that the relations the Board sustained to American slavery were not right in the sight of God,'" 104.

26. A letter "circulated" to many people.

which we requested an expression of their views, in the hope of using their replies for the furtherance of our cause as identical in spirit and aim with that of the world's evangelization."[27]

The six questions are:

"1. Let us inquire how far you regard this cause as identical in spirit and results with your own, and how far the former as essential or tributary to the latter.

"2. To what extent has the practice of war among nations reputedly Christian, prejudiced the unevangelized against the gospel, and obstructed its spread, or neutralized its saving power?

"3. What influence, in your judgment, would a general war in Christendom, or a protracted war between two such countries as England and America,[28] be likely to have on the missionary cause?

"4. What do you think would be, or what have you found actually to be, the effect of war on the immediate field of missionary operations?

"5. Since the gospel has been preached in Christendom for fifteen centuries without abolishing war in a single nation, and as we must all desire to prevent so long a delay in accomplishing this part of its promised results among the heathen, what can be done, or what should be attempted, by Christians at home, and by missionaries, to make sure henceforth of having peace go hand in hand with the gospel over the whole earth?

"6. Is there, on this part of Christianity, any special defect, and if so, what, in the education of Christian missionaries for their work?"

In addition, the Circular casts a broad net by then asking that "if you see fit, dear Sir, to answer these inquiries in detail or to make any other suggestions on the general subject that may serve to guide or encourage us in the great Christian enterprise entrusted for the present to our care, you will oblige us." Also, if the missionaries would like to request from the Peace Society volumes, tracts, and the "monthly periodical, we shall be glad to forward one copy or more of each and all for your mission in any way you may direct."

The reason why Green and Coan are included in this piece is that "we have just received the first response." Green avails himself of the invitation to make suggestions on the general subject of peace. His letter is one and a half pages in length.[29] "I must no longer delay the performance of a duty which I have owed you and your Society, a long time, viz., the duty of writing you, and assuring you of my sympathy and co-operation, so far as I may be able to co-operate with you in your most interesting work."

---

27. Note the equating and importance of peace with world evangelization.
28. Was such a hypothetical war really considered a possibility in the early 1850s?
29. From the bottom of 340 through the top of 341.

Echoing Coan's equating being a Christian with being a "peace man," Green avers, "I see not how any good man can be indifferent to the speedy success of the cause of peace." He makes reference to writings in the July and August 1851 *Advocate of Peace* and then notes, "It seems amazing that a single follower of the Son of God, of the Prince of Peace, should hesitate a moment as to his duty of engaging in this cause, of devoting a portion of his time and strength and resources to the good work of causing men to beat their swords into plow-shares, and their spears into pruning-hooks" [Joel 3:10; Isa 2:4].

He addresses the "excuses in self-justification" that people bring forward. "How many seem to expect that evils are to be expelled from the earth by a process so quiet, that every one around can sleep as soundly as he might have done, had sin never entered our poor, distracted world."

He then contrasts this view with that of the Prince of Peace. "So thought not Christ." In an interesting twist on a Bible verse, Green writes that Christ "came to send a fire on the earth, 'to send not peace but a sword' [Matt 10:34]. So his gospel, when faithfully preached, is a very different thing from what many regard it. It comes down upon *specific* evils like 'the fire and hammer which break in pieces the flinty rock'" [Jer 23:29].

Green concludes his letter with encouragement and exhortation to those who are pressing forward the cause of peace. "Go on, friends, of the Redeemer, in the good though arduous work in which you are engaged. The promises of the Bible may well cheer you, though multitudes refuse at present to co-operate with you in so good a work. Soon all the great and wise of the land, and the world, will be with you, and you will see the nations with one heart and soul 'sitting at the feet of Jesus in their right mind.'"[30]

While Coan's letter is similar in sentiment to Green's, there are a number of contrasts: 1) it is longer;[31] 2) after an introduction, it addresses itself to each of the six questions; 3) it includes a specific allusion to missions elsewhere in the Pacific; and 4) he indicates[32] the publications most helpful to him.

He gives the example of peace furthering missions, in this case Micronesia.[33] Next Coan replies to each of the journal's questions in the order posed.

"I. The cause of peace I regard as identical with the cause of Christian missions, or, more comprehensively, Christianity itself, from the fact that the origin, objects,

---

30. This is a reference to the demoniac whom Jesus heals, as related in Mark 5:15 and preceding verses. Apparently this was the first letter by Green published by *The Advocate of Peace*, because the editors close with the expressed "hope for more from the same source." Green in *Advocate of Peace* 13 (September 1853) 340–41. No other letter from Green to this publication is known to exist.

31. It is six and a half pages in length.

32. Per the Circular.

33. *Advocate of Peace* 13 (September 1853) 342–43.

spirit, and results are identical." He develops that statement in almost one page of typed text.

"II. Your second question is too broad for my narrow limits and my limited time. It calls for facts and illustrations from the four quarters of the globe. If the annals of Christian warfare (what a misnomer!)[34] could be *spread out* before us, fearful, and soul-stirring tales would be of bitter and ruinous prejudices, which the worse than savage wars of nominally Christian nations have excited among the unevangelizing tribes." He lists many groups from around the world who do not respond well to Christianity because of warfare.

"III. As to your third question, the influence of a general war in Christendom on the missionary cause, I answer, *most disastrous*, undoubtedly in every respect.

"IV. The effects of war on the immediate field of missionary operations have been, and they always will be, vastly unhappy. Many of the remarks under the foregoing heads, are equally apposite here, and need not be repeated.

"V. It is a painful reflection that, for the last fifteen centuries, the gospel has not abolished war in a single nation where it has been preached." In answer to the question, "What can be done?" Coan provides five points:

"1. Let every minister *review his theology*, without commentary, on this point, and see to it, that he fully understand the import and the objects of the gospel of peace.

"2. Let him kindly, fearlessly, wisely, and uniformly preach 'the truth, the whole truth, and nothing but the truth,' on this subject.

"3. Let him illustrate all 'the fulness of the blessing of the gospel of peace' [Rom 15:29][35] in his own life and conversation.

"4. Let him never receive to his church any one who holds to the doctrine of war and revenge, and who will not subscribe to that blessed 'New Covenant,' 'Love your enemies, bless them that curse you, do good to them that hate you, and *pray* for (not fight them) that spitefully entreat you'[36] [Matt 5:44].

"5. Let him promptly, wisely, consistently call to account any member who teaches or acts inconsistently with these heavenly rules; and if, after kind, faithful and patient instruction and admonition, this belligerent member will not be reformed, let him be severed from the church, as one who cannot be forgiven of his Heavenly Father, because he refuses to forgive his own enemies.

---

34. Unless otherwise noted, all parentheses in this section are by Coan.
35. In the verse it is "the gospel of Christ," with peace being mentioned later in the verse.
36. It appears that hear Coan the Presbyterian is veering toward an Anabaptist position, namely that all war and peace verses apply equally to nations as well as individuals.

"VI. On the sixth question I have little to say which has not been anticipated in foregoing remarks. There is nothing peculiar in the education of missionaries. They are educated like other Christians, and other ministers of the gospel."

Coan concludes his response to George Beckwith with these words: "I have written hastily, and amidst many interruptions; but, if anything here stated shall give comfort and encouragement to you and your dear coadjutors in the cause of peace, then may God only be praised for it.

"In behalf of Christ, I am, dear brother, most faithfully and fraternally yours, in the gospel of peace, Titus Coan."[37]

Returning to the beginning of Coan's response to Beckwith's circular, he indicates that a "kind note was included with the Circular, and answers the question about the most helpful publications: "Nothing comes amiss; but what we value most are, *The Book of Peace, Peace Manual, Review of Mexican War*, by Livermore and Jay, and *Advocate of Peace* (the journal itself)."[38]

The Book of Peace contains sixty-four essays and an index. There are eighteen named authors, including Erasmus. The diversity of the repeat authors with the number of essays in parenthesis indicates the eclectic nature of the work: W[illiam] Ellery Channing[39] (four); Jonathan Dymond[40] (four); Howard Malcom[41] (two); and Charles Sumner[42] (two).

The following are selected essay titles:

1. "Cause of Peace"

2. "A Sketch of War: What It Is and What It Does"

3. "Testimonies against War"

4. "War and the Bible"

9. "Erasmus on War"

23. "The Early Christians and War"

45. "Inefficacy of War"

49. "Peace and Government"

51. "War a Destroyer of Souls"

52. "War and Hearth, or the Influence of War on Domestic Happiness"[43]

37. *Advocate of Peace* 13 (September 1853) 343–46.

38 *Advocate of Peace* 13 (September 1853) 342. See also passages in the two chapters in *Life* on his journeys to the Marquesas Islands.

39. Unitarian theologian and Transcendentalist poet, 1780–1842.

40. English Quaker and ethical philosopher, 1796–1828.

41. American educator and Baptist pastor, 1799–1879.

42. Massachusetts abolitionist senator 1811–74.

43. Beckwith, *Book of Peace*, 3.

Beckwith is the compiler and editor of *The Book of Peace: A Collection of Essays on War and Peace*.[44] In the Preface, Beckwith writes, "There has been, since the time of the gifted Erasmus, a great deal of eloquent writing on peace; and the following pages contain the best productions on the subject not only of past ages, but of our own."[45] He notes that "no theme has ever waked a purer or loftier inspiration [than has peace]; and on no topic in the whole range of morals, theology, or general literature, can there be found finer specimens of taste and experience."[46]

The second book Coan mentions to Beckwith is another book put together by Beckwith, *The Peace Manual: or War and Its Remedies*. It has two parts: "I. Physical Evils of War" and "II. Moral Evils of War." The Reverend Mr. Jeffries[47] writes that "America has the honor of inventing two of the most valuable institutions that ever blessed mankind,— the Peace Society and the Temperance Society." Beckwith continues on the same page, if "every American viewed them as I do, *he would join them immediately*."[48]

The third book Coan mentions to Beckwith is *The War with Mexico Reviewed*. While Coan speaks of Livermore and [William?] Jay, it was only written[49] by Abriel Abbot Livermore. Writing in Keene, New Hampshire, on September 11, 1849, Livermore notes in the preface, "War, the great spiritual injury, must fall in due time before the progress of the gospel. To doubt this result seems to presume that the Prince of Peace has come in vain, and that finite creatures can eventualy [sic] frustrate the plan of the infinite Creator."[50] It appears that Coan selected this work as important because of the timely nature of it—with the relatively recent conclusion of that war. The previous two books could better endure the test of time.

In one of Coan's earliest letters to *The Advocate of Peace*, he expresses his passion. "I feel an unutterably deep and deathless interest in this cause, for it is the cause of Christ. It is heaven's true mission to man; and I feel pained at my very heart, I feel grieved and ashamed that, for more than a thousand years, the gospel of peace should have been so misread and misinterpreted as to give sanction to the diabolical practice of war, and to lead otherwise good and generous minds to sleep under the dark delusion that the '*Prince of Peace*' may be propitiated with the sacrifices of the bloodstained, or may preside with complacency over the pomp, and the rage, and the fiendish carnage of the battle-field."[51]

---

44. In an ironic twist, this volume is available from Barnes and Noble online as part of the War College Series.
45. Beckwith, *Book of Peace*, 3.
46. Beckwith, *Book of Peace*, 4.
47. Characterized as a "distinguished English Missionary in India."
48. Beckwith, *Peace Manual*, 14.
49. According to all bibliographies checked.
50. Livermore, *War with Mexico*, viii.
51. Coan letter, January 14, 1851, in *Advocate of Peace* 12 (February 1852) 29.

Except for the next section, most of the rest of the chapter draws from Coan's letters to this publication.

CORRESPONDENCE WITH QUAKERS

During the 1860s a mutually enjoyed correspondence commenced between Titus Coan and Joel and Hannah Bean.[52] Lydia provides in the *Memorial Volume* four letters from Titus and one from Joel. In a letter written to Lydia after Titus's death, Joel shares how he first learned of Titus and when they first met.

Joel learned of Titus through the Royal British Navy participant turned globe-trotting Quaker evangelist Daniel Wheeler.[53] Long before he and Hannah met him, "we had read of him and his fellow-laborers, in the journal of Daniel Wheeler; and the warm welcome extended by these dear fathers of the Sandwich Islands Mission to members of our society who visited the islands, as ambassadors for Christ, brought them into esteem in our section of the church, both in England and America."[54]

Bean also writes of his and Hannah's first meeting with Fidelia and Titus at the Emerald Bower in 1862. He provides a touching description of his nervousness at meeting them. "Our first meeting with dear Titus Coan was in his own home, in the spring of 1862."[55]

Lydia returns the esteemed regards within the parentheses before the first letter from Titus to the Beans found in the *Memorial Volume*: "*widely known and esteemed members of the Society of Friends.*" In that letter, Coan starts with a recurring theme in his correspondence with the Beans: Christian unity that transcends denominations. "My very pen seems to rejoice in dropping thoughts of love to Christian friends so congenial and so dear to us as our precious brother and sister, Joel and Hannah."

He emphasizes unity and expresses the hope that he would never inadvertently write anything that would break their Christian fellowship. "Your united letters came loaded with fragrant odors from the hills of Zion. There is not in them a sentiment or a word which does not meet a cordial welcome and a warm response. And so deep is our respect, so tender and true our love for you, and for all the consistent members of your society, that you might ever express any sentiment in which we may accidentally

---

52. Joel Bean (1825–1914) was a Quaker (Religious Society of Friends) minister whose name has been associated with a branch of Quakerism that some label "Beanite." The Beans favored revival within the Society of Friends, but during the 1870s they decided that the revival had gone beyond foundational Quaker teachings. Nevertheless, they did not join with the more conservative reaction to the revival. Regardless of the intramural strife within their quintessential Peace Church, the Beans maintained cordial relationships with the Coans through and after Titus's death. Wikipedia, "Joel Bean."

53. Wheeler, *Extracts*.

54. Joel Bean to Lydia Coan, 1883, in Coan, *Memorial Volume*, 240. The visit by Daniel Wheeler to the Sandwich Islands occurred in late 1835 and early 1836. Wheeler first met with Hiram Bingham, who gave Wheeler letters of introduction to Titus Coan and David Lyman.

55. Joel Bean to Lydia Coan, 1883, in Coan, *Memorial Volume*, 240.

and honestly differ without the least fear that our Christian fellowship would be interrupted. 'How good and how pleasant it is for brethren to dwell together,' not in *uniformity*, but in 'unity'" [Ps 33:1].

Coan next makes reference to the Beans' letter reference to their visit to Hilo. "Your reference to your visit to our tropical shores kindles our love and awakens our kindest reminiscences; and the elevation of your spiritual telescope to the heavenly hills where faith and hope shall inherit a fruition of love and joy stimulates us to plume our wings for upward flight."

Having re-established their mutual friendship and Christian unity, Coan moves to the heart of their communion. Referring to the end of the Civil War, he writes, "The news of peace rolled a wave of joy over our islets. Our hearts swelled in gratitude, and our lips burst in thanksgiving to God. The old Pacific seemed more peaceful, and her broad bosom swelled with joy, and her radiant face was kissed by the soft breezes and lighted by the smiles of heaven. 'The trees of the woods sang out, the floods clapped their hands and the hills were joyful' [Ps 96:12] at the glad news."[56]

Then came the tragic news of the assassination of Abraham Lincoln. That situation will be discussed in the transition to the next topic of this chapter. The next recorded letter in the *Memorial Volume* from Coan to the Beans is three years later, on July 15, 1868. He first rejoices in the Quaker publication on the subject of peace. "I hail with delight the news that 'Friends' are publishing in Chicago *The Herald of Peace*. Such papers should be greatly multiplied, or, better still, all moral and Christian periodicals should, in my humble judgment, hang out the flag of peace, that on all proper occasions they should be known as opposed to war and strife, and bear their testimony on the side of peace and good-will."

Coan next focuses on the pulpit and peace. "The pulpit should especially speak out in no indistinct notes, and the gospel trumpet should give no uncertain sound" [1 Cor 14:8]. He returns to a focus on the journal. "Your paper has a good title—*Herald of Peace*. Let it go forth on the wings of all winds; let its notes be the echo of angel voices; let it proclaim the advent of the Prince of Peace; let it show the real fruits of the Spirit of Peace; and let it paint, in the pure light of heaven, the glorious future as flashed upon us in the rapt glow of prophets, 'when nothing shall hurt or destroy' [Isa 11:9], when 'nation shall no more lift up sword against nation' [Isa 2:4], when 'the Tabernacle of God shall be with men' [Rev 21:3], and John's vision of a new heaven and a new earth [Rev 21:21] shall be realized."

Coan proclaims that all the prophecies will come to pass. "All this must come to pass, and its coming will be hastened just in proportion as Christians one by one come out of cruel and bloody Babylon [Rev 17:5], and by word and deed, and by patient suffering, if called to it, bear witness against the heathenish and the brutal customs of war."

---

56. Coan to Beans, August 22, 1865, in Coan, *Memorial Volume*, 95–96.

Coan inveighs against those who criticize the ardent peace promoters. "War will never be abolished by the timid, the conservative and the wise men of this world, who call peace men and Peace Societies foolish and fanatical; who say 'you must take the world as you find it;' 'you cannot stop war, and all your theories on the subject of peace are utopian, because impracticable, and you may as well let the matter take care of itself.'"

He responds to these critics. "But war will cease in spite of these reasons, and it would cease at once over all Christendom if every professor of the Christian religion would arise and shake himself from the blinding dust of the war system, and resolve to have no more to do with the bloody code, but to obey the Royal Law, 'Thou shalt love thy neighbor as thyself'" [Matt 22:39].

Coan seems sarcastic when he next writes about forked tongue pastors helping lead the peace movement. "Such a united and decided testimony from the Church, headed by her cloven-tongued ministers and her thunder-toned presses, would silence all the batteries of our enemies, and staunch the red blood that flows in broad waves over the world."

Showing that their friendship and correspondence were not solely on the subjects of peace and Christian unity, he concludes the letter by responding to a theological question from Mrs. Bean. "Sister H. asks our opinion as to the condition of the soul between death and the general judgment. We believe in no intermediate state, such as purgatory or insensibility,[57] but that spirits go to their final award.[58] Judas went to his *own place* [Acts 1:25], and the penitent thief to *Paradise* [Luke 23:43]. Paul believed that for him to be 'absent from the body was to be present with the Lord'"[59] [2 Cor 5:8].

In his next to last[60] reported missive to them, Coan addresses himself to the subject of Christian unity in a letter to the Beans during his trip to the United States. Writing from the capital of the Quakers, the City of Brotherly Love, Coan writes that nothing "short of the full orbed glory of Jesus and the completed fruition of heaven affords so much joy and satisfaction as the true communion of saints on earth. Why is it that all the professed disciples of the God of peace and love do not more freely exercise and more fully enjoy this heavenly gift. To dwell in God is to dwell in love, for 'God is love' [1 John 4:8b]. I am prompted to write thus to-day by a precious visit last evening at the house of your and our dear brother and sister [in Christ], Samuel R. and Anna Shipley. Your mother and sister were present with other dear friends,

---

57. In his Greek ascetical treatise *Ladder of Divine Ascent* or *Ladder of Paradise*, the early seventh century, John Climacus places insensibility—"On insensibility, that is, deadening of the soul and the death of the mind before the death of the body"—as rung number eighteen on the way up to number thirty—"the linking together of the supreme trinity among the virtue." Wikipedia, "Ladder of Divine Ascent."

58. Also called "reward."

59. Coan to Beans, July 15, 1868, in Coan, *Memorial Volume*, 120–22.

60. The last being October 9, 1878, in Coan, *Memorial Volume*, 162–63.

among whom was Sarah F. Smiley, just returned from her mission in the Orkney and Shetland Islands."

He shares that they talked and prayed, and their souls rejoiced. "We conversed and prayed together; and I am sure that our souls sung out, and we made melody in our hearts [Eph 5:19] to the Lord. How often we spake of you and wished that if it were the will of God, we might have you with us." He writes about the two times he visited with the Beans in person. "We recounted the pleasure we enjoyed in those hours and days in Hilo and in Iowa. West Branch bloomed and fruited again as the 'garden of the Lord' [Isa 51:3]. How we love to live over these joys and to revive their fresh fragrance as we pass along our pilgrim path to the 'land of pure delight.'[61] Shall we not meet there soon? I am sure that *our* earthly journey is nearly ended, and we desire to return to the dear people God has given us, not to live there *always*, but to finish our course, to set our house in order, and to await the call of our dear Lord to give account of our stewardship. Will he not be 'gracious to our unrighteousness,' [Heb 8:12] and not enter into judgment with us?"[62]

While rejoicing in Christian unity across denominations, Coan views that harmony as strong enough to sustain differences. Nowhere is that more evident in his dialogue with the Beans than his views on the War of Rebellion.

AN EXCEPTION TO THE RULE: SUPPORT OF UNION IN THE WAR OF REBELLION

In his August 22, 1865, letter to the Beans, Coan writes that they may "honestly differ" on various subjects and still maintain their Christian friendship. Later in the same letter, Coan abruptly pivots from rejoicing at the end of the war to devastation upon hearing the news of President Lincoln's assassination. He is at his most vivid pen-painter best in his intense remarks.

"But suddenly all was changed. The sea, the sky and the fields darkened—a sigh of sorrow, a wave of woe swept over us. Our sunny islands were draped in mourning. Abraham Lincoln is *dead!* 'A prince and a great man is fallen!' [2 Sam 3:38]. *Treason* has murdered *Mercy*. Thus we wept. But still we looked up to the high throne of heaven and saw our Father there."[63]

Three years before, Coan's letter to George Beckwith was published in *The Advocate of Peace*. "While events thicken, and clouds darken, and thunders roar, and while the great bell of time rings its changes, no subject more interests my heart than the cause in which you labor."[64] One year later he writes, "We watch with sad and solemn interest the progress of the war in our own beloved father-land. May that bleeding

---

61. Isaac Watts's hymn, "Land of Pure Delights."
62. Coan to Beans, February 18, 1871, in Coan, *Memorial Volume*, 130–31.
63. Coan to Beans, August 22, 1865, in Coan, *Memorial Volume*, 95–96.
64. *Advocate of Peace* 22 (September 1862) 138.

nation come forth of this awful furnace, purified seven times. The fiery trial will not then have been in vain. I apprehend that the conflict will not cease, until the rulers and the people are made to feel and confess that 'there is a God in heaven' who *rules* among the nations, and who doeth his pleasure in all the earth.'"[65]

In a January 21, 1862, letter[66] published in August of the same year, Coan writes very vividly of the conflict. "It is a year since I wrote you. And *what* a year! How sad, how eventful, how awful the tale it records! 'The rod has blossomed, pride has budded, violence has broken forth' [Exod 7:11]. Oppression, rebellion, and treason have culminated. Cabals, dark plots, and midnight conspiracies have ripened into deadly deeds, and the revengeful and bloody blow falls everywhere. Over all the land we hear the roll of the drum, the blasts of the trumpet, the sound of clarion."

Though he would support the Union in its efforts, Coan writes of war as a demon. "The demon of war is unchained, and his foot-prints are marked with 'tears and ashes and blood.'[67] On every hand we hear the sigh of the sister, the parent, the brother, and the wail of the widow. Grief and woe sell into thunder-notes, and roll over the land. Vials of wrath [Rev 16:1] are being poured upon the nation."

Coan notes that God has moved from mercy to judgment of the nation. "Her judgment has come. 'It is the time of Jacob's trouble' [Jer 30:7]. The long-abused mercy and forbearance of God have been exhausted. 'His sword is bathed in heaven' [Isa 34:7]. His hand takes hold on judgment. He is rendering 'vengeance to his adversaries' [Nah 1:2], and 'tribulation and anguish' [Rom 2:9] take hold on evil doers."

Coan next addresses his views on peace as they relate to the facts of war and the occasional necessity of war. "But perhaps you are asking, What now is your opinion of war? Just what it has ever been. War is *stern fact*. This is a truism. It is also a *necessary and inevitable fact*, so long as Christendom remains what it is."

Coan interacts with peace and millennium. "But we anticipate better days. We believe in a reign of peace. It is *promised*, it is *sure*, it *will come*. To this abstract doctrine the millions of Christendom assent. In theory there is unity. Our difference and our difficulty is *practical*. A few testify against war in word and in deed; the many have little to say, less to do, and nothing to give to check this enormous evil. What we desire, and all we ask, is that ministers and Christians everywhere lift up the voice of instruction, and warning, and supplication on this subject; that they unite in one solid phalanx to oppose the sin, and that they contribute enough of their substance to

---

65. *Advocate of Peace* 23 (July 1863) 304–05. The quotation appears to be a combination of various verses from the Old Testament, including the Psalms and Daniel.

66. Nowhere in this letter, other correspondence, or other known writings does Coan make reference to the February 1861 peace conference held at the Willard Hotel. Instigated and guided by "former president John Tyler, referred to sometimes as 'His Accidency' . . . [the] goal of the conference was to 'negotiate how to avoid disunion and war.'" Though a religious-based gathering, the index provides no mention of Coan, Quakers, the American Board, or Congregationalists. Tooley, *Peace That Almost Was*, ix. Chapter 4 is entitled "The Clergy and Churches," 85–116.

67. No single Bible verse found for these three words together.

secure the circulation of all necessary light among all reading classes in all nations. Let them once do this, and war ceases in Christendom of *necessity*. With such a rampant opposition against it, it would be an *impossibility*."

Coan lays out the origin of the Civil War and indicates that pastors in both sections of the country are at fault. "Here was the origin of the calamity now upon our country. Had the professed Christians of the United States, North and South, taken this stand twenty, or ten, or even five years ago, this awful war would, in my humble opinion, never have rolled its waves of fiery ruin over the land. The true spirit which rises in intelligent opposition to war, involves in it the elements of opposition to all the *causes* of war. It is the spirit which 'deals *justly*, loves *mercy*, and *walks humbly with God*' [Mic 6:8]. Ministers and disciples of 'the Prince of Peace' should have this spirit; and they should have it in full and glowing action."[68]

Coan finds another outlet to express his views on the War of Rebellion in the midst of the conflict through a letter to an admiral in the United States Navy. In a September 20, 1862, letter to Samuel Francis DuPont, Coan begins, "With your pressing and overwhelming cares it may seem intrusive for me to write you. But I cannot forbear to assure you of the deep and full-souled sympathy your old Hilo friends feel in the great cause in which you are engaged. Though we should prize a line from you more than gold, yet we will not ask or expect such a favor just now. Your head and hands and heart are too full of a *nation's* weal to turn aside to private friends."

After referring to a recent letter from Mrs. DuPont, Coan continues, "And now, my dear Admiral, allow me to say that I look upon this fraternal strife with awe and with anguish. How great must be our national wickedness which calls down such bolts of wrath and which scatters such a tempest of sulphur and fire [Luke 17:29] and blood over the land. Did ever cloud darken and thicken and thunder with more fearful portent over a people? Did ever the baleful fires of civil strife burn more fiercely? Was ever a conquest more sanguinary or more desperate?"

Coan pours himself out to his friend on the subject of the South's rebellion. "The proportion, the magnitude of this rebellion are, perhaps, unparalleled in man's history. Will not the result be correspondent in magnitude?" He addresses his views on war in theory. "You know my views on war in the abstract: I preach and pray and labor against it, as against all other sins: theft, robbery, murder, etc. Its origin is in the lusts and wickedness of the human heart, and as I desire the removal of idolatry so I pray that this gigantic evil may cease."

He next addresses himself to the fact of war in the midst of a fallen world. "I do, nevertheless, accept war *as a fact*, and we must meet it when it comes, in the wisest and best manner possible to our present state and to the state of our fallen world. Powers, governments, laws are of God—ordained and sustained by him. He has put the sword into the hand of rulers [Rom 13:4], and they are bound to use it in protecting the right and in terror to evil-doers."

---

68. *Advocate of Peace* 22 (August 1862) np.

He focuses in on the specifics of this war. "I look upon the present rebellion as a premeditated, a haughty, wanton, diabolical treason against law and constitutional right. Our Southern brethren do not see it in this light, and I would feel a sad pity for them and pray that their eyes may be opened; as a man and a Christian I would feel for them and treat them with all proper kindness, but as a loyal and law-loving citizen I must sustain my government with my prayers and sympathies, my treasure and my life if need be."

Coan encourages DuPont in his Christian service and specific acts in the war. "We have read, dear sir, with great interest of your toils and cares, your sacrifices and your heroic deeds in this day of darkness and of peril. And we bless God who has given you wisdom and strength and other places, we rejoiced deeply. And we do follow you in our prayers constantly. It is a matter of great joy to us that so many of our best naval and military commanders are men who fear God and who look to him for help. My heart is full and I know not how to stop."[69]

In his autobiography, Coan writes of his visit to the Gettysburg battlefield in 1871. While lamenting the death and destruction of the Civil War, he provides his opinion that the battle of Gettysburg and the entire war were necessary. Echoing Lincoln he writes, "the scars of war are everywhere... But our country needed this fiery chastisement, and it will be better in the end if it so be that the North and South understand and profit by the lesson."[70]

The Civil War forces Coan to clarify his position on war and peace. In the two following letters he delineates his view, adhering to his passion for peace while providing necessary nuances. He makes clear his opposition to the "Rebellion" and his support of the Union in a letter published in *The Advocate of Peace*, "You can imagine with what keen and earnest interest we watch the bloody and unnatural strife in our fatherland. Probably no rebellion of such gigantic proportions, so unprovoked, and so diabolical in character, ever before cursed our world. We are against it unequivocally, unreservedly, and emphatically.[71] We are against it in all our powers of being, material and spiritual. And as we believe in government and law, we are with the President and his Cabinet, in every necessary measure[72] to put down this wicked rebellion, and to restore peace and joy in our bleeding country. And with all my opposition to war, and my strong and ever strengthening convictions of its essential wickedness, yet I pray God, that this conflict may not cease without those results which shall be commensurate with the magnitude of the sacrifices and sufferings it has cost. Let the fire burn, the lightnings flash, thunders break [Rev 4:5] until the atmosphere is purified of its deadly malaria. It is an awful ordeal; but God is in it. The social, political, and

---

69. Coan to DuPont, September 20, 1862, in Coan, *Memorial Volume*, 90–92.

70. Coan, *Life*, 215.

71. Note that he is against the Southern Rebellion, not the Union's military response to it.

72. It would appear that Coan supports Lincoln's suspension of the writ of *habeas corpus*, which he did on May 25, 1861.

moral atmosphere was too corrupt, too foul, to sustain the vigor and vitality of 'the body politic' with this fiery tempest. The state of the atmosphere invites the thunder, and beckons for the hurricane."

He continues to blame the Christian leaders in the South for allowing slavery to continue and for the outbreak of the war. He recognizes that his views on war and peace in this matter may appear paradoxical. "Our sentiments may appear paradoxical; but we must still say, that we hate war and we reaffirm and reiterate the opinion that, if all professed Christians [agreed to unified opposition to war, conflict in any of the] lands would be *impossible*. Why is the South so confident, so fierce, so earnest, so obstinate in this wicked struggle? Simply because their church creeds and their religious teachers approve their cause, urge them on to deeds of darkness, perfidy, and blood, and proclaim the most damnable acts *virtuous* and *heroic*, and wicked, blood-stained perjurers *heroes, saints,* and *martyrs!* Had the religious teachings at [in?] the South been what they *should* have been, slavery, with its blinding, defiling, and maddening power, had long since disappeared from that fair heritage of our fathers, and this awful rebellion would never have been."

Coan next expands to consider war around the world, exhorting pastors, and how it relates to the gospel. "So it is everywhere. Only let ministers and Christians go forth as 'salt' and 'light' [Matt 5:13–16], and 'in the *fullness* of the blessing of the gospel of peace'[73] [Rom 15:29] teach and live as our blessed Redeemer taught and lived; and the war trump would cease to alarm the nations, 'the sword would be beaten into a plowshare' [Joel 3:10] and the nations would 'learn war no more' [Isa 2:4]. If there is one truth in the blessed gospel which shines into my soul with more clearness and glory than any other, it is the one just stated. It comes to me like *intuition*; and all the sophistry, and all the logic of the schools, naval, military, civic, legislative, diplomatic, scientific, and theological, can never dislodge it. And this rebellion and all wars, on whatever pretext or whatever scale, serve only to confirm my principles, and quicken my zeal in the cause of peace."

Coan encourages the readers through the use of capital letters. "AND NOW, MY DEAR FRIEND, TAKE HEART. We are not to be discouraged, because we *are not discomfited*. In patience we are to possess our souls [Luke 21:19], and 'in the meekness of wisdom' [James 3:13] do what we can to convince and convert others. If we die while the shock of war rages over the earth, we shall, at some future day, look down from the heavenly hills, and see our world, so long seared, blackened, and desolated by war, clothed in beauty, resting in peace, and rejoicing in love. For this consummation we will pray and toil."

He concludes with a peroration. "We are, I trust, thankful to our God that, while the earth is in commotion, and war rages around, we are permitted to live in peace and safety, under the precious vine which 'the Prince of Peace' has planted in this land.

---

73. Once again, the actual verse speaks of the gospel of *Christ*, with peace mentioned later in the verse.

No where on earth is liberty more perfect, life and property more secure, and peace and happiness more general than on the Sandwich Islands. 'The Lord hath done great things for us' [Ps 126:3]; and we owe him everlasting praise.

"Yours in the bonds of peace, T. COAN"[74]

He wrote the above letter on May 3, 1865. He had not yet heard of the end of the war or death of Abraham Lincoln, as he had by his August 25 letter to the Beans. In an undated letter in *The Advocate of Peace* he writes more about war and peace near the end of the Civil War. "Yes, I sigh and long for peace, not in my dear bleeding country alone, but over all the earth." He next notes that there is no peace without purity. There can be no reliable peace without truth, righteousness, and love. "In looking over the world, my eye affects my heart, and both melt together; but my tears are not generated in a copperhead, nor is my heart so soft as to wish to see peace without purity. There can be no reliable peace without truth, righteousness, and love."

He does not want peace at the expense of hell fire. "I want no peace that slumbers over infernal fires." He relates it to the metaphor of a volcano. "I have just returned from a visit to a 'lake of fire and brimstone' [Rev 20:10]. At first sight the lake seemed congealed on its surface, with a stratum so firm that horsemen and chariots might have rushed over it; but in thirty minutes all was changed. The slumbering lake below began to boil, and the fiery flood burst upward from its awful abyss, rending the superincumbent crust into fragments, dashing its burning waves against its sides, and vomiting its jets of incandescent minerals far into the air. The whole surface of the lake, some five hundred feet in diameter, was now one raging sea of fire, and the heat, the glare, the tossing, the hissings, the mutterings, the belching, the spoutings, and the lashings filled the beholder with awe, and led him to desire a place of safety. What peace, what safety, to a house built on the banks of such a lake? And just so it is in the *moral world*. 'Is it peace Jehu? What peace, so long as the wholesome of thy mother, Jezebel, and her witchcrafts are so many? There is no peace, saith my God, to the wicked'" [2 Kgs 9:22].

He restates the question of paradox and adds that of principles. "Perhaps you begin to think that my principles are changed, or that they are paradoxical. Not a whit. I have always advocated law and order, and preached submission to authority; and I have ever felt that righteous and wholesome laws *must* be maintained at all hazards. God has so ordained, as a universal *necessity*, in family and in state, on earth and in heaven. *He* has clothed men with authority, and holds them responsible for its use. The parent holds the rod [Prov 13:24]. The ruler, too, holds the sword [Rom 13:4] as well as the shield. So it is in heaven. God holds the golden crown for the loyal, and the thunderbolt for the rebel. Satan found law, wrath, and crushing thunders, even in paradise, all issuing from the throne of 'the Prince of Peace.'"

Coan makes it clear how vehemently he is against war, while making a distinction. "Still I abhor war. Its *cause* is always wrong; its origin is in wickedness; and never,

---

74. *Advocate of Peace* 25 (July 1865) 106–07.

since Satan fell from heaven, was a war more wicked, more diabolical, than that which the South has waged against their country. No human language can express the intensity and malignity of its wickedness; and *I see not how our paternal government could have avoided the awful conflict without a violation of its most sacred oaths*, an abandonment of all our dearest interests, and the giving over of our peaceful citizens to be trodden down by proud and haughty rebels, without regard to justice or mercy."

He discusses war as a fact and how to deal with it. "We accept war in this case as a *fact*, and we must deal with it as best we can. 'It is impossible but that offences come; but woe to him through whom they come' [Luke 17:1]. Our work, and the work of all good men, is to endeavor to remove the *causes* of war; and what these causes are we well know. 'The fruit of righteousness is sown in peace of them that make peace' [James 3:18]. Instead of being disheartened, and giving up the holy cause, I feel more deeply in earnest than ever. I wish to see Christian zeal and love intensified, and Christian efforts multiplied in this work."

Coan writes of the Civil War being a motive to continue working for peace. "The present war illustrates the horrors of the code, and gives great force to the arguments for peace. We wish to make all men feel that, to prevent or extinguish war, the selfish and diabolical passions must be restrained, and man must understand and feel and practice the golden rule" [Matt 7:12]. While his sentiments are laudable, Coan does not seem to understand the depth of the sin nature in humanity, as well as how Jesus speaks the Golden Rule to individuals not to nations.

"But [with] the unrighteousness and all the horrors of war, I would preach peace, but I would preach it to the transgressor, and not sadden the heart of the righteous by laying the sin at his door. I have great hope that the awful sorrows which have come upon the nation will prepare multitudes to listen with less prejudice and a deeper interest to the arguments on behalf of peace."

He uses the metaphor of atmospheric conditions to continue to explain his views on peace. "There are certain conditions of the atmosphere [that] cannot be corrected without thunder. Electricity must be discharged, and there must be burning and the smell of sulphur. Sometimes a tempest or a cyclone must sweep and howl, and carry terror and devastation in its track. These and other calamities come through the action of physical laws. We know not but that the time may come when, by the action of these same laws, such direful scourges may cease."

He returns to the need for purity, as well as the volcano analogy. "Now, though freighted with terror, they act as purifiers, and on the whole as healthful and necessary preservers. So it is with volcanoes. They give vent to the subterranean steam, gases, and fires of the earth; and, though their local and immediate effects are often terrific, yet they are necessary, in the present state of our planet, to preserve it from universal explosion and wreck. So, then, there is mercy even in seeming wrath."

Coan weaves together the atmosphere and volcano metaphors with eschatology. "When the Lord 'makes all things new' [Rev 21:5], a new heaven and a new earth [Rev

21:1]; when the baleful fires shall have burned out, and all the disturbing elements of the atmosphere shall have been consumed, and the ocean shall no more be lashed to fury by the tempest, then some of the physical calamities of our race may cease. Whether such a speculation will or will not be realized in the future, one thing is true: that the *moral* atmosphere of our world will be renovated, the baleful fires of human passion will cease to burn, disturbing and explosive elements of depravity will have been extinguished, and Peace will spread her wings over the earth; 'nation shall not lift up sword against nation, neither shall they *learn war any more*' [Isa 2:4; Mic 4:3],

> Come, thou Prince of Peace, oh, come quickly!
> Erect thy throne of light and love on earth.
> Unfold thy banner, and wave it round the world.
> Come the blest day, the joyful hour,
> When earth shall feel they saving power."[75]

Coan continues with exhortation and a pivot to eschatology. "Let all who love peace take courage. Let all who are children of 'the God of love and peace' [2 Cor 13:11] take down their harps and tune them for a song, such as waked the seraph and the church, and tuned the lyres of heaven, when our Emmanuel was born. We shall not always sigh and mourn. War has raged, and the earth has run red with human gore. Its crashing thunder and its flashing fires have formed an horizon of wrath; its groans and its wails have rolled over the land, and the whole earth has been darkened by its sable clouds, and swept by its fiery tempests. Under its furious wheels and its iron hoofs the world still shakes, and the mountains tremble at the blast of its trumpet."

Coan extends his tying together of end times and the Civil War. "But Peace, also, shall have her time. Her jubilee is sure. Her love is now abroad on the dark surface of the deluge, but she will at length return with the 'olive leaf' [Gen 8:11]. We shall yet sing, 'The winter is past, the rain is over and gone, the flowers appear [?] the earth'" [Song 2:11].

After relating the press of his duties, Coan returns to the theme of the Civil War. He writes of specific news and the nearing of the end of the war. "When news of the fall of Richmond, Petersburg,[76] etc., reached us, a shout of joy rang along our shores. We are inspired with the hope that peace is near, that slavery is dead, and that our nation is saved."[77]

Coan follows up his discussion of the Civil War in a letter published in *The Advocate of Peace* in June of 1868. He provides perspective and shares lessons learned. "The great 'Prince of Peace' was a law-abiding and law-upholding character. He upholds right, and puts power into the hands of rulers to avenge wrong and protect innocence.

---

75. Isaac Watts, "Let all the earth their voices raise."

76. General Grant took Richmond and Petersburg in early April of 1865, with the surrender at Appomattox taking place on April 9.

77. *Advocate of Peace*, np, nd, 297–301.

On this plain principle, our Society cannot condemn our federal government for putting down an unprovoked, unscrupulous, and remorseless rebellion.

"But that such a rebellion should have been *possible* in a country so enlightened and professedly so Christian as ours, is amazing." Perhaps Coan should look to the doctrine of Original Sin[78] and the sin nature to understand that it does not matter the civilization or culture of any nation.

"It shows a vast and awful deficiency in the moral religious training of our people." See Revelation 2 and 3 for the deep flaws of various churches. "Few believed such an unparalleled catastrophe, such a diabolical onslaught, to be possible; yet it came. From an almost cloudless sky, on a serene day,[79] a storm of 'hail and fire, mingled with blood' [Rev 8:7] burst upon our land. A tempest, a cyclone, of wrath swept over the nation. The bloody hoof of rebellion trampled on all that was sacred in altar, constitution, law, moral sentiment, and domestic happiness, and scattered with ruthless ferocity its billions of material treasures to the winds and flames. Under the furious tread of war, the whole land trembled, and the nation surged like the great ocean in a tempest. God has brought us up out of this sea of blood, and fire, and sorrow, bruised, mangled, bleeding, with a load of debt sufficient to crush almost any nation on earth."

Coan examines the primary lesson to be learned from this conflict. "Surely, we should learn a lesson from this sore and solemn experience. And this lesson should sound out from all our pulpits and presses, from all our forums and legislative halls, from all our stages and platforms, from all our schools of instruction, from all our associations, civil, political, literary, scientific, social, commercial, and religious, and from every nursery in the land. The voice of the nation should rise and swell into one mighty thunder-note, and roll over every sea and land, *in condemnation of the cruel, reckless, heaven-insulting system of war.*"

He interacts with other articles published in *The Advocate of Peace* and other journals. "I read with great interest *The Advocate of Peace*, and all articles wisely written on the subject of peace. Whatever others may think, I am sure the subject has been handled carefully, thoughtfully, logically, and in a most earnest Christian spirit."

Coan denies the claim that peace advocates have their heads in the clouds and are of no earthly good. "Whatever some may think or say, all the advocates of peace were not born or educated in Utopia.[80] Many of them are men who have lived in this war-cursed world, have contemplated *verities*, have seen, felt, and handled statistical *facts* . . . The evils are so gigantic as to defy all human measurement, and the sins so deep, and dark and diabolical, as to stun the human soul with horror."

---

78. Or "Inherited Sin," as Wayne Grudem phrases it in his *Systematic Theology*.

79. Was Coan unaware of the tensions building in the nation for decades, especially during the decade leading up to the war?

80. In Sir Thomas More's novel, *Utopia* is a place. That work is sarcastic in nature, but the words "utopia" and "utopian" have entered into the lexicon of languages.

While mixing in a sentence on the millennium, Coan turns his attention to pastors. "I have great fears that many of my dear brethren in the church and in the ministry do not give themselves time to read, and think, and reason, and pray candidly and earnestly on this awful theme. The subject is heavy and oppressive, and nature might wish to throw it off, and excuses are many and at hand. We all have much important work to do. We must try to Christianize the world, and leave war to rulers. It will, of course, cease in the millennium. I find it difficult, even here, to get Christians to read some of the most lucid, eloquent, and able articles on the subject; and sometimes feel amazed at the apparent ignorance of, or indifference to, the arguments which so clearly show *how* this evil may be checked, and finally rooted out of Christendom . . . Will not the clergy and the conductors of our presses take hold of the subject in earnest? It is a simple and natural duty, and such service can do no harm, while it may dry up fountains of tears, staunch rivers of blood, and quench continents of fire."[81]

Eight years later, at the age of seventy-six, Coan compares abolitionists and those working for peace. His letter is preceded by an editor's introduction. "We are happy to grace our editorial columns with the following ringing letter from the veteran missionary at the Sandwich Islands. Would that its words of fire might burn their way into the hearts of the disciples of the Prince of Peace, until a voice go forth from the Christian church, making wars not only difficult, but impossible; and the good time be hastened of universal peace and righteousness."

Coan writes, "Well do I remember when good men in the Northern United States were insulted and threatened for advocating anti-slavery principles. I once heard a popular minister of the gospel in the city of Rochester, New York, speak decidedly against allowing an anti-slavery lecturer to speak in the city. 'We do not want these fanatical fellows,' said he, 'to come among us to disturb our peace, and if this man shall be mobbed and tarred and feathered it will be his own fault!'[82] But in spite of the indifference, the contempt and the bitter opposition of very many worldly-wise and self-satisfied Christians in the North, the principles of freedom gained hearers and hearts, and the call for abolition swelled into such thunder-notes, that the fiat of earth and heaven went forth, the earthquake of the Eternal rocked the prison; the doors were opened, and every chain of slavery was broken.[83] And thus it will be with war. The leaven of peace and righteousness will work against all indifferences, sarcasm, contempt, and open opposition, until the crisis shall come, when the seventh angel shall sound his trumpet [Rev 8:6–7], and there shall be 'great voices in heaven' [Rev 11:15] proclaiming the joyful fact that 'the kingdoms of this world are become the

---

81. *Advocate of Peace* 28 (June 1868) 82–84.

82. As is often the case in Coan's time, he provides no name, no citation, no date. Nothing other than "I heard" (in person? If so in the early 1830s? Surely not during his visit to the United States in 1870 or 1871. Or did he hear about this second hand through a letter? The pastor is not named.).

83. Coan uses the analogy of Paul and Silas being freed from the prison in Philippi, as related in Acts 16:26.

kingdom of our Lord' [Rev 11:15] and that 'the Prince of Peace' shall sway his eternal scepter over all the earth."[84]

In the 1862 station report, Coan reflects on the turmoil abroad, peace and prosperity in Hilo, yet violence hitting close to home. "Amidst the visitudes [sic] of time and the convulsions of empires, Hilo has enjoyed a year of peace and prosperity." Sadly, however, murder mars the peacefulness of Hilo for the first time since Coan's arrival there. "For the first time during a residence of twenty-seven years has the blood of murder stained our soil—The tragic death of John Ely and wife filled us with surprise and consternation."[85]

PASTOR OF PEACE

Donations

The chief object of Coan's first letter to *The Advocate of Peace* is to inform the American Peace Society's Corresponding Secretary that a donation of one hundred dollars[86] is on the way from the Haili church. "It is but a mite that we are able to cast into your treasury; but be assured, dear Sir, we do it with cheerful hearts, and with many prayers and warm desires, that the principles your Society advocates may spread and prevail until they fill the earth with peace and goodwill."[87]

Before[88] and after[89] Coan's letter, the American Peace Society used the letter to appeal for the cash-strapped organization. After the letter the editor sought to challenge[90] his American readers: "We ask the special attention of our friends at home to this instance of liberality from a church whose members were heathens a few years ago. Have they mistaken our common Christianity on this point? Do they think too highly of its pacific principles and aims? Have they done for our cause too much for persons in their circumstances? If not, how deficient the professed followers of the Prince of Peace in our land! Few, very few churches can be found here that are not better able than 'the native church at Hilo,' to give us one hundred dollars; but what, in comparison with this spontaneous liberality, are *any* of our churches, even the richest of them, doing for this cause? How many *individuals* among our friends here could give us even five hundred dollars more easily than this church could one hundred! We

---

84. *Advocate of Peace* 9 (November and December 1877) 44.
85. 1862 Hilo station report, 1/140. HMH.
86. 100 dollars in 1850 might have been equivalent to twenty-eight hundred to dollars in 2007.
87. Coan to Beckwith, *Advocate of Peace* 9 (February 1849) 23.
88. Coan to Beckwith, *Advocate of Peace* 9 (February 1849) 22.
89. Coan to Beckwith, *Advocate of Peace* 9 (February 1849) 23–24.
90. Shame?

beg our friends, especially at a time when we are so much in need of funds, to ponder this example till they are ready to go and do likewise" [Luke 10:37].[91]

In the February 1852 *Advocate of Peace,* under the heading "PEACE OPERATIONS," a letter is introduced "from Rev. Titus Coan" with a paragraph that includes a reference to Coan's 1849 letter sent with a donation from the Haili church. It mentions other donations received since then.[92]

In an 1855 publication, Coan writes about a fifty-dollar donation. "We wish to send you one hundred dollars now; but, as we are striving to collect funds for a good meeting-house, and as there are many objects we wish to help, fifty dollars are all we can appropriate to your cause at this time."[93] Perhaps referring to the fifty-dollar payment of 1855, Coan writes in his April 1856 journal: "Enclosed you will see a Bill of Exchange[94] (No. 1) for one hundred dollars . . . With this draft, the native church at Hilo redeems its pledge for one hundred dollars, towards making out the sum of five hundred dollars, as a premium to be awarded by a competent committee for the best history of the present European war,[95] to be published so soon as may be, after the close of said war. We earnestly hope that the five hundred dollars will be made out without delay. Should this expectation fail, and should the gift of our poor Hawaiian Christians not 'provoke to emulation'[96] [Rom 11:14] their more enlightened brethren in America, then we again pledge ourselves to make up what is lacking on their part, whether it be one, two, three, or four hundred dollars. If left by our American friends to make up the last mentioned sum (four hundred dollars), we will try to do it in early installments of two hundred dollars each. But I trust this work will not be left to us, for your Christian community cannot afford to allow the Hawaiians all the blessedness of the act; for as the words of the Lord Jesus are true—'It is more blessed to give than to receive'" [Acts 20:35].[97]

In 1858, the journal publishes the gift of one hundred dollars and possibly another one hundred dollars from Coan.[98] It is preceded by financial faith challenges

91. Coan to Beckwith, *Advocate of Peace* 9 (February 1849) 23.

92. *Advocate of Peace* 12 (February 1852).

93. *Advocate of Peace* 15 (July 1855) 309.

94. Wikipedia explains a Bill of Exchange as follows: "A bill of exchange is essentially an order made by one person to another to pay money to a third person. A bill of exchange requires in its inception three parties—the drawer, the drawee, and the payee. The person who draws the bill is called the drawer. He gives the order to pay money to the third party. The party upon whom the bill is drawn is called the drawee. He is the person to whom the bill is addressed and who is ordered to pay. He becomes an acceptor when he indicates his willingness to pay the bill. The party in whose favor the bill is drawn or is payable is called the payee." Wikipedia, "Negotiable Instrument."

95. "The Crimean War (October 1853–February 1856) was a conflict in which Russia lost to an alliance of France, the United Kingdom, the Ottoman Empire, and Sardinia." Wikipedia, "Crimean War."

96. Victorian challenge/shaming?

97. *Advocate of Peace* 16 (April 1856) 56.

98. See Coan lists of donations and payments, LOC.

by the American Peace Society.[99] "Hilo must do something for you this year. Your cause is dear to us. It is *our* cause; it is the cause of all men; it is the cause of God. I think we shall send you one hundred dollars by-and-by from our native church; and if I feel able, I may send another one hundred dollars from my own private stipends. How I wish I could count you out *thousands*; but you and Christ will not despise 'two mites.'[100] Our native church is struggling hard to build a good meetinghouse at a cost of twelve thousand dollars. This is a heavy and almost crushing work; but we have commenced, the contracts are drawn, and the carpenters are at work. We shall, therefore, not be able to do all we wish for other objects; *but your cause we cannot put off*. Your reasoning is good; viz., *if the mass of Christians will contribute to other societies, and leave yours to languish, it is the duty of the friends of Peace to devote* MORE *than they otherwise would to your cause*. My own reflections lean to the same conclusion. I love the great sisterhood of benevolent societies. Strongly and deeply do I sympathize with them all, and ardently do I desire their success; but as we need to use all our funds this year in our church edifice, we shall probably devote to no other society except yours, and our own Hawaiian Missionary Association for sending the gospel to the dark isles beyond us."[101]

In 1859, the Hilo church was not able to give anything. "I know not when we shall be able to send you another mite. Our new church has cost us more than we anticipated, yea, twice as much. Our bills are not yet all brought in; but we think the building, bell, and other appurtenances have cost some fifteen thousand dollars. Our people have given nobly, and out of what Americans would call deep poverty."[102]

Coan writes in the shadow of the looming war in America. Fifty dollars are given by "native church officers." "In our Annual Convention of native church officers we appropriated fifty dollars to the American Peace Society, for which see enclosed order . . . We desired to send you more; but as we have the Marquesas mission on our hands, beside other objects of care, we could not well go higher now. This church has just given seven hundred dollars to support our native missionaries in the Pacific, besides four hundred dollars for other objects which call on our benevolence. You will accept the mite we send with the assurances of our warm sympathies, and continued prayers for the blessed cause of peace; and may the God of love and peace bruise Satan under your feet [Gen 3:15] shortly."[103]

In the midst of the Civil War, Coan sent money from the church and a donation of his own. "As a small token of our continued interest in the cause of peace,

---

99. *Advocate of Peace* 18 (March 1858) 42.
100. An allusion to Jesus' talking about the two "widow's mites" in Luke 21:1–4.
101. *Advocate of Peace* 18 (March 1858) 43.
102. *Advocate of Peace* 19 (September 1859) np.
103. *Advocate of Peace* 21 (May 1861) 235.

the church of Hilo sends you fifty dollars, and I take the liberty to add the trifle of twenty-five dollars."[104]

Near the end of the war Coan indicates that he hopes to send a donation soon. "I intend to aid your cause more so soon as I can attend to getting a draft, etc., which I cannot do now. We rejoice to give, as the Lord prospers us, to every good cause."[105] Seven years later he writes, "Eight days ago I wrote you and [sic] enclosed draft . . . for one hundred dollars, in favor of the American Peace Society."[106] He also explains his wanting copies for the children and encloses an order for five dollars. "I add this supplement to confess my 'sin of omission,' viz. I neglected to order fifty copies of *The Angel of Peace*. I want to give this light-winged messenger to the girls and boys in our foreign Sabbath-School, and I herewith enclose an order . . . for five dollars."[107]

In approximately 1871, Rev. S. Hopkins Emery twisted Coan's nuanced view to fit his without-exception pacifist views. He imposed a pacifist cast upon Coan in his statements concerning his work in general, and especially the teachings of the mission from the beginning on the subject of war. Emery was impressed by Coan's ability to persuade the violent and cruel Hawaiians "in favor of peace. The mission appears to have adopted the principle of the early Christians, that it is unchristian to fight."[108]

The last recorded donations from the church and Coan is found in the late 1877 *Advocate of Peace*. "Please find enclosed an order . . . for fifty dollars on behalf of the American Peace Society. Of this trifling sum thirty dollars are a donation from our native church, and twenty dollars are a mite from me."[109]

Preaching

In an 1880 letter to *The Advocate of Peace*, Coan relates how peace is warp and woof in his sermons and for the life of the Hawaiian people. Preaching the Prince of Peace

---

104. *Advocate of Peace* 24 (July 1864) 108.

105. *Advocate of Peace* 7 (July 1875) 300–301.

106. *Angel of Peace* 15 (July 1882) 3.

107. *Angel of Peace* 15 (July 1882) 3. This shows the development of English-speaking families in Hilo.

108. Non-sourced (1871?) article, a copy of which was provided to the author by the Library of Congress. There are two military assistance paradigms in two next-to-each-other books in the Old Testament. Ezra chose not to have a military escort when he went to Jerusalem, while Nehemiah did. John the Baptist told soldiers to be ethical. He did not tell them to stop being soldiers. Jesus counseled his disciples to carry a sword near the end of his earthly ministry, though he did not want them used to defend him. He also said that he came "with a sword." Paul shared the gospel with his Roman soldier escorts and home arrest watchers, but did not tell them to stop being soldiers. Some reasons for most early Christians not having a military career include: most Jews did not join the military; Christians were a minority within the Roman Empire; at some times and in some places a pagan bull ritual was required to become a soldier. Additionally, Coan was friends with many Navy personnel. His passion was for them to know and follow Christ. There is no evidence that he sought to persuade them to leave military service.

109. *Advocate of Peace* 9 (November and December 1877) 45.

is what has held together the Hawaiian nation and the mission endeavor. "I have instructed them much on this subject, and they feel that their independence, national life, social, civil, and religious privileges, with all their personal safety and general prosperity, are the fruits of the peace principles, inculcated by the gospel of peace; and that the principles are their only safeguard for the future. At the present there is no people or nation on which the sun shines that enjoys more peace and safety or more true freedom than the Hawaiian nation. Had we preached a patriotic and honorable war gospel, the nationality of the Hawaiians would long ago have ceased and our missionary labors have ended. The peace doctrines here taught have been to this people and to us a factor and bulwark of superhuman power, which have resisted the fiery darts of the wicked, the assaults of Satan, and threatened thunders of four war ships, to say nothing of the mad rage of other enemies. To him who relies and thunders through the skies, and who has said 'Vengeance is mine,' we look for protection, while we refuse to strike with carnal weapons."[110]

Mobilizing Children

As in any area of life, Coan worked with children on practical ways to grow up favoring peace. He provides alternatives to the trappings of the military. In the 1852 station report, Coan writes about how he organized children as the "Cold Water Army" for peace. "This has been again called out in ten grand divisions, numbering about two thousand children in all. Each division has had its banners—its mottos—its uniforms—its marchings—its songs—its festival—its speeches—its bright faces and its joyous hearts. Each succeeding anniversary shows a decided improvement on the former in dress and in the comforts of life."[111]

Micronesia

Less than two years before he died, Coan passed along a letter from a Hawaiian missionary in Micronesia on the subject of war and peace. Coan included it in a letter dated January 24, 1880. Published in the May 1880 *Advocate of Peace*, it is a remarkable letter on revival and peace. It shows the internalizing of Coan's teachings on peace and following through on them in very gritty ways.

"I just read to my church and congregation[112] letters from a Hawaiian missionary now laboring on one of the islands of Micronesia, called Tapiteuca, of the Gilbert group, about two weeks' sail from Honolulu. It has been very savage, and many a white man has been slain there."

---

110. *Advocate of Peace* 12 (May 1880) np.
111. 1852 Hilo station report, 6/18. HMH.
112. Two words for the same thing or to English church and Hawaiian congregation?

A "remarkable awakening has occurred" on the island of Tapiteuca of "the Gilbert group." Before leaving for Toneana the native Christians "who accompanied the missionaries were charged not to take sword, musket, or any offensive weapon: but that each man take a Bible—the New Testament, translated by Mr. Bingham[113]—in his hand to go peaceably and to use no harsh or threatening words, but to trust in the Lord Jesus. Other boats accompanied them . . . When the boats were beached, [the Hawaiian] missionaries Malimu and Kapu[114] were seized by their arms and held fast." They were released.

"This same night they came to fight us and they left us. This was on June 13. On the fifteenth, Sabbath, as the friendly party were called for worship, the cry of war, war, was sounded when fifty savages with muskets and others armed with deadly weapons appeared in battle array. The congregation was broken up, and the people fled, but numbers of the friendly party (I do not understand them to have been of the Christian party that came with the missionaries)[115] withstood the heathen band, and Kapu says, as none of their muskets would bang or go off, they fled and were pursued, and sixteen of their number were killed by the friendly party, one only of said party being killed, all this having transpired in ten minutes."

Coan continues relating the letter. "After this, continues the narrative, the opposing parties met in cordial harmony and warm love; peace was re-established, obstacles removed, and the work of the Lord went forward. So the battle of ten minutes was decisive. Would to God that no battles may hereafter be allowed to last over ten minutes, and may the time be reduce[d] to five, two, one and zero, and savages and bloodstained Christians cease this deadly strife, and the 'nations learn war no more' [Isa 2:4]. (Amen, and amen.—Ed.) I have translated this narrative as another illustration of the power of the 'weapons of our warfare' and to give glory to the 'Prince of Peace.'"[116]

Violence and Peace in the Marquesas Islands

Coan writes of fighting among the clans in Marquesas, as well as French attacks. There is violence among the Marquesans. "It was hoped that the presence of our missionary would prevent all further hostilities. Our hopes were fain. Before my second visit to the Marquesas, a fiendish quarrel arose among the cannibals; Kauwealoha's[117] fine house was plundered and torn down, and he with his heroic wife fled the valley never

---

113. Hiram Bingham II completed the "translation of the New Testament into Gilbertese, April 11, 1873," Judd, *Missionary Album*, 45.

114. See Nancy Morris dissertation and book(s) on Hawaiian missionaries.

115. Parentheses by Coan.

116. Coan letter in *Advocate of Peace* 12 (May 1880) np.

117. See Forbes et al., *Partners in Change*, 399–400; and Morris and Benedetto, *Nā Kahu*, 149–53.

to return. Thus the savages extinguished the rays of light which had begun to dawn upon them."[118]

Notwithstanding "the success which has attended the gospel and the school at Omoa, the large heathen party are still bloodthirsty cannibals, and always at war with the people in Hanavave, a valley five miles distant."[119]

In his journal, Coan writes of people coming to a gospel meeting with weapons. At Puamau, "Brother Parker,[120] the native missionaries, and myself came on shore to hold service. More than a hundred people collected under the trees, to whom we preached the gospel of the kingdom. Many came with spears, war-clubs, and harpoons, axes, muskets, and knives; and during service little circles of three or five would light their pipes, have a delicious smoke, and then listen again to the speaker."[121]

Coan was militantly against potential and actual French naval actions in the Pacific. He wrote of one battle on a small island: "The French did not conquer it without loss of blood and treasure." He asked several rhetorical questions: "Why should the professed disciples of the 'Prince of Peace' endeavor to propagate the Christian religion by the use of fire and sword? And why do men who call themselves 'priests of the Most High God' call in the aid of weapons, and go and come and live under the cover of cannon? Did the Captain of our salvation teach his disciples such doctrines?"[122]

NUNC DIMITTIS

In what would be the last words Titus Coan would ever publish in *The Advocate of Peace*, he writes the following in his conclusion. Fittingly, he has written about Hawaiian missionaries prior to what could be his benediction to the peace movement of his time. "Please give my warmest love to all your associates and fellow-workers in the cause of peace, and may the blessing of the God of love and peace rest upon all your efforts to turn back the footsteps of the bloody Moloch of war, and to eradicate the bitter root of strife in the human heart.

"Most fraternally yours, in 'brotherly love.' TITUS COAN."[123]

During its almost two millenia of existence, the Roman Catholic Church has held various positions on war and peace. The Church was persecuted off and on during its first two centuries. After Constantine the Great became the emperor,[124] Christianity

---

118. Coan, *Life*, 169.
119. Coan, *Life*, 173.
120. Benjamin Wyman Parker. See Forbes et al., *Partners in Change*, 499–504.
121. Coan, journal entry, May 19, 1869, in Coan, *Memorial Volume*, 113.
122. Coan, *Life*, 166.
123. Coan letter in *Advocate of Peace* 12 (May 1880) np.
124. In AD 306.

and warfare were, at times, combined. Aurelius Augustinus[125] lived between 354 and 430. In his *City of God*, he wrote about what would come to be called "The Just War Theory."

Over the millenia, some Roman Catholics have held to pacifist views. One such was Francis of Assisi, who wrote a poem entitled "The Peace Prayer." It opens with "Lord, make me an instrument of Thy peace."

By contrast, a new religion started—in the same area (Upstate New York) and period (from the early 1820s onward, with the official establishment of the church in 1830) as Titus Coan before he went to the Sandwich Islands—that both experienced and engaged in bloodshed. The Church of Jesus Christ of Latter-day Saints would eventually become part of the American mainstream, including having its members serve in the military.

Titus Coan would interact with a Catholic Bishop in South America on his way to Hawai'i in early 1836. A small Catholic church was started at Hilo in approximately 1839. From then on he would interact with and write about Catholics. The first LDS missionaries arrived in Hilo and the other major Hawaiian Islands in 1850. Coan and other ABCFM missionaries interacted with these Mormons and their affect on the islanders through 1858. These two groups and Coan's interactions with them are the subject of the next chapter.

---

125. Most commonly known in English as St. Augustine.

14

Other Religions

INTRODUCTION

Titus Coan served long before Vatican II and its aftermath. He ministered even more years before the advent of Mormon-Evangelical dialogues—both in one-on-one discussions[1] and small-group scholarly discussions.

He shared the outlook of other Evangelical leaders of his time both of the centuries old Roman Catholic Church and the over two decades old Church of Jesus Christ of Latter-day Saints. He viewed both as being religions other than the faith to which he ascribed and which he proclaimed. Representatives of both religions came to the Hilo area within fifteen years of Coan's arrival.

ROMAN CATHOLICS

"Romanism is using all the efforts which flattery, subtlety, malice, bigotry, and terror can command to overthrow the faith of the people and to supplant the religion of the Bible on these shores. Eight or ten Popish priests are said to be already here, and fifteen more are expected soon. They will soon plant themselves at all our important posts. As yet they have not gained a large number of proselytes, but their old leaven is diffusing and poisoning the minds of many. But one of our greatest evils is that the government has signed a treaty to admit ardent spirits into the land, and this has rolled back the flood of intemperance upon the nation from which they had but just escaped, and now the chiefs can make no laws to protect their people from the burning scourge without being branded by the French consul, and others of his stamp, with a breach of treaty and threatened with a war of swift retribution. So drunkenness has

---

1. Millet and Johnson, *Bridging the Divide*.

returned with bloated visage and fiery eyeballs, and seating himself on his magazines of death, deals out his vials of burning wrath."[2]

Whether stopping in Peru on his way to the Sandwich Islands or during his tours of the Marquesas islands,[3] Titus Coan could be pleasant while on the home turf of Roman Catholics. Similarly, he could be civil with Mormons while in Salt Lake City,[4] while continuing to make observations about which he would write.

On the way to Hawai'i, the *Hellespont* spent twenty-one days in the harbor of Callao, Peru. This stay gave them the "opportunity of going on shore as often as we desired, of visiting Lima, of attending the gorgeous ceremonies of Passion Week, of looking into the grand Cathedral and their splendid churches, and of noticing the monuments of art, and the scars of revolution in that renowned, but often suffering, desecrated, and vandalized city."

He writes of the Roman Catholic Passion Week ceremonies as "gorgeous," the Catholic Cathedral "grand," the Catholic churches "splendid," and the Catholic works of art "monuments" in a positive sense. He continues on to write of the hospitality of the Bishop of Lima while observing the bishop's Catholic habits. "With the courteous Bishop of Lima, we went through the Cathedral, he bowing and crossing himself as he passed by the various pictures and statues, telling us of the guardian care of the different saints over the city."[5]

Many years later—during his second visit to the Marquesas Islands—Coan writes positively of his conversations with Catholic officials in a location where, as in Peru, Catholicism was the dominant religion at the time. Coan notes that the bishop is polite and that they engage in open conversation[6] with each other. The Lady Superior of a nunnery also engages in a mutually respectful exchange with Coan as she welcomes him. "We called on the bishop, who received us politely, and entered into free conversation with us, and with the two English gentlemen, residents, we visited the French nunnery. The Lady Superior received us with great urbanity, and introduced us to the two Sisters."

Coan notes with apparent approval the equality of the grounds and schooling of the girls at the Catholic school. He does note, however, that the expense of the school was borne by the French government.[7]

While he could be civil with Catholics on their home turf, when it came to Catholics in Hawai'i and arriving on the Big Island, the situations became confrontational and hostile on both sides.

---

2. Titus Coan to his brother Ezra Coan, January 20, 1841, in Coan, *Memorial Volume*, 61–62.
3. See second chapter on Missions.
4. See chapter on trip to the United States.
5. Coan, *Life*, 22.
6. Dialogue?
7. Coan, *Life*, 200–01.

There is some uncertainty as to the precise time Roman Catholicism arrived at the Hawaiian Islands.[8] Some point to the arrival of Don Francisco de Paula Marin[9] during the early 1790s. While he lived less than the ideal Catholic life, there are several reports of his baptizing over three hundred Hawaiians, both royalty and common people.[10]

At this point of the chapter, Peter T. Young's blog on Catholicism in Hawai'i is contrasted with Titus Coan's autobiography.

"In 1819, Kalinimoku was the first Hawaiian Chief to be formally baptized a Catholic." A pioneer French Catholic mission arrived in Honolulu on July 7, 1827. "It consisted of three priests of the Order of the Sacred Hearts of Jesus and Mary: Father Alexis Bachelot, Abraham Armand, and Patrick Shorty." Six Frenchmen supported the priests in their efforts. In an ironic twist, the first mass was celebrated "on Bastille Day, July 14."

Coan relates the arrival of the Catholics in his autobiography: "The pioneer Catholic missionaries arrived in 1827 and were rejected by the rulers." He does not indicate the influence of the Board missionaries on those same rulers.

He continues with his information and commentary by noting that this "company was led by Rev. John Alexius Augustine Bachelot, was commissioned by Pope Leo XII, as 'Apostolic Prefect of the Sandwich Islands.'[11] They landed without permission and refused to depart, under the delusion that the Pope as the Viceregent of Heaven had dominion over all earthly principalities and powers, as if the earth were his footstool."[12]

In his blog, Young notes that the "American Protestant missionaries and the French Catholics did not get along. The Congregationalists encouraged a policy preventing the establishment of a Catholic presence in Hawai'i. Catholic priests were forcibly expelled from the country in 1831. Native Hawaiian Catholics accused King Kamehameha III and his government of imprisoning, beating, and torturing them."

Later in 1831, "Commodore John Downes, of the American frigate *Potomac*, made a plea for freedom of religion, telling the Hawaiian court that civilized nations did not persecute people for their religion." This appeal led to a brief let up. At the end of September in 1836, almost four months after Titus Coan arrived in Honolulu, a French Navy ship *La Bonte* forced the king to restrict a Catholic priest's ministry to foreign Catholics. In 1837, two other Catholic priests were allowed to come on shore for good.

---

8 Young, "Ho'okuleana: To Take Responsibility."

9 "Manini."

10. Young, "Ho'okuleana: To Take Responsibility."

11. Note the similarity to the title Coan would later informally receive, "Apostle to the Sandwich Islands."

12. Coan, *Life*, 93. The pope is no longer viewed as having "dominion over all early principalities and powers."

OTHER RELIGIONS

The major event of the 1830s took place in 1839, when the French Navy frigate *l'Artemise* under the command of Captain Cyrille-Pierre Theodor Laplace sailed into Honolulu Harbor and pressured the "Hawaiian leadership to get along with the Catholics—and the French." Fearing a French attack on his kingdom, King Kamehameha III issued an Edict of Toleration on June 7, 1839,[13] "permitting religious freedom for Catholics in the same way as it had been granted to the Protestants."

In May of 1840, the Vicar Apostolic of the Pacific arrived with three priests, "one of whom, Rev. Louis Maigret, had been refused a landing at Honolulu in 1837. The King donated land for what would become the Cathedral of Our Lady of Peace."[14]

Coan explains those tumultuous years in his autobiography. "Then followed a long struggle, in which arrogance, intrigue, and duplicity were freely exercised, and which conflict has continued until this day. One step of aggression followed another until the power of the French Government was invoked by the priests, and in 1839, Captain Laplace, commander of the French frigate *l'Artemise*, appeared and made charges and demands which, it was then supposed, meant a seizure of the Islands. But the Lord spared us."[15]

Sarah Acheson[16] wrote a masterful undergraduate thesis in 1969 that shows the interaction of Catholicism and geopolitics, particularly with France. She includes such appendices as: "Secret instructions to Capt. of the *Blonde*, the Right Honorable [George Anson] Lord Byron, RN"; Father Reginald Yzendoorn, who presents negative views of Coan; four letters from Fidelia Coan;[17] and nine letters[18] from Titus Coan.[19]

Reginald Yzendoorn published[20] in 1926 *History of the Catholic Mission in the Hawaiian Islands*. In the Preface he sounds somewhat contradictory[21] in his explanation of the treatment of American Board representatives. "Unlike many other ecclesiastical histories, this history is neither apologetic nor controversial. No such needs have prompted the writing of its pages. As it is the duty of every man to oppose error, when its toleration would not be for the greater good, I have not reproached nor condemned the Protestant missionaries for opposing with all their might what in their

---

13. King Kamehameha III had previously refused to allow Catholic missionaries to establish themselves in Hawai'i for fear that it would divide the kingdom into two conflicting camps, typical of the divisions that existed before unification of the Islands." Forbes et al., *Partners in Change*, 348.

14. Young, "Ho'okuleana: To Take Responsibility." See also Forbes et al., *Partners in Change*, 348.

15. Coan, *Life*, 93.

16. A direct descendant of Titus Coan. Married name Stephens.

17. Fearing the Catholic takeover of the Sandwich Islands.

18. Within months of writing this thesis, Sarah and her family donated to the Library of Congress the Fidelia and Titus letters as part of the Titus Coan Papers.

19. Acheson, "Scramble for Hawaii."

20. With the usual Catholic *imprimatur* and *nihil obstat*.

21 Yzendoorn, *History of the Catholic Mission*, v. On a cover page with two quotations, he relates the Letter of Leo XIII, August 18, 1883: "This, above all, writers should keep in mind: that the first law of history is that no one dare say anything false, and next, that no one be afraid to say anything which is true; les[t] there be a suspicion that the writer seeks to curry favor or is actuated by malice."

opinion is the error of errors. If the Reverend Messrs. Hiram Bingham and C. M. Hyde have been handled with severity, it is not because of their opposition was more violent, but because ungentlemanly they made use of unfair weapons."[22]

Yzendoorn's second chapter is entitled "A Protestant Mission" and has the following headings: "The American Board of Foreign Missions.—First Mission to the Sandwich Islands.—First School.—Bibliopathy.[23]—Printing Press Started.—Ellis's First Visit.—Reinforcement.—Ellis's Second Visit and Tour around Hawaii.—Foundation of Missions at Kailua and Lahaina.—Death of Kaumualii.—Rebellion on Kauai.—Kaahumanu's Interest in the Mission.—Incipient Success."[24]

Other chapters include: "Persecution,"[25] "The Death-Spasm of Persecution,"[26] and "L'Artemise."[27] The latter chapter provides the Catholic perspective on the frigate incident. The themes of that chapter include: "The Manifesto.—No Protection for Missionaries.—Committee of Vigilance.—Armistice.—The $20,000 Guarantee.—Grant of Religious Liberty.—Military Mass.—The Commercial Treaty.—An Apology for Laplace.—Whatever we have done to Others, do not do it to us.—The US East-India Squadron.—A Diplomatic Roman Candle."

The Coan letters in Acheson's Appendix C[28] provide a contrast to Yzendoorn's emphases. In what appears to be a reference to Catholicism and the Eucharist, Titus writes Fidelia in 1839: "It is now morning, and I am waiting a little for assembling of the 'Sacramental Host' and for the mustering of the troops of hell in order to bring on a general engagement, and once more to test the 'weapons of our warfare' [2 Cor 10:4]. Thus far the Lord of Hosts has been with us [Ps 46:7]—signally so: and 'he that is faithful and true' [Rev 19:11]. He whose arm is omnipotent, and whose spear gleams lightening—He who judges and makes war in righteousness, will not fail us nor forsake us."[29]

Four days before, Fidelia writes her sister Maria Robinson in Bangkok on the subject of the frigate. "A French man-of-war is in the Pacific, settling the grievances of Catholic subjects. It has made the Society Islands government pay two thousand dollars for—I don't know what. The frigate is expected here next. You perhaps know that this government has forbidden Romish priests to disseminate their doctrines at these islands. I fear the time is coming when this doctrine will be propagated by the sword among us."[30]

---

22. Yzendoorn, *History of the Catholic Mission*, xiii–xiv.
23. No definition for "bibliopathy" can be found in Yzendoorn's book or online.
24. Yzendoorn, *History of the Catholic Mission*, 21–25.
25. Yzendoorn, *History of the Catholic Mission*, 44–59.
26. Yzendoorn, *History of the Catholic Mission*, 121–33.
27. Yzendoorn, *History of the Catholic Mission*, 134–40.
28. Acheson, "Examples of Missionary Experience," in "Scramble for Hawaii," 62–66.
29. Titus Coan to Fidelia Coan, March 16, 1839, in Acheson, "Scramble for Hawaii."
30. Fidelia Coan to Maria Robinson, March 12, 1839, in Acheson, "Scramble for Hawaii," 66.

Six months later, Fidelia Coan writes to her sister Amanda Church about Laplace's demands, the resulting treaty, and demonstrates that the Hilo missionaries are not aware of any imprisonment of native Catholics. She writes of the treaty, "It was doubtless got up by villains nearer us than France." She expresses disapproval of the manipulative power of military war ships. If "a French frigate can frighten them once to repeal their best laws, it can do so again, and so can any other frigate. The Catholics have commenced their work—have a number of proselytes—some eight or ten from the churches on Oahu. A few have burned their Bibles and hymnbooks,[31] which act seems to be their initiation into the Catholic faith. What bearing all these things will have on us as a mission no one can tell. With the Catholic religion stalking abroad, and ourselves virtually under the French government, we may I think apprehend some trials. But oh, this people! What will become of them! Romanism is just the thing to take with them; for it allows them to sin, and they can buy a pardon. The doctrine is already spreading among them, and the proselytes glory in it, that there is no sin which the priest cannot pardon."[32]

Sarah Lyman writes her sister of her concerns at the time of the French frigate's presence in the islands. The "natives have always viewed Romanism as a species of idolatry; the King of France on hearing of this and they had expelled Romish priests belonging to his kingdom, from their dominions, sent out a frigate of seven hundred men to bring the nation to terms, or make war upon them. On the arrival of the frigate a manifesto was sent on shore proclaiming war, if the chiefs did not within forty-eight hours comply with all the requirements of the French commander . . . The chiefs felt themselves in a dilemma and knew not what to do; after consultation they concluded that it would be better to *yield* (their independence) than to subject their people and the proscribed missionaries to the ravages of war . . . A few weeks after the French frigate departed, the English man-of-war *Sparrowhawk*, Capt. Shepherd, touched here on her way to Honolulu.

"Capt. S. and officers, while here, spoke freely *against* the proceedings of the French and unhesitatingly said that Capt. Laplace undoubtedly had acted contrary to the instructions of his government. Be that as it may, the mischief they have done cannot be retrieved, the ruinous influence they have exerted on this nation can never be done away."[33]

On page 94 and the first part of 95 of his autobiography, Coan continues his "hasty sketch of the introduction of Catholicism into these Islands." For more information he refers "the reader to the histories of the Rev. Hiram Bingham[34] and James J.

---

31. Both translated by Board missionaries, with some, such as Lorenzo Lyons, writing original hymns in Hawaiian. Judd, *Missionary Album*, 144.
32. Fidelia Coan to Amanda Church, September 16, 1839, in Acheson, "Scramble for Hawaii," 65.
33. Sarah Lyman to Melissa Joiner, September 19, 1839, in Martin, *Sarah Joiner Lyman*, 104–06.
34. Bingham, *Residence*, 311–13.

Jarvis, Esq."[35] Coan sets forth two reasons why these two books are of benefit on this subject. "These histories were written mostly at the times and place of the troubles, and they present a fair and truthful statement of the facts."[36]

Coan continues in his autobiography with his specifics of Catholics coming to and affecting the Hilo and Puna areas. "Of this persistent aggression of the Catholics, Hilo and Puna have had their full share. Priests were early[37] stationed in these and the adjoining districts and they at once took a bold and defiant stand."[38]

Yzendoorn's Preface opens with unspecified years in Hilo. "During my four years' stay at Hilo, in the Island of Hawaii, I once visited the neighboring district of Puna, where my congenial confrere, Father Ulrich Taube,[39] conducted his flock heavenward with music and with song."

At the Pahoa mission in Puna, Yzendoorn is told about another undated prophecy by Kahapuu that "one day there was to come a man dressed in a 'kapa loloa,' a long garment; he and his companions were the ministers of the true religion." Absent specifics, it was said that she "died a martyr[40] to the unknown faith."[41]

According to the online "History of St. Joseph Church," "Catholic Christian worship in Hilo was as early as 1839." The first chapel was located on the bayfront and was made from pili grass. It was called Saint Martin de Tours.[42] The "History" continues, "Father Charles Pouzot, SCC became the first pastor of the parish in 1845. By 1848 the small grass chapel was replaced by a new wooden structure. The Tabernacle to preserve the Eucharist was placed in the sanctuary in 1849. Gradually the worship space was adorned with statues and stations of the cross. A bell, donated in 1850, was a gift from sailors serving on the American man-of-war *Independence*. In 1852 the chapel was enlarged due to the generosity of sailors from another American warship whose spiritual needs had also been served in Hilo.""

By 1862 a larger church was built, using "stones and rocks." "On July 9, 1862, Bishop Luis Maigret, Bishop of Honolulu, dedicated the new church to Saint Joseph.[43] That same day thirty more people were baptized and about three hundred more were

---

35. Jarves, *History of the Hawaiian Islands*, 275–302; Coan, *Life*, 94–95.

36. Coan, *Life*, 95.

37. While Coan gives no specific date, he means that Catholic priests came to early in his tenure in Hilo.

38. Coan, *Life*, 95.

39. Apparently during the early 1900s.

40. By whose hand?

41. Yzendoorn, *History of the Catholic Mission*, xiii.

42 "St. Martin of Tours (Latin: *Sanctus Martinus Turonensis*; 316 or 336–November 8, 397) was Bishop of Tours, whose shrine in France became a famous stopping-point for pilgrims on the road to Santiago de Compostela in Spain. He has become one of the most familiar and recognizable Christian saints. As he was born in what is now Szombathely, Hungary, spent much of his childhood in Pavia, Italy, and lived most of his adult life in France, he is considered a spiritual bridge across Europe." Wikipedia, "Martin of Tours."

43. Husband of Mary, the mother of Jesus.

confirmed to become full members of the Saint Joseph Catholic Community."[44] In his 1863 station report, which covered the period of the dedicated Catholic church in Hilo, Coan writes that never "has the papal power made such determined demonstrations at Hilo as during the past year."[45] During the decade of Coan's death, "Portuguese immigrants doubled the size of the church."[46]

By early 1842 Coan was seeking assistance because he wanted to teach the church members about Catholicism. He desperately wrote Levi Chamberlain: "Can you procure McGavin's *Protestant* for me, either 'for love or money'. There are several copies in the mission, and perhaps in the mission library. If you could buy me a copy at a fair price I should prefer it. If not can you not call in one belonging to the library that I may have a share in its profits? Perhaps no one needs the work just now more than your servant. I am trying to enlighten my people on the subject of Popery, skirmish, we are expecting a formal attack from 'the Beast'[47] every day. Walsh's expressed plan is to build two or three houses of 'imagery'[48] in Hilo shortly."[49]

Between 1818 and 1822, William McGavin "contributed to the *Glasgow Chronicle* a series of letters on major points of controversy between the Roman and Reformed churches under the general title of *The Protestant*."[50] The full title is *The Protestant, Essays on the Principal Points of Controversy Between the Church of Rome and the Reformed*, 2 Volumes. The 1834 edition has engravings. Volume 1 has 103 chapters/essays and is over seven hundred pages. Volume 2 has 436 pages.

Coan addresses what he characterizes as confrontations initiated by the Catholics. "These emissaries confronted me everywhere. I often heard of them as having gone just before me on my tours. They appointed meetings near by my appointments, and at the same hour; they even came to my congregations in anger to command some of their claimed neophytes to leave the house" of worship.

Coan laments the confusion and frustration he claims the priests caused the Hawaiian people. "Everywhere they perplexed and vexed the simple natives by telling our best and most tried Christians that they were outside the true Church and on their way to perdition. They taught the people that the Protestants were all heretics and deceivers, that their ordinations were invalid, their pretended marriages adultery, and their teachings delusive."

Coan points out how the priests significantly lowered the level of personal behavior required for Hawaiians to become Catholics in contrast to Protestant missionaries.

---

44. St. Joseph Catholic Church, "History."
45. Coan, 1863 station report, HMH, digitized 1/147.
46. St. Joseph Catholic Church, "History."
47. See Revelation 13.
48. Coan and other Protestant missionaries viewed as idolatrous representations in a Catholic worship room such as statuary of Jesus on the cross or any representation of Mary and saints.
49. Titus Coan to Levi Chamberlain, January 16, 1841, HMH.
50. Wikipedia, "William McGavin."

Remember how many months Coan took before admitting adults to membership, with one of the disqualifiers being immoral and unrepentant behavior, as well as church discipline. Responsible participation through giving and labor was offered to any Hawaiian who would become Catholic. "They also appealed to the selfish and baser feeling of the natives to carry their point, encouraging them in the cultivation and use of tobacco, and assuring them that if they would turn Catholic they would never be called on to give to the priests, to assist in building churches, to contribute at monthly concerts, or be taxed in any way to support religion. Thus they gained weak followers. But when the priests changed their policy and began to call on their proselytes for help in building churches and supporting their teachers, many of the natives saw the duplicity and left them at once."

On the subject of Hawaiians under discipline in the Protestant church being wooed away by the priests, Coan wrote that "'daubing with untempered mortar' [Ezek 13:10] and crying 'Peace, peace, when there was no peace' [Jer 6:14 and Jer 8:11] was a bold and impudent opposition to sound church discipline, encouraging delinquents to harden themselves in sin. It became a refuge of lies, a hiding-place of transgressors, a snare to catch souls."

Coan admits to the affect all of these efforts had on him as a pastor. "This determined and unrelenting attack of the papal powers upon the church of Hilo and Puna greatly increased the cares and labors of the pastor." He indicates the prodigious number of public lectures he gave on the subject. "I delivered more than thirty public lectures on the history, character, and predictions of the papacy."

He shares both the burden and comfort he experienced in the course of these ongoing endeavors in the midst of everything else going on at and through the Hilo station. "I had continuous and wearied private efforts with those who were perplexed by the sophistry of the priests. And I had the comfort of knowing that many of my people became more than a match for the priests in faith and argument."[51]

Coan provides specific examples of confrontations between priests and Hawaiians. "A priest one day assailed one of the native Christians by asserting that all the American missionaries came to the Islands to get money.

"'Ah!' Said the native, 'you believe that, do you?' 'Most certainly,' said the priest. 'Well, your belief is marvelous. We Hawaiians think that those who are in search of gold and silver avoid such poor people as we are and go where money is plenty. Bingham, Mr. Thurston, and others came here to get money in this country. Do you think them such *fools*?'"[52]

Some descendants of the early missionaries—and even a few of the missionaries—did develop significant financial holdings and wealth in Hawai'i. But anyone who examines the commitment and lives of the vast majority of ABCFM missionaries to Hawai'i will see that they certainly were not in it for the money.

51. Coan, *Life*, 95–97.
52. Coan, *Life*, 97.

After another page and a half of priest versus Hawaiian, Coan shares one "of their most audacious acts," which was perpetrated against Coan by some Hawaiian Catholics as led by a priest. "I had once visited Mr. [John Davis] Paris,[53] at Kau, on the occasion of transferring those members of my church from that district to the care of Mr. Paris.

"On Monday I was returning toward Hilo. When near the center of Kau, as I was passing a Catholic church under the foot-hills of Mauna Loa, I was stopped by about two hundred Catholics, headed by a French priest, who challenged me then and there to a debate. This was in a narrow pass along the road which was so completely obstructed by the collected Catholics as to prevent my passing on. The challenge I respectfully declined, and as it was late in the afternoon, and I had some eight or ten miles of rough road to travel before I slept, I begged the mob to open the road, and suffer me to pass peacefully on my way.

"This the priest refused, commanding the people to keep the passage blocked, and with lifted hands and clenched fists, he declared that this Coan, this opposer of the Catholics, should never pass until he had accepted the challenge for debate. Again and again I calmly declined, and asked for a passage through the crowd. The priest became furious and his whole frame trembled with excitement, while the people around him seemed fierce as wolves.

"Not being able to proceed, I dismounted and tried to elbow my way through, leading my horse. The priest kept right before me, with hands quivering, and voice roaring: 'Who is the head of the Church? Who is the head of the Church?' For a time I made no reply, but quietly tried to work my way along, till at last I spoke out in full and clear tones, 'The Lord Jesus Christ, he is the Head of the Church.' Immediately the priest roared out at the top of his voice, 'That is a lie. Peter is the head of the Church.'"

Coan explains how he got out of the situation. "Several faithful natives were with me, watching with intense interest the scene. When this assertion of Peter's headship thundered from the priest, one of the men named Sampson, a bold and powerful man, could hold it in no longer, and said with a loud voice, 'Clear the road, and let my teacher pass,' and with the word came the act; with his strong arms he scattered the mob to the right and left, and I followed on through the passage thus opened. As I mounted my horse and rode quietly on, the howling crowd shouted: 'He flees! He flees! He is a coward.'"

Coan also explains the aftermath and denouement of this event. "Some of the leaders of this mob afterward left the Catholics, and repented with tears." On the next day, the priest behaved very differently. "This priest, recognizing me upon the road one day afterward, at once turned into the bushes, rather than to meet me. I never met him again, and it was not many months before the strong man was dead."[54]

---

53. Forbes et al., *Partners in Change*, 493–98.
54. Coan, *Life*, 99–101.

Coan transitions from Catholics to Mormons by writing the following, "Not many years after the introduction of the papal priests came a drove of Mormon emissaries. These spread themselves in squads all over the group like the frogs of Egypt."[55]

LATTER-DAY SAINTS

"[The Mormons] made an early descent upon Hilo. At first they employed flattering words. They called at once on me, asserted their divine commission, affirmed the heavenly origin of their order, enlarged on the new and sure revelations made to Joe Smith . . . [W]hen I produced my copy of *The Book of Mormon*, and showed them I knew more than they about the doctrines of the faith to which they were trying to make me a proselyte, they were confounded, and went away despairing of my becoming a convert.

"Finding that they could not prevail by flattery, they assumed a bold front, denounced the American missionaries as false pretenders, deceivers, and blind guides, without baptism, without ordination, and without credentials from heaven. One of their number came into our congregation on a Sabbath, and when I arose at the close of the service to dismiss the assembly, the Mormon arose, and with a loud voice gave notice that he would preach immediately. The great congregation moved quietly toward the church door, when he placed himself in the door-way to prevent their egress, demanding in loud, boisterous language that they all remain and hear '*the true gospel*.' Steadily the crowd moved to the door, and pressing the arrogant intruder aside, returned to their homes."[56]

The Mormon road to Hawai'i went through California's Gold Rush. Sam Brannan was one of the first Americans "to publicize the discovery of gold at John Sutter's Mill in early 1848." Brannon along with other "discharged members of the Mormon Battalion[57] were on hand when Sutter's partner James Marshall found the first flakes." Hundreds of Mormons poured into California to work in the gold fields. As with some other enterprising businessmen, Brannan made his fortune not through gold mining but "through an impressive merchandising operation."

Brigham Young demanded that Brannan send ten percent of his profits in tithing for the "Lord's treasury." Young also demanded thousands of dollars' worth of gold dust. Brannan, who had already become disillusioned with Young and the church,

---

55. Coan, *Life*, 101.

56. Coan, *Life*, 101–03.

57. "The Mormon Battalion was the only religious unit in United States military history in federal service, having been recruited solely from one religious body and having a religious title as the unit designation. The volunteers served from July 1846–July 1847 during the Mexican-American War of 1846–1848. The battalion was a volunteer unit of between 534 and 559 Latter-day Saint men, led by Mormon company officers commanded by regular US Army officers." Wikipedia, "Mormon Battalion."

did not respond to Young's demand. But the arrival of gold dust bags in Salt Lake City "further stoked Mormon gold fever."[58]

"Brigham Young was strongly opposed to the Saints running off to California in the pursuit of riches. Yet he was willing to make an exception, for it was agreed that the Mormon missionaries would bring home to Utah whatever treasure they gleaned." It was to those missionaries that Young turned. In the fall of 1850,[59] "Elder Charles C. Rich of the LDS Church Council of the Twelve Apostles called on a company of LDS ... gold miners working on the American River near Sacramento, California. The miners had been sent from Utah the previous year on a 'gold mission.'"

Fred Woods[60] describes the visit to the gold-mining missionaries. "On September 25, 1850, Henry W. Bigler recorded [in his journal][61] that Rich had visited him and his gold-mining brethren. The result was that Rich made a practical decision to send some of these missionaries to Hawai'i:

"'This morning the bretheren[62] [sic] was called together at the tent of Bro. [Rich], he stated he wanted some of us to go on a mission to the Sandwich Islands to preach the gospel, that his opinion was that it would cost no more to spend the winter there than it would here, that we could make nothing in the wintertime in consequence of so much water in the streams, and another thing provisions would be much higher in the mines and it would cost us more money to stay here and make nothing than if we went to the islands to preach.'"[63]

Fred Woods sketches the response and the journey. "As a result of this counsel, ten men[64] accepted the call to preach Mormonism in what came to be known as

---

58. Turner, *Brigham Young*, 179. The Pioneer Company of Mormons reached Salt Lake City in 1847.

59. Chad Orton precisely dates George Q. Cannon's departure from Great Salt Lake for California as October 11, 1849. Cannon reaches "Williams's ranch in southern California on December 13, 1849." Cannon and the others worked in the California gold fields for most of 1850. The call from "apostle" Rich to "serve a mission in the Sandwich Islands" is dated September 24, 1850. The eight missionaries left San Francisco on "the bark *Imaum* [Imam] *of Muscat*." The group landed in the Hawaiian Islands on December 12, 1850. Cannon, *Journals*, xxix.

60. The author would like to thank several CJCLDS friends and scholars for their very helpful advice and materials. They have made this second part of the chapter very strong.

61. Beginning with the religion's founder Joseph Smith, Mormons have placed large store in keeping journals. A "Mormon Wiki" site notes that keeping "a journal is something that members of [the CJSLDS] have been asked to do. President Spencer W. Kimball said, 'every person should keep a journal and every person can keep a journal,'" Mormon Wiki, "Keeping a Journal." Turner in *Brigham Young*, xviii, writes about the sources he used in the Young biography, listing journals first: "These sources—journals, minutes, correspondence, and sermon transcripts—proved an often-intimate window into Young's personality and leadership." It will be recalled that Titus Coan and many of the ABCFM missionaries kept journals or diaries as well.

62. Most Mormon journal entries have fluid spelling and grammar. Instead of placing a "[sic]" after each instance, the journals will be quoted as is.

63. Woods, "Most Influential Mormon Islander," 135–36.

64. In addition to George Q. Cannon, the ten included the eventual President Hiram Clark and Elders Henry Bigler, Hiram Blackwell, John Dixon, William Farrer, James Hawkins, James Keeler,

the Sandwich Islands Mission. Embarking from San Francisco on November 12, they landed in Honolulu on December 12, 1850, after a successful voyage of a month's duration."

Woods also describes the difference between the Mormon missionaries and the Catholic and Protestant missionaries. "Two decades after the founding of the Church of Jesus Christ of Latter-day Saints (LDS) in 1830, Mormonism was introduced to the Hawaiian Islands. Unlike Catholics or Protestants, who had tried to reform the mother church, the message the Latter-day Saints proclaimed was that the primitive Christian church had fallen into apostasy and that there had been a restoration of the gospel of Jesus Christ, which called for modern-day prophets and apostles."[65]

George Q. Cannon[66] was the leader of the first ten Mormon missionaries to arrive in the Sandwich Islands. Cannon writes of their arrival in Hawai'i. "The monotonous character of their language, their rapid utterance, their numerous gestures, caused us to watch them with interest. We thought them a strange people. I little thought at that time that I would ever learn their language . . . Though we had been sent on a mission to the Islands, we supposed our time would be occupied in preaching to the whites."'[67] Eventually Cannon changed his mind. "The language barrier was frustrating. But citing inspiration to do so, he focused his energy on the native islanders rather than the few white men and slowly made progress."[68] Following the Mormon custom of casting lots,[69] the ten missionaries cast lots twice: to determine who was going with whom; and to which island (Kauai, Oahu, Molokai, Maui, or Hawai'i) the pairs would go. Cannon went to Maui. Cannon writes about the first two missionaries sent to the Big Island of Hawai'i. He writes of "James Hawkins, who chose Hiram Blackwell as his companion, and to whom the island of Hawaii fell as a field of labor."[70]

Thomas Morris, and Thomas Whittle. *Deseret News*, "George Q. Cannon."

65. Woods, "Most Influential Mormon Islander," 135.

66. George Q. Cannon would go on to leadership both spiritual and political in the Mormon Church, including: the Quorum of the Twelve Apostles, the First Presidency, and the United States House of Representatives. He was jailed as a polygamist under the Edmunds Act and served almost six months. He authored a number of works, including his journal, *The Journals of George Q. Cannon: Hawaiian Mission, 1850–1854*, and *My First Mission*. See also Wikipedia, "George Q. Cannon"

67. Cannon, quoted in Turner, *Brigham Young*, 136.

68. *Deseret News*, "George Q. Cannon." This July 21, 2009, *Deseret News* summary of the first 10 Mormon missionaries to Hawai'i appears to draw from Cannon's *My First Mission*.

69. Cannon, *My First Mission*, 10. From the LDS Bible Dictionary: "Lots, casting of. There are many instances in scripture of the use of lots for the purpose of making a choice (Lev 16:8; Num 26:55; 33:54; 34:13; Josh 13:6; 14:1–2; Judg 20:9; 1 Sam 10:20–21; 14:40–42; 1 Chron 24:5, 31; 25:8; 26:13–14; Acts 1:26). Prov 16:33 expresses a feeling on the subject of the Lord's hand in the matter." LDS Bible Dictionary, "Lots, casting of." NB: There is no record of casting lots in the New Testament after the selection of Judas's replacement, Matthias, in Acts 1:26.

70. Cannon, *My First Mission*, 11. Cannon gets more specific in his journal. Discussions were held and lots were cast two days after their arrival in the Sandwich Islands. On Saturday, December 14, 1850, he writes, "This evening we got into conversation about staying here and going to the other Islands . . . [Thomas] Morris thought we had better stay here a week or two and try and get acquainted

OTHER RELIGIONS

It is not known whether Hawkins and Blackwell were included in "the squads"[71] to which Coan refers descending upon Hilo. But within the quotations from Coan's autobiography at the beginning of this section, Coan relates a dialogue or debate he had with the missionaries. The subject of signs comes up. "I asked, 'What signs?' They replied, 'Speaking with tongues, healing the sick, and all miracles.' I then said, 'Let us take up the '*signs*,' in order, and see if you Mormons have them. Can you cast out devils?' 'Yes.' 'But, if testimony is true, many of your people, like other sinners, act as if the devil were still in them.' 'They shall speak with tongues.' 'Can you do it?' 'Oh, yes, we can at Utah.' 'And why not here, where you need the gift more? And why do you ask for a teacher of the native language?'[72] Do you believe you could handle poisonous serpents, and drink deadly things with impunity?' 'We can heal the sick.' 'And so can I. But do not Mormons die?' 'Oh, yes.' 'Can you raise the dead?' 'The Mormons at Salt

---

with the situation of things and the language this was overruled by the rest; their plea was that [we] were using up our means here and it would take just as long on the rest of the Islands to get acquainted with things as it would on this. Bro. Clark said we might go into pairing off this evening and selecting our Islands, this was unanimously agreed to; various plans were proposed as to the mode of selecting partners and islands; Bro. Clark in the mean time had chosen Bro. [Thomas] Whittle to stay with him on this island if we thought best (this was joyfully assented to) it was finally left to Bros. C & W to select four and let them cast lots for the first second & third choice of the remaining four; we retired while they made choice; the four chosen were Bro. Hy. [Henry] Bigler, Bro. Hawkins, Bro. Discon, and myself I never in my life felt my weakness so sensibly as I [did] at this time my inability to do anything unless aided by the Spirit of the Lord. We cast lots for the first choice and it fell to me; the second to Bro. Bigler; Bro. D. third; and Bro. H. fourth. I was non-plussed for a minute or two not knowing . . . [who to] take; the spirit dictated to me very plainly to [choose] Bro. [James] Keeler, he said he was willing Bro. B. chose Bro. Morris; Bro. D. Bro. [William] Farrer; Bro. H. Bro. [Hiram] Blackwell. We then cast lots for the Islands; Maui fell to Bro. Keeler and me; Molokai . . . to [Bros.] Bigler and M.; Kauai . . . to Bros. Disxon and F.; Hawaii . . . to Bros. Hawkins & B{lackwell}, I had a desire to go to Maui and I got my desire when it fell to my lot. After this business was got thro' with we all felt better satisfied as we could each attend to getting off." Cannon, *Journals*, 29–30. Also on 30, editor Orton quotes from Cannon's *My First Mission*, 10–11. Orton introduces it by writing, "Cannon later provided a more extensive account of their casting lots:

"'The president did not like to pair us off, nor to say which of the islands we should go to; but he consented, with his partner, to select four out of the eight to preside, one on each of the islands . . .

"'My mind had not rested on any one as my choice for partner, and I was at a loss for a few moments whom to select. Then the spirit of the Lord plainly told me to choose Bro. J. K. I did so. I was both surprised and pleased at the manner in which he received my choice; for I, being so young, and he so much my senior, had thought that he would prefer a partner of more mature years and experience. He afterwards told me that when the four were chosen, and he found that I was one of them, he had slipped out and prayed to the Lord that I might be led to elect him to go with me. His prayer was heard and answered, and we both were gratified.

"'In casting lots for islands, Maui fell to us. When we were sailing past it my feelings were drawn towards that island, and I felt that I would like that to be my field of labor."

71. Though they probably were, being the first to arrive on the Big Island. And they could well have been the two with whom Coan conversed, as reported next by him.

72 " In the Church of Jesus Christ of Latter-day Saints the gift of tongues is manifested every day among the thousands of missionaries serving around the world. Missionaries learn foreign languages and the interpretation thereof with astonishing ease, and words come to them that they have not mastered." Mormon Wiki, "Speaking in Tongues."

Lake can do it.' 'Well, if you will go with me to a fresh grave near by, and raise a dead body to life, I will join you to-day.' This silenced them on miracles and signs."[73]

At the end of the opening quotation, Coan explains how the Hawaiian congregants dealt with a Mormon missionary who tried to start preaching. Mormon missionary John Stillman Woodbury reports a similar effort. Blackwell is mentioned, so one wonders whether it took place on the Big Island. "After breakfast we went to attend meeting and after their meeting was closed we the congregation repared [sic] to the outside to hear us preach." The "old deacon thought he would break it up so he ordered the church members into the house to attend to Sunday school or something else and said we must go off some hundred and fifty feet from the meeting house to preach . . . We had already commenced the meeting and Bro. Hawkins was just going to give out his text, but we quit off and removed our quarters off down towards the sea beach, a part of the congregation followed and part remained and some did not like it because we were driven from the meet-ing house." Enough stayed that Woodbury writes that "it kneeded the voice of a Lion to make them all hear." He also speaks of fear of retribution from the Congregational missionaries. *"Many of them seemed afraid to come up very near fearing they might be reproched for coming to a mormon meeting."*[74]

In May of 1854, George Q. Cannon makes the following entry about Coan and prejudice "against the truth" of Mormonism: "Mr. [Rev. Titus] Coan is missionary here, and another by the name of [Rev. David B.] Lyman has charge of a seminary here [Hilo Boys' Boarding School]. The people appear to be much prejudiced against the truth, through the efforts of the Calvinist and Catholic Priests, who have and are doing all they can to stop its influence."[75]

John R. Young talks about being denied permission to preach in a Calvinist church. Many Mormons referred to the ABCFM missionaries as "Calvinists" and their churches as "Calvinist Churches."[76] In a journal entry after meeting Lorenzo Lyons in Waiemea, Smith writes, December 15, 1856: "Monday returned to Waipio to day. On our way we met the Rev. Mr. [Lorenzo] Lion [sic], he shook hands with us very agreeably and went on, we said nothing to him and he said nothing to us. Found all well at Waipio. Some four of the 'Mormons' had left the Church and gon back to the 'whore of the Sandwich Islands,' their excuse for leaving, 'it is not popular.'"[77] In a footnote, Ricks explains that "Joseph F. probably means the Protestant churches; in the Book of

---

73. Coan, *Life*, 101–02.

74. Emphasis added. Woodbury, journal entry, May 1, 1853, 95–96.

75. Cannon journal entry, May 7–9, 1854, in Cannon, *Journals*, 465. Bracketed information provided by Chad Orton, editor. "Calvinist" is Mormon shorthand for Protestant.

76. See Young journal entry, April 25, 1856, in Young, *Memoirs*, np, while on Molokai: "Attended meeting in the Calvinist Church. Asked permission to preach, was refused." See Smith, *"My Candid Opinion,"* 102, "Calvinist minister." Smith uses the word in a derogatory manner several times. Joseph F. is a nephew of the founder of the LDS church.

77. Smith, *"My Candid Opinion,"* 68–69.

Mormon 1 Ne[phi] 14:10, those churches that oppose Christ's church are described thus: 'Behold there are saved two churches only; the one is the church of the Lamb of God, and the other is the church of the devil; wherefore, whoso belonged not to the church of the Lamb of God belonged to that great church, which is the mother of abominations; and she is the whore of all the earth.'"[78]

On July 26, 1851, Cannon writes about a confrontation on Maui with a Hawaiian leader of a Congregational or "Calvinistic" church. "Held meeting in the morning a prayer meeting. I spoke exhorting the saints to diligence. After this meeting this morning I baptized twelve; some of these were brethren of the Calvinistic Church. The luna[79] met me as I was returning and asked me the reason for my baptising[80] some of their members—I told them I did not know their members from any body else—they had come to me and demanded baptism at my hands and professed their willingness to live up to the requirements of the gospel—and I could not refuse them—He said he thought I had done wrong he was somewhat excited—he said I had said that their was only one baptism in the Church and I had baptised these making two—I told him that there was but one baptism in the Church—but these people had never been baptised until this morning—for their former baptism they had no authority from the scripture nor from the Lord for it—and it therefore was nothing."

Next, Cannon warns[81] the luna. "I told him he had better take care and not try to oppose the work of the Lord for it might crush him.—I then left him."[82]

In 1854, Mormon leaders divided the Big Island into two Conferences: "Hilo and Kohala, the boundaries to be Laupahoehoe Gulch and the boundary line between Kona and Kohala; the Conference of Hilo to include the districts of Hilo, Puna, Kau[83] . . . And Kona; the Conference of Kohala to include Kohala and Hamakua; Bro. [Thomas] Karren was appointed to take charge of Hilo Conference and Bro. R[eddick] N[ewton] Allred to Kohala."[84]

Karren writes of his arrival in Hilo in 1854. In his journal he writes about opposition by "the Catholick priest." He makes no mention of Coan, Lyman, or any "Calvinists."[85]

Chad Orton notes that by early 1854, the following LDS missionaries had been called to the Sandwich Islands: "John T. Caine, William W. Cluff, Sixtus E. Johnson, William King, M. D. Merrick, Simpson M. Molen, Edward Partridge, Ward E. Pack,

78. Ricks, ed., footnote in Smith, *"My Candid Opinion,"* 69.

79. "A *luna* is a supervisor or officer given the specific responsibility and control of something. Because the Congregationalist missionaries in this part of Maui traveled a circuit, they sometimes appointed local church members as lunas to oversee church-related affairs," in Cannon, *Journal*, 104.

80. Cannon was born and raised in England, hence the spelling?

81. Threatens?

82. Cannon journal entry, July 26, 1851, in Cannon, *Journal*, 106–07.

83. These three comprised Coan's area of mission.

84. Cannon journal entry, July 26, 1854, in Cannon, *Journal*, 513.

85. Karren journal entry, May 9, 1854, in Cannon, *Journal*, 466.

Joseph A. Peck, Henry F. Speirs, Smith B. Thurston, John A. West, Orson K. Whitney, and John R. Young." All but Merrick would make it to Hawai'i. He was assigned "to labor in the area around Sacramento instead."[86]

The nephews of two LDS luminaries served as missionaries in Hilo during the 1850s. John R. Young, a nephew of Brigham Young, "labored six months" in Hilo, under the presidency of "my cousin, Henry P. Richards. I was then called to preside over the Molokai conference."[87] He would write a letter to founder Joseph Smith's nephew, Joseph F. Smith, that Hilo was one of his least favorite places. Whether because of the Congregational hold on the town and region or the rain or some other reason(s), he wrote Joseph F. Smith, "'I presume that you see some rather disagreeable times up in Hilo, I know I used to, and I will acknowledge that it was the most lonesome hole that ever I've been in.'"[88]

The son of Joseph's brother Hyrum, Joseph F. Smith arrived in Hawai'i when he was fifteen. Drawing from the journal, Nathaniel R. Ricks provides the following chapter headings:

"1. 'It Is Allmost Heart Brakeing to Any Lover of Vertue': Maui, 1856 [3–22]"

"2. 'I Have Not Finished My Mission Yet': Hilo, Hawai'i, 1856–1857 [23–60]"

"3. 'I Am Not Worth "Two Bits" Alone': Kohalaa, Hawai'i, 1856–1857 [61–92]"

"4. 'My Folks at Home Would Think Me Lazy to Read My Journal': Molokai, 1857 [93–114]"

"5. 'I Could Hardly Bear to Leave the Little Fellow': Lanai, 1857 [115–134]"

Ricks provides many helpful insights to Smith and his time in the Islands. "Shrouded in myth and romance, Joseph F. Smith's first mission to the Sandwich Islands (later Hawaiian Islands) is perhaps best known today for its bookends: leaving home at the unusually young age of fifteen, then three years later returning to Utah as a 'dyed-in-the wool, true blue, through and through' Mormon."[89] Ricks notes that Smith struggled "to love the native islanders despite what he perceived as their many shortcomings."[90] While his transparency is admirable, one cannot help but contrast this outlook with Titus Coan's enduring love of Hawaiians. Perhaps if Smith had stayed on the Islands, that perspective might have changed.

Ricks also reports that nothing "is recorded regarding Joseph F.'s[91] early feelings regarding his mission call, which was announced over the pulpit during the Church's general conference. His great-uncle John Smith (1781–1854), the Church's Presiding

---

86. Cannon, *Journal*, 524.
87. Young, *Memoirs*, np.
88. John R. Young to Joseph F. Smith, June 9, 1856, in Smith, *"My Candid Opinion,"* 24.
89. Smith, *"My Candid Opinion,"* vii.
90. Smith, *My Candid Opinion*, vii.
91. To distinguish him from his uncle, Mormons usually use the shorthand of "Joseph F."

Patriarch, had blessed Joseph F. in June 1852,[92] that he would serve as a powerful missionary for the Church."[93]

In his journal, Smith notes the decision for him to head up the Hilo Conference. "April 7, 1856; Monday. I was chosen to preside over the Hilo Confrance on the Island of Hawaii, and Bro. Richards was sent to my old stomping ground [Maui]."[94] Two months later he writes of the baptism of a sick Hawaiian woman. "June 5, 1856. We were called upon last evening to administer to a sick woman by the name of Kaʻnapu, and I counseld her to be baptized as soon as she could muster strength and courage to undertake it. There fore this morning we went and by the assistance of her husband (who was a faithful Calvinist member, hence, bit[t]er against Mormonism) we accomplished her baptism tho' it was some distance to the watter and a very rainey and disagreeable morning."[95]

When it comes to the Puna District, Coan in his station reports[96] indicates very little Mormon activity. Only two pages of Smith's correspondence refer to that region. "We attended three meetings thro' the day. I ucupied most of the time as bro. [Washington B.] Rogers is still somewhat deficient in the preaching line, and the two native Elders who ware with us have gon[e] to Puna, to try and open a field in those parts . . . June 22, 1856; Sunday. Received a letter from Bro. Ward E. Pack by which we learn they ware well, had opened a way into Puna, had Baptised fifteen persons and organized a Branch."[97]

Smith writes of picking up and reading some mail in Hilo.[98] Mail provides a link to his one reference to Titus Coan and his church. "August 25, 1856; Monday. Baptized one person this morning, and left for Kawainui, bro. Wiliam [W. Cluff] and I took a strole thro' the City visited the Post Office and Rev. Mr. Coan's [church] and returned and persued our way to Kawinui, and arrived here in safty, found the folks all well, spent the evening preaching, teaching, arguing with some 'outsiders' &c, converted one."[99]

It was Cannon who secured the most notable Hawaiian convert to Mormonism during the 1850s. Woods uses early baptisms in Hawaiʻi to transition to the subject of the article: Jonathan Napela. "One of the early baptisms was John H. (Hawaii)

---

92. When he was ordained to the "Aaronic Priesthood"?
93. Smith, *"My Candid Opinion,"* vii.
94. Smith, *"My Candid Opinion,"* 21.
95. Smith, *"My Candid Opinion,"* 30.
96. See HMH digitized collection.
97. Smith, *"My Candid Opinion,"* 36. In the LDS organization, the basic meeting unit is a "ward." A "branch" is a smaller meeting unit than a ward.
98. Smith, *"My Candid Opinion,"* 49–50.
99. Smith, *"My Candid Opinion,"* 51.

Napela, who is considered by many to be the most influential Hawaiian convert to Mormonism."[100]

Though Napela is nowhere mentioned by Coan, the Board missionaries no doubt felt especial pain at this conversion. Napela had been among the first graduates of the Board's Lahainaluna school on Maui. Lahainaluna is up a hill from the coastal town of Lahaina. He went on to practice law and become a judge. He married Kitty Keliʻikuaʻaina Richards.[101]

Napela attended the Lahainaluna school while the founder and first principal Lorrin Andrews[102] was still the leader. He was the principal from 1831 through 1842.[103] Andrews might have influenced Napela in his choice of profession, because after Andrews resigned from the ABCFM over the issue of slavery,[104] he first "took charge of the printing office and bindery at Lahainaluna and taught music and penmanship from 1842 to 1843. In 1842 he also opened a school in Lahainaluna for his own children and those of other families and served as seamen's chaplain, Lahaina, 1833–1845." But then he entered the legal field: "He was appointed by the King and Chiefs as Judge of the Court of Oahu in Honolulu in 1845; and later was appointed member of the Superior Court of Law, made Secretary of the Privy Council, and was appointed the first Associate Justice of the Supreme Court" through 1855.[105]

While Andrews might have been in the background, Cannon's journal indicates Napela was removed from his judgeship after "his conversion to the Church of Jesus Christ of Latter-day Saints"[106] by a petition initiated by Jonathan Green. Cannon avers that the removal was already in the works before the conversion to Mormonism because of his drinking. "I heard to-day (Saturday) that Mr. Napela had been discharged from his office of *Luna Kanawai* or Judge and a many by the name of *Kaauwai*, his

---

100. Woods, "Most Influential Mormon Islander," 136.

101. Woods, "Jonathan Napela."

102. Coan refers to Andrews in the context of the school in Coan, *Life*, 232. "This school was in operation when we arrived at the Islands, under the care and instruction of the Revs. Lorrin Andres, E. W. Clark, and Sheldon Dibble."

103. Judd, *Missionary Album*, 24–25; and Forbes et al., *Partners in Change*, 62–67.

104. In an email to the author, the now Executive Director (Tom Woods) of the Mission Houses provides the following perspective on Andrews's departure from the ABCFM: "Although his concern about slavery played a role in his resignation from the mission, I don't think that was the major impetus, and I think it is sometimes overplayed. His primary reason that comes out very clear in his correspondence and relationships with other missionaries was the issue of lack of support for his engraving enterprise at Lahainaluna. He received very little financial support or equipment to do the amazing work he and the Hawaiian boys did there with engravings. The common stock system was still in place until 1842, just when Andrews was in his final struggle to make ends meet and using his own money to support the engraving business. There was a high degree of animosity about his desire to make some money from engraving to pay for the work and equipment. In complete frustration, he finally 'jumped ship.' David Forbes does a good job of describing the outlines of Andrews's break with the ABCFM in his *Engraved at Lahainaluna*."

105. Judd, *Missionary Album*, 25.

106. Wikipedia, "Jonatana Napela."

brother-in-law put in his place. From the best information I could get, they considered N. did not set a very good example indulging a little oftener than they considered consistent in drinking beer; no good brother in their church tasting the article. Mr. Green I understand made out a petition and had . . . it signed by his members to have him removed. I cannot find out that his being friendly to me has had any particular effect except probably to bring it to a head a little sooner: the avowed causes of dissatisfaction are of older standing than our acquaintance."[107]

Descended from the *ali'i*,[108] Napela and Cannon first met in early March of 1851. Napela hosted Cannon. In conversing with Napela, Cannon notes that Napela "said if their principles were wrong and ours were right he would embrace them; this made me feel good and I prayed to the Lord that prejudice that might be instilled into his mind might not turn . . . him from the truth. He was an influential man[, a] Judge of this side of the Island."[109]

Cannon baptized Napela into membership of the Church of Jesus Christ of Latter-day Saints on January 5, 1852.[110] Cannon's journal entry is brief on this subject. "Napela came over to be baptised this morning. I baptised him and three more and confirmed them at the water's edge."[111] The event this short entry records led to a long letter of concern from Maui ABCFM missionary Jonathan Green to fellow missionary Dwight Baldwin a month later.[112]

In addition to the facts that he was a well-educated professional descended from the *ali'i*, Napela would make his greatest mark on Mormonism in the islands by working with George Cannon on the Hawaiian language translation of *The Book of Mormon*. They began the translation on January 27, 1852.[113] Within three years Cannon, with assistance from Napela, had completed the translation. In a March 19, 1852, journal entry, Cannon notes: "Engaged Bro. Napela and myself revising what had been translated."[114] On July 22, 1853, they finished the translation.[115]

---

107. Cannon, *Journal*, 91–92.
108. Hawaiian royal line.
109. Cannon journal entry, March 7, 1851, in Cannon, *Journal*, 60.
110. Cannon, *Journal*, xxix.
111. Cannon journal entry, January 5, 1852, in Cannon, *Journal*, 149.
112. Cannon, *Journal*: "In early February 1852, the Reverend Jonathan S. Green wrote to the Reverend Dwight Baldwin decrying the success Cannon was having around Wailuku and making specific reference to the recent baptisms of Napela, [H. K.] Kaleohano, and [David] Rice." Orton notes that on 43 of Cannon's *My First Mission*, he (Cannon) reflects "on the highly charged religious atmosphere during this time." Orton also suggests for "an overview of the tensions between the Latter-day Saints and Congregationalists," to see Bishop, "Waging Holy War."
113. Cannon, *Journal*, xxix.
114. Cannon journal entry, March 19, 1852, in Cannon, *Journal*, 162.
115. Cannon, *Journal*, xxx.

On July 25, 1854, Cannon was released from the Hawaiian mission by the conference at Honolulu. He left four days later and arrived in San Francisco on August 12.[116] Once in California, he saw to the printing of the Book of Mormon. In late 1856, he wrote a letter to "Saints and Friends," providing an eight-page summary of the Book of Mormon. The first twelve cases of unbound Hawaiian Book of Mormon copies were reportedly received by Henry Bigler on "November 24, 1857." The copies bound in red[117] cost $1.25, while the remainder went for one dollar.[118]

Although he did not apparently live up to Titus Coan's church membership standards,[119] Napela was "chosen to the high Office of President of the Twelve of the Church in the Hawaiian Islands." This is the top position of any stake, or group of wards, within the Mormon church.[120] In 1869, Napela travelled to Salt Lake City to receive his Temple endowment.[121]

Cannon records two discussions[122] with American Board missionaries. They are told from his perspective as Coan's is told from his. Bitton indicates that the Latter-day Saint missionaries had quite regular contact, with Cannon relating occasional conversations with Catholic priests. He also notes that "tension was inevitable" between the Mormon and Congregational missionaries.[123] One Cannon conversation with a Board missionary was with Daniel Conde, who was stationed in Wailuku, Maui, between 1848 and 1856.[124]

Under the heading "Relationship with Christian Clergy," Britton relates the conversation. Cannon meets Daniel Conde[125] in March of 1851. "A moderately friendly chat ensued and Cannon offered Conde a copy of Parley P. Pratt's *Voice of Warning*.[126] Conde, however, 'condemned the principles before he had read or heard.' In particular,

---

116. Cannon, *Journal*, xxx.

117. "An attractive color to the natives."

118. Whittaker, "Placing the Keystone."

119. There is significant evidence of Nepala having a problem with alcohol. In response to the author regarding a Joseph F. reference in *"My Candid Opinion,"* Chad Orton, researcher at Brigham Young University and lead editor of *Journals of George Q. Cannon: Hawaiian Mission, 1850-54*, wrote in a May 8, 2013, email to the author: "You asked about Napela and drinking. In April 1851, Cannon reports that Napela had been 'drinking a little' and that Reverend Conde 'held a trial' for Napela for his drinking and associating with Cannon. In June 1851 Napela was released as a judge because he drank beer a little more often than he should have. They might have let the drinking slip if it was not for his association with Cannon. Of course, this was before he was baptized. I do not find other references for the remainder of Cannon's journal to Napela's drinking, but we do know that since he shared a similar background with so many in the islands it wouldn't be surprising for him not to continue to be challenged by alcohol as noted in the published account of Smith's journals."

120. Woods, "Jonathan Napela," 30.

121. http://ldsmag.com/article-1-11975/.

122. Arguments? Polemics?

123. Bitton, "George Q. Cannon."

124. Judd, *Missionary Album*, 72.

125. Forbes et al., *Partners in Change*, 190-95.

126. First published in 1837.

he rejected out of hand the possibility of modern revelation. Conde's approach frustrated Cannon: 'I could not get him to show me my errors from the scriptures if I had any but it was all I think, I think, I think, no proof.' Conde had no hesitation in rejecting the Latter-day Saint claims: 'He said he would rather belief Mahomet than Joseph Smith.'"

Conde's comment is interesting, since Mormonism shares some similarities with both Islam and Catholicism. On the last Sunday of March, Cannon attended Conde's service in Wailuku. Because Cannon was mastering the basics of the Hawaiian language, he could tell that Conde was inveighing against Mormonism and its founder. "A major part of his discourse was a diatribe against the Latter-day Saints. Joseph Smith had pretended to see angels, Conde said, and claimed that an angel had taken away the plates from which the Book of Mormon was translated, which, if genuine, should have been left for all the world to see."

Conde related common claims of the day against Joseph Smith. He "called Joseph Smith 'a notoriously bad character,' a thief, a lawbreaker, a dissolute rake with 'many wives or concubines'—in short, 'a very wicked man.' If Joseph Smith had truly seen angels, Conde taunted, why did they not deliver him from death?"

Understandably, Cannon's emotions were churning as he listened to this attack. He did not feel proficient enough yet in the language to challenge Conde in front of the congregation. He realized that Conde "had the pulpit and could out-talk." Nevertheless, after the meeting Cannon confronted Conde and asked him "'if he could inform him better in regard to the things he had told this people' so that Conde could 'disabuse the people of the lies he had told them.'"

Conde replied, "'I do not think they are lies. It is my duty to warn the people.'" Britton indicates that Cannon then responds "tactlessy, speaking rapidly, his heart pounding": "'I dare you to prove Mormonism wrong from the scriptures . . . I can prove before this whole people that what you preach is not the gospel of Jesus Christ according to the scriptures.'"

Alluding to his previous observation of tension between Board missionaries and Mormon missionaries, Britton notes in an understated way that it "was not a genial conversation." Cannon relates how Hawaiian congregants who knew some English had listened to the conversation. He goes back to his home of the opinion that the Hawaiians have been hurt spiritually by Conde's teachings. "Some of the congregation had gathered around to listen, but they only understood English about as well as Cannon did Hawaiian. Upon returning to his lodgings, realizing that the people 'had been so much hurt listening to [Conde's] slanders,' Cannon 'wept like a whipped child.'"[127]

Britton next relates an even more raw conversation between Cannon and Jonathan Green. In April of the same year he went to Hamakua Loa to meet with Green the day before he was scheduled to preach. They shook hands and Green invited him to a nearby house. "After some polite small talk, the two men quickly engaged in an

---

127. Bitton, "George Q. Cannon."

argument with each other. What, Green asked, was Cannon's purpose in coming? Hadn't the gospel already been preached here? Cannon did not mince words. He was there to preach the gospel of Jesus Christ and to tell all people that the Lord had again established his church as it was anciently. 'I do not think the gospel is preached here or I would not have been sent here,' he declared."

If possible, the conversation went downhill from there. "'Have you read any of our publications?' Cannon inquired.

"'Yes,' said Green.

"When Cannon insisted to know what they were and who had written them, it turned out that they were exposés written by ex-Mormons. But, Cannon continued, 'Have you read any of ours?'

"'No,' replied Green, 'nor would I read anything that Joe Smith or any of his followers would write.'

"'Then you are incompetent to judge whether we are right or wrong,' declared Cannon. 'A wise man hears both sides of the question and then judges.'

"Cannon next asked Green if his church had apostles.

"'No,' Green answered, 'but the church is built upon their foundation.'

"'But they were meant to continue for the perfecting of the saints.' Cannon was quoting the epistle to the Ephesians chapter 4.[128] 'You don't claim to be perfect, do you?'

"'No, we do not,' Green answered.

"'Well, then,' Cannon pressed his conclusion, 'you are not the Church of Christ or you would have these offices.'"

The argument reaches an explosive conclusion. "Green paced back and forth. Grabbing his hat, he said, 'God curse you,' and strode out of the room.

"Cannon followed. 'You do not have the authority to curse me.'

"'I did not curse you but I prayed to God to curse you,' Green said.

"'Well, I do not think he will hear your prayers.'

"Poor Green was trying to get away. As he mounted his horse, he had to listen to one more sentence: 'Mr. Green, you would do well to take Paul's advice [to] "prove all things and hold fast that which is good."'[129]

"Spurring his horse, the Protestant missionary said, 'I have proved Mormonism,' and rode away. Just moments before, though, he turned to a group of Hawaiian onlookers and warned, 'This man is ae enemi keia.'[130]

"'No I am not,' replied Cannon in Hawaiian, 'and he cannot prove me one from the Bible.'"[131]

---

128. Cannon was extrapolating from Ephesians 4:12.
129. 1 Thess 5:21.
130. "I declare that this man is an enemy demon"?
131. Britton, "George Q. Cannon."

Britton may well have drawn this from Cannon's journal. It is found almost *verbatim* in his Sunday, April 6, 1851, entry. He provides the context of the discussion. "To-day the [Latter-day Saint] Church is twenty-one years old, it [the weather] is very wet and disagreeable. I went to the meeting house with my host, we sat there several *hours* at last Mr. G. made his appearance he was *passed* me without seeing me. He is an elderly man very plain in his appearance after getting [settled]; he commenced asking questions, first the decalogue[132] and then other questions on various subjects.—He then commenced his discourse, he expatiated upon the sufferings of the savior &c. &c. and repentance. After he had finished his discourse I went out for a few minutes Mr. G. still sitting in the stand while I was out he went out and was followed by my host who I suppose told him who I was and what I wanted what their conversation was I did not know. They returned after some time & then they attended to the Sacrament, after which Mr. G. came and shook hands with me and said he was going to stay for a few minutes at a house a short distance and invited me to go with him. As we were going he asked me if I intended staying long at the islands, &c. & said he supposed he had heard of me at Wailuku."[133]

Then begins the conversation related above. While not scoring the debate on points, the reader sees the conflict between two kinds of missionaries—Mormon and Protestant. This interfaith strife did not stop Mormon missionaries from making rather unique requests.

Cannon, along with most nineteenth-century Mormon missionaries[134] around the world, sought permission to speak in Protestant churches. As portrayed in an introductory quotation to this section, Coan writes about the attempt of a Mormon missionary to hijack the Protestant church's facility for preaching purposes. Britton writes from a Mormon perspective that Cannon "did not disrupt meetings and could be low-key in setting forth basic biblical teachings, but he did not hesitate to set forth the claims of the Restoration. If some of his comments seem a bit confrontational for modern tastes, it is important to remember that he was responding to the denunciations of churchmen who did not hesitate to poison the minds of their congregations against the Latter-day Saints. 'I have found that nothing is ever lost by Elders standing up for their rights,'[135] Cannon later wrote. 'People respect others who are spirited in claiming the privileges[136] which belong to them; and no Elder should ever forget that

---

132. The Ten Commandments.

133. Cannon journal entry, April 6, 1851, in Cannon, *Journal*, 74.

134. Young journal entry, April 25; 1856, in Young, *Memoirs*, np: "Attended meeting in the Calvinist Church. Asked permission to preach, was refused."

135 One wonders what Cannon means by "rights." Did he have the right to speak in a house of worship different from his? Did he grant such a right to Protestant missionaries requesting to meet at Mormon meetings?

136. Is it a right or a privilege?

he is the ambassador of the King of heaven, and that he should maintain his calling. If he is firm and respectful, he will be respected."[137]

Cannon held firm to his calling. Joseph F. Smith returned to the continent with a stronger belief in his religion. Most Mormon missionaries retained their religious views after concluding their service in the islands. One who did change his views was John Hyde, who would become a thorn in the side of Mormons and an encouragement to the Congregational missionaries and other Protestants in English-speaking countries.

In his Hawaiian journal, Joseph F. Smith notes that in November of 1856 he and brother John Brown "went to Pololu where we found the saints very backward and they were greatly affected by the report of John Hydes [sic][138] Jun[e] had left the Church, and was doing all in his power against it."[139]

The editor provides background to Hyde in a footnote. "Called as a missionary to the islands, John Hyde Jr. had a change of heart on his journey from California and began preaching and publishing anti-Mormon articles almost immediately upon his arrival in Honolulu. One of his earliest diatribes appeared in the *Polynesian*, October 18, 1856. Hyde left the islands and traveled to New York, where he published the following year his famous critique of the LDS Church, *Mormonism: Its Leaders and Designs*.[140] Hyde's apostasy—and Joseph F.'s efforts to counter its effects among the natives—is discussed in numerous entries herein." Ricks then lists the entries.

Citing an October 29, 1856, letter from Edward Partridge to Joseph F. Smith, Ricks notes that "Partridge declared, 'I do not think he can do any harm for the people already begin to become disqu[ie]ted[141] with him altho' he took well at first, and does yet with some, but the honest in heart if there are any can see what his aim[142] is without being uninformed.'"[143]

John R. Young has a November 5, 1856, journal entry of attending and responding to Mr. Hyde making a presentation at the Presbyterian Church at Waialua.[144] "Several clergy men and about fifty white people were seated on the stand, while the body of the church was packed with natives. Mr. Hyde lecture on the Evils of Mormonism." Young relates that Hyde talks about polygamy. Hyde relates how he went to France as a missionary "and converted thousands of the French people to the Mormon faith. Alas, today, I awake, as from a dream, and find Mormonism to be false."

137. Britton, "George Q. Cannon."
138. Misspelling noted because of proper name.
139. Smith journal entry, November 15, 1856, in Smith, *"My Candid Opinion,"* 64–65.
140 See Lynne Watkins Jorgensen, "John Hyde, Jr.: Mormon Renegade." *Journal of Mormon History* 17 (1991) 120–44.
141. Brackets by Ricks.
142. Partridge does not state what Hyde's aim is.
143. Ricks in Smith, *"My Candid Opinion,"* 64.
144. Did Young mean Congregational? No reference can be found to a Presbyterian Church in Waialua.

Young requests permission to reply, but the chairman refuses to let him.

Several "gentlemen demanded fair play. At length the chairman gave me fifteen minutes' time. Young later notes that this was his first experience in debate. "Opposition strengthened my faith, and added members to the church."[145]

The actual title of Hyde's 1857 book is *Mormonism: Its Leaders and Designs*. After a frontispiece picture of Brigham Young, Hyde dedicates the book to "Honest Believers in Mormonism." The chapter titles are: "The Author," "Salt Lake City," "Practical Polygamy," "Mormon Mysteries," "Education," "Brigham Young at Home," "Brigham the Prophet," "Chronological History of Mormonism," "Analysis of Internal Evidences of Book of Mormon," "Real Origin of the Book of Mormon," "Theoretical Polygamy," and "The Suppression of Mormonism."[146] For a thorough online thread of the Mormon controversy in Hawai'i, one can go to Uncle Dale's Readings in Early Mormon History (Hawaii Newspapers).[147]

While the two are not related, the first period of Mormon missionaries in Hawai'i ended the same year Hyde's book was published. The missionaries left because of the Utah War in 1857. In 1861, Walter Murray Gibson arrived at an LDS colony that had been established in 1854 on the island of Lanai.[148] Gibson would cause damage to the Mormon cause, eventually being excommunicated in 1864, "having deceived many of the Hawaiian Saints,"[149] "for preaching false doctrine," "maladministration of the colony, and embezzlement of church funds."[150]

Jonathan Napela turned to the Salt Lake City leaders for assistance. Joseph F. Smith returned to try to sort things out. In the process, the Lanai property was lost. Eventually the LDS Church would regroup and develop branches, wards, and a stake.

While there is now a ward in Hilo, Titus Coan reported very little enduring Mormon activity through the 1860s, when the station reports ended. He does note in his autobiography that "for years numbers of this deluded sect traveled over these districts, using all their powers of persuasion, not excepting lying and deceit, to draw the people after them. When once they succeeded in making a disciple they would quarter themselves in his house until he had cooked the last pig, goat, or fowl, and until his taro, potatoes, and bananas were gone, all the while boasting of their great love, and comparing themselves with the American missionaries, who they said came here to get salaries and to oppress the people.

---

145. Young, *Memoirs*, 83–86.

146. Hyde, *Mormonism*.

147. Uncle Dave's Readings.

148. Wikipedia, "The Church of Jesus Christ of Latter-day Saints in Hawaii."

149. Woods, "Jonathan Napela," footnote 25: "For more information on Walter Murray Gibson, see Gwynn Barrett, 'Walter Murray Gibson: The Shepherd Saint of Lanai Revisited,' *Utah Historical Quarterly* 40.2 (Spring 1972) 142–162; and R. Lanier Britsch, 'Another Visit with Walter Murray Gibson,' *Utah Historical Quarterly* 46.1 (Winter 1978) 65–78."

150. Wikipedia, "The Church of Jesus Christ of Latter-day Saints in Hawaii."

"I met the Mormons often on my tours, and had abundant evidence from repeated conversations, and from the testimony of the most reliable members of the church, of their ignorance, bigotry, impudence, and guile."[151]

Elias Bond, American Board missionary for fifty-five[152] years in Kohala,[153] provides information and analysis about the Mormons in his station reports. In his 1853 station report he transitions from smallpox to what he viewed as a spiritual scourge. "The smallpox was the immediate precursor of another disease whose distinctive power seems greater just in proportion to its abominable absurdity—I mean Mormonism." He writes that Hawaiians,[154] "together with several foreigners, have been diligent in the work of making proselytes. Their chief measures are a villifying[155] of the Missionaries—promises of healing the sick and promises of reliving the people of taxes."[156]

Bond provides census numbers and paints Catholics and Mormons with the same brush. "The recent census of this district gives in all Mormons 248 Papists 328 Protestants 2859 giving 3413[157] as the entire census." Bond writes of the disreputable nature of some of the early converts to other religions. He points out that Catholics and Mormons fight over the same people for converts. "The papists and Mormons have been having a battle on their own account in consequence of the turning of the former in considerable number to the latter."

He points out that for some Hawaiians, conversion to Mormonism is like a game. "It is a curious fact to be noted, that many of the Mormon converts turn 'just for the fun of it' as they say—they are coaxed until tired and then consent to be baptized."

Bond then presents a trenchant analysis of Mormonism while claiming to have little to do with the group and retaining some humility on the matter. "With the exception of exposing the delusion to our people I have, personally, had little to do with it—because reasoning and warning, where absurdity and bare-faced falsehood are more than evident to all minds, seem out of place."

He returns to the theme of coaxing as well as using the Mormon derogatory word for the Protestant missionaries—"Calvinists." "As to the *coaxing* people to be religious or to be *called* Calvinists in distinction fr[om] Papists or Mormons, I have no gift in that direction, not having so learned Christ" [Eph 4:20].

Bond points out that there is "nothing new under the sun" [Eccl 1:9] and that contemporary heresies are simply recycled old ones. "Mormonism is one of the facts of the cycle to wh. we belong—an Anti-type of corresponding facts in previous cycles

---

151. Coan, *Life*, 101–02.
152. Judd, *Missionary Album*, 54; and Forbes et al., *Partners in Change*, 147–53.
153. The northern section of the island of Hawai'i.
154. Several from Maui, including Napela?
155. Note that any Protestant journal misspellings are retained in this chapter as well.
156. Kohala station report, 3. HMH digitized online.
157. Apart from the first one, Bond does not use commas in this sentence.

of human affairs." Bond avers that Mormonism's "very absurdity appears to be its chief merit whereby it commends itself to many, perhaps most minds. A mince of the Spiritual and sensual, it possesses a delicious flavor for the palates of the sensual natures and in this but follows Mohammedanism, the refined systems of paganism, and not doubtfully Romanism."

With an understanding of human nature, he indicates at least a temporary positive trajectory for Mormonism around the world. It will have its day in the sun. It "will have its day as its types had in their day—& when we see it gathering its converts by thousands in Great Britain, Prussia, and the U. States, we need not wonder that amongst these credulous Hawaiian children it makes considerable progress." To that end, Bond notes that six "or eight of our church members have been drawn off by the agency of friends to this delusion."[158]

While he does not record interaction with Catholic leaders or missionaries on his trip to the United States, he does so with regard to Mormons and his time in Salt Lake City. It is to the Titus and Fidelia 1870–71 trip that we now turn.

---

158. Kohala station report, 3. HMH digitized online.

15

The Coans Visit America, 1870–71

"I HAVE SEEN MAUNA Kea veiled with the mantle of night, and casting its gigantic shadow of darkness upon us. Again I have seen it when the first rays of the rising sun began to gild its summit. Watching it for a little while, the light poured down its rocky sides, chasing the night before it, until the mighty pile stood out clothed in burnished gold, and shining like a monarch arrayed in robes of glory.

"And when I gazed upon that platform in Brooklyn, and cast my eyes upon the great assembly which filled the house, I said in my heart, 'When will Polynesia and Micronesia display such a gathering of wisdom, piety, and moral power? A brighter than a natural sun begins to illume the darkness of those lands, chasing away the night of ages; but when will the full-orbed Sun of Righteousness ascend to the zenith and pour a flood of light and glory over all our benighted islands?' And then I reflected that even these lights of the Christian churches were yet to flicker as distant tapers before the coming glories of Zion, as predicted in the sixtieth chapter of Isaiah [Isa 60:1, 14d][1]."

In 1880, a brief article in the *New York Evangelical Journal* noted, "Dr. Coan, the venerable missionary . . . visited his native country, and spent some months seeing old friends and old places, and making many new friends who had come up amid the old surroundings to fill the places of their fathers. Whoever saw him then will have delightful memories of that beloved patriarch." He told the story of his life "with childlike simplicity."[2]

"Mr. and Mrs. Coan made a long visit to the United States in 1870 to 1871 that was intended to [improve] Mrs. Coan's health, and it also provided Titus a chance to

---

1. Coan, *Life*, 218. Coan wrote this about the annual meeting of the American Board of Commissioners in Brooklyn, New York.
2. *New York Evangelical Journal* (188[0?]), np.

visit old haunts and friends and to lecture widely on his mission work in Hawai'i, for which he had become a celebrity among the American mission community."[3]

FROM HILO TO ARRIVAL IN SALT LAKE CITY

Titus Coan resisted visiting the United States. He had been invited by the American Board as early as 1867, but he pleaded pressing church service in Hawai'i. In a November 30, 1867, letter to his sister-in-law, he wrote, "I see that you and other friends are indulging strong expectations of seeing us again in the land of our birth. We do not yet feel confident on the subject. Cares seem to thicken and labors to multiply as life advances. It now looks as though we could not go before 1869, and before that time who can tell what will be?"[4]

One thinks of Moses's father-in-law Jethro who counseled Moses with the virtues of delegation [Exod 18:17–26]. Granted, the Hilo area was a challenging situation for staffing, but at least temporary assistance in various areas of service had been provided prior to this time.

In the next letter in the *Memorial Volume* ("To Mrs. G[eorge] Coan") he writes on December 18, 1867, of the challenges of selecting, teaching, training, and ordaining Hawaiians for ministry. Many of them do not make it for various reasons: death, incompetence, taking other work and so on. Coan laments that it "often seems as if our earthly pilgrimage would close ere this reconstruction and reorganization [of Christian work in Hawai'i] is done. I have given a vacation to a class of fifteen in theology, which I taught five days in a week besides spending two hours daily in revising and correcting a commentary on Matthew in the Hawaiian language. And now our anniversaries are coming on . . . Our work never seemed heavier or more responsible and absorbing than now. Do not think that our Hawaiian Christians are full grown and mature. They are all children and need paternal care. I doubt whether our American friends realize this fact. If it is hard for parents to leave a family of five or ten small children how much more so for us to leave our five thousand?"[5]

A turn in thinking begins with increased concerns over Fidelia's health and the possibility of professional medical attention in the United States that might result in a diagnosis and relief, if not a cure. Titus puts it this way in his autobiography: "The

3. Forbes et al., *Partners in Change*, 187. NB: the word in the text before "Mrs. Coan's health" is "recruit," which might have meant "recoup." As will be seen in this chapter, a goal of the trip was to consult with stateside physicians about Fidelia's health. As a result of his "celebrity" and actual work, he would receive an honorary doctorate while in the United States.

4. Coan, *Memorial Volume*, 115.

5. Coan, *Memorial Volume*, 116. And Coan writes this more firm letter to the Rev. J. D. Paris in a December 28, 1869, "O! this going to the United States! It is a constant trouble to me. It seems like breaking up life. How to leave my people, and what to say and do if we go, are great questions for a small man. Others rush one even to Europe, but I cannot get on such light wings. Pray for us, that our dear Lord will direct in this matter, and we do pray that 'If the Lord go not with us, He will not suffer us to go'" [Exod 33:15]. Coan, *Memorial Volume*, 123.

health of Mrs. Coan being precarious, and no medical skill at the Islands affording relief, it seemed the more desirable to go."[6] On February 17, 1870, Titus wrote his future brother-in-law Hiram Bingham II. Hiram had encouraged Titus to stay in Hilo during 1870. In that letter he connected travel and the introduction of the need for medical advice for Fidelia. "I thank you, beloved armor-bearer of our Great Captain, for the kind things you are pleased to say of an unworthy fellow-laborer, and I feel your plea that we remain at our post this year. But we had accepted the second invitation of the Board, and the numerous and urgent calls of personal friends to visit the States. Our hearts and treasures are here, and our minds sung heavily over to assent to go. At our time of life, it appears to us that not to go this year is not to go at all. And as a new factor in our plans for going Mrs. C. needs medical advice."[7]

While Fidelia had had some sort of health problems since early after arrival in Hilo, there is evidence as early as 1869 of the disease that ultimately led to her death. In a February 8, 1870, letter from Mrs. Hiram Bingham II, Clara addresses Fidelia as "My Dear Hilo Mother." On Fidelia's behalf, Clara had consulted with Dr. Sangenwald (in Honolulu?) on a treatment for pain. The doctor dismissed it as "humbug."

Continuing on regarding the third-party consultation with Dr. Sangenwald, Clara writes, "In regard to the swelling on your neck, he at first seemed reluctant to express an opinion without touching and seeing it. But, in the course of conversation, he said, unless there were evidence of inflammation, such as heat pain and redness, he should not advise poulticing. When I mentioned that there was also a swell further down toward the shoulder, he said that was encouraging. A second swelling, in such cases, was a hopeful indication."[8]

The author of this book wonders whether she had some form of cancer. Was it lymphoma? Could those two areas of swelling be indications of tumors? After consulting with several doctors via email, the consensus does appear to be a diagnosis of cancer, even though each of the three physicians who responded to my email pointed out other possibilities. Of the three, one was rather emphatic that cancer was not his first choice. See the next chapter for a description of Fidelia's final days.

According to Clara's letter, the Coans were scheduled to take "the April steamer" so she could see the doctor. By early 1870, the Coans had decided to go to the United States. They begin discussing specifics with their son Samuel Latimer Coan. Latimer's February 9, 1870, letter is touching in its solicitousness and practicality. He suggests that they leave Hawai'i in early May to escape the cold weather (of San Francisco? Salt Lake City? Elsewhere?). He addresses the dread of packing and traveling. He encourages his parents to see the trip as a vacation.

He talks about clothing, the cold, train, and "investing" (depositing for interest) money in a San Francisco bank. "Regarding clothing [etc.] you will probably do well

---

6. Coan, *Life*, 213.
7. Titus Coan to Hiram Bingham II, February 17, 1870. Yale Bingham papers, Box 4.
8. Titus Coan to Hiram Bingham II, February 17, 1870. Yale Bingham papers, Box 4.

to wait about buying anything more than is necessary till you get east. What you need for the journey you can get here . . . It will be early enough for I suppose you wish to escape the cold weather."

Latimer talks about daughter Hattie being able to provide advice and suggestions. He encourages them to bring as little baggage as possible because "trunks are a great nuisance . . . I suppose you dread somewhat the idea of breaking up, [packing] and leaving, but this feeling will wear off, and after you get over the sea voyage, I think you will enjoy every hour."

Latimer also encourages his parents to come to America to enjoy themselves. He provides a refreshing call to his parents to set aside their duties and have fun on the trip, or else cancel the trip. "If [you] can[,] [throw?] off all anxiety and care for the time being and spend the year as school children do a vacation . . . But I have no doubt you will take the philosophical view of it[?] seeing it is right and best for you to come [?] it is right and best to enjoy all you can and forget for the time being all the cares and duties behind . . . If I thought that you did not look at it in such a light I should be sorry to see you leave Hilo. But you will I think."[9]

They arrived in San Francisco on May 5.[10] In the introduction to *Adventures in Patagonia*, Henry F. Field writes about Coan's visit to the United States. "Mr. Coan and his wife remained on the islands thirty-five years before revisiting their native country. When they came back in 1870, they found another world than that which they had left. All things had become new.[Rev 21:5]. They had made their outward voyage in a small sailing vessel. They returned in a steamship. When they landed in San Francisco they had scarcely seen a railroad. Now they were whirled in fire-drawn cars up the mountains and over the plains, across the whole breadth of the continent."[11]

They stay in San Francisco at Mrs. Thompson's boarding house. On February 10, Latimer writes, "You will hardly like the noise and excitement of a hotel, and I know of no better boarding house than Mrs. Thompson's. But as she is generally pretty full, in order to have pleasant quarters here it will be necessary to write beforehand. If you will let me know I will call up there and see what arrangements I can make." Latimer plans on showing them the city and its culture, including the San Francisco music festival with "Carmella Urso the renowned violinist."[12]

After spending two weeks with Latimer, they boarded a train on May 19. In a letter to Hattie he writes of leaving San Francisco and arriving in Sacramento. "We left San Fran. day before yesterday at a.m."[13] The western terminus of the Pacific Railroad was first Sacramento, then Alameda, and ultimately Oakland Point in Oakland,

---

9. Samuel Latimer Coan to Titus Coan, February 9, 1870, LOC Box 10.
10. Coan, "Waymarks," and *Life*, 213.
11. Field, in Coan, *Patagonia*, xii-xiii.
12 Samuel Latimer Coan to Titus Coan, February 9, 1870, LOC Box 10.
13. Titus Coan to Harriet Coan, nd, LOC Box 10.

California. Wherever they boarded the Pacific Railroad they took a train to and through Sacramento.

In a bridge passage in the *Memorial Volume*, Lydia Bingham Coan writes, "An almost playful prophecy on the part of Mrs. Coan when about to leave the United States in 1834, that they would return when a railroad across the continent should be completed, had its fulfillment in the spring of 1870."[14] Titus brings up the anticipated completion of the Transcontinental Railroad in a letter to James Dana. He talks about how relatively quickly Dana could travel from his home to the Coans in Hilo. "When the Pacific railroad shall have been completed, it will be but a step from the Elm City to the Emerald Bower of Hilo. That step will be over the eastern Pacific. Would not such a vacation rejuvenate you?"[15]

As they continue east, Coan notes to Hattie that the "[shale?] over which we passed is of volcanic origin and much of it [structurally? stunningly?] resembles some parts of Hawaii."[16] Almost to the day one year after the Golden Spike was driven in at Promontory Summit (May 10, 1869), the Coans traveled from the Bay area to the Utah territory. In 1870 the Transcontinental Railroad did not go through Salt Lake City, but they transferred at some point.

Not pleased with it being bypassed, Brigham Young oversaw the funding and building of a spur to Salt Lake City. Under "Young's leadership of hundreds of Mormons helped grade the railroads that finally met in May 1869 at Promontory Summit, thirty miles west of Brigham City. Though it did not prevent him from bidding on the work, Young was disappointed that the railroads bypassed the Mormon capital by taking the northern route around the Great Salt Lake. Although the contracts had proven an economic boon, the Union Pacific—in financial straits despite years of lavish government subsidies—failed to meet its obligations to Young.

"Young attempted to overcome his financial difficulties by moving ahead with plans for a railroad to connect Salt Lake City with Ogden where the transcontinental intersected. The Union Pacific agreed to contribute iron rails and other materials, and church members contributed their labor to settle tithing or emigration debts or for payment in stock or railroad tickets. Young sold bonds for what became the Utah Central Railroad, intending to use the proceeds to pay off his Union Pacific subcontractors . . . At an August 1870 meeting of the School of the Prophets, the apostle George Q. Cannon[17] referenced 'a wide spred feeling of discontent and distrust in relation to monetary matters in connexion with President Brigham Young and the Railroad.' Predicting the railroad's profitability, Young nevertheless insisted that

---

14. Coan, *Memorial Volume*, 126. No quotation or citation regarding Fidelia's "Prophecy." Could it perhaps have been spoken by Fidelia to Lydia, or by Titus to Lydia during the 1870s?

15. Coan to Dana, August 31, 1866, in Coan, *Memorial Volume*, 98.

16. Coan, *Memorial Volume*, 98.

17. For Cannon as the leader of the first LDS missionaries in Hawai'i beginning in 1850, see "Other Religions" chapter.

profits were beside the point. 'We ought to take hold of it for the sake of building up the Kingdom of God.'"

In January of 1870—four months before the Coans' travel on the railroad—church leaders "celebrated the railroad's completion in January 1870 . . . The railroads facilitated everything from Utah's internal commerce to the construction of the Salt Lake City Temple."[18]

Titus writes to Hattie that our "ride from Ogden this morning was splendid. The air was cool and pure; the lands are grown and beautiful . . . The valley through which we rode looked a paradise surrounded with giant hills . . . We saw numbers of Indians on the way, but all were [?] in the extreme, and most of them were incessantly beggars. '*Two bits*' is their countersign, and you are sure to hear it so soon as you come in hearing distance."[19]

SALT LAKE CITY

On Saturday May 21,[20] the Coans debarked their train after riding the short Mormon spur from Ogden. Titus writes about the "great basin" and notes that after dinner "I sallied out with the Hon. Mr. Barstan to see one of the Twelve Apostles [of the Lamb?] and to call on President Young."

Indicating that "dinner" might have been lunch, Coan writes to Hattie that we "visited the great Tabernacle and saw the foundation of the new Temple which, as I was told, the cost ten millions of dollars."[21] Coan next tells his daughter that the "Apostle [George Q. Cannon], on whom we were to call with a letter of introduction from the [?] was not in [?], and suddenly a great shower of hail and rain fell [?] from us [?] and we retired into a telegraph office and waited for it to cease." Someone came into the office to get out of the storm. The visitor spoke of the weather, but Coan did not realize that it was Brigham Young until after he had left! "We shall, D. V.,[22] see him and the apostle prophets and elders tomorrow as we purpose to be in the Tabernacle. Paper and time fail so must close."[23]

18. Turner, *Brigham Young*, 353–54. 478n31: "SOPM {School of the Prophets Minutes, 1867–74, CR 390/6, CHL (Church History Library) (Church Archives), Church of Jesus Christ of Latter-day Saints, Salt Lake City, Utah), 6 Aug. 1870; 'mind and will' in WWJ [Scott G. Kenney, ed., *Wilfred Woodruff's Journal, 1833–1898: Typescript*, 9 vols. (Midvale, UT: Signature Books, 1983–84), 7 Oct. 1870m 6:574; *Utah Reporter* [Corinne, Ut.], 15 January 1870."}.

19. Titus Coan to Harriet Coan, May 21, 1870 [see context of letter, "the ride *this morning*"], LOC Box 10.

20. Titus Coan, "Waymarks," LOC Box 1, indicates being in Salt Lake City May 21–23.

21. Titus Coan to Harriet Coan, LOC Box 10. The Salt Lake Temple(http://www.utah.com/mormon/salt_lake_temple.htm) confirms that the Tabernacle took forty years to build (from 1853–93) and provides other details, including a cost of $3.5 million. The latter amount would be over $64 million in 2015 dollars.

22. *Deus Volent*, "God willing."

23. Titus Coan letter to Harriet Coan, LOC Box 10.

Coan picks up the Sunday narrative in his autobiography. He combines his usual trenchant observations with searing commentary. We "spent a Sabbath at Salt Lake City, saw the Prophet and several of his apostles, met several of the Mormon missionaries whom we had seen in Hilo." We do not know if he saw the Prophet and Apostles from afar or if a Sunday meeting worked out. He nowhere provides the names of the Mormon missionaries who had been in Hilo between 1850 and 1859. It is possible that Joseph H. Smith was in Salt Lake City that weekend and year.[24]

We "attended service in the Great Tabernacle, heard much bold assertion without proof, and witnessed a singular observance of the Lord's Supper, the elements being distributed by laughing boys, while a speaker was haranguing the audience without making a single allusion to the death of Christ."[25] The Tabernacle, completed three years before in 1867, was the location of the service Coan attended. The laughing boys would have been the younger (12 and older) "Aaronic" priesthood, as opposed to the older (18 and older) "Melchizedek" order.[26]

As for the "haranguing" address, a typed summary of the principals and subject matter for May 22, 1870, from the *Deseret Evening News* of May 23:

"May 22, 1879.

"Sunday, May 22. Meetings were held at the new Tabernacle, S. L. City, as usual. Elder Nathaniel H. Felt and Pres. Geo. A. Smi[t]h preached in the forenoon and Pres. Daniel H. Wells in the afternoon."[27] Elder Felt "occupied a portion of the time in relating his experiences during his mission in the east, from which he has just returned." He was followed by President Smith, "who briefly described the organization of the Church, the early history of the Church, the driving, privations of the Saints and their settlement and progress in these valleys."[28]

Coan writes that we "also saw the foundation of the great temple [on Saturday and Sunday?], which a bold declaimer said was a literal fulfillment of the prophecy of Isaiah 2:2: that 'the mountain of the Lord's house shall be established in the top of the mountains, and shall be exalted above the hills; and all nations shall flow unto it.'

"The speaker affirmed that this prediction was now fulfilled before the eyes of the Mormons, and all the people shouted *Amen*."[29] Coan makes no reference to the second part of President George Smith's presentation. Smith, who was a polygamist

---

24. While the author has not been able to definitely pinpoint Smith, who had been on the Big Island of Hawai'i and, at times picked up his mail in Hilo, as being in Salt Lake City that weekend in 1870, the circumstantial evidence points to that being the case.

25. Coan, *Life*, 213–14.

26. An LDS friend confirms to the author that at times the teenage Aaronic priests can be rather rambunctious. He emphasizes that they are repeatedly instructed to be somber and quiet. The one such service the author observed had serious and quiet servers of the elements.

27. *Deseret News* 19:186.

28. *Deseret News* 19:186.

29. Coan, *Life*, 214.

with seven wives, talked about polygamy.[30] "Referring to the repugnance the world professes to entertain for polygamy, President Smith said."[31]

President Smith might have selected the subject of polygamy because of efforts earlier in 1879 by Congress to further limit polygamy in the Utah territory. Even though the passage in its strongest form was not passed and it did not make it out of the Senate, it continued to be of concern to LDS leaders.[32]

HEADING EAST

From Salt Lake City, the Coans headed east. The train arrived in Omaha on May 25. On the twenty-sixth, they "crossed the great mud ditch Missouri" on a boat or a raft.[33]

---

30. George A. Smith, 1817–1875, was part of the LDS Presidency. Brigham Young was the First President from 1847 until his death in 1877. "Known for his somewhat bombastic speaking style, Smith once said: 'We breathe the free air, we have the best looking men and handsomest women, and if [non-Mormons] envy us our position, well they may, for they are a poor, narrow-minded, pinch-backed race of men, who chain themselves down to the law of monogamy, and live all their days under the dominion of one wife. They ought to be ashamed of such conduct, and the still fouler channel which flows from their practices; and it is not to be wondered at that they should envy those who so much better understand the social relations.'" Reynolds, "Work of the Lord."

31. *Deseret News* 19:186.

32. In "early 1870, the writer and editor John Beadle and Robert Baking eagerly testified before the Republican-dominated Congress about everything from Mormon juries to Young's public profanity. In February, Representative Shelby Cullom of Illinois introduced sweeping anti-polygamy legislation. The bill proposed to limit the jurisdiction of the territory's probate polygamy legislation. The bill proposed to limit the jurisdiction of the territory's probate courts, strip voting and preemption rights from those who refused to swear under oath that they neither practiced nor believed in polygamy, give federally-appointed officials the authority to impanel juries, and convict men on the basis of 'cohabitation . . . with more than one woman as husband and wives.' As an enforcement mechanism, the bill would have authorized the president to send up to forty thousand troops to Utah, which boasted a population of slightly more than one hundred thousand." Turner, *Brigham Young*, 361–62. See also 479n51: "Testimony in *Execution of the Laws in Utah*, House Report 21, Forty-First Cong., Second Sess.; draft of Cullom bill in *Congressional Globe*, House of Representatives, Forty-First Cong., Second Sess., 1367–69. See Bigler, *Forgotten Kingdom*, 281–85; Gustav Larson, *The Americanization of Utah for Statehood*, 64–72. Turner continues with "Utah's Mormon population was predictably outraged at the proposed legislation," calling it crushing bondage similar to Southern slavery. "In another sign of Young's shrewder political approach, thousands of Mormon women gathered at the tabernacle to affirm their commitment to 'Celestial Marriage.' The assembled women pledged themselves, in the event the Cullom Bill became law, 'to aid in the support of our own State Government' . . . Shorn of its most draconian provisions, a weakened version of the Cullom Bill passed the House in March 1870, but the measure died in the Senate. Mormon Utah had narrowly escaped the federal government's cudgel once again." Something else that occurred a little while before Coan's arrival was the arrival of a new territorial governor. "In the absence of new legislation, President Grant expected his Utah appointees to assert federal control over the territory through other means. In the spring of 1870, new territorial governor J. Wilson Shaffer reached Utah. A former aide to General Benjamin Butler during the Army's occupation of New Orleans, Shaffer [who would die on October 31, 1870, at the age of 43—Wikipedia, "J. Wilson Shaffer."] determined to make himself governor in fact as well as in name, and he regarded his new wards much as he and Butler had viewed obstinate Confederates." Turner, *Brigham Young*, 361–63.

33. Titus Coan letter, May 28, 1870, LOC Box 10.

The Missouri River was the last place a railroad bridge was built. Completed in 1873,[34] the bridge was available a year after the Coans returned to Hilo.

"We spent a little time in Iowa."[35] It appears that they were in West Branch,[36] which is near Iowa City in southeastern Iowa. They were in Iowa from May twenty-seventh through the thirtieth. From there, they continued to Chicago, staying there from June first through the fourteenth.

After almost a month of visiting and observing, Titus begin to hit his ministering stride in Chicago. "Here I was called to labor more abundantly, and here we met many warm friends, and two sons of our esteemed associations Mr. and Mrs. D. B. Lyman . . . In this marvelous city we spent two weeks, and then came eastward."[37]

In his autobiography, Coan next provides an overview of how many states and territories he visited. "In all, we visited more than twenty states and territories, everywhere finding multitudes of Christian friends; many of whom we had seen before, and many more whom we had not seen in the flesh, but who were fathers and mothers, brothers and sisters and friends in Christ Jesus."[38] Later he notes the number of times he spoke, "My talks in large and smaller assemblies during the eleven months we were in the States numbered two hundred and thirty-nine."[39] That would be an average of speaking twice every three days. When one factors in train travel, the average could well be once a day.

He writes about his "opportunities to meet Christian conventions and associations, Sabbath-schools, Monday meetings of clergymen, meetings of benevolent societies, of working-women, etc." as "numerous and exhilarating." He most appreciated "the fact that partition-walls were gradually giving way between different evangelical denominations." He lists some of the denominations, the members of whom he spoke to and met with: Episcopalians, Presbyterians, Baptists, Methodists, Congregationalists, "and many others." Because of this he said that "my tongue longed to sing with David: 'Behold how good and how pleasant it is for brethren to dwell together in unity'"[40] [Ps 133:1].

At one point, Coan says he does not need to list the many the seminaries and female seminaries to which he was invited. Then he lists several of them: "Andover, Bradford, Vassar, Union, Auburn, and Princeton." He indicates "Our great enjoyment

---

34. Wikipedia, "Union Pacific Missouri River Bridge."

35. Coan, *Life*, 214.

36. Coan, *Memorial Volume*, 131. Where their Quaker friends, the Beans, lived.

37. Coan, *Life*, 214.

38. Coan, *Life*, 214.

39. Coan, *Life*, 216. Quoted without citation (except that Titus had written it and in quotation marks) in Coan, *Memorial Volume*, 128. Ehlke, "Enthusiastic Religion," paraphrases and quotes from the *Memorial Volume,* 128, without any reference to *Life*.

40. Coan, *Life*, 216.

on these occasions."[41] He received an Honorary Doctor of Ministry degree from Dartmouth College, which led to his occasionally being addressed as "Dr. Coan."[42]

Coan writes about the United States as he found it in 1870: "We found our country broad, fertile, populous, and wealthy. It had extended from ocean to ocean; its villages, towns, and cities had multiplied, and its population increased beyond a parallel in history. Its schools, its colleges, its churches, and its humane and benevolent institutions had multiplied marvelously. Its railroads formed a web-work work over all the land, and its telegraphic wires were quivering through the atmosphere. Its progress in science, in art, in discovery, in intelligence, in invention, in wealth, and in Christianity, seemed to make it the pride of all lands."

But he next describes "the scars of war."[43] Returning to the Coans' travel east, they proceeded from Chicago to Niles, Michigan, at the invitation of Mr. Humphrey of the ABCFM.[44] But Titus spent only the night of June 14 before returning for three weeks after attending the annual Congregational annual meeting in Oberlin.[45]

OHIO GENERAL CONGREGATIONAL CONFERENCE IN OBERLIN

Ehlke characterizes Coan's time in Oberlin as "one of the highlights" of his visit to America. There at the invitation of the new[46] James Harris President Fairchild and the President Emeritus Charles Grandison Finney,[47] Coan comes full circle by his participation in this event. Having come to a saving knowledge of Jesus under Finney's ministry in Upstate New York and then having become known for leading the Hawaiian Great Revival using Finneyesque New Measures (such as protracted meetings and Concerts of Prayer), Coan spoke and co-officiated communion with Finney as an equal and colleague. He would also get to visit with some Hawaiian mission veterans and relatives.

---

41. Coan, *Life*, 216.

42. LOC, single page. Printed Seal, "Dartmouth College, and Hanover, N. H." Next to location in hand writing is written "August 5, 1871." Since Titus and Fidelia returned to Hilo on May 2, 1871, this page was prepared well after the fact (perhaps at Titus's request?). Evidence suggests that they were in New England in December of 1870 and early January of 1871, so he may well have received this degree at that time. If it was conferred after the Coans had returned to Hawai'i it would have been conveyed to him by ship. Handwritten wording: "This certifies, that the Honorary Degree of Doctor of Divinity was confirmed on the Rev. Titus Coan by the Trustees of Dartmouth College, at their last Annual Meeting." It is signed by "Asa D. Smith, *President*."

43. Coan, *Life*, 214–15.

44. Titus Coan to Harriet Coan, June 20, 1870, LOC Box 10.

45. Coan, *Memorial Volume*, 128.

46. Harris served as President of Oberlin College from 1866 through 1889.

47. Ehlke, "Enthusiastic Religion," 256.

On June 15, Coan took "the [train] cars for Oberlin, more than two hundred miles. There the Ohio Conference (Congregational) of more than two hundred members[48] was in session, and here I remained until the twentieth."[49] He notes that "I was received with open arms by presidents Fairchild and Finney and professors Maya, Charles and many others. My intercourse with these and with *many* of the clergy of Ohio was precious."[50]

On Thursday June 16, Coan was joined by fellow (now retired) missionary to Hawai'i Peter Gulick[51] and Mr. Bates of Ceylon "for a great missionary meeting" between 7 and 10 p.m.[52] Coan also writes that "in Oberlin I found Brother Gulick," probably Peter's son. Luther Halsey Sr. had served as a physician in Polynesia between 1852 and February of 1870.[53] Clifford Putney notes that "Luther Sr.'s daughter married an Oberlin Professor and her brother went to the school.[54] Oberlin was a stopping point for many of the Gulicks (and other Congregational missionaries) as they traversed the country."[55] In addition to a Gulick reunion, Titus "found a brother and sister of Mr. [Samuel Northrup] Castle."[56]

Peter Gulick left the same day, the Friday on which at "2 p.m. the Lord's Supper was celebrated and I was invited with President Finney and Bro. Porter from Texas [to] assist in the administration" of the elements.[57] Coan's co-officiating a Communion service provides insight on his development from a revival convert to an equal with the world-renowned Dr. Finney. "Rosell T. Cross remembered a meeting in the Second Church in Oberlin in June 1870 when 'the Communion was administered

---

48. "Ministers and delegates," see below.

49. Titus Coan to Harriet Coan, June 20, 1870, LOC Box 10. NB: During five years of service in Ohio, the author attended one June an Ohio Conference annual meetings of the United Church of Christ, which is the structural heir of the Congregational Churches of Ohio and the nation.

50. LOC Box 10.

51. Peter and Fanny were part of the Third Company of ABCFM missionaries to arrive in the Sandwich Islands. They arrived at Honolulu on March 30, 1828, Judd, *Missionary Album*, 100; and Forbes et al., *Partners in Change*, 292–97. For an excellent biography of the husband-and-wife team, see Putney, *Missionaries in Hawai'i*.

52. Titus Coan to Harriet Coan, June 20, 1870, LOC Box 10.

53. Forbes et al., *Partners in Change*, 284–88.

54. Judd, *Missionary Album*, 106.

55. Clifford Putney, email to author, July 2014.

56. Titus Coan to Harriet Coan, June 20, 1870, LOC Box 10. Judd, *Missionary Album*, 59, indicates that Samuel and Angelina Loraine Tenney arrived at Honolulu with the Eighth Company at Honolulu on April 9, 1837—almost two years after the Coans had arrived. The company of Castle and Cooke had been in operation for nineteen years in 1870, Wikipedia, "Castle & Cooke." For more on Samuel Northrup Castle and his family, see *Partners in Change*, 156–65.

57. LOC Box 10. "Brother Porter" is probably Jeremiah Porter who, along with his wife Eliza Emily Chappell, was an active reformer and abolitionist. After the Emancipation Proclamation, Jeremiah and Eliza established a Sunday School for freed slave children in Austin, Texas. Wikipedia, "Eliza Emily Chappell Porter."

by Mr. Finney and Titus Coan, the great Hawaiian missionary. Probably no two men then living had led more souls to Christ. It was an impressive communion service.'"[58]

The collegiality continued on the Sunday Sabbath Services. He writes Hattie that on the Sabbath June 19 the seventy-two-year-old Finney in the morning preached at "10 ½ a.m. and . . . I preached to children in the presence of two thousand people at 7 p.m. I addressed the two[59] united . . . churches—the students, nearly a thousand, and others in a great congregation on the subject of missions."[60] He points out that Oberlin College people, with their already growing reputation for sending forth missionaries, "do not tire of hearing" about missions.

He summarizes his time in Oberlin in a letter to one of his sons. "I had a most interesting season and saw about two hundred ministers and delegates of the first order of intelligence and piety. I was the guest of Presidents Fairchild[61] and Finney, of Professors Cowles[62] and Morgan.[63] On the Sabbath I spoke four times. The last time, in the evening, [I] was before an assembly of some two thousand five hundred. I have never met a more enlightened, attentive and appreciative audience than in

---

58. Roselle Theodore Cross, "Memories of Charles G. Finney," in Dupuis and Rosell, *Restored Memoirs*, 313. See Corr, "Titus Coan," 261–62.

59. First and Second Churches of Oberlin. The First Church of Oberlin (United Church) is the facility Finney had built in 1834 with thin round poles holding up the balcony so no one could escape the gaze of Finney's sharp blue eyes. www.firstchurchoberlin.org and author's personal tour of church received from pastor in 1980s.

60. Titus Coan to Harriet Coan, June 20, 1870, LOC Box 10.

61. "When Oberlin opened its doors in 1834, Fairchild entered as a freshman. He graduated in 1838. The year after graduation he was appointed tutor in the college, was ordained in 1841, and in 1842 became professor of Latin and Greek. In 1847, he was transferred to the chair of mathematics, and in 1858 to that of theology and moral philosophy.

"A committed abolitionist, Fairchild played a role in the famous Oberlin-Wellington Rescue. In September 1858, he hid fugitive slave John Price in his home. A short time later, rescuers took Price to freedom in Canada.

"In 1866, Fairchild became the third president of Oberlin College. During his tenure, the faculty and physical plant of the college expanded dramatically. In 1889, he resigned as president but remained as chair of systematic theology. In 1896, Fairchild returned to the Oberlin leadership as acting President, serving until 1898." Wikipedia, "James Fairchild."

62. "Biblical scholar, teacher, anti-slavery advocate and founding member of Oberlin's Theological Department, Henry Cowles was born April 24, 1803, in Norfolk, Connecticut, to Samuel Cowles and Olive (Phelps) Cowles. After a boyhood spent in farm labor and in diligent study, Cowles entered Yale College in 1822, intending a career in the Congregational ministry. He graduated from Yale in 1826 and enrolled in Yale's Theological Department, where he came under the tutelage of revival preacher Nathaniel William Taylor (1786–1858), a follower of the Rev. Timothy Dwight (1752–1817). In 1828, Cowles was licensed to preach by the Litchfield North Association and ordained in Hartford in the same year. Hillsdale College in Michigan awarded Cowles the honorary DD degree in 1863." http://www.oberlin.edu/archive/holdings/finding/RG30/SG27/biography.html.

63 John Morgan earned an AB from Williams College in 1826 and an honorary DD from Williams College in 1857. "Professor of the Literature of the New Testament, and of the History of the Christian Church, 1835–37; Professor of the Literature of the New Testament, 1837–48; Professor of Biblical Literature, 1848–70; Professor of the New Testament Literature and Biblical Theology, 1870–80; Professor Emeritus, 1880–84." http://www.seeking4truth.com/professor_john_morgan_of_oberlin.htm.

Oberlin. The college is a great success, and Oberlin is a place of marked intelligence and goodness."[64]

Coan spoke in Oberlin even though he had received invitations from many Congregational Ohio pastors. During most of his time in the United States he had to choose some speaking engagements from among many. "Four ministers from Cleveland, one from Hudson,[65] one from Twinsperg,[66] and many from other places urged me to go . . . with them to address their people, but I had promised to remain in Oberlin over the Sabbath and to return to Niles on Monday."[67]

FROM NILES TO BROOKLYN

As already mentioned, Coan travelled to Niles at the invitation of Mr. Humphrey. On Tuesday, June 22, Titus and Fidelia attended a "gathering of about thirty of the Coan tribe." He writes to one of his sons that our "three weeks in Niles have been one continued ovation. You know the friends here. We were received with open doors and arms, and with such enthusiastic love as no one ever feigns. Since I have been here, I have been called to speak in public eight times. I pray the Lord that good may follow in the name of Jesus."[68]

Writing in the introduction to Coan's *Adventures in Patagonia* the ABCFM's Henry Field concurs with the reception Titus and Fidelia received across the country. "The fame of the missionary had gone before him, and wherever he came among the churches he was welcomed with an enthusiasm such as had not been manifested since the heroic [Adoniram] Judson came back from Burma, years before."[69]

His fame went before him as he spent three weeks in the Albany, New York, area. He visited various other places, including his birthplace in Kilingworh, Connecticut. "Our visit to Killingworth, my native town, was full of interest. Tender memories of childhood and youth often drew tears. Sixty-nine years had swept along the flood of time since my eyes first saw the light of day, and forty-four since I had left the home where I was born and nourished. The homestead where my father taught his boys to plow and harrow, to plant and hoe, to sow and reap, to cradle and bind, to mow and rake, and pitch and gather into the barn the winter's feed for cattle, was there. The

---

64. Titus Coan to to unspecified son, July 2, 1870, in Coan, *Memorial Volume*, 128.
65. 40 miles east of Oberlin.
66. Twinsburg.
67. Coan, *Memorial Volume*, 128.
68. Titus Coan to unspecified son, July 1870, in Coan, *Memorial Volume*, 128.
69. Field, in Coan, *Patagonia*, xiii. NB: Judson had been a member of the ABCFM's first group of missionaries sent forth from America's shores in 1812. He arrived in the Indian subcontinent a convinced Baptist and continued on his own to Burma, becoming the patron saint of American Baptist missions. He returned only once to the United States in 1845–46 before dying while on a boat in the Bay of Bengal in 1850. Wikipedia, "Adoniram Judson." The founder of Gordon Divinity School, now Gordon-Conwell Theological Seminary, was named after Judson: Adoniram Judson "A. J." Gordon.

orchard, where we children gathered apples and other fruits was there; but many of the choice trees were gone and the great sugar-maple and the nut-bearing trees where we had contested with the squirrel for our winter stores had disappeared. The cottage, where eight children had been reared, and where, as years passed on, we gathered at our annual thanksgivings, was desolate and silent, and no living voice came up from lawn and meadow and field which once echoed with the shout and merry laughter of childhood. The cool waters of the well were unruffled, and the sweep and 'the old oaken bucket' were no more. The 'Cranberry Brook' sung and babbled amidst the alders and witch-hazels, but with no response from eager, gleesome anglers and bathers. Birds built their nests and sang and reared their broods without disturbance."[70]

During his time in the United States, Coan visited at least four seminaries, including his alma mater of Auburn. He eventually arrived in New York City for the October Annual meetings of the American Board of Commissioners for Foreign Missions.

AMERICAN BOARD ANNUAL MEETING IN BROOKLYN, NEW YORK

While giving ahead of time his New York City address as "Care of Rev. Geo. W. Wood DD, [W?]ilde House, Astor Place,"[71] Field indicates that when the Coans "visited New York they were guests in the house of the writer, where we were charmed alike by the intelligence, sprightliness, and animation of the veteran missionary, and the sweetness of her who had been his faithful companion during his long exile" from the United States.[72] Fidelia would have attended the women's meeting that took place before the official opening of the Board meeting.

"The meeting of the American Board for 1870 was held in Brooklyn, and for the first time we had the privilege of attending this annual gathering." This meeting would be a combination of looking out at others and being looked at by them. "Here we met missionaries and men of distinction from the Orient and the Occident, from every continent,[73] and from many an island of the globe. Never shall I forget that

70. Coan, *Life*, 219–21.

71. Titus Coan to "Jane," dated September 7, 1870, np, LOC Box 10.

72 Field, *Patagonia*, xiii.

73. Coan probably included Australia but not Antarctica in his mentioning of "every continent." As for the naming of what are now called the seven continents, Wikipedia, "Continent," has the following: "From the late eighteenth century some geographers started to regard North America and South America as two parts of the world, making five parts in total. Overall though the fourfold division prevailed well into the nineteenth century. Europeans discovered Australia in 1606 but for some time it was taken as part of Asia. By the late eighteenth century some geographers considered it a continent in its own right, making it the sixth (or fifth for those still taking America as a single continent). In 1813 Samuel Butler wrote of Australia as 'New Holland, an immense island, which some geographers dignify with the appellation of another continent' and the *Oxford English Dictionary* was just as equivocal some decades later. Antarctica was sighted in 1820 and described as a continent by Charles Wilkes on the United States Exploring Expedition in 1838, the last continent identified,

great congregation of glowing faces and earnest listeners. I have seen larger and more compact assemblies on Hawaii, but they were like a sea of shining silver. It was mind and soul looking out of its windows; it was intelligence, culture, piety, beaming like sunlight from human faces."[74]

Two organizations published reports on the Board's proceedings: one local, the other national; one secular, the other Christian; one daily, the other monthly; one the newspaper *The Brooklyn Eagle Daily Newspaper*,[75] the other the journal *The Missionary Herald*.[76] *The Herald* as the publication of record for the American Board opens with the following information: "Sixty-First Annual Meeting at Brooklyn, NY, in the Academy of Music, commencing on Tuesday, October 4, at 3 o'clock, p.m., and closing on Friday, October 7, at half-past 10 o'clock."[77] While various meetings and services were held at nearby large churches, the Brooklyn Academy of Music on Montague Street held the plenary sessions. Characterized as a "large theater seating 2,200," it was inaugurated in early 1861 "with a program including Mozart and Verdi."[78]

The Eagle reported on the opening meetings and addresses from October 4, including noting the cost of the Sandwich Islands Mission as being $21,359.41, which is below the average of all the missions.[79] *The Eagle* further reports that on the opening evening the "Rev. J[onathan] F. Stearns, DD, of Newark, preached an eloquent sermon from Matthew 27 [sic, should be 28], [verses 18–20], on the duty of Christians to preach the gospel."[80]

The Herald reports under "Missionaries": "Rev. Titus Coan, Sandwich Islands."[81] *The Eagle* on Thursday evening, October 6, has as its top headline in bold: "**FOREIGN MISSIONS**." One of the subheadings is "**The Mission on Sandwich Islands**." Under "**THE AFTERNOON SESSION**," the unnamed reporter writes, "The Rev. Dr. Clark,

---

although a great 'Antarctic' (antipodean) landmass had been anticipated for millennia. An 1849 atlas labeled Antarctica as a continent but few atlases did so until after World War II."

74. Coan, *Life*, 217–18.

75 Newspapers.com, "Brooklyn Daily Eagle." Reports begin Wednesday Evening 5 October 1870 for October opening meetings and addresses through Saturday Evening October 8 for closing morning of Friday October 7. The *New York Times* also had articles but the author did not purchase a "subscription" to access those archived digital online articles.

76 *Missionary Herald* 66.6 (November 1870). Begins on 337 of volume.

77. *Missionary Herald* 66.6 (November 1870), 337.

78. Wikipedia, "Brooklyn Academy of Music." The *New York Times* abstract indicates that at the Academy of Music, the "lower floor of the edifice, holding about six hundred people, was well filled with members and delegates from all parts of the country"—and, should be added, the world—in addition to the distinguished persons "on the platform," October 5. The *Times*'s abstract of October 8 reports that the Board's audience attendance the annual meeting closing exercises at the Music Academy "was the largest that had been gathered together during the conference."

79. NB: The lower cost could be because of the transition that had already occurred from the ABCFM to the Hawaiian Evangelical Association.

80. *Brooklyn Eagle*, October 5, 1870, evening.

81. *Missionary Herald* 66.6 (November 1870), 343.

Foreign Secretary of the Board, presented a report of his visit to the Hawaiian Islands, to the Hawaiian Islands, where he found fifty-eight self-supporting churches, forty-four in charge of a native ministry, with a membership of 14,850—about one fourth of the native population." There follows a long paragraph with more details of Secretary Clark's report.[82]

The *Herald* takes part or all of four pages to summarize Secretary Clark's report. Clark, who had followed the transformational generational leadership of Rufus Anderson,[83] reports that he took his trip to Hawai'i for two reasons: for his health and "to attend the Jubilee Celebration"[84] of missionaries in Hawai'i. Clark indicates how long it took at that time to travel by train across the United States, showing how long it would have taken if the Coans had travelled nonstop. It took him sixteen and a half days to go from Boston to Chicago to San Francisco. From that west coast city he took a "commodius [sic] steamer" to Hawai'i. While he does not provide the total number of days,[85] he does compare it to the 163-day trip of the Coans' trip on the "little brig" *Thaddeus*. Clark concludes his report by calling the listeners to celebration of the completion of the work on those islands: "Let us rejoice today in our finished work."[86]

Building on Secretary Clark's report, *The Eagle* continues its reporting on the October fifth session by talking about three speakers. The first is Dr. Leonard Bacon who "presented resolutions congratulating the Board upon the success of the mission to the Sandwich Islands, where at the end of fifty years the mission will no longer appear in the Board's report." *The Missionary Herald*, as the Board's journal of record, also reports on the resolutions. The second of two "be it resolved" sections includes the following: "That inasmuch as the proper work of the Board in those islands are now virtually completed, so that there remains only the duty of sustaining the few veteran missionaries in comfort and continued usefulness till they shall enter into rest, and the name of that mission will henceforth disappear from our Annual Reports, we record once more our reverent and thankful acknowledgement of the success with which God, in his providence and by his spirit, has crowned the work of our missionaries in that field, and by which a race of barbarians . . . has been transformed into a Christian nation, civilized and free, under a government of laws, with free schools for all children, and with the [translated] Bible in the homes of the people."[87]

---

82. *Brooklyn Eagle*, October 6, 1870, evening.

83. Anderson, the Board's General Secretary from 1832 and 1866, wrote a book on the Board's work in Hawai'i [provide title and year]. See Anderson, *Heathen Nation*; Beaver on Anderson writings in *To Advance the Gospel*; Schneider, "The Senior Secretary"; and Harris, *Nothing But Christ*.

84. This gathering commemorated the arrival of the First Company of missionaries, led by Hiram Bingham.

85. Clark probably traveled to Hawai'i in less than a third of the time it took the Coans to get there.

86. *Missionary Herald* 66.6 (November 1870), 359.

87. *Missionary Herald* 66.6 (November 1870), 350.

Luther H. Gulick, "Secretary of the Hawaiian Board, followed with an eloquent address upon the missionary work in the Sandwich Island [sic]."[88]

"The Rev. Titus Cohen [sic],[89] who has been a Sandwich Island missionary for thirty-five years, spoke next upon the wonderful progress of the gospel in those Islands, and cited many instances of the practical as well as the moral benefits that have accrued to the natives from the labors of the missionaries." The reporter tacks on the name of a fourth speaker—President Hopkins—who pronounced a brief eulogium upon the apostolic character and labors of the Rev. Mr. Cohen, and the audience arose and sung a hymn[90] in honor of that veteran missionary."[91]

The annual meeting of the Board continued into Thursday through Friday morning. "The sacrament of the Lord's Supper was administered Thursday afternoon, in three churches, to a very large number of communicants." One of the three services was at "Lafayette Avenue Church,[92] Dr. S[amuel] G. Buckingham[93] presided, assisted by Rev. H[enry] Allon,[94] of London, and Rev. Titus Coan, of the Sandwich Islands."

On Friday morning, the closing meeting included farewell addresses "of much interest . . . by Rev. S. B. Fairbank, of the Mahratta Mission, Rev. A. A. Sturges, of the Micronesia mission, and Rev. Titus Coan, who has labored thirty-five years at the Sandwich Islands . . . The usual parting hymn—'Blest be the tie that binds'—was sung, and the benediction was pronounced by Dr. [Rufus] Anderson."[95]

---

88. *Brooklyn Eagle*, October 6, 1870, evening.

89. One marvels that the unnamed reporter could misspell Coan's last name. Granted, the one syllable Irish name ["cone"] became two syllables ["Co-uhn"]—in the Hawaiian language that pronounces every vowel—that sound very close to the last name "Cohen." However, given the prominence of the speaker and the likely fact that the reporter had his own copy of the session's program, the mistake seems egregious.

90. The hymn was probably drawn from *Hymns for the Meeting of the American Board*.

91. *Brooklyn Eagle*, October 6, 1870, evening. One notes that by 1870, colleagues and others already viewed his missionary efforts as apostolic in nature. No doubt it was because of the Great Awakening, followed by his pastoring of the Hilo church, as well as his mission trips beyond the Hawaiian Islands and other forms of Christian leadership as enshrined in many of his writings and the writings of others.

92. Founded in 1857 when Brooklyn was one of the largest cities in the country, this Presbyterian church "was known from the outset as a 'temple of abolition.' Both the Presbyterian nature and abolitionist nature of the church would have appealed to Coan the Presbyterian in a predominantly Congregational organization." Coan was strongly anti-slavery, even leading him as a near pacifist to support the putting down of the slave states in what he characterized as "The War of Rebellion." Lafayette Avenue Presbyterian Church.

93. Pastor of South Congregational Church in Springfield, Massachusetts, for forty-four years beginning in 1847. Historic Buildings of Massachusetts, "Rev. Samuel G. Buckingham House (1875)."

94. Allon served Union Chapel in Islington for 48 years until his death in 1892. Wikipedia, "Henry Allon."

95. *Missionary Herald* 66.6 (November 1870), 350.

The Coans Visit America, 1870–71

BROOKLYN TO THE DISTRICT OF COLUMBIA

On the Thursday a week after the conclusion of the meetings, Titus preached at Plymouth Church, where Henry Ward Beecher was the pastor. Within two years Beecher would become embroiled in a scandal. Though tainted by the controversy, he would continue as pastor at Plymouth until his death in 1887.[96] Coan anticipated speaking the next evening, October 14, at Dr. Eddy's church. The following Sunday he planned on spending a Sabbath in Hartford, Connecticut. Then he was off to Worcester to meet Dr. Trent "and with him to move here and there."

After the meetings, the Coans hopscotched across the northeastern United States for four months. Then they would head back to Hilo. Their pining for the Emerald Bower is evident even while at the Brooklyn meetings. Titus writes Lydia Bingham from there on October 13, "O! the busy racing life we are leading; we sigh for repose and a quiet evening with loved friends. But we are in a whirl all the time. I can't think because we have so much to think of, and we can't talk because we have so many things to say, nor can we see anybody because there are so many bodies in the way. We are a little weary and we long to get back to our nest in the Bower."

He continues discussing his travels. "Our friends here are legion and they almost kill us with kindness. We had a blessed season in Rochester, in dear old Auburn, in New Haven and in the place of my birth. In New Haven I saw the grave of your beloved and honored father's dust. I collected a few leaves and a little grass from the peaceful sleeper's grave, and enclose the simple memorials to his beloved children."

He concludes the letter to his future wife with: "Not much rest in prospect, but there remaineth a rest" [Heb 4:9].[97] In a letter to "Mrs. E. Coan"[98] from New Bedford on November 4, Coan refers to his visit to Killingworth. Because he writes about it after the Brooklyn meeting, his reflections on visiting his hometown are included here. "On and on we go, leaving the past behind, and yet we do not, we cannot, leave it. On it comes after us, surrounding and flooding us with its deep-traced memories. Our visit to Killingworth, O! how short! The house you lived in, the rock whence I was hewn, the churchyard, the departed, the living, the changes, the unchanged and changeless. Dear childhood's memories came crowding in flocks to the soul—the scenes and friends of youth—love, joy, sorrows, sins, how they came back on wings."[99]

Titus is equally poignant in his relating of his time in Killingworth in his autobiography. Prior to departing for the United States, Titus wrote Mr. M. Lord and, among other things, wrote the following with regard to his anticipated visit to his hometown. "Please be so kind as to give my great love to all friends in Killingworth, and also to

96. Wikipedia, "Henry Ward Beecher."

97. Titus Coan to Lydia Bingham, Coan, *Memorial Volume*, 129.

98. While this letter is quoted in Coan, *Memorial Volume*, the original at the LOC indicates that it is to "Fanny," Coan's sister. The reference to "the house you lived in" would certainly indicate that he is writing to a sister of his.

99. Coan, *Memorial Volume*, 129–30.

the rocks and the rills, to the vale and hills[100] of my still cherished native town. Shall I recognize one face there? How changed all will appear. Changed for the better I trust, and many are changed from 'the corruptible to the incorruptible, from the mortal to the immortal, and from glory to glory'"[101] [1 Cor 15:53].

Returning to his autobiography, he indeed does indicate new people in his hometown and the passing of others. In an extended paragraph about the old schoolhouse and "barn-like meeting-house," where a new church building was "in its stead." He observed the new congregation of people and the new pastor. He visits the cemetery, "where each of the departed ones slept alone unconscious of his proximity to the dust of his dearest earthly friend. On the marble I read the sober epitaph of father, mother, sister, neighbor, and friend. Stones in the other grave-yards already marked the resting-places of all my brothers save one, and he has since that time departed."

The visit to the graveyard brings one more sentence of thought. "Thankful for one more view of my boyhood's home, with chastened reflections I turned from it for the last time."[102] Coan's report in his autobiography on his visiting his home town is the last section on his trip to the United States. But in various letters, especially one that became two articles on his visit to Washington City, he continues to write about his sojourn.

Returning to his letter to his sister Fanny, Titus writes that our "reception in New Haven was wonderfully warm, and we spent a most wakeful and happy week there. How unworthy we are to receive such favors. Surely God *is* good, even to the unthankful."

He reflects on the gathering in Brooklyn. "I hope the papers have told you of many things done and said in Brooklyn. It was a great and good meeting. But there was too much at a time. It surfeits and overwhelms one. I love detail, to eat slowly, to see distinctly, to do and think deliberately, to enjoy calmly, to hear and feel intelligently. But 'there is a time for all things' [Eccl 2:1], even for crowds and rushings and mass-meetings. So Brooklyn has its time and place memories."

He continues on, once again noting that there are too many invitations to speak and too little time. Additionally he talks about how the nearness of winter is taking its toll and the yearning to return to their Hilo home and the people he loves so dearly. "The calls from Fall River, Boston, Providence, Springfield, and very many other places look formidable. Meanwhile winter comes on apace and we begin to shiver. We love our country and our hearts yearn over our precious friends, and yet we often long for the balmy air and the dear home in the Emerald Bower. Our hearts cling to the Hawaiians as our dear children in the Lord, and should the blessed Master say to us, 'Go return to the land of your adoption,' we will hail the day with delight."[103]

100. Reference to hymn "This is my Father's World."
101. February 1870, in Coan, *Memorial Volume*, 126.
102. Coan, *Life*, 219–221.
103. Coan, *Memorial Volume*, 130.

The Coans Visit America, 1870–71

Not long after the letter to his sister, American Board missionary Elias Bond in Kohala[104] writes what could be taken as a "sour grapes" letter about Coan's US honors to fellow missionary J. W. Pogue: "Bro. Coan didn't tell them that he baptized his '1700 in a day' with a *paint brush*! Had he told full the *modus operandi*, he [would] have caused the nerves of many a conservative admirer to twinge sorely!"[105]

In a January 11 letter, Titus wrote to "My dear Mrs. DuPont" of Delaware that since she last heard from him they had been in many places, including New York, Connecticut, Rhode Island, Massachusetts, and New Hampshire.[106] During February the Coans spent a significant amount of time in Philadelphia.

On February 17, Coan pens a newsy letter to his son Latimer. He indicates that on that day he received a letter from Dr. Wetmore in Hilo. Once again he writes of his overwhelming speaking schedule and even more overwhelming number of invitations to speak. "I have lately spoken in Phillie eight times within four days. I am now urged to go to [Marietta], Springfield, Columbus, Cincinnati, and other places in Ohio to address the people. So far as we can now see, we might be here three years in this land and be constantly engaged in speaking to churches." He further indicates that the eighteenth is a Sabbath and I have already some five or six invitations to preach in Phila[.] I accept[ed] three."

Titus and Fidelia enjoyed a visit with son Munson in Philadelphia. The day before they had "a blessed visit with the Phila[delphia] Friends" [Quakers].[107]

Returning to his letter to son Latimer, Titus writes his son of his wife's feebleness, winter causing her more illnesses, and all that increasing their desire to return to Hilo. "Your mother suffers from colds and general feebleness, and I long for the day when we shall feel that we have really started for the Hawaiian islands." He shares a tentative itinerary for the return trip east. Though he does not mention it, this return trip would commence after their visit to Washington, DC. "We may go from Baltimore to Detroit, Niles, and Chicago. Thence to Lexington, Lafayette County, Missouri. It may be well for you to send us a letter in triplicate one copy to Niles, care of your cousin Geo. M. Another *Chicago*, Care of H. M. Lyman MD, 26 North Reuben St., and a third to Lexington. Lafayette Co. MO, Care of Jared B. Church, DD." He then sketches his

---

104. Elias and Ellen Mariner Howell arrived in Honolulu on May 21, 1841, as part of the Ninth Company. He "labored unremittingly [in the northern Hawai'i region of Kohala] for fifty-five years until his death" at the age of eighty-five in 1886. *Memorial Volume*, 54. John Fawcett Pogue arrived in Honolulu on July 15, 1844 as part of the Eleventh Company, which included Maria Kapule Whitney, whom he would marry in 1848. They both served on the big island from 144 until 1850, when they moved to Lahaina. At the time Bond wrote Pogue, Pogue was the Secretary of the Hawaiian Board, from which he resigned in 1877 because of ill health. He died the same year at the age of 63 due to ill health. Judd, *Missionary Album*, 158.

105. Elias Bond to J. W. Pogue, November 28, 1870, Missionary Letters, 1816–1900, HMH, in Ehlke, "Enthusiastic Religion," 257.

106. Titus Coan to Mrs. DuPont, January 11, 1871, LOC Box 10.

107. Titus Coan to Samuel Latimer Coan, February 17, 1871, LOC Box 10. See also "Peace" chapter for a discussion of his time with the Bean family.

Missouri to San Francisco plans. "We suppose that our last visit on this side the Rocky Mountains will be at your Uncle [Jared's?] in Lexington, MO. And, that we shall leave that place for San Francisco as early as Monday the third ["first" is crossed out] of April, if not before."[108]

IN AND AROUND WASHINGTON CITY

Between February 24 and March 4, the Coans visited Washington City[109] and its environs. Titus devotes two paragraphs in his autobiography to his Washington visit, while Lydia quotes a section of one paragraph in a letter to "his son," probably Latimer. Whereas Ehlke had characterized Titus's time at the Oberlin meeting as "one of the highlights" of his trip to America, Titus himself characterizes his and Fidelia's[110] time in Washington as one "of our happiest weeks" of their American sojourn.

"Every day was full of interest. We looked in upon our institutions, legislative, civil, literary, benevolent, and religious, and were cheered to see so much of good sense, philanthropy, and earnest piety modifying and refining life in the metropolis of the Union."[111]

Titus writes a tantalizing summary to his son. "We had a most interesting week in Washington and received many kind attentions. We met the President twice and also many of the Senators and Representatives. We were greatly interested in Gen. Howard and his grand University for the Freedmen. We visited the Capitol, the Patent Office, the Soldiers' Rest and the Soldiers' Cemetery. We also went over to Arlington Heights, into the desolate house of the rebel, Gen. Lee, over his estate, and through the cemetery where some fifteen thousand soldiers lie buried in ranks. One day we spent in visiting Mt. Vernon."[112]

Titus could be brief and Lydia economic perhaps because they both knew of the letter by Titus published in two parts in *The Pacific Commercial Advertiser*.[113] Coan is

---

108. Titus Coan to Samuel Latimer Coan, February 17, 1871, LOC Box 10.

109. Coan, *Life*, index, 340, lists "Washington City, visit to." In Stephen L. Carter's alternate history mystery novel, *The Impeachment of Abraham Lincoln*, 51, Washington is described as a modern city in 1867, "alive with sound; streetcars rattling, horses whinnying, shopkeepers shouting their prices through half-open doors, machinery thudding and pumping in the factories, crowds thronging the avenues in hopes of glimpsing the rich and the powerful in their grand homes, trains rumbling through the middle of town on their way soon and the others rumbling north, beggars calling as you passed, builders, constructing ever-larger edifices for the government and its departments."

110. Fidelia probably stayed in Niles, Michigan, while Titus traveled to and from Oberlin.

111. Coan, *Life*, 217.

112. Coan, *Memorial Volume*, 132. In a letter to Mrs. DuPont dated April 1, 1871, in Omaha, HMCS Eleutherean Mills Historical Library, Titus complements the letter to Latimer. "Our visit to Washington was precious. Very many friends rallied around us and we felt quite at home . . . Commodore Reynolds and Lady made an early call on us, and we dined with them. He spoke with great admiration of your husband and affirmed all of his official services."

113. No vol, no issue, no page. Under the heading **A WEEK IN WASHINGTON**, it is dated

at his pen-painter best in the letter that begins with February 25, the day after their arrival in Washington City. Knowing this letter would be published he has his audience in mind as he narrates their arrival to Washington and arrival at the home of the Reverend John W. Alvord. What might be too much information for some and trite for some in the twenty-first century is of interest to the first readers and sincere in his writing.

"Here we are in this Mecca of the great American people. We arrived last evening, and found Mr. and Mrs. [J. W. Alvord] at the station waiting to take us to their home. Those of us who followed the war through its darkest phases will remember how Mr. Alvord[114] followed the soldiers with food for body and soul, and never deserted them, under any circumstances. And those of us who have watched the fate of the freed negroes know with what devotion he had sought their interests up to the present moment. He is now President of the National Freedmen's Savings and Trust Company."

On the twenty-fifth, Coan noted that this "morning being a very fine one, it was thought best to make sure of a visit to the Capitol. Our view of it from the railway station last evening was not imposing. We saw it through a vista of poor buildings, and over a road of deep clay mud. It reminded us[115] of that 'jewel' which Solomon speaks of [Song 4:9?]. But this morning we approached it through Pennsylvania Avenue—which made all the difference in the world. We not only saw the dome, which is seen everywhere in the city, but the immense pile of white marble on which it rests; and the beautiful trees, and grounds which redeem the whole from the rawness of the other view. Our visit commenced with the pictures, and other objects of interest in the vast circular room beneath the dome, and extended to other room and pictures, and statues, and wonders. At length we made our way to the House of Representatives. The bills before the House were on appropriations, and not very exciting. But we saw the honorable members in their seats—saw them rise and speak—but the sovereign

---

"Honolulu, March 29, 1871," and has the following explanatory note: "To the Editor of the *Pacific Commercial Advertiser*:

"The accompanying most interesting letter was written for the columns of *The Friend* but unfortunately it was received too late for insertion in the April number. It is at your disposal, as I should hardly feel justified in delaying its publication until my next issue.

"Yours, EDITOR OF THE FRIEND [Samuel Damon]."

This letter was published in two parts because another undated issue notes, "Concluded from last week."

114. Rev. Alvord had actually retired two months before the Coans' arrival, US Archives, "Records of the Education Division." "The Freedman's Saving and Trust Company, popularly known as the Freedman's Savings Bank, was a private corporation chartered by the US government to encourage and guide the economic development of the newly emancipated African-American communities in the post-Civil War period. Although functioning only between 1865 and 1874, the company achieved notable successes as a leading financial institution of African-Americans. Its failure was devastating to the newly emancipated black community. Its archives are valued as an exhaustive collection of information regarding the African American community and its socio-economic life in the immediate aftermath of emancipation." Wikipedia, "Freedman's Savings Bank."

115. Is Titus using the royal we here or is it something he and Fidelia discussed together?

people in the galleries talked, laughed, and made so much noise generally that we heard but little."

"From the House we went to the Senate Chamber. Here we found a body of men, which impressed me as being worthy of their high position, dignified, earnest, gentlemanly, even in the Senate Chamber." After noting the high quality of the senators as a group, Coan focuses on the African-American senator from Mississippi, the Reverend Hiram Rhodes Revels. The colored Senator Revel [sic] sat directly below us. We did not hear him speak, further than to say *no*, to some of the appropriation measures under consideration. But I saw what I believed to be an elegant autograph album, brought to him by one of the little runners[116] (who jumped about the room as thick as grasshoppers) and in which write his name."

Coan initially expresses disappointment that Vice President Schuyler Colfax Jr. was not in the seat of the President of the Senate.[117] For whatever reason, Coan refers to him as "Speaker" instead of the Vice President or the President of the Senate. The presiding senator had difficulty in determining the majority of ayes or nays, so he had the senators rise in their seats for determining the outcome of votes. Coan writes that "this appeared to us just as it should be. But when Colfax came in half an hour after, we had the rare treat of seeing how *he* put business through. It seemed easy for his practiced ear to detect the excesses of a single vote on one side or the other. In no case did he call on the members to rise in their seats. On the instant the vote was taken, he called out in clear yet rapid tones 'The ayes appear to have it. The ayes have it.' Or, 'The noes appear to have it. The noes have it.' The members might ring out their 'ayes' or their 'noes' ever so loudly thinking to make amends for the fewness of their votes, by the loudness of their voices. But no such dodge could succeed with such a man in the chair, and in no instance was his rapid declaration of the votes challenged by either party."

Coan writes disappointedly how nothing of great moment occurred during their time on Capitol Hill and expresses the hope that they will be able to visit the Hill again while still in Washington City. "There was no measure of great importance before the Senate, 'Retrenchment'[118] seemed just then to be a sort of party cry, by a party not much given to the practice of that virtue; and it turned out that several thousand dollars were deducted from the appropriations for twine and wrapping paper, for the

---

116. Pages?

117. Shuyler Colfax was Speaker of the House of Representatives from late 1863 until 1869, when he became Grant's Vice President. He served in that office for one year. NB: Colfax came within one vote of becoming President in the impeachment vote of President Johnson. Wikipedia, "Schuyler Colfax."

118. Retrenchment apparently refers to the policy of cutting back on military spending after a war. Wording similar to Coan's is found online: "Want to know how devastating post-war budget cuts can be? The Civil War is a good example . . . retrenchment had been the political cry of both parties." www.defenseone.com/ideas/2014/04/heed-historical.

use of members. We stayed out our time and left the Capital with regret, yet hoping to visit again."

Coan next relates his visit with General Oliver Otis Howard, who helped found and lead the newly formed university of the same name.[119] In the *Pacific Commercial Advertiser* published letter, Titus goes deeper than in his autobiography about his visit with General Howard at the university. "Monday morning twenty-seventh. Our first visit this morning was to the Howard University for the education of colored people, in every department of learning known or taught in our best American colleges. The institution is in an important sense, the creation of Gen. O. O. Howard. Within four years he, and a few men of like mind towards the freedmen, have converted an old tenantless rebel farm, which was ground into one great mud hole during the war— converted it into 'the garden of the Lord' [Isa 51:3]. The locality is now known as University Hill—lies just without the city limits—opposite the Capitol and of about the same elevation." Coan mentions that someone two years ago built a home on University hill and there are now "scores of elegant houses, growing up around the University buildings, which are the central figures of the place."

"Of those are five huge and elegant beyond most of our small college buildings in any part of the country . . . at present gathering within their walls more than four hundred students of both sexes, and every shade of color." He then describes those shades, including the fact that there are a few "non-colored" students, "who stand side by side the late slave for the honors of the legal and medical professions."

The Coans went to Howard University to attend the morning prayers of the students. This prayer time was always led by General Howard. They first step into the general's "room for a few moments . . . There was a gentle-looking girl in that room of twelve years old, I should judge, whom he introduced us as his daughter 'Gracie.'"[120]

With regard to the prayer gathering, "General Howard read the scriptures, and prayed in the most earnest simple manner, and a few remarks were made by others, when the students went to their recitation rooms. The General had no difficulty in making us understand that his whole soul was in this work. It was touching to hear him lament that he did not see results, as he desired while we were wondering in our hearts what magician's wand had brought forth the grand results then before our eyes."

Coan next transitions to his visit at the "Soldier's Rest." "We hastened through the university halls, and then went out to find Mr. Alvord's carriage waiting to take us two or three miles beyond this place to a still higher hill, quite in the country. Here are the fine buildings known as the 'Soldier's Rest'—where the old [remnants? A line through 'old' and this word] of the War of 1812 and the Mexican War are spending

---

119. Carpenter, *Sword and Olive Branch*. Howard was a Medal of Honor recipient for action in 1862 and knows "as the 'Christian general' because he tried to base his policy decisions on his deep religious piety, Wikipedia, "Oliver O. Howard."

120. Grace Ellen.

Titus Coan: "Apostle to the Sandwich Islands"

their last days in peace and comfort. Here too is the modest house, to which Lincoln[121] loved to retire during the summer heats, and spend a few months in comparative quiet. Farther down the hills, and among the trees, is the summer residence of the late Sec. Stanton."[122]

Here are his comments on another cemetery that is not Arlington: "But there is still another 'Soldier's Rest' on this [slight?] hill, not provided for in the elegant buildings of the living. There is a cemetery for the nation['s] dead,—'*only five thousand,*' they tell us, were buried here. 'Arlington and Gettsyburg, contained more.' But we thought that five thousand graves, with their pathetic little white head boards, and all they suggested would be sufficiently impressive, and convey to us a lesson we should not lose. So we alighted, and wound about among the graves, until the war, once so many thousand miles away seemed very *near*. The *system* of hills in this vicinity is beautifully graded for carriages, and is the summer drive for the Washingtonians. It [illegible word. provides? affords?] a magnificent view of the city below—the Potomac—Arlington heights—Alexandria—and other places."

The Coans returned from their drive and had lunch. Returning from their trip to Capitol Hill, Coan discusses his time with Dr. Parker[123] and the doors he opened for them. "We returned from our drive . . . then repaired by appointment to the house of Dr. Peter Parker and Mr. Alvord, we enjoyed many rare pleasures in Washington, and among the rest, was that of being presented to the President."

Thus begins the explanation of his having indicated meeting twice with President Grant in the letter to Latimer Coan. "Dr. Parker lives near the White House, and is extensively and favorably known for his public services in China. He had arranged to bring us [there?][124] [black mark over word] [three fuzzy words] to the White House at a certain hour, which he did. The President received us with a cordial shake of the hand, and we had a few words with that man of a few words, who looks more than he says." We then learn of how and when the second "meeting" with the President came about. "He told Dr. Parker that he was to have a reception the next day, when we would be presented to [Mrs. Grant]. We took our leave, as we entered by a shake of the hand, and we left the President to his writing, and his cigar, both of which he laid down as we entered the door."

---

121. The Soldiers' Rest or Home was where President Abraham Lincoln would get away from the cares of the war and the pressure of life in the White House. Lincoln, his wife Mary, and son Tad stayed in a cottage during the oppressive summers of 1862, 1863 and 1864. President Lincoln at the Soldiers' Home, President Lincoln's Cottage. One time while riding his donkey "Old Abe" to the Soldiers' Rest, a bullet flew through his stove top hat. After that he took more care for his security, but his bodyguard let him down on the night he was assassinated.

122. Edwin McMasters Stanton had died on December 24, 1869, at the age of fifty-five. Wikipedia, "Edwin McMasters Stanton."

123. See "Education, Medicine, and Social Concern," in Corr, *"Field Is the World."* For some years, Peter Parker was an ABCFM medical missionary in eastern China.

124. The LOC image of the *Pacific Commercial Advertiser* in the column relating this meeting has some blurred words and a black dot over one word.

The Coans Visit America, 1870-71

On Tuesday, February 28, Coan writes about a gentleman who was once well-known in the Hawaiian Islands. He does not provide a name, however. Titus and Fidelia were "much gratified for a morning visit from the gentleman." Is he so well known at that time for introducing the rose apple and alligator pear[125] that Titus does not need to mention his name? Again possibly indicating how well known this gentleman is, Coan writes that he "has since held high positions of [illegible] under the government, and has the rare reputation of a thoroughly honest man. He brought his wife with him. They both feel much interest in the islands."

On Tuesday afternoon the Coans visited the Patent Office "and saw its immensity."[126] "From our hasty visit to the Patent office we went again to Dr. Parker's. He took us to the White House, and presented us again to the President and Mrs. Grant, who with sundry ladies in elegant toilettes, and long trains, stood to be victimized for the benefit of the glorious democracy of this glorious country."

Titus moves to a description of Mrs. Grant's external and internal beauty. "Mrs. Grant is a plain but pleasant looking woman, who puts on no airs, and is much respected for her social Christian character." After Mrs. Grant, the Vice President's recent wife enters the report. "We were introduced to sundry people during the hour we remained—but no one who interested us more than the wife[127] of [S]peaker Colfax—a sweet, refined looking woman whom Colfax found, not in New York or Washington, but in Ohio, I was told—and brought her to the Capital, without asking consent of the belles of Washington—which I am sure he never would have obtained." Coan is already engaging in gossip. He next says one should not gossip and then does! "It will not do to gossip, but there are certain stories afloat about letters to him with long dark tresses inclosed [sic]." He worsens his gossip by alluding to an unnamed friend of theirs as being someone who could provide further information. One of the tresses "at least, which the lady referred to a well-known friend of ours in Boston, for further information." Coan concludes his discussion of Mrs. Colfax by indicating she gave them an offer they could not refuse. "Mrs. Colfax told us she was to have a reception the next day, her 'last for the season,' and invited us to be present, which of course we should desire whether invited or not."

On Wednesday morning, March 2, "we set out early for Arlington Heights. After crossing the Potomac, we ascended its gently sloping bank for a mile or two, when we came to the hill which is crowned by the mansion of the late Confederate Gen. Lee.[128] The white pillars of the immense portico in front of the house[129] contrasted exquisitely

---

125. "Alligator pear" is another word for avocado.

126. This where the second installment of Coan's running letter about their visit to Washington City resumes in the next unidentified and undated issue of the *Pacific Commercial Adviser*.

127. Ella Marie Wade was a niece of Senator Benjamin Franklin Wade. Wikipedia, "Schuyler Colfax."

128. Lee had died a few months before on October 12, 1870.

129. The Custis-Lee mansion.

with the fine forest trees through which we saw them, as the carriage wound slowly up the hill. The situation of the house, the grounds, the view from the portico across the broad Potomac—all are magnificent; and as we stood almost spellbound by the beauty of the scene we could not help exclaiming: O! how much the rebels lost by their own folly!" [Prov 19:9].

Both Coan the tourist and Coan the host makes vivid observations and quotes apt Bible passages on a regular basis. "On looking through the house, you find it plain and cheap—and if its walls and porches could whisper out their secrets, they would no doubt become immortalized in the annals of treason." Perhaps Coan is too close to the conflict and convinced by his perspective of being a peace man to understand any complexities in the life and views of General Lee.

Former slaves on site provide first-person perspective. The lens broadens from the Lees to the Custisses and the entire institution of slavery as seen through the eyes of an individual. "We went all over the house, which is entirely unfurnished, but kept clean by an attendant on the place. Our driver was once a slave of Gen. Lee, and has an aged grandmother once a slave, now living on the place. There is another notable, 'Aunt Saltie,' to whose house the driver was told by our friends to take us—which he did. We found her in a very ancient black cabin, kept neat and clean by her granddaughter. She is over eighty years old—was 'raised all over the place' as she said—had borne nineteen children into the kingdom of slavery! I asked her if Lee sold them from there. 'Old Custis did that,' she said. The father of Mrs. Lee, and relative of Martha Washington. They were scattered everywhere. One went to Africa, and of the rest, she knew not where they were, or whether they were alive, with [?] exception of three, who had found their way back to her since the war. She told of her 'Jim,' dragged out of the whipping-house in chains to be sold farther south, saying in a choked voice, 'O! I wish they had taken a gun and shot him.' As the poor creature swayed continually back and forth in her seat, and wiped her nearly sightless eyes, it was plain that the hot iron of slavery was still burning into her soul."

Heading toward the elderly woman's home, the Coans saw "more of the beauty and extent of the Arlington estate. We saw something else, too—something calculated for by the chivalrous owner—the cemetery where fifteen thousand Union soldiers hold quiet possession of these magnificent grounds. Acres upon acres of graves—as far as the eye can discern the little white spots which mark the soldier's hat [illegible] place. The sight was overpowering. It must be seen to be felt. There was a fascination about the place, and we wanted to linger till sundown, but other engagements hurried us away."

The next engagement was at 2 p.m. at "a meeting of a Woman's Board of Missions, lately organized in Washington."[130] The Coan's had a recent commitment to make at 3,

---

130. Wikipedia indicates that the Christian Woman's Board of Missions was started on October 21, 1874, so this might have been an immediate precursor to this organization. Wikipedia, "Christian Woman's Board of Missions."

the reception of the Vice President's wife—Mrs. Colfax. They spent most of their brief visit there visiting Mrs. Colfax's mother-in-law. She was "a venerable lady whom we all remember to have read of—as giving receptions, and doing all the honors of her son's house, with admirable grace, until the advent of the bride, some two or three years ago. The fine old lady was elegantly but appropriately dressed, and *sitting* at some little distance from the daughter, and her group of younger women, who were of course standing."

The Coans followed the reception with dinner at General Whitelsey's, prior to the first graduating class of medical doctors at Howard University. General Whitelsey being a professor at that school, Titus notes that the "class was small—about equally divided between white and colored students; but one of the latter took the valedictory. The address was highly applauded, and was very creditable to the 'colored gentleman' and to the University."

The Coans spent all of Thursday March third traveling to, visiting at, and returning from Mt. Vernon. That morning "found us on board a little steamer, bound for Mount Vernon—that shrine of every true American heart." The weather was a lamb rather than a lion in early March. "The day was mild and perfect in every respect, and the boat was crowded with fine-looking people, on the same pilgrimage ourselves." After two hours, the Coans and others arrive at "the sacred grounds" and ponder Washington's tomb. "Was it a reality or was it a dream, that only a slab of marble separated us from all that remained of one whose body is mortal. We stood long before the iron grating, over which is the simple inscription, 'Within this vault lie the remains of George Washington.'"

They drank "of the old spring from which Washington drank. It seemed like a sacrament." They tour the grounds and inside the home. Coan goes into great detail about musical instruments and many other items. "We passed reverently from room to room, looking into closets, pantries, sleeping apartments, &c., not without some slight compunctions, as if we were invading sanctuaries of the dead." All visitors were respectful. "There was no levity . . . in our large company—especially were the voices hushed, as one and another entered the chamber where Washington died."

Before departing, Titus experiences a melancholic moment with the beauty of the day and grounds providing a strong contrast to his emotions. "The buildings, garden, green houses, and grounds are all well kept, and the combined whole must be supremely lovely in this summer. Yet a sense of utter loneliness possesses one, in wandering through this earthly Paradise. Gone; dead; past; last; are the words crowding upon the mind with a terrible reality, as your feet echo through the bare and silent rooms where once all was intense life, thought, action."

He is called back to the present by the "imperative whistle" of the steamer "to quit the spot around which the love of a nation centres." They collect souvenirs of leaves that previously hung over the front door. On the way back, Coan describes forts and guns along the banks of the Potomac that put one in mind of war. He notes that "everything in and about Washington recalls the war. It is the first place we have visited where we have *felt* the war. It is in the very atmosphere, though it takes a newcomer to perceive it."

He continues his reflections on "the war," which everyone reading his letter installment knew to be the Civil War or War of Rebellion. "The war is interwoven into the very life of the people . . . The war enters into every public address. The most effective speech I have heard in the city, was one of which the burden was these three words, 'Ten years ago.' What could, and what could not be done in Washington ten years ago. And here are the scarred and maimed. A few evenings since, two gentlemen, a General and a Colonel walked in, in company to make us a call. Each had lost a right arm to the war. Yes, in Washington we become fully convinced that there has been a war."

Coan concludes his letter published in two installments in the *Pacific Commercial Advertiser* with this paragraph. "Our visit to Mount Vernon was a fitting close to our week in the capital of this great country. We left more hopeful than we entered it, for there is deep and healthful religious life in the city. There is a noble army of workers who have not forgotten the lessons of heroism they practiced during a five years'[131] struggle for the nation's life. And more, there are good men and true in our Capitol. The Senators especially, as a body, stand high in the estimations of the citizens. With such men at the helm, and with our motto, 'In God we Trust,' we may hope that our nation is saved." Signed "T. Coan."[132]

RETURN TO HILO

Having arrived in Washington City on the evening February 24, the Coans take their leave on March 4. As they felt an almost physical need for correspondence during their early months in Hilo, so now Titus and Fidelia feel a great need to return to Hilo for the warmth of weather and friends. Ehlke writes that "their lack of tolerance for cold weather and the rapid decline of Fidelia's health made it necessary for them to return to their Hilo home as soon as possible."[133] They would debark San Francisco in approximately one month and arrive in Hilo approximately one month after that.

From Washington, the Coans took a short train trip to Baltimore, where they "spent a Sabbath."[134] On February 17, Titus had written his son Latimer with a tentative itinerary: "We may go from Baltimore to Detroit, Niles, and Chicago. Thence to Lexington, Lafayette County, Missouri." In that same letter he writes, "We suppose that our last visit on this side the Rocky Mountains will be at your Uncle [Jared's?] in Lexington, MO. And, that we shall leave that place for San Francisco as early as Monday

---

131. On installment text, ink says "four."
132. Titus Coan, *Pacific Commercial Advertiser*, second installment.
133. Ehlke, "Enthusiastic Religion," 257.
134. Titus Coan to [unnamed] sister, Eleutherian Mills Collection, HMH.

the third ["first" is crossed out] of April, if not before." Father asks son to "let us know, as near as possible, on what day in April the steamer will leave for Honolulu."[135]

Less than two weeks before the letter to Latimer, Titus had written Mrs. DuPont that "Mrs. Coan sends much love—her health is not firm."[136] Less than a month before that he wrote Mrs. DuPont that we "are everywhere received with very great kindness and cordiality.—and calls to visit and make addresses are greatly multiplied. For all this we bless the dear Lord. But we do sigh for our dear Island home, for our work in the Pacific, and for the people of our adoptive" nation.

"Mrs. Coan suffers much from the cold weather and from colds."[137] Fidelia appears to have a compromised immune system. While she had gone decades without the change of seasons and frigid weather of her younger years, the disease affecting her body compounded her medical difficulties and made her susceptible to almost any illness to which she was exposed.

On March 10 he writes that cold "weather and bleak winds are too rude and rough for your precious mother."[138] Then from Omaha on April 1 he writes his sister that my "precious angel, Fidelia, is upon her couch weak and languid, and I cannot forbear ourselves while I sit by her . . . Fidelia is unwell . . . We arrived here yesterday—and we purpose, if the Lord will, to leave for San Francisco . . . She [takes to her bed here], but is resolute to go on, because we feel that our only hope is to get into a milder clime. She does not recuperate here. Her courage is good, and you will pray the Lord to lead her gently. All is done for her which can be."[139]

Lydia provides a "beautiful tribute" and retrospective of the Coans' time in America from one "of the public papers of the day": "We do not believe there are many men in this world, going down into the vale of years, to whom there are more precious memories of the past, or to whom a review of life can be more agreeable than to that honored servant of God, Rev. Titus Coan . . .

"For nearly a year he has been a most welcome guest among the friends of missions all over the country, and tens of thousands of people have listened to the simple story of the triumphs of God's Word. For thirty-six years, and with never-faltering vigor, he sowed the precious seed of divine truth . . .

"Having given to his countrymen the most striking of all possible testimony to the value of the missionary work—having given an inspiration to the cause in this land scarcely any other man has ever done—having lifted up that great work to a noble pre-eminence by showing the moral grandeur of its results in the isles of the sea, having given the most delightful and animating view of the joy of the missionary work proved by his own personal and most happy experience, and having taken leave of his

---

135. Titus Coan to Samuel Latimer Coan, February 17, 1871, LOC Box 10.
136. Titus Coan to Mrs. DuPont, February 6, 1871, Eleutherian Mills Collection, HMCS.
137. Titus Coan to Mrs. DuPont, January 11, 1871, Eleutherian Mills Collection, HMH.
138. Coan, *Memorial Volume*, 132.
139. Titus Coan to sister, April 1, 1871, HMH.

countrymen with his most fervent benedictions upon them, he is now on his way of return to the Sandwich Islands to finish up what is left of his work, and find his grave among those whose fitness for heaven has been the labor of his life. A blessed welcome on his return awaits him there, and a more blessed one to the realms of light, when a long life of eminent usefulness is closed."[140]

The Coans have experienced several full circles during the trip. They journeyed to the Sandwich Islands around a cape; they returned via steamship from Hilo to San Francisco, then took trains across the land. They had gone up against Mormon missionaries on the Big Island; they visited with some of them in Salt Lake City. Coan had entered into a relationship with Jesus and been inspired to enter missionary work under the ministry of Charles G. Finney. He co-officiated the Lord's Supper with Finney for the large Ohio Congregational gathering. He spoke in Finney's church. The American Board had sent him first to Patagonia, then to the Sandwich Islands. In Brooklyn leaders and delegates of the Board welcomed him and hailed him as a leader of the global mission effort, having him speak and serve Communion. He returned to the place of his birth, which had 2,342 residents as he approached the age of twenty in 1820. When he visited there at the age of sixty-nine, the town's population had declined to 856.[141] When he was born there Thomas Jefferson was one month away from being inaugurated the President of the United States of America. In Washington City he twice met briefly with President Ulysses S. Grant. They experience the ultimate full circle when they return to the place where the journey had begun: Hilo and their beloved Emerald Bower.

Lydia writes a bridge passage near the end of the United States chapter: "The rapid decline of Mrs. Coan's health became alarming, and they hastened their return to the quiet home in the tropics, leaving much unseen and unsaid, but followed by many prayers and remembered in loving appreciation."[142] In early April of 1871, the Coans would embark the steamship *Nevada* and arrive early May in Hilo, where Fidelia and Titus would embark on the final chapters of their lives. Fidelia would endure a short chapter of a little over a year, while Titus would prosper for most of his remaining chapter of ten and half years.

---

140. Coan, *Memorial Volume*, 132–33.

141. Wikipedia, "Killingworth, Connecticut." 1820 is the first year with a recorded census in Killingworth.

142. Coan, *Memorial Volume*, 132.

16

Final Years, 1872–82

"It is time to bring these imperfect sketches to a close. The foregoing pages have been written among interruptions and anxieties, but they make some partial record of a life preserved by its Giver in many scenes of danger and crowned with many blessings. And among its chief blessings I would recognize God's goodness in granting me precious partners in my lifework. My second marriage, October 13, 1873, was to Miss Lydia Bingham, daughter of the Rev. Hiram Bingham. This faithful helpmeet is the strength and support of my age. But for her suggestions, and her patient labors in copying the manuscript of this volume, I should not have undertaken, at my time of life, the task of writing it.

"As I lay aside the pen, our anxieties have passed away.[1] If again, while I remain, the rocks should melt and flow down at the presence of the Lord [Mic 1:4], again we 'will look unto the hills whence our help cometh.'"[2]

In *The Last Volcano*, John Dvorak writes of the quest over the years by Thomas Jaggar to visit one more volcano. Ultimately, the 1912 founder of the Hawaiian Volcano Observatory overlooking Kilauea would visit what was his last volcano. In the case of Titus Coan's life, he had many "lasts," many final milestones, in his life: the last days of his first wife's life; the last page of his autobiography, the last lava flow he would see, the last sign of revival, his last letter, his last spoken words, and his last breath. This chapter presents many "lasts" for Titus Coan in a decade that was both vibrant and poignant as he sojourned through his valedictory years.

---

1 Coan, *Life*, 335. The pen painter laid aside his autobiographical writing instrument in "Hilo, August 15, 1881," at the age of eighty. A lava flow had recently threatened Hilo. Some residents had sent their goods to Honolulu and some abandoned their homes, while others arrived to sightsee. Coan, *Life*, 329–31, 335.

2. Coan, *Life*, 335. NB: Coan quotes the KJV of Ps 121:11. Most English translations—preceded by Martin Luther's German Bible—end that sentence with a question mark, with the focus on the next verse: "My help comes from the LORD."

455

Titus Coan: "Apostle to the Sandwich Islands"

FINISHING WELL: FIDELIA'S LAST MONTHS AND DAYS

When the Coans returned to Hilo in early May of 1871, Fidelia was physically spent. Though the specter of death hung over the Emerald Bower for some months, she was faithful and fruitful until her Lord called her home. At the conclusion of his United States tour chapter in his autobiography, Titus writes that on "our return to Hilo we met a cordial welcome from all, and the church and people were in a prosperous state. But a heavy shadow darkened over our home. The dear one who had been its light and joy for thirty-six years was growing feebler day by day, and the signs of her departure could not be mistaken.

"Calmly she began to set her house in order, to be ready to welcome the coming messenger. She assured us of her unshaken faith in Christ, and prepared farewell suggestions for the dear ones she was soon to leave."[3]

Her condition permeates most correspondence by and about her. She writes Titus on August 24, 1871, while he is away on a Puna tour. His absence surprises the later reader, though the couple continued to maintain their patterns of life and ministry as best they could. "My dear husband . . . We have got on very well since you left. I thought I was getting bravely over the week since you left, but for a day or two I have been warned of the approach of one of my old-fashioned colds, which sometimes last me a month. If sweating will carry off a cold mine ought to go forthwith. My heavy night sweats[4] are a great drawback to my strength and comfort. No special change in my neck since you left. I am thinking much of you as you pass over the battlefields of Puna . . . Hattie is helpful and thoughtful as ever, she would send her love did she know I am writing. I shall probably be in bed before her company leaves.[5] Poor child! She gets no time for reading or writing."[6]

Fidelia was in Titus's thoughts. The next day he wrote her. The couple's letters passed each other. Titus wrote, "My dearest . . . Send me a line by return of mail on Monday. It will meet me at Keaau, or Makuu, if taken outside of the mail bag. I hope to hear that you are better."[7]

Almost a year later, Fidelia's love of God and family shines through her June 24, 1872, letter to her firstborn son Munson. She appeals to him with regard to his belief, the importance of the family getting along after her death, and the challenges of liberal theology creeping into Protestant evangelical seminaries and beyond.

---

3. Coan, *Life*, 221; Coan, *Memorial Volume*, 134 (both paragraphs combined into one paragraph).

4. Excessive sweating can be a sign of cancer, in particular leukemia. Mayo Clinic, "Excessive Sweating."

5. Frances Johnson was visiting Hattie in the parlor of the Emerald Bower.

6. Fidelia Coan to Titus Coan, August 24, 1871, HMH (typescript). Ehlke notes that during her mother's last years, Hattie "was called upon to run the household." Ehlke, "Enthusiastic Religion," 288.

7. Titus Coan to Fidelia Coan, Opihikau, August 25, 1871, HMH (typescript).

She opens her letter to her physician son with a discussion of her condition. "My dear Munson, It has been a long time since I wrote you or Sarah.[8] The others[9] have written you and told you that I have been home poorly for three months. Whether they have excited any serious alarm or not I do not know." Terminal cancer patients can have their ups and downs, their plateaus. Fidelia next describes symptoms that could be cancer markers. "For two or three weeks past I have had a good appetite and to that in part I must attribute an increase in strength, though the *tumors* and *all the discomfort attending them*[10] maintain this ground."

She expresses her intimation of impending death and bases her appeals upon this uncertainty. "I know not how much I shall be able to write you in the future. Not much of course. But while I can write I want you and Sarah to know that your mother is *happy*[11]—not in the sense of having lost my [?] in everything but in the bright world beyond." She comments on the happiness of her home of decades. "Hilo home is as cheerful as it ever was." She gives herself to God's care. When earthly comforts fail there still remains the "house of God, eternal in the [everlasting?] arms."[12]

Fidelia shows herself to be a pen painter in her own right as she appeals for family unity in a way that will be echoed by Titus in a paragraph of his "Last Will and Testament."[13] "I charge you all, not to let the family become dismembered in heart and affection because one link has dropped out. Write to each other of the little incidents which go to make up life and which we should all immediately begin to talk about could we meet. Failing to do that you will soon feel 'there is nothing to write about,' for great experiences are of rare occurrence. We are hoping soon to hear from you abroad.[14] May the town be all that you anticipated . . . Your loving mother."[15]

Writing perhaps two days later, she writes Munson words that further continue descriptions of what could well be cancer-caused symptoms.[16] "I write these things in weakness and not without suffering yet without acute pain. When that comes upon me as it must sooner or later I do not expect to rejoice in it. My system is exceedingly intolerant of pain and when it comes upon me my mind is chiefly occupied with it."

---

8. Daughter Sarah Eliza Coan (who married Edward Emerson Waters), Judd, *Missionary Album*, 71; and Forbes et al., *Partners in Change*, 189.

9. Other Coan children?

10. Emphasis added.

11. Fidelia's emphasis.

12. Deuteronomy 33:27?

13. Hawai'i State Archives microfilm (printed copy of "Last Will and Testament of Titus Coan." Paragraph VII, "divide my library among Fidelia and my children 'amicably.'" Paragraph IX, praying "for unity [of? In?] spirit, harmony and prosperity on earth, and a unity of bless and glory in heaven." For more, see Legacy chapter.

14. The Philippines?

15. Fidelia Coan to Titus Munson Coan, June 24, 1872, LOC.

16. Perhaps indicating the genetic nature of cancer in the church family, Ehlke notes that Hattie died of cancer. Ehlke, "Enthusiastic Religion," 288.

Having acknowledged a low threshold of pain, she writes of acceptance. "But I hope to be able to *acquiesce* when I cannot enjoy it and say in deepest spirit 'Thy will *be done*'" [Luke 22:42].

In March of 1872, Titus had written his sister-in-law Fanny about Fidelia being an invalid. "Fidelia has written you in her weakness. For once in her life she is an invalid—But God spares her graciously and we *do* feel thankful. 'He knoweth our frame' [Ps 103:14] and he will not lay a load upon us which we cannot bear."[17]

As she had with Titus, Fidelia writes Munson about Hattie's loving attention to detail. "Hattie keeps the home in the *nicest order*,[18] [including] two or three vases of the choicest flowers.[19] I am happy in her blessed ministrations and in the untiring devotion of your dear Father who spares nothing that can contribute to my comfort. I might enumerate many more *temporal blessings* which often seem like sacraments knowing that *I shall not need them long*."[20]

However it happened and whomever made the challenges, some of the theological strife post-Civil War had reached Hilo. Perhaps Titus and Fidelia had learned more of these post-Civil War controversies while visiting seminaries and talking with pastors on their visit to the United States.[21] "More than all I am happy in having the sting of death taken away.[1 Cor 15:55]. I believe that he is just what he claimed to be. 'The Son of God [sic—'Son of Man' in this verse] who came to save that which is lost' [Luke 19:10]. Theologians may quarrel on as to what his precise claims were, but to me he is . . . 'God Manifest.'"[22]

"On the Sabbath, September 29, 1872," Titus Coan "wrote[23]: 'The solemn hour has struck—a great wave of sorrow has rolled over me. My precious Fidelia, my companion, counselor, friend, my loving and faithful wife, ascended at half-past one today, with the celestial escort and a shout of victory, to the heavenly hills. She was full prepared, and God's grace was *sufficient* [2 Cor 12:9] unto the end. Thanks be to God who gave her the victory through our Lord Jesus Christ [1 Cor 15:57]. Pain and long

---

17. Titus Coan to Fanny Coan, March 15, 1872, LOC, in Ehlke, "Enthusiastic Religion," 257.

18. Fidelia's emphasis.

19 Possible flowers used: "From white kukui blossoms to pink cottage roses, these native Hawaiian flowers provide color and allure to each of Hawaii's main islands . . . The official flower of the Big Island is the red ohia, which is the blossom of the native ohia tree. Lehua blossoms can also be orange, yellow, or white. The flower is often used for leis." Aloha Hawaii, "Hawaiian Flowers."

20. Emphasis added.

21. See Taylor, "Great Debate," as well as Taylor, "That Obnoxious Dogma." The proponent of Future Probation, Egbert Smyth, also led the "Progressive Orthodoxy" or "New Theology" at the Board's foundational Andover Seminary, Taylor, "The Great Debate," 11. The Great Debate took place in the late 1880s, but the liberal theology of European theologians such as Dorner surged into the Evangelical seminaries after the Civil War.

22. Fidelia Coan to Titus Munson Coan, June 26 [?], 1872. LOC. There are missing lines on this page—torn or ripped off.

23. No indication of correspondence is given. Perhaps Lydia draws this quotation form Titus's journal. She provides it after his death.

disease had wasted her dear frame to a skeleton,[24] but her pure spirit triumphed over all. Her faith was calm, clear, and firm; not a doubt, not a shadow came over her soul. She rested *on* Jesus, and *in* Jesus with entire trust and perfect peace. She was at *his feet* always. Now she wears a starry crown."

Coan quotes a hymn:

> No shadows yonder!
> All light and song.
> No weeping yonder!
> All fled away.[25]

On the next day, a Monday, there "were tender and solemn funeral services in our church . . . but the day was stormy and it was not till the following morning that the dust of our beloved one was laid to rest in the cemetery on Prospect Hill, where hers was the first grave. On the marble that marks the spot, these words are inscribed:

> 'Faithful unto death,'
> Crowned with life" [Rev 2:20].

Coan next reflects on the beauty of the location of the cemetery. "The cemetery is in a beautiful place; the towering mountains are upon the west and south. East and north stretches the ocean, and a glorious emerald landscape is on every side. The soft breezes that rustle the leaves, and the murmurs of the distant surf, do not wake the sleeping form that awaits the behest of him who is 'the Resurrection and the Life' [John 11:25]. The soul unfettered, unchained, has drawn nearer than they to the throne."

He closes his reflection on Fidelia with two paragraphs on her abilities, character, and capacity to love. "The dear one was an extensive and eclectic reader, a clear and logical thinker. Her mind and heart were well prepared to take an active part in the literary and religious discussions and activities of the age, but she freely chose the life of a missionary to the heathen. To me she was a peerless helper."

After restating her self-sacrifice for his going to Patagonia, as well as his perilous journeys in Hawaii, as well as his two trips to the Marquesas Islands, "when I expostulated with her against remaining alone in the house, as she sometimes did, she would answer, 'I am not afraid.'

"To her tender love, her faithful care, her wise counsels, her efficient help, and her blameless life, I owe under God the chief part of my happiness, and of my usefulness if I have had any, as a laborer in the Master's vineyard."[26]

Coan's grief expressed in his autobiography is public in nature. The memorials to Fidelia published in *The Friend* border on the hagiographic. There is an opening

---

24. Further evidence of cancer?

25. Titus Coan, September 29, 1872, in Coan, *Memorial Volume*, 134–35. The hymn "No Shadow Yonder," lyrics by Horatius Bonar in 1856 based upon "Her light was like unto a stone most precious, even like a jasper stone" (Rev 21:11).

26. Coan, *Life*, 221–22.

obituary that summarizes some of her life. The second part of it includes these words: "During her residence on these islands of over thirty-five years, Mrs. Coan has been an active, an earnest, and a patient laborer in the missionary field. None knew her but to love, none knew her but to praise. She was endeared to all classes of the community who were brought within reach of her gentle influences, but more particularly to the natives, by whom she will be held in grateful remembrance."

Following the obituary written by *The Friend* editor, Samuel C. Damon, comes a letter penned by "the Reverend F. Thompson of Hilo"[27] that provides "a tribute to the excellence and worth of Mrs. Coan." Alluding to the lingering nature of the illness he begins with, "At last our beloved Mrs. Coan is gone." He continues to extol her virtues, concluding with, "The strength and beauty of a godly life are rarely exhibited in this world of ours as they have been in the life and character of the late Mrs. Coan."

The section on Fidelia concludes with an ode simply entitled "In Memoriam." While anonymous, the theme of angels and the phrase "Emerald Bower" would appear to point to Titus as the author.

> An angel bright on joyful wing,
> At God's behest set forth
> To find amid his wide domain,
> A spirit lent to earth.
>
> For God required his own once more—
> Amid the seraph choir
> A strain was mute—a seat was void—
> There was an unstrung lyre . . .
>
> Within a cool sweet *Emerald Bower*
> Bedewed with God's rich grace,
> The angel found a waiting soul
> Ripe for heavenly peace.
>
> Long had her wings been plumed for flight,
> Her eye been fixed above;
> The furnace had been seven times tried,[28]
> The gold refined in love . . .
>
> A nation mourns the spirit rare,
> Transplanted thus from the Earth—
> Lord grant our end like hers, may be
> Triumphant over Death.[29]

---

27. Frank Thompson served as pastor of Hilo's English-speaking residences for five years, beginning in early 1869. Coan, *Life*, 135.

28. Dan 3:19, King Nebuchadnezzar orders the furnace heated seven times hotter than usual.

29. *The Friend*, 29.11 (November 1872) 90.

Final Years, 1872–82

TITUS GRIEVES, THEN REMARRIES

Titus would write an agonizing multipage ode to Fidelia, perhaps never thinking it would see the light of day. It is at a private level of agony and repetition that may have assisted Titus in the grieving process.

In "Recollection," Titus Coan appears to refer to Fidelia's likely cancer with such words as "wasting sickness," "sweat of death," and "emaciated frame." He writes of hope though he knew she would die.

The first section begins

>*This day five years I saw her die.
>*The march of Death had warn'd me, but I did
>*Not take the token. Slow, wasting sickness,
>*Because 'twas slow, was full of hope. I watched.
>*I pray. I trusted she would live again.
>*Even when I took her in my arms, and she
>*Could scarcely whisper: softly her spirit
>*Resting on God, and her emaciated frame,
>*Leaning on me even, even then I was deceived.
>
>*She told me she must die. And so did others.
>*In such a prospect we had talked and prayed.
>*Often at her request I knelt beside
>*Her bed, when utterance failed me and I wept
>*And sobbed my prayer: Preserve her life, O God!"
>*She is "scarcely able to whisper."
>
>*This day five years I stood beside her bed.
>*And saw and felt the sweat of death come on.
>*Hope vanished, anguish expectation mock.
>*She sunk into my arms—she looked unearthly—
>*She gasped and all was hushed as death. 'Twas death.

He writes three more sections about friends encouraging him to behold her in death, with a pleasant, serene, and intelligent countenance. He thanks his brother for being with him and praying during that occasion.[30]

"The Last Visit at The Grave of A Wife" opens with

>*It was an hour of anguish, and yet dear
>*To one long nurtured in the school of woe,
>*For then he came to shed the farewell tear
>*O'er the lone grave of all he loved below.
>*Thither he oft had come with no vain show
>*Of grief it was a luxury to pour

---

30. Coan, "A Recollection," LOC.

*Affections tears. And how when forced to go
*Where he could [?] her [?]-grown grave no more,
*He came to weep to mournful pleasures [over?].³¹

Titus wrote Fidelia's sister Maria Robinson, "Hattie and I have written so fully to our friends, of the last days and departure of my most precious angel, that I need add nothing for your information."³² Not long after the time it would take for Titus's letter to reach Maria on the eastern part of the mainland and for Maria to write back, Maria writes Titus and Hattie from West Rush, New York. "I have just heard of your great bereavement, and tho I had expected it, still I thought not quite yet, but I so rejoice that *her sufferings are over, pain from which she had not been free for years,*³³ but now ceased and she is at rest with her dear Savior." Marie seeks to comfort Titus and Hattie while recognizing the weight and pain of grief. "For her we will be comforted but for you that are left behind, what shall we say. I know how the heart will [mourn?] . . . how desolation seems written on very thing, how night and day awake or asleep there is a heaviness of heart, as if the life and light and joy of life were removed."³⁴

A little over seven months after Fidelia's death, Titus writes a missionary friend of his who lost his wife many years prior. Mrs. Mary Grant Paris "labored six years in the isolated district of Kau,³⁵ Hawaii. Her burial place was in the cup of Halai Hill, Hilo."³⁶ Coan laments that he has not heard from or seen Paris since Fidelia's death. "Where art thou, beloved disciple, my brother and companion in tribulation and in the kingdom and patience of Jesus Christ? For long months I have not heart that voice which used to cheer me, or seen a note from that pen which used so often to greet me. I do not chide thee, but I wish to inquire after thy welfare and to remind thee of olden times when we worked and prayed and rejoiced and wept together.³⁷ You are busy, and things around and near you occupy your time and thought."

Coan turns to the heart of his missive by referring to Paris's first wife and Coan's beloved Fidelia. "But you do, I doubt not, sometimes think of your brother in the solitary Bower, and of the precious dust, thine and mine, so calmly sleeping near each

---

31. "Last Visit at the Grave of a Wife," LOC.

32. Titus Coan to Maria Church Robinson, nd, LOC.

33. Emphasis added, to focus on possible clue of cancer.

34. Maria Church Robinson to Titus Coan, November 30, 1872. LOC Box.

35. Kau is the region east of Puna. Titus went by boat to Kau and toured through that district back through Puna and then home to Hilo.

36 Judd, *Missionary Album*, 153. She died in 1847. Paris would marry Mary Carpenter four years later. "Mr. Paris's reminiscences were published in 1926 [thirty-four years after his death] under the title of *Fragments of Real Missionary Life*," Judd, *Missionary Album*, 152. Porter et al., *Fragments of Real Missionary Life*.

37. Paris began serving in Waiohinu, Kau, in 1841. At the time of Coan's letter, Paris had been in Kealakekua (approximately five miles south of Kaiulua in the Kona area of the Big Island) for over twenty-one years. He remained stationed there until his death in 1892. Judd, *Missionary Album*, 152; and Forbes et al. *Partners in Change*, 493–98.

other in their rural beds. *I am permitted the mournful pleasure to go often to the place where all that is mortal of my precious companion sleeps its last, long sleep. This is a comfort, and*

> It gives me solace in my heavy grief.
> The dear lone spot where her loved form doth lie
> Yields to my stricken, aching heart relief,
> Chastens my sorrow, while it wakes a sigh,
> Tells me she has gone, yet speaks her presence nigh."[38]

Coan concludes by tying together the memory of the two wives, again referring to his beloved Fidelia as he characterized her when he first saw her over forty years before. "I rarely think of the *calm trust* and the perfect triumph of my shining angel without thinking of the very similar triumph of your precious one. The two have met and reviewed the way in which they were led til they left the same tabernacle, mounting on like wings, and pursuing the same shining track to the realms of 'pure and perfect day.'"[39]

Titus continues to process his grief while getting on with his life. That life includes the courting of Lydia Bingham, whom he had first met in her mother Sybil's arms in June of 1835 when he and Fidelia arrived in Honolulu for the first time. When Lydia returned to the Islands from the States, the Coans made her adult friendship. One time Titus brought Lydia by the Emerald Bower for an unannounced visit. After the visit was over, Fidelia wrote him a letter admonishing him: "I very much wish Lydia Bingham could come up with you while the house was clean, the supplies fresh and the peaches not quite gone." Without suggestion of suspicion or scandal, Lydia once "accompanied him on an excursion to the volcano. Coan continued on to Kalapana from the volcano" and sent a letter with Lydia for Fidelia.[40]

Records do not indicate when Titus began courting Lydia. She had admired him throughout her life.[41] In his undated "Waymarks," Coan writes "October 13, 1873. Married to Lydia Bingham at 11 a.m. by Rev. Mr. [?]"[42] While Titus provides the date and time of his wedding, one looks in vain in his autobiography for any mention of it. All one reads is, "When Miss Bingham came to Hilo."[43] It is in the context of her leaving the seminary in Honolulu and her sister taking over the administration of that school and the school using the facilities of the second Hawaiian Church of Honolulu.

---

38. Unsourced poem.
39. Titus Coan to John Paris, May 9, 1873, in Coan, *Memorial Volume*, 135–36.
40. Ehlke, "Enthusiastic Religion," 258.
41. She kept a picture of him in her room.
42. Coan, "Waymarks." The name is difficult to read. It looks like "Frean," but there is no such person associated with Hawai'i. Could it be the Reverend Jonathan Green of Maui?
43. Coan, *Life*, 243.

There is no mention of the purpose of her coming to Hilo, namely to be Titus Coan's wife!

Which leads one to wonder whether Munson Coan did not approve of his father's marriage to a woman only two years older than he was. Munson identifies himself in a "Note"[44] as the reader of the proofs of the autobiography. So it is possible that Munson deleted any specific references to the wedding ceremony that his father might have made. Titus prepared "Waymarks" to remind himself of key events in his life in preparation for writing his autobiography. Even with the one mention of "Miss Bingham," she is not listed in the index, whereas her brother Hiram Bingham II[45] is mentioned once and Bingham I three times in the index.

Even more intense in opposition to her father's second marriage is daughter Harriet or "Hattie," whose middle name is that of her mother, Fidelia. Ehlke reminds the reader of Hattie's care of her mother in Fidelia's last years and notes that the "housekeeper role was often assigned to spinster daughters in nineteenth-century America." Ehlke opines that perhaps "Hattie felt cheated out of this cherished and accepted role" by her father's marriage to a spinster only three years her senior.[46]

Ehlke writes that Harriet "found it difficult to accept a younger woman in her mother's place, a view shared by some in the missionary community."[47] Ehlke provides a frame by which to understand the opposition by some family members and by some missionaries. In a letter dated to her father one day before the wedding that shows either a major lapse of memory or a colossal Freudian slip, Hattie writes her father about not being aware he had arrived in Honolulu. The entire letter cries out for comment. "Dear Papa, It never once entered my head till some one told me last evening, but what you were to be here this week." Certainly she must have known that he was coming to get married since she knew enough not to attend the wedding. "I feel perfectly 'done up,' as the saying is to discover my mistake." Does she actually want to talk about his mistake in remarrying? "It came about by my thinking of there always being a full two weeks between the steamer arrivals in Hilo, and it never occurred to me that it was different at this end." Was this a justification? Excuse? How could she not know the difference in shipping regularity in the hub of Honolulu? According to Hattie, Mrs. Church had proposed "that you should come up and spend the afternoon today after church and go down in the evening." Was this proposed by a personal messenger? Was the letter delivered by a personal messenger? "You can have a bath . . ."[48]

Samuel Castle agonizes over the situation in a letter to his children. "Her father's remarriage greatly disturbed Hattie Coan who was then teaching at Punahou. She refused to attend the wedding, supported by 'others who feel that the step is such an one

---

44. Coan, *Life*, np.
45. Called "Bingham, Hiram Jr.," in the index.
46. Ehlke, "Enthusiastic Religion," 288.
47. Ehlke, "Enthusiastic Religion," np.
48. Harriett Coan to Titus Coan, October 12, 1873, TOC. The rest of the letter is unreadable.

as they would not take,' reported Mr. Castle to his children. Mr Castle felt sorry for all concerned as he felt it to be a 'perfectly right and proper' step if 'the parties choose.'"[49]

Even though *The Friend* regularly published marriage notices, the editor Samuel Damon chose not to print a notice of the Coan-Bingham nuptials. This omission and written silence were a source of pain to the tenderhearted Lydia. She writes to "Julie" from Hilo in December of 1873. "Julie, my dear, dear friend . . . *Hattie doesn't write me*,[50] so it is only thro' you that I have known the things you mentioned connected with [the] Co[u]s[in's] Society. About the 'exception' made in Mr. C.'s case, we both think it is all right just as we could prefer. But; Jule dear, it did make me wear a sober face, or a *sad*,[51] for some time after reading your letter to think that an honorable mention of 'the wedding could not be made in the pages of the *Maile*.' After six years and a half service as an employee of the Soc. I withdraw from active service and no mention of my marriage can be made for fear of touching a dangerous subject! *Rather a bitter pill*[52]—but—I try to swallow it patiently, because the hand that gave it has always been extended lovingly and helpfully heretofore and didn't *mean* to wound me now I'm sure. You have had more letters from *abroad*[53] and I am wondering whether any of them give more light upon the mooted question."[54]

The *Partners in Change* encyclopedia notes without citation that it "was a marriage not approved of by some of his family and friends, who thought it disrespectful for him to marry so soon after his beloved wife's death, and who were disturbed by the difference of thirty-three years in their ages. But the marriage was a success, and by all accounts they were very happy together."[55]

Mentioning both Fidelia and Titus Coan, Ehlke puts in perspective Titus's marriage to Lydia. "The loss of his loving wife and companion left her husband without his ever-present sounding board. Their love and devotion to each other was deeply rooted, but the void left by her passing was too much for the loving human being to face. The marriage of bereaved ministers to young women seemed to be the ordinary thing to do in the nineteenth century.[56] Charles G. Finney married three times, although no one doubted his love for his first companion, Lydia Andrews Finney.[57]

Lydia would speak to history through the *Memorial Volume*, which is overwhelmingly in Titus's words. She would also indirectly share about the quantity as well as the quality of their relationship in a letter to her sister-in-law Clara less than one month

---

49. Samuel N. Castle to his children, October 12, 1873, in Ehlke, "Enthusiastic Religion," 258–59.
50. Emphasis added.
51. Emphasis in original.
52. Emphasis added.
53. Emphasis in original.
54. Lydia Bingham Coan to "Julie," December, 1873. HMH.
55. Forbes et al., *Partners in Change*, 187.
56. See some examples in Judd, *Missionary Album*.
57. Ehlke, "Enthusiastic Religion," 267.

after his massive stroke and less than two months before his death. Writing from the Emerald Bower and dated October 12, she notes that "I do not write this date without going back in [this?] to nine years ago when an untried future was before me on the eve of one of life's most important steps carrying a burden of bitter grief yet bearing it for the sake of the two, three, perhaps four years of companionship that might be mine. And now I look back to nine years of such precious partaking together. How wonderful that such 'goodness and mercy' [Ps 23:6] have been allowed me."[58]

Titus brings the loving relationship between them home in a letter he wrote to Lydia the day she departed for a short trip to Honolulu. He is at his eloquent best when he writes her on December 3, 1875: "You steamed out of the bay splendidly at 4 p.m. *I gazed at the vessel which bore away the dearest earthly treasure of my heart*, till she was far off from her anchorage and yet close to the moss-mantled and fern-fringed shore. I then walked meditatively to the empty tabernacle. *All was now solitude where so late the voice of love*,[59] of prayer, of intelligent conversation, and of Christian communion was heard."

Lydia does include more from his letter and upon what subject he was meditating. He writes of friendship, raiment, everything that God provides, yet focuses on being consumed by and focused on the love of God. "I trust I hold all love and all friends in subordination to God, and with this belief I could give up all for Jesus."[60]

CONTINUATION OF LIFE AND MINISTRY AS REFLECTED IN LETTERS[61]

In the midst of his renewed marital bliss, Titus Coan found time to productively use the days and years left to him on earth. He continued to pastor, take tours of the Puna and Hilo districts, to press the cause of peace, and, of course, write letters.

He gives Professor Dana cordial "thanks for your very kind and appreciative congratulations on my new social relations.[62] To me it seems a boon of mercy from God to cheer and help during the balance of my mortal state, otherwise desolate and sad."

In the same letter he writes of the compatibility of the Bible and science. "I regard all Scripture as divine, and all true science none the less so; and the student and teacher of the one should ever be the student and teacher of the other. Both are filled with lofty and profound mysteries, and both proclaim the Infinite, Eternal, and All-wise God. Both are and must be reconcilable, and it has always been a joy to me that,

---

58. Bingham Papers, Box 4.
59. Emphases added.
60. Coan, *Memorial Volume*, 151.
61. From Coan, *Memorial Volume*.
62. At this point, Lydia places an asterisk and rather distantly explains the new social relations without mentioning her name: "Mr. Coan's second marriage was to a daughter of the Rev. Hiram Bingham."

in all your multiplied and varied labors in the department of natural science, you have recognized the divine hand."

After noting that his health is "remarkably good" and that he is "able to do as much work on the Sabbath as in former years, besides continuous labor during the week," he shares that "Mrs. Coan and I purpose to make the tour of Puna next week, and perhaps visit the volcano." He continues to show himself to be both revivalist and Renaissance man as he answers a question about coral reef rock.[63]

Writing about the mode of writing he observes to Rev. Lowell Smith, "Did we, as in olden times, get our pens from the geese, we might say that we keep our quills flying. We now change the phrase and say we keep our metal warm.[64] Well, I am glad of it, for we love to talk, and if we cannot do it face-to-face with our lips, let us do it apart with our metallic pens."

He notes that he is both ready to keep living on earth while being ready to go to haven. "I am not tired of this world, nor weary of its work, and yet I do desire 'a better country' [Heb 11:16] if the amazing grace of our Savior shall bring me there."[65]

He writes his Quaker friend Joel Bean from Makawao on the flank of the dormant volcano Haleakala about the value of Christian unity. Referring to his wife as his "precious L.," Titus relates their travel after the annual meetings of the Hawaiian Evangelical Association how they traveled to Maui to visit the girls' seminary, visiting the residents, and planning to "ascend to the great crater Haleakala."[66]

He writes a leader of a Quaker school near Richmond, Indiana—the Reverend Joseph Moore, President of Earlham College, of scaling Haleakala's long yet gentle side and the beauty of sunrise over the dormant volcano. It is remarkable how a seventy-four-year-old man is able to accomplish such a feat. He and friends ascended the gentle slope on the first day to the village of Makawao. The second day they reached the summit, enjoying sunset, night time, and sunrise at the summit. His scientific precision combined with biblical references is vintage Coan. "We, with nine others spent a night on the summit of Haleakala. The day was warm—mercury at 70°—the night stinging cold, mercury at 30°. The sky was clear, the stars brilliant, and the great vault above glorious. The scenery around was grand and magnificent. As the sun went low in the west, the fleecy clouds, moving up from the sea, came like heaven's light cohorts, gathering around the bases of the mountains, spreading like eider-down over the isthmus which divides East and West Maui, resting on hill and dale, hamlet and plantation, and reposing like a soft gossamer mantle on all objects below us. In this fleecy sea of exquisite beauty, the great orb of heaven dipped and bathed, shedding forth such a flood of golden glory—such flashing rays, such brilliants, such sparkling tints of beauty as I had never seen surpassed. In the morning this inimitable picture

---

63. Coan to Dana, October 6, 1874, in Coan, *Memorial Volume*, 137–38.
64. By this point, pens had changed form natural quills to metal-tipped.
65. Coan to Lowell Smith, December 15, 1874, Coan, *Memorial Volume*, 140–41.
66. Coan to Joel Bean, June 26, 1875, Coan, *Memorial Volume*, 143–44.

was repeated on the other side of the island, with ravishing beauty. The sun rose from the ocean depths, pierced the white canopy of drapery, shook his golden locks, and sent out such flashes of quivering radiance as to dazzle mortal vision, and to awaken unutterable admiration, calling for the adoration of devout souls, and lifting the spirit to those higher realms of glory where the 'Sun of Righteousness' [Mal 4:2] forever shines, and where life and immortality reign without night, or sorrow, or end. We descended from the mount, like Moses, feeling that we had been dazzled by the glory of God"[Exod 34:29].[67]

He writes Lydia a letter of a tour through the Puna district. The letter covers September 13 through September 20, 1875. Coan mentions Puula, Opihikao, and Kalapana as places visited. His age begins to show as he relates hip pain. He relates how the "pain in the hip joint was keen and piercing, but rest and *lomiing*[68] have abated it." Two days later he indicates that the "journey, with all its jostle and jar, has done me good." He writes that "bitter herbs act as tonics."[69] He writes of the challenging weather throughout the journey, but writes of God's blessing and the beauty of God's creation. "My heart rejoices in him who has clothed these heavens with such glory, and adorned the earth with such beauty." He also notes the occasional salubrious nature of the weather. "The air is balmy and pure, just pure enough and just vitalizing enough to send the oxygenated blood in sparkling currents through all the channels of the animal frame, and by a mysterious and gracious sympathy, to touch and cheer and vivify the soul."[70]

In 1875 and at age seventy-six, Coan laments the focus on material gain in the Islands. He introduces that by contrasting word of a "spiritual wave" in the United States with a lack of donations to "missionary treasuries." Then he writes of what causes celebrations in the Islands. "When we hear of the conquests of the gospel of a thousand born in a day, we are not deeply moved, but let the trumpet sound the final passage of *The Treaty* and the rising prospects of the planters, of sugar, or business at the Islands; flags run up and flutter, bells ring, powder takes fire, men shake hands, embrace, congratulate, drink healths (?),[71] and shout hosanna to the coming dollar."[72]

Eight months later he writes his son,[73] "The present grasping for wealth on these islands is great beyond anything we have hitherto seen. There will be many sad failures in the end. Kau is troubled with drouth [sic] and with subterranean dynamics. Wealth

---

67. Coan to Joseph Moore, June 26, 1875, in Coan, *Memorial Volume*, 244–45.
68. Massage? Pukui, *Hawaiian Dictionary*, 212.
69. As painkillers?
70. Titus to Lydia Coan, September 13–20, 1875, in Coan, *Memorial Volume*, 146–49.
71. Coan the temperance man puts the question mark in his letter to note the irony of drinking alcohol being tied with health.
72. Coan to Rev. Dr. Smith, July 10, 1876, in Coan, *Memorial Volume*, 156.
73. Munson? Latimer? Context would appear to be Latimer because of his repeated efforts at getting ahead in business, with many failures.

may come, or disappointment and disaster. I would rather have you possess Godliness, with contentment [1 Tim 6:6], than all the winged wealth of the world."[74]

In 1877, Titus writes "his son" a description of a great tidal wave on May tenth.[75] More than three months later he writes his nephew George Whitfield Coan.[76] Most notable about this letter is the footnote provided by Lydia Coan. It speaks to the vagaries of correspondence and other documents.[77] "Mr. Coan's correspondence with this beloved nephew began in his earliest years, but letters previous to this date were lost through accident on the removal of G. W. C.'s family from one home to another."[78]

In a late-1878 letter to the Beans, Titus wishes that he could be a missionary to so many people of the world: Native Americans, those in Africa, India, Turkey, China, and Japan: "My heart yearns to go forth again to the heathen, and, if it might be, to spend another life in laboring to win them to the love of Christ." He concludes the letter by proclaiming, "The wrath, the cupidity, the curiosity and the ten thousand schemes of sinful men will be over-ruled in the end to accomplish God's redeeming purposes in the earth."[79]

Coan often wrote his Quaker friends, the Beans, about peace.[80] In his last years, Coan continued to passionately preach on the value and necessity of living peacefully. Coan wrote to *The Advocate of Peace* on "February 2 . . . Yesterday was my seventy-ninth birthday. The gracious Master has so preserved my life and health that I preach with almost as little weariness as I did forty years ago. My subject very naturally included a glance of what had been done in obedience to this command, the present state of the world, and what remains to be done, as the quenching of the baleful fires of war, the extinction of intemperance, the overthrow of idolatry, of oppression, persecution, caste, and the universal diffusion of true knowledge and evangelical piety."[81]

The same letter also includes a key sentence as to how preaching the Prince of Peace is what has held together the Hawaiian nation and the mission endeavor. "I have instructed them much on this subject, and they feel that their independence, national life, social, civil, and religious privileges, with all their personal safety and general prosperity, are the fruits of the peace principles, inculcated by the gospel of peace; and that the principles are their only safeguard for the future. At the present day there is no people or nation, on which the sun shines, that enjoys more peace and safety, or more true freedom than the Hawaiian nation. Had we preached a patriotic and honorable

74. Titus "to his son," March 23, 1877, Coan, *Memorial Volume*, 157.

75. See "Science" chapter in "Renaissance Man" section.

76. Named after the great Evangelist of the first Great Awakening of the English-speaking world.

77. For instance, Titus Coan's numerous lectures appear to be lost to time, perhaps because of the 1930s fire of the Haili Church structure. They are not found in any of the known repositories of Coan's papers.

78. Lydia Coan footnote, Coan, *Memorial Volume*, 159.

79. Coan to Joel and Hannah Bean, October 9, 1878, Coan, *Memorial Volume*, 163.

80. See "Peace" chapter.

81. Coan letter, January 24 and February 2, 1880, in *Advocate of Peace* 12 (May 1880).

war gospel, the nationality of the Hawaiians would long ago have ceased and our missionary labors have ended. The peace doctrines here taught have been to this people and to us a factor and bulwark of superhuman power, which have resisted the fiery darts of the wicked, the assaults of Satan, and threatened thunders of four war ships, to say nothing of the mad rage of other enemies. To him who [?] and thunders through the skies, and who has said 'Vengeance is mine' [Deut 12:35; Rom 12:19], we look for protection, while we refuse to strike with carnal weapons."[82]

ENTERTAINING A VISITOR IN 1878

In or near 1878, Leavitt H. Hallock paid Titus Coan a visit. He met with the Coans at the Emerald Bower. He accompanied Coan to observe Kilauea and the Halemaʻumaʻu crater. He attended church. He listened to Coan's reminiscences and was in awe as Coan prayed for a half hour. Some of these items have already been related in previous chapters.[83]

At church, he tells of those still living who were part of the Great Awakening. "I saw many, with grey locks on their brown brows but with souls white within, who were born then and there and have proven their royal son-ship unto this day. It was touching to sit and worship with those . . . believers in their own church whose timbers were dragged by hand from the forest, miles away: whose mortar was lifted by divers from coral reefs beneath the sea. I tried to address the congregation, with Father Coan interpreting, but the odd liquid, mellow tones of his voice quite disconcerted my thought and I said in despair, 'I think you will have to finish this,' and he did!

"One of the early converts bears the honored name of 'Paul' and after praying in the Hawaiian tongue for me and for other sinners and saints, he said: 'When you get back to your people please give them Paul's love!' I give you the tender message now. Many and hearty handshakes testified their cordiality, and with extreme reverence and affection they hung upon Father Coan's words as he told them over and over the story of peace through Jesus Christ. Would you ask, What has the Christian faith done for the native character? It has transformed it."[84]

Hallock also notes that the gospel can transform anyone. "I gladly affirm that the Hawaiians are an eternal witness to the power of Christ to renew and revolutionize the life of low-down men. Some relapse, even as some white men do within our parishes, but the nation is regenerate."[85]

He also knew that the "story of redemption of Hawaii remains. It covers but a single generation, from 1820 to 1853. Only thirty-three years from the landing of the

---

82. *Advocate of Peace* 12 (May 1880).

83. The first Great Awakening chapter; "Science"; "Volcanoes" 1 and 2; and "Ministry to Expatriates."

84. Hallock, *Hawaii under King Kalakaua*, 64–65.

85. Hallock, *Hawaii under King Kalakaua*, 66.

first missionary to the accomplished evangelization of the race and the withdrawal of missionary aid.[86] It was indeed a signal instance of a 'nation born in a day' [Isa 66:8]. In round numbers we spent a million dollars, and sent out a hundred and forty Christian workers; the result? Seventy thousand men and women baptized, nearly all of whom have gone to sing the new song in their Father's house."

Hallock continues with comparisons to New England and further statistics. "One in four of the present population (1878) are members of the church. New England cannot match that after two hundred and fifty years of gospel privilege. Father Coan alone received upwards of twelve thousand into his church at Hilo, married over three thousand couples and baptized forty-five hundred infants. If we seek returns in kind for our outlay, the church in Hilo, during Father Coan's life, contributed a hundred thousand dollars for missionary work beyond."

Hallock notes that, even though the Hawaiians of Hilo have dwindled and been "reduced by repeated colonization,"[87] the church members continue to give annual gifts that average $1200. He relates the sacrificial giving of people of all ages. "I saw the monthly concert offering taken. Every man, woman, and child marched down the aisle and past the table where the venerable missionary sat, and each laid a gift upon the table; poor people they were, but their gifts exceeded a hundred dollars for that month alone."[88]

Hallock concludes his short book by apparently drawing from his journal and addressing his readers. Our "good ship *Zealandia*[89] is already hauling her cables for San Francisco. The cheery 'Aloha' is ringing from deck and wharf and we are off. Our dream of the tropics is over. Now the islands lie astern. Their amethystine peaks, studding the golden sea, are watching the setting sun and our flying ship. Farewell! Hawaii! Farewell to the sunny land and the happy people. Farewell to its unrivalled beauties and dread baptisms of fire. Farewell to Father Coan and all the *kanakas*[90]! Aloha nui, Isles of the Pacific! Aloha nui, fair reader!"[91]

---

86. In 1850, the Hawaiian Evangelical Association was formed to move forward the gospel.

87. Not to mention illness.

88. Hallock, *Hawaii under King Kalakaua*, 60–61.

89. From MaritimeHeritage.org, "RMSS *Zealandia*, SS *Zealandia*": "February 10, 1876, *Daily Alta California*, San Francisco, California, USA. The following will be interesting to our Australian neighbors and all intending passengers on the Australian route, as descriptive of the two British steamers of the service: The *Zealandia* and *Australia* are sister steamships, built specially by the well-known firm of John Elder & Co., Glasgow, for the new mall service between San Francisco and the Colonies of New South Wales and New Zealand. For the purposes of the service five powerful steamships are required; three of these the *City of San Francisco*, *City of New York*, and *City of Sydney*, each 3,500 tons, six hundred horsepower, have been built by the Pacific Mall Company, at Chester, Delaware, USA. The *Zealandia* and *Australia* complete the fleet, and have to proceed by the Cape of Good Hope to Australia to take up their stations on the mail route. They are expected to make the voyage to Melbourne within forty-three days."

90. People.

91. Hallock, *Hawaii under King Kalakaua*, 72.

WRITES TWO BOOKS

While Coan continued to write letters, he took up his pen to write the first of two books. Drawing on his journal and other writings, he put together his *Adventures in Patagonia: A Missionary's Exploring Trip*. He dates the Preface as 1879, with Henry M. Field dating his Introduction as March 1880.[92] The chapter in this biography discusses the differences between the original diary and what is related in the published book, as well as other matters.

In a bridge section, Lydia writes about Titus's quiet composition of his first published book. "To the many guests who through the passing years had been entertained with cordial hospitality at the Emerald Bower, Mr. Coan had sometimes related his experiences as a missionary explorer in the wilds of Patagonia. The story, as it fell from his lips, was full of interest, and the listeners often asked why he did not publish it."

Coan made the most of time he had when he no longer felt strong enough to tour the districts as much as he had before. "While he had strength for touring he never felt that he had time to write a book, but when, by reason of advancing age, he was not able to go as often as aforetime to the outskirts of his parish, he thought he might, perhaps, be doing good by responding to the wish of those who desired 'to see the simple narrative in print.'

"It was thus that he came, in 1879, to prepare his first volume, *Adventures in Patagonia*. To very few of his correspondents and to almost none of his island neighbors did he speak of this work while engaged upon it." But Lydia knew.

The Seamen's Bethel Church chaplain wrote and spoke the following about the Patagonia book. Arms's and Coan's "tour is aptly and graphically described in the recent volume written by Mr. Coan . . . Theirs was a daring enterprise and worthy of being recorded beside that of the most perilous missionary tours since Paul, Peter, and the other apostles traversed the Roman empire, from Palestine to far-away Britain and Spain, and distant Arabia and India."[93]

In the rest of the bridge section, Lydia credits the enthusiastic response to the *Patagonia* book for his deciding to write an autobiography. "The favor with which [*Adventures in Patagonia*] was received by his friends, and their solicitations that he should give a sketch of his life, in its earlier and later periods, led him, after much hesitation, to write his autobiography. This was in 1881, when he had reached his eighty-first year." Lydia explains his physical and mental state as being strong while writing the book, as well as his maintaining the everyday and seasonal habits developed over of forty-five years in and around Hilo. "This was in 1881 when he had reached his eighty-first year. At this time his form was still erect, his step alert, and his characteristic ardor in work was unabated. Seldom lying down during his active day of sixteen or seventeen waking hours, he kept up his correspondence, and met the daily

---

92. Coan, *Patagonia*, 8, xiv.
93. Damon, "Living for the Good of Others," in *The Friend* 40.1 (January 1, 1883).

duties of his position with his habitual cheerfulness and patience."[94] One is reminded of what he writes near the beginning of the first chapter of the autobiography. "My physical constitution was good, my health was perfect, and my childhood happy."[95]

To help jog his mind for the writing of his autobiography, Coan prepared a small string-bound notebook he called "Waymarks." Neither an outline nor a skeleton for the work, various dates, names, and or events are listed.[96]

In the autobiography's Preface, Titus explains why he wrote his autobiography. Beginning with allusions to Bunyan's *Pilgrim's Progress* he begins, "A pilgrim of fourscore years, standing near the margin of the border land, essays to give a sketch of his life—and why?" In the next sentence he answers the rhetorical question just posed and states his purpose for writing the book. "Because many personal and Christian friends have long urged it as a duty to my beloved Master to leave my testimony behind me of his faithfulness and grace."

He notes that he had had no intention of writing such a book. "To publish my autobiography was far from my thoughts." He recognizes the challenging nature of such an endeavor. "It is a difficult, delicate, and dangerous task. One does not choose to publish his own follies and sins, and surely it is not modest for one to proclaim his own goodness. I will, therefore, only say in the words of the great Apostle, 'Unto me, who am less than the least of all saints, is this grace given, that I should preach among the Gentiles the unsearchable riches of Christ'" [Eph 3:8].

He next interacts with the reader. "Let me then ask, if in reading this narrative there shall seem to be the weakness of egotism or of vain boasting, that the fault may lie at the door of the writer, or be pardoned on account of the great difficulty of relating one's own experiences and observations without often repeating the pronoun *I*."[97]

Titus Coan concludes his Preface with a typical clarion declaration. "On the other hand, if it shall appear that during a ministry of almost half a century a blind man has been led into the light, a lame man has been helped to walk in the way of life, a leprous soul has been washed in the fountain opened for sin and uncleanness; if a heathen has found the true God, and cast away his dead idols, if fierce cannibal has been persuaded to cease to eat the flesh of his enemies, and taught to trust the Son of Man for pardon, or if some who were dead in trespasses and sins have been raised to life by the quickening power of the gospel, then let God have all the glory."[98]

Coan organizes his autobiography as follows. He places the first thirty-plus years of his life into chapter I. Chapter II runs from his marriage to arrival in Hilo to "first labors." Chapter III introduces the mission field, including the Hilo and Puna Districts. While chapter IV discusses the "Great Awakening," Coan devotes seven chapters (VI,

94. Coan, *Memorial Volume*, 168–69.
95. Coan, *Life*, 2.
96. LOC.
97. Emphasis in the original text.
98. Coan, *Life*, "Preface," np.

XVIII–XXIII) to volcanic eruptions over the years. This disparity in chapters and pages (19, 86) devoted to the revival and volcanoes could be explained by the Great Awakening being much better known by most of his readers.[99]

Coan also writes about Catholics and Mormons, notes on the mission stations and the state of the church, and ministries to non-Hawaiians, and the trip to the United States. With some mixture of various subjects (as is the case in many chapters), he writes multiple chapters about missionary family life, Hawaiians, and missions (including two on trips to the Marquesas Islands).

As he concludes the autobiography, Titus thanks Fidelia for her indispensable assistance in writing the book.[100] In the *Memorial Volume*, Lydia reiterates how Titus wrote his autobiography while a lava flow from Mauna Loa threatened Hilo. "For seven months of this year he watched with others, sharing in their anxiety, that threatening lava flow from Mauna Loa, which, beginning on the fifth of November, 1880, continued until the tenth of August, 1881, without any abatement of action."[101] Titus put down his autobiographical pen five days after the lava flow ends.[102]

Perhaps sensing that he had not long before shuffling off his mortal coil,[103] approximately two months before his stroke, Coan wrote a one-page letter[104] of resignation as President of the Hawaiian Evangelical Association. It provides a window to his servant-leader soul.

"To the Board of the Hawaiian Association Evangelical Association.

"Beloved brethren.

"By the annual suffrage of this Board I have[105] been elected to the honourable office of president of your body for which favor I desire to render to you my heartfelt thanks. Although living at a distance from Honolulu, so that I could meet with you for consultation only at our annual assemblings, yet through your Christian courtesy I have sustained the office of president for nineteen years.[106] During all these years my heart and soul have been with you in the blessed task to which we have been called of God, and our relations and intercourse, so far as I can remember, have been of the most cordial and amicable nature, without friction or jar.

---

99. The irony is that when this Coan biography was being written, the focus was reversed with most people interested in his volcanic writings.

100. Coan, *Life*, 335. See opening quotation of this chapter.

101. Coan, *Memorial Volume*, 169."

102. Coan, *Life*, 335. Charles Darwin, who engaged in some correspondence with Titus through son Munson, "acquired a copy [of *Life* that] is still on the Darwin Archive in Cambridge University Library," University of Cambridge Charles Darwin Correspondence Project.

103. Shakespeare, *Hamlet*, Act 3, Scene 1, Line 67.

104. Undated, but a separate/later hand wrote "1882" in the upper right corner. See below re: notation after letter with date.

105. Inserted with a caret above the line.

106. Starting with the organization's founding in 1853. See second "Missions" chapter.

"For your body, for the Hawaiian Evangelical Association and for all the churches under its care: I feel an undying interest, and while *I now offer to you my resignation*,[107] it is with the assurance that my heart and prayers shall be with you always, and my efforts to assist the funds of the Board, and help in all practicable ways in the blessed evangelistic work[108] in which it is engaged is, by divine help, pledged.

"In 'Brotherly Love' of union

"Yours for the [?]

"Titus Coan."

After the letter[109] Coan wrote:

> Resignation of
> Rev. T. Coan as
> President of the
> Hawaiian Board
> Presented June 13, 1882[110]
> Not accepted, &
> withdrawn by request
> of the Board.[111]

LAST CORRESPONDENCE

Lydia provides examples of correspondence during the writing of the autobiography and the flow from the volcano. She also shares information about the last several letters Titus Coan wrote before suffering his massive stroke. On August 14, 1882, he wrote to the Reverend E. P. Goodwin, DD, to answer the latter's question on "my impressions as to the correctness of 'President Washburn's convictions that the American churches are losing their interest and faith in foreign missions.'" Coan hopes that the proposition is not true. Using rivers as an analogy and Ezekiel 47 as his Bible reference, he writes that the "church must be the channel of conveyance, and, as God has now removed all formidable obstacles, and provided the means of rapid and universal communication with the nations and peoples of the earth, it is, doubtless, the solemn duty and the precious privilege of the children of Zion to carry the water of life to all the families of men; and with trump of jubilee, sounding from every hilltop and along every valley, to call a thirsty and perishing world to come to the gushing fountain, to drink and live" [John 7:37–39].

---

107. Emphasis added.
108. Written to the left of the left side margin.
109. Visible dimly through the page of the letter.
110. Lines (about five words long) above and below "Presented . . ."
111. Coan, letter, June 13, 1882, HMH.

He turns to his visit to the United States, where and when he "felt assured that many ministers of the gospel, and many churches were earnest and faithful in this work. I also felt that many were delinquent, that they had never understood the marching orders of Zion's King; that a veil was upon their hearts; that the god of this world had blinded their minds to the great, and *only* great life-work of the church, viz.: to '*disciple all nations.*'"[112]

Coan turns to a consideration of the Hawaiian Christians and missions. "The Hawaiians are poor, and yet as to their percentage of giving, there is no comparison between our native churches and the wealthy members of your churches in the United States. They give a thousand per cent more than your rich men. And they often do it with shining faces and jubilant hearts. But all do not give."

He notes that "I usually preach a missionary sermon, or something connected with generosity, on the first Sabbath of every month, giving my people such facts as keep them informed on what God and his children are doing to evangelize the nations." He sums up the Great Commission with three words. "Three words embrace our whole commission to the heathen, viz: *Pray! Give! Go!* And how can a man pray 'Thy kingdom come,' while he gives nothing, or nothing worthy of a man, to help the conquests and enlargements of this kingdom?"

He concludes as follows: "Please let me know if I have in any way answered your questions satisfactorily.

"With great respect and brotherly love, I am your fellow-laborer in the kingdom and patience of Jesus Christ."[113]

In a bridge section to the last recorded[114] full letter written by Titus Coan, Lydia notes that "Mr. Coan had sometimes said that if God would grant him once more to see life among 'the dry bones' [Ezek 37:3], he thought he could pray 'now lettest thou thy servant depart in peace'[115] [Luke 2:29]. When the blessing came in the reviving influences of the Holy Spirit, which attended his own labors among his people after his return from Honolulu, and which continued to be manifested during the gospel meetings held by the evangelists, his soul rejoiced and blessed the Lord. But he was still eager, while strength remained, to be about his Father's business" [Luke 2:49].

Lydia continues the narrative of Titus Coan's last days before his stroke. "Early in September, the East Hawaii Association met in Hilo. With cheerful endurance he daily attended its long, wearying sessions until they closed." On September fifteenth—the day after the meetings were over—Coan said, "Now the pressure is lifted somewhat, I am going to break out to-day. I will go among the people to find a little exercise and recreation."

---

112. Emphases by Coan.

113. Coan to Goodwin, August 14, 1882 Coan, *Memorial Volume*, 191–97.

114. In Coan, *Memorial Volume*.

115. *Nunc Dimittis*, from the Latin *Vulgate* Bible, of Simon's first words to the Lord once he has seen the infant Jesus in the Temple. Luke 2:29–32.

During a family worship time,[116] Coan read with feeling from Psalm 103. He paused a little "to talk about the Lord's putting our sins from us 'as far as the east is from the west' [verse 12], and about the precious thought of the Heavenly Father's pity for his children. A tender pathos was in his voice while he read, 'As for man, his days are as grass; as a flower of the field, so he flourisheth. For the wind passeth over it, and it is gone; and the place thereof shall know it no more' [verses 15 and 16]. Yet he knew not, as he laid down the family Bible, that he should never again read from its sacred pages, and that the place at which he knelt to pray would know him no more."[117]

On the afternoon of September fifteenth, he "repaired to his study. Unanswered letters were on his table; he would reply to those from two young nephews, sons of the missionary to Persia. He wrote to each; and to the elder thus: "My dear nephew Fred: If you are filled with the spirit of love and obedience to Christ, and an earnest, pure desire to win souls for the Master, your life will be useful and happy." He uses himself as an example to share the Christian faith regardless of age of life or profession. "I would not make myself an example of fidelity, but would bless the Lord for inclining me, long before my decision to study for the ministry, and during my theological course, to watch for souls, and to improve opportunities by the wayside and everywhere, as Providence gave them, to speak a word for Jesus." He concludes with, "My prayer shall ever be that you may be fully consecrated, and meet for the work and warfare of life, having put on the whole armor of God."[118]

The last letter he ever began was to his decades-long co-laborer in the mission field of the Big Island. Starting with the Great Awakening, Titus Coan and Lorenzo Lyons were as close as any two missionaries could be. "Once more he dipped his pen and wrote a few lines to his 'ever dear brother Lyons,' but the letter was never finished. Reading and sweet discourse[119] filled the evening hours of that day."[120]

STROKE, FINAL MONTHS, AND DEATH

On the morning of September 16, 1882, Titus Coan suffered a massive stroke or some other form of significant illness from which Titus would die in less than three months. Lydia phrases it this way: "On the following morning a messenger came, bearing summons from the master. Mr. Coan seemed to have caught some vision of him; he called him 'a beautiful messenger,' and told us he had come to bid him away. He said he believed it was his time to go, and with solemn earnestness he repeated Paul's memorable words, 'The time of my departure is at hand. I have fought a good fight; I have

---

116. Was anyone besides Lydia present?
117. Coan, *Memorial Volume*, 197–98.
118. Coan, *Memorial Volume*, 199–200.
119. With Lydia?
120. Coan, *Memorial Volume*, 200.

finished my course. I have kept the faith; henceforth there is laid up for me a crown of righteousness'"[121] [2 Tim 4:7].

Lydia notes that "The bodily powers failed rapidly; but his soul triumphed."[122] Within a month she is writing to Hiram Bingham II's wife Clara about how far Titus's physical condition has declined and how draining the care has become. She writes of Lizzie, her sister, having written Clara about the situation and about how Lizzie is helping with Titus's care. After expressing a hope that is not fulfilled that Clara could visit, she notes that "Lizzie has answered your question. She does the lifting—the especial lifts out of and back into bed are made, have to be, by stronger arms than mine, but there are different turnings, the daily baths &c, that call for every inch of strength I have and back, neck, and arms feel constantly strained."

Next, Lydia makes a comment that breaks one's heart. It possibly shows the Victorian resolve to show a brave front to the public. It might have to do with Lydia's upbringing in a leading missionary family house and the pedestal upon which members of such a family are placed. Whatever the reason, she admonishes Lizzie, "You will not repeat this."[123]

During his last months, Lydia notes in the *Memorial Volume* that "as wearisome days and nights were appointed him, he bore witness often to the presence of the Comforter" [John 14:16]. Without mentioning Lizzie, Lydia lists the four people who were at Titus's side during his last months. "The faithful physicians, Drs. Wetmore and Kittredge, and Mr. Coan's son, who lived near, together with her with whom he had 'walked in loving fellowship,' watched by him though all that day and night, believing that the end was very near."[124] But his death was not to be at once.

Munson Coan, who was residing at some nearby location other than the Emerald Bower, Dr. Wetmore—Titus's friend of over thirty years, and Dr. Kittredge—all provided loving attention as well as medical care. The Library of Congress has a somewhat difficult to decipher handwritten document by Munson relating his observations of his father's last season on earth.[125]

Lydia notes that despite his being a physical "invalid," his mind remained sharp. "A remarkable degree of memory and great clearness of mind were granted to the dear invalid through all those weeks of waiting. He retained an unfailing interest in the world's progress, and listened to all that could be read to him." He listened to "the three closely printed sheets of *The Portland*[126] *Press*, not wishing to have one paragraph omitted of that paper's report of the meeting of the American Board."[127]

121. Coan, *Memorial Volume*, 200.
122. Coan, *Memorial Volume*, 200.
123. Lydia Bingham to Clara Bingham, October 12, 1882, Yale University Archives, Box 4.
124. Coan, *Memorial Volume*, 200–01.
125. LOC Box 17.
126. Maine.
127. Coan, *Memorial Volume*, 202.

Titus also enjoyed having read to him the recently published *Life and Times of Mrs. Lucy G[oodale] Thurston, Wife of Rev. Asa Thurston, Pioneer Missionary to the Sandwich Islands, Gathered from Letters and Journals, Extending over a Period of More Than Fifty Years. Arranged by Herself.*[128] Lucy and Asa[129] were part of the Pioneer/First Company with Lydia's parents and others. Lucy and Asa served many years in Kailua, which is on the island of Hawai'i and is now known as Kailua-Kona.[130] "As we read to him from Mrs. Thurston's "Book of Reminiscences," he delighted in recalling the experiences of missionary toil through which they both had passed."[131]

Appropriately enough, Coan was interested in another recently published book: James William Kimball's *Heaven, "My Father's House."*[132] Chapters in Mr. Kimball's book on heaven gave him great comfort, while letters from beloved friends were welcomed as often as they came.

But he was, nevertheless, in decline. "Yet he was not inclined to talk at any length, and would sometimes say that he was not thinking much, only found it 'sweet to lie passive in his hands and know no will but his.' Sometimes, in reply to inquiries how he felt, he would answer, 'I feel pretty well, as if I ought to be up and at work;' and then would tell of his dreams, in which he had been culling over long lists of names, assigning to each one some task to be done. Once he said, 'I can't rest; with my Redeemer. The Redeemer doesn't rest; he works always.'"[133]

Hawaiian friends, students, co-laborers, and others came to say their farewells. "There were many touching scenes through all those days. Aged men, who in their prime had been the companions of the beloved missionary in his tours, came long distances to speak once more with their revered teacher. Leaving their shoes at an outer door, they stepped softly into the room where he lay, and with tears coursing down their cheeks, pressed the hand that had so often been extended to them. Then kneeling by the bedside they would pour out their grief in tender prayer to God."[134]

Another touching scene took place on November 1, when Papa Coan requested that candidates for admission to the church be brought to the Emerald Bower. They "assembled in the parlor of his home. Unable, himself, to take active part in the examination held, he listened to it as conducted by the venerable Father Lyman and the assistant Hawaiian minister. At its conclusion, as the eighteen candidates passed from the room, he gave his left hand to each and spoke a word of gracious benediction, his own face radiant with holy peace, while others wept."

---

128. Thurston, *Life and Times*.
129. For both Thurstons, see Frobes et al., *Partners in Change*, 598–608.
130. Judd, *Missionary Album*, 190.
131. Coan, *Memorial Volume*, 202.
132. Kimball, *Heaven, "My Father's House."*
133. Coan, *Memorial Volume*, 202.
134. Coan, *Memorial Volume*, 202–03.

As many terminal patients do, Coan rallied not long before his death. "About the eighth week of his sickness there began to be so much gain of strength and vitality in the prostrated frame that hopes of his recovery revived in the hearts of his friends. A comfortable *manele*, or reclining chair, was made for him, and in this, borne on the shoulders of strong men, he was carried about the village." Papa Coan made a few last tours around Hilo. "Those who saw him on these occasions spoke of his beautiful, bright smiles, and of his courteous greetings as they met him. Ever thoughtful of others, he sometimes directed the bearers to rest by lowering the *manele* to the ground; and while they thus halted, natives from houses near by gathered about him. Their plaintive wails were touching, but in his placid eyes there was a wondrous look of heavenly love and calm. *Heaven was not far away.*"[135]

During his last month, Titus continued to be fervent in prayer. "Not infrequently during the last month Mr. Coan was able to lead in prayer at the morning or evening devotions. And he prayed as if in the very presence of the Father. As a trustful child sure of forgiveness, he confessed his sins and quietly committed his soul to the faithful Keeper."

To others Coan appeared to improve on the morning of Friday, December 1. We "thought him better than he had been at any time before since his attack." But the moment had arrived. "As his head leaned upon the pillow fitted to it a pallor and look of pain passed over his face, and to the anxious inquiry, 'What is it, darling?' he answered, 'I am going.' Yes, the hour to go had come. The heavenly visitant, whose first coming had been at dawn, September 16, had tarried for a while that precious seasons in the land of Beulah[136] might, to the survivors, give glimpses of glory to be revealed. Now he was ready to take the beloved toiler to higher service."

Lydia continues to describe the scene. Good-byes had already been spoken and closure secured. "Tender counsels and blessed testimonies had long been uttered. What need of more? Three words of 'farewell,' spoken calmly—slowly; the name of Jesus whispered with the latest breath, and then he stood before the King,

"Faultless in his glory's presence![137]

"Faultless in that dazzling light."

Mourning in the Hilo area was immediate. With Titus Coan laying in state at the church, numerous leaders—Hawaiian and missionary—led, read and spoke two days later on the Sunday. "The third of December was a Sabbath of most exquisite loveliness. Something of the beauty of those heavenly fields 'in living green,' and of the brightness of the upper courts seemed reflected upon the earth. But in Hilo flags were for the third day at half-mast, and a slow-tolling bell called together a company of weeping mourners. The precious remains of the departed pastor were borne to the

---

135. Coan, *Memorial Volume*, 203.

136. Beulah Land, Isa 62:4.

137. Jude 24.

church, and once more his people looked upon the noble face so calmly beautiful in death.

"Occupying the draped pulpit of their revered pulpit of their revered friend, the Reverends Mr. Lyman, Mr. Baker,[138] and Mr. Oleson,[139] with the Hawaiian pastors, Mr. Kalana and Mr. Pahio, took their assigned parts in reading the Scriptures, in prayers and in addresses. The sweet hymns, 'There is a land of pure delight,'[140] and 'Nearer, my God to Thee,'[141] were sung."

The Sunday service was a funeral, with a procession afterwards to the cemetery where Fidelia's earthly remains reposed. "Then a long procession followed the hearse, drawn by many kindly hands, to the place of burial. No more fitting spot on all the earth could be a quiet resting place for the sainted dead. Into a flower-strewn grave the sacred dust was lowered, while tearful voices sang,

"'Asleep in Jesus, blessed sleep,
From which none ever wake to weep.'"[142]

David Lyman offered a concluding graveside prayer. "The venerable Father Lyman offered one more prayer, and then 'all that love the deepest, the tenderest, all that respect and honor, the highest and truest could do, had been done; and in undoubting hope of a glorious resurrection we left him there.'"[143]

Titus Coan had prepared ahead of time what would go on his tomb stone—except for his date of death, of course. Preaching to the end . . . and beyond.

---

138. Referring to the 1881 eruption, Coan writes, "Visitors to the stream were now frequent; and the crater on Mauna Loa was reached, on a third attempt, by the Rev. Mr. Baker, of Hilo." Coan, *Life*, 329.

139. William B. Olseson headed up the Lyman school. "Mr. Lyman, feeling obliged through declining health to resign his office as Principal, the Rev. W. B. Oleson was appointed in September 1878 as his successor." Coan, *Life*, 28.

140. Isaac Watts, 1709.

141. Sarah Flower Adams, 1841.

142. Margaret Mackay, 1832.

143. Coan, *Memorial Volume*, 204–05.

TITUS COAN.
FEBRUARY 1, 1801.
DECEMBER 1, 1882.
HE LIVED BY FAITH.
HE STILL LIVES.
BELIEVEST THOU THIS?
JOHN 11 26[144]

---

144. Coan, *Memorial Volume*, 248. See also Paragraph IX of Coan's Last Will and Testament, in "Legacy" chapter.

17

Legacy

"His name and life are identified with God's marvelous work of grace in these islands, the overthrow of pagan cruelty and superstition, the spread of Christian truth and love, the upbuilding of the institutions of piety and philanthropy."[1]

"He loved to preach the gospel. He was no ordinary preacher, but was often truly eloquent, in both English and Hawaiian. As a platform speaker few were more ready and eloquent.

"Some men are distinguished in their public career, but fail when viewed in the home circle and by their neighbors. We believe it was the good fortune of our departed brother to appear at his very best at home and among his familiar friends. He was most considerate and thoughtful of those with whom he came in familiar intercourse. How often have we heard guests refer to the home of the missionary, Coan, in Hilo, and have there ourselves experienced his kindness. I am happy to bear my testimony to the purity, refinement and ideal beauty and excellency of that home." It was one of the homes "so enthusiastically described by the Rev. Dr. Chaney in his [1879] volume entitled *Aloha*."[2]

OBITUARIES

News of Papa Coan's death spread as fast as 1882 and 1883 transportation and communication capabilities would allow. By foot and word of mouth the people of the Big Island became aware of the homegoing of the Apostle to the Sandwich Islands. Ships would carry the news to other islands. Steamers took written news to San Francisco where it would be telegraphed across the United States of America. Obituaries appeared in many newspapers and journals.

---

1. Coan, *Memorial Volume*, 214. Undated letter from Rev. C. M. Hyde, DD (President of the North Pacific Theological Institute), to Mrs. Coan.

2. George Leonard Chaney, *Alo'ha!*, Coan, *Memorial Volume*, 216. Rev. Samuel C. Damon, DD.

Perhaps the first published obituary appropriately appeared in the Honolulu based newspaper *The Friend* on January 1, 1883, still edited by Titus's long-time friend Samuel Damon. Found under the heading "Died," Coan's entry is the longest of the listed group. It begins simply with, "At Hilo, Hawaii, December 1, Rev. Titus Coan, aged eighty-one years and ten months." Sharing sadness and listing him as a pioneer missionary even though he arrived fifteen years after the first Pioneer Company arrived, it notes that he has passed away. "It is with sincere regret that we publish the death of Rev. Titus Coan of Hilo, one of the pioneer missionaries of these Islands. He passed away at the ripe old age of eighty-one."

Damon notes the date and place of his birth and points out Coan's teaching school for five years. His entering Auburn Seminary is mentioned along with his becoming "a licensed minister of the gospel in 1833." It makes reference to Coan going with "a friend"[3] to Patagonia, as well as Coan's return home, marriage to Fidelia Church, and departure for the Hawaiian Islands.

Damon precisely notes the Coans' arrival in Honolulu on June 6, 1835. He writes of their arrival in Hilo, "where they ever after lived, and where both now lie in the long sleep of death." Reference is made to his two visits to the Marquesas Islands "to inspect the missions there" and an 1870 revisiting of "his old home in America."[4] Damon notes the date of Fidelia's death, "after his return from the States." He provides the specific date of Coan's marriage to "Miss Lydia Bingham of Honolulu,[5] who survives him." Damon points out that for many years Coan was "a contributor to several of the leading American scientific and other magazines"[6] and reminds the readers of Coan's two books. Damon concludes with evidence that Titus Coan suffered a stroke and the sadness experienced by all who knew him. "In August [sic][7] last he was stricken with paralysis, and his death, though not unexpected, has filled the hearts of his friends with sorrow."[8]

Four days later, the publication that thirty years later would be called "the paper of record"[9] printed "The Late Dr. Coan. Brief Sketch of the Life of an Old Missionary." The unnamed *New York Times* obituary writer pens a sympathetic rendering of Coan's life. It even has some Christian overtones. While it gets some facts wrong, the article does give the gist of Coan's life.

3. William Arms.

4. While he did visit Killingworth in late 1870, they were in America from early May 1870 through April of 1871.

5. Did Lydia return to live in Honolulu the same month of Titus's death? It would appear so in this obituary, meaning she worked on the *Memorial Volume* with materials she took to Honolulu. If such was the case, she would return to Hilo for the second, full memorial service in late March.

6. That would include, among others, *The Missionary Herald* and *The Advocate of Peace*.

7. In Coan, *Memorial Volume,* 198 and 200, Lydia indicates that the medical event occurred on September 16.

8. *The Friend* 40.1 (January 1, 1883) 5.

9. Wikipedia, "The New York Times."

It begins with a summary sentence that refers to a preliminary death notice published the previous day in the *Times*.[10] "The Rev. Dr. Titus Coan, whose death at his home in Hilo, Sandwich Islands, on December 1 last, was reported in yesterday's *TIMES*, was one of the oldest missionaries in point of service rendered that ever bore the cross to heathen lands." The writer notes Coan's forty-eight years of service and as "regarded by the natives with a feeling of affection and veneration."

The *Times* obituary gets the date of the medical episode correct and characterizes it as "a severe stroke of paralysis." It is not completely accurate in its claim that Coan recovered enough to take exercise every day until the day of his death. "He rallied from this attack, and became so much improved that he was able to take daily exercise in the open a[i]r up to the very day of his death." Funeral services are correctly listed as being "held on the morning of Sunday, December 3, in the native church at Hilo," with the added detail that the services "were held in both the Hawaiian and English languages."

The article mentions Coan's age at the time of his death, then backs up to give his date and place and birth, followed by a summary of his life. Perhaps referring to Titus's autobiography, the writer says that Coan's "father was a farmer, and after attending the village school until he had reached the age of twelve years, Titus, who was the youngest of seven sons, was put to work on the farm to aid his father[11] . . . He showed an earnest inclination to continue his studies, however, and private tutors were engaged to teach him at his home."

In contrast to *The Friend*, *The Times* indicates that Coan taught school for eleven years.[12] *The Times* obituary writer summarizes his graduating with "highest honors" from Auburn Theological Seminary, time in Patagonia, marriage to Fidelia, sailing from Boston on the "ship *Hellespont* for the Sandwich Islands. From this date the life work of Dr. Coan began. He was stationed with his wife at Hilo, and in addition to preaching the gospel to the natives as a missionary he was obliged to act as a physician of the town for fourteen years of his labors."

The article points out that he began his work at Hilo by learning the Hawaiian language. After "he had mastered this his success in making converts was wonderful." Commenting on Coan's personality, the writer reveals that Coan was of "a singularly mild and affectionate disposition," leading him to win "the confidence of the Hawaiians at the beginning."

Crediting the co-labors of Fidelia, who "established a school for girls," the two are said to have "succeeded in converting 12,113 of the native men and women at the

---

10. Perhaps news arrived by telegraph on January 2 and the writer took a day or two to gather information on Coan.

11. Perhaps as part of the times, no mention is made of Titus's mother, to whom Titus lovingly and with praise refers in Coan, *Life*, 1.

12. Based on a review of the first chapter of Coan, *Life*, Coan taught for five years in New York.

beginning of 1880."¹³ The writer wrongly avers that Coan established the Hilo church, when the church, though small, pre-existed Coan's arrival by some years. Wrongly indicating that it was a "short time" within which Coan had trained "missionaries among their own people," the article next has Coan in America for six months instead of the actual eleven.

The article concludes by noting Coan's Renaissance man and revivalist natures. "In addition to his missionary labors, he added a great deal to the knowledge of the world in regard to volcanic eruptions, by his contributions to the *American Journal of Science* and *The Missionary Herald*. He also published a book entitled *A Life in Hawaii*, in which he gave an interesting history of his experiences in the island."¹⁴

The next known published obituary is in the Hawaiian language. Entitled "Ka Nupepa Kukoa,"¹⁵ there follows capital letters that conclude with "REV. TITO KOANA" and the word for "gospel."¹⁶ The last sentence is "E hoolahaia keia mau olelo hooholo ma ka olelo Hawai a me ka olelo Haole. Ma ke kauoha a ka Papa Hawaii."¹⁷

The longest Titus Coan obituary is found in the February 1883 *Missionary Herald*. By this time the *Herald* has very clean print and includes a fine photograph-like sketch of Titus Coan. After the centered "THE REV. TITUS COAN," there is an asterisk that refers to the bottom of the page with a paragraph summary of his life: "Titus Coan, son of Gaylord and Tamza (Nettleton) Coan, born at Killingsworth [sic], Conn., February 1, 1801; united with the church in Riga, NY, March 2, 1828; graduated at Auburn Theological Seminary, 1833; ordained in Park Street Church, Boston, July 28, 1833; on a voyage of exploration to Patagonia, 1833–34; married Fidelia Church, of Riga, NY, November 3, 1834 (she died September 29, 1872); embarked at Boston for Sandwich Islands, December 5, 1834, arriving at Honolulu, June 6, 1835; reached Hilo, Hawaii, in August, 1835, where he lived as pastor until his death, December 1, 1882. Mr. Coan married Miss Lydia Bingham, daughter of the Rev. Hiram Bingham, October 13, 1873. His widow and four children, two sons and two daughters, survive him."

Returning to the main body of the obituary, the writer speaks of Coan's death as a "veteran missionary" passing "from his earthly service to the rest and reward of heaven." The article notes that "his life was more remarkable for what was accomplished through it than for its length." He is held up as without peer. "No pastor of modern times—perhaps none of any time—has been permitted to receive into the Church of Christ a larger number of persons on their confession of faith, than did this

---

13. It is not known whence this statistic came.
14. "Brief Sketch of an Old Missionary," *New York Times* January 5, 1883, np.
15. Pukui, *Hawaiian Dictionary*, 184.
16. "Euanelio."

17 Google translation provided by Ed Coan: "These resolutions shall be published in the Hawaiian and English languages. By order of the Hawaiian Board." Obituary in Hawaiian from Papakilo database. "Ka Nupepa Kukkoa," Papakilo Database.

pastor of Hilo. Under his leadership over twelve thousand souls have avouched the Lord to be their God."

The second paragraph begins with his birth and moves forward. Characterizing him as the "son of a plain Connecticut farm, Titus Coan enjoyed no advantages in early life beyond those found in a Christian home and in common schools, yet he taught in these schools at various times during a period of eight or ten years." Once again there is uncertainty as to the number of years he taught.

The article notes that despite his relation to the evangelist Asahel Nettleton and "often deeply impressed by his preaching, he did not feel assured of his hope in Christ until he was twenty-seven years of age." While no mention is made of Charles Finney, the turning point in his deciding on the matter of his salvation was "a revival which occurred in the school he was teaching, during the winter of 1829–30."

Entering Auburn Seminary and journeying to Patagonia[18] are noted. He "undertook and prosecuted with devotion and efficiency" his trip to Patagonia. "But finding that part of the world wholly unpromising for missionary effort, he returned to the United States." With his wife he "formed a part of the sixth re-enforcement for the Sandwich Island Mission."

The year of arrival in Honolulu and Hilo are noted. Words about the parish are described along the lines of the autobiography. "Up and down this line he passed, for years on foot, there being neither houses nor roads, the people often coming about him in crowds to listen to the word of life."

From 1836 through 1839 the islands "witnessed a wonderful outpouring of the Spirit," and thousands were converted to Christ. Gone is any "hasty admission" to membership controversy. The July 1838 date of 1,705 baptisms based on profession of faith took place "after prolonged and careful scrutiny."

The opening of the paragraph at the top of the second page of the obituary reads a bit like John commenting on how all the libraries cannot contain all that Jesus did and taught [John 21:25]. "There is not room in these pages to give even a summary of the history of the succeeding years, which were marked by patient and devoted toil for the flock he loved and that loved him." The reader is referred to Coan's autobiography.

"During the last year, as far as his strength would permit, he visited among his people, but finding it difficult to mount his horse and dismount, he would ride through the various districts, and summoning a little company by his clear-ringing 'Aloha!' he would carefully inquire after their bodily and spiritual state."

Noting his partial and temporary recovery during his last weeks, the writer notes that "since he was quite unable to walk, that a reclining chair be arranged so that it could be easily borne by attendants; and in this way he went first of all to the church, where he rested in silence in the aisle before the sacred desk,[19] a spot so inexpressibly

---

18. A cross at the bottom of the page writes an "interesting account of these explorations is given in his volume entitled *Adventures in Patagonia*."

19. Pulpit.

dear to him, and afterwards from day to day he visited such neighbors as he could reach, giving his counsels and benedictions."

The author retells Coan's last day in a way similar to Lydia's bridge passage in the *Memorial Volume*.[20] "He was being lifted into his chair preparatory to one of these visits, just at noontime of December 1, when the messenger came to call him instantly into the presence of the King."

Reference is made to two ABCFM representatives, "Messrs. Hallenbeck and Forbes," who made an evangelistic tour of Hawaii in August of 1882. The eulogy writer notes that Coan's "constant attendance upon these special daily services, together with his anxiety for souls, told upon his health." Maintaining the positive theme that Lydia publically kept, the writer proclaims that Coan "rejoiced in the work and blessed God that he had been spared to see it."

In a way similar to the *Memorial Volume*, the writer relates Coan's focus on the next world and the tenderness of his nature. "During the last year, as well as during his protracted period of invalidism, he was manifestly preparing for the better world. One who stood nearest to him[21] writes: 'His saintly patience was wonderful. His graces ripened, and his conversation was more and more in heaven. Always gentle and courteous, it seemed as if his heart overflowed with love. I noted this in his prayers. Often as he prayed, deep emotion for a moment overcame him as some view of the Saviour's great love filled his soul, and he asked that he might be like him.'"

He prayed for everyone. "His prayers were wonderful for breadth of thought, going out for all peoples and for every righteous cause. When asked during his sickness if he had any fears, he answered, 'When I look at myself, I see no reason why I should be in heaven. When I look at Jesus, I see such a Saviour I have no fears, not one, not one!'"

The *Missionary Herald* eulogy concludes with the ongoing positive theme of the article, bordering on the hagiographic. "And so a triumphant life was crowned by a triumphant death. Among all who have known 'Father' Coan there cannot be one who will question his right to use the memorable words of Paul, as he did in humble tone but with solemn earnestness shortly before his death: 'The time of my departure is at hand. I have fought a good fight, I have finished my course, I have kept the faith: henceforth there is laid up for me a crown of righteousness' [2 Tim 4:6–8]. The answering utterance of a great multitude will be: 'They that be wise shall shine as the brightness of the firmament; and they that turn many to righteousness as the stars for ever and ever'"[22] [Dan 12:3].

The three summarized English obituaries, one secular with strong Christian overtones, the other two in Christian publications,[23] provide a three-strand strong

---

20. Coan, *Memorial Volume*, 204.
21. Could this be anyone but Lydia and perhaps a letter she sent to the ABCFM offices in Boston?
22. *Missionary Herald* 89.2 (February 1883) 48–49.
23. Both missions related.

[Eccl 4:12] look at the life and legacy of Titus Coan. His legacy is further solidified by the memorial service held in Hilo almost two months after *The Missionary Herald* obituary.

MEMORIAL SERVICE

Titus Coan died on December 1, 1882. Two days later on a Sunday the worship service was a funeral, with a committal held afterwards. Many felt a desire for more than what took place that day. "As Mr. Coan's Hilo friends desired another occasion when in some public way they might still witness to the esteem and affection in which his memory was cherished, they held a Memorial Service in Haili Church on the twenty-fifth of March, 1883."[24]

William B. Oleson provided an overview and summary of this memorial service in the April 2, 1883, issue of *The Friend*. Under the heading of "Communicated," Oleson wrote that a "service in commemoration of the life and labors of the late Rev. Titus Coan, DD,[25] was held in Hilo church, March 25, the foreign and native churches uniting in the service. The order of exercises was quite full and of so interesting a character that the great audience sat quietly and patently [sic] for three and a half hours to the close."

Oleson proceeds to indicate each paper read and speech given. "The two papers prepared respectively by Dr. S[amuel] C. Damon[26] and Professor W[illiam] D. Alexander[27] were read by Rev. W. B. Olesen; as were two pages written[,] one by Mrs. Bingham [II],[28] and one by Mrs. Coan.[29] The letters from abroad were by Rev. Dr. Clark of the American Board, Dr. Goodwin of Chicago, Prof. Bingham[30] [sic] of Harvard, and Mr. Halsey of Connecticut.[31] Letters were also read from Rev. Hiram Bingham [II],[32] Rev.

---

24. Coan, *Memorial Volume*, 204.

25. "Doctor of Divinity." See honorary Doctor of Divinity degree granted while in the United States in the trip to America chapter.

26. Coan, *Memorial Volume*, 215–17.

27. Coan, *Memorial Volume*, 217–21.

28. Coan, *Memorial Volume*, 214–15.

29. Not found in *Memorial Volume*. Not in due to modesty? Personal nature of content? Combination of the two?

30. Should be William T. Brigham. Coan, *Memorial Volume*, 206–07.

31. Those four letters not in *Memorial Volume*.

32. Coan, *Memorial Volume*, 214–15.

S[ereno] E[dwards] Bishop,[33] Rev. Mr. [Lorenzo] Lyons,[34] Dr. Lowell Smith,[35] Rev. D[wight] Baldwin,[36] and Hon. S[amuel Northrup] Castle."[37]

Oleson notes what is already indicated in a footnote, namely the letter from Titus written to Bishop. "A most valuable feature of the programme was a copy of a letter written by Rev. Dr. Coan a few months before his death." His letter "seemed like his last word on the religious condition of Hawaii nei."[38]

Oleson continues with his summary of the service. He notes that a "Memorial poem[39] of great merit written by Mrs. M. C. Kittredge[40] enhanced the interest of the occasion." He continues on with other letters read, as well as in-person addresses. "Letters from Hon. Kahane, and others,[41] were read by Hon. J. Nawahi. Addressed in English and Hawaiian by D. B. Lyman, Judge D[avid] H[oward] Hitchcock,[42] Hon. J. E. Austin, Dr. C. H. Wetmore,[43] Hon. J. Nawahi, ended the service."

In his will, Titus Coan asked that he have a "modest marble slab."[44] Oleson notes that at the Memorial Service it "was announced that about three hundred dollars had

---

33. Coan, *Memorial Volume*, 221–23, including Coan letter, December 24, 1881, Coan, *Memorial Volume*, 223–26.

34. Coan, *Memorial Volume*, 226–27.

35. Judd, *Missionary Album*, 178; and Forbes et al., *Partners in Change*, 564–70. He and Abigail arrived with the Sixth Company in 1833. He served in various ways, including as pastor of the Second Church (Kaumakapili). "He retired from the pastorate in 1869 but still labored in various ways for the welfare of the Hawaiians for the rest of his life." He died in 1891 at the age of eighty-eight. Mentioned in Coan, *Life*, 238 and 243.

36. Judd, *Missionary Album*, 36–37; Forbes et al., *Partners in Change*, 91–94. Member of the Fourth Company with Charlotte. Experienced partial paralysis in 1868. Died in 1886 at the age of eighty-seven. Mentioned in Coan, *Life*, 231.

37. Judd, *Missionary Album*, 59; and Forbes et al., *Partners in Change*, 256–60. Member of Eighth Company, arriving in 1837. In 1851 he started Castle and Cooke. Died 1894 at the age of eighty-five.

38. Pastor Brian Welsh indicates in March 2013 emails to the author that "nei" is a specifier that is used for emphasis. In this case could it be equivalent to an exclamation point?

39. Coan, *Memorial Volume*, 236–37.

40. Wife of one of the three doctors who attended Titus Coan during his last illness. See previous chapter.

41. Perhaps two of the other Hawaiian letters were from Paakaula, "a Native Parishioner," Coan, *Memorial Volume*, 227–28; and Ili, "another native parishioner," Coan, *Memorial Volume*, 228–29.

42. Judd, *Missionary Album*, 115. Oldest child of Harvey and Rebecca Howard Hitchcock, who arrived with the Fifth Company in 1832. Judge Howard (1831–99) had a son who was born in Hilo and bore the same name and therefore went by D. Howard. D. Howard (1861–1943) "was an American painter of the Volcano School" and was known for his depictions of Hawai'i. The Wikipedia article includes a digital representation of his oil painting entitled "Halemaumau, Lake of Fire," 1888. Wikipedia, "D. Howard Hitchcock."

43. Compare Coan, *Memorial Volume*, 229–31, with material found in Wetmore Lyman House document.

44. See below.

been subscribed and paid towards a monument to be placed in the cemetery to the memory of the deceased missionary."[45]

Oleson provides a very helpful overview of the service, including the listing of names and words not found in the *Memorial Volume*. What follows are some quotations from the service from the *Memorial Volume*.[46] Before presenting voluminous material, Lydia concludes her bridge section with the following words: "Portions of papers and letters read at that time, together with some of later dates, are gathered into this *thesaurus*, in the hope that to many who knew and loved the friend thus mourned and honored, these tributes may be valuable."[47]

This book with the "thesaurus" provides material from some people not mentioned by Oleson.[48] These *Memorial Volume* only contributors include: Rev. J. R. Boyd,[49] Mrs. Edward E. Waters,[50] S. J. Humphrey, E. K. Alden,[51] and C. M. Hyde.[52] Coan's legacy is moved forward by Lydia's chapter entitled "In Memoriam."

Chapter XIV begins with a poem:

> When the weary ones we love
> Enter on their rest above,
> Seems the earth so poor and vast,
> All our life joy overcast?
> Hush! Be every murmur dumb,
> It is only 'till He come.[53]

The first letter in the chapter is from William T. Brigham[54] of Harvard to the Reverend E. P. Baker. He covers some of the areas most of the speakers will discuss:

---

45. *The Friend* 40.4 (April 2, 1883) 27.

46. Once again, to understand Titus Coan as fully as possible, the reader is encouraged to purchase via Print on Demand both his *Life* and Lydia's *Memorial Volume* with many letters from and journal entries from Titus Coan, as well as thirty-one pages based on the memorial service and eleven pages after that.

47. Coan, *Memorial Volume*, 206.

48. It appears that everything from 206 through 237 was received and/or read at the Memorial Service. It is possible that Lydia tucked some letters in to this section that were not read during the service, since it was so long as it was.

49. Coan, *Memorial Volume*, 208.

50. Coan, *Memorial Volume*, 209–10. Titus and Fidelia's daughter, Sarah Eliza, 1843–1916, Judd, *Missionary Album*, 71.

51. Coan, *Memorial Volume*, 212–13. Corresponding Secretary of the ABCFM, Boston, January 30, 1883. To "Miss Bingham."

52. Coan, *Memorial Volume*, 213–14. President of the North Pacific Theological Institute. Coan, *Life*, 251. Coan characterizes him as "a minister and pastor of ripe experience."

53. Coan, *Memorial Volume*, 206. Verse two of "'Till He Come," lyrics by Edward H. Bickerstaff, 1861. See 1 Cor 4:5.

54. "William Tufts Brigham (1841–1926) was an American geologist, botanist, ethnologist and the first director of the Bernice P. Bishop Museum in Honolulu ... He taught biology for a year at Harvard and over the next dozen years lectured and published books and articles on classical art, volcanology,

Coan's kindness, his being a mentor, his ministry transcending geographic bounds, and his scientific contributions, especially in the area of volcanoes. "I look back to those very happy days when he was my mentor in exploring Puna and Kilauea, and my kind host in the Emerald Bower; to the later years when he was aiding science so effectually by his wise correspondence; to the visit he made me in my own home; to our last meeting two years ago in Hilo; and to the last letter I had from him so full of kindness and love."

Brigham continues with a common verse stated at such gatherings, "Can we doubt that he has heard the blessed words, 'Well done, thou good and faithful servant, enter into the joy of thy Lord?'" [Matt 25:23]. Brigham also notes that no "narrow bounds confined his work, and while acting as a true bishop to his flock, and a wise citizen and friend, he yet found time to do more for science in watching and recording the wonderful fiery work of Kilauea and Mokuaweoweo than all other men united. Today, wherever the phenomena of volcanoes are studied, the name of Titus Coan is familiar, and no work on the Hawaiian volcanoes would have much value that did not quote largely from his reports. Science will enroll his name among the illustrious dead of the departed year, and in the name of my fellow scientists here I hasten to offer a tribute to his memory."

That tribute request was as follows: "Will you lay upon the new-made grave a wreath of maile, as I would do if present, as an offering from me, who loved, honored and never doubted Titus Coan? May its leaves be a token that here, so many thousand miles away, we will keep his memory green."[55]

Sarah Coan Waters writes as a grieving daughter who appears to have inherited her father and mother's pen-painting abilities: "There are many incidents of my childhood connected with Father which I can never forget, but the present sorrow is too great to think of much but the magnitude of our loss. That which stands out most clearly and brightly before me now is his whole character, to which I would reverently and affectionately pay a few words of tribute. As a father he was firm, but his firmness was so tempered of gentleness born of love, as to 'cast out fear' [1 John 4:18]. Not a day passed without some expression of his deep affection. It might be a bright smile, and a gest about his little bird, made to a little girl swinging in the top of a guava tree, or a snatched kiss as the same little girl flew past him in the romp of a game. In childhood, girlhood and womanhood to think of him was to say to one's self, 'Papa loves me.' And to the boundless love of his nature I think you, his townsmen, can bear witness. 'With malice toward none, with charity for all'[56] might fittingly be his epitaph, for it was the sin and not the sinner against which he battled.

---

geology, seismology, and botany ... Brigham authored forty-six articles and monographs on Hawaiian botany, geology, and material culture such as mat weaving, tapa cloth, feather work, and stone and wood carvings." Wikipedia, "William Tufts Brigham."

55. Coan, *Memorial Volume*, 206–07.
56. From Lincoln's Second Inaugural Address.

Legacy

"I can remember no angry word, no impatience amid all the trials of life, nor even a complaint that life had its hardships, of which he endured many in his long career." She concludes with a childhood incident that illustrates what he wished to have on his tomb. "He was endeavoring to make clear the meaning of perfect faith, and wished to illustrate it, as was his custom, by a practical application. I was to stand on the top of a high wardrobe and jump, without injury, he assured me, into his arms. It was some time before his affectionate coaxings and promises of safety could overcome to my mind the obstacle of that hard floor beneath onto which I might fall. But I finally jumped unhurt, and the lesson on faith went home with lasting force.

"He had faith, hope, charity; but the greatest of these was charity"[57] [1 Cor 13:13].

S. J. Humphrey rejoices that some of Coan's last work was in assisting an evangelistic outreach. "It is a very delightful thought that a life which had witnessed such scenes of revival should have given its last labors in special efforts for lost souls, and that in the midst of the toils of a season of refreshing from the Most High the tense bow should have broken. There was a divine and delightful fitness that the spirit of the aged warrior should ascend to its reward from the battle-field where the gracious conflict was still raging, and where such amazing triumphs of infinite love had been achieved."

He gives his benediction to those gathered at the memorial service. "I trust that your memorial service will be one of great spiritual profit, and that in rendering due respect to the friend and father departed, there will come fresh honor to the blessed King and Lord whom it was his highest ambition to serve."[58]

Lydia shares the following specific memories from her brother Hiram Bingham II. "I can never forget the great hospitality of Mr. Coan when I have visited Hilo. I cannot forget his cordial manner and pleasant smiles; his deep interest in the foreign work in Micronesia; his thorough work as a delegate of the Hawaiian Board, in the Marquesas in 1867; his zeal in collecting funds for missionary purposes; his promptness in meeting his appointments; his regular attendance at the annual meetings of the Association in Honolulu, and his great liberality. Did my memory serve me well, I would go back forty-five years to the days when Brother Coan's words of love to the mission children thrilled our young ears, and made us realize the love of Jesus, and the duty we were under of giving our hearts to him in our childhood. Will the fading past re-appear in vivid distinctness when we drink of the waters of life above?"[59]

Samuel Damon, long-time friend, pastor to seamen, and publisher of *The Friend* weighs in next. He puts preaching to the Hawaiians first, as Coan indicates in his various writings, while wishing he could spend more time with sailors and nautical officers. "The grand business of Mr. Coan's life has been to preach the gospel among Hawaiians, and right nobly has he performed his life-work. But he had broad sympathies,

---

57. Coan, *Memorial Volume*, 210–11.
58. Coan, *Memorial Volume*, 211.
59. Coan, *Memorial Volume*, 214–15.

which led him to labor efficiently for his fellow-men of all races, so far as they were brought under his influence. For many years he has been a most efficient seamen's chaplain. Assisted by the Rev. Mr. Lyman, a chaplaincy was sustained at Hilo, by their voluntary, well-directed efforts, which for usefulness equaled almost any chaplaincy in any other part of the world."

Damon drills down in this area of his expertise as it relates to Titus Coan and his legacy that lasts for eternity in the lives of many. "Upon this subject I can speak with great freedom and assurance, for during the past forty years I have been in the most intimate correspondence with Mr. Coan. I feel sure the spiritual interests of seamen attached to the whaling fleet and vessels of war could not have been more thoughtfully cared for if a chaplain had been sent out from America or England for this special field of labor; yet this extra service was discharged with the most hearty cheerful consideration. Many masters, officers, and seamen must have good reason to bless God to all eternity that they touched at Hilo in their long voyages, and came under the happy influence of Mr. Coan and other resident missionaries at that port."

Damon next addresses Coan's abilities as a preacher and as a family man.[60] He begins his peroration with a Latin phrase, moves to put him on the Olympus of other modern missionaries, and ends with a poetic quotation. "In contemplating his life and character I am forcibly reminded of the old Roman saying, '*Mens sana in corpora sano*.'[61] With these he was right royally endowed by the Author of his being, and when we reflect that to these were added a good education, a naturally poetic temperament, and an emotional, spiritual nature, it is apparent that Rev. Titus Coan stands forth as a man of no ordinary abilities and endowments. He will be remembered as one of the noble men who have in modern times been leaders in the world's evangelization. Such men may have been sustained by some local or national missionary society or organization, but they belong to the church universal, the catholic church. Carey, Williams, Livingston, Pattison, and Moffat head the list of English Protestant missionaries, while Judson,[62] Mills, Goodell, Bingham, Thurston, and others lead off in the noble phalanx of those who have left America.

"Among those noble men our friend who has just passed away will have his allotted place.

> Servant of Christ, well done,
>   Praise be thy new employ;
> And, while eternal ages run,
>   Rest in thy Savior's joy."[63]

60. See quotation at the beginning of this chapter.

61. "A healthy mind in a healthy body."

62. All five Americans listed were affiliated with the American Board, though Adoniram Judson became a Baptist on his way with the first Board group. He would go on to establish a Baptist mission in Burma.

63. "Servant of God, Well Done!," James Montgomery, 1819, in Coan, *Memorial Volume*, 215–17.

Professor W. D. Alexander mostly rehearses Coan's achievements with regard to volcano observations and writings. "The sublime volcanic phenomena which he witnessed were to him but manifestations of the power and glory of the Creator, and with the inspired poet of old he would exclaim, 'He looketh upon the earth and it trembleth; he toucheth the hills and they smoke; he uttered his voice and the earth melted. The hills melted like wax at the presence of the Lord' [Ps 104:32].

"Although he had not enjoyed any special scientific training, and made no pretensions to the character of a professional geologist, he was a good observer and of sound judgment; while for physical vigor and endurance he had few equals."

Professor Alexander suggests that Coan could have been a member of an elite international mountain climbing organization: "As a mountain climber he would have qualified for admission into the Alpine Club."[64] He ties in Coan's physical prowess with a similar excellence in describing his trips and observations. "In addition to these qualities he had a natural gift of language, and his descriptions are remarkably vivid and true to nature."

Professor Alexander concludes by putting the focus on the overriding purpose and legacy of Titus Coan's life: saving souls. "But these were only episodes in a most laborious and useful life. Our departed friend thought little of them in comparison with his main object, to bring immortal beings to a saving knowledge of Jesus Christ, and to lead them gradually upward to higher stages in Christian civilization. It is this part of his work which be lasting as eternity."[65]

Samuel Castle notes that he first made the acquaintance of "Mr. Coan in the spring of 1828. We were both employed in adjoining stores in Western New York, and we boarded at the same house, sitting at the same table." He met him again when he passed through the same place on his way to Auburn Seminary. He knew of his being "a most acceptable and successful worker and assistant in some of the great revivals which at that time so largely blessed Western New York." He knew of Titus's Patagonia expedition.

The two met again when he and his wife Angeline arrived in Honolulu in 1837. "You can imagine the deeper interest which I felt in renewing, under such changed circumstances and in a foreign land, the acquaintance begun nine years earlier in our far-off native country.

"Here I found him engaged in that loved life-work[66] from which he never ceased till the message from the Master came, bidding him 'come up higher' [Rev 11:12]. Castle also explains that Coan "possessed fine conversational powers, and spoke and wrote acceptably with equal facility on sacred and secular subjects, as those well know

---

64. The first Alpine Club, founded in London in 1857, was once described as: "a club of English gentlemen devoted to mountaineering, first of all in the Alps, members of which have successfully addressed themselves to attempts of the kind on loftier mountains." Wikipedia, "Alpine Club."

65. Coan, *Memorial Volume*, 218–20.

66. The Hawaiian Great Awakening had begun by this time.

who have read the productions from his facile pen." Castle shares about Coan's volcanic observations and writings. He concludes with, "He fascinated men, as I have occasion to know, who have heard so many testify of him. He had unusually diversified powers, but he consecrated them all to Christ."[67]

Sereno Edwards Bishop summaries the "chief portions" of a letter "the beloved Father Coan" had sent him, dated December 24, 1881. Particular "circumstances led him to make what was to me a very wonderful revelation of his inner experience in preaching the word of salvation. Bishop also addresses, however indirectly, opponents to the intensity of the revival.

It "is to be observed that he asserts an intense and habitual consciousness during the earlier period of his ministry to the Hawaiians, of a divine *power* resting upon him in speaking the word." Referring to the Great Awakening, Bishop writes, "To those who witnessed his speech in those days, or who were familiar with the wonderful effects produced, such an assertion will not seem strange or improbable, unless they are disbelievers in the Savior's promise of such power of the Holy Ghost to his messengers."

Bishop shares reflections similar to those found in his autobiography, namely what he observed as a child during the Great Awakening and after. Bishop, who in addition to Coan "came under the stringent intellectual and spiritual force of Finney, and felt the piercing power of the Spirit's sword, in his hands, but never have known a winning power of love in any preacher like that of the spiritual father of our childhood."

Before introducing Coan's letter into the memorial record, Bishop provides this paragraph: "God has vouchsafed many peculiar mercies to the people of the Hawaiian Islands, both temporal and spiritual, to which they owe their present high vantage ground of liberty and prosperity. It seems to me that we may estimate as among the most remarkable of these mercies God's gift to the Hawaiian people of a man of such extraordinary evangelistic power as Titus Coan."[68]

Lorenzo Lyons, Coan's close friend and co-laborer in the Big Island field of revival, provided material about his dear friend—both his prodigious correspondence and protean labors. "After Mr. Coan reached his location at Hilo in August 1835, our correspondence commenced and was continued sometimes weekly and sometimes less frequently until that fatal stroke of paralysis terminated it. O, how I wept when the tidings came that I must lose such a correspondent! In the time of the great revival his letters were frequent, and his soul was all on fire, kindled by the Holy Spirit. They were very cheering and very stimulating to me. How earnestly he preached and prayed and wrestled in prayer for the salvation of souls. How he moved vast assemblies by his fervent and overwhelming preaching and praying. There was work enough for two preachers and pastors in the large field of Hilo and Puna—yes, more than enough. Yet Brother Coan, being a strong young man and full of missionary fire, thought he could

---

67. Coan, *Memorial Volume*, 220–21.
68. Coan, *Memorial Volume*, 221–23.

do the work of two pastors and preachers and thus allow Brother Lyman to devote himself more exclusively to school-teaching."

Later, Lyons returns to correspondence, then moves on to his humility. "Brother Coan's correspondence was extensive, embracing the world. O! ye recipients of his cheering, comforting, soul-stirring letters, join with me in mourning over the loss of this prince of correspondents.

"Though he was the pastor of the largest church in the world, he was not proud of it. Though he received the degree of DD, he wished to be addressed simply as Rev. T. Coan. Though a very holy man, in his letters to me he would express himself as a great sinner, and, if saved at all, it would be by grace."[69]

The *Memorial Volume* material on the memorial service next turns to two letters written by Hawaiian members of Coan's church.[70] "Before giving expression to any testimony relating to him, I would express my great love for Mr. Coan, a true worker for Christ, a faithful laborer in the garden of the Lord throughout the districts of Hilo and Puna; and in his separation from us we all grieve in the loss of a laborer for the kingdom of Christ in Hawaii.

"He was strong, without discouragement, in the work of the Lord, with all meekness, content, and deep reverence. He treated with kindness the poor, the afflicted, the sick; and to all he was constant in the preaching of the kingdom of God. I can see that he did his work without the desire of man's approbation, but was strong in the work of the Lord even to the end. I am sure that we of Puna as well as of Hilo are under a great debt for Mr. Coan's instruction in Christian uprightness, as also as regards many other good works. And I believe that some of us who have gone before have found the life eternal in the heavens, and that they now are meeting Mr. Coan, rejoicing greatly. I desire that I may die the death of the righteous."[71]

Ili picks up on the theme of uprightness and being just. He continues through the physical challenges of travel in the early days, on to his preaching and his good works, concluding with Coan now being in heaven. "He was an upright man before God and man, and his works were just. He was a faithful minister of the great God, and his thoughts were ever of him up to the time of his death. He was full of love and gentleness, and his hand was ever ready to clasp the hands of the men, women and children of Puna.

"During the first years of his pastorate, while the roads were exceedingly bad, with great patience he made his journeys through Puna on foot, instead of on horseback.

"He showed to the people of Puna his very great love for them in that he kept up his intercourse with them during all of his long residence in Hilo.

---

69. Coan, *Memorial Volume*, 226–28.

70. Paakula and 'I'i. NB: Forbes et al., *Partners in Change* writes about two with that name, but both died well before Titus Coan died.

71. Coan, *Memorial Volume*, 227–28.

"Through his preaching of the word of God, doubtless those that believed in Jesus found life. I doubt not that because of his labors in turning souls to Jesus, he himself has found life everlasting in heaven.

"These are a few of my thoughts of him, but there remain untold many of his good works. 'Blessed are the poor in spirit, for theirs is the kingdom of heaven' [Matt 5:3]. Mr. Coan is there."[72]

The two Hawaiians are followed by a Hilo friend of over thirty years, one of the three doctors who attended Coan in his last days—Dr. Charles Wetmore. After mentioning how much while still in America he read Coan's letters in *The Missionary Herald* and how his father-in-law always read Coan's letters and reports first and asked his son-in-law to tell Coan "I wish there was a multitude of other missionaries like him." Wetmore talks about how Coan ministered to "the souls and bodies of his parishioners until Wetmore arrived. He speaks of Coan's help with the Hawaiian language, but Coan's relief when Wetmore could take care of the medical needs of the people, so that Titus could "devote himself more efficiently 'to the ministry of the word'" [Acts 6:4].

Wetmore was uniquely positioned to comment upon Coan, because they were neighbors. "As neighbors—living as we did almost within 'a stone's throw' of each other—we were, of course, intimate; not even a fence was needed to keep us from quarreling. Seldom have families lived so near to each other for so long a time, in such pleasant and happy relations."

Echoing Damon, Dr. Wetmore concludes with, "He had 'a sound mind in a sound body'; it was this that helped to make him so cheerful, hopeful, and active in his long and faithful career. He labored diligently in his Master's vineyard, aiming constantly at perfection. His work is finished, and already he has heard the commending words, 'Well done, good and faithful servant, enter thou into the joy of thy Lord'"[73] [Matt 25:23].

Lydia's sister-in-law, Mrs. Hiram Bingham II weighs in next. Her memories of Titus Coan go back twenty-five years when she first arrived in Honolulu with her husband. "For more than twenty-five years it was permitted me to know this noble man, 'one of God's great men,' and under varied circumstances to note the excellence of his Christian character."

She notes that when Titus and Fidelia first arrived in Hawai'i more than twenty years before that, they stayed first "at the old Mission House, then the Bingham home, and during the month spent there, while awaiting opportunity to go to his appointed station in Hilo, was commenced the life-long friendship, so prized in both families."[74] She goes on to describe many of his characteristics. "Courtesy, urbanity, consideration

---

72. Coan, *Memorial Volume*, 228–29.

73. Coan, *Memorial Volume*, 229–31.

74. As has been previously noted, Lydia was less than a year old when the Coans stayed with the Binghams. Hiram Bingham II would have been four years old at the time.

for others, abounding hospitality, faithfulness in every department of domestic and social life, are words that but feebly convey an idea of what he was." She gives specific examples.

She spends a paragraph on the legacy of his warm greetings for one and all. "How kindly his greeting always was! Long will last the memory of the gentle 'How do you do, my little friend?' as he lovingly took the hand of some child whom he met upon the street, or in the home. Was it some lowly Hawaiian who wanted a few words with the pastor so revered and loved? The hearty 'Aloha,' the warm grasp of the hand were ever ready."

She notes his focus in the study during the morning on "the many sermon briefs, the essays for associations, the accurate church records, the annual reports and sermons, always ready in time, the glowing accounts of nature phenomena, and the many letters to friends both across the ocean and at the Islands." And yet, he was always ready for divine appointments, never impatient when someone came by wanting to visit with him.[75]

Mrs. Kitteredge's "Memorial Poem" takes up two pages, with eight stanzas. Here is the first stanza:

> Toll, softly toll, oh! Swinging bell,
> And from thine airy church-tower tell
> In what strange mystery of rest—
> Hands folded on a marble breast,
> Closed eyes and frozen lips, whose calls
> But lately thrilled these sacred walls—
> He lies encoffined, 'gainst whose door
> Love pleads in vain forever more.

And the last:

> At last the night!—ah! No, the morn!
> God touched him—and for him the dawn!
> 'He walked with God, and he was not';[76]
> Like Enoch's is the story wrought.
> Toll, softly, oh! Swinging bell,
> And from thy airy church-tower tell
> That he who helped a race from sin
> 'Mid welcoming hosts has entered in![77]

Except for a paper and the very end of the book with a short bridge paragraph and the wording of Coan's grave marker,[78] Lydia concludes the *Memorial Volume* with

75. Coan, *Memorial Volume*, 231–35.
76. Gen 5:24.
77. Coan, *Memorial Volume*, 236–37.
78. Coan, *Memorial Volume*, 248. For grave marker inscription, see the next section in this chapter

two letters that arrived after the March memorial service. Elias Bond writes "Mrs. Coan" a letter on May 26, 1883, from his field of service in Kohala.[79] After a brief introductory paragraph, the rest of the letter recalls a visit Titus and Lydia made to Kohala the year before.[80] As he looks back at that visit, it "does seem to me a fittingly tender and last adieu, as though he were leaving for his heavenly home, as indeed he was."

He concludes the letter as follows: "And so, substantially, closed a period of fraternal Christian intercourse which had, at that time, run on through forty-one years. And now, in the retrospect, it affords me great and tender satisfaction that in all that long season of very frequent epistolary intercourse, not one shadow of unhappy disagreement ever came between us. He loved peace, was ever a peacemaker, and now lives in the full fruition of the blessedness promised to such [Matt 5:9].

"Good-bye, dear brother, till again we meet, face to face, in the blessed Master's presence."[81]

The last letter in the book is, fittingly, from an ecumenical friend—Joel Bean, a member of the Society of Friends—with whom Titus had exchanged many loving letters especially on the subject of peace. He writes to Mrs. Coan of his first in person meeting "with dear Titus Coan . . . in his own home in the spring of 1862. Long before, we had read of him and his fellow-laborers, in the journal of Daniel Wheeler;[82] and the warm welcome extended by these dear fathers of the Sandwich Islands mission to members of our Society who visited the islands, as ambassadors for Christ, brought them into esteem[83] in our section of the church, both in England and America."

Bean reveals his nervousness at approaching the threshold of the Coan home with Titus's reputation preceding him. "Not without some little trepidation did I approach the threshold of one whose praise in the gospel was throughout all the churches. But when we met, the grasp of his hand, the benignity of his countenance, and the gentleness and sweetness of his spirit dispelled it all, and my heart was at once drawn to him, as a Father[84] in Christ."

---

as well as the conclusion of the previous chapter.

79. Northern area of the Big Island.

80. In *Life*, 224, Coan refers to one visit to Kohala with Brother Lyons. Referring to a second visit to Kohala (but before the referenced visit in his letter because the latter would have been after Coan finished writing his autobiography), Coan writes, "I have visited this field again, since the arrival of its present faithful and successful occupant, the Rev. Elias Bond, and rejoiced in all its fruit-bearing prosperity." Mr. and Mrs. Bond arrived in Kohala in 1841 until her death in 1881 and his death in 1896. Judd, *Missionary Album*, 54–55; and Forbes et al., *Partners in Change*, 147–53.

81. Coan, *Memorial Volume*, 238–40.

82. Daniel Wheeler, British Quaker, minister, teacher and missionary in Russia and the South Pacific. Wikipedia, "Daniel Wheeler (Missionary)." Wheeler, *Extracts*, 1840. Wheeler, *Tract*, 33, about Wheeler visiting Honolulu in late December of 1835. After hearing Hiram Bingham preach, Bingham recommended Wheeler to "Lyman [sic] and Coan."

83. No doubt Titus's peace position endeared him to the Friends.

84. Mr. Bean was twenty-four years Mr. Coan's junior.

He writes of both Coan's hospitality and the fellowship he and his wife had with them during the subsequent ten years, as well as after Fidelia's death. "What their letters have been to us, these twenty years, can only be estimated by those who shared the warmth and wealth of their affection, and the intellectual and spiritual impulse they were gifted so largely to impart through the pen." He writes of Titus's contributions to periodicals, "especially those on the subject of peace, were very acceptable to the Society of Friends; and his books . . . have found delighted readers among our people."

He concludes with, "Dear and noble veteran of the cross! In the Spirit of the Master, and by the grace of God, he did large and blessed service, and in no common degree he possessed and exhibited that catholicity of spirit, that breadth and depth of Christian love which brings into joyful realization the fact attested in the gospel, that the children of God, of every nation and denomination, are 'all brethren,' and one church and one body in Christ Jesus, the head"[85] [Col. 1:18?].

The final document in the *Memorial Volume* is a paper by Rev. E. P. Baker "at the monthly concert in the Hilo Foreign Church." It is written in early July 1883, on the occasion of the forty-fifth anniversary of Titus Coan's receiving "1,705 persons to membership." Characterized as perhaps the largest ingathering to the church since the day of Pentecost, "it seems fitting that we should speak of him whose personality occupied so large a place in the Christian past of Hawaii."

"Mr. Coan was, first of all, a man of practical efficiency in dealing with external circumstances and handling material things." Mr. Baker calls forth evidence to prove the claim:

"Witness those perilous months of abode he and his companion spent in Patagonia.

"Witness Father Coan's foot tours around Hawaii, involving excessive weariness, and his persistent inspections of the great eruptions of Mauna Loa, involving more or less of danger.

"Witness, also, that carefully devised and efficiently executed plan and method, by and according to which, for long years, he carried forward Christian work in his chosen field.

"Father Coan, moreover, had a certain versatility of nature which enabled him to encounter any and every environment with which he might find himself beset, in the best possible temper, and as it seems to us, looking at what he did through the perspective of the past, in the best possible way."

Soaring into Victorian metaphor to describe Coan's essential nature, Baker writes, "But though encircled with ivy and exteriorly variegated and adorned with many beautiful and brilliant flowers, his essential personality was a tower of the solidest description: conjoined with great gentleness of disposition and irrepressible cheerfulness of demeanor was an interior rectitude of the very toughest adamant—he

---

85. Joel Bean, San Jose, California, 1883, to Mrs. Coan. in Coan, *Memorial Volume*, 240–41.

literally loved righteousness and hated iniquity [Heb 1:9]—while his philosophy of existence was scarcely less than the sternest."

Baker concludes after reflecting on Coan's last visit to contemplate the "sacred desk," the pulpit at the church. "And though looking for the last time in the flesh upon the dear old spot where he used to tell of Christ's love, he was too near the home where God shall wipe away tears from every eye [Rev. 21:4], to gaze otherwise than with steadfast, undimmed vision, we who look upon the grave that marks his last earthly resting-place are able to see it only imperfectly on account of weeping.

> Go stand on the hill where he lies;
> The earliest ray of the golden day
> On that hallowed spot is cast,
> And the evening sun as it leaves this world
> Looks kindly on that spot last."[86]

IN HIS OWN WORDS: TITUS COAN'S WILL AND TESTAMENT

One month after Titus Coan's memorial service, his Last Will and Testament completed the probate process.[87] It is truly a holographic, that is, handwritten will. There are no printed items or lines. No fill-in-the-blanks. No printed form such as a law office might have—with its logo, etc., on it. The only noted printed areas are justified lines, with the odd pages having a line down the left line and the even pages with a line down the right side. It looks like there are lines with which to write straight across the page. Some words can be difficult to make out because of ink bleeding through.

Except for page 7 from the Hawaiian archives, all but the last two are in Titus Coan's hand. The remaining two paragraphs are the last one on the document itself, apart from the office filing notation. Those two paragraphs are written by F[rederick] S[chwarz] Lyman, a son of David and Sarah Lyman. Frederick was both a judge and a practicing attorney.

Paragraph one in Lyman's hand has to do with the witnesses to the will, followed by their signatures. The third of three signatures was that of Lyman, with the first two being Coan's long-time physician friend "Cha[rle]s H. Wetmore" and his wife "Lucy S[heldon]."

---

86. Pierpont, "The Pilgrim Fathers," lines 28–32, in Coan, *Memorial Volume*, 242–48.

87. The following information is from the Judicial District Court of the Hawaiian Islands (Hilo), Book 5, 131–34, microfilm from the State Archives of Hawai'i turned into paper of seven legal-sized pages, with the original taking up part or all of four pages. Numbered lower left, odd pages; lower right, even pages. The number 214 is mechanically written to the right of "Will." All such items were sent years ago from the island counties to the State Archives where they were placed on microfilm.

Legacy

The first page[88] with the number "214" on the upper right hand corner has perhaps an inch and a half from the top before the handwriting starts. It contains the formulaic beginning of a will from that time. It begins:

"Know All Men by these Presents;

"That I, Titus Coan, of the town of Hilo, Island of Hawaii, Hawaiian Islands, at the present time Pastor of the First Hawaiian Church of Hilo, of the age of [blank rest of line] years, and being of sound mind and memory, do make, publish, and declare this my last will and Testament."[89] It is known that Titus Coan was eighty-one when he signed and sealed the will: "this eighth day of April, 1882."[90] This was approximately five months before he suffered a stroke and less than eight months before his death. By way of context, he had completed the draft of his autobiography the previous year on August 15, 1881—after lava had come within a half mile of Hilo.

Coan then writes out ten[91] paragraphs in the will, as follows.

"I. To my faithful and beloved wife, Lydia Bingham Coan, I give and devise my dwelling house with all its furniture, and the lot of land on which it stands, commonly called the House [lot?], Extending from the House lot of C. H. Wetmore, MD, on the Mauka,[92] to a parcel of land owned by my wife L. B. Coan on the Mauko[93] side, with all its appurtenances and privileges, to have and to hold,[94] and to enjoy without let or hindrance[95] so long as she shall see fit to remain in the town of Hilo. And whenever she shall be called away by death or to reside permanently in any other part of the world, then those [these?] premises and buildings, with furniture shall revert jointly to my daughter Harriett Fidelia, and my son Samuel Latimer."

Commentary on I. This paragraph shows his prioritizing in taking care of his second wife, Lydia. However, it raises many questions. Why did Lydia return to Honolulu to live the rest of her life so soon after Coan's death,[96] if the home, furnishings, and surrounding property were hers to use until her death if she wished? Also, it is ironic that half-ownership would have reverted to Harriett,[97] who so strongly opposed her father marrying Lydia. Samuel was married. Note later in the will both the provision for another location for Hattie and the fact that Titus named Samuel Latimer "Lattie"

---

88. Based on the microfilmed pages.

89. The underlining is by hand, with the underlining of various lengths under "Testament" broken up with six spaces between each.

90. Paragraph X.

91. Using Roman numerals.

92. Pukui, *Hawaiian Dictionary,* "toward or by the sea."

93. "Mountain side, toward the mountains."

94. Echoing wedding vows?

95. A phrase used regarding unencumbered preaching.

96. After completing the *Memorial Volume*?

97. Forbes et al., *Partners in Change,* notes that Harriett Fidelia Coan died in Hilo approximately 10 years before Lydia died in Honolulu. It does not say where Samuel Latimer died.

co-executor with Lydia. In the months leading up to his father's death, Dr. Titus Munson Coan was living near his father and his family home.[98]

Paragraph II has to do with the church Titus Coan served for so long.

"II. I give and bequeath to the First Hawaiian Church of Hilo, Hawaii that portion of a lot of land called [unintelligible][99] lying makai of portion of land owned by C. J. Wetmore MD and extending seaward [blank space] feet to the foundation of an old stone wall, and bounded on the Puna side by the house lot now occupied by W. L. Rose, and by a piece of land owned by me, and on the Hilo side by Pūhona to have and to hold by said church as a parsonage so long as the church shall remain in harmony, and in the faith in which they have been taught by their missionary fathers and in the observance of the rules of their charter.

"If these rules shall by violated by the church the land shall revert to my son Samuel Latimer Coan, or in case of his death, it shall be given in trust to the Board of the Hawaiian Evangelical Association, as a permanent legacy."

Commentary on II. After his wife, Coan prioritizes his church. He gives a portion of land and a house as a parsonage. Recognizing that churches can fall away from the historic Christian faith, he lists three qualifications for the church keeping the land and building: remaining in harmony, following the teachings of the missionaries, and observing the rules of the charter. Section/paragraph VIII will be a call to all to live in harmony. The teachings of the missionaries are related and examined elsewhere in this volume. To this day, the church Coan pastored holds to the historic Christian faith. It is interesting that the property would revert to Samuel Latimer Coan and not his oldest brother. Perhaps this is because Munson was more financially secure. Apparently both were living in Hilo at the time.[100]

Note that in the event of Samuel L. Coan's death, the property reverts to the Hawaiian Evangelical Association, which was formed after the ABCFM closed shop in Hawai'i in the early 1850s. Titus Coan was the first president of the HEA and was so for many years. The HEA continues today as sort of a subset of the Hawaiian Conference of the United Church of Christ. Coan provides a bequest to the HEA in section/paragraph VI.

The church no longer has a parsonage on that site due to the first level being on the Hilo tsunami plain. The church is putting to good use the facility on that property.[101]

"III. I give and bequeath to my daughter Harriet Fidelia all that parcel of lot No. 3 situated in Hilo, Hawaii, and bounded as follows. On the Makai side by a house lot

---

98. Coan, *Memorial Volume*, 200.

99. Looks like three letters or so. Something "b"?

100. It is assumed that Lattie lived in Hilo at the time because he will be named co-executor in Section/Paragraph X. In those days it was difficult to be an executor while living a significant distance from the person writing the will.

101. Per information from Pastor Brian Welsh.

now owned and occupied by W. L. Rose,[102] on the Mauka side by a house now occupied by Akau Hapa.

"On the Puna side by Church Street, and on the Hilo side by the lot bequeathed to the First Hawaiian Church of Hilo."

Commentary on III. Did Harriet move into the Emerald Bower after Lydia returned to Honolulu? If so, what became of the property? Again, transferences could be checked though it might be a rather lengthy process for a minimal gain in knowledge. It is intriguing how the borders are described: seaside, mountainside, Puna side, Hilo side. Certainly everyone back then knew what he meant. Some in Hilo continue to understand to a lesser extent what is meant.

"IV. I give and bequeath to my sons Titus Munson and Samuel Latimer, and to my grandson Philip Munson Coan,[103] in equal divisions, all that parcel of land styled No. 3, situated in Hilo, Hawaii and bounded as follows. On the *mauka* side by a house lot now owned and occupied by William L. Rose, and by a parcel of land bequeathed by me to the First Hawaiian Church of Hilo, on the Makai side by the Front Street, on the Puna side by Church Street and the house lot of W. L. Rose, and on the Hilo side by land owned and now occupied for a drugstore by C. H. Wetmore and by Puhona."

Commentary on IV. This parcel was given to three males: two sons and grandson Philip Munson Coan.[104] Philip was two years old at the time of the writing and signing of this will; three years old when his grandfather died. Did the young Philip make the trip to Hilo with his father? Since it is probably unlikely, Munson might have brought photographs of the toddler.

"V. I give and bequeath to my daughter Sara Elisa Coan Waters, all that parcel of lot 3 lying at the makai side of Front Street and extending seaward to [two undecipherable words], near [four undecipherable words] by L. Akaniu (Chinaman)[105] and Joseph Nanaki (Hawaiian)."

Commentary on V. First Coan gives a bequest to an unmarried daughter. Next he gives property to three males. Lastly with regard to family members, he gives a bequest to his married daughter.

"VI. Lot No. 4 commonly called W[eod?]—land and pasture lot (see [undecipherable]) and area described on the royal[106] patent I give and bequeath to the Board

102. See William L. Rose obituary in April 24, 1903, *Hilo Tribune*.

103. Philip Munson Coan was Titus Munson Coan's son and Sarah Acheson Stevens's grandfather. Sarah is the one who donated the Titus Coan Papers to the Library of Congress and holds the literary rights to those papers.

104. Born May 14, 1879, in New York City, and died in 1969.

105. "While a few score enterprising Chinese came to Hawai'i after Captain Cook's time on the Islands, the great influx of tens of thousands of Chinese men started arriving in the islands after 1850. This was in large part as a result of the sandal wood market. Because of that business, Chinese Hawaiians to this day call the islands Tan Heung San, Sandalwood Mountains." Initially Chinese boys then also girls attended the mission schools, followed by the public schools. Clarence Glick, http://hawaiiguide.com/origins/chinese.htm.

106. "The term 'Royal' indicates that the document was issued during the Monarchy (up to 1893)."

of the Hawaiian Evangelical Association the land to be leased by said board, or their Agent, and the yearly [unclear] to be appropriated to missionary work in Micronesia or other islands of the Pacific. Said land to remain in the care of said board as a permanent fund so long as it shall continue to act as an Evangelical Missionary Board.

"Should this board ever be dissolved, or cease to act as an Evangelical mission board, the land shall become the property of the ABCFM for the furtherance of the evangelistic work among the heathen."

Commentary on VI. As understood by the author, the Titus Coan fund continues to assist churches that belong to the Hawaiian Evangelical Association.[107] Patricia Bjorling worked with such churches to help them get grants from the fund.[108] But Coan's expressed wishes and qualifications raised some potentially interesting questions during the second decade of the twenty-first century. The income from the investment is to be used to do missionary work in the islands of the Pacific. If the HEA is dissolved[109] or ceases to act as an evangelical mission board,[110] the bequest goes to the American Board of Commissioners for Foreign Missions. While no one wants to deprive the churches of their funds,[111] how much if any of the funds are being used for missions in the Pacific?

The ABCFM no longer exists. In the late 1950s it became the United Church Board for World Ministries[112] which has since combined with the Disciples of Christ world ministry. Even though pioneering cross-cultural missions continue around the world,[113] most Americans involved with the current expression of global outreach would bristle at the thought of furthering "the evangelistic work among the heathen" as understood by Titus Coan.

As this book goes to press, the situation essentially has been resolved in favor of the Hawai'i Conference of the United Church of Christ.

"VII. My library. I give and bequeath to my precious wife Lydia and my four beloved children, to be divided amicably among the five, or to be sold and the proceeds to be equally divided."

Commentary on VII. Lydia is mentioned by name. Note the word "amicably." Was the division done amicably? How did the five divide his library? Did his library include any of his correspondence, sermons, lectures, or other documents? Were any items of his library sold? Is it possible that the books in the Library of Congress collection,

---

Hawaiideptland.custhelp.com.

107. I.e., churches started by Congregational missionaries among Hawaiians.
108. See later in this chapter.
109. Which is not the case at this writing.
110. The churches of the HEA are among the most evangelical in the United Church of Christ.
111. In the early part of the 2010s, a leader of the HEA asked for a review of the use of the funds in light of the Titus Coan will.
112. Note the substitution of the word "Ministries" for "Missions."
113. Including in the United States.

which include Munson's books, are only those which Munson received in the division of the Titus Coan library? Did Lydia take any books to Honolulu with her?

"VIII. To all my beloved ones, to my precious and faithful wife, my dear children, and all relatives and friends, and to the church of Christ in Hilo, over which the Holy Ghost made me overseer,[114] I beg we all [remember] that which is 'more precious than gold that perisheth' [1 Pet 1:7], my steadfast faith, and my fervent imperishable love, praying for unity [of or in?—no word here] spirit, harmony and prosperity on earth, and a unity of bliss and glory in heaven."

Commentary on VIII. This is a spiritual bequest. How did this work itself out between Lydia and the four siblings? Did Samuel get along fine with Lydia? Sarah? Did Hattie ever reconcile with her? How did Munson and Lydia get along?

"IX. For my dust I desire a quiet and decent burial in a plain coffin, by the side of the remains of my departed angel, Fidelia, with a modest marble slab to mark the resting place of my mortal [indecipherable word], with this inscription

<u>Titus</u> Coan

Feb. 1, 1801_____

He lived by Faith.

He Still Lives.

"Believest Thou This?"

John 11:26

Commentary on IX. This involves funeral and burial requests. "Ashes to ashes, dust to dust" [Job 30:19] is a traditional graveside committal phrase. There is the basic phrase that every human being deserves "a decent burial." A plain coffin speaks to his simplicity. The first time he saw his future first wife as he rode by a school room and beheld her through the window, he said he had seen "the face of an angel." "During this summer of 1826 I often rode by a school-house in a western district of Riga,[115] and through the windows I saw a face that beamed on me like that of an angel. The image was deeply impressed, and is still ineffaceable."[116] Lydia concludes the *Memorial volume* with this inscription and the date of death added.

"X. I appoint my wife, Lydia Bingham Coan, and my son Samuel Latimer Coan[117] Executors of this Will.

---

114. The New Testament Greek work is *episcopes*, which means overseer and also came to be "bishop" as well.

115. Approximately ninety miles from Auburn, where Titus and Fidelia would join the Presbyterian church and Titus would study at the seminary.

116. Coan, *Life*, 9. He wrote that page nine months before penning his Last Will and Testament.

117. Latimer is written above in between the lines after the "u" in Samuel and until the "o" in Coan.

"In witness whereof I hereunto set my hand and seal[118] this eighth day of April, 1882. Titus Coan."[119]

The next two paragraphs are in Judge Lyman's hand as previously noted. Also as previously noted, the first of those paragraphs has to do with the witnesses to the document. "Signed and sealed and declared by the said Testator as and for his last Will and Testament in the presence of us, who, at his request, and in his presence, and in the presence of each other, do now set our names hereto as subscribing witnesses.[120]

Chas. H. Wetmore

Lucy S. Wetmore

F. S. Lyman

[121]"The foregoing Instrument was proven in the probate Court Third Judicial District, Hawaiian Islands, at Hilo, Hawaii, February 23, AD 1883, to be the last Will and Testament of Titus Coan of Hilo, Hawaii, deceased, and admitted to Probate.

F. S. Lyman

Circuit Judge, Third

Judicial District. H. Is."[122]

MEMORIAL VOLUME

When it comes to Lydia's compiling, writing, and publishing the homage to her husband, *Titus Coan: A Memorial*, one needs to ask the questions of a journalist: who, what, when, where, and why? The "who" and "what" are easily dealt with. Lydia Bingham Coan wrote a memorial volume about her husband, based mostly on his own writings—letters and journal entries. She provided numerous helpful bridge passages.[123] She provides a fitting conclusion with material from the March 1883 memorial service and concludes with a paper written on the occasion of the anniversary of the largest recorded baptism service in one day since Pentecost.

In a March 31, 1883, letter that she wrote to S. E. Bishop, Lydia shares her desire to publish a memorial volume that will have a great deal of Titus Coan material,

---

118. The seal—black in the photocopy—is to the right of his signature, with the top being as high as the capital letters of his name and the bottom taking up the line below, the rest of which line is blank. The seal is approximately one inch in diameter and has diagonal marks all the way around the circle on the outside of the seal's circle.

119. Date already noted. Standard wording.

120. Appears to be boiler plate language. Already discussed.

121. With different pen, darker ink.

122. Previously commented upon. Given the exigencies of the day, a witness of the Will also accepted the Will in Court. Probate was concluded after the second memorial service.

123. Because Coan lived such an inexhaustible life and Lydia herself was a gifted writer, one yearns for more, even a full volume written solely by Lydia.

Legacy

including that which was presented and read at the Coan service. "My dear Friend Mr. Bishop. I must not be judged in these sad carefull days, unappreciative of kindness and sympathy because I am tardy in answering the letters of friends . . . I felt very grateful to you for your kind favor of January 23 with its enclose, the copy of my precious, honored husband's last letter to you.[124] And last Sabbath when I heard at the Memorial services your beautiful tribute to him, my heart was full of deep appreciation and of gratitude for this contribution from your pen. *It is a cherished purpose of mine to publish a memorial volume which shall embody much of the material prepared for the service.*[125] And you will be quite willing that I should use your letter for that occasion? I wish I knew how to tell you in what manner I particularly valued your tribute. Much that has been said and written of Mr. Coan, while good and just, has left me unsatisfied. It has seemed only what might be said of almost any other faithful worker in the vineyard—it has not somehow portrayed the man. But in your sketch of him, as the preacher, reaching and winning the hearts of youth, and in your vigorous outlines of his soul,[126] God-given during his earlier ministry."[127]

With regard to the time period of the preparation of the book, there is a window between Titus Coan's death in early December 1882, and the publication year of 1884. Lydia might have worked on the volume for approximately two years. While much of the material was already at hand, she began work on the book in 1883.[128] She would have written everything out by hand. Ultimately it was sent to the American mainland where it would have been typeset and printed.

Did she send it to S. J. Humphrey, the District Secretary of the ABCFM? He writes a short introduction to the volume. Perhaps he sent the manuscript to the Fleming H. Revell publisher on 148 and 150 Madison Street in Chicago.[129] The portrait on the frontispiece is the same one as in *Life*. In the autobiography his name is typed in capital letters. In the *Memorial Volume* his signature is beneath the picture.

A late 1884 issue of *The Friend* provides an anonymous and effusive "Review of Lydia Bingham Coan's *A Memorial*. Just as our paper was going to press, arrived a book with the above title. The book meets our highest expectations. It is difficult to imagine how the compiler could have so restrained her desire for publishing the vast amount of materials at her disposal, and sent for a volume of only 248 pages.[130] She

---

124. Titus Coan to Sereno Edwards Bishop, December 24, 1881, in Coan, *Memorial Volume*, 123–26, with Bishop's writing to Lydia about in letter, 221–23 (see above).

125. Emphasis added.

126. Added with caret.

127. Lydia Coan to S. E. Bishop, March 31, 1884, 83, in File #2 of the Bishop collection, HMH.

128. See Bishop letter, March 31, 1884, above.

129. Coan, *Memorial Volume*, cover page, which also notes that Revell is a publisher of evangelical literature. Revell is now a division of Baker Books. Coan, *Life,* was published by Anson D. F. Randolph in New York.

130. When one considers the thousands of pages of letters and journal entries, the word "restrained" is an understatement.

has allowed Mr. Coan to tell the story of his life in brief but choice paragraphs, from his correspondence, to which is added testimonials from the numerous friends of the departed. Thus she has culled, adjusted, and arranged choice 'bits' of correspondence to form a biographical mosaic as beautiful as any oriental ever made from the most costly and brilliant jewels. It is a marvel how much and how varied are the materials thus condensed and arranged. The volume lying before us is a most admirable supplement to the previous volumes, *Patagonia* and *Life in Hawaii*. The three should go together, forming a graceful trio. If anything is needed to make the historic sketch of the Coan family complete, it would be a memoir of the first Mrs. Coan, from the easy, facil[e] pen of Dr. [Titus Munson] Coan of New York."[131]

The Library of Congress has a handwritten manuscript of *Life*, perhaps one proof read by Munson. It is not known whether Lydia's manuscript is extant.

Where did she compile and write the volume? While she might have returned to Honolulu for a season, she apparently returned to the Emerald Bower for the memorial service. She wrote Sereno Edwards Bishop from the Emerald Bower on March 31, 1883, six days after the service.

Whence the material she used? Much of it is at the Library of Congress, while some is at the Mission Houses Library. Some of the material might be lost to posterity. The chain of custody of the Titus Coan papers is murky, especially in the early years after his death. The material that the family donated to the Library of Congress was returned to the family at the time of Munson's death in 1921.

What is known is that the *Memorial Volume* is of immense value to anyone wanting to learn more about the life and labors of Titus Coan. *Life* and the *Memorial Volume* are a complete set, providing mutual insight and information. While Titus writes a traditional autobiography, Lydia provides journal entries and many letters. Both books are of great help to scholars and those interested in spiritual matters and the church.

COAN ENDOWMENT HELPS CHURCHES

Titus Coan's legacy continues to help churches in Hawai'i, based on paragraph VI of his will. A 2014 Press Release by the Nature Conservancy indicates that Coan acquired land "through the American Board of Commissioners for Foreign Missions during the Great Mahele in 1849." The land is described as "a 922-acre conservation easement along the Saddle Road above Hilo, a site that includes a two-hundred-acre kīpuka with a disappearing stream and a diverse ancient forest."[132]

---

131. Sadly, such a project never happened, due in large measure to Munson having departed from his parents' belief and behavior systems.

132. December 2, 2014, Nature Conservancy Press Release, http://hilo.hawaii.edu/depts/biology/TNC.php.

The Release also states that in 1899 Coan's "widow granted title to the Hawaiian Evangelical Association, now the Hawaii Conference UCC and Hawaii Conference Foundation." The preceding paragraph presents some difficulties. Coan's will was probated in 1883 and the land should have been turned over to the Hawaiian Evangelical Association that year, not sixteen years later. A further difficulty is that while the HEA is within the Hawaii Conference UCC, it is not the same as the Conference. The HEA has its own board and is comprised of a group of churches within the Conference.

It is not known how the funds were used in the early years or exactly when the transition occurred to grants being provided to churches in the Hawai'i Conference.

As for the land itself, the Press Release quotes from Coan's autobiography: "Coan clearly appreciated the specialness of the area, referring in his book *Life in Hawai'i* (1882) to the 'winding, rocky gorge, the cascades, basins, caves, and natural bridges of this wild and solitary stream . . . velvet masses, luxuriant creepers, hanging in festoons.'"[133]

At one point the Coan property provided 25 percent of the water for Hilo. The water comes from the 'Ōla'a Flume Spring, which is six miles west of Hilo and has an elevation of 1,978 feet.[134]

The November 28, 2008, Water District Minutes include the following agenda item with notes:

"A. OLA'A FLUME SPRING SOURCE: A presentation will be given by Pural Water Specialty Co., Inc., on the potential use of the Ola'a Flume Spring source located near the Kaumana City subdivision. They will be presenting their relationship with the land owner (Hawai'i Conference Foundation United Church of Christ), as well as the treatment process and the financial aspect of producing water for potable use in our existing water system. This source was in use in our existing system up until approximately 2001 after the Saddle Road Well was completed."[135]

The minutes also explain that the spring is "on conservation land on the slopes of Mauna Kea above Kaumana City, [and] was *bequeathed to the Foundation*[136] [sic?] by missionary Titus Coan."[137]

KILLINGWORTH

While Titus Coan's legacy continues to make a major difference in Hawai'i—through his spiritual heirs and financial endowment—he has a more modest yet significant legacy in his hometown of Killingworth, Connecticut. This legacy includes a plaque

---

133. The Press Release provides an exhaustive description of the flora and fauna of the acreage.
134. Statistics are from Mapcarta.com, "Ola'a Flume Spring," per Ed Coan.
135. http://www.hawaiidws.org/2%20water%20board/2ba%20agendas/11-25-08~Agenda.htm.
136. Emphasis added. It is understood that Water Board minutes cannot be expected to be precise on the stages of the organizations having custody of the Coan endowment.
137. http://www.hawaiidws.org/2%20water%20board/2ba%20agendas/11-25-08~Agenda.htm.

at the site where Titus's home stood, a Titus Coan Road, and a Titus Coan Trail. It also includes the Congregational Church of Killingworth's unveiling on June 5, 1912, a memorial tablet dedicated to Titus Coan, which reads: "Firm in the faith, diligent in service, he baptized in the name of Christ more than fourteen thousand souls."[138]

SCHOLARSHIP AND INSPIRATION

Titus Coan's legacy expands and endures when one factors in ongoing scholarship and inspirational reading. This book has introduced the reader to the scholarship on Titus Coan spanning parts of three centuries. This volume has advanced Coan scholarship by examining previous topics in further detail and opening up new areas of research by mining primary and secondary sources. *Partners in Change* summarizes Coan's legacy in its opening sentence: He "is remembered both as a charismatic preacher and as an engaged amateur volcanologist."[139] *Partners* describes his preaching as "evangelistic and dramatic."[140] In between we learn of Fidelia and Titus's kindness, welcoming, hospitality, and his medical ministrations before the arrival of Dr. Wetmore.[141]

As far as Coan's volcano legacy, *Partners in Change* puts it this way: "Even today, his observations form an immensely valuable record."[142] Sarah Acheson Stephens, a descendant of Coan, testifies to his enduring legacy, as quoted earlier in this text.[143] In the 1990s, USGS scientists requested that second-great-grandson Edward J. Coan digitize Coan's autobiography, primarily for the six chapters that primarily examine volcanic eruptions.[144]

When it comes to inspiration, there are those who hope that a rediscovery of the life and labors will spark a revival in Hawai'i and renewal around the world—including Stan Aoki, a long-time resident in the Hilo area. With the advent of Facebook, he posted a musical tribute performed in slack key entitled "Makua Koana."[145]

As a labor of love, Beryl Walter shepherded Coan's unabridged autobiography into an easy-to-hold and -read paperback in 2002. She writes in her dedication, "Being a native of Hawaii Island where I lived most of my life, and as a descendant of the missionary Shipman family and the family of Henry Opukahaia, and a member of Haili Congregational Church, I dedicate this reprint . . . to all his descendants and

---

138. Forbes et al., *Partners in Change*, 187.
139. Forbes et al., *Partners in Change*, 184.
140. Forbes, et al., *Partners in Change*, 185.
141. Coan, "Rev. Titus Coan and Mrs. Fidelia C. Coan," in Forbes et al., *Partners in Change*, 186.
142. Forbes, et al., *Partners in Change*, 187.
143. Sarah Stephens, September 21, 2018, email to author.
144. Though the author, Paul Rapoza, and others have begun using it to research the Great Awakening.
145. Aoki, "Makua Koana."

the descendants of those who were blessed by 'Kahu' Coan's ministry so many years ago."[146]

Referring to the aftermath of the big day of baptisms, Walter quotes Coan's reflections[147] of the permanency of the Great Awakening: "He later wrote, 'The question naturally follows, "do these results abide?" After careful examination, the permanence of the results seem almost as marvelous as the revival itself.'"[148]

As previously mentioned, Paul Rapoza has used the Ed Coan digitized version to have his own digitized version of *Life* and the *Memorial Volume*. He continued on to digitize every known book by or about ABCFM missionaries to and in Hawai'i.

One year before this book went to press, two documentaries were released to celebrate the bicentennial of the arrival of the Pioneer missionaries at the Islands: *A Witness to Aloha*;[149] and one about 'Ōpūkaha'ia.[150]

In an early 1887 issue of *The Friend* celebrating the Jubilee event commemorating the arrival of the Company that arrived in 1837, Lydia notes that the "portraits of Rev. H. Bingham, the pioneer, and of Rev. Titus Coan, one of Hawaii's most devoted apostles, [were] garlanded with maile."[151]

Characterizing her father and husband as apostles echoes the words of the writer of the preliminary death notice, which characterized Titus Coan as "The Apostle to the Sandwich Islands."[152]

---

146. Walter reprint of Coan, *Life*, np.

147. Perhaps with the hope that revival fires would once again be kindled in Hilo, Puna, and beyond.

148. Walter reprint, Coan, *Life*, np. No Coan citation.

149. Produced by the Kawaiaha'o church in Honolulu.

150. Produced by Michael Leinau. He hopes to develop funding to do a documentary on Titus Coan and the brother sister/priest/priestess of Pele who became Christians under Coan's ministry.

151. *The Friend* 45.1 (1887) 37.

152. *New York Times*, January 4, 1883.

Bibliography

PRIMARY AND ARCHIVAL SOURCES

ABCFM papers at Harvard (some digitized on Hollister Archival Discovery, formerly OASIS catalog).
Advocate of Peace 9 (1849)–15 New Series (1883) (microfilm and digitized).
American Bible Society Tracts.
American Peace Society Tracts.
Angel of Peace.
The American Journal of Science and Arts.
Congressional Globe.
Deseret News and *Deseret Evening News.*
First Things.
The Friend (digitized).
Hawaiʻi Voyager Collection, University of Hawaiʻi at Manoa.
Hawaiian Historical Society.
Hawaiian Mission Houses Archives and Library.
Hilo Tribune.
Library of Congress, Titus Coan Papers.
Lyman Museum in Hilo (Lymans, Wetmores, etc.).
The Missionary Herald, 1837–83 (hard copy and digitized).
Missionary Station Reports, Hilo, Hawaii, 1835–63.
National Archives, Washington DC.
New York Evangelical Journal.
New York Times (digitized).
Pacific Commercial Advertiser.
Sailor's Magazine.
Scribner's Magazine.
Wilkes Family Papers, Duke University.
Yale Bingham Collection.

BOOKS, ARTICLES, AND ONLINE SOURCES

Acheson, Sarah. "The Scramble for Hawaii: 1820–1850." Senior thesis, McGill University, 1969.

Bibliography

Adams, John Quincy. *History of Auburn Theological Seminary, 1818–1919*. Auburn, NY: Auburn Seminary Press, 1918.

Alexander, James M. *Mission Life in Hawaii: Memoir of Rev. William P. Alexander*. Oakland, CA: Pacific Press, 1888.

Alexander, W. D. *A Brief History of the Hawaiian People*. New York: American Book Company, 1891.

Aloha Hawaii. "Hawaiian Flowers." http://www.aloha-hawaii.com/hawaii/flowers/.

Anderson, Rufus. *A Heathen Nation Evangelized: History of the Sandwich Islands Mission*. Boston: Congregational Publishing Society, 1870.

Andrew III, John A. *Rebuilding the Christian Commonwealth: New England Congregationalists and Foreign Missions, 1800–1830*. Lexington, KY: University Press of Kentucky, 1976.

Aoki, Stan. "'Makua Koana' by Stan Aoki (Done in Slack Key)." https://www.youtube.com/watch?v=9vx8Nud24Zw.

Associated Press. "At Sacred Hawaiian Site, Veneration Looks a Lot Like Litter." *New York Times* April 22, 2007. https://www.nytimes.com/2007/04/22/us/22Volcano.html.

Back to the Bible. "Security in Storms." www.backtothebible.org/devotions/security-in-storms.

Baker, Albert S. *Morning Stars and Missionary Packet*. http://www.trussel.com/kir/mstar.htm.

Ballou, Howard M., and George R. Carter. "The History of the Hawaiian Mission Press, with a Bibliography of the Earlier Publications." *Papers of the Hawaiian Historical Society* 14 (1908) 10–11.

Barrett, Gwynn. "Walter Murray Gibson: The Shepherd Saint of Lanai Revisited." *Utah Historical Quarterly* 40.2 (Spring 1972) 142–62.

Bartlett, Samuel Concord. *Historical Sketch of the Hawaiian Mission: and the Missions to Micronesia and the Marquesas Islands*. Boston: American Board of Commissioners for Foreign Missions, 1869.

Beaver, Pierce, ed. *To Advance the Gospel: Selections from the Writings of Rufus Anderson*. Grand Rapids: Eerdmanns, 1967.

Beckwith, George Cone. *The Book of Peace: A Collection of Essays on War and Peace*. Philadelphia: Perkins and Purves, et al, 1845.

Bible History. https://www.bible-history.com/index.php.

———. *The Peace Manual: or, War and Its Remedies*. Boston: American Peace Society, 1868.

Bigler, David. *The Forgotten Kingdom: The Mormon Theocracy in the American West, 1847–1896, Volume 2*. Kingdom in the West: The Mormons and the American Frontier Series. Logan, Utah: Utah State University Press, 2005.

Bingham, Hiram. *Bartimeus, of the Sandwich Islands*. New York: New York Tract Society, 1855.

———. *A Residence of Twenty-One Years in the Sandwich Islands*. Canandaigua, NY: H. D. Goodwin, 1855.

Bird, Isabella L. *Six Months in the Sandwich Islands. The Hawaiian Archipelago: Among the Palm Groves, Coral Reefs, and Volcanoes of the Sandwich Islands*. Tokyo: Charles E. Tuttle Company, 1974.

Bishop, M. Guy. "Waging Holy War: Mormon-Congregationalist Conflict in Mid-Nineteenth-Century Hawaii." *Journal of Mormon History* 17 (1991) 110–19.

Bishop, Serano Edwards. *Reminiscences of Old Hawaii*. Honolulu: Hawaiian Gazette Company, 1916.

BIBLIOGRAPHY

Bitton, Davis. "George Q. Cannon in Hawai'i, 1850–54: Relationship Challenges of a Young Missionary." In *Pioneers of the Pacific*, edited by Grant Underwood. Provo, Utah: Brigham Young University Press, 2005.

Blomberg, Craig L., and Stephen E. Robinson. *How Wide the Divide: A Mormon and an Evangelical in Discussion*. Downers Grove, IL: IVP Academic Press, 1997.

Boston University School of Theology. "Coan, Titus (1801–1882)." http://www.bu.edu/missiology/missionary-biography/c-d/coan-titus-1801-1882/.

Bourne, Benjamin Franklin. *The Captive in Patagonia; or, A Personal Narrative of the Capture, Sufferings, and Escape of Benjamin Franklin Bourne, Mate of the Schooner John Allyne, of New Bedford*. Boston: Gould and Lincoln, 1853.

Bradley, James, and Richard Muller. *Church History: An Introduction to Research, Reference Works, and Methods*. Grand Rapids, MI: William B. Eermans, 2016.

Brecher, Jeremy. *Cornwall in Pictures: A Visual Reminiscence, 1868–1941*. Hartford: Connecticut Historical Society, 2001.

Brigham, William T. *The Volcanoes of Kiluea and Mauna Loa*. Bishop Museum Memoirs. Honolulu: Bishop Museum Press, 1909.

Britsch, R. Lanier. "Another Visit with Walter Murray Gibson." *Utah Historical Quarterly* 46.1 (Winter 1978) 65–78.

Brown, Kathy. "Titus Coan: 'The Prince of the Penn Painters." *HK-Now* April 4, 2020. https://hk-now.com/2020/04/04/titus-coan-the-prince-of-penpainters/.

Burke, Libby. Presentation on Wetmore women. Lyman Museum, Hilo. No date, unpublished.

Bunyan, John. *The Pilgrim's Progress from This World, to That Which Is to Come: Delivered under the Similitude of a Dream*. Edited by Roger Charrock and J. B. Wharey. Oxford: Oxford University Press, 1975.

Cannon, George Q. *The Journals of George Q. Cannon: Hawaiian Mission, 1850–1854*. Edited by Chad M. Orton, Adrian W. Cannon, and Richard E. Turley Jr. Salt Lake City: Deseret Book Company, 2014.

———. *My First Mission: Designed for the Instruction and Encouragement of Young Latter-Day Saints*. Faith Promoting Series. Salt Lake City: Juvenile Instructor Office, 1879.

Carpenter, John A. *Sword and Olive Branch: Oliver Otis Howard*. New York: Fordham University Press, 1999.

Carter, Stephen L. *The Impeachment of Abraham Lincoln*. New York: Alfred A. Knopf, 2012.

Chaney, George Leonard. *Alo'ha!: A Hawaiian Salutation*. Boston: Roberts Brothers, 1880.

Charlot, John. "Two Early Hawaiian-Christian Chants." *Anthropos* 105 (2020) 29–46.

Citizendum.org. http://en.citizendium.org/wiki.

Climacus, John. *Ladder of Divine Ascent*. Boston: Holy Transfiguration, 2012.

Coan, Fidelia Church. "Eruption from the summit of Mauna Loa, Hawaii." *American Journal of Science* 2.14 (1852) 106–07.

———. "Letter of Mrs. Coan." In *Mother's Magazine* 5 (October 1837) 236–40.

———. "Scientific Intelligence." *American Journal of Science* 14 (September 1852) 106–07.

Coan, Lydia Bingham. "A Brief Sketch of the Missionary Life of Mrs. Sybil Mosely Bingham." Honolulu: HMCH, 1895.

———. *Titus Coan: A Memorial Volume*. Chicago: Fleming H. Revell, 1884.

Coan, Titus. *Adventures in Patagonia: A Missionary's Exploring Trip*. New York: Dodd, Mead, and Company, 1880.

———. "The Appropriate Duties of Christian Females, in Public and Social Worship." Honolulu, 1862.

———. "The Last Visit at the Grave of a Wife," LOC.

———. "Last Will and Testament." State Archives of Hawai'i, Judicial District Court of the Hawaiian Islands, Book 5, 131–34.

———. *Life in Hawaii: An Autobiographic Sketch of Mission Life and Labors (1835–82)*. New York: Anson D. F. Randolph and Company, 1882. https://www.soest.hawaii.edu/GG/HCV/COAN/coan-intro.html.

———. *Missionary Herald*, 1834–83—letters, articles, Station Reports, obituary.

———. "A Recollection," LOC.

———. "A Sailor's Sabbath: or, A Word from a Friend to Seamen." LOC Box 26. Honolulu, 1846.

Conservative Congregational Christian Conference, Micronesia. ccccusa.com/conference-services/micronesia/.

Cook, Christopher L. *Preparing the Way: A Pictorial History for the Hawai'i Mission Bicentennial*. Waimea, HI: Pa'a Studio, 2020.

———. *Providential Life and Heritage of Henry Obookiah: Why Did Missionaries Come To Hawai'i from New England and Tahiti?* Waimea, HI: Pa'a Studios, 2015.

———. "When Revival Swept Hawaii: A Decade after the Missionaries Arrived, the Gospel Tore across the Islands in the 1830s." *Christian History/Christianity Today* 2019.

Cooper, George. *Seamen's Chaplain: Reflections on the Life of Samuel C. Damon*. Hong Kong: C. F. Damon Jr., 1992.

Corr, Donald Philip. "The Coan Chronicles." Escondido, California. Unpublished research document. 2012–15.

———. *"The Field Is the World": Proclaiming, Translating, and Serving by the American Board of Commissioners for Foreign Missions*. William Carey Library Dissertation Series. Pasadena: William Carey University Press, 2009.

———. "Titus Coan and Me." Escondido and McFarland, California. Unpublished series of chronological essays on the research endeavor, 2011–20.

———. "Titus Coan: 'Apostle to the Sandwich Islands.'" In *The Role of the American Board in the World: Bicentennial Reflections on the Organization's Missionary Work, 1810–2010*, edited by Clifford Putney and Paul Burlin. Eugene, OR: Wipf & Stock, 2012.

Cross, Whitney R. *The Burned-Over District: The Social and Intellectual History of Enthusiastic Religion in Western New York, 1800–1850*. Ithaca: Cornell University Press, 1950.

Damon, Ethel M. *Samuel Chenery Damon: Chaplain and Friend of Seamen, Historian, Traveler, Diplomat, Doctor of Divinity, Journalist, Genial Companion, Genealogist*. Honolulu: Hawaiian Missionary Children Society, 1966.

Damon, Samuel Chenery. *Damon Memorial*. Reading, MA: John Damon, 1882.

Damon, Samuel Chenery, and Cooper, George. *Seamen's Chaplain: Reflections on the Life of Samuel C. Damon*. Google book, 1992.

Dana, James Dwight. *Characteristics of Volcanoes, with Contributions of Facts and Principles from the Hawaiian Islands, Including a Historical Review of Hawaiian Volcanic Action for the Past Sixty-Seven years, a Discussion of the Relations of Volcanic Islands to Deep-Sea Topography, and a Chapter on Volcanic-Island Denudation*. New York: Dodd, Mead, and Company, 1890.

———. *Creation; Or, The Biblical Cosmogony in the Light of Modern Science*. Oberlin, OH: E. J. Goodrich, 1885.

———. "History of Changes." *American Journal of Science* 36.212, 81–112.

———. *Manual of Geology: Treating of the Principles of the Science with Special Reference to American Geological History, for the Use of Collectors, Academies, and Schools of Science.* New York: Ivison, Blakeman, Taylor, and Company, 1863.

———. "Science and the Bible: A Review of 'The Six Days of Creation' of Prof. Taylor Lewis." Andover, MA: Warren F. Draper, 1856.

Darlow, T. H., et al, compilers. *Historical Cotologue of the Printed Editions of Holy Scripture in the Library of the British and Foreign Bible Society, Volumes 1–2.* London: Bible House, 1903.

Darwin, Charles. *Voyage Around the World.* New York: D. Appleton and Co., 1873.

Davis, Lynne Ann. *Na Paiʻi iʻi: The Photographers in the Hawaiian Islands, 1845–1900.* Honolulu: Bishop Museum Press, 1980.

Daws, Alan Gavan. "Evangelism in Hawaii: Titus Coan and the Great Revival of 1837." *Hawaiian Historical Society Annual Report* 69 (1960) 20–34.

———. *Shoal of Time: A History of the Hawaiian Islands.* Honolulu: University of Hawaiʻi Press, 1989.

Day, A Grove. "Pioneer Presses of Hawaii." *Journal of the American Institute of Graphic Arts* 4 (1952) 33–40.

Day, A. Grove, and Albertine Loomis. "Ka Paʻi Palapala: Early Printing in Hawaii." Pamphlet. Lihuʻe, HI: Printing Industries of Hawaii, January 1, 1973.

Demetrion, George. *In Quest of a Vital Center: An Ecumenical Evangelical Perspective.* Eugene, OR: Wipf & Stock, 2014.

Deseret News. "George Q. Cannon among 10 first missionaries to Hawaii." July 21, 2009. http://www.deseretnews.com/article/705318137/George-Q-Cannon-among-10-first-missionaries-to-Hawaii.html?pg=all.

Diamond, *Guns, Germs, and Steel: The Fate of Human Societies.* New York: W. W. Norton, 1999.

Dibble, Sheldon. *A History of the Sandwich Islands.* Lahainaluna, Hawaii: Press of the Mission Seminary, 1843.

Dictionary.com. https://www.dictionary.com.

Dorn, Peter. "The Three-Self Principle as a Model for the Indigenous Church." MDiv Thesis. Condordia Seminary, 1982.

Doughty, Andrew. *Hawaiʻi: The Big Island Revealed. The Ultimate Guidebook.* Lihuʻe, HI: Wizard Publications, 2018.

Dudley, Michael Kioni. *A Hawaiian Nation I: Man, Gods, and Nature.* Honolulu: Nā Kāne O Ka Malo Press, 1990.

Dupuis, H. G., and Garth M. Rosell. *Memoirs of Charles G. Finney, the Complete Restored Text.* Grand Rapids, MI: Zondervan, 1989.

Dutton, Clarence E. *Hawaiian Volcanoes.* Honolulu: University of Hawaiʻi Press, 2005.

Dwight, Edwin Welles. *Memoirs of Heneri Opukahiaia (Henry Obookiah) A Native Hawaiian 1692–1818.* Titus Coan Memorial Library. http://www.tc-lib.org.

Edwards, Jonathan. "The Distinguishing Marks of a Work of the Spirit of God Applied to That Uncommon Operation That Has Lately Appeared on the Minds of Many of the People of This Land: With a Particular Consideration of the Extraordinary Circumstances with Which This Work Is Attended. A Discourse Delivered at New Haven, September Tenth, 1741. Being the Day after the Commencement." In *The Great Awakening*, edited by Harry S. Stout and C. C. Goen. Works of Jonathan Edwards 4. New Haven: Yale University Press, 1972.

———. "Part II. Shewing What Are No Certain Signs That Religious Affections Are Truly Gracious, or that They are Not." In *Religious Affections,* edited by Harry S. Stout and John E. Smith. Works of Jonathan Edwards 2. New Haven: Yale University Press, 1959. 125–90.

———. "Part III. Shewing What are Distinguishing Signs of Truly Gracious and Holy Affections." In *Religious Affections,* edited by Harry S. Stout and John E. Smith. Works of Jonathan Edwards 2. New Haven: Yale University Press, 1959. 125–90.

EH.net. https://eh.net/.

Ehlke, Margaret S. "Enthusiastic Religion and the Lives of Titus and Fidelia Coan, Missionaries to Hilo." Master's Thesis. University of Hawai'i at Manoa, 1986.

Ellis, William. *Journal of William Ellis: Narrative of a Tour of Hawaii, or Owhyhee: With Remarks on the History, Traditions, Manners, Customs, and Language of the Inhabitants of the Sandwich Islands.* Honolulu: Honolulu Advertiser, 1963.

———. *Owhyhee: With Remarks on the History, Traditions, Manners, Customs, and Language of the Inhabitants of the Sandwich Islands.* Honolulu: Advertiser Publishing, 1963.

———. *Vindication and Appeal: The American Mission in the Sandwich Islands.* Saint Helens, OR: Helps Communications / Titus Coan Library, 2016.

Emens, Etta A. *Descendants of Captain Samuel Church of Churchville, New York.* Rochester, NY: Emens, 1920.

Emerson, Nathaniel B. *Unwritten Literature of Hawaii: Sacred Songs of the Hula.* Smithsonian Institution Bulletin of the Bureau of American Ethnology 38. Washington, DC: Smithsonian Institution, 1909.

Encyclopedia Britannica. https://www.britannica.com/.

Erskine, Charles. 2006. *Twenty Years Before the Mast: With the More Thrilling Scenes and Incidents while Circumnavigating the Globe under the Command of the Late Admiral Charles Wilkes, 1838–1842.* Chicago: Lakeside Press, 2006.

Find Latitude and Longitude. "Marquesas Islands." https://www.findlatitudeandlongitude.com/l/?=loc=Marquesas+Islands&id=208085#.Vv2Ddnr-mUk.

Finney, Charles G. *The Memoirs of Charles G. Finney: The Complete Restored Text.* Edited by Garth Rosell et al. Grand Rapids, MI: Academie Books, 1989.

———. *Holy Spirit Revivals.* Reprint. New Kensington, PA: Whitaker House, 1999.

Forbes, David W., et al. *Partners in Change: A Biographical Encyclopedia of American Protestant Missionaries in Hawai'i and their Hawaiian and Tahitian Colleagues, 1820–1900.* Honolulu: Hawaiian Mission's Children Society, 2018.

Fornander, Abraham. *An Account of the Polynesian Race: Its Origin and Migrations.* North Clarendon, VT: Tuttle, 1989.

———. *Ancient History of the Hawaiian People.* Honolulu: Mutual, 1996.

Freedictionary.com. https://www.freedictionary.com/.

The Friend. "Obituary of Fidelia Coan." *The Friend* 21.11 (November 2, 1872).

Fulton, Ruth. *Coan Genealogy, 1697–1982: Peter and George of East Hampton, Long Island, and Guilford, Connecticut, with Their Descendants in the Coan Line as well as Other Allied Lines.* Kanpur, India: Library Bot, 2010.

Grace-Paz, Gladys. "Patagonia Bookshelf." https://patlibros.org/.

Gray, William R. *Voyages to Paradise: Exploring in the Wake of Captain Cook.* Washington, DC: National Geographic Society, 1981.

Green, Jonathan S. *Notices of the Life, Character, and Labors of the Late Bartimeus L. Puaaiki, of Wailuku, Maui, Sandwich Islands*. Lahanaluna, HI: Press of the Mission Seminary, 1844.

Grudem, Wayne. *Systematic Theology*. Grand Rapids, MI: Zondervan Academic, 2020.

Gulick, Orramel, et al. *The Pilgrims Of Hawaii; Their Own Story Of Their Pilgrimage From New England And Life Work In The Sandwich Islands, Now Known As Hawaii*. New York: Revel, 1918.

Hallock, Leavitt H. *Hawaii under King Kalakaua from Personal Experiences of Leavitt H. Hallock*. Portland, ME: Smith and Sale, 1911.

Haskell, Daniel C. Haskell. *The United States Exploring Expedition, 1838-1842, and Its Publications, 1844-1874*. New York: New York Public Library, 1942.

Hawaii Fruit. "Figs." http://www.hawaiifruit.net/figs.htm.

Alexander, William P. "The Duty to Evangelize." Pamphlet. Honolulu: Hawaiian Islands Mission, 1836.

Hawley, Emily C. *The Introduction of Christianity into the Hawaiian Islands and the Development of These Islands through the Agency of the Missionaries and Their Descendants, 1820-1920*. Brattleboro, VT: Press of E. L. Hildreth, 1922.

Hibler, Anita M. *The Publication of the Wilkes Reports, 1842-77*. Washington, DC: George Washington University Press, 1989.

Historic Buildings of Massachusetts. "Rev. Samuel G. Buckingham House (1875)." http://mass.historicbuildingsct.com/?p=2619.

Hitchcock, Charles Henry. *Hawaii and Its Volcanoes*. Honolulu, Hawaii: The Hawaiian Gazette, 1909.

———. "Mohokea caldera," *Geological Society of America Bulletin* 17, 485-96.

Hotel Del Nómade. "Elephant seals in Peninsula Valdes." https://ecohosteria.com.ar/en/elephant-seals-in-peninsula-valdes-argentine-patagonia/.

Howe, K. R., ed. *Vaka Moana Voyages of the Ancestors: The Discovery and Settlement of the Pacific*. Honolulu: University of Hawaii Press, 2007.

Humphrey, Simon. "Titus Coan: Missionary Explorer." New York: New York American Tract Society, 1890.

———. "VI. Titus Coan," in *American Heroes on Mission Fields*. New York: American Tract Society, 1890, 3-26.

Hutchison, William R. *Errand to the World: American Protestant Thought and Foreign Missions*. Chicago: The University of Chicago Press, 1997.

Hyde, John Jr. *Mormonism: Its Leaders and Designs*. Whitefish, MT: Kessinger, 2006.

Hymnary.org. "The Happy Land." http://www.hymnary.org/text/there_is_a_happy_land_far_far_away.

Jarves, James Jackson. *History of the Hawaiian Islands*. Honolulu: C. E. Hitchcock, 1847.

Johnson, Paul E. *A Shopkeeper's Millennium: Society and Revivals in Rochester, New York, 1815-1837*. New York: Hill and Wang, 2004.

Johnson, Rossiter. *The Twentieth-Century Biographical Dictionary of Notable Americans*. Boston: The Biographical Society, 1904.

Jones, Pei Te Hurunui. *King Potatau: An Account of the Life of Potatau Te Wherowhero the First Maori King*. Wellington, New Zealand: Polynesian Society, 1959.

Judd, Albert F., II. *Missionary Album: Portraits and Biographical Sketches of the American Protestant Missionaries to the Hawaiian Islands*. Honolulu: Hawaiian Mission Children's Society, 1969.

Judd, Gerrit Parmele. *Fragments: Family Records, House of Judd*. Honolulu: Honolulu Star Bulletin, 1928.

Judd, Laura Fish. *Sketches of Life in Hawaii*. St. Helens, Oregon: Helps Communications, 2016.

Kane, Herb Kawainui. *Ancient Hawaii*. Captain Cook, HI: Kawainui Press, 1997.

Kaohi, Aletha, Stanly Lum, Sharon Matsuyama, and Boyd Magsuyama, eds. *Celebrating Advocacy: Past, Present, and Future*. Honolulu: State Council of Hawaiian Congregational Churches, 2008.

Kay, E. Alison. "Missionary Contributions to Hawaiian Natural History." *Hawaiian Journal of History* 31 (1997) 27–52.

Kimball, James William. *Heaven: "My Father's House."* Charleston, SC: Andesite Press, 2015.

Kuykendall, Ralph S. *The Hawaiian Kingdom: Volume 1: Foundation and Transformation, 1778–1854*. Honolulu: University of Hawai'i Press, 1938.

Lacy, Creighton. *The Word-Carrying Giant: The Growth of the American Bible Society*. Pasadena: William Carey Library, 1985.

Lafayette Avenue Presbyterian Church. http://www.nycago.org/Organs/Bkln/html/LafayetteAvPres.html.

Lamaina, John Kalei Jr. "Hawaiians Begin Learning the Palapala." In *Bedroom Annex/Print Shop: Language, Literacy, and Meaning*, edited by Thomas A. Woods, 27. Honolulu: Hawaiian Mission Houses Historic Site and Archives, 2017.

Larsen, Timothy. "Austin Henry Layard's Nineveh: The Bible and Archeology in Victorian Britain." *Journal of Religious History* 33.1 (March 2009) 66.

Larson, Gustav. T*he Americanization of Utah for Statehood*. San Marino, CA: Huntington Library, 1971.

Latter-day Saint Bible Dictionary. "Lots, casting of." https://www.churchofjesuschrist.org/study/scriptures/bd/lots-casting-of?lang=eng.

Library of Congress. "Titus Coan Family Papers." http://rs5.loc.gov/service/mss/eadxmlmss/eadpdfmss/uploaded_pdf/ead_pdf_batch_17_june_2010/ms009306.pdf.

Lingenfelter, Richard E. *Presses of the Pacific Islands, 1817–1867: A History of the First Half Century of Printing in the Pacific Islands*. Los Angeles: Plantin Press, 1967.

Livermore, Abiel Abbot. *The War with Mexico Reviewed*. BiblioLife Reproduction Series. New York: Wentworth, 2019.

Lockwood, John P., and Richard W. Hazlett. *Volcanoes: A Global Perspective*. Oxford: Wiley-Blackwell, 2010.

Lockwood, John P., and Lipman, Peter W. "Holocene eruptive history of Mauna Loa Volcano." In *Volcanoes in Hawaii*, edited by R. W. Decker, T. L. Wright, and P. H. Stauffer, 509–36.

Loomis, Albertine. *Grapes of Canaan: Hawaii 1820. The True Story of Hawaii's Missionaries*. Honolulu: Hawaiian Mission Children's Society, 1984.

———. *To All People: A History of the Hawaii Conference of the United Church of Christ*. Honolulu: The Hawaii Conference of the United Church of Christ, 1970.

Lyman, Chester Smith. *Around the Horn to the Sandwich Islands and California, 1845–1850: Being a Personal Record Kept by Chester S. Lyman*. New Haven: Yale University Press, 1924.

Lyman, Nettie Hammond, Kathryn Lyman Bond, and Ethel M. Damon, eds. *The Lymans Of Hilo: A Fascinating Account of Life in Nineteenth-Century Hawaii*. Hilo: Lyman House Memorial Museum, 1979.

Lyon, Jeffrey. "*No Ka Baibala Hemolele*: The Making of the Hawaiian Bible." *Palapala* 1 (2017) 113–51.
Manuscript Finding Aids. "HEA." https://sites.google.com/site/manuscriptfindingaids/hea.
Mapcarta.com. "'Ola'a Flume Spring," https://mapcarta.com/24049010.
Maps of World. "Micronesia Lat-Long." http://www.mapsofworld.com/lat_long/micronesia-lat-long.html.
MaritimeHeritage.org. "RMSS Zealandia, SS Zealandia." https://www.maritimeheritage.org/passengers/RMSS-Zealandia.html.
Marocco, James. *Hawaii's Great Awakening*. Kahuli, HI: Bartimeus Publishing, 1991.
Marsden, George. *Jonathan Edwards: A Life*. New Haven: Yale University Press, 2003.
Marsh, John W., and W. H. Stirling. *The Story of Commander Allen Gardiner, RN, with Sketches of Missionary Work in South America*. London: Nisbet and Co., 1857.
Martin, Margaret Greer, et al., eds. *The Lymans of Hilo: A Fascinating Account of Life in Nineteenth-Century Hawaii*. Hilo: Lyman House, 1979.
Martin, Margaret Greer, ed. *Sarah Joiner Lyman of Hawaii: Her Own Story*. Hilo: Lyman House, 2009.
Maui Hawaii.org. "Liohi." https://www.mauihawaii.org/loihi/.
Mayo Clinic. "Excessive Sweating." http://www.mayoclinic.org/symptoms/excessive-sweating/basics/causes/sym-20050780.
McBride, Likeke R. *The Kāhuna: Versatile Masters of Old Hawaii*. Hilo: Petroglyph Press, 2000.
McGavin, William. *The Protestant: Essays on the Principal Points of Controversy Between the Church of Rome and the Reformed*. Hartford, CT: Hutchison and Dwier, 1834.
McLoughlin, William. *Modern Revivalism: Charles Grandison Finney to Billy Graham*. Santa Fe, NM: Ronald Press, 1959.
Merriam Webster Online Dictionary. https://www.merriam-webster.com.
Miller, Char. *Fathers and Sons: The Bingham Family and American Mission*. Philadelphia: Temple University Press, 1982.
———. *Selected Writings of Hiram Bingham, 1814–1869: "To Raise the Lord's Banner."* Studies in American Religion 31. Lewiston, NY: Edwin Mellen, 1988.
———. "Text in Context: The Journal of a Nineteenth-Century American Missionary." *Yale University Gazette* (October 1991) 47–63.
———. "'The World Creeps In': Hiram Bingham III and the Decline in Missionary Fervor." *Hawaiian Journal of History* 15 (1981). http://scholarship.claremont.edu/cgi/viewcontent.cgi?article=1183&context=pomona_fac_pub.
Millett, Robert L., and Gregory C. V. Johnson. *Bridging the Divide: The Continuing Conversation Between a Mormon and an Evangelical*. Rhinebeck, NY: Monkfish Press, 2007.
Minutes of the Hawaiian Association, Held at Honolulu, May and June, 1839.
"Mission Station Reports - Hawaii - Hilo - 1835–1863." *Hawaiian Mission Houses Digital Archive*. https://hmha.missionhouses.org/items/show/845.
Montgomery, James. *Selection of Psalms and Hymns*. London: Longmun, Hurst, Rees, Orme, and Brown, 1819.
More, Thomas. *Utopia: A Little, True Book, Not Less Beneficial Than Enjoyable, About How Things Should Be in a State and about the New Island Utopia*. 1514.
Mormon Wiki. https://www.mormonwiki.com.

Morris, Nancy Jane. *Hawaiian Missionaries Abroad, 1852–1909.* Manoa, HI: University of Hawaii Press, 1987.

Morris, Nancy Jane, and Robert Benedetto. *Nā Kahu: Portraits of Native Hawaiian Pastors at Home and Abroad, 1820–1900.* Honolulu: University of Hawai'i Press, 2019.

Morse, Jedidah. *The Universal American Geography.* Charleston, SC: Nabu Press, 2011.

Newspapers.com. "Brooklyn Daily Eagle." https://bklyn.newspapers.com/image/50436884/?terms=Brooklyn+Daily+Eagle+Board.

New World Encyclopedia. http://www.newworldencyclopedia.org.

New York Times. Preliminary death notice of Titus Coan. January 5, 1883, "Brief Sketch of an Old Missionary."

Nida, Eugene. *The Book of a Thousand Tongues.* New York: United Bible Societies, 1972.

———. *Toward a Science of Translating: With Special Reference to Principles and Procedures Involved in Bible Translating.* Boston: Brill, 1964.

Oden, Thomas. "General Introduction" to *The Ancient Christian Commentary Series*, 29 volumes. Downers Grove, IL: IVP Academic, 2014.

O'Driscoll, Jeff. "Hyrum Smith: An Example of Faithfulness." Speech, Brigham Young University, Laie, HI. January 26, 2010.

'Opukahai'ia. 2020; Kaila-Kona, Hawai'i, and Seattle, Washington; Michael Lienau, Global Net Productions. Documentary.

Ostlings, Richard, and Joan K. Ostings *Mormon America: The Power and the Promise.* New York: Harper Collins, 2007.

Oxford Dictionaries Online. http://www.oxforddictionaries.com/us/.

Pacific Commercial Advertiser. *Kalakaua's Tour Around the World.* Honolulu: Pacific Commercial Advertiser, 1881.

Papakilo Database. https://www.papakilodatabase.com/.

Paul Rapoza's Helps Communications. http://www.helps7.com/Books/paperback.html.

Philbrick, Nathaniel. *The Private Journal of William Reynolds: United States Exploring Expedition, 1838–42.* New York: Penguin Classics, 2004.

———. *Sea of Glory: The Epic South Seas Expedition 1838–42.* New York: Harper Perennial, 2005.

———. *The Scientific Legacy of the US Exploring Expedition.* New York: Viking Penguin, 2003.

Phillips, Clifton Jackson. *Protestant America and the Pagan World: The First Half-Century of the American Board of Commissioners for Foreign Missions.* Cambridge, MA: Harvard University Press, 1969.

Piercy, LaRue. *Hawaii's Missionary Saga: Sacrifice and Godliness in Paradise.* Honolulu: Mutual Publishing, 1992.

Plumley, G. S. *The Presbyterian Church Throughout the World: From the Earliest to the Present Times, in a Series of Biographical and Historical Sketches.* New York: D. W. C. Lent & Company, 1875.

Porteus, Stanley D. *A Century of Social Thinking in Hawaii.* Palo Alto, CA: Pacific Books, 1962.

Porter et al. *Fragments of Real Missionary Life: From the Recollections of the Rev. John D. Paris.* Honolulu: The Friend, 1926.

President Lincoln's Cottage. www.lincolncottage.org.

Puku'i, Mary Kawena. *Hawaiian Dictionary. Hawaiian-English. English-Hawaiian.* Honolulu: University of Hawaii Press, 1980.

———. *Hawaiʻi Island Legends: Pikoi, Pele, and Others*. Honolulu: Kamehameha School Press, 1996.

Putney, Clifford. *Missionaries in Hawaiʻi: The Lives of Peter and Fanny Gulick, 1797–1883*. Boston: University of Massachusetts Press, 2010.

Richardson, Don. *Eternity in their Hearts*. Bloomington, MN: Bethany House Publishers, 1981.

Reynolds, George. "The Work of the Lord in the Sandwich Islands and New Zealand." *Journal of Discourses* 26 (1885) 157–63. https://jod.mrm.org/26/157.

Reynolds, William Cleaver, Anne Hoffman, and E. Jeffrey Stann, eds. *Voyage to the Southern Ocean: The Letters of Lieutenant William Reynolds from the US Exploring Expedition, 1838–1842*. Annapolis, MD: Naval Institute Press, 1988.

Rieu, E. V. and J. B. Phillips. *Translating the Gospels*. London: Penguin Books, 1954.

Schmitt, Robert C. *Demographic Statistics of Hawaiʻi, 1778–1965*. Honolulu: University of Hawaiʻi Press, 1968.

Schneider, Robert Alan. "The Senior Secretary: Rufus Anderson and the American Board of Commissioners for Foreign Missions, 1810–1860." PhD dissertation. Harvard University, 1980.

Schültz, Albert J. *Hawaiian Language: Past, Present, and Future: Things Every Teacher and Student of the Hawaiian Language Might Like to Know*. Honolulu: University of Hawaiʻi Press, 2020.

Smith, Edward, et al. *Polynesian Religion*. Bernice P. Bishop Museum Bulletin 34. Honolulu: Bernice P. Bishop Museum. Reprint, Millwood, NY: Kraus Reprint Co., 1978.

Smith, Joseph F. *"My Candid Opinion": The Sandwich Islands Diaries of Joseph F. Smith, 1856–1857*. Edited by Nathaniel R. Ricks. Faith Promoting Series 1. Salt Lake City: Juvenile Instructor Office, 1879.

Spaulding, Thomas M. "The adoption of the Hawaiian alphabet." *Papers of the Historical of the Hawaiian Historical Society* 17 (1930) 28–33.

Spargo, Chris. "Breathtaking moment Hawaiian volcano explodes as crater wall collapses causing flaming lava lake blast." *Daily Mail*, May 4, 2015. https://www.dailymail.co.uk/news/article-3067326/Breathtaking-moment-Hawaiian-volcano-explodes-crater-wall-collapses-causing-fiery-lava-lake-blast.html.

Spring, Leverett W. *A History of Williams College*. Boston: Houghton Mifflin, 1917.

St. Joseph Catholic Church. "History." http://www.stjoehilo.org/history.php.

Stanton, William Ragan. *The First Great United States Exploring Expedition of 1838–1842*. Oakland: University of California Press, 1975.

Stauffer, Peter H., et al. *Volcanism in Hawaii*. Washington, DC: US Government Publishing Office, 1987.

Steigerwald, Bill. "Biggest, Deepest Crater Exposes Hidden, Ancient Moon." NASA Goddard Space Flight Center, March 4, 2010. https://www.nasa.gov/centers/goddard/news/features/2010/biggest_crater.html.

Sterman, Paul "Retiring But Not Shy." *Pomona College Magazine*. https://magazine.pomona.edu/2015/summer/retiring-but-not-shy/.

Stevenson, Robert Louis. *In the South Seas*. Edited by Sidney Colvin. New York: Charles Scribner's Sons, 1896.

Stimson, Frank J. *The Cult of Kihotumu*. Bernice P. Bishop Museum Bulletin 111. Honolulu: Bernice P. Bishop Museum, 1944.

Tamashiro, Alan. "The Original Monotheism of the Hawaiians and their Receptivity to the Gospel through Special Revelation with Relevant Applications to Puna Baptist Church in Pahoa, Hawaii." Doctor of Ministry Dissertation. Southwestern Baptist Theological Seminary, 2013.

Tate, Merze. "Sandwich Islands Missionaries Train a Native Pastorate." *The Journal of Religious Thought* 17 (Winter–Spring 1960): 33–39.

Taylor, Sharon. "That Obnoxious Doctrine: Future Probation and the Struggle to Construct an American Congregational Identity." PhD thesis. Boston College, 2004.

Taylor, Sharon. "The Great Debate." In *The Role of the American Board: Bicentennial Reflections on the Organization's Missionary Work, 1810–2010*. Eugene, OR: Wipf & Stock, 2012. 11–26.

Thurston, Lucy Goodale. *Life and Times of Mrs. Lucy G. Thurston: Wife of Rev. Asa Thurston, Pioneer Missionary to the Sandwich Islands*. Whitefish, MT: Kessinger, 1872.

Titus Coan Memorial Library. http://www.tc-lib.org.

Tooley, Mark. *The Peace That Almost Was: The Forgotten Story of the 1861 Washington Peace Conference and the Final Attempt to Avert the Civil War*. Nashville: Thomas Nelson, 2015.

Tracy, Joseph. *History of the American Board of Commissioners for Foreign Missions*. New York: M. W. Dodd, 1842.

Traditional Music Library. http://www.traditionalmusic.co.uk/.

"Translating the Gospels." BBC Radio. April 1, 1954. https://genome.ch.bbc.co.uk/2e860b35 82f9495da72cfda9e95ab13d.

Turner, John G. *Brigham Young: Pioneer Prophet*. Cambridge, MA: Belknap, 2012.

Uncle Dave's Readings in Early Mormon History. http://sidneyrigdon.com/dbroadhu/HI/mischawi.htm.

United Methodist Church Discipleship Ministries. "Changing Wine into Grape Juice: Thomas and Charles Welch and the Transition to Unfermented Fruit." https://www.umcdiscipleship.org/resources/changing-wine-into-grape-juice-thomas-and-charles-welch-and-the-transition.

University of Cambridge Charles Darwin Correspondence Project. http://www.darwinproject.ac.uk/titus-coan.

US Archives. "Records of the Education Division of the Bureau of Refugees, Freedmen, and Abandoned Lands. " https://www.archives.gov/files/research/microfilm/m803.pdf.

US Climate Data. "Hilo–Hawaii." https://www.usclimatedata.com/climate/hilo/hawaii/united-states/ushi0022.

US Geological Survey. "Volcano Watch: New Book Reintroduces Old Terminology." Hawaii 24/7. https://hawaii247.com/2010/09/03/volcano-watch-new-book-reintroduces-old-terminology/.

———. "Volcano Watch: Strong Ties Between Volcanoes and Religion." Hawaii 24/7. https://hawaii247.com/2010/01/07/volcano-watch-strong-ties-between-volcanoes-and-religion/.

US Geological Survey Earthquakes. https://earthquake.usgs.gov/earthquakes/.

US Geological Survey Hawaiian Volcano Observatory. https://www.usgs.gov/observatories/hawaiian-volcano-observatory/active-volcanoes-hawaii.

US Geological Survey Volcano Watch. http://hvo.wr.usgs.gov/volcano-watch/.

US National Park Service. https://www.nps.gov/index.htm.

Warren, Jane S. *Morning Star: History of the Children's Missionary Vessel, and of the Marquesan and Microneisian [sic] Missions*. New York: American Tract Society, 1860.

The Weather Channel. "Kilauea Volcano Shoots Out Thin Glass Threads Called Pele's Hair." Weather.com. June 26, 2018. https://weather.com/science/nature/video/kilauea-volcano-shoots-out-thin-glass-threads-called-peles-hair.

Webster, Noah. *The Webster Bible in the Common Version. With Amendments of the Language.* New Haven: Durrie & Peck, 1832.

Webster, Noah, and Samuel Austin. *Universal Geography of the United States.* 1833.

Welch, John W. "The Book of Mormon as the Keystone of Church Administration." In *A Firm Foundation: Church Organization and Administration,* edited by David J. Whittaker and Arnold K. Garr. Salt Lake City: Deseret Book, 2011. 15–57.

Westervelt, W. D. "The Story of the Hawaiian Board." *The Friend* 24.4 (April 1, 1916) 83–84.

Wetmore, Charles Hinckley. "The Revival of 1837 at Hilo." In *Jubilee Celebration of the Arrival of the Missionary Reinforcement of 1837. Held April 9th, 10th, and 11th, 1887.* Honolulu: Daily Bulletin Stream Print, 1887. 61–75.

Whatahoro, H. T. *The Lore of the Whare-Wananga.* Translated by P. Smith. Memoirs of the Polynesian Society. New Plymouth, New Zealand: Thomas Avery, 1913.

Wheeler, Daniel. *Extracts from the Letters and Journals of Daniel Wheeler. While Engaged in a Religious Visit to the Inhabitants of Some of the Islands of the Pacific . . . Accompanied by His Son, Charles Wheeler.* London: Harvey and Darton, 1839.

———. *Tract.* London, 1907.

Whittaker, David J. "Placing the Keystone: George Q. Cannon's Mission and Translating the Book of Mormon in the Hawaiian Language." In *Revelation, Reason and Faith: Lessons in Honor of Truman G. Madsen,* edited by Parry Donald W., et al. Provo, UT: BYU Maxwell Institute, 2002.

Wikipedia. "Alpine Club." https://en.wikipedia.org/wiki/Alpine_Club_(UK).

———. "Architectural Metals." https://en.wikipedia.org/wiki/Architectural_metals.

———. "Brooklyn Academy of Music." https://en.wikipedia.org/wiki/Brooklyn_Academy_of_Music.

———. "Chester Lyman." https://en.wikipedia.org/wiki/Chester_Lyman.

———. "Christian Woman's Board of Missions." https://en.wikipedia.org/wiki/Christian_Woman%27s_Board_of_Missions.

———. "Continent." https://en.wikipedia.org/wiki/Continent.

———. "Daguerreotype." https://en.wikipedia.org/wiki/Daguerreotype.

———. "Daniel Wheeler (Missionary)." https://en.wikipedia.org/wiki/Daniel_Wheeler.

———. "François Fénelon." https://en.wikipedia.org/wiki/François_Fénelon.

———. "Freedman's Savings Bank." https://en.wikipedia.org/wiki/Freedman%27s_Savings_Bank.

———. "George Q. Cannon." https://en.wikipedia.org/wiki/George_Q._Cannon.

———. "Grammar School." https://en.wikipedia.org/wiki/Grammar_school.

———. "Great Awakening." https://en.wikipedia.org/wiki/Great_Awakening.

———. "Guanaco." https://en.wikipedia.org/wiki/Guanaco.

———. "Haleakalā." https://en.wikipedia.org/wiki/Haleakal%C4%81.

———. "Henry Allon." https://en.wikipedia.org/wiki/Henry_Allon.

———. "Henry Ward Beecher." https://en.wikipedia.org/wiki/Henry_Ward_Beecher.

———. "Hilo, Hawaii." https://en.wikipedia.org/wiki/Hilo,_Hawaii.

———. "Hiram Bingham I." https://en.wikipedia.org/wiki/Hiram_Bingham_I.

———. "James Dwight Dana." https://en.wikipedia.org/wiki/James_Dwight_Dana.

———. "Kīlauea." https://en.wikipedia.org/wiki/https://en.wikipedia.org/wiki/Kīlauea."

———. "Killingworth, Connecticut." https://en.wikipedia.org/wiki/Killingworth,_Connecticut.

———. "King James Version." https://en.wikipedia.org/wiki/King_James_Version.

———. "Ladd and Co." https://en.wikipedia.org/wiki/Ladd_%26_Co.

———. "List of Earthquakes in Chile." https://en.wikipedia.org/wiki/List_of_earthquakes_in_Chile.

———. "Louis McLane." https://en.wikipedia.org/wiki/Louis_McLane.

———. "Mauna Loa." https://en.wikipedia.org/wiki/Mauna_Loa.

———. "Maui." https://en.wikipedia.org/wiki/Maui.

———. "Mother Carey." https://en.wikipedia.org/wiki/Mother_Carey.

———. "Negotiable Instrument." https://en.wikipedia.org/wiki/Negotiable_instrument.

———. "New York Times." https://en.wikipedia.org/wiki/The_New_York_Times.

———. "Noah Webster." https://en.wikipedia.org/wiki/Noah_Webster.

———. "Oliver O. Howard." https://en.wikipedia.org/wiki/Oliver_Otis_Howard.

———. "Omoʻa." https://en.wikipedia.org/wiki/Omo%27a.

———. "Patagonia." https://en.wikipedia.org/wiki/Patagonia.

———. "Puna, Hawaii." https://en.wikipedia.org/wiki/Puna,_Hawaii.

———. "Rod (unit)." https://en.wikipedia.org/wiki/Rod_(unit).

———. "Rufus Anderson." https://en.wikipedia.org/wiki/Rufus_Anderson.

———. "Shuyler Colfax." https://en.wikipedia.org/wiki/Schuyler_Colfax.

———. "United States Exploring Expedition." https://en.wikipedia.org/wiki/United_States_Exploring_Expedition.

———. "USS Guerriere." https://en.wikipedia.org/wiki/USS_Guerriere_(1814).

———. "Wikipedia." https://en.wikipedia.org/wiki/Wikipedia.

———. "William Tufts Brigham." https://en.wikipedia.org/wiki/William_Tufts_Brigham.

———. "Valparaíso." https://en.wikipedia.org/wiki/Valparaíso.

Wilkes, Charles. *Voyage Round the World: Embracing the Principal Events of the Narrative of the United States Exploring Expedition, in One Volume: Illustrated with One Hundred and Seventy-Eight Engravings on Wood*. Philadelphia, George W. Groton, 1849.

A Witness to Aloha. 2020; Honolulu: Kawaiahaho Church and Cornerstone Multimedia. Documentary.

Wood, Reverend James, ed. *The Nuttall Encyclopædia: Being a Concise and Comprehensive Dictionary of General Knowledge*. London: Frederick Warne, 1907.

Woodbury, John Stillman. *Journals*. BYU Library. http://archives.lib.byu.edu/repositories/14/resources/5077.

Woods, Fred. "A Most Influential Mormon Islander: Jonathan Hawaii Napela." *The Hawaiian Journal of History* 42 (2008) np.

Woods, Fred E. "Jonathan Napela: A Noble Hawaiian Convert." In *Regional Studies in Latter-day Saint Church History: The Pacific Isles*, edited by Reid L. Neilson et al. Regional Studies in Latter-day Saint History 8. Provo, UT: BYU Religious Studies Center, Provo, 2008.

Wright, Thomas L., et al. *Hawaii Volcano Watch: A Pictorial History, 1779-1991*. Honolulu: University of Hawaiʻi Press, 1992.

Wyss, Max, et al. "The Lyman Hawaiian Earthquake Diary, 1833–1917." In *The US Geological Bulletin* 2027. Denver: US Geological Society, 1992.

Young, John Ray. *Memoirs of John Ray Young on His Sixtieth Birthday*. Salt Lake City: Deseret News, 1920.

BIBLIOGRAPHY

Young, Peter. "Hoʻokuleana: To Take Responsibility." http://totakeresponsibility.blogspot.com/2013_06_01_archive.html.

Yzendoom, Reginald. *History of the Catholic Mission in Hawaii*. Honolulu: Honolulu Star Bulletin, 1927.

Zamudio, A, Jesus Berrocal, and Celia Fern. "Seismic hazard assessment in the Peru-Chile border region." https://core.ac.uk/display/104018272.

Index of Scripture

OLD TESTAMENT

Genesis

1	198
1:9–10	362
6–9	360
8:11	385
9:24	275
14:18–20	110
18:25	277
19:11	360
32:26	15

Exodus

7:11	379
10:21	263
13:21	247, 265, 292
14:15	292
17:12	130
18:17–26	425
19:18	269
20:8	355
24:17–21	270
33:15	425n5
34:29	468
34:29–35	345

Leviticus

16:8	408n69
19:11	289
19:34	343
25:11–12	154

Numbers

26:55	408n69

Deuteronomy

12:35	470
29:5	205

Joshua

1:11	293
13:6; 14:1–2	408n69
24:15	144, 348

Judges

20:9	408n69

1 Samuel

7:2	297–98
10:20–21	408n69
18	119

2 Samuel

1:16	49
3:38	378

2 Kings

9:22	383

1 Chronicles

24:5,31	408n69
25:8	408n69
26:13–14	408n69

Ezra

48:35	133

Index of Scripture

Job

9:6	68
30:19	507
38:7	303
38:11	277
41:1	356
41:24	147

Psalms

7:11	156
8:4	283
16:6	68
18:18	151
20:5	155
22:12	268
23:6	466
29:3	85
29:3–4	168
31:23	277
46:1	220
46:7	179, 400
49:8	96
51:12	166
51:15	95
63:4	171
74:20	320
90:10	206
93:4	73
95:7	100
97:5	267
103	477
103:14	458
104:32	495
110:7	305
119:126	147
126:3	383
126:6	155
127:3	341
132:2	26
133:1	432
147:15	352
150:6	171

Proverbs

4:14	145
10:15	334
13:24	383
16:9	145
16:33	408n69
19:9	446
28:19	347
28:20	361

Ecclesiastes

1:9	422
2:1	442

Song of Solomon

2:11	385
2:15	48
4:9	445
5:6	15

Isaiah

1:18	347
2:2	430
2:4	371, 382, 385
2:22	172
3:11	143
9:6	365, 367n11
12:3	305
21:28	100
22:16	291
24:15	165
30:33	234
34:7	379
40:15	283
51:3	378, 445
54:2	292, 293
59:2	15
60:1, 14d	423
64:11	220
66:8	471

Jeremiah

3:1	15
6:14	404
6:26	240
8:11	404
8:16	220
13:29	371
23:24	152
23:29	139, 148
30:7	379
51:20	139

Ezekiel

3:17	155
4:12	489
13:10	404
30:3	146
33:4	49
36:26	348

Index of Scripture

37:3	476
47	475

Daniel

12:3	488

Joel

3:10	371, 382
4:13	157

Amos

7:5	172

Micah

1:4	455
4:3	385
6:8	380

Habakkuk

2:3	59
3:2	165

Zephaniah

3:17	156

Zechariah

2:5	61

Malachi

4:2	467

NEW TESTAMENT

Matthew

3:8	346
5:3	498
5:9	500
5:13–16	381
5:44	372
5:48	179
6:9–13	284
6:19–20	210
6:24	357, 361
7:12	384
7:26	210
9:37	334
9:38	80
10:34	371
11:28–30	100
12:8	355
12:33	151
13:1–23	144
13:45–46	352
16:2–3	165
16:24	305
17:20	172
22:39	377
24:38	146
24:39	146, 206
24:44	146, 207
25:23	49, 490, 498
25:35	343
28:19	159
28:20	155, 305

Mark

1:3	146
1:6	53
2:27	361
4:29	157
5:15	320, 371
11:12–25	145

Luke

2:10	119
2:20	166
2:29	476
2:49	476
6:28	189
7:38, 44	15
9:62	42
10:37	389
10:38–42	26
10:39	320
13:24	143
14:13	343
14:17	100
15:11–32	331
17:1	384
17:26–27	255
17:29	380
18:13	151
19:1–10	167
19:10	458
19:40	95
21:19	382
22:42	456
23:43	377
23:56	356

Index of Scripture

John

1:9	347
1:12	144
1:29	100, 155, 347
3:14	145
3:19	144, 362
4:8b	377
4:35	29, 80
5:24	144
5:25	143, 150
5:25, 28	147
6:37	347
7:37–39	475
8:12	46
10:14	159
11:25	459
14:16	478
21:25	495

Acts

1:25	377
1:26	408n69
2:37	142
2:38	142
2:39	160
5:1–11	360
6:1	288
6:4	498
8	170
8:4	288
9:6	301
10:44	148
16:25–40	167
16:26	387n83
16:30	96
17:30	98
18:6	49
19:19	149
20:21	133, 151
20:26	49
20:27	49
20:35	389
26:20	149

Romans

1:16	139, 154, 155
1:20	110
2:9	379
2:14	54
6:22, 23	289
8:1	129
8:13	144
11:14	389
12:19	470
13:4	380, 383
14	353n118
15:29	372, 381
16:27	171

1 Corinthians

2:16	130
6:1	289
12:21	68
12:31b	171
13:13	491
15:53	442
15:55	458
15:57	458
15:58	132
16:22	98, 99, 100
2 Corinthians	377
3:17	289
5:8	377
5:17	145
7:10	133, 151
10:4	400
12:9	458
13:11	385

Galatians

2:10	343
4:19	156
6:9	305

Ephesians

2:1	151, 166
3:8	97, 473
4	418
4:10	422
4:15	289
4:30	174
5:4	289
5:19	378
6:10–18	156
6:16	367

Philippians

2:12	220
3:14	156

Colossians

1:18	500

1 Timothy

6:6	369
6:9	361
6:10	361

2 Timothy

1:5	98
2:3	367n11
2:14	289
3:15	130
4:2	132
4:5	26
4:6–8	496
4:7	478

Titus

2:13	155

Hebrews

3:7	100
4:9	441
4:12	148
4:12–13	139
8:12	378
10:29	347
11:10	89
11:16	72, 467
12:24	347
12:25	144
13:2	343

James

1:27	348, 355
3:13	382
3:18	384

1 Peter

1:7	507
1:8	153
4:18	353

2 Peter

1:19	63
1:21	288

1 John

4:8b	377
4:18	490
5:20	54

Jude

1:23	154
1:25	171
7	360
25	155

Revelation

2, 3	386
2:20	459
2:28	46, 291
4:5	381
5:6	100
6:2	155
7:9, 10, 13–17	73
8:6–7	387
8:7	386
9:2	256
11:12	495
11:15	387, 388
16:1	379
19:8	367
19:11	400
20:10	383
20:13	327
21:1	305, 384–85
21:3	168
21:4	502
21:5	384, 427
22:7	144
22:16	46, 291, 295
22:17	99

Index of Subjects

Abeel, David, 97n164
abolitionists, 387
Abraham, 110
Abraham (Natua), 321
Acheson, Sarah, 225, 399
Adams, John Quincy, 183
Admiral Cockburn (whaler), 206, 346–47
Adventures in Patagonia, 34, 436, 472
The Advocate of Peace, 368–75, 378, 381, 383, 469
afterlife, Patagonian perception, 60
albatross (*Diomedia exulans*), 45
Alden, E.K., 491
Alexander, William D., 489
Alexander, William P., 165, 230, 315, 330, 495
aliʻi (chiefs), 113
aliʻi-kapu, 113
Allon, Henry, 440
Allred, Reddick Newton, 411
alphabet, Hawaiian, 121
Alpine Club, 495n64
"altitude sickness," 187
Alvord, John W., 445
American [Bible] Society, 125
American Board of Commissioners for Foreign Missions (ABCFM), 2, 4, 5, 17, 284, 285–88, 506
    annual meeting 1870, 6, 437–41
    control by, 70
    Damon application to, 338
    Eleventh Company, 443n104
    Hawaiʻi mission completion, 286
    land owned by, 189
    missionaries' first arrival in Hawaiʻi, 4
    Pioneer Company, 285
    Prudential Committee, 31, 64, 310
    Third Company, 434n 51
American Journal of Science, 5, 199, 230, 268
American Journal of Science and Arts, 264
American Missionary Society, 129
American Peace Society, 369
    donations for, 388–89

American Philosophical Society, 185
    The Wilkes Exploring Expedition of the United States Navy, 1838–1842, 185
American Seamen's Friend Society, 336, 351
Anderson, Rufus, 135, 137, 164, 172
    at annual meeting, 440
    caution on conversions, 173
    and Coan ordination, 34
    Coan visit with, 39–40
    correspondence with Coan, 4, 35–36, 70, 286
    Hawaiian mission termination, 287
    letter to Sandwich Islands, 176
    on Patagonia project, 36–37
    response to Lyons, 173
    Seventh Company letter, 79–80
    Titus commendation for Goodrich, 87
    visit to Hawaiian Islands, 288, 344
Andes mountains, 47
Andres, Robert W., 82–83
Andrews, Lorrin, 124, 179, 414
The Angel of Peace, 366, 391
animals, 86
Antarctic (schooner), 61–62
Anthony, Thomas, 91
Aoki, Stan, 512
Apaiang, Gilbert Islands, 300, 304
archaeology, 202
Argentina, 47. *see also* Patagonia
Arica, Peru, earthquake, 213n93
aristocracy, 112
Armand, Abraham, 398
Arms, Mrs., 38
Arms, William, 2, 17, 33, 34, 36, 61, 285
    threats to, 62
Armstrong, Richard, 77, 164, 165, 167, 177, 286, 315
l'Artemise (French Navy frigate), 399
Ashurbanipal, library, 202
Auburn
    Coan work in prison, 26–27
    revival at First Church, 28

Index of Subjects

Auburn Presbyterian Church, 2, 17
Auburn Seminary, 2, 17, 285
   Coan entry into, 23–24
   courses, 25
Auna, 116n57
Auona in Marquesas Islands, 331–32
Aurelius Augustinus, *City of God*, 395
Australia, 437n73
Australia (steamship), 470n89

Bachelot, Alexis, 398
Bacon, Leonard, 439
Bailer, Edward, 201
Baker, Albert S., 282, 307, 312, 481
Baking, Robert, 431n32
Baldwin, Dwight, 165, 169, 176, 415, 490
banyan, 329
baptism
   by Bishop, 163–64
   of children, 160
   by Coan, 158–61, 170, 513
   Coan views, 180
   by Mormons, 411, 413
bark cloth (tapa), 315n16
Barstan, Mr., 429
Bates, Mr., 434
Bay of Hilo, 67–68, 206
Beadle, John, 431n32
Beagle (ship), 196–97
Bean, Hannah, 344, 375, 377
Bean, Joel, 344, 375, 467, 500–501
Beckwith, George Beckwith, 369, 373
   Coan letter to, 378
   The Peace Manual, 374
Beecher, Henry Ward, 441
Beecher, Lyman, 27
Benedict, Daniel, 180n117
Bethel Church in Honolulu, 339
Bethel Seamen's Chapel, 340, 341
Bible. *see also separate scripture index*
   burning, 401
   Coan and, 26
   distribution, 363–64
   Hawaiian translation, 97, 123–25
   and science, 195, 234, 466–67
   for seamen, 353
Bibline, xxi
Bickerstaff, Edward H., 491n53
Bicknell, Mr., 327
Bigler, Henry W., 407, 407n64, 408, 415
Bill of Exchange, 389n94
Bingham, Clara, 296, 426
   pregnancy, 306
Bingham, Clarissa, 300
   death, 308

Bingham, Hiram, 82, 135, 175–78, 400, 401
   on annual meeting, 1837, 150
   on Awakening, 126, 168, 175–78
   and Coan arrival in Hawai'i, 77
   death, 299n77
   and Hawaiian translation of Bible, 124
   in Hilo, 1830, 128–29
   on Kilauea, 241
   leadership of Pioneer company, 4
   on learning of revival, 128
   marriage to Sybil Mosley, 117
   on spelling book, 122
   on tsunamis, 207
   Twenty-One Year Residence in the Sandwich Islands, 297
   visit to Mauna Kea, 236
   on volcanoes, 227
   writings, 137
Bingham, Hiram II, 296–97, 489
   correspondence with Coan, 305, 426
   death, 308
   first view of Hawai'i, 294
   health, 306
   in Honolulu, 306
   inclusion in *Memorial Volume*, 230
   memories of Coan, 493
   on Morning Star crew member conversions, 293–94
   pressure on, 297, 298
   The Story of the Morning Star: The Children's Mission Vessel, 300
   translations by, 308
   trip to Marquesas Islands, 326–27, 333
Bingham, Hiram III, 304, 489
   birth, 306, 308
Bingham, Lydia, 77, 85, 160, 182–83, 441. *see also* Coan, Lydia Bingham; *Memorial Volume* (L. Coan)
   excursion to volcano, 229
   marriage to Titus, 6–7, 455
   retrospective on Coans' U.S. visit, 453–54
   Titus courting of, 463
   on Titus' gift with children, 78
Bingham, Mrs. Hiram II, 498–99
Bingham, Sybil, 297
Binghams, 3
Bird, Isabella, 83–84, 280, 343
birds, 45, 201
Bishop, Artemas, 163, 226
Bishop, Sereno Edwards, 171, 490, 496
   on baptisms by Coan, 160
   on Coan, 191
   Coan's impact on children, 78
   on great revival, 126, 135, 137, 162–63, 168
   Lydia letter to, 508–9

Index of Subjects

on preaching, 139
weather observation, 203
"Bishop's Rings," 203-4
Bistante, 58
Bitton, Davis, 416
Bjorling. Patricia, 506
Blackwell, Hiram, 407n64, 408
"Blind Bartimaeus." *see* Pua'aiki, Lalana (Blind Bartimaeus)
Boarding Schools, in Marquesas Islands, 333
Bonar, Horatius, "No Shadow Yonder," 459n25
Bond, Elias, 422, 443, 500, 500n80
La Bonte (French Navy ship), 398
The Book of Mormon, 406
    Hawaiian language translation, 415
books, 348-49
bookshelves, 91
Borneo, 36
Boruck, Henry, 57
Boston, 73-74, 176
Boyd, Dr., 344
Boyd, Geneva, 344
Boyd, Rev. J.R., 491
Bradley, James, *Church History: An Introduction to Research, Reference Works, and Methods*, 7
Brannan, Sam, 406
Bray, Isaiah, 309, 310, 367
Brigham, William Tufts, 228, 343, 491-92
    The Volcanoes of Kiluea and Mauna Loa, 225
Brinsmade, Peter A., 182, 186, 188
Brooklyn
    American Board annual meeting, 437-41
    Coan in, 423
Brooklyn Academy of Music, 438n78
Brooklyn Eagle Daily Newspaper, 438
Brown, John W., 293, 316, 319
Brown, Lydia, 71
Buckingham, Samuel G., 440
bull on Mauna Loa, 268
Burchard, Samuel Dickerson, 24
burial customs
    in Patagonia, 58
    at sea, 327
Butler, Benjamin, 431n32
Byron, George Anson Lord, 67, 399
Byron's Bay, 82. *see also* Hilo

Caine, John T., 411
California Gold Rush, 350, 406
Callao, Peru, 76, 397
Calvinists, 422
Campbell, Douglas S., 35
cancer, 457, 461
canefields, 188

cannibalism, 320, 323, 325, 393-94
Cannon, George Q., 417, 428, 429
    arrival in Hawai'i, 408
    attempt to speak in Protestant churches, 419
    on Coan and prejudice, 410
    departure from Great Salt Lake, 407n59
    Hawaiian conversion to Mormonism, 413-15
    Hawaiian *Journals*, 22-23n50
    Hilo description, 84-85
    and J. Green, 417-19
    Maui confrontation, 411
    in San Francisco, 415
    visit to Kilauea, 241-42
    visit to Mauna Loa, 228
    volcano description, 242
Cape Horn, *Morning Star* trip around, 297-98
Cape pigeons, 45
Caroline (ship), 301
caste system, 112
casting lots, 408
Castle, Samuel, 464-65, 490, 495-96
Catholic missionaries, in Marquesas Islands, 316
Celestial Marriage, 431n32
cemetery
    near Washington, 448, 450
    Prospect Hill, 459
census, 422
Chamberlain, Levi, 77, 90, 91, 92, 94, 147, 172, 214n97, 363, 403
Chamberlain, Maria Patton, 214n97
Chapin, Dr. and Mrs., 82
Chappell, Eliza Emily, 434n 57
Chatwin, Bruce, 47
Checo, 58
Cheeseman, Lewis, 23, 27
Chicago, Coans in, 432
children, 157, 178
    fundraising for mission ship, 292-93, 310
    and language, 89n127
    in Omoa, 320
    in Patagonia, 53, 61
    special attention to, 150
    spiritual state of, 145
    Titus' care of, 79, 80
    Titus' concern for missionary, 78-79
    visits to Coan home, 345
    work for peace, 392
Chile, 47. *see also* Patagonia
Christian baptismal name, 164
Christian Woman's Board of Missions, 450n130
Christianity
    Ka'ahumanu and, 118

Index of Subjects

Christianity *(continued)*
   Marquesas inhabitants opposition, 316–17
   in Micronesia, 301
   power over traditional beliefs, 223
   religious challenges to, 142
   spread of, 118
   and warfare, 372
Christmas day in Patagonia, 57
Church, Abigail (Munson) (Fidelia's mother), 20
Church, Amanda, 93–94, 401
Church, Fidelia, 2–3, 16–17. *see also* Coan, Fidelia Church
   call to mission, 29
   influence on Titus' Hawai'i decision, 3
   Patagonia mission discussion with Titus, 38–41
   physical appearance, 30
   physical needs, 30–31
   relationship with Titus, 30
   Titus' first sight of, 20
   Titus reunion after Patagonia, 64
Church, Samuel (Fidelia's father), 20
Church, S.C., 97
church building, 390
   cost of, 362–63
   in Hilo, 148–49, 163
Church History: An Introduction to Research, Reference Works, and Methods (Bradley and Mueller), 7
Church of Jesus Christ of Latter-day Saints, 395, 406–23
   critique, 420
   missionaries, 84–85
   Napela baptism, 415
   Quorum of the Twelve Apostles, 408n66
church planting, 288
churches
   Expedition impact on members, 182
   flaws, 386
   formation in Hanamenu, 331
   response to whaling, 358
Civil War (U.S.), 351
   Coan's opinion, 6, 380, 381–82, 452
   Coan's support of union, 378–87
   donations for peace, 390–91
   end times and, 385
   southern pastors and, 358
Clark, Ephraim, 124, 130, 287, 300, 312, 438–39, 489
Clark, Hiram, 407n64
Clark, Mary, 130
clergy
   ordination of Hawaiian, 287
   and peace, 387

Clift, Captain, 38, 42–43, 65
Climacus, John, 377n57
climate
   Coan's observations, 203
   of Micronesia, 304n108, 306
clothing, in Patagonia, 53–54
Cluff, William W., 411, 413
Coan, Edward J., 225, 512
Coan, Ezra, 73
Coan, Fidelia Church, 227
   on arrival in Hilo, 85
   cancer, 426, 457, 461
   death, 6, 458–59
   family unity, 457
   on frigate, 400–401
   health, 443, 452, 453, 454
   journey description, 74
   last days, 456–60
   letter to sister, 93–94
   letter to son Munson, 456–57
   Mauna Loa eruption description, 1852, 268–69
   obituary, 460
   view of Anderson letter, 176–77
Coan, Gaylord (father), 17
Coan, George, 71
Coan, George Whitfield, 468
Coan, Harriet Fidelia ("Hattie"), 201, 456, 458, 503
   opposition to Titus' second marriage, 464–65
   Titus' will and, 503, 504–5
Coan, Latimer, 444
Coan, Lydia Bingham, 23, 26, 27, 70, 134, 138, 146, 227. *see also Memorial Volume* (L. Coan)
   on 1877 tsunami effects, 210–12
   on appointment to Hawai'i, 69
   correspondence, 92, 93
   correspondence after Titus' stroke, 477
   journal, 296
   return to Honolulu, 503
   on Titus' business talents, 21
   on Titus' childhood, 16
   Titus giving of Hilo house, 503
   on Titus' in Auburn, 24
   on Titus' Patagonia trip, 34, 65
   Titus' relationship, 466
Coan, Mabel, 71
Coan, Munson, 97–98, 443, 464, 478
Coan, Philip Munson, 505n103
   Titus' will and, 505
Coan, Samuel Latimer (son), 6, 426–27, 504
   Titus' will and, 503, 505

Index of Subjects

Coan, Titus
  ABCFM land for, 189
  assistance with revivals, 23
  birth, 15, 18
  call to missions, 2, 32
  childhood, 15–16
  chronology, xvii–xviii
  confrontations with Catholics, 403
  conservative stance on doctrine, 192
  conversations with crews and officers, 363–64
  daily schedule, 144
  death, 18n20
  description of Mrs. Grant, 449
  education, 15, 18–19
  evangelization, 133, 191
  expatriate ministry, 335–64
  first tour of Hawaii, 140
  forgiveness, 15–16
  "God was there" theme, 168
  on God's presence, 144
  heiau description, 111
  Hilo residence. *see* Emerald Bower [Coan home]
  Last Will and Testament, 457n13, 490, 502–8
  lectures on papacy, 404
  library division, 506–7
  licensure to preach the gospel, 32
  love for Hawaiians, 192
  memorial service, 489–502
  as mentor, 285
  in militia, 367
  on missionaries and warfare, 317
  obituaries, 483–87
  opposition to coffee trees, 189–90
  as "Papa Coan," 78
  "peace man" perspective, 61
  personal qualities, 16
  physical appearance, 30
  preaching in Hawaiian, 95
  primary source material, 11–13
  prison work, 26–27
  "Recollection" ode to Fidelia, 461
  as Renaissance man, 19
  as revival leader, 191–92
  as seamen's chaplain, 335
  select-school opened in Riga by, 21
  statistics on ministry, 157–58
  as teacher, 19–21
  vocational options, 21–22
  "Waymarks" notebook, 463–64, 472
Coan, Titus, correspondence, 466–70
  to American Board, 1842, 178
  to Anderson, 286
  to Bingham, 305
  with brother Ezra, 182–83
  on Catholicism, 400
  with DuPont, 348–49
  to E. Hall, 182
  with Fidelia, 29, 171, 178
  last, 475–77
  "Letter to the Children," 366, 367
  to Lyons, 168, 170
  during NY canal travel, 71
  on Patagonia, 33, 35–40
  with Quakers, 375–78
  to son Latimer, 443
  on volcanoes, 230
Coan, Titus, health
  hip pain, 468
  illness and spiritual experience, 22–23
  medical care, 204–5
  stroke, 475
  stroke, last days before, 476
  stroke, months after, 477–81
Coan, Titus, personal relations
  on Fidelia, 459
  first sight of Fidelia, 20
  grief over Fidelia's death, 463
  marriage to Lydia Bingham, 455
  relationship with Fidelia, 30
Coan, Titus, scientific observations
  climatological observations, 203
  on earthquakes vs. volcanoes, 220
  on Kilauea eruption, 1840, 251
  lava flow study, 277–78
  at Mauna Loa summit, 265, 267
  preparation for Mauna Loa ascent, 265
  on science and the Bible, 234
  scientific interests, 4, 44–45, 202–4
  trip to lava flow, 1843, 271–73
  visit to Kilauea, 243
  volcano observations, 224, 495, 512
Coan, Titus, travels
  arrival at Patagonia camp, 51–52
  journey to Hilo, 66
  in Marquesas Islands, 1860, 316–26
  passport for travel to Patagonia, 41
  Patagonia mission discussion with Fidelia, 38–41
  recommendation on Patagonian mission, 56, 62, 64–65
  return to U.S. from Patagonia, 63–66
  trip to U.S. (1870–1871), 6
Coan, Titus, writings
  Adventures in Patagonia, 34, 436, 472
  autobiography (*Life in Hawaii*), 13, 472–73, 511
  autobiography organization, 473–74

541

Index of Subjects

Coan, Titus Munson, 227, 504
   Titus' will and, 505
"The Coan Chronicles," 1
Coans' visit to US (1870-71), 423-54
   American Board annual meeting, 437-41
   arrival in San Francisco, 427
   desire to return to Hilo home, 441, 442
   in District of Columbia, 441-44
   heading east, 431-33
   in Killingworth, 436-37
   medical attention for Fidelia, 425-26
   from Niles to Brooklyn, 436-37
   at Oberlin, 444
   Ohio General Congregational Conference, 433-36
   return to Hilo, 452-54
   in Sacramento, 427
   in Salt Lake City, 425-31
   states visited, 432
   travel planning, 426
   in Washington city, 444-52
coffee, 189
"Cold Water Army" for peace, 392
Colfax, Schuyler Jr., 446
   wife, 449, 451
commentaries, Hawaiian translation, 289n30
common sense of Coan, 25
communication. *see also* languages
   between Hawai'i and Boston, 176
communion, 160, 180-81, 321
   at Brooklyn national meeting, 440
   Coan officiating at Oberlin, 434
   in Salt Lake City, 430
Conde, Andelucia, 165
Conde, Daniel T.J., 352, 416, 417
Congo (Chief in Patagonia), 55-56, 57, 59
Congregationalists
   and natural theology, 201
   policy on Catholic presence, 398
Congress (whale ship), 323
Conservative Congregational Christian Conference, 312
constellations, southern, 45
conversions, 157-58, 162, 169, 179
   assimilation plan after, 192
   Bartemeus on, 167
   evidence of, 170
   methods for assuring genuine, 176
   of Morning Star crew members, 293-94
Cook, Captain, 3, 204
Cook, Christopher L., 136
   Preparing the Way, 115-16
Cook, James, 113
Cooke, Juliette, 168
coral polyp, 328n87

coral reef-rock, 198
Cornwall school, 116
correspondence, slowness of, 92-93
Cowles, Henry, 435n62
Cowman, Mrs. Charles, *Springs in the Desert*, 84n94
Cox, Doak C., 214-21
Crimean War (1853-4), 389n95
Crook, Mr., 315
Cross, Rosell T., 434
Cullom, Shelby, 431n32

dagguerotypes, 343n53, 344n56
Damon, Andrew M., 337
Damon, Ethel M., *Samuel Chenery Damon*, 337
Damon, Julia, 339, 351
Damon, Samuel Chenery, 224, 336-53, 460, 465, 489, 493-94
   Coan obituary, 484
   initial step toward missions, 338
   ordination, 338
   Seamen's Chaplain, 336-37
Dana, James. D., 182, 197-98, 210, 223, 238, 243, 248, 277, 428, 466
   Characteristics of Volcanoes, 224
Darling, Mr., 315
Darlow, T.H., 124
Dartmouth College, 433
Darwin, Charles, 2, 34, 55, 63, 196
"Darwin Project," 34
Daws, Gavan, 135-36, 138, 146, 155, 169, 173, 190-91
   The Hawaiian Kingdom, 105-6
de Neyra, Mendaña, 314
de Paula Marin, Don Francisco, 398
deliverance, 277
denominations, 432
Deseret Evening News, 430
Devlin, Philip R., 230
Diamond, Jared, *Guns, Germs, and Steel*, 204
Dibble, Sheldon, 113, 114, 117, 118, 164, 169, 350
Dido (ship), 66n111
Diell, John, 351, 363-64
digitization, 8-9, 13-14, 513
Dimond, Henry, 71, 76
Dimond, Mrs. Henry, 71
disasters, 355
Disciples of Christ world ministry, 506
District of Columbia, Coans in, 441-44
"divine afflatus," 163
Dixon, John, 407n64
documentaries, 513
domestic helpers, 89n127

Index of Subjects

Dominis, John, 212
Dominis, Lydia, 212
Don Quixote (ship), 93
Doughty, Andrew, 107n9, 228, 235
Downes, John, 398
Druery, Nicholas, 57–58
Dudley, Michael Kioni, *A Hawaiian Nation I: Man, Gods, and Nature*, 109
Duff (ship), 315
DuPont, Mrs., 348n85, 453
DuPont, Samuel F., 197, 202, 348–49, 353
    Coan letter to, 341, 380
Dutton, Clarence, 257
Dvorak, John, *The Last Volcano*, 455
Dwight, Edwin W., *Memoirs of Henry Obookiah*, 115
Dwight, Timothy, 116, 435n62
Dyaks, 36
"dynamic equivalent" translation, 98

E. Davidson (ship), 66n111
The Eagle, 439
earthquakes, 68, 89, 198n21, 214–21
    Arica, Peru, 213n93
    Coan's theory on cause, 218–19
    diaries, 214–15
    Kau, 1868, 216, 218
    and tsunamis, 4–5, 208
    and volcano eruption, 279
East Hawaii Association, 476
Edict of Toleration, 399
Edinburgh, Duke of, 346
Ehlke, Margaret, 7, 19, 22, 34, 90, 136, 140, 172, 175, 176–77, 286, 336, 354
    on Great Awakening protracted meeting, 149
    on Kauai revival, 127
    on opposition to Titus marriage to Lydia, 464
Ellis, William, 84, 121–22, 124, 226
    Journal of a Tour Around Hawaii, 227
Ely, John, 185, 388
Emerald Bower [Coan home], 3, 69, 83, 88–89, 101
    Hallock on, 345
    Titus work on, 91
    visitors, 342–48
Emery, Samuel Hopkins, 368–69, 391
end times, Civil War and, 385
Erasmus, 374
Erskine, Charles, 185, 186, 187
    Twenty Years before the Mast, 184
evangelization, 133, 191. *see also* missions
evil spirits, Patagonian perception, 58
Ewa, 163, 165

exchange rate, 199n26
expatriate ministry, 335–64
"expatriates," 334
Exploring Expedition (ExEx), 4, 181–91, 201–2, 248, 328
    activities on Sabbath, 359
    costs, 183
    Library of Congress on, 184
    mixed value of, 183
    secondary sources, 185
    working conditions for Hawaiians, 187
Ezra, 391n108

Fairbank, S.B., 440
Fairchild, President, 435n61
Falkland Islands, 63
Farrer, William, 407n64
Felt, Nathaniel H., 430
Field, Henry F., 436
Fifth Company, 132
Finney, Charles, 2, 6, 17, 27, 149, 177, 192, 433, 465
    and Perfectionism, 179–80
Finney, Lydia Andrews, 465
firearms. *see* weapons
First Church of Hawai'i, Hilo, 3
First Church of Oberlin (United Church), 435n59
First Congregational Society of West Pultney, 20
First Foreign Church of Hilo, 342
First Hawaiian Church of Hilo, 504
fissure in volcano, 271–72
flora of Hawai'i, 458n19
    Darwin on, 199
food, 65
    in Patagonia, 59
Forbes, Anderson Oliver, 342
Forbes, Cochran, 178
Forbes, David, 414n104
Foreign Mission School, 116
forest, destruction by lava, 271
forgiveness, 15–16, 347
Fornander, Abraham, 203n46
    An Account of the Polynesian Race, 108–9
Francis of Assisi, "The Peace Prayer," 395
Freedman's Saving and Trust Company, 445n114
Freedman's Savings Bank, 445n114
freedom of religion, 398
French
    Coan against naval actions, 394
    garrison in Marquesas Islands, 325
    law enforcement in Marquesas, 326

Index of Subjects

The Friend, 12, 137, 223, 276, 287, 299, 311, 322, 339, 340–41, 509, 513
Friends (Quakers), 375n52
   Coan correspondence with, 375–78
funding
   for Micronesia missions, 290
   for mission ship, 310
   for *Morning Star*, 301
   for *Morning Star III*, 308–9

Galatea (steam frigate), 346
Galilee fishing vessel, 128n146
Gallaudet, Thomas H., 117
gap theory of creation, 198, 229n73
Gardiner, Capt., 65–66n111
Garland, George F., 309
gases, from volcano, 256
Gelett, Charles W., 293, 309
General Meeting, discontinuation, 287
general readers, interests, 2–7
"gentiles," xxi
Gettysburg, PA, Coan visit in 1871, 381
Gibson, Walter Murray, 421
Gilbert Islands, 285, 306
"Gilbertina," 299f
girls, arrival for school examinations, 324
Glasgow Chronicle, 403
God. *see also* Supreme Being
   presence on Mauna Loa, 265
   revelation to Hawaiians, 110
   words for attributes, 98
Goetzmann, William H., *New Lands, New Men: America and the Second Great Age of Discovery*, 185
gold mission, 407, 408
Golett, Captain, 319
gonorrhea, 204
Goodfellow, Stephen, 344
Goodrich, Joseph, 86–87, 128, 188, 189, 226
   and Coans' Hilo residence, 90–91
Goodrich, Martha Barnes, 86–87
Goodrich family, 3
Goodwin, E.P., 475, 489
Goodwin, Maria S., 36
gospel, transformation by, 470
gospel meeting, weapons in, 394
Grace-Paz, Gladys, 35
grammar schools, 15n2
Grant, Ulysses, 448
grape juice, pasteurization, 180–81n117
Gray, William R., *Voyages to Paradise*, 109, 113
Great Awakening, 3, 4. *see also* Second Great Awakening
Great Revival, 134–36. *see also* Hawaiian Great Awakening

Green, Jonathan, 129, 165–66, 167, 369, 370–71, 415
Green, Theodotia, 129, 130
Gregory Bay (now in Chile), 34, 65
   potential mission-house at, 61
Griggs, J. D., *Hawai'i: A Pictorial History, 1779-1991*, 226
guanacos, 53
Gulick, Luther H., 440
Gulick, Peter J., 127, 135, 301, 434
Gulick, Rev. and Mrs. Orramel Hinckely, 135

Haili Church, 84, 88n123
   donations for peace from, 388–89
Hakahekau valley, 328–29
Hakatu, Coan visit in 1867, 330–31
Haleakala volcano, 223n8, 232–36
   Coan at summit, 467–68
   cones, 233f
   hazard map, 233–34, 233f
   USGS summary, 234–35
Halemaumau, 242
   lava lake in crater, 243
Hall, Edwin, 71, 182, 203n46
Hall, Mrs. Edwin, 71
Hallett, William B., 309
Hallock, Leavitt, 160, 207, 217, 220, 270, 279, 283, 344–45
   trip to Halemaumau, 246–47
   visit with Titus, 470–72
Halsey, Herman, 22, 349, 489
Halsey, Luther Sr., 434
Hamakua, 149
Hamakua Loa, 417
Hanahi valley in Marquesas Islands, 323–24
Hanamenu, 331
Hanavave, 394
Handy, E. S. Craighill, 111
   Polynesian Religion, 109
Hapuku, Zachariah, 319, 332
Harris, Mr., 315
Hassel, Harry, 57
Hawai'i Conference of the United Church of Christ, 506
Hawaiian Association of ABCFM missionaries, 175
Hawaiian Board of Missions, 313
Hawaiian clergy, 288
   ordination, 287, 288–89
Hawaiian Evangelical Association, 5, 284, 311, 312
   Coan as first president, 288
   established, 285, 287
   The Friend as journal, 340–41. *see also The Friend*

Index of Subjects

as Micronesia mission sponsor, 299
missionaries for the Marquesas, 317
Titus Coan Fund, 21, 506
in Titus' will, 504, 510–11
Hawaiian Great Awakening, 28, 153–57
   beginning, 123, 138–47
   Coan's description of Hilo, 148–49
   end of momentum, 190–91
   foreshadowing, 100, 101
   foundations, 105
   Hawaiian Bible translation and, 124
   Hawley description, 165
   Hilo and Puna districts (1836–40), 133–61
   name for, 134–36
   New Measures, 149–52
   opposition and response, 169–81, 496
   permanency, 513
   physical demonstrations, 150–51
   sources, 137–38
   spread between islands, 162–67
   statistics, 157–58
Hawaiian Islands, 107
   Chinese arrival, 505n105
   church leadership, 289–90
   Coan meeting of chiefs and people, 77–78
   Coans' description, 77
   coastal area growth from lava, 252–53
   communication between Boston and, 176
   hotspots, 235f
   Kekela lecturing, 322
   Marquesas missionaries from, 317
   missions in, 286
   natural history, 199
   needed materials for, 69–70
   and peace, 392, 469–70
   pre-Europeans/Americans, 107–13
   report at 1870 annual meeting, 439
   voyagers influence on culture, 120–21
Hawaiian Islands Mission, annual meeting, 1836, 139n49
Hawaiian language
   Coan obituary in, 486
   Coans and, 3, 95
   learning, 95–101
   preaching in, 98–99
Hawaiian missionaries. *see also* Pioneer Company
   Third Company, 434n51
   Fifth Company, 132
   Seventh Company, 71–72, 79–80, 140
   Eleventh Company, 443n104
   annual General Meeting, 76–77
Hawaiian Missionary Society, 5, 285, 290–91, 301
Hawaiian orthography, 122

Hawaiian royalty
   kapu system and, 111–12
   missionaries and, 80, 118
Hawaiian Spectator, 208–9
Hawaiian Volcano Observatory, 220, 455
Hawaiian Volcanoes, 257
Hawaiians, 285
   Christians like children, 425
   church gifts, 470
   Coan medical care for, 204–5
   Coan's love for, 192
   confrontations with Catholics, 404–5
   conversion to Mormonism, 422
   Expedition working conditions, 187
Hawkins, James, 407n64, 408
Hawley, Emily, 135, 165
Hazlett, Richard W., *Volcanoes: A Global Perspective*, 227
heat, from volcano, 246, 266–67
Heber, Regina, 293n47
heiau (temple), 3, 111
Hellespont (merchant ship), 3, 69, 70, 76, 397
   description, 72–73
hemolele (holiness), 98
Henderson, David, *The Hidden Coasts*, 185
Henry, Captain, 74
Heteani, 325
Hewahewa (priest), 117
Hill, C.W., 342, 350
Hillsdale College, 435n62
Hilo, 69, 82–91, 127, 165
   as American Board station, 82–83
   Catholics in, 402
   census, 1910, 148
   church building survival after earthquake, 219–20
   church membership at Coan's arrival, 147
   Coan's church as world's largest, 286
   Coans' journey to, 66
   Coans' return to, 452–54
   congregation size, 173
   and Fidelia's physical needs, 30–31
   First Foreign Church, 342
   Great Awakening (1836–40), 133–61
   history, 84
   home. *see* Emerald Bower [Coan home]
   language learning and early ministry, 95–101
   lava flow threat, 223, 269, 270–71, 274–75, 282
   loneliness, 92–94
   and Mauna Loa, 239
   missionaries in, 4
   as missionary station, 81, 128
   murder, 388

Index of Subjects

Hilo (continued)
    response to *Morning Star* arrival, 295–96
    ships increase, 349–51
    tidal waves, 146–47, 209–10
    Titus description, 99–100
    travel to, 82
    tsunami, 1868, 213–14
    Vancouver in, 113
    worship center losses from earthquake, 220
Hilo, Bay of, 67–68, 206
Hilo Conference (Mormon), 413
Hilo station report, 12
    1862, 289
Hind, Rolph, and Co., Inc., 311
Hiram Bingham (gasoline launch), 310
historian, business of, 106
Historical Commission of the Territory of Hawaii, 106
Hitchcock, Charles E., 203n46
Hitchcock, Charles Henry, *Hawaii and Its Volcanoes*, 224
Hitchcock, David, 281
Hitchcock, Elizabeth, 71
Hitchcock, Harvey, 28, 167
Hiva Oa in Marquesas Islands, 317, 317n27
    population, 318
Hoapilli, 124
holiness (*hemolele*), 98
Holy Spirit, 134, 155, 163, 169, 288, 293
    Coan on, 178
Honaaula, 167
Honoli'i (John Honoore), 119
Honolulu, 76–81, 118, 127, 165, 294
    Bethel Church, 339
    Coans' arrival, 3, 76–77
    journey to, 72–76
    revival in, 168
    sendoff, 73–74
Honolulu Sailors' Home, 340
Honoore, John (*Honoli'i*), 119
Honorary Doctor of Ministry degree, 433
Hooker, Joseph Dalton, 199
Hooper, William Northey, 188
Hopkins, Charles G., 203n46
Hopkins, Samuel, 39
Hopoo, Thomas (*Hopu*), 119
hospitality, in Patagonia, 52
House of Sacred Learning, 109
housing in Hilo, 86. *see also* Emerald Bower [Coan home]
Howard, Oliver Otis, 447
Howard University, 447, 451
Howe, K. R., *Vaka Moana Voyages of the Ancestors*, 109
Howell, Elias, 443n104

Howell, Ellen Mariner, 443n104
hula, 119
human sacrifice, 3, 111
humans, volcano eruption effects, 255–56
Humphrey, S. J., 134, 491, 493, 509
Humphrey, Simon, 63
Hunnewell, James, 321
Hutchison, William R., 116
Hyde, C.M., 400, 491
Hyde, John, 420
Hyde, John, Jr., 420
hymns
    in *Morning Star* celebration, 301
    "No Shadow Yonder," 459n25
    "Till He Come," 491n53
hypocrisy, 151

Iaea, 142n66
idolatry, Romanism and, 401
'I'i, 124
Ili, 497
immersion (baptism), 180
Independence (ship), 341
India, British officer in, 347
indigenous people
    Expedition impact on, 182
    illnesses from Europeans, 204
infanticide, Darwin's interest in, 197
influenza, 204
Ingraham, Capt., 314
insensibility, 377n57
Internet, 13–14
'Io (supreme being), 109
    killing of priests, 110
    link to God of Bible, 110
iron gall ink, 22–23n50

Jackson, Andrew, 183
Jagger, Thomas, 455
Jarves, James J., 203n46
Jay, *The Book of Peace*, 373–74
Jeffries, Rev., 374
John the Baptist, 391n108
Johnson, Charles, 29
Johnson, Sixtus E., 411
Jones, Ap Catesby, 346
Jones, Pei Hurinui, *King Potatau*, 109
Jose, David, 330, 332
Jubilee Celebration, 135
Judd, Gerrit, 122, 186, 201–2
Judson, Adoniram, 436
Junkin, George, 177
"Just War Theory," 395

Ka'ahumanu (queen regent), 112

Index of Subjects

and Christianity, 118
Kaawaloa, 127
Kahapuu, 402
Kahatech, 58
Kahuna, 110
Kailua, 127
Kaiu, 127
Kaiula, 118
Kaivi, Isaiah, 319–20
Kaivi, J.W., 319
kake, 119
Kalana, Mr., 481
Kalapana, 143
Kalinimoku, baptism, 398
Kamehameha I, 3, 111, 112, 113–14
    Coan on, 114–15
    Vancouver conversation on potential missionaries, 113–14
    war to unite islands, 114
Kamehameha II (Liholiho), 112
    Coan on, 115
    end of kapu system, 114
Kamehameha III, 152–53, 340, 351, 398, 399
Kanaloa (Hawaiian god), 111
Kane (Hawaiian god), 111
Kanooa, Paulo, 128
Kanui (William Tennooe), 119
Kapiolani (Chiefess), 128, 223
Kapohaku, Paul, 325, 325n71
kapu system, 111–13
    ending, 114
Karren, Thomas, 411
Kashumanu, 127
    visit to Hilo, 129–30
Ka'u, 213
    earthquake, 1868, 216, 218
    earthquake and lava flow, 279–80
    worship center losses from earthquake, 220
Kauai, 165
    Wiamea, 113
Kauhane, license renewal, 289
Kaukau, Alexander, 320
Kauwealoha, Hana, 320, 393
Kauwealoha, Samuel, 317–18, 319, 332
    Coan on home and ministry, 318
Kawaiaha'o Church, 115, 298, 299, 300
Kawainui, Herb, *Ancient Hawaii, Voyage: Discovery of Hawaii, and Voyagers*, 109
Kay, E. Alison, 198, 199, 200, 226, 227
Keeler, James, 407n64
Kehena, 147
Kekai ("Salt Sea"), 265
Kekela, James, 321–22, 332, 333
    missionary to Marquesas Islands, 322
    trip to Micronesia, 322

Kekela, Naomi, 321
Kekuhoupio, 99
Keopuolani, 112, 118
Keoua, 239
Kilauea, 230, 237–47, 278
    Bingham on, 241
    crater sink, 255
    earthquake, 217–19
    eruption, 1790, 239
    eruption, 1840, 248–57
    eruption, 1868, 278–80
    eruption effect on water, 242
    eruption frequency, 235
    lava flows, 225, 251–52
    size, 241
    trip up summit, 1846, 257
    varied nature of activity, 242
    visitors, 246
Killingworth, Conn., 18
    Coans in, 436–37
    Coan's legacy, 511–13
    Titus in, 441–42
Killingworth Dome, 230, 366
Kimball, James William, *Heaven, "My Father's House,"* 479
Kimball, Spencer W., 407n61
King, William, 411
Kittredge, Dr., 478
Kittredge, Mrs., 490
    "Memorial Poem," 498
Kohala, 149, 155, 422, 500n80
Kona, 149
Koyanagi, Robert Y., 214–21
Krakatoa Island, destruction, 203
Ku (Hawaiian god), 111
Kuakinni, 124
Ku-kailimoku (war god), 111
Kuolo, 100
kupana, 98
Kusaie, 311
Kuykendall, Ralph S., 106–7, 111, 118, 120, 121, 135, 138, 186, 229
    Presses of the Pacific Islands, 125n128
Kuyunjik mound, 202

Ladd and Co., 188
Lafon, Dr., 244
Lahaina, 82, 127, 129, 165, 169
Lahainaluna, Maui, 164n17
Lahainaluna school, 414
Lahainaluna Seminary, 126
Laioha, 329, 330
    school, 330–31
Lanai, LDS colony, 421

languages, 15n2, 65, 307, 409n72
   and children, 89n127
   Hawaiian translation of commentary, 289n30
   Hawaiian translation *The Book of Mormon*, 415
   importance of written, 121
   learning Hawaiian, 95–101
   learning Spanish, 55
   as Mormon missionary barrier, 408
   in Patagonia, 52–53
   for preaching in Hawai'i, 69
   Spanish in Patagonia, 50
   words for God's attributes, 98
Laplace, Cyrille-Pierre Theodor, 399
Larsen, Timothy, 202
"The Last Visit at The Grave of A Wife," 461–62
Lausanne, 351
lava chimneys, 256–57
lava flows, 107
   Coan on, 231
   Coan study, 277–78
   Coan trip to,1843, 271–73
   depth, 253–54
   destruction by, 280
   from Kilauea, 225, 251–52
   light from, 254
   from Mauna Loa, 260, 281
   and ocean, 252
   Pele's hair from, 246
   threat to Hilo, 269, 270–71, 274–75, 282
   visitors, 282
law of compensation, 278
Layard, Austen Henry, 202
Lee, Robert E., mansion, 449–50
Lee, William L., 228
leeward islands, 314
Leo XII (pope), 398
Library of Congress
   Coan collection, 368
   on Exploring Expedition, 184
licensure, renewal of, 289
Life in Hawaii, 79
lightning, 261
Liholiho (Kamehameha II), 112
   Coan on, 115
   end of kapu system, 114
Lima, Peru, 76
   Bishop, 397
Lincoln, Abraham, 323, 448n121
   assimilation, 378
Lipman, Peter W., 224
Litchfield North Association, 435n62
literacy, 105, 121, 122–23

Livermore, Abiel Abbot, *The Book of Peace*, 373–74
Lockwood, John P., 224
   Volcanoes: A Global Perspective, 227
Loihi, 107
London Missionary Society, 121, 226
   Tahiti station, 116n57
loneliness, 92–94, 304n108
   of sailors, 338
Longley, William, 187
Lono (Hawaiian god), 111
Loomis, Elisha, 125
Lord, M., 441–42
Lord's Prayer, in Gilbertese, 307
Lord's Supper. *see* communion
love, 191
   Coan's concept of, 192
lua, 119
luna, 411n79
Lyman, Chester Smith, 135, 137, 147, 198, 246, 257, 290, 343, 346, 351–52
   Coan as friend, 197
Lyman, David, 3, 80, 81, 100, 132, 133, 137, 143, 335, 410, 481
   ABCFM land for, 189
   and seaman's chaplaincy, 335
Lyman, Frederick, 213, 214, 215, 216–17, 219, 502
Lyman, Isabella, 214, 215
Lyman, Josie, 216
Lyman, Sarah, 3, 13, 81, 132, 183, 207–8, 214, 228, 401
   on 1841 tsunami, 209
   about home, 86
Lyman, Sarah Joiner, 200
Lyons, Jeffrey, *Na Ka Baibala Hemolele*, 124
Lyons, Lorenzo, 4, 28, 145, 150, 153, 173, 410, 477, 490, 496–97
   Coan letter to, 168, 170
   on membership, 173
Lyons, Mrs. Lorenzo, 28

Magellan, 46–47
Magellan nebula, 45
Magnificant Voyagers (Smithsonian Institute), 185
Maigret, Louis, 399
Maigret, Luis, 402
makaainana (mass of the people), 113
Makawao church, 129
Malo, 124
Manini. *see* Mann, Francisco de Paula
Maori, first king, 109
Maria (Queen in Patagonia), 51, 56, 62
   Coan first meeting with, 58

Index of Subjects

Marin, Francisco de Paula, 112n33, 118
Marquesans, in Oahu, deaths, 327
Marquesas Islands, 5, 108, 197, 229, 285, 302, 313–34
    cannibals, 315, 320, 323, 325, 394
    Coan with Catholic officials, 397
    Coan's description, 314
    early missionaries, 315–16
    European discoveries, 314
    general meeting of mission, 314
    mission disadvantages, 292
    missionaries for, 317
    missionary convention, 324
    Morning Stars impact, 311
    mountain climb, 325
    residents, 314–15
    statistics, 326
    violence and peace in, 393–94
    visit, 1867, 326–34
    western illnesses impact, 315
    worship services, 319
marriage
    of Coans, 70
    in Patagonia, 58
    of Sybil and Hiram Bingham, 117
Marshall, James, 406
Mary Jane (schooner), 44
Massey, Gerald, "Jerusalem the Golden," 84n93
material gain, Titus on, 468
Matthews, Nathaniel, 309
Matuunui (Marquesan chief), 322
Maui, 82
    Kekela lecturing, 322
    Mormon missionaries, 408
MauiHawaii.org, 230
Mauna a Wakea, 236
Mauna Kea, 236
    eruption frequency, 235
Mauna Loa, 185, 230, 234n94, 237–47
    after earthquakes, 279
    climbing, 260–62
    Coan at summit, 265, 267–68
    Coan's descent, 262–63
    eruption, 1839, 247
    eruption, 1843, 259–64
    eruption, 1852, 264–69
    eruption, 1855–56, 269–78
    eruption, 1868, 278–80
    eruption, 1880–81, 280–83
    eruption, 1984, 237
    expedition to summit, 181–91
    and Hilo, 239
    lava flows, 260, 281
    map, 237f
    slope, 231, 238
    snow on, 262
    statistics, 277
    summit crater, 238
    USGS summary, 237
    visitors, 228
Mauna Roa, 68
McBride, R., *The Kahuna: Versatil Masters of Old Hawaii*, 110
McDowell, James, 38
McGavin, William, *Protestant*, 403
medical care
    by Arms and Coan, 54
    by Coan, 204–5
medicine man, battle against Pele, 282
Melchizedek, 110
Melville, Herman, *Typee*, 329
membership
    admission, 169
    candidates for, 157–58
    Coan on accepting, 170
    probationary period, 171
Memorial Volume (L. Coan), 13, 137, 314, 326, 348, 375, 425, 428, 478
    E.P. Baker paper, 501–2
    conclusion, 499–500
    contributors, 491
    Lydia's preparation of, 509
    on memorial service, 497
    quotations from service, 491
    review, 509–10
mentor, Coan as, 285, 288–90
Merrick, M. D., 411, 412
Methodist Episcopal Church, 20
Methodists, 178, 179, 180, 181n117
Mexican American War, 406n57
Micronesia, 285, 302
    Bingham II and, 300
    Christianity in, 301
    climate of, 306
    missionaries' difficulties, 304
    missionary effort, 290
    Morning Stars impact, 311
    war and peace on, 392–93
Micronesia Mission Committee, 285
Micronesian people, 285
migration, from Polynesia, 108
Mikahala (steamer), 311
militia, Coan in, 367
millenium, 173n67
Miller, Char, 124, 136, 137, 296, 298, 304, 306
Mills, Henry, 25
mission field, as sacrifice, 29
Mission House library, 11–12

Index of Subjects

missionaries. *see also* Mormon missionaries
  cultivating students as, 28
  earthquake observations, 226
  Kamehameha and Vancouver conversation, 113–14
  Micronesia indifference to gospel message, 305
  Mormon, 6, 84–85, 241–42, 407
  permission for first to land in Hawai'i, 117
  scientific interests, 199–202
  Titus wish to be, 469
  and warfare, 317
  weapons and, 329n91
Missionary Album, 344n56
The Missionary Herald, 5, 42, 64, 122, 137, 207, 248, 249, 250, 254, 255, 286, 438, 439
  Coan obituary, 486–88
  Coan on mission work, 174
missionary sermons, 284
missionary spirit, 291
missions of conquest, 312
Mississippi River, 253
Moku'aweoweo (summit crater), 238, 273
Molaki, Kekela lecturing, 322
Molen, Simpson M., 411
mollemoke (*Procellaria glacialis*), 45
Molokai, 167
monothesim, 110
Moore, Samuel G., 293, 295, 344
moral code, Patagonian perception, 54
Morgan, John, 435n63
Mormon Battalion, 406n57
Mormon missionaries, 6, 84–85, 241–42, 407
  on ABCFM missionaries as Calvinists, 410
  baptism by, 411
  Big Island division into 2 Conferences, 411
  preaching by, 410
Mormonism. *see also* Church of Jesus Christ of Latter-day Saints
  Hawaiian conversion to, 413–15
Mormonism: Its Leaders and Designs, 420, 421
Morning Star, 285, 291–312, 295f, 327
  arrival in Hawai'i, 294, 299, 302
  Bingham II's discussion of first, 306–7
  Coan on, 334
  cost, 293
  Hilo response to, 295–96
  naming, 293
  need for second, 307
  steamer as goal, 310
Morning Star II, 307f
  Coan on, 307–8
Morning Star III, 308–9, 309f
  shipwreck, 309
Morning Star V (steamer), 310

Morning Star IV, 310
Morning Star Institute, 312
Morrell, Benjamin, 37–38, 42
Morris, Nancy, 136, 291, 317, 330
Morse, Jedidiah, 18n26
Mother Casey's Chickens, 45n58
Mount Vernon, Coans at, 451
mountain fever, 187
Mueller, Richard, *Church History: An Introduction to Research, Reference Works, and Methods*, 7
Munson, Henry, 80
Munson, Samuel L., 228
murder, in Hilo, 388
Murray, Lindley, 18

Napela, Jonathan, 413, 415, 421
  travel to Salt Lake City, 416
Nash, James S., 62
National Geographic Magazine, 311
native guides, with Coan on Mauna Loa, 260, 261–62, 263
native pastors. *see* Hawaiian clergy
native room, 89n127
Natua (Abraham), 321
natural theology, 201
Nature Conservancy, press release, 510–11
nature worship, 110–11
Nehemiah, 391n108
Nettleton, Asahel, 2, 17, 149, 192
Nettleton, Tamza, 17–18
Nevada (steamship), 454
New Measures of the Second Great Awakening, 27, 149–52
New Review of Spanish Philology, 46
New Years 1834 in Patagonia, 57
New York City, Coans in, 71
New York Evangelical Journal, 424
New York Times, obituary, 484–86
Newton, Alfred, 199n27
Newton, Rev., 26
Nimitz, Chester W., 312
Nineveh, 348–49
  excavations, 202

Oahu, 208–9, 294
  Kekela lecturing, 322
Oahu Bethel Church, 351
Oberlin, Ohio General Congregational Conference, 433–36
Oberlin Wellington Rescue, 435n61
Obookiah, Henry, 116–17
ocean, lava flows and, 252
Ocean Queen (ship), 65–66n111
Ohio (ship), 341

Index of Subjects

Ohio Congregational annual meeting, 6
Ohio General Congregational Conference, 433–36
Oleloa, Daniel, 128
Oleson, William B., 481, 489
Oliphant, Sarah, 69, 71
Omoa on Fatuiva island, 316, 332
    cannibalism, 320
    Coan's description, 320
    deaths of students, 319–20
    General Meeting, 333
    hostility of people, 319–20
    mission school, 321
    war nature, 321
Ontario Female Seminary, 21
Opukahai'ia, Henry, 105, 115
ordination, concerns, 289–90
Original Sin, 386
Orton, Chad, 22–23n50, 407n59, 411, 416n119
Oucas tribe in Patagonia, 60

Pa'ao (Tahitian high priest), 110
Pacific Commercial Advertiser, 444, 447, 452
Pacific Railroad, 427–28
Pack, Ward E., 411, 413
Page, David, Coan assistance with revivals, 23
Pahio, Mr., 481
pahoehoe (field lava), 261, 276
pain, Fidelia on, 457
Pandanus, 108n11
Paris, J.D., 260, 425n5
Paris, John, 213, 238, 405
    Titus letter to, 462–63
Paris, Mary Grant, 462
Park Street church (Boston), 71–72
Parker, Benjamin, 315, 327
Parker, Peter, 448
Parpon, 58
Partners in Change, 124, 223, 465, 512
Partridge, Edward, 411, 420
passport for travel to Patagonia, 41
pastoral school, Coan and, 291
Patagonia, 2–3, 17, 33–66, 285, 354
    arrival at camp, 51–52
    background, 46–47
    book on, 34, 346, 472
    children in, 53
    Coan and Arms agreement with natives, 51
    Coan correspondence on, 33, 35–40
    Coan description of native people, 49–50
    Coan interaction, 54–55
    Coan learning about land, 59–60
    Coan on, 75, 196–97
    departure from, 61–62
    eastern vs. western coasts, 45
    food, 52, 59
    geographic description, 47
    journey to, 43–46
    land sighting, 45
    languages, 52–53
    map, 48f
    medical care by Arms and Coan, 54
    physical appearance of indigenous people, 56–57
    reactions to religious tracts, 62
    Sabbath in, 54
    Sandwich Islands vs., 31
    Titus and Fidelia's decision on trip, 38–41
    Titus Coan's journal, 34–35
    tribes, 56
"Patagonia Bookshelf," 35
Patagonian Missionary Society, 65–66n111
Paul (apostle), 391n108
Paumau, 322–23
Paumotu Archipelago., 327–28
peace, 469. *see also* war
    children's work for, 392
    Coan against criticism of promoters, 377
    Coan preaching on, 391–92
    in Marquesas Islands, 393–94
    purity and, 383
peace advocates, Coan on, 386
The Peace Book, 369
peace celebration, 366
peace man, Coan as, 366–68
Peck, Joseph A., 412
Pehe, license renewal, 289
Pele (goddess of the volcano), 111, 241–42, 247
    defiance of, 128
    High Priest, 100
    medicine man battle against, 282
    priest and priestess conversion, 142, 222
"Pele's hair," 245–46
Penny, H., 61
Perfectionism, Finney and, 179–80
Perrine, Matthew LaRue, 25
Philbrick, Nathaniel, 184
Philbrick, Thomas, 184
    Sea of Glory, 185
Philpo, license renewal, 289
photography, 344
physical demonstrations in revival, 139, 150–51, 169
Pigafetta, Antonio, 46
"pillar of fire," 247
"pine-tree appendage," 281
Pioneer Company, 105, 128, 175, 285
    preparation for, 115
    royalty's acceptance of missionaries, 114

Pioneer Company *(continued)*
   sailing from Boston, 117
poetry, 121
Pogue, John, 330, 352, 443n104
polygamy, 420, 430–31
   in Patagonia, 58
Polynesia. *see also* Voyagers
   migration from, 108
The Polynesian, 203, 420
Polynesian people, 284–85
polytheism, 3, 110–11
pono (repent; wash), 98
Porter, Jeremiah, 434n 57
Potomac (frigate), 398
Pouzot, Charles, 402
power encounters, 142
Pratt, Parley P., *Voice of Warning*, 416
prayer, 74, 133, 255, 345, 480
   at Auburn Seminary, 285
   Fidelia for language learning, 98
   and Hilo protection from lava, 270, 275–76
   at Howard University, 447
   volume of, 178
prayer meeting, 149
preaching, 100–101, 469
   by Bartimeus, 120
   by Coan, 145
   Coan on, 96, 139
   in Hawaiian language, 98–99
   missionary sermons, 476
   by Mormons, 410, 419
   against Sabbath whaling, 357
   special measures, 164
   visitors from other islands to hear Coan, 148
Preble (ship), 342
Presbyterian Church, 178
   Waialua, 420
Presbyterian General Assembly, 22, 27
Price, John (fugitive slave), 435n61
Price, Willard, 311
Primaleón of Greece, 46
printed material
   demand for, 123
   for sailors, 363
printing presses, 125
Prospect Hill, cemetery, 459
Protestants, Catholic description, 403
Puaʻaiki, Lalana (Blind Bartimaeus), 4, 105, 119–20, 129–31
   efforts for salvation, 166, 167
   Green and, 130, 131–32
Puamau in Marquesas Islands, 321, 331, 333
Pukui, Mary Kawena, *Hawaiʻi Island Legends: Pikoi, Pele, and Others*, 110
Puna, 100, 497

Catholics in, 402
Coan tour of, 101, 141–42, 155
Great Awakening (1836–40), 133–61
Great Awakening, beginning, 139–40
locations on tour, 140–41
preaching tour in, 4
tour through, 468
worship center losses from earthquake, 220
Puna District (Mormon), 413
purgatory, 377
purity, need for, 384
Putney, Clifford, 135, 434
pyroduct, 227, 231
pyrometer, 243–44

Quakers, 375n52
   Coan correspondence with, 375–78
Queen (Maria in Patagonia), 51, 56, 62
   Coan first meeting with, 58

railroad, spur to Salt Lake City, 428
Rapoza, Paul, 35, 89n127, 225, 513
reader assistance
   audience similarities, 13–14
   general readers, 2–7
   scholars, 7–13
Reed, Newton, 24, 25
refrigeration process, 278
religious liberty, 398
Renaissance man, Coan as, 19, 25, 195
repent (*pono*), 98
repentance, Bartemeus on, 167
Resolution Bay (Vaitahu) Tahuata, 316
retrenchment, 446n118
Revels, Hiram Rhodes, 446
revivals, 27–28, 136. *see also* Hawaiian Great Awakening
   at Auburn First Church, 28
   Coan as leader, 191–92
Reynolds, William, 184
Rich, Charles C., 407, 408
Richards, Henry P., 412
Richards, James, 25
Richards, Kitty Keliʻikuaʻaina, 414
Richards, Mr. and Mrs., 82
Richards, William, 124, 286
Ricks, Nathaniel, 412
Robbins, Samuel P., 36
Robert W. Logan (schooner), 310
Robinson, Charles, 29, 178
Robinson, Maria, 462
Rochester, NY, 32
   churches, 69
Rogers, Edmund Horton, 71, 71n27, 88n118
Rogers, Washington B., 413

Index of Subjects

The Role of the American Board, 1
Roman Catholic Church, 396–406
    Coan confrontation with, 403
    controversy between Reformed church and, 403
    Hawaiian confrontations with, 404–5
    in Hilo, 395
    Passion Week ceremonies, 397
    personal behavior required for membership, 403–4
    positions on war and peace, 394–95
Roy, Fitz, 196
Rubin, Ken, 225
Ruggles, Samuel, 128, 188

Sabbath, 353n118
    absence from Marquesas Islands, 323–24
    arguments against observing, 359
    Expedition and Hawaiians' work, 190
    hypocrisy regarding, 357
    on journey to Sandwich Islands, 297–98
    Lyman at Seamen's Chapel, 352
    during Mauna Loa exploration, 273–74
    on Mauna Loa Paumotu Archipelago., 328
    in Patagonia, 54
    protection of, 186
    in Salt Lake City, 430
    services in Oberlin, 435
    ship owners and, 361
sailors
    Coan outreach to, 5
    gospel preaching to, 350
    in Hawai'i, 95, 96
    nursing sick, 353
    in Patagonia, 57
    printed material for, 363
    worship services for, 341–42
Sailor's Magazine, 275, 353
"Sailor's Sabbath," 353–63
Saint Joseph Catholic Community, 403
Saint Martin de Tours chapel, 402
Salt Lake City, Coans arrival, 425–29
salvation, Coan and, 26
Samoan Islands, 208
Samuel (Old Testament), 297
sanctification, 179
Sandwich Islands. *see also* Hawaiian Islands
    Coans request for posting to, 68, 69
    commissioning for Seventh Missionary Company, 71–72
    Cook and, 113
    journey to, 72–76
    Patagonia vs., 31
    success of mission, 439
Sandwich Islands Institute, 351

Sandwich Islands Mission, 408
    General Letter of 1838, 173
Sangenwald, Dr., 426
Santa Maria. *see* Maria (Queen in Patagonia)
Santiago, Chile, 76
Sappho (schooner), 61
Saturday Evening Post, 311
"savages," on Marquesas Islands, 319
Schmitt, Robert C., *Demographic Statistics of Hawai'i*, 123n110
scholars
    assisting, 7–13
    online and digitized material, 8–9
School of the Prophets, 1870 meeting, 428
schools, 130
science. *see also* earthquakes
    Bible and, 195, 234
    Coan's climatological observations, 203
    Coan's interests, 4, 44–45, 196–99. *see also* Coan, Titus, scientific observations
scoria, 253
Scribner's Weekly, 219
Seaman's Chapel, donations for, 348
seamen. *see* sailors
Seamen's Chaplain, 350, 351
    Coan as, 335
Second Great Awakening, 2
    Au and, 24
seminaries, 432
Sennacherib, 202
sennit, 108n11
Seventh Company
    Anderson letter, 79–80
    commissioning, 71–72
    instructions, 140
Severance, Judge, 282
Shaffer, J. Wilson, 431n32
Sheldon, Henry, 339
Shepherd, Capt., 401
Shipley, Anna, 377–78
Shipley, Samuel R., 377–78
ships
    for missions, 292–93
    port departure timing, 355
    of war, 349
shipwrecks
    letters lost, 92–93
    of *Morning Star III*, 309
Shorty, Patrick, 398
signs, 409
Silliman, Benjamin, 198, 223
Silliman, Benjamin Jr., 198, 199
Silliman Journal, 198, 224
slavery, 450
smallpox, 204, 329, 330, 422

Index of Subjects

Smiley, Sarah F., 378
Smith, Daniel, 58
Smith, George, 430, 431n30
Smith, George A., 430
Smith, John, 412–13
Smith, Joseph F., 228, 275, 407n61, 412, 420, 421
    Conde claims, 417
Smith, Lowell, 29, 31, 490
smoke, from volcano, 256
Snow, Mr., 301
snow, 187
    on Mauna Loa, 262
social classes, kapu system and, 112
Society Islands (Tahiti), 108, 121
Society Island indigenous Christians, 315
Society of Friends, 375n52
    Coan correspondence with, 375–78
"Society of Inquiry," 28, 285
"Soldier's Rest," 447, 448n121
soul, 377
sound
    from lava flow, 282
    from volcano, 250, 252, 265
Southern Elephant Seal colony, 36n21
Spanish language in Patagonia, 50, 55
Sparrowhawk, 401
Spaulding, Ephraim, 101, 339, 352
Spaulding, Mr. and Mrs., 82
Speirs, Henry F., 412
spelling book, 122
spiritual battle, 156
spiritual experience of Coan, illness and, 22–23
sprinkling (baptism), 180
Stangenwald, Hugo, 343–44
Stanton, William R., 183, 187–88, 190
State Council of Hawaiian Congregational Churches, 287
statistics on Hawaiian Great Awakening, 157–58, 165
Stearns, Jonathan F., 438
Stennett, Samuel, 67n3
Stephens, Sarah Acheson, 512
Stevenson, Robert Louis, Kauweloha description, 317–18
Stewart, Charles, 122
Stimson, Frank J., *The Cult of Kihotumu*, 109
storms
    on Mauna Loa, 261
    at sea, 75
stormy-petrel, 45
Strait of Le Maire, 75
Stranger's Friend Society, 340
Strong, Mrs. M. D., 302

studding sails, 75n42
Sturges, A.A., 301, 440
sugar cane, 189
    bill for Expedition damage, 190
    plantation, 188
sulphur crystals, 251
sulphurous acid gas, 246, 272
sun, rings around, 203
Supreme Being, 111. *see also* God
    Hawaiians worship of, 109
    Patagonian perception, 54, 60
Sutter, John, 406
syphilis, 204

Tabernacle in Salt Lake City, 429
tabu system, 111–13
    of Marquesas Islands, 325–26
    in Omoa, 320
Tahiti (Society Islands), 108
Taiohae, 329
Takahashi, Taeko Jane, *Hawai'i: A Pictorial History, 1779-1991*, 226
Talmud, 1n4
Tamashiro, Alan, 3, 108–9, 115, 136, 138, 192
Tan Heung San, Sandalwood Mountains, 505n105
tapa (bark cloth), 315n16
Tapiteuca island, Micronesia, 392–93
Taube, Ulrich, 402
Taylor, Emma Ahueana, "The Cult of *Iolani*," 109
Taylor, Nathaniel William, 435n62
teacher, Coan as, 19–21
teaching, 97
Tehuelches in Patagonia, 46
Temperance Advocate, 339
temperance movement, 181n117
temperature, at volcano summit, 232
temple (*heiau*), 3
Tenney, Angelina Loraine, 434n56
Tenney, Samuel, 434n56
Tennooe, William (*Kanui*), 119
tents, in Patagonia, 53
Thaddeus (brig), 117
Thompson, Frank, 342, 460
thunder, 261
Thurston, Asa, 226
Thurston, Lucy Goodale, 479
Thurston, Smith B., 412
tidal waves. *see* tsunami
Tierra del Fuego, 47
Tiiekai, Joseph, 313
Tiietai, Joseph, 327
Toldos (Patagonian residents), 34
Toleration, Edict of, 399

Index of Subjects

Tomlinson, Antoinette, 164n17
Tomlinson, Maria, 164n17
tongues, gift of, 409n72
Toorloon, 58
Transcontinental Railroad, completion, 428
translations, by Hiram Bingham II, 308
Transport (schooner), 57
trees, lava impact, 255, 274
tsumami, 205–14
    1837, November, 206–9
    1841, 209
    1868, 212–14
    1877, 209
    earthquakes and, 4–5
    in Hilo, 146–47
tuberculosis, 204
Tyler, David B., *The Wilkes Expedition*, 185
typhoid epidemic, 204

Union Pacific, 428
United Church Board for World Ministries, 506
United States
    Coan's description in 1870, 433
    Navy, 350
    Navy, Coan letter to admiral, 380
United States Congress, Coan's observations, 445–46
United States (frigate), 346
US Exploratory Expedition (Ex Ex). *see* Exploring Expedition (ExEx)
US Geologic Society, Haleakala volcano summary, 234–35
US National Park rangers, 223n8
U.S. Patent Office, 449
Utah Central Railroad, 428
Utah War (1857), 421

Vaitahu (Resolution Bay) Tahuata, 316
Valparaíso, Chile, *Hellespont* in, 76
Vancouver, George, 113–14
    Kamehameha conversation on potential missionaries, 113–14
Vázquez, Francisco, 46
Velocity (schooner), 82
Vicar Apostolic of the Pacific, 399
Vincennes (USS), 181, 183, 185
violence, in Marquesas Islands, 393–94
vog, 266n17
volcanic eruptions
    distinctive, in Hawai'i, 224n13
    effects, 255–56, 279
    major, by year, 247
Volcanic Explosivity Index, 241, 241n124
volcanic waves. *see* tsunami

Volcano House, 228
Volcano Museum, 225
volcanoes, 107, 222–58. *see also* Pele (goddess of the volcano)
    Coan's scientific on-site observations, 224
    cooking food over steam vents, 343
    crust cooling, 254
    description, 229–31
    heat from, 250, 266–67
    major, by year,
        1840, Mauna Loa, 248–58
        1843, Mauna Loa, 259–64
        1852, Mauna Loa, 264–69
        1855-56, Mauna Loa, 269–78
        1868, Kilauea, 278-80
        1880-81, Mauna Loa, 280–83
    as metaphor, 383, 384
    "Pele's hair," 245–46
    smoke and gases from, 256
    sound from, 250, 252
    sources, 224–29
Voyagers, 3, 105, 108
    and Hawaiian culture, 120–21
    monothesim, 109

Wahineomao, 142n66
Waiakea, 84
Wailuku, Maui, 129, 132, 165, 166, 167
Waimea, Kauai, 113, 118, 127, 128, 149, 153, 155, 173
Walter, Beryl, 512–13
war. *see also* peace
    and Christianity, 372
    Coan on, 380–81
    as demon, 379
    as fact, 384
    in Marquesas Islands, 319
    missionaries and, 317
    ships of, 349
war and peace, 365–95
    on Micronesia, 392–93
War of 1812, 366
War of Rebellion. *see* Civil War (U.S.)
Warren, Jane S., *Morning Star: History of the Children's Missionary Vessel, and of the Marquesan and Micronisian [sic] Missions*, 300
Waters, Mrs. Edward E., 491
Waters, Sarah Coan, 492–93, 505
"Waymarks" notebook, 463–64, 472
weapons
    Coan's views, 61
    in gospel meeting, 394
    missionaries and, 329n91
weeping, 151

Index of Subjects

Welch, Charles, 181n117
Welch, Thomas Bramwell, 180n117
Wells, Daniel H., 430
Welsh, Brian, 88n123, 188
Wesley, Charles, 87n117, 154n132
Wesley, John, 179
West, John A., 412
Westerners
    greed of, 322
    views of other cultures, xxi
Westervelt, W.D., 287
Westminster Shorter Catechism, 18–19
Wetmore, Charles, 4, 135, 201, 204, 205, 265–66, 478, 498
    ABCFM land for, 189
whalers, 350, 353, 364n145
whaling industry, 338
    Coan on, 354–55
    ship owners, 356
Whalon, Mr., rescue from cannibals, 323
Whatahoro, H. T., *The Lore of the Whare-Wananga*, 109
Wheeler, Daniel, 344, 375
Whitelsey, General, 451
Whitney, Maria Kapule, 443n104
Whitney, Orson K., 412
Whittlesey, Mr. and Mrs., 71
Wilcox, Mrs., 176
Wilkes, Charles, 181, 183, 208
    Narrative of the United States Exploring Expedition, 184
Williams College, 435n63
winter, impact on Coans, 442, 453
Wisner, Benjamin B., 32, 69, 70
Witness to Aloha (documentary), 112, 115, 121, 122–23, 123n110, 513

Woman's Board of Missions, 450
women, travel restrictions, 324
Woodbury, John Stillman, 410
Woods, Fred, 407, 408
World Affairs, 369n20
World Affairs Institute, 369
worship centers, loss from earthquakes, 220
worship services
    absence in Patagonia, 60
    changes, 114
    in Hawai'i, 79
    on *Hellespont*, 74
    in Hilo, English, 336
    during Patagonia journey, 44, 48–49
    places for. *see heiau*
    for sailors, 341–42
Wright, Thomas L., *Hawai'i: A Pictorial History, 1779–1991*, 226
written language, importance of, 121
Wycliffe Bible Translators, 97
Wyss, Max, 214–21

Yale College, 116, 435n62
Young, Andrew, "The Happy Land," 331n103
Young, Brigham, 406, 428, 431n30
Young, John, 114, 117, 118, 410, 412, 420
Young, Peter T., 398
Yzendoorn, Reginald
    History of the Catholic Mission in the Hawaiian Islands, 399–400
    stay at Hilo, 402

Zealandia (steamship), 470
zinc, for roof, 90

www.ingramcontent.com/pod-product-compliance
Lightning Source LLC
Chambersburg PA
CBHW080529300426
44111CB00017B/2656